Edwardian and Georgian Fiction, 1880 to 1914

Titles in the CRITICAL COSMOS series include

THE CRITICAL COSMOS SERIES

Edwardian and Georgian Fiction, 1880 to 1914

Edited and with an introduction
by *HAROLD BLOOM*
Sterling Professor of the Humanities
Yale University

CHELSEA HOUSE PUBLISHERS
New York ◇ *Philadelphia*

© 1990 by Chelsea House Publishers, a division of
Main Line Book Co.

Introduction © 1990 by Harold Bloom

Printed and bound in the United States of America

10 9 8 7 6 5 4 3 2 1

Library of Congress Cataloging-in-Publication Data

Edwardian and Georgian fiction, 1880 to 1914 / edited and
with an introduction by Harold Bloom.
    p. cm. — (The Critical cosmos series)
    Bibliography: p.
    Includes index.
    Summary: Critical essays on British fiction produced
    during the Edwardian and Georgian period, 1880–1914.
    ISBN 0–87754–982–6
    1. English fiction—19th century—History and criticism.
2. English fiction—20th century—History and criticism.
[1. English literature—History and criticism.] I. Bloom,
Harold.
    II. Series: Critical cosmos.
PR873.E38 1988   823′.8′09—
dc19   87–27462   CIP   AC

Contents

Editor's Note

This volume of the Critical Cosmos series brings together a representative selection of the best critical essays on British fiction of the Edwardian and Georgian period, 1880–1914. As a book, this forms a companion volume to the Critical Cosmos on Victorian fiction, which covers the years 1830–80. The critical essays are arranged in the chronological order of the authors' birth. I am grateful to Shawn Rosenheim and Susan Laity for their erudition and judgment in helping me to edit this book.

My introduction begins with Thomas Hardy's last novel, *Jude the Obscure*, and then continues with an appreciation of Oscar Wilde's fairy tales and prose poems. I then discuss Joseph Conrad's *Heart of Darkness*, *Lord Jim*, and his masterpiece, *Nostromo*, after which I conclude with a reading of Rudyard Kipling's *Kim* and an analysis that centers upon *A Passage to India*, E. M. Forster's most celebrated novel.

Carole Silver discusses three of William Morris's late prose romances—*The Story of the Glittering Plain*, *The Wood beyond the World*, *The Well at the World's End*—with particular emphasis upon his employment of mythology and folklore. The great Edwardian critic, Walter Pater, is then viewed in his critical fiction *Marius the Epicurean* by his disciple, the editor of this volume.

Thomas Hardy, the great transitional figure between Victorian and Edwardian fiction, was represented most fully in the Critical Cosmos volume on Victorian fiction. Here he is studied by Mary Jacobus, who examines the reception of *Tess of the D'Urbervilles* and then charts the ways in which Hardy altered and edited his novel in order to present poor Tess as a "pure" woman. Together with my commentary on *Jude the Obscure* in the introduction, this gives us readings of Hardy's last two major novels, the reception of which caused him to abandon prose fiction and return to the composition of poetry.

An overview on women and the new fiction of this period, by Penny

Boumelha, provides the background for Hardy's final novels by exploring the way in which both male and female writers were examining the issue of "womanliness." Problems of sexuality and class distinctions are involved in Geoffrey Wall's approach to Bram Stoker's famous shocker, *Dracula*.

Alastair Fowler, distinguished Scottish critic, discusses Robert Louis Stevenson, centering upon *Treasure Island* and *The Ebb-Tide* and their moral ambiguities. A social analysis of the rather different receptions accorded to Oscar Wilde's short stories and to his novel *The Picture of Dorian Gray* is provided by Regenia Gagnier.

In a consideration of three novels of the 1880s by the realist George Gissing, John Goode compares Gissing to Dickens as a portraitist of the London lower classes. Joseph Conrad, surely the major novelist of his era, receives three essays, in addition to the coverage in this volume's introduction. Aaron Fogel discerns in the great mid-period of Conrad's fiction a preoccupation with what he calls "coercion to speak": the forcing of dialogue between characters, seen with particular clarity in *Heart of Darkness*. Robert Penn Warren follows with his classic appreciation of Conrad's masterpiece, *Nostromo*, while the eminent Marxist critic Fredric Jameson centers upon the *Patna* episode in *Lord Jim* and concludes that Jim does attempt to learn from history.

The Adventures of Sherlock Holmes by Arthur Conan Doyle is read by Stephen Knight both as a unified collection and as individual stories. Rudyard Kipling receives two critiques, the first by Robert L. Caserio on the undervalued *The Light That Failed*, seen here as related to Swinburne's vision of William Blake, and the second by Stephen Prickett, who considers the fantasy world of Kipling's fiction in conjunction with the fantasies of E. Nesbit, since both fantasists create deep social commentaries in their visionary projections. Another fantasist, the utopian H. G. Wells, is examined by Frank McConnell, who concentrates upon the relation of *The Time Machine* to Romantic literary tradition.

Arnold Bennett's *The Old Wives' Tale* is defended for its realistic fidelities by John Lucas, while James Gindin analyzes John Galsworthy's *The Man of Property*, the first novel in *The Forsyte Saga*. *Zuleika Dobson*, a work of delight, is read by Robert Viscusi as a grand instance of Max Beerbohm's notions of Form , after which Stephen Medcalf gives us an overview of the entire achievement of G. K. Chesterton, rather surprisingly comparing the English Catholic master of paradox to the much stronger Danish Protestant ironist, Søren Kierkegaard.

Barbara Rosecrance centers upon E. M. Forster's *Howards End*, with some consideration of *A Passage to India*, in a study of their common subject: a growing sense of existential impasse. P. G. Wodehouse's early fiction is examined by Richard J. Voorhees, who finds in Wodehouse's Edwardian novels the prototypes for Bertie Wooster, Freddie Threepwood, and even Jeeves. This book then ends fittingly with Kate Fullbrook's exegesis of the early, feminist short stories of Katherine Mansfield, who carries us into a different world, that of World War I and its aftermath.

Introduction

I

For Arthur Schopenhauer, the Will to Live was the true thing-in-itself, not an interpretation but a rapacious, active, universal, and ultimately indifferent drive or desire. Schopenhauer's great work, *The World as Will and Representation*, had the same relation to and influence upon many of the principal nineteenth- and early twentieth-century novelists that Freud's writings have in regard to many of this century's later, crucial masters of prose fiction. Zola, Maupassant, Turgenev, and Tolstoy join Thomas Hardy as Schopenhauer's nineteenth-century heirs, in a tradition that goes on through Proust, Conrad, and Thomas Mann to culminate in aspects of Borges, and Beckett, the most eminent living writer of narrative. Since Schopenhauer (despite Freud's denials) was one of Freud's prime precursors, one could argue that aspects of Freud's influence upon writers simply carry on from Schopenhauer's previous effect. Manifestly, the relation of Schopenhauer to Hardy is different in both kind and degree from the larger sense in which Schopenhauer was Freud's forerunner or Wittgenstein's. A poet-novelist like Hardy turns to a rhetorical speculator like Schopenhauer only because he finds something in his own temperament and sensibility confirmed and strengthened, and not at all as Lucretius turned to Epicurus, or as Whitman was inspired by Emerson.

The true precursor for Hardy was Shelley, whose visionary skepticism permeates the novels as well as the poems and *The Dynasts*. There is some technical debt to George Eliot in the early novels, but Hardy in his depths was little more moved by her than by Wilkie Collins, from whom he also learned elements of craft. Shelley's tragic sense of eros is pervasive throughout Hardy, and ultimately determines Hardy's understanding of his strongest heroines: Bathsheba Everdene, Eustacia Vye, Marty South, Tess

Durbeyfield, Sue Bridehead. Between desire and fulfillment in Shelley falls the shadow of the selfhood, a shadow that makes love and what might be called the means of love quite irreconcilable. What M. D. Zabel named as "the aesthetic of incongruity" in Hardy and ascribed to temperamental causes is in a profound way the result of attempting to transmute the procedures of *The Revolt of Islam* and *Epipsychidion* into the supposedly naturalistic novel.

J. Hillis Miller, when he worked more in the mode of a critic of consciousness like Georges Poulet than in the deconstruction of Paul de Man and Jacques Derrida, saw the fate of love in Hardy as being darkened always by a shadow cast by the lover's consciousness itself. Hugh Kenner, with a distaste for Hardy akin to (and perhaps derived from) T. S. Eliot's in *After Strange Gods*, suggested that Miller had created a kind of Proustian Hardy, who turns out to be a case rather than an artist. Hardy was certainly not an artist comparable to Henry James (who dismissed him as a mere imitator of George Eliot) or James Joyce, but the High Modernist shibboleths for testing the novel have now waned considerably, except for a few surviving high priests of Modernism like Kenner. A better guide to Hardy's permanent strength as a novelist was his heir D. H. Lawrence whose *The Rainbow* and *Women in Love* marvelously brought Hardy's legacy to an apotheosis. Lawrence, praising Hardy with a rebel son's ambivalence, associated him with Tolstoy as a tragic writer:

> And this is the quality Hardy shares with the great writers, Shakespeare or Sophocles or Tolstoi, this setting behind the small action of his protagonists the terrific action of unfathomed nature; setting a smaller system of morality, the one grasped and formulated by the human consciousness within the vast, uncomprehended and incomprehensible morality of nature or of life itself, surpassing human consciousness. The difference is, that whereas in Shakespeare or Sophocles the greater, uncomprehended morality, or fate, is actively transgressed and gives active punishment, in Hardy and Tolstoi the lesser, human morality, the mechanical system is actively transgressed, and holds, and punishes the protagonist, whilst the greater morality is only passively, negatively transgressed, it is represented merely as being present in background, in scenery, not taking any active part, having no direct connexion with the protagonist. (Œdipus, Hamlet, Macbeth set themselves up against, or find themselves set up against, the unfathomed moral forces of nature, and out of this unfathomed force comes their death. Whereas Anna Karenina, Eustacia, Tess, Sue, and Jude find themselves up against the established system of human government and morality, they cannot detach themselves, and are brought down. Their real tragedy is that they are unfaithful to the greater unwritten morality, which would have bidden Anna

Karenina be patient and wait until she, by virtue of greater right, could take what she needed from society; would have bidden Vronsky detach himself from the system, become an individual, creating a new colony of morality with Anna; would have bidden Eustacia fight Clym for his own soul, and Tess take and claim her Angel, since she had the greater light; would have bidden Jude and Sue endure for very honour's sake, since one must bide by the best that one has known, and not succumb to the lesser good.

(Study of Thomas Hardy)

This seems to me powerful and just, because it catches what is most surprising and enduring in Hardy's novels—the sublime stature and aesthetic dignity of his crucial protagonists—while exposing also his great limitation, his denial of freedom to his best personages. Lawrence's prescription for what would have saved Eustacia and Clym, Tess and Angel, Sue and Jude, is perhaps not as persuasive. He speaks of them as though they were Gudrun and Gerald, and thus have failed to be Ursula and Birkin. It is Hardy's genius that they are what they had to be: as imperfect as their creator and his vision, as impure as his language and his plotting, and finally painful and memorable to us:

> Note that, in this bitterness, delight,
> Since the imperfect is so hot in us,
> Lies in flawed words and stubborn sounds.

II

Alone among Hardy's novels, *Jude the Obscure* has three strong figures, all triumphs of representation: Sue, Jude, Arabella. Unfortunately, it also has little Father Time, Hardy's most memorable disaster in representation. Even more unfortunately, it is a book in which Hardy's drive to go on telling stories gives way to his precursor Shelley's despair that there is one story and one story only, the triumph of life over human integrity. As the most Shelleyan of Hardy's novels (except perhaps for *The Well-Beloved*, which precedes it in initial composition, though not in revision and publication), *Jude the Obscure* has a complex and perhaps crippling relation to *Epipsychidion*. Sue Bridehead is more Shelleyan than even Shelley's Emilia in that poem, and would have been better off married to Shelley than to Jude Fawley, which is not to say that poor Shelley could have survived the union any better than the unhappy Jude.

D. H. Lawrence, inevitably, was Sue's most articulate critic:

Her female spirit did not wed with the male spirit: she could not prophesy. Her spirit submitted to the male spirit, owned the priority of the male spirit, wished to become the male spirit.

Sue needs no defense, least of all in 1986 when she has become prevalent, a subtle rebel against any dialectic of power founded wholly upon mere gender. Yet, within the novel, Sue is less a rebel than she is Jude's Shelleyan epipsyche, his twin sister (actually his cousin) and counterpart. She can live neither with Jude, nor without him, and their love is both narcissistic and incestuous, Hardy's metaphor for the Will to Live at its most destructive, because in Jude and Sue it destroys the most transcendent beings Hardy had ever imagined.

It will not suffice to call *Jude the Obscure* a tragedy, since what is most tragic in Jude and Sue is their Shelleyan transcendence. When Shelley attempted tragedy in *The Cenci*, he succeeded only by diverting the form into a lament for the descent of Beatrice Cenci to her father's level. But Jude and Sue cannot be said to descend, any more than Eustacia, Henchard, and Tess descend. The Will to Live in Hardy's cosmos is too terrible and too incessant for us to speak of it as debasing its subjects or victims. In a world dominated by drive, a spirit like Jude's is condemned to die whispering the Jobean lament: "Let the day perish wherein I was born." *Jude the Obscure* is Hardy's Book of Job, and like Job is too dark for tragedy, while unlike Job it is just the reverse of theodicy, being Hardy's ultimate declaration that the ways of the Immanent Will towards man are unjustifiable.

Few interchanges in literature are at once so pathetic and so charming as the intricate, Shelleyan dances of scruple and desire intertwined that involve Sue and Jude:

> He laughed. "Never mind," he said. "So that I am near you, I am comparatively happy. It is more than this earthly wretch called Me deserves—you spirit, you disembodied creature, you dear, sweet, tantalizing phantom—hardly flesh at all; so that when I put my arms round you, I almost expect them to pass through you as through air! Forgive me for being gross, as you call it! Remember that our calling ourselves cousins when really strangers was a snare. The enmity of our parents gave a piquancy to you in my eyes that was intenser ever than the novelty of ordinary new acquaintance."
>
> "Say those pretty lines, then, from Shelley's 'Epipsychidion' as if they meant me," she solicited, slanting up closer to him as they stood. "Don't you know them?"
>
> "I know hardly any poetry," he replied, mournfully.
>
> "Don't you?" These are some of them:
>
> " 'There was a Being whom my spirit oft
>   Met on its visioned wanderings far aloft.
>
> . . . .
>
>   A seraph of Heaven, too gentle to be human,
>   Veiling beneath that radiant form of woman . . . ' "
>
> "Oh, it is too flattering, so I won't go on! But say it's me!—say it's me!"

"It *is* you, dear; exactly like you!"

"Now I forgive you! And you shall kiss me just once there—not very long." She put the tip of her finger gingerly to her cheek, and he did as commanded. "You do care for me very much, don't you, in spite of my not—you know?"

"Yes, sweet!" he said, with a sigh, and bade her good-night.

It is Sue, right enough, and it is disaster. The true epigraph to *Jude the Obscure* comes at the climax of *Epipsychidion*:

> In one another's substance finding food,
> Like flames too pure and light and unimbued
> To nourish their bright lives with baser prey,
> Which point to Heaven and cannot pass away:
> One hope within two wills, one will beneath
> Two overshadowing minds, one life, one death,
> One Heaven, one Hell, one immortality,
> And one annihilation.

That "one will beneath" the "two overshadowing minds" of Sue and Jude is the Immanent Will of Thomas Hardy, and it indeed does become "one annihilation."

III

Oscar Wilde was essentially a man of action displaced into a man of letters. In some curious sense, there is a sickness-unto-action in Wilde's life and work, a masked despair that led him to the borders of that realm of fantasy the Victorians called "nonsense" literature, the cosmos of Edward Lear. Wilde stands between a doctrine of momentary aesthetic ecstasies, phantasmagoric hard gemlike flames, and a vision of lyric simplification through aesthetic intensity, what Yeats called the Condition of Fire. Nonsense is the truest rejection of mere nature, and the strongest program for compelling nature to cease imitating itself and to imitate art instead.

In his collection of stories, I turn with pleasure to Wilde at nearly his most delightful, the nine fairy tales published originally as two volumes, *House of Pomegranates* and *The Happy Prince and Other Tales*. "The Young King" is a visionary narrative in the mode of Walter Pater's *Imaginary Portraits*, and suffers from being both too ornate and a touch too sentimental. But its hero, questing always for beauty crossed by the shadow of mortality, is one of Wilde's luminous Christ figures, and almost redeems the story from its baroque elaborations. Far better is the cruel and provocative "The Birthday of the Infanta," where the dancing dwarf's first sight of his own reflection is necessarily self-destructive, and represents Wilde's great theme of the narcissistic element in the death drive, beyond the pleasure principle. The story's closing outcry, the Infanta's "For the future let those who come to play with me have no hearts,'' can be considered one of Wilde's veracious if ironic mottoes.

"The Fisherman and His Soul," a much more ambitious story, is one of the authentic weird tales in the language, worthy of E. T. A. Hoffmann and better than anything by Poe. Its great figure is not the young Fisherman but his equivocal and dangerous Soul, or shadowy double, and its most ironic and telling moment, extraordinary in context, is the reunion between self and soul in the act of dying:

> And his Soul besought him to depart, but he would not, so great was his love. And the sea came nearer, and sought to cover him with its waves, and when he knew that the end was at hand he kissed with mad lips the cold lips of the Mermaid, and the heart that was within him, brake. And as through the fulness of his love his heart did break, the Soul found an entrance and entered in, and was one with him even as before. And the sea covered the young Fisherman with its waves.

The last story to appear in *A House of Pomegranates*, "The Star-Child," may invest too much of its intensity in pathos, yet the hidden meaning redeems the hyperbolic sentiment, as this is clearly one of Wilde's allegories of his own malaise and quest for the mother. Freud's reading of the psychosexuality of Leonardo da Vinci is wholly relevant to "The Star-Child," where the child is Oscar and the mother is a displaced version of Lady Jane Wilde, who wrote poems and revolutionary articles for the Irish cause under the name Speranza and who was famous as the author-translator of *Sidonia the Sorceress*, a dubious work yet greatly admired by William Morris.

Freud, in his study of Leonardo, remarks that all great men must retain something of the infantile throughout their whole life, and certainly this was true of Wilde. But the sublime Oscar knew this of himself; what after all, whether of himself or others, did he not know? This may account for the marvelous bitterness that ends the tale of "The Star-Child." Though reconciled to this mother, and his father, the star-child Oscar cannot live and rule happily ever after:

> Yet ruled he not long, so great had been his suffering, and so bitter the fire of his testing, for after the space of three years he died. And he who came after him ruled evilly.

IV

Four of the five fairy stories in *The Happy Prince and Other Tales* are Wilde's masterpieces in this genre, being short, swift, and eloquently ironic. Only "The Devoted Friend" yields to its own bitterness, while "The Happy Prince" and "The Remarkable Rocket" are perfectly balanced between irony and pathos, and "The Nightingale and the Rose" and "The Selfish Giant" are more mixed successes, the first inclining too much to disillusion, while the second falls finally into Wilde's Christological obsessions.

The title story, "The Happy Prince," is consistently superb, but my own favorite passage in it comes with the introduction of the hero, the insouciant little Swallow, who comes upon a beautiful Reed and is "so attracted by her slender waist" that, for a time, he falls in love with her:

> "Shall I love you?" said the Swallow, who liked to come to the point at once, and the Reed made him a low bow. So he flew round and round her, touching the water with his wings, and making silver ripples. This was his courtship, and it lasted all through the summer.
>
> "It is a ridiculous attachment," twittered the other Swallows, "she has no money, and far too many relations"; and indeed the river was quite full of Reeds. Then, when the autumn came, they all flew away.
>
> After they had gone he felt lonely, and began to tire of his lady-love. "She has no conversation," he said, "and I am afraid that she is a coquette, for she is always flirting with the wind." And certainly, whenever the wind blew, the Reed made the most graceful curtsies. "I admit that she is domestic," he continued, "but I love travelling, and my wife, consequently, should love travelling also."
>
> "Will you come away with me?" he said finally to her; but the Reed shook her head, she was so attached to her home.
>
> "You have been trifling with me," he cried. "I am off to the Pyramids. Good-bye!" and he flew away.

Delicious in its urbane control, the passage belongs to the higher sphere of nonsense literature, with Edward Lear and Lewis Carroll and *The Importance of Being Earnest*. What Wilde wrote of his greatest play is true also of the story of the Swallow and the Reed: "It is exquisitely trivial, a delicate bubble of fancy, and it has as its philosophy . . . that we should treat all the trivial things of life seriously, and all the serious things of life with sincere and studied triviality."

In "The Nightingale and the Rose," as I have already intimated, Wilde unfortunately concludes by treating all the trivial matters trivially and all the serious issues too seriously, so that the tale falls short of the sublimities of true Nonsense. "The Selfish Giant" is better, if slighter, and has about it the Paterian sadomasochism that always attends Wilde when he celebrates "the wounds of Love." Bitterness, never much below the surface of Wilde's work, breaks through too strenuously in "The Devoted Friend," which, however, is saved by its beginning and end, where we inhabit the cosmos of the old Water-rat, the Duck, and the Green Linnet. In that world, prophetic of *The Wind in the Willows*, the divine Oscar cannot go wrong.

I am delighted to conclude my consideration of these stories with Wilde at his strongest, in "The Remarkable Rocket," perhaps the best of all his fairy tales. With earnest originality, Wilde places us in the psychic realm of royal fireworks, where we listen to the conversation of Roman Candles, Catherine Wheels, Squibs, Bengal Lights, and the Remarkable Rocket himself, a veritable paragon of vainglory and self-importance. The Remarkable Rocket cannot be bothered to keep himself dry, since he is too concerned with giving pleasure only to himself: "The only thing that sustains one through life is the consciousness of the immense inferiority of everybody else, and this is a feeling that I have always cultivated."

Incapable of going off at the right time, the Remarkable Rocket fails to shoot up into the sky at the royal fireworks display. In a descending slide worthy of Thomas Pynchon, the Remarkable Rocket goes out to no effect whatsoever:

> Then he began to feel a curious tingling sensation all over him.
>
> "Now I am going to explode," he cried. "I shall set the whole world on fire, and make such a noise, that nobody will talk about anything else for a whole year." And he certainly did explode. Bang! Bang! Bang! went the gunpowder. There was no doubt about it.
>
> But nobody heard him, not even the two little boys, for they were sound asleep.
>
> Then all that was left of him was the stick, and this fell down on the back of a Goose who was taking a walk by the side of the ditch.
>
> "Good heavens!" cried the Goose. "It is going to rain sticks"; and she rushed into the water.
>
> "I knew I should create a great sensation," gasped the Rocket, and he went out.

The great line of Nonsense writers, from Lear and Carroll through Perelman and Pynchon, would not disown this grand epiphany, this fit conclusion to the narcissistic ego's orgy of self-love. Freud, who has his own recondite place among the seers of Nonsense, taught us that the ego must fall in love with an object other than itself in order to avoid becoming very ill indeed. "The Remarkable Rocket" is Wilde's parodistic presentation of this dark Freudian truth, and certainly is part of Wilde's permanent literary legacy, worthy of the genius who also gave us *The Importance of Being Earnest* and "The Decay of Lying."

V

The prose-poem is a notoriously difficult genre to transpose into English, and Wilde, at his best, superbly understood that to succeed in English it must become more parable than poem. His first prose-poem, "The Artist," fails because it lacks parabolic force, since its insight is too obvious. The reader performs no labor of understanding in moving from the image of "The Sorrow that Endureth for Ever" to the new image of "The Pleasure that Abideth for a Moment," or more simply, from the ideology of realism to the humane hedonism of Walter Pater.

But the next prose-poem, "The Doer of Good," is an extraordinary parable, celebrated by Yeats, though he regretted that Wilde may have spoiled it in the passage from oral recital to the ornate diction of the text. Jesus comes to four people he had healed or saved—the leper, the blind man, Mary Magdalen, and Lazarus—and they reply to the Christ in unanswerable paradoxes. The healed leper, now a reveler and a drunkard, asks: "How else should I live?" The cured blind man, now an idolator of the forgiven Magdalen, asks: "At what else should I look?" The Magdalen, who will not walk the way set forth by the normative Torah, is beyond asking anything and laughs that her own way "is a pleasant way." Finally, the resurrected Lazarus asks the overwhelming rhetorical question "What else should I do but weep?"

Yeats may have been too concerned about the ornateness of diction to have seen how subtly Wilde has arranged this poem in prose. Each time, Jesus touches again the person he has healed, saved, or resurrected by a previous laying on of hands, but each time the touch is different. He touches the former leper on the shoulder, the restored blind man on the hand, the Magdalen on her painted raiment, and the resurrected Lazarus, most erotically, on "the long locks of his hair." Each touch is precise, because each is a clear displacement of desire, as though Wilde's Jesus were restrained by his normative Judaic allegiances from yielding to his own true nature. The leper's shoulder is a displacement of his Dionysiac mouth or lips, now freed of sores, while the hand of the man formerly blind substitutes for his eyes. Painted raiment and the long hair of Lazarus manifestly become fetishes, in each case for sexual parts. Drink, sexual excess, despair of life itself; these are the reality that the Christ himself cannot abolish, the reality everywhere underlying Wilde's fantasy and wit.

Oscar Wilde's best prose poem, "The Disciple," written in 1893, represents the consummate expression of Wilde's psychological and spiritual sense of the abyss. It is difficult to see how a poem in prose could be better. The diction and prose rhythm, far from being ornate, are of a limpid clarity, graciously mitigating the savage irony of "The Disciple's" awareness of both natural and human limits.

> When Narcissus died the pool of his pleasure changed from a cup of sweet waters into a cup of salt tears, and the Oreads came weeping through the woodland that they might sing to the pool and give it comfort.
>
> And when they saw that the pool had changed from a cup of sweet waters into a cup of salt tears, they loosened the green tresses of their hair and cried to the pool and said, "We do not

wonder that you should mourn in this manner for Narcissus, so beautiful was he."

"But was Narcissus beautiful?" said the pool."

Who should know better than you? answered the Oreads. "Us did he ever pass by, but you he sought for, and would lie on your banks and look down at you, and in the mirror of your waters he would mirror his own beauty."

And the pool answered, "But I loved Narcissus because, as he lay on my banks and looked down at me, in the mirror of his eyes I saw ever my own beauty mirrored."

Kierkegaard might have called this "The Case of the Contemporary Disciple Doubled." Narcissus never saw the pool, nor the pool Narcissus, but at least the pool mourns him. Wilde's despair transcended even his humane wit, and could not be healed by the critical spirit or by the marvelous rightness of his perceptions and sensations. Wilde, like Pater both a contemporary of Freud and a Freudian before Freud, as it were, anticipates the fundamental Freudian formula. All love initially is self-love, and can return to the ego when the object is withdrawn. The ego is always a bodily ego, and is necessarily a narcissistic ego, and so partly unconscious or repressed. These realizations, which in Pater and Freud led to Stoicism, in the more emotional and flamboyant Wilde could lead only to authentic despair.

Something of the same despair oddly vitalizes "The Master," where the despair mounts up to become a horror, where the homoerotic and masochistic would-be Christ weeps not for Jesus but for himself: "All things that this man has done I have done also. And yet they have not crucified me." Wilde, having rushed towards his own crucifixion by British society, in his long letter to Lord Alfred Douglas from Reading Gaol, January–March 1897 (*De Profundis,* as we now call it), insisted that Jesus, like Wilde himself, had created his own catastrophe out of profound imaginative need:

> And it is the imaginative quality of Christ's own nature that makes him this palpitating centre of romance. The strange figures of poetic drama and ballad are made by the imagination of others, but out of his own imagination entirely did Jesus of Nazareth create himself. The cry of Isaiah had really no more to do with his coming than the song of the nightingale has to do with the rising of the moon—no more, though perhaps no less. He was the denial as well as the affirmation of prophecy. For every expectation that he fulfilled, there was another that he destroyed.

This Jesus is High Romantic rather than nihilistic, as though Wilde does not quite dare wholly to assimilate the Christ to himself. The fifth prose-poem, "The House of Judgment," embraces nihilism, when the Man assures God that he cannot be sentenced to Hell by the Deity "because in

Hell have I always lived," or to Heaven, because it is unimaginable by men. When we reach the final prose-poem, "The Teacher of Wisdom," Wilde's complex bitterness gives us a parable of the sorrows of influence, of the loss that tuition causes in the teacher, rather than in the taught. "The Teacher of Wisdom" confirms Lord Henry Wotton's remark to Wilde's Dorian Gray that all influence is immoral, necessarily including Lord Henry's instruction of Dorian:

> Because to influence a person is to give him one's own soul. He does not think his natural thoughts, or burn with his natural passions. His virtues are not real to him. His sins, if there are such things as sins, are borrowed. He becomes an echo of someone else's music, an actor of a part that has not been written for him.

Closer even to "The Teacher of Wisdom" is Wilde's own bitterness in "The Portrait of Mr. W. H." "Influence is simply a transference of personality, a mode of giving away what is most precious to one's self, and its exercise produces a sense, and, it may be, a reality of loss. Every disciple takes away something from his master."

This is the loss experienced by the Teacher of Wisdom, who finally gives away completely his knowledge of God, only to be rewarded by the perfect love of God. If this seems sentimental to us, that may be because Wilde was enough of a Gnostic not to be able to convince himself that knowledge of God and love of God were antithetical to one another. We can believe that Wilde's deathbed conversion to the Church was simply a reaffirmation of his lifelong belief that Christ was an artist, not in Wilde a frivolous belief but an heretical one, indeed an aesthetic version of Gnosticism. Hence Wilde's preference for the Fourth Gospel, which he shrewdly regarded as Gnostic:

> While in reading the Gospels—particularly that of St. John himself, or whatever early Gnostic took his name and mantle—I see this continual assertion of the imagination as the basis of all spiritual and material life, I see also that to Christ imagination was simply a form of Love, and that to him Love was Lord in the fullest meaning of the phrase.

This is Wilde speaking out of the depths in *De Profundis*. G. Wilson Knight, startlingly linking Wilde and Christ, hints that the ideology of Wilde's homosexuality was its dominant element, involving the raising of love to the high realm of aesthetic contemplation. Without disputing Knight (or Wilde), one can observe that such an elevation is more like Pater than Plato, more like the lying against time that is the privileged moment than the lying against mortality that is the realm of the timeless Ideas. As Pater's most dangerous disciple, Wilde literalizes Pater's valorization of perception over nature, of impression over description.

VI

In Conrad's "Youth" (1898), Marlow gives us a brilliant description of the sinking of the *Judea:*

> Between the darkness of earth and heaven she was burning fiercely upon a disc of purple sea shot by the blood-red play of gleams; upon a disc of water glittering and sinister. A high, clear flame, an immense and lonely flame, ascended from the ocean, and from its summit the black smoke poured continuously at the sky. She burned furiously; mournful and imposing like a funeral pile kindled in the night, surrounded by the sea, watched over by the stars. A magnificent death had come like a grace, like a gift, like a reward to that old ship at the end of her laborious day. The surrender of her weary ghost to the keeper of the stars and sea was stirring like the sight of a glorious triumph. The masts fell just before daybreak, and for a moment there was a burst and turmoil of sparks that seemed to fill with flying fire the night patient and watchful, the vast night lying silent upon the sea. At daylight she was only a charred shell, floating still under a cloud of smoke and bearing a glowing mass of coal within.
>
> Then the oars were got out, and the boats forming in a line moved round her remains as if in procession—the longboat leading. As we pulled across her stern a slim dart of fire shot out viciously at us, and suddenly she went down, head first, in a great hiss of steam. The unconsumed stern was the last to sink; but the paint had gone, had cracked, had peeled off, and there were no letters, there was no word, no stubborn device that was like her soul, to flash at the rising sun her creed and her name.

The apocalyptic vividness is enhanced by the visual namelessness of the "unconsumed stern," as though the creed of Christ's people maintained both its traditional refusal to violate the Second Commandment, and its traditional affirmation of its not-to-be-named God. With the *Judea,* Conrad sinks the romance of youth's illusions, but like all losses in Conrad this submersion in the destructive element is curiously dialectical, since only experiential loss allows for the compensation of an imaginative gain in the representation of artistic truth. Originally the ephebe of Flaubert and of Flaubert's "son," Maupassant, Conrad was reborn as the narrative disciple of Henry James, the James of *The Spoils of Poynton* and *What Maisie Knew,* rather than the James of the final phase.

Ian Watt convincingly traces the genesis of Marlow to the way that "James developed the indirect narrative approach through the sensitive central intelligence of one of the characters." Marlow, whom James derided as "that preposterous magic mariner," actually represents Conrad's swerve away from the excessive strength of James's influence upon him. By always "mixing himself up with the narrative," in James's words, Marlow guarantees an enigmatic reserve that increases the distance between the impressionistic techniques of Conrad and James. Though there is little valid comparison that can be made between Conrad's greatest achievements and the hesitant, barely fictional status of Pater's *Marius the Epicurean*, Conrad's impressionism is as extreme and solipsistic as Pater's. There is a definite parallel between the fates of Sebastian Van Storck (in Pater's *Imaginary Portraits*) and Decoud in *Nostromo*.

In his 1897 Preface to *The Nigger of the "Narcissus,"* Conrad famously insisted that his creative task was "before all to make you see." He presumably was aware that he thus joined himself to a line of prose seers whose latest representatives were Carlyle, Ruskin, and Pater. There is a movement in that group from Carlyle's exuberant "Natural Supernaturalism" through Ruskin's paganization of Evangelical fervor to Pater's evasive and skeptical Epicurean materialism, with its eloquent suggestion that all we can see is the flux of sensations. Conrad exceeds Pater in the reduction of impressionism to a state of consciousness where the seeing narrator is hopelessly mixed up with the seen narrative. James may seem an impressionist when compared to Flaubert, but alongside of Conrad he is clearly shown to be a kind of Platonist, imposing forms and resolutions upon the flux of human relations by an exquisite formal geometry altogether his own.

To observe that Conrad is metaphysically less of an idealist is hardly to argue that he is necessarily a stronger novelist than his master, James. It may suggest though that Conrad's originality is more disturbing than that of James, and may help explain why Conrad, rather than James, became the dominant influence upon the generation of American novelists that included Hemingway, Fitzgerald, and Faulkner. The cosmos of *The Sun Also Rises*, *The Great Gatsby*, and *As I Lay Dying* derives from *Heart of Darkness* and *Nostromo* rather than from *The Ambassadors* and *The Golden Bowl*. Darl Bundren is the extreme inheritor of Conrad's quest to carry impressionism into its heart of darkness in the human awareness that we are only a flux of sensations gazing outwards upon a flux of impressions.

VII

Heart of Darkness may always be a critical battleground between readers who regard it as an aesthetic triumph and those like myself who doubt its ability to rescue us from its own hopeless obscurantism. That Marlow seems, at moments, not to know what he is talking about is almost certainly one of the narrative's deliberate strengths, but if Conrad also seems finally not to know, then he necessarily loses some of his authority as a storyteller. Perhaps he loses it to death—our death, or our anxiety that he will not sustain the illusion of his fiction's duration long enough for us to sublimate the frustrations it brings us.

These frustrations need not be deprecated. Conrad's diction, normally flawless, is notoriously vague throughout *Heart of Darkness*. E. M. Forster's wicked comment on Conrad's entire work is justified perhaps only when applied to *Heart of Darkness:*

> Misty in the middle as well as at the edges, . . . the secret casket of his genius contains a vapour rather than a jewel. . . . No creed, in fact.

Forster's misty vapor seems to inhabit such Conradian recurrent modifiers as "monstrous," "unspeakable," "atrocious," and many more, but these are minor defects compared to the involuntary self-parody that Conrad inflicts upon himself. There are moments that sound more like James Thurber lovingly satirizing Conrad than like Conrad:

> We had carried Kurtz into the pilot house: there was more air there. Lying on the couch, he stared through the open shutter. There was an eddy in the mass of human bodies, and the woman with helmeted head and tawny cheeks rushed out to the very brink of the stream. She put out her hands, shouted something, and all that wild mob took up the shout in a roaring chorus of articulated, rapid, breathless utterance.
> "Do you understand this?" I asked.
> He kept on looking out past me with fiery, longing eyes, with a mingled expression of wistfulness and hate. He made no answer, but I saw a smile, a smile of indefinable meaning, appear on his colorless lips that a moment after twitched convulsively. "Do I not?" he said slowly, gasping, as if the words had been torn out of him by a supernatural power.

This cannot be defended as an instance of what Frank Kermode calls a language "needed when Marlow is not equal to the experience described." Has the experience been described here? Smiles of "indefinable meaning" are smiled once too often in a literary text if they are smiled even once. *Heart of Darkness* has taken on some of the power of myth, even if the book is limited by its involuntary obscurantism. It has haunted American literature from T. S. Eliot's poetry through our major novelists of the era 1920 to 1940, on to a line of movies that go from the *Citizen Kane* of Orson Welles (a substitute for an abandoned Welles project to film *Heart of Darkness*) on to Coppola's *Apocalypse Now*. In this instance, Conrad's formlessness seems to have worked as an aid, so diffusing his conception as to have made it available to an almost universal audience.

VIII

Lord Jim (1900) is the first of Conrad's five great novels, followed by what seems to me the finest, *Nostromo* (1904), and then by the marvelous sequence of *The Secret Agent* (1906), *Under Western Eyes* (1911), and finally *Victory* (1915). Of these, it seems clear that *Lord Jim* has the closest to universal appeal; I have rarely met a reader who was not fascinated by it. Martin Price, the subtlest of Conrad's moral critics, prefers *Lord Jim* to *Nostromo* because he finds that both the author's skepticism and the author's Romanticism are given their full scope in *Lord Jim* rather than in *Nostromo*. Doubtless this is true, but Jim himself lacks the High Romantic appeal of the magnificent Nostromo, and I prefer also the corrosive skepticism of Decoud to the skeptical wisdom of Marlow and Stein. Not that I would deprecate *Lord Jim*; had Conrad written nothing else, this single novel would have guaranteed his literary survival.

Aaron Fogel, writing on *Nostromo,* sees it as marking Conrad's transition from an Oedipal emphasis (as in *Lord Jim*) to a representation of the self's struggle against more outward influences. Certainly Jim's struggle does suit Fogel's formulation of the earlier mode in Conrad: "the denial, by internalization, of the Oedipal order of forced dialogue in the outside world—the translation of inquisition into an inner feeling of compulsion to quarrel with a forebear or with oneself." Though there is much of Conrad in Marlow, and a little of him in Stein, his true surrogate is surely Jim, whose dialectics of defeat are in some sense a late version of Polish Romanticism, of the perpetual defeat of Polish heroism. This is only to intimate that Jim's Byronism is rather more Polish than British. Jim rarely demands anything, and he never demands victory. One way of understanding the novel is to see how incomprehensible it would be if Conrad had chosen to make his hero an American.

Marlow, our narrator, becomes something like a father to Jim, in an implicit movement that has been shrewdly traced by Ian Watt. There is an impressive irony in the clear contrast between the eloquent father, Marlow, and the painfully inarticulate son, Jim. The relation between the two poignantly enhances our sense of just how vulnerable Jim is and cannot cease to be. Marlow is a survivor, capable of withstanding nearly the full range of human experience, while Jim is doom-eager, as much a victim of the Romantic imagination as he is a belated instance of its intense appeal to us.

Albert J. Guérard associated *Lord Jim* with *Absalom, Absalom!* (a not un-Conradian work) as novels that become different with each attentive reading. Jim's "simplicity" takes the place of the charismatic quality we expect of the Romantic protagonist, and Guerard sees Jim as marked by a conflict between personality and will. But Jim's personality remains a mystery to us, almost despite Marlow, and Jim's will is rarely operative, so far as I can see. What we can know about Jim is the enormous strength and prevalence of his fantasy-making powers, which we need not confuse with a Romantic imagination, since *that* hardly excludes self-knowledge. Indeed, the deepest puzzle of Jim is why should he fascinate anyone at all, let alone Marlow, Stein, Conrad, and ourselves? Why is he endless to meditation?

Everyone who has read *Lord Jim* (and many who have not) remember its most famous statement, which is Stein's:

A man that is born falls into a dream like a man who falls into the sea. If he tries to climb out into the air as inexperienced people endeavour to do, he drowns—*nicht wahr?* . . . No! I tell you! The way is to the destructive element submit yourself, and with the exertions of your hands and feet in the water make the deep, deep sea keep you up.

That describes Stein's Romanticism, but hardly Jim's, since Jim cannot swim in the dreamworld. When he seems to make the destructive element keep him up, as in Patusan, there would always have to be a Gentleman Brown waiting for him. An imagination like Jim's, which has little sense of otherness, falls into identification as the truly destructive element, and the error of identifying with the outrageous Brown is what kills Jim. Tony Tanner deftly compares Brown to Iago, if only because Brown's hatred for Jim approximates Iago's hatred for Othello, but Brown has a kind of rough justice in denying Jim's moral superiority. That returns us to the enigma of Jim: why does he make such a difference for Marlow—and for us?

We know the difference between Jim and Brown, even if Jim cannot, even as we know that Jim never will mature into Stein. Is Jim merely the spirit of illusion, or does there linger in him something of the legitimate spirit of Romance? Marlow cannot answer the question, and we cannot either, no matter how often we read *Lord Jim*. Is that a strength or a weakness in this novel? That Conrad falls into obscurantism, particularly in *Heart of Darkness*, is beyond denial. Is *Lord Jim* simply an instance of such obscurantism on a larger scale?

Impressionist fiction necessarily forsakes the Idealist metaphysics of the earlier Romantic novel, a metaphysics that culminated in George Eliot. Marlow beholding Jim is a concourse of sensations recording a flood of impressions; how can a sensation distinguish whether an impression is authentic or not? Yet Marlow is haunted by the image of heroism, and finds an authentic realization of the image in Stein. The famous close of Marlow's narrative invokes Jim as an overwhelming force of real existence, and also as a disembodied spirit among the shades:

"And that's the end. He passes away under a cloud, inscrutable at heart, forgotten, unforgiven, and excessively romantic. Not in the wildest days of his boyish visions could he have seen the alluring shape of such an extraordinary success! For it may very well be that in the short moment of his last proud and unflinching glance, he had beheld the face of that opportunity which, like an Eastern bride, had come veiled to his side.

"But we can see him, an obscure conqueror of fame, tearing himself out of the arms of a jealous love at the sign, at the call of his exalted egoism. He goes away from a living woman to celebrate his pitiless wedding with a shadowy ideal of conduct. Is he satisfied—quite, now, I wonder? We ought to know. He is one of us—and have I not stood up once, like an evoked ghost, to answer for his eternal constancy? Was I so very wrong after all? Now he is no more, there are days when the reality of his existence comes to me with an immense, with an overwhelming force; and yet upon my honour there are moments, too, when he passes from my eyes like a disembodied spirit astray amongst the passions of his earth, ready to surrender himself faithfully to the claim of his own world of shades.

"Who knows? He is gone, inscrutable at heart, and the poor girl is leading a sort of soundless, inert life in Stein's house. Stein has aged greatly of late. He feels it himself, and says often that he is 'preparing to leave all this; preparing to leave . . .' while he waves his hand sadly at his butterflies."

Stein's sadness is that he had hoped to find a successor in Jim and now wanes into the sense that he is at the end of a tradition. Enigmatic as always, Marlow cannot resolve his own attitude towards Jim. I do not suppose that we can either and I wonder if that is necessarily an aesthetic strength in Conrad's novel. Perhaps it is enough that we are left pondering our own inability to reconcile the authentic and the heroic.

IX

Endlessly enigmatic as a personality and as a formidable moral character, Conrad pervades his own books, a presence not to be put by, an elusive storyteller who yet seems to write a continuous spiritual autobiography. By the general consent of advanced critics and of common readers, Conrad's masterwork is *Nostromo*; where his perspectives are largest, and where his essential originality in the representation of human blindnesses and consequent human affections is at its strongest. Like all overwhelming originalities, Conrad's ensues in an authentic difficulty, which can be assimilated only very slowly, if at all. Repeated rereadings gradually convince me that *Nostromo* is anything but a Conradian litany to the virtue he liked to call "fidelity." The book is tragedy, of a post-Nietzschean sort, despite Conrad's strong contempt for Nietzsche. Decoud, void of all illusions, is self-destroyed because he cannot sustain solitude. Nostromo, perhaps the only persuasive instance of the natural sublime in a twentieth-century hero of fiction, dies "betrayed he hardly knows by what or by whom," as Conrad says. But this is Conrad at his most knowing, and the novel shows us precisely how Nostromo is betrayed, by himself, and by what in himself.

It is a mystery of an overwhelming fiction why it can sustain virtually endless rereadings. *Nostromo*, to me, rewards frequent rereadings in something of the way that *Othello* does; there is always surprise waiting for me. Brilliant as every aspect of the novel is, Nostromo himself is the imaginative center of the book, and yet Nostromo is unique among Conrad's personae, and not a Conradian man whom we could have expected. His creator's description of this central figure as "the Magnificent Capataz, the Man of the People," breathes a writer's love for his most surprising act of the imagination. So does a crucial paragraph from the same source, the Author's Note that Conrad added as a preface thirteen years after the initial publication:

> In his firm grip on the earth he inherits, in his improvidence and generosity, in his lavishness with his gifts, in his manly vanity, in the obscure sense of his greatness and in his faithful devotion with something despairing as well as desperate in its impulses, he is a Man of the People, their very own unenvious force, disdaining to lead but ruling from within. Years afterwards, grown older as the famous Captain Fidanza, with a stake in the country, going about his many affairs followed by respectful glances in the modernized streets of Sulaco, calling on the widow of the cargador, attending the Lodge, listening in unmoved silence to anarchist speeches at the meeting, the enigmatical patron of the new revolutionary agitation, the trusted, the wealthy comrade Fidanza with the knowledge of his moral ruin locked up in his breast, he remains essentially a man of the People. In his mingled love and scorn of life and in the bewildered conviction of having been betrayed, of dying betrayed he hardly knows by what or by whom, he is still of the People, their undoubted Great Man—with a private history of his own.

Despite this "moral ruin," and not because of it, Conrad and his readers share the conviction of Nostromo's greatness, share in his sublime self-recognition. How many persuasive images of greatness, of a natural sublimity, exist in modern fiction? Conrad's may be the last enhanced vision of Natural Man, of the Man of the People, in which anyone has found it possible to believe. Yet Conrad himself characteristically qualifies his own belief in Nostromo, and critics too easily seduced by ironies have weakly misread the merely apparent irony of Conrad's repeated references to Nostromo as "the magnificent Capataz de Cargadores." Magnificent, beyond the reach of all irony, Nostromo manifestly is. It is the magnificence of the natural leader who disdains leadership, yet who loves reputation. Though he is of the People, Nostromo serves no ideal, unlike old Viola the Garibaldino. With the natural genius for command, the charismatic endowment that could make him another Garibaldi, Nostromo nevertheless scorns any such role, in the name of any cause whatsoever. He is a pure Homeric throwback, not wholly unlike Tolstoy's Hadji Murad, except that he acknowledges neither enemies nor friends except for his displaced father, Viola. And he enchants us even as he enchants the populace of Sulaco, though most of all he enchants the skeptical and enigmatic Conrad, who barely defends himself against the enchantment with some merely rhetorical ironies.

Ethos is the daimon, character is fate, in Conrad as in Heracleitus, and Nostromo's tragic fate is the inevitable fulfillment of his desperate grandeur, which Conrad cannot dismiss as mere vanity, despite all his own skepticism. Only Nostromo saves the novel, and Conrad, from nihilism, the nihilism of Decoud's waste in suicide. Nostromo is betrayed partly by Decoud's act of self-destruction, with its use of four ingots of silver to send his body down, but largely by his own refusal to maintain the careless preference for glory over gain which is more than a gesture or a style, which indeed is the authentic mode of being that marks the hero. Nostromo is only himself when he can say, with perfect truth, "My name is known from one end of Sulaco to the other. What more can you do for me?"

X

Toward the end of chapter 10 of part 3, "The Lighthouse," Conrad renders his own supposed verdict upon both Decoud and Nostromo, in a single page, in two parallel sentences a paragraph apart:

> A victim of the disillusioned weariness which is the retribution meted out to intellectual audacity, the brilliant Don Martin Decoud, weighted by the bars of San Tomé silver, disappeared without a trace, swallowed up in the immense indifference of things.

> The magnificent Capataz de Cargadores, victim of the disenchanted vanity which is the reward of audacious action, sat in the weary pose of a hunted outcast through a night of sleeplessness as tormenting as any known to Decoud, his companion in the most desperate affair of his life. And he wondered how Decoud had died.

Decoud's last thought, after shooting himself, was "I wonder how that Capataz died." Conrad seems to leave little to choose between being "a victim of the disillusioned weariness which is the retribution meted out to intellectual audacity" or a "victim of the disenchanted vanity which is the reward of audacious action." The brilliant intellectual and the magnificent man of action are victimized alike for their audacity, and it is a fine irony that "retribution" and "reward" become assimilated to one another. Yet the book is Nostromo's and not Decoud's, and a "disenchanted vanity" is a higher fate than a "disillusioned weariness," if only because an initial enchantment is a nobler state than an initial illusion. True that Nostromo's enchantment was only of and with himself, but that is proper for an Achilles or a Hadji Murad. Decoud dies because he cannot bear solitude, and so cannot bear himself. Nostromo finds death-in-life and then death because he has lost the truth of his vanity, its enchanted insouciance, the *sprezzatura* which he, a plebeian, nevertheless had made his authentic self.

Nostromo's triumph, though he cannot know it, is that an image of this authenticity survives him, an image so powerful as to persuade both Conrad and the perceptive reader that even the self-betrayed hero retains an aesthetic dignity that renders his death tragic rather than sordid. Poor Decoud, for all his brilliance, dies a nihilistic death, disappearing "without a trace, swallowed up in the immense indifference of things." Nostromo, after his death, receives an aesthetic tribute beyond all irony, in the superb closing paragraph of the novel:

> Dr. Monygham, pulling round in the police-galley, heard the name pass over his head. It was another of Nostromo's triumphs, the greatest, the most enviable, the most sinister of all. In that true cry of undying passion that seemed to ring aloud from Punta Mala to Azuera and away to the bright line of the horizon, overhung by a big white cloud shining like a mass of solid silver, the genius of the magnificent Capataz de Cargadores dominated the dark gulf containing his conquests of treasure and love.

XI

Twenty years after writing his essay of 1943 on Kipling (reprinted in *The Liberal Imagination*, 1951), Lionel Trilling remarked that if he could write the critique again, he would do it "less censoriously and with more affectionate admiration." Trilling, always the representative critic of his era, reflected a movement in the evaluation of Kipling that still continues in 1988. I suspect that this movement will coexist with its dialectical countermovement of recoil against Kipling, as long as our literary tradition lasts. Kipling is an authentically *popular* writer, in every sense of the word. Stories like "The Man Who Would Be King," children's tales from the *Jungle Books* and the *Just-So Stories*; the novel *Kim*, which is clearly Kipling's masterwork; certain late stories and dozens of ballads—these survive both as high literature and as perpetual entertainment. It is as though Kipling had set out to refute the sublime function of literature, which is to make us forsake easier pleasures for more difficult pleasures.

In his speech on "Literature," given in 1906, Kipling sketched a dark tale of the storyteller's destiny:

> There is an ancient legend which tells us that when a man first achieved a most notable deed he wished to explain to his Tribe what he had done. As soon as he began to speak, however, he was smitten with dumbness, he lacked words, and sat down. Then there arose—according to the story—a masterless man, one who had taken no part in the action of his fellow, who had no special virtues, but who was afflicted—that is the phrase—with the magic of the necessary word. He saw; he told; he described the merits of the notable deed in such a fashion, we are assured, that the words "became alive and walked up and down in the hearts of

all his hearers." Thereupon, the Tribe seeing that the words were certainly alive, and fearing lest the man with the words would hand down untrue tales about them to their children, took and killed him. But, later, they saw that the magic was in the words, not in the man.

Seven years later, in the ghastly Primal History scene of *Totem and Taboo*'s fourth chapter, Freud depicted a curiously parallel scene, where a violent primal father is murdered and devoured by his sons, who thus bring to an end the patriarchal horde. Kipling's Primal Storytelling Scene features "a masterless man" whose only virtue is "the necessary word." But he too is slain by the Tribe, or primal horde, lest he transmit fictions about the Tribe to its children. Only later, in Freud, do the sons of the primal father experience remorse, and so "the dead father became stronger than the living one had been." Only later, in Kipling, does the Tribe see "that the magic was in the words, not in the man."

Freud's true subject in his Primal History Scene was the transference, the carrying-over from earlier to later attachments of an overdetermined affect. The true subject of Kipling's Primal Storytelling Scene is not so much the Tale of the Tribe, or the magic that was in the words, but the storyteller's freedom, the masterless man's vocation that no longer leads to death, but that can lead to a death-in-life. What Kipling denies is his great fear, which is that the magic indeed is just as much in the masterless man as it is in the words.

Kipling, with his burly imperialism and his indulgences in anti-intellectualism, would seem at first out of place in the company of Walter Pater, Oscar Wilde, and William Butler Yeats. Nevertheless, Kipling writes in the rhetorical stance of an aesthete and is very much a Paterian in the metaphysical sense. The conclusion of Pater's *Renaissance* is precisely the credo of Kipling's protagonists:

> Not to discriminate every moment some passionate attitude in those about us, and in the brilliancy of their gifts some tragic dividing of forces on their ways, is, on this short day of frost and sun, to sleep before evening. With this sense of the splendour of our experience and of its awful brevity, gathering all we are into one desperate effort to see and touch, we shall hardly have time to make theories about the things we see and touch. What we have to do is to be for ever curiously testing new opinions and courting new impressions.

Frank Kermode observed that Kipling was a writer "who steadfastly preferred action and machinery to the prevalent Art for Art's Sake," but that is to misread weakly what Pater meant by ending the conclusion to *The Renaissance* with what soon became a notorious formula:

> We have an interval, and then our place knows us no more. Some spend this interval in listlessness, some in high passions, the wis-

est, at least among "the children of this world," in art and song. For our one chance lies in expanding that interval, in getting as many pulsations as possible into the given time. Great passions may give us this quickened sense of life, ecstasy and sorrow of love, the various forms of enthusiastic activity, disinterested or otherwise, which come naturally to many of us. Only be sure it is passion—that it does yield you this fruit of a quickened, multiplied consciousness. Of this wisdom, the poetic passion, the desire of beauty, the love of art for art's sake, has most; for art comes to you professing frankly to give nothing but the highest quality to your moments as they pass, and simply for those moments' sake.

Like Pater, like Nietzsche, Kipling sensed that we possess and cherish fictions because the reductive truth would destroy us. "The love of art for art's sake" simply means that we choose to believe in a fiction, while knowing that it is not true, to adopt Wallace Stevens's version of the Paterian credo. And fiction, according to Kipling, was written by daemonic forces within us, by "some tragic dividing of forces on their ways." Those forces are no more meaningful than the tales and ballads they produce. What Kipling shares finally with Pater is a deep conviction that we are caught always in a vortex of sensations, a solipsistic concourse of impressions piling upon one another, with great vividness but little consequence.

XII

Kipling's authentic precursor and literary hero was Mark Twain, whose *Huckleberry Finn* and *Tom Sawyer* are reflected inescapably in *Kim*, certainly Kipling's finest achievement. "An Interview with Mark Twain" records Kipling's vision of the two hours of genial audience granted him, starting with Twain's "Well, you think you owe me something, and you've come to tell me so. That's what I call squaring a debt handsomely."

Kim, permanent work as it is, does not square the debt, partly because Kim is, as David Bromwich notes, both Huck Finn and Tom Sawyer, which is to confuse essentially opposed personalities. Since *Kim* is founded upon *Huckleberry Finn*, and not on *Don Quixote*, the mixing of Huck and Tom in Kim's nature brings about a softening of focus that malforms the novel. We cannot find Sancho Panza in Kim, though there is a touch of the Don, as well as of Nigger Jim, in the lama. Insofar as he is free but lonely, Kim is Huck; insofar as he serves the worldly powers, he is Tom. It is striking that in his "Interview with Mark Twain" Kipling expresses interest only in Tom Sawyer, asking Twain "whether we were ever going to hear of Tom Sawyer as a man." I suspect that some anxiety of influence was involved, since *Kim* is the son of the *Adventures of Huckleberry Finn* and not of the lesser novel.

Kim is one of the great instances in the language of a popular adventure story that is also exalted literature. *Huckleberry Finn* is too astonishing a book, too nearly the epic of the American consciousness, together with *Leaves of Grass* and *Moby-Dick,* to be regarded as what it only pretends to be: a good yarn. *Kim* stations itself partly in that mode which ranges from Rider Haggard, at its nadir, to Robert Louis Stevenson, at its zenith: the boy's romance crossing over into the ancient form of romance proper.

There are many splendors in *Kim,* but the greatest is surely the relation between Kim and his master, the lovable, half-mad Tibetan lama, who proves to be Kim's true father, and to whom Kim becomes the best of sons. It is a triumph of the exact representation of profound human affection, rather than a sentimentality of any kind, that can move us to tears as the book ends:

> "Hear me! I bring news! The Search is finished. Comes now the Reward. . . . Thus. When we were among the Hills, I lived on thy strength till the young branch bowed and nigh broke. When we came out of the Hills, I was troubled for thee and for other matters which I held in my heart. The boat of my soul lacked direction; I could not see into the Cause of Things. So I gave thee over to the virtuous woman altogether. I took no food. I drank no water. Still I saw not the Way. They pressed food upon me and cried at my shut door. So I removed myself to a hollow under a tree. I took no food. I took no water. I sat in meditation two days and two nights, abstracting my mind; inbreathing and outbreathing in the required manner. . . . Upon the second night—so great was my reward—the wise Soul loosed itself from the silly Body and went free. This I have never before attained, though I have stood on the threshold of it. Consider, for it is a marvel!"
>
> "A marvel indeed. Two days and two nights without food! Where was the Sahiba?" said Kim under his breath.
>
> "Yea, my Soul went free, and, wheeling like an eagle, saw indeed that there was no Teshoo Lama nor any other soul. As a drop draws to water, so my soul drew near to the Great Soul which is beyond all things. At that point, exalted in contemplation, I saw all Hind, from Ceylon in the sea to the Hills, and my own Painted Rocks at Suchzen; I saw every camp and village, to the least, where we have ever rested. I saw them at one time and in one place; for they were within the Soul. By this I knew the Soul had passed beyond the illusion of Time and Space and of Things. By this I knew that I was free. I saw thee lying in thy cot, and I saw thee falling down hill under the idolater—at one time, in one place, in my Soul, which, as I say, had touched the Great Soul. Also I saw the stupid body of Teshoo Lama lying down, and the *hakim* from Dacca kneeled beside, shouting in its ear. Then my

dark predicate that there is nothing else. The extravagant fiction of the great love between an Irish boy gone native in India, half a Huck Finn enthralled with freedom and half a Tom Sawyer playing games with authority, and a quixotic, aged Tibetan lama is Kipling's finest invention, and moves us endlessly. But how extravagant a fiction it is, and had to be! Kipling refused to profess the faith of those who live and die for and by art, yet in the end he had no other faith.

XIII

E. M. Forster's canonical critic was Lionel Trilling, who might have written Forster's novels had Forster not written them and had Trilling been English. Trilling ended his book on Forster (1924) with the tribute that forever exalts the author of *Howards End* and *A Passage to India* as one of those storytellers whose efforts "work without man's consciousness of them, and even against his conscious will." In Trilling's sympathetic interpretation (or identification), Forster was the true antithesis to the world of telegrams and anger:

> A world at war is necessarily a world of will; in a world at war Forster reminds us of a world where the will is not everything, of a world of true order, of the necessary connection of passion and prose, and of the strange paradoxes of being human. He is one of those who raise the shield of Achilles, which is the moral intelligence of art, against the panic and emptiness which make their onset when the will is tired from its own excess.

Trilling subtly echoed Forster's own response to World War I, a response which Forster recalled as an immersion in Blake, William Morris, the early T. S. Eliot, J. K. Huysmans, Yeats: "They took me into a country where the will was not everything." Yet one can wonder whether Forster and Trilling, prophets of the liberal imagination, did not yield to a vision where there was not quite enough conscious will. *A Passage to India*, Forster's most famous work, can sustain many rereadings, so intricate is its orchestration. It is one of only a few novels of this century that is *written-through*, in the musical sense of thorough composition. But reading it yet again, after twenty years away from it, I find it to be a narrative all of whose principal figures—Aziz, Fielding, Adela Quested, Mrs. Moore, Godbole—lack conscious will. Doubtless, this is Forster's deliberate art, but the consequence is curious; the characters do not sustain rereading so well as the novel does, because none is larger than the book. Poldy holds my imagination quite apart from Joyce's *Ulysses*, as Isabel Archer does in James's *Portrait of a Lady*, or indeed as Mrs. Wilcox does in Forster's *Howards End*, at least while she is represented as being alive. The aesthetic puzzle of *A Passage to India* is why Aziz and Fielding could not have been stronger and more vivid beings than they are.

What matters most in *A Passage to India* is India, and not any Indians nor any English. But this assertion requires amendment, since Forster's India is not so much a social or cultural reality as it is an enigmatic vision of the Hindu religion, or rather of the Hindu religion as it is reimagined by the English liberal mind at its most sensitive and scrupulous. The largest surprise of a careful rereading of *A Passage to India* after so many years is that, in some aspects, it now seems a strikingly *religious* book. Forster shows us what we never ought to have forgotten, which is that any distinction between religious and secular literature is finally a mere political or societal polemic, but is neither a spiritual nor an aesthetic judgment. There is no sacred literature and no post-sacred literature, great or good. *A Passage to India* falls perhaps just short of greatness, in a strict aesthetic judgment, but spiritually it is an extraordinary achievement.

T. S. Eliot consciously strove to be a devotional poet, and certainly did become a Christian polemicist as a cultural and literary critic. Forster, an amiable freethinker and secular humanist, in his *Commonplace Book* admirably compared himself to Eliot:

> With Eliot? I feel now to be as far ahead of him as I was once behind. Always a distance—and a respectful one. How I dislike his homage to pain! What a mind except the human could have excogitated it? Of course there's pain on and off through each individual's life, and pain at the end of most lives. You can't shirk it and so on. But why should it be endorsed by the schoolmaster and sanctified by the priest until
>
> > the fire and the rose are one
>
> when so much of it is caused by disease or by bullies? It is here that Eliot becomes unsatisfactory as a seer.

One could add: it is here that Forster becomes most satisfactory as a seer, for that is the peculiar excellence of *A Passage to India*. We are reminded that Forster is another of John Ruskin's heirs, together with Proust, whom Forster rightly admired above all other modern novelists. Forster too wishes *to make us see*, in the hope that by seeing we will learn to connect, with ourselves and with others, and like Ruskin, Forster knows that seeing in this strong sense is religious, but in a mode beyond dogmatism.

XIV

A Passage to India, published in 1924, reflects Forster's service as private secretary to the Maharajah of Dewas State Senior in 1921–22, which in turn issued from his Indian visit of 1912–13 with G. Lowes Dickinson. It was not until 1953 that Forster published *The Hill of Devi*, utilizing letters he had written home from India both forty and thirty years before. *The Hill of Devi* celebrates Forster's Maharajah as a kind of saint, indeed as a religious genius, though Forster is anything but persuasive when he attempts to sustain his judgment of his friend and employer. What does come through is Forster's appreciation of certain elements in Hinduism, an appreciation that achieves its apotheosis in *A Passage to India,* and particularly in "Temple," the novel's foreshortened final part. Forster's ultimate tribute to his Maharajah, a muddler in practical matters and so one who died in disgrace, is a singular testimony for a freethinker. *The Hill of Devi* concludes with what must be called a mystical apprehension:

> His religion was the deepest thing in him. It ought to be studied— neither by the psychologist nor by the mythologist but by the individual who has experienced similar promptings. He penetrated into rare regions and he was always hoping that others would follow him there.

What are those promptings? Where are those regions? Are these the questions fleshed out by *A Passage to India?* After observing the mystical Maharajah dance before the altar of the God Krishna, Forster quotes from a letter by the Maharajah describing the festival, and then attempts what replies seem possible:

> Such was his account. But what did he feel when he danced like King David before the altar? What were his religious opinions?
> The first question is easier to answer than the second. He felt as King David and other mystics have felt when they are in the mystic state. He presented well-known characteristics. He was convinced that he was in touch with the reality he called Krishna. And he was unconscious of the world around him. "You can come in during my observances tomorrow and see me if you like, but I shall not know that you are there," he once told Malcolm. And he didn't know. He was in an abnormal but recognisable state; psychologists have studied it.
> More interesting, and more elusive, are his religious opinions. The unseen was always close to him, even when he was joking or intriguing. Red paint on a stone could evoke it. Like most people, he implied beliefs and formulated rules for behaviour, and since he had a lively mind, he was often inconsistent. It was difficult to be sure what he did believe (outside the great mystic moments) or what he thought right or wrong. Indians are even more puzzling than Westerners here. Mr. Shastri, a spiritual and subtle Brahmin, once uttered a puzzler: "If the Gods do a thing, it is a reason for men not to do it." No doubt he was in a particular religious mood. In another mood he would have urged us to imitate the Gods. And the Maharajah was all moods. They played over his face, they agitated his delicate feet and hands. To get any pronouncement from so mercurial a creature on the subject, say,

of asceticism, was impossible. As a boy, he had thought of retiring from the world, and it was an ideal which he cherished throughout his life, and which, at the end, he would have done well to practise. Yet he would condemn asceticism, declare that salvation could not be reached through it, that it might be Vedantic but it was not Vedic, and matter and spirit must both be given their due. Nothing too much! In such a mood he seemed Greek.

He believed in the heart, and here we reach firmer ground. "I stand for the heart. To the dogs with the head," cries Herman Melville, and he would have agreed. Affection, or the possibility of it, quivered through everything, from Gokul Ashtami down to daily human relationships. When I returned to England and he heard that I was worried because the post-war world of the '20's would not add up into sense, he sent me a message. "Tell him," it ran, "tell him from me to follow his heart, and his mind will see everything clear." The message as phrased is too facile: doors open into silliness at once. But to remember and respect and prefer the heart, to have the instinct which follows it wherever possible— what surer help than that could one have through life? What better hope of clarification? Melville goes on: "The reason that the mass of men fear God and at bottom dislike Him, is because they rather distrust His heart." With that too he would have agreed.

With all respect for Forster, neither he nor his prince is coherent here, and I suspect that Forster is weakly misreading Melville, who is both more ironic and more Gnostic than Forster chooses to realize. Melville too distrusts the heart of Jehovah and consigns the head to the dogs precisely because he associates the head with Jehovah, and identifies Jehovah with the Demiurge, the god of this world. More vital would be the question: what does Professor Godbole in *A Passage to India* believe? Is he more coherent than the Maharajah, and does Forster himself achieve a more unified vision there than he does in *The Hill of Devi*?

Criticism from Lionel Trilling on has evaded these questions, but such evasion is inevitable because Forster may be vulnerable to the indictment that he himself made against Joseph Conrad, to the effect that

> he is misty in the middle as well as at the edges, that the secret casket of his genius contains a vapour rather than a jewel; and that we need not try to write him down philosophically, because there is, in this particular direction, nothing to write. No creed, in fact. Only opinions, and the right to throw them overboard when facts make them look absurd. Opinions held under the semblance of eternity, girt with the sea, crowned with the stars, and therefore easily mistaken for a creed.

Heart of Darkness sustains Forster's gentle wit, but *Nostromo* does not. Is there a vapor rather than a jewel in Forster's consciousness of Hinduism, at least as represented in *A Passage to India?* "Hinduism" may be the wrong word in that question; "religion" would be better, and "spirituality" better yet. For I do not read Forster as being either hungry for belief or skeptical of it. Rather, he seems to me an Alexandrian, of the third century before the Common Era, an age celebrated in his *Alexandria: A History and a Guide* (1922), a book that goes back to his happy years in Alexandria (1915–19). In some curious sense, Forster's India is Alexandrian, and his vision of Hinduism is Plotinean. *A Passage to India* is a narrative of Neoplatonic spirituality, and the true heroine of that narrative, Mrs. Moore, is the Alexandrian figure of Wisdom, the Sophia, as set forth in the Hellenistic Jewish Wisdom of Solomon. Of Wisdom or Sophia, Forster says: "She is a messenger who bridges the gulf and makes us friends of God," which is a useful description of the narrative function of Mrs. Moore. And after quoting Plotinus (in a passage that includes one of his book's epigraphs): "To any vision must be brought an eye adapted to what is to be seen," Forster comments:

> This sublime passage suggests three comments, with which our glance at Plotinus must close. In the first place its tone is religious, and in this it is typical of all Alexandrian philosophy. In the second place it lays stress on behaviour and training; the Supreme Vision cannot be acquired by magic tricks—only those will see it who are fit to see. And in the third place the vision of oneself and the vision of God are really the same, because each individual *is* God, if only he knew it. And here is the great difference between Plotinus and Christianity. The Christian promise is that a man shall see God, the Neo-Platonic—like the Indian—that he shall be God. Perhaps, on the quays of Alexandria, Plotinus talked with Hindu merchants who came to the town. At all events his system can be paralleled in the religious writings of India. He comes nearer than any other Greek philosopher to the thought of the East.

Forster's Alexandria is in the first place personal; he associated the city always with his sexual maturation as a homosexual. But, as the book *Alexandria* shrewdly shows, Forster finds his precursor culture in ancient Alexandria; indeed he helps to teach us that we are all Alexandrians, insofar as we now live in a literary culture. Forster's insight is massively supported by the historian F. E. Peters in the great study *The Harvest of Hellenism*, when he catalogs our debts to the Eastern Hellenism of Alexandria:

> Its monuments are gnosticism, the university, the catechetical school, pastoral poetry, monasticism, the romance, grammar, lexicography, city planning, theology, canon law, heresy, and scholasticism.

Forster would have added, thinking of the Ptolemaic Alexandria of 331–30 B.C.E., that the most relevant legacy was an eclectic and tolerant liberal humanism, scientific and scholarly, exalting the values of affection over those of belief. That is already the vision of *A Passage to India*, and it opens to the novel's central spiritual question: How are the divine and the human linked? In *Alexandria*, Forster presents us with a clue by his account of the Arian heresy:

> Christ is the Son of God. Then is he not younger than God? Arius held that he was and that there was a period before time began when the First Person of the Trinity existed and the Second did not. A typical Alexandrian theologian, occupied with the favourite problem of linking human and divine, Arius thought to solve the problem by making the link predominately human. He did not deny the Godhead of Christ, but he did make him inferior to the Father—of *like* substance, not of the *same* substance, which was the view held by Athanasius, and stamped as orthodox by the Council of Nicaea. Moreover the Arian Christ, like the Gnostic Demiurge, made the world;—creation, an inferior activity, being entrusted to him by the Father, who had Himself created nothing but Christ.
>
> It is easy to see why Arianism became popular. By making Christ younger and lower than God it brought him nearer to us—indeed it tended to level him into a mere good man and to forestall Unitarianism. It appealed to the untheologically minded, to emperors and even more to empresses. But St. Athanasius, who viewed the innovation with an expert eye, saw that while it popularised Christ it isolated God, and he fought it with vigour and venom. His success has been described. It was condemned as heretical in 325, and by the end of the century had been expelled from orthodox Christendom. Of the theatre of this ancient strife no trace remains at Alexandria; the church of St. Mark where Arius was presbyter has vanished: so have the churches where Athanasius thundered—St. Theonas and the Caesareum. Nor do we know in which street Arius died of epilepsy. But the strife still continues in the hearts of men, who always tend to magnify the human in the divine, and it is probable that many an individual Christian today is an Arian without knowing it.

To magnify the human in the divine is certainly Forster's quest and appears to be his interpretation of Hinduism in *A Passage to India*.

> Down in the sacred corridors, joy had seethed to jollity. It was their duty to play various games to amuse the newly born God, and to simulate his sports with the wanton dairymaids of Brindaban. Butter played a prominent part in these. When the cradle had been removed, the principal nobles of the state gathered together for an innocent frolic. They removed their turbans, and one

put a lump of butter on his forehead, and waited for it to slide down his nose into his mouth. Before it could arrive, another stole up behind him, snatched the melting morsel, and swallowed it himself. All laughed exultantly at discovering that the divine sense of humour coincided with their own. "God is love!" There is fun in heaven. God can play practical jokes upon Himself, draw chairs away from beneath His own posteriors, set His own turbans on fire, and steal His own petticoats when He bathes. By sacrificing good taste, this worship achieved what Christianity has shirked: the inclusion of merriment. All spirit as well as all matter must participate in salvation, and if practical jokes are banned, the circle is incomplete. Having swallowed the butter, they played another game which chanced to be graceful: the fondling of Shri Krishna under the similitude of a child. A pretty red and gold ball is thrown, and he who catches it chooses a child from the crowd, raises it in his arms, and carries it round to be caressed. All stroke the darling creature for the Creator's sake, and murmur happy words. The child is restored to his parents, the ball thrown on, and another child becomes for a moment the World's desire. And the Lord bounds hither and thither through the aisles, chance, and the sport of chance, irradiating little mortals with His im-mortality. . . . When they had played this long enough—and being exempt from boredom, they played it again and again, they played it again and again—they took many sticks and hit them together, whack smack, as though they fought the Pandava wars, and threshed and churned with them, and later on they hung from the roof of the temple, in a net, a great black earthenware jar, which was painted here and there with red, and wreathed with dried figs. Now came a rousing sport. Springing up, they struck at the jar with their sticks. It cracked, broke, and a mass of greasy rice and milk poured on to their faces. They ate and smeared one another's mouths and dived between each other's legs for what had been pashed upon the carpet. This way and that spread the divine mess, until the line of schoolboys, who had somewhat fended off the crowd, broke for their share. The corridors, the courtyard, were filled with benign confusion. Also the flies awoke and claimed their share of God's bounty. There was no quarrelling, owing to the nature of the gift, for blessed is the man who confers it on another, he imitates God. And those "imitations," those "substitutions," continued to flicker through the assembly for many hours, awaking in each man, according to his capacity, an emotion that he would not have had otherwise. No definite image survived; at the Birth it was questionable whether a silver doll or a mud village, or a silk napkin, or an intangible spirit, or a pious resolution, had been born. Perhaps all these things! Perhaps none!

Perhaps all birth is an allegory! Still, it was the main event of the religious year. It caused strange thoughts. Covered with grease and dust, Professor Godbole had once more developed the life of his spirit. He had, with increasing vividness, again seen Mrs. Moore, and round her faintly clinging forms of trouble. He was a Brahman, she Christian, but it made no difference, it made no difference whether she was a trick of his memory or a telepathic appeal. It was his duty, as it was his desire, to place himself in the position of the God and to love her, and to place himself in her position and to say to the God, "Come, come, come, come." This was all he could do. How inadequate! But each according to his own capacities, and he knew that his own were small. "One old Englishwoman and one little, little wasp," he thought, as he stepped out of the temple into the grey of a pouring wet morning. "It does not seem much, still it is more than I am myself."

Professor Godbole's epiphany, his linkage of Mrs. Moore's receptivity toward the wasp with his own receptivity toward Mrs. Moore, has been much admired by critics, deservedly so. In this moment-of-moments, God-bole receives Mrs. Moore into Forster's own faithless faith: a religion of love between equals, as opposed to Christianity, a religion of love between the incommensurate Jehovah and his creatures. But though beautifully executed, Forster's vision of Godbole and Mrs. Moore is spiritually a little too easy. Forster knew that, and the finest moment in *A Passage to India* encompasses this knowing. It comes in a sublime juxtaposition, in the crossing between the conclusion of "Part II: Caves" and the beginning of "Part III: Temple," where Godbole is seen standing in the presence of God. The brief and beautiful chapter 32 that concludes "Caves" returns Fielding to a Western and Ruskinian vision of form in Venice:

Egypt was charming—a green strip of carpet and walking up and down it four sorts of animals and one sort of man. Fielding's business took him there for a few days. He re-embarked at Al-exandria—bright blue sky, constant wind, clean low coast-line, as against the intricacies of Bombay. Crete welcomed him next with the long snowy ridge of its mountains, and then came Venice. As he landed on the piazzetta a cup of beauty was lifted to his lips, and he drank with a sense of disloyalty. The buildings of Venice, like the mountains of Crete and the fields of Egypt, stood in the right place, whereas in poor India everything was placed wrong. He had forgotten the beauty of form among idol temples and lumpy hills; indeed, without form, how can there be beauty? Form stammered here and there in a mosque, became rigid through nervousness even, but oh these Italian churches! San Giorgio standing on the island which could scarcely have risen from the waves without it, the Salute holding the entrance of a canal which, but for it, would not be the Grand Canal! In the old undergraduate days he had wrapped himself up in the many-coloured blanket of St. Mark's, but something more precious than mosaics and marbles was offered to him now: the harmony between the works of man and the earth that upholds them, the civilization that has escaped muddle, the spirit in a reasonable form, with flesh and blood subsisting. Writing picture post-cards to his Indian friends, he felt that all of them would miss the joys he experienced now, the joys of form, and that this constituted a serious barrier. They would see the sumptuousness of Venice, not its shape, and though Venice was not Europe, it was part of the Mediterranean harmony. The Mediterranean is the human norm. When men leave that exquisite lake, whether through the Bosphorus or the Pillars of Hercules, they approach the monstrous and extraordinary; and the southern exit leads to the strangest experience of all. Turning his back on it yet again, he took the train northward, and tender romantic fancies that he thought were dead for ever, flowered when he saw the buttercups and daisies of June.

After the muddle of India, where "everything was placed wrong," Fielding learns again "the beauty of form." Alexandria, like Venice, is part of the Mediterranean harmony, the human norm, but India is the cosmos of "the monstrous and extraordinary." Fielding confronting the Venetian churches has absolutely nothing in common with Professor Godbole confronting the God Krishna at the opposite end of the same strip of carpet upon which Godbole stands. Forster is too wise not to know that the passage to India is only a passage. A passage is a journey, or an occurrence between two persons. Fielding and Aziz do not quite make the passage together, do not exchange vows that bind. Perhaps that recognition of limits is the ultimate beauty of form in *A Passage to India*.

William Morris:
The World beyond the World

Carole Silver

William Morris's last romances, *The Story of the Glittering Plain*, *The Wood beyond the World*, *Child Christopher and Goldilind the Fair*, *The Well at the World's End*, *The Water of the Wondrous Isles*, and *The Sundering Flood* are journeys to worlds beyond the ordinary world in search of love and fellowship. Designed as much for the socialist utopia of the future as they are for Morris's own unregenerate age, they represent Nowherian ideals of art; they are tales to be depicted on the walls of the communal dining halls of Nowhere or to be told around the fireplace of a rejuvenated Kelmscott Manor. Their objectivity, fantasy, and vitality are qualities Nowherians would enjoy, and their sources, derived from the "Bibles . . . of the people" and the romance tradition of the Middle Ages, are those Nowherians would appreciate.

Even the themes of Morris's final romances are rooted in the ideology of Nowhere, for all the works trace the movement from individual alienation and social discord to union, harmony, and reconciliation. Yet, Morris emphasizes new aspects of this process. Employing the pattern of the quest, long a favorite vehicle for his ideas, but perhaps made more significant to him by his translation of Homer's *Odyssey* in 1887, Morris increasingly explores the problem of human maturation, the drama of spiritual death and rebirth, and the psychic miracle of the integration of the personality. Weaving together his literary, social, artistic, and psychological concerns, Morris makes of his last romances fascinating webs of much that he had felt and of much that he had read.

Morris was, first of all, an exceptionally knowledgeable reader of medieval romance, a literary genre he had loved since his Oxford days and had richly utilized in such poems as *The Earthly Paradise*. In addition to

From *The Romance of William Morris*. © 1982 by Carole Silver. Ohio University Press, 1982.

translating romances for his own use, he had written a redaction of *Havelock the Dane* and, in 1892 and 1893, translated and published a group of *Old French Romances*. Along with perennial favorites like *Le Morte D'Arthur*, *Amadis of Gaul*, *Parzifal*, and *Sir Gawain and the Green Knight*, Morris knew and owned such medieval works as *Joseph of Arimathea*, *The History of the Holy Grail*, *Percival le Gaulois*, *Palmerin of England*, *Sir Eger and Grime*, *Lancelot du Lac*, *Le Chevalier de la Tour Landry*, *Le Chevalier Bayard*, *Ogier le Danois*, *Amadis et Ydoine*, *Houon de Bordeaux*, *Tristram de Lyones*, and *The Romance of Alexander*. He possessed important compilations of romance materials such as Lady Charlotte Guest's *Mabinogion*, Bishop Percy's *Folio Manuscript*, Ritson's *Ancient English Metrical Romances*, Weber's *Metrical Romances*, Hunt's *Popular Romances of the West of England*, Ashton's *Romances of Chivalry*, and Joyce's *Old Celtic Romances*.

His equally rich knowledge of the "Bibles . . . of the people" has already been examined [elsewhere]. These works, as previously mentioned, included ancient epics, myths, legends, and folk tales—many of which had become part of the romance tradition. Familiar, as well, with the important scholarly studies of mythology and folklore both previous to and current in his era, Morris considered Jacob and Wilhelm Grimm's *Teutonic Mythology* among his "Bibles," and greatly admired such works as John Brand's *Observations on Popular Antiquities*, Lady Wilde's *Ancient Legends, Mystic Charms, and Superstitions of Ireland*, and Eugene O'Curry's *On the Manners and Customs of the Ancient Irish* with its notes by W. K. Sullivan. He used other important scholarly works as "tools." Although he does not always mention their titles, he employs incidents and descriptions drawn from them. In addition, Morris's last romances show his awareness of still other major studies—a knowledge derived either through reviews and critical articles about them or through volumes he did own and read. In all, Morris was fully cognizant of the various theoretical methods and systems which attempted to demonstrate the interconnections among history, myth, folklore, literature, and life.

Morris was, however, especially interested in the emerging disciplines of comparative mythology and cultural anthropology which sought to explain the origin, transmission, and significance of myth, folklore, and romance. His thorough grasp of Max Müller's philological and etymological method, and of Müller's thesis that all myth is solar has already been documented. His agreement with the Grimms' treatment of folklore and fairy tale as important survivals of a great Indo-European mythological system is manifested both in his admiration for *Teutonic Mythology* and in his use, in the last romances, of materials drawn from it. A knowledge of the euhemeristic approach to mythology, utilized in his era by two of his heroes, Carlyle and Ruskin, may be assumed—since he had read virtually all their works—and his awareness of Ruskin's and Pater's aesthetic and humanistic approaches to the analysis of myth (demonstrated by such works as Ruskin's *Queen of the Air* [1869] and Pater's *Greek Studies* [1875–89] is equally apparent.

The final romances, however, reveal a fact which is less evident: Morris was cognizant of the new interpretations of myth and folklore which were flowering in the last quarter of the nineteenth century. Lewis H. Morgan's views of the life and beliefs of the ancient world, as described in *Ancient Society* (1877), had shaped Morris's ideas about the heroic peoples; E. B. Tylor's comparative method, demonstrated by his major work, *Primitive Culture* (1871), and Tylor's thesis that cultures pass through the same stages of development so that one may study modern primitive societies to understand ancient civilizations, had influenced both Andrew Lang, Morris's acquaintance and admirer, and Morris himself. Lang, in such books as *Custom and Myth* (1884), was interpreting ancient materials by comparing them to rituals employed in contemporary primitive societies. Challenging Müller's solar thesis, Lang was also seeking the roots of myth in vegetative and fertility cults, again influencing Morris. And, whether Morris knew James George Frazer's *Golden Bough* (1890) through Andrew Lang, through reviews of the work, or directly, he employs themes and descriptions clearly derived from Frazer in his own final works of art.

Even the language of Morris's last romances, though often attacked as quasi-archaic and unreadable "Wardour Street" English, is partially a result of his study of the past. It is his attempt to capture the qualities of the prose of epic and romance. Imitating more than the "whiloms" and "nonces" of medieval English, Morris tries to recreate what for him was the rich word-building and freshness of the language before it became merely "a dialect of French." Believing that if the English "could only have preserved our language as the Germans have theirs . . . we . . . would have made the world richer than it is now," he utilizes the complex syntax and archaic vocabulary he associates with Anglo-Saxon poetry, Icelandic saga, and the work of Chaucer and his predecessors. Although Morris's archaisms are sometimes pure inventions and the syntax of his sentences is sometimes obscure, his unique language serves an important aesthetic function in the final romances. Initially difficult to comprehend, it pulls the reader away from the words and objects of a modern, commercial society, gradually drawing him into the remote world of which it is a manifestation. Furthermore, words selected by Morris primarily for their connotative or root meanings become memorable. Because the reader is forced to analyze linguistic meaning, he must progress slowly; thus, he becomes aware of the romances' symbolic intentions and begins to participate in their events.

What is most significant about the ways in which Morris manipulates language and utilizes manifold and varied source materials is how they enhance his private vision. For, while Morris analyzes and interprets the sources he uses in varied ways, according to the theoretical structure he is following, he is always concerned with the same interlocking mythic patterns. Thus, he depicts the "green world" of medieval romance, but places within it groups living in various stages of social evolution or moving from savagery to barbarism or civilization, as described by anthropologists like Morgan or Tylor. For the structure of his plots, he utilizes the pattern of the quest, derived from epic and romance and from his contemporaries' analyses of them; for his major characters, he draws upon the conventions of romance and upon the speculations of his era as to their nature. Assimilating a remarkable range of source materials, utilizing them without pedantry or self-consciousness, Morris creates a new personal and social mythology for himself and for his audience.

The framework of Morris's final romances is the world depicted according to ancient and medieval romance conventions, a realm in which the ordinary laws of nature are slightly rather than radically suspended. Morris's basic terrain is the woodland and forest, well supplied with castles and hermitages, and broken, occasionally, by small medieval towns or larger (and almost always evil) cities. Morris's world includes false paradises, places of illusion and artifice where the hero may be trapped, natural valleys and gardens of love and education, and realms of negation symbolized by wastelands. Blue Calhoun, analyzing the landscape of the romances, describes how Morris evaluates different views of nature and natural life by moving from the simple pastoral setting, through the supernatural complexity of the wilderness and the sophisticated complexity of the city, back to the idyllic pastoral. Morris's convictions as a socialist and as a romancer coalesce in his preference for places where nature requires that man must work. His beliefs again merge in his depiction of cities which manifest the evils of capitalism and of small Nowherian communities which are filled with the spirit of the golden age.

Yet the world of the last romances is animistic, full of elemental spirits, not all of whom are benevolent. The evil witches, wise old men and crones, saintly hermits and fairy folk common to the genre of romance are present. In addition, savages, barbarians, and civilized men fill the landscape. Abandoning the essentially historical treatment of "upper barbarism" he had employed in *The House of the Wolfings* and *The Roots of the Mountains*, Morris turns to depicting anthropologically identifiable groups at various levels of social development coexisting within the same imaginary time and place. Using anthropological sources mythically and psychologically, he demonstrates how cultures in various stages of growth may aid or injure each other.

The heroes of the final romances also demonstrate the fusion of many strands of Morris's thought, for they are drawn from the romance tradition, the nineteenth-century idea of the cultural hero, and the Morgan-Engels description of the ideal upper barbarian. Essentially, they are modeled upon the simplified, idealized figures of medieval romance, men superior to others not in kind but in degree, yet they are not of aristocratic birth or lineage. Clearly manifesting his socialist sensibilities, Morris makes Walter, in *The Wood beyond the World*, merely the son of a merchant and Osberne, in *The Sundering Flood*, the child of a freeholder. Ralph, in *The Well at the World's End*, is the figure highest in rank, but he is only the youngest of the four sons of a minor ruler. All the heroes are strong and courageous warriors who joust, battle, and rescue damsels in the best medieval manner. Yet, they fight only when they deem it necessary to preserve their lives or those of others. Their courage is coupled with humility and wisdom, and they have often been educated in these values by supernatural figures. They themselves are not divine or even demi-gods; instead, they are culture heroes, figures who represent the highest ideals of their given social groups. Like the culture heroes described by John Rhys in his *Lectures on the Origin and Growth of Religion as Illustrated by Celtic Heathendom* (1888), Morris's heroes add to their anonymous or obscure parentage courage in war, wisdom, and "creative powers." The mothering or fathering force of imagination is theirs.

In this way, they show their cultural inheritance of the best qualities of "upper barbarism," even when, like Ralph, they are nominally Christian. They retain the simplicity, vitality, and sense of duty to home and kindred of the barbaric peoples; they have the barbarians' sense of their correct role in a rightfully constituted group, and they possess, as well, that barbaric inheritance which Morris believed would again blossom in the future: "that higher form of conscience that would impel . . . [men] to action on behalf of the future of the race."

But the heroes must leave their groups; as culture heroes, all are wanderers journeying on quests for life-giving goals. Their quests are richly symbolic, and Morris derives the structure, imagery, and symbolism of the journey from many sources: the bridequests seem drawn from folklore, the *Mabinogion,* and ancient epic and saga; the grailquests from the Sangraal romances he knew and admired. Devising a series of journeys whose goals are the bride, the grail, or both, Morris dismisses the alternative aims of questers—treasure and empire—as unworthy of socialists. Instead the goals of his journeys are happiness through wisdom and love, and the quests are metaphors for the process of regeneration. Whether they are land journeys or *imrama*—the sea-voyages of Celtic legend—their stages follow the same basic pattern and the experiences within them constitute what Joseph Campbell calls "the monomyth of the hero" (*The Hero with a Thousand Faces*). F. A. C. Wilson, in analyzing the structure of the quest in *The Well at the World's End* [in his study of *Yeats's Iconography*], virtually describes the basic design of all the last romances. All Morris's heroes are called to adventure, sometimes by a vision, as in *The Wood beyond the World,* or by a rumor, as in *The Well at the World's End,* or by a direct challenge to them or their loved ones. Leaving the world of common day, they enter a supernatural realm; here, they undergo their "Katabasis" or initiation by ordeal. Separated from others, they undergo the experience of evil and the confrontation with death. Hallblithe, in *The Story of the Glittering Plain,* must voyage to the Isle of Ransom: Birdalone, the female hero of *The Water of the Wondrous Isles,* must encounter the ordeals imposed on her at several of the islands; Golden Walter must traverse the varied dangers of *The Wood beyond the World.*

All the male heroes survive their initiation by ordeal to encounter the Virgin—often a figure for both the Great Mother and the anima in Morris's romances—and to free the pure anima and emanation who is the female part of their soul. The women (or, in the case of Birdalone, the men) with whom they unite are the images of their marriage with self and of their union with the life-force. The bride *is* the grail, even in *The Well at the World's End,* where the objects of the quest are ostensibly twofold; the quests always culminate in success. When the hero and his anima unite, what Charlotte Oberg calls "the pattern of separation and isolation ended by union and generation" is not yet complete. The lovers do not live in isolation but return, instead, to the world to exercise the widsom and grace they have gained. They may discover and rule a new society as in *The Wood beyond the World,* create their own utopian community as in *The Water of the Wondrous Isles,* or simply return to their pastoral homes. Wherever they end their journey, they bring to their final residence both personal and societal regeneration.

While all of Morris's last romances follow the pattern outlined above, they are richly various in incident and setting. They do not replicate each other in the emphases they place on stages in the pattern of the quest or on specific major themes. Instead, each romance may be thought of as representing Morris's last words on an issue that has preoccupied him throughout his literary career. Thus, *The Story of the Glittering Plain* contains Morris's final repudiation of escape, while the literary works which follow it illustrate Morris's metamorphoses of the figure of the dark anima, his increased understanding of the nature of erotic passion, and the many facets of his vision of the world rejuvenated through the individual, male and female, reborn to new heroic stature.

I

The Story of the Glittering Plain, or the Land of Living Men is Morris's final study of the human desire to avoid the limitations imposed by age and death by finding an earthly paradise in which the golden age survives intact. In the romance, Morris returns to the motifs he had first explored in "The Hollow Land" and *The Defence* volume and had fully developed in *Jason* and in the "Prologue" and a number of the tales of *The Earthly Paradise.* Yet, in *The Glittering Plain,* the drive for such escape is unambivalently condemned and the alternative to it—life working for and in the purely human world—is roundly praised.

Published in 1891, *The Glittering Plain* is closest in theme, detail, and heroic tone to the historical romances of the 1880s. However, the world of the romance is no longer that of an identifiable place or time. The people Morris describes resemble the Norse and some dwell in lands reminiscent of Iceland, but the work is as much influenced by Celtic folklore as by Norse saga. Morris derives elements of his story from the tales of "Connla of the

Golden Hair" and "Oisin in Tirnanoge," as retold in P. W. Joyce's *Old Celtic Romances* (1879) and from O'Curry's account of the Druid Dallan's rescue of Queen Edain from the earthly paradise of the fairies. Perhaps speculating on the historical connections between the Norse and the Irish, Morris makes his hero, Hallblithe, a member of a northern gens, the House of the Raven, and Hallblithe's betrothed, the Hostage, a member of another gens "wherein it was right and due that the men of the Raven should wed," but sets some of the book's action in a realm drawn from Irish legend. When the Hostage is kidnapped by Vikings, Hallblithe embarks on a quest to find and free her. Seeking her first on the Isle of Ransom, a land described as an underworld and modeled on Iceland, he next journeys to a terrestrial Eden, patterned after Tir-na-mbeo, "The Land of the Living" visited by Oisin and Connla.

The quest in *The Story of the Glittering Plain* leads from an ideal pastoral home through a realm of death to a paradise exposed as false and, finally, back to home. Hallblithe—the hearty spirit of his House—must triumph over the forces that oppose life and natural fertility, but are disguised as their counterparts. Again utilizing the bridequest, Morris further develops the motif he had employed in "Rapunzel," "The Land East of the Sun," and *Love Is Enough,* concentrating even more explicitly on how the hero finds himself through the search for a fulfilling woman. The romance is essentially a *Bildungsroman,* an account of how Hallblithe, in maturing, learns to separate appearances from realities.

In search of his beloved, Hallblithe must leave Cleveland by the Sea, a natural land where things are as they seem, and journey to the Isle of Ransom, a "land of lies." Hallblithe's first initiation by ordeal occurs in Ransom, after an almost classic descent to the underworld. The island, a realm of black-robed figures, strange rituals, and false values, can be approached only through a dangerous underground cave. Modeled on those aspects of Iceland which, during his journey of 1871, became for Morris the symbols of the bare and terrible in life, Ransom contains high mountains, glacial rocks, and a wasteland of black volcanic sand marked only by a few dwarfed, wind-bitten trees. Like the Iceland of Morris's day, it lies beyond the edge of the ordinary world and suggests experience beyond the norm. Like the Iceland of Morris's mind—before the restorative journey of 1873—it is a place of despair and death which must be confronted and finally conquered.

Puny-Fox, Hallblithe's guide, honored among the Ransomers as "chief liar," subjects Hallblithe to a series of trials, deserting him in the wilderness and subjecting him to tests of silence and self-control. Only when Hallblithe has proved himself, may he resume his journey. But he is sent on a false quest, that of accompanying Sea-Eagle, a dying chieftain, to the land of the Glittering Plain. The Plain or "the Land of Living Men" is the other half of Morris's psychological underworld and the second site of Hallblithe's initiation. Ruled by an immortal king, called the "Glittering Plain" because its unchanging sun shines even in the depths of winter, this "Acre of the Undying" is a terrestrial Eden in all externals:

> A land of youth, a land of rest,
> A land from sorrow free;
> It lies far off in the golden west,
> On the verge of the azure sea.

But Hallblithe learns to see and, thus, to reject the land for its internal flaws: exclusivity, sloth, and false eroticism.

Those who enter the land regain their youth and are granted personal immortality. But only the few (the oldest chiefs of the Ransomers) may go and, of these, some refuse. Not seeking to separate their fates from those of their people, the best of the chieftains prefer death and a return to the earth to the death in life the Glittering Plain actually offers. For, once on its shores, men lose their memories of the past, forgetting kinsmen, deeds, and communal responsibilities. The Plain, however benevolent it appears, is in reality a tyranny, in which the old structures and customs of the gentes have been abrogated; it offers its inhabitants an existence devoid of adventure and even of change. Lacking both the natural processes of growth and decay and the external goads to action, it lures men to sloth, a vice, which to Morris the socialist is as insidious as exclusivity. Hallblithe learns that the "plenty and peace and good will and pleasure without cease" within the borders of this Lotos Land are goods whose price is the relinquishment of manhood and duty.

But the lack that Hallblithe finds most troubling is the absence of the correct variety of love. The Glittering Plain is filled with beautiful and eager women; it permits spontaneous relationships and promises the fulfillment of desire. The ladies of the land are revealed as sirens, made for pleasure only, and its princess, condemned to unrequited love, is shown as born to grieve. Hallblithe rejects them all. Not only are they not of the Houses into which he may wed, but they seem to him alien to "the old laws of marriage" in which he believes. With them, he cannot find the friendly love which must be the basis of a true union of body and soul. He is never even really tempted to forget the woman he considers his appropriate and rightful bride.

After Hallblithe has confronted death, rejected immortality in a realm devoid of fellowship, and repudiated inappropriate erotic passion, he is free to seek and find the Hostage. Returning to the Isle of Ransom, he rescues her through his truthfulness and the constancy of his love. When he publicly admits that his victory over the Ransomers' champion has been based on fraud, he moves his hosts to help him. When he rejects the beautiful maidens offered to him, he convinces the Ransomers to restore his bride. Demonstrating the strength of his values to his hosts, he begins to reform them. Once he has infused his civilizing power into their culture, he may return, with his bride and his blood brother, Puny-Fox, to the ordinary land of normal life, Cleveland by the Sea. There, where "men die when their hour comes . . . and they [the hours] are long enough for the doing of deeds that shall not die," he may wed the Hostage amid promises of good and fertile life to come.

Thus, Morris, through his account of Hallblithe's experiences, offers a final statement on the matter of the earthly paradise. Showing that "the quest for immortality ends in living death and that true life is experienced only through acquiescence to natural process," he drives home the point he had announced in his earlier works. Though, as in *Jason* and *The Earthly Paradise*, he reveals his understanding of the human urge to avoid the limitations of mortality, he no longer sees escape as even mildly tempting or attractive. Like Hallblithe, Morris seeks "no dream but rather, the end of dreams," finding man's true life in participation in the joys, sorrows, and struggles of the mortal world. For Morris, man's role lies in improving himself, others, and the world in which he lives, in accepting his death as life's just end, and in finding his immortality in"the continuous life of the world of men" and of the world of nature.

While *The Story of the Glittering Plain* emphasizes the problems one faces in choosing the correct mode of human life, *The Wood beyond the World*, begun in 1891 and published in 1894, concentrates on the issue of differentiating between appearance and reality in selecting the correct partner in romantic love. Having effectively dealt with man's need to accept the processes of change and death, Morris moves to what to him seemed the more complex question of the constructive and destructive aspects of erotic passion. Like *The Glittering Plain*, *The Wood beyond the World* is structured as a bridequest. Again, Morris depicts a hero undergoing trial and temptation and eventually moving from falsehood to truth and from death to life as he obtains union with the virgin who is his soul. Following the strategy of *The Glittering Plain*, Morris keeps his canvas small, emphasizing the fortunes of a few individuals whom he names symbolically and characterizes archetypally. Morris's recognition that he is using archetypal figures and his clear depiction of them is already evident in such characters as the Friend and the Bride in *The Roots of the Mountains* and in the Hostage of *The Glittering Plain*. But the depiction of all the major characters as archetypes differentiates *The Wood beyond the World* from its predecessors among the romances. The intensification of archetypal figures and patterns in this romance may have been due to Morris's increased contact with the contents of his subconscious mind—the last romances were written during his bouts of insomnia—to the aging artist's impulse to universalize his fictions, or to his readings in comparative mythology which emphasized the pervasiveness and underlying similarity of seemingly disparate deities and culture heroes. Whatever the causes, types, especially female archetypes, dominate the romance.

The hero and heroine of *The Wood beyond the World*, Golden Walter and the Maid, though not dissimilar to Hallblithe and the Hostage in appearance and actions, are even more reduced to their central and essential characteristics. Golden Walter, so named to associate him with the brightness of the sun (perhaps as a vestigial tribute to Max Müller's solar theory), is the only figure in the book who bears a Christian name. The others are designated by their characteristics and functions. The Maid's name connotes her magical virginity and her condition of servitude, the Lady's name indicates her roles as goddess, witch, and ruler of the wood beyond the world. The King's Son is the Lady's royal, if temporary, consort and a child both in terms of his maturity and of her power. The Dwarf, a Browning-esque Caliban, is a representative of the primitive, demonic forces in the world.

The most striking figures in the romance are the two women with whom Golden Walter becomes erotically involved. Each is an aspect of his inner self; the Lady is his dark anima, the Maid, his pure anima or emanation. Each is envisioned in terms of fertility and vegetative power, for, deriving the connections from the Grimms, Lang, and Frazer, Morris links human sexuality and the processes of nature. Indeed, beyond its general similarity to folklore, *The Wood beyond the World* specifically resembles *The Golden Bough*. Like Frazer's book, Morris's romance is a quest in search of the explanations of a mystery. Like *The Golden Bough*, it begins with a re-enactment of a ritual of love, pain, and death, while each of the two women between whom the hero is caught is eventually revealed as an aspect of one goddess, the Great Mother. At the beginning of Morris's romance, Golden Walter finds himself involved in a mysterious rite of fertility and death, for his first meeting in the woods is with an old man who functions as a Frazerian priest of Nemi. The old man describes his former participation in a bloody ritual, telling Walter that he has slain his predecessor and supplanted him in order to possess the Lady. His warnings, that evil has come of his act, and that he too would have been killed (were it not for the Maid), are meant to discourage Walter from entering the forbidden precincts of the valley. But Walter, called to adventure by a vision of the Lady, feels compelled to explore the mystery. He too is almost lured to his death, for the Lady wishes him to kill and replace the King's Son as her consort. She will, in turn, eventually tire of Walter and persuade her next male victim to destroy him.

Walter's first series of ordeals ensues partially from his initial failure to clearly ascertain the meaning and goal of his quest. He is in search of the wrong woman. The Lady he believes he is seeking is only a more potent version of the cruel and unchaste wife from whom he is in flight. Not a man whom all women love, Walter has already married and been betrayed:

When they had been wedded some six months he found by manifest tokens, that his fairness was not so much to her, but that she must seek to the foulness of one worser in all ways; wherefore his rest departed from him, whereas he hated her for her untruth and her hatred of him, yet would the sound of her voice . . . make his heart beat; and the sight of her stirred desire within him, so that he longed for her to be sweet and kind with him, and deemed that, might it be so, he should forget all the evil gone by.

Walter is as attracted to the Lady as he had been to his wife and equally unable to see her true nature. The Lady, however, is more powerful and seductive than an ordinary mortal woman. She is an Acrasia, modeled on Spenser's character, luring men to her artificial Bowre of Bliss and leaving them dishonored and destroyed. More significantly, she is a passionate and cruel fertility figure whose love demands the shedding of blood, a Diana of Nemi who represents the fearsome aspects of the Great Mother. She is described both as Diana, appearing garbed like "the hunting-goddess of the Gentiles" in a tunic and sandals, with a bow and arrows slung across her back, and as the carnal Venus, arising from the bed of love, clothed only in her flowing golden hair. Hunting or loving, men are her prey. Her wantonness, "a disordered abundance like that of weedy places," is a form of natural fertility run wild.

At first, unable to break the masochistic pattern of his past, Walter succumbs to the Lady. When he is overpowered by his mixed passion and fear, he yields to her advances. But he is not destroyed, for, aided by the Maid, he begins to purge the elements within him which have prevented him from loving appropriately and from integrating his psyche. The Maid, his pure anima, represents the creative life-giving aspects of the Great Mother. Her potency, like the Lady's, is that of a nature goddess, but she is associated with the Maiden Korê and her magic powers depend on her remaining chaste. Employing both her supernatural and her human powers, she destroys the Lady and the King's Son and leads Walter out of "the wilderness fruitful of evil."

In the realm through which she takes him, she must employ her power as a fertility figure, for the two—friends but not lovers—must pass through the valley of the People of the Bear. The Bear tribesmen are enormous figures, larger and stronger than civilized men, ignorant of iron weapons and even of the bow, and dressed only in the skins of beasts. They have evolved to what Morgan and Engels categorize as "middle savagery," worshipping an Ancient Mother of Tribes to whom they offer human sacrifices. Using only their primitive bone and flint tools, they have built a doom-ring and an altar to their goddess. Since they have worshipped the Lady as her incarnation, they must be persuaded by the Maid that she, not the Lady, is "the new body" of their "God." Thus, she appears to them as Korê or Demeter, clothed in a flower-bedecked gown. When they demand proof of her powers, she makes the faded blossoms that adorn her bloom again. Like Frazer's May Spirit or May Queen, she manifests herself as the "Mother of Summer," a vegetative force who can send rain from the mountains to make the earth bear fruit and whose very footsteps on the meadows will make them thrive. Though virgin, she is the bringer of fecundity, "the very heart of the year's increase." Serving as an Isis figure or civilizer, she issues new edicts which will raise the Bears from savagery to ideal barbarism. No longer are they to practice the customs of slaying all aliens or offering them as sacrifices to the Great Mother. Instead, they are to adopt into their tribe the strong and worthy and to enthrall only the weak or degenerate among their captives. The Maid's final gift to the People of the Bear assures their gradual evolution to "upper barbarism"; she sends them iron tools, seed corn, and the men to educate them in the art of tillage.

Only after this second set of trials do the Maid and Golden Walter find the realm in which they are to live. Still led by the Maid, Walter sees from afar the land of Stark Wall. By arriving from the hills where local legend indicates the people's tribal heritage began, by being unflawed in body, and by selecting the correct role in life—symbolized by his choice of the worn battle garb of deeds as opposed by the opulent robes of peace—Walter becomes the ruler of the land. The Maid's work done, she may renounce her chastity and magic and become, as Walter's bride, a fully mortal woman. When Walter consummates his friendly love with the Maid, he achieves union with his anima. Thus, he becomes a whole man, ready to transmit his wisdom to a new society. The type of the good king, he creates within Stark Wall a realm of justice and mercy based on the finest aspects of barbarism. The ultimate fruit of the personal love of Walter and the Maid is a kingdom rooted in fellowship and growing toward utopia.

To explore the problem of escape in *The Story of the Glittering Plain* and to examine the nature of love in *The Wood beyond the World*, Morris synthesizes elements derived from his own psyche, the romance tradition, myth and its study, and socialist doctrine. Morris creates an especially powerful amalgam of these in *The Wood beyond the World*. From his subconscious mind comes the projection of submerged parts of himself as benign and malign female figures. Reinforced by the experiences of his life, these figures emerge as images of the sexually unfaithful wife-mistress and the loving friend who becomes the ideal beloved. Following the tradition of medieval romance, in which life may be viewed as a quest for love, the same female figures are metamorphosed into those of the enchantress, who must be defeated, and the maiden, who must be rescued and wed. Through the mythological and folkloric motives embedded in romance, the hero becomes the representative of the force, be it solar or cultural, which undergoes the processes of birth and death through an encounter with a dual-natured goddess who is the symbol of the earth. A successful encounter leads, in Morris's socialist view, to the hero's return to and rejuvenation of the ordinary world. Ideal erotic love helps forge an ideal world, for the integrated man can transform his private passion into acts of general benevolence.

Morris enriches these patterns, through variation and expansion, in the next of the romances, *The Well at the World's End*. No longer seeing the feminine components of the self in the form of two opposing figures, he creates a female character whose dichotomous nature incorporates the qualities of each. Developing his social theme, he broadens his focus to describe the rise, fall, and rebirth of a series of communities. Depicting an entire imaginary world, he demonstrates how the power of human love transforms both those who share it and the realms through which they pass.

II

Written between 1892 and 1894 and published in 1895, *The Well at the World's End*, Morris's most elaborate and detailed romance, is again structured as a bridequest. Beginning with the *enfance* of the hero and depicting his education through preliminary adventures and ordeals, the romance carefully develops the twofold pattern of a search: first, for an appropriate woman and the love she represents; second, for the secular grail of the well at the end of the world. The romance centers on the triumph of the hero once he has passed through temptation, a confrontation with death, and the experience of rebirth. Significantly, however, *The Well at the World's End* concentrates as much on the societal aspects of life as it does on the destinies of individuals, showing the hero's impact on his world after the integration of his personality. Filling a huge canvas, Morris shapes a myth about the connections between romantic love and communal fellowship and demonstrates how both are forces which can conquer evil and, thus, redeem the earth.

The characters and incidents in the romance are derived from such disparate sources as the Grimms and Frazer, the medieval romances of Alexander and of the holy grail, Celtic folklore, and contemporary adventure tales like Rider Haggard's *She*. While *The Well at the World's End* is not allegorical, it is a "romance of types," in which sections of pure narrative are interspersed with symbolic incidents and descriptions. A "stream of conscious symbolic intention" runs through the work, as images of the inner life are projected by means of the exterior world. One of the main sources of the romance is autobiography; much of the inner life depicted in it is Morris's own—distilled into fiction. Like *News from Nowhere, The Well at the World's End* obliquely depicts Morris's feelings and experiences, here, his childhood joy, his somewhat aimless and frustrated youth, his rejection of the ministry, his call to social activism, and the problems of his twofold love: initially, for a fatal woman who brings both joy and sorrow; later, for a friend who becomes his love and finer spirit. Though Ralph, the hero of the romance, is a man all women love and, thus, something of a compensatory figure for Morris, he displays a number of his creator's essential traits—bluntness, rapid shifts of mood, a passionate love of the world of nature, and a concern with political and economic justice.

Morris's own preoccupations with social evolution and revolution are embodied in Ralph's travels to various lands, many of them countries of the mind. Ralph moves from the pastoral world of Upmeads, modeled on Kelmscott Manor and its neighboring villages, through cities, the places of corruption which reflect Morris's hatred of Victorian London, through the realms of romance, the forest and the wasteland—the latter derived from the Iceland Morris perceived on his 1871 sojourn—and then to the place of reward, an Iceland transformed by the journey of 1873. Not content with depicting the attainment of the goal, Morris shows how Ralph, on his return trip to his home, witnesses or aids in the rejuvenation of the societies through which he passes.

Upmeads, Ralph's first and final home in this circular romance, is one of the most tenderly depicted of Morris's peaceable kingdoms. A medievalized Nowhere by which all other communities are measured, it is a land of simple living, firmly independent people, whose rulers have "but scant dominion save over their horses and dogs." Although Ralph, leaving Upmeads in search of adventure, is attracted to Higham-on-the-Way because of its wealth, culture, and well developed guild system, he is repelled by its theocratic rule and by the priestly vocation itself. In terms reminiscent of Morris, Ralph observes that those who choose the church do so not because they find the world lacking, but because it finds them so. His rejection of Higham and priesthood leads him to the Wood Perilous, the green world threatened, and to the Burg of the Four Friths. A capitalistic tyranny built on slavery, the Burg exploits its female captives, the Wheatwearers. These beautiful women lack all legal and personal rights and are forced to serve as laborers or are purchased as concubines. Yet, even the Burg's free citizens are not truly so; they cannot openly criticize their government or buy and bear weapons. Corrupted by the system under which they live, they resent Ralph's "manly bearing," "free tongue," and hatred of "cruel deeds and injustice" and force him to flee the city.

Ralph next enters the magic realm of the Land of Abundance, a beautiful place of fertility and propagation, though one not devoid of their darker aspects. Abundance must be left behind, however, and, grieving at the loss of love, Ralph must confront the land of Whitewall. Imaginatively depicting England gone wrong, Morris shows how the countryside of Whitewall has been deformed. Ralph cannot even locate a yeoman's cottage or farmer's house; all dwellings are either the manorial estates of the rich or the foul slave barracks and "long rows of ugly hovels" of the impoverished laborers. Goldburg, whose name connotes its dedication to Mammon as well as its role as the chief mercantile and commercial city of Whitewall, is still more diseased. In a city that is "half marble and half slums," the sumptuous houses of the rich are juxtaposed with the miserable hovels of the poor, while the "two nations" live in mutual enmity. The poor lack even the care that Scott's Garth the thrall received from Cedric the Saxon:

> They belong not to a master, who must at worst feed them, and
> to no manor, whose acres they might till for their livelihood, and

on whose pastures they might feed their cattle; nor had they any to help or sustain them against the oppressor and the violent man; so that they toiled and swinked and died with none heeding them, save that they had the work of their hands good cheap; and they forsooth heeded them less than their draught beasts whom they must needs buy with money, and whose bellies they must needs fill; whereas these poor wretches were slaves without a price, and if one died another took his place on the chance that thereby he might escape present death by hunger, for there was a great many of them.

Ruled by an ineffectual queen, perhaps a Morrisian caricature of Victoria in medieval dress, Goldburg encourages commercial anarchy, the exploitation of labor, and the inhumane treatment of the poor. While Whitewall embodies the worst corruptions of the civilized world, it also marks its terminus, and Ralph leaves Christian and feudal realms to journey back into history.

One of his first encounters in the uncharted lands beyond Whitewall is with a group of living barbarians, the vigorous Kindred of the Bull. The members of this gens are pagans who dwell in the hidden places of the fell, worshipping their ancestral totem and the forefathers of their clan. In the tradition of "upper barbarism," they follow a blood code and adopt worthy aliens into their tribe. But they are slavers, and Ralph must later wean them from this vice. In selling Ralph as a slave in Utterbol, they bring him into a city resembling the early despotisms Morris and Bax had described in *Socialism*. Ralph escapes from Utterbol and, after adventures in a supernatural wilderness, is finally succoured by the Innocent Folk. They are the people of the age of gold. Dressed in wool and feathers, ignorant of iron, they are noble savages who live in peace and harmony and neither need nor desire the water of the Well at the World's End. As they tell Ralph:

> Ye of the World beyond the Mountains are stronger and more godlike than we, as all tales tell; and ye wear away your lives desiring that which ye may scarce get; and ye set your hearts on high things, desiring to be masters of the very Gods. Therefore ye know sickness and sorrow, and oft ye die before your time, so that ye must depart and leave undone things which ye deem ye were born to do; which to all men is grievous. And because of all this ye desire healing and thriving. . . . Therefore ye do but right to seek to the Well at the World's End.

The Innocent Folk are the last human beings Ralph encounters; the earliest children of the earth, they partake of the spirit of the golden age and of the nature of the prelapsarian realm of the Well, at which Ralph finally arrives.

The lands through which Ralph travels function both as cultural and historical symbols and as images of Ralph's psychological transformation. They and the people who live within them indicate stages in Ralph's life journey. When, for example, Ralph leaves home and childhood behind, he enters the Wood Perilous, the world of uncertain but exciting growth. There he first meets Ursula, the anima he is not mature enough to recognize, and the Lady of Abundance, an incarnation of the mother of the earth.

The Lady, connected by her title and attributes to Frazer's corn goddess and the Grimms' *domina Abundia,* rules both the region of the Dry Tree and the fecund Land of Abundance. The Lady's paradoxical nature is manifested by more than the differing characteristics of her two provinces. Though the folk of the Land of Abundance believe that "when she came . . . increase became more plenteous," other peoples see her as "devil" and "mahmet," the evilest woman who ever spat upon the blessed Host of the Altar." The Lady is an embodiment of the Great Mother, a personification of the earth in all its aspects. "From her hands goeth all healing," but also the inadvertent destruction of men and their kingdoms. The Lady is seen as creator and destroyer, enemy and kindly guide, mother and harlot. Although she is wed to the Knight of the Sun, she freely gives herself to Ralph; her actions, like the processes of fertility, are unconditioned by the usual morality.

Morris's Lady of Abundance is somewhat reminiscent of Rider Haggard's She, in the popular romance of the same name. Like She-who-must-be-obeyed, the Lady is feared and hated by most women but fatally charming to all men. Protected from change and age by the magic of the Well, she has lived long past the ordinary span of life. "Lovely as no woman was lovely or ever had been," she is loved by the Black Knight, the Chief of the Dry Tree, and the Knight of the Sun, yet causes the demise of each. But she does no injury to Ralph, who, like Leo Vincy in Haggard's tale, is the handsome man all women love. Like Leo, Ralph, despite his passion, has an unsettling sense of his beloved's power and mystery. When he asks her if she is good or evil, she replies: "Whatsoever I have been, I am good to thee," thus evading, while answering, his question. Ralph's illicit sexual union with the Lady is described by Morris, in startlingly Laurentian terms, as utterly fulfilling:

> He drew her down to him as he knelt there, and took his arms about her, and though she yet shrunk from him a little and the eager flame of his love, the might not be gainsayed, and she gave herself to him and let her body glide into his arms, and loved him no less than he loved her.

Initiating the hero into love and manhood, the Lady tells him of her past, in which she has been victim and victimizer both, and indicates the nature of the future life he is to lead. Through an act provoked by her fatal beauty, the Lady is slain, but, like the corn goddess and the fertile grain, she dies to be reborn in a new form. Although Ralph grieves for her, he senses that she is not the mate intended for him and learns that he must move beyond the memory of her.

Only after he has left the Land of Abundance is Ralph prepared to begin his quest. *Enfance* and first love are behind him, and he is now ready to recognize the woman who is his soul. She is Ursula, named after the saint who is "the Friend of Maidens," and a fully mortal "sending" of the Lady of Abundance. Frank, courageous, and natural, a child of the woodlands which bore her, Ursula incarnates only the benevolent aspects of the Great Mother. Like Ellen in *News from Nowhere*, whom she resembles in body and spirit, she is the Jungian anima in all her positive attributes. Kidnapped and enslaved in Utterbol—a hell on earth that is a metaphor for the life of lust and violence on the outmost promontory of existence—she is capable of evading the desire of its rapacious lord and of engineering her own escape. When she joins Ralph, himself endangered by the lord of Utterbol's determination to castrate him, she becomes the hero's sworn companion on the quest. As Ralph's friend—for their love begins as friendship—she aids in his plans and deeds. As his anima, she senses and responds to the inner workings of his mind. As his guide, she leads him through all barriers to the well of life, herself unprotected by the talisman she wears.

In the finest section of the romance, "The Road to the Well at the World's End," Morris's use of symbolic landscape illuminates Ralph's gradual transformation: the death of his old egocentric self, the birth of an altruistic identity, and the integration of the personality. Ralph and Ursula are initially educated and purified in preparation for their perilous journey by the Sage of Swedenham, the wise old man of romance. Accompanied by the Sage, who takes them as far as he may go, the couple undergo a test of courage and endurance as they traverse the barren Sea of Molten Rock, modeled on an Icelandic lava sea, and pause beside the statue of "The Fighting Man," a figure carved from living rock and an emblem of dedication to a life of deeds, which guards the passage to an unknown world. Then, bidding farewell to their teacher, they enter the pass, the long and narrow way to a new world and life. Spending fall and winter within its confines, they emerge from the pass in the spring to find themselves, appropriately, within the land of the Innocent Folk. There, they become one flesh. Sexually united, they are ready to undertake their last symbolic trail—the journey through the Thirsty Desert to the Dry Tree.

Ralph has read of the Dry Tree, for he is cognizant of the deeds of Alexander the Great, who, according to medieval romance, had been to see it. But neither he nor Ursula is prepared for its horrors or for those of the barren wasteland they must cross to reach the Tree. Entering the desert of negation whose sands are strewn with desiccated corpses, they look upon the remains of those who have sought and failed, of those dead of their frustration and despair:

So came they to the brow and looked over it into a valley, about which on all sides went the ridge, save where it was broken down into a narrow pass on the further side, so that the said valley was like to one of those theatres of the ancient Roman Folk, whereof are some to be seen in certain lands. Neither did those desert benches lack their sitters; for all down the sides of the valley sat or lay children of men; some women, but most men-folk, of whom the most part were weaponed, and some with their drawn swords in their hands. Whatever semblance of moving was in them was when the eddying wind of the valley stirred the rags of their raiment, or the long hair of the women.

Finally, Ralph and Ursula confront the Dry Tree—an image of death itself:

But a very midmost of this dreary theatre rose up a huge and monstrous tree, whose topmost branches were even the horns which they had seen from below the hill's brow. Leafless was that tree and lacking of twigs, and its bole upheld but some fifty of great limbs, and as they looked on it, they doubted whether it were not made by men's hands rather than grown up out of the earth. All round about the roots of it was a pool of clear water, that cast back the image of the valley-side and the bright sky of the desert, as though it had been a mirror of burnished steel.

Death's other kingdom is before them: the dead who, like the mummified corpses in *The Earthly Paradise*, ironically appear alive in death, the water which, though clear, is poisonous, and the Tree itself, a perversion of the force of life from which it sprang. Leafless, twigless, barren, death's trophies hung upon its rigid boughs, it is the Tree of Life transformed into the Tree of Death. With burning cheeks and sparkling eyes, the lovers go to investigate its mysteries. Although they see that "each of the dead leathery faces [of its victims] was drawn up in a grin, as though they had died in pain and yet beguiled," they are unaware of their own enthrallment. Ursula first prevents Ralph's destruction by noticing that although the wind blows, the water surrounding the Tree remains unrippled and, thus, according to medieval lore, is poisoned. Subduing her own attraction to death, she next saves Ralph from his desire to die by pretending that a more heroic doom awaits him in the form of horsemen waiting to attack. Functioning as his anima, Ursula rescues Ralph from his temptation by death, and, having successfully confronted the specter, the two lovers may traverse the remainder of the Thirsty Desert. When they cross the Wall of the World, a range of mountains based on those Morris saw in Iceland, they find themselves in a small valley filled with living trees and intersected by a flowing river—a memory of the peaceful spots that Morris found on his return to the Icelandic world. At the edge of the sea, they find the Well. At last, they are fully ready to drink of the water of life.

The Well at which they do so is pagan. Their quest for it has been condemned by a priest as "a memory of the customs of the ancient gentiles and heathens," and the talisman that each wears, though derived from Sarras, the city of the Christian Grail, may not be blessed or exchanged for a rosary. The rituals necessary to prepare them for their quest include pagan rites of purification, the wearing of toga-like garments, and the study of ancient books which must be pursued in the groves where the old gods of earth were worshipped. Even the sign of the quest which is carved on rocks and trees, found in the wasteland, and marked on the sacred Well, is the ancient pagan emblem of a sword crossed by a three-leaved bough. A symbol known only to initiates, it is the Golden Bough of the *Aeneid* and, possibly, of Frazer's book.

The Well itself has the properties of the many Irish wells that confer the blessings of wisdom or eternal youth; its description is derived from O'Curry's account of Connla's Well, O'Grady's passage on the fountain of youth located at Slieve Gullian, and Lady Wilde's depiction of St. Seenon's Well, whose curative waters run close to the sea but remain untouched by salt. In Morris's romance, however, the Well is clearly a new and secular grail to be enjoyed by humanists. It does not grant men physical immortality—an ignoble goal to Morris—but it offers long and happy life devoid of sorrow, weariness, and sickness. It is a fountain of love; to Ursula, its water tastes as if Ralph's "love were blended with it." A spring of wisdom, it enables those who drink to see into the life of things, offering them "the Clearing of the Eyes that they might behold." Its symbol, the interwoven sword and bough, is the sign of its ability to integrate the human personality, but for an end beyond the merely personal.

When Ralph and Ursula drink the water of the Well they experience a brief epiphany and fall into a profound sleep. Their physical regeneration manifests itself when, after their immersion in the sea, they discover that their scars and blemishes have vanished; the merging and regeneration of their spirits is demonstrated by their sense of oneness, their ability to love each other totally. Because "they are one which were twain,"

> The Tree bloometh again,
> And the Well-spring hath come
> From the waste to the home.

The Well's gifts of wisdom, love, and wholeness will help them redeem the societies through which they pass. As the Tree of Death becomes the Tree of Life, the water of goodness and fellowship, which is no longer inaccessible to men, begins to irrigate the entire created world.

Thus, Morris indicates how the integration of the personality leads naturally to the betterment of society. When Ralph drinks the Well's waters, he does not toast either himself or his beloved, but "the Earth and the World of Manfolk." In drinking of the Well, Ralph knowingly assumes a responsibility to society, for its waters are only for those who love the earth and its inhabitants. The Well carries with its gifts the obligations to "be the friends of men," to "succour the oppressed," and to create a better world, thus bringing "Heaven to the Earth for a little while." Ralph willingly accepts his duty to "serve . . . [his] fellows and deliver them from the thralldom of those that be strong and unwise and unkind." Now leading Ursula, he and his beloved both directly and obliquely aid in reforming the corrupt and blighted regions through which they had previously passed. They arrive at Utterbol to find that Bull Shockhead, the barbarian they have reformed, has conquered it and eliminated its cruel and decadent practices. They discover that Goldburg and the land of Whitewall have improved, for, driven by her unrequited love for Ralph, The Queen of Whitewall has either fled or killed herself. A successful revolution, helped by Ralph, makes the Burg of the Four Friths a free land. The Wheat-wearers and the Men of the Dry Tree have captured the city and banished its old masters. The two groups, united in marriage, will generate a new and uncorrupted people. The Kindred of the Bull, the Men of the Dry Tree, and the Shepherds—a semi-barbaric people who remember their ancient customs and their descent from a clan of the Bear (perhaps from the old savage tribe depicted in *The Wood beyond the World*) join with Ralph to help him free his threatened homeland.

Thus, the end of the romance demonstrates that the product of an integrated personality is the liberation of others and the development of fellowship with them. Ralph and Ursula return to a life of dedication within Ralph's small realm filled with the power, wisdom, and love to revitalize and live purposively within their world. "They have learned to love the world almost as abundantly as they love each other, almost as naturally as they love themselves" (Talbot).

In all, *The Well at the World's End* represents both the fruition of Morris's consciously held views of what constitutes the correct life in this world—ideas that he had suggested in his two previous romances and in *News from Nowhere*—and the flowering of Morris's less conscious examination of his past inner history. In symbolically recounting the experiences of his life, Morris depicts his gradual acceptance of the flaws in his love relationships and of the fate that seemingly ordains that one must suffer on the road to wisdom. Accepting his fears of physical extinction and psychic paralysis, he vividly describes—through a quest in which he imaginatively relives his two Icelandic journeys—both the dark night of the soul and the dawn which he now knows will follow it. Moreover, accepting the destructive power of passion, he explores his infatuation with the dark anima, both as a projection of the self and a figure for the faithless but alluring mistress-wife. Significantly, when the Lady of Abundance dies, the writer who created her is born again. The figure of the *femme fatale* is put to rest and although there are enchantresses in the remaining works, they are grotesque or sexually unappealing characters whose power is never really felt as menacing. Even the Lady, though seen as dichotomous in nature, is not perceived as intentionally malevolent. Rather, she is a necessary tutor, an essential predecessor of the woman who will be the soul and rightful partner of the integrated man. In the same vein, Morris no longer sees romantic love and social fellowship as separate or opposing forces. Instead, he carefully delineates the process by which passion generates the fellowship of all and shows how the two forces can work together to create more truly human lives within a fully humane world. Thus, Morris's examination of the truths of existence becomes, for him, purgation leading to a sense of renewed life.

The Place of Pater:
Marius the Epicurean

Harold Bloom

The Aesthetic Movement in England (*circa* 1870–1900) is usually tracked to its sources in the literary Paris of the 1850s. The poets Théophile Gautier and Charles Baudelaire are thus viewed as being the inventors of the new sensibility exemplified in the life and work of Algernon Swinburne, James Whistler, Walter Pater, and their immediate followers—George Moore, Oscar Wilde, Aubrey Beardsley, Simeon Solomon, Ernest Dowson, Lionel Johnson, Arthur Symons, and the young William Butler Yeats. Whistler, an American and a painter, rightly felt that he owed everything to Paris and himself and nothing to English tradition. But behind Swinburne and Pater were three generations of English Romanticism, from the poetry of Blake and Wordsworth on through to the Victorian Romanticism of the Pre-Raphaelite poets and painters. In the midst of this tradition one finds a more direct source of English Aestheticism: the literary theories of Arthur Henry Hallam, as set forth in a review of his friend Alfred Tennyson's poetry some twenty years before Gautier and Baudelaire created their sensibility out of Delacroix, Poe, and their own complex natures.

Yeats remarked that he had found his literary aesthetics in Hallam before coming under Pater's influence. Hallam contrasted Shelley and Keats as "poets of sensation" with Wordsworth as a "poet of reflection":

Susceptible of the slightest impulse from external nature, their fine organs trembled into emotion at colors, and sounds, and movements, unperceived or unregarded by duller temperaments . . . So vivid was the delight attending the simple exertions of eye and ear, that it became mingled more and more with their trains of

From *The Ringers in the Tower: Studies in Romantic Tradition.* © 1971 by The University of Chicago. University of Chicago Press, 1971.

active thought, and tended to absorb their whole being into the energy of sense.

Marshall McLuhan observed that the theme of Hallam's essay is usually the theme of Pater and of T. S. Eliot: the Copernican revolution in poetry that saw a change in the direction of poetic art, from "the shaping of the poetic object . . . to the shaping of psychological effects in the reader," as McLuhan phrases it. Eliot disliked Pater's work, as he disliked most of the romantic tradition, but critics tend now to agree that he has a place in that tradition despite himself.

Walter Pater's place in Romantic tradition was a consciously chosen one, and only recently have readers begun to see again what that place was. In his lifetime Pater was a shadowy but famous figure, vaguely blamed by the public as being the half-sinister and withdrawn theorist whom extravagant disciples—Wilde, Beardsley, Moore—would cite as the authority for their more extreme stances in art and in life. This Pater of popular tradition is so vivid a part of literary folklore that any critic ought to be wary of clearing away the myth. We would lose the "tremendous Ritualist" who had lost all faith, and who burned his poems because they had been too pious, but who felt frustrated nonetheless when he was prevented (by his friends) from being ordained. A still greater loss would be the Pater who is reputed to have walked the Oxford meadows in the cool of the evening, murmuring that the odor of the meadow-sweet gave him pain: "It is the fault of nature in England that she runs too much to excess."

Aside from his assured place in the great line of English eccentrics, Pater is one of the central figures in the continuity between Romanticism, Modernism, and the emergent sensibility still in the process of replacing Modernism today. Pater's most ambitious and extensive work, the historical novel *Marius the Epicurean*, is in itself one of the more remarkable fictional experiments of the later nineteenth century, but it has the added value now of teaching us something about our own continuity with the past that otherwise we could not wholly know.

Currently fashionable sensibility, two-thirds of the way through the century, is perhaps another ironic disordering of Paterian sensibility. Pater is halfway between Wordsworth and ourselves. But he is more than a link between, say, the sensibility of Keats and that of the late Yeats or late Stevens; he is a kind of hinge upon which turns the single gate, one side of which is Romantic and the other modern poetry. Marius himself may be little more than an idealized version of Pater's own self-consciousness, and yet Marius, more than any fictional character of our age, is the representative modern poet as well as the representative man of literary culture who remains the only audience for that poet. If one holds in mind a handful of our age's lyrical poems at their most poignant, say Yeats's "Vacillation" and "The Man and the Echo," with Stevens's "The Course of a Particular" and "Of Mere Being," and imagines a possible poet who might make those poems into a story, one gets the sensibility and even the dimmed, half-willing, self-defeated fate of Pater's Roman quester.

"His Sensations and Ideas" is the subtitle of *Marius the Epicurean*. At the center of the novel is the flux of sensations; at its circumference whirl a succession of ideas of the good life, all of them inadequate beside the authenticity of the central flux. This inadequacy is highly deliberate:

> . . . with this sense of the splendour of our experience and of its awful brevity, gathering all we are into one desperate effort to see and touch, we shall hardly have time to make theories about the things we see and touch. What we have to do is to be for ever curiously testing new opinions and courting new impressions, never acquiescing in a facile orthodoxy. . . .

That is Pater at his most central, in the famous "Conclusion" to *The Renaissance*, written in 1868. Thinking of this "Conclusion," and of its effect on the "Tragic Generation" of Wilde, Aubrey Beardsley, Ernest Dowson, Lionel Johnson, and their companions, Yeats eloquently complained that Pater "taught us to walk upon a rope, tightly stretched through serene air, and we were left to keep our feet upon a swaying rope in a storm." Pater's reply is more eloquent still:

> While all melts under our feet, we may well catch at any exquisite passion, or any contribution to knowledge that seems by a lifted horizon to set the spirit free for a moment, or any stirring of the senses, strange dyes, strange colours, and curious odours, or work of the artist's hands, or the face of one's friend. Not to discriminate every moment some passionate attitude in those about us, and in the brilliancy of their gifts some tragic dividing of forces on their ways, is, on this short day of frost and sun, to sleep before evening.

Eliot complained that Pater was neither a critic nor a creator but a moralist, whether in *Marius*, *The Renaissance*, or elsewhere. Clearly Pater, whenever he wrote, was all three, like Eliot himself. The confusion of purposes, in both men, was well served by a late version of Romantic art, the usual mode for each being a flash of radiance against an incongruous or bewildering background. In this "privileged" or "timeless" moment of illumination, the orthodox religious quest of the later writer found its equivocal conclusion, but the skeptical, more openly solipsistic Pater tended to remain within a narrower vision, confined to what he himself naturalistically could see.

Because of this restraint, *Marius* is a surprisingly unified narrative for all its surface diversity. At first reading one can feel that its motto might well be the tag from Nennius affixed by David Jones to his *Anathemata*: "I have made a heap of all that I could find," or perhaps Eliot's line in *The Waste Land*: "These fragments I have shored against my ruins." Pater gives us the tale of Cupid and Psyche from Apuleius, an impressionistic account of the *Pervigilium Veneris,* a supposed oration of Cornelius Fronto, a version of a dialogue of Lucian, and a paraphrase of selected meditations of Marcus Aurelius. Critics have suspected his motives: they argue that Pater resorted to imitation because he could not invent a story, create a character, dramatize a conflict, or even present a conversation. This is true enough. We hardly *hear* anything said in Pater's novel, and few events occur that are not historical. Critics less prejudiced than Eliot have also questioned the accuracy of Pater's summations of philosophical creeds, and others have indicated the absence of all theological content from the presentation of Christianity in the closing pages of the book. All true, and all irrelevant to the achievement of *Marius,* which remains a unified reverie or aesthetic meditation upon history, though a history as idealized and foreshortened as in Yeats's *A Vision,* a thoroughly Paterian work.

Pater and Yeats made magical associations between aspects of the Renaissance and their own times. Yeats extended the parallel to different phases of Byzantine culture, with an arbitrariness justified by his needs as a lyrical poet not content with the limitations of lyric. Pater's *Marius* is founded on a more convincing and troubling resemblance, between Victorian England in the 1880s and Rome in the Age of the Antonines, two summits of power and civilization sloping downward in decadence. The aesthetic humanism of Marius, poised just outside of a Christianity Pater felt to be purer than anything available to himself, is precisely the desperately noble and hopeless doctrine set forth in the "Conclusion" to *The Renaissance.* Like Pater, Marius is committed to the universe of death, loving it the better for every evidence of decay. "Death is the mother of beauty" in Pater as in his immediate ancestor, the poet of the "Ode to Psyche" and the "Ode on Melancholy," and in his immediate descendant, the poet of "Sunday Morning" and "Esthétique du mal." There is a morbidity in Pater, not present in Keats or in Stevens, the spirit of sadomasochism and inversion, the infantile regressiveness of his "The Child in the House," and the repressed destructiveness that emerges in some of his *Imaginary Portraits.* Something of this drifts into *Marius the Epicurean,* through the subtly evaded homosexuality of the love of Marius first for Flavian and then for Cornelius, and in the reveries on human and animal victims of pain and martyrdom. But what morbidity there is distracts only a little from the central theme of the book, which is Pater's own version of Romanticism, his individual addition of strangeness to beauty. For Wordsworth the privileged moments, "spots of time," gave precise knowledge of how and to what extent his power of mind reigned over outward sense. "I see by glimpses now," Wordsworth lamented, but the glimpses revealed the glory of human imagination, and recalled a time when the poet stood alone, in his conscious strength, unaided by religious orthodoxies. For Pater the spots of time belonged to the ascendancy of what Wordsworth called "outward sense," and the dying Marius is still an "unclouded and receptive soul," sustained by "the vision of men and things, actually revealed to him on his way through the world." The faith, to the end, is in the evidence of things seen, and in the substance of things experienced. Certainly the closest analogue is in the death poem of Stevens, "Of Mere Being," where the palm that rises at the end of the mind, the tree of mere being, has on it the life-enhancing aureole of an actual bird:

> The bird sings. Its feathers shine
>
> . . . .
>
> The bird's fire-fangled feathers dangle down.

The burden of *Marius the Epicurean* is the burden of modern lyric, from Wordsworth to Stevens, the near solipsism of the isolated sensibility, of the naked aesthetic consciousness deprived of everything save its wavering self and the flickering of an evanescent beauty in the world of natural objects, which is part of the universe of death. As a critic, Pater derived from Ruskin, and went further in alienation. This stance of experiential loss and aesthetic gain is familiar enough to contemporary analysts in several disciplines. It was while Pater labored at the composition of *Marius* that the unconscious was formally "discovered" (about 1882), and thus the Romantic inner self received its definitive formulation. Societies (Victorian and Antonine) disintegrate, and individuals (Pater and Marius) lose all outward connections. Pater would have understood immediately the later description of the unconscious proposed by the phenomenologists: an index of the remoteness in the self's relationships with others. The famous description of the Mona Lisa in Pater's *Renaissance,* anthologized by Yeats as the first modern poem, is just such a vision of the unconscious: what J. H. Van den Berg, the phenomenological psychiatrist, defines as "the secret inner self, the innerworld in which everything the world has to offer is shut away." Van den Berg, as it happens, is referring to Rilke's account of Leonardo's lady and her landscape, but Rilke writes of the painting much in Pater's spirit. The landscape, Rilke observes, is as estranged as the lady, "far and completely unlike us." Both represent what Van den Berg calls "things-in-their-farewell," a beauty purchased by estrangement.

This, I think, is the most relevant context in which to read *Marius the Epicurean. Marius* is the masterpiece of things-in-their-farewell, the great document in English of the historical moment when the unconscious came painfully to its birth. Where Wordsworth and Keats, followed by Mill and Arnold, fought imaginatively against excessive self-consciousness, Pater welcomes it, and by this welcome inaugurates, for writers and readers in English, the decadent phase of Romanticism, in which, when honest, we still find ourselves. What Pater, and modernist masters following him, lack is not energy of apprehension, but rather the active force of a synthesizing imagination, so titanic in Blake and Wordsworth. Yet this loss—in Yeats, Joyce, Stevens—is only an honest recognition of necessity. Except for the phenomenon of a last desperate High Romantic, Hart Crane, the faith in the saving, creative power of the imagination subsides in our time. Here too Pater is the hinge, for the epiphanies of Marius only help him to live what life he has; they do not save him, nor in the context of his world, or Pater's, or ours, can anyone be saved.

As an artist, Pater was essentially a baroque essayist, in the line of Sir Thomas Browne and De Quincey, and the aesthetic achievement of Marius is of a kind with the confessions of those stylists. Yeats, at least, thought *Marius* to be written in the only great modern prose style in English. One can add Yeats, in his still undervalued prose, to the line of Browne, De Quincey, and Pater, and indeed the influence of Pater remains to be traced throughout all of Yeats's prose, early or late, particularly in the marvelous *Autobiographies*. Criticism has said little to the purpose about this late tradition of highly mannered prose, whose elaborate and conscious harmonies have an affinity with the relatively more ascetic art of James, and reach their parodistic climax in Joyce. Our expectations of this prose are mistaken when we find it to be an intrusion, of any kind, between ourselves and its maker; it is as much of his vision as he can give to us, and its self-awareness is an overwhelming attempt to exorcize the demon of discursiveness. The marmoreal reverie, whether in *Marius* or in Yeats's *Per Amica Silentia Lunae* and *A Vision*, is allied to other modernist efforts to subvert the inexorable dualism of form and content.

Pater has the distinction of being one of the first major theorists in the modern phase of this effort. He rejected the organic analogue of Coleridge, by which any work of art is, as it were, naturalized, because he feared that it devalued the intense and solitary effort of the artist to overcome natural limitation. In his essay on "The School of Giorgione" he could speak of art as "always striving to be independent of the mere intelligence, to become a matter of pure perception, to get rid of its responsibilities to its subject or material." This ideal is impossible, and prompts the famous and misleading formula: "All art constantly aspires towards the condition of music." What stimulated Pater to this extravagance was his obsessive concern with what Stevens states so simply in one of his *Adagia:* "One has a sensibility range beyond which nothing really exists for one. And in each this is different." The peculiar structure of *Marius the Epicurean* emanates from the primacy Pater gives to sensibility, in his own special sense of that complex faculty.

Paterian "sensibility" is nothing less than the way one sees, and so apprehends, everything of value in human experience, or in the art that is the best of that experience. Poetry and *materia poetica*, Stevens says, are the same thing. *Marius* is a gathering of *materia poetica*, taken out of one moment of European history, on the chance of illuminating a later moment. The late Victorian skeptic and Epicurean, of whom Pater and Wilde are definitive, is emancipated from his immortality, and suffers the discontent of his own passion for ritual. Pater, as was notorious, studied the nostalgias of religion only in terms of form and ceremony. The passionate desire for ritual, in Pater and in his Marius, as in the Yeats of "A Prayer for My

Daughter," is not a trivial matter, because the quest involved is for the kind of innocence and beauty that can only come from custom and from ceremony. The social aspect of such innocence may be pernicious, but fortunately Pater, unlike Yeats, offered only visionary politics.

Marius the Epicurean is constructed as a series of rituals, each of which is absorbed into its successor without being destroyed, or even transcended. As art was ritual for Pater, so life is ritual for Marius, the ordering principle always being that no form or possibility of life (or of art) is to be renounced in favor of any other. This could be described, unkindly and unfairly, as a kind of polymorphous perversity of the spirit, a refusal to pay the cost of choosing a single aim for culture, or of meeting the necessity of dying by a gracious yielding to the reality principle. What can be urged against Pater, fairly, is that he evaded the novel's ultimate problem by killing off Marius before the young man grasps the theological and moral exclusiveness of Christianity. Marius could not remain Marius and renounce; forced to make the Yeatsian choice between perfection of the life and perfection of the work he would have suffered from a conflict that would have destroyed the fine balance of his nature. Whether Pater earns the structural irony of the novel's concluding pages, as a still-pagan Marius dies a sanctified Christian death, is quite legitimately questionable.

But, this aside, Pater's novel is unflawed in its odd but precise structure. The four parts are four stages on the life's way of Marius, but the continuities of ritual pattern between them are strong enough to set up a dialectic by which no apparent spiritual advancement becomes an aesthetic retreat. The consequence is that the spiritual quest is not from error to truth, but only from alienation to near-sympathy. Thus the first part opens with the most humanly appealing presentation of a belief in the book, as we are given the ancestral faith of Marius, "the Religion of Numa." Here there is no skepticism, but a vision of home and boyhood, the calm of a natural religion that need not strain beyond the outward observances. The world of sense is at home in the child and his inherited faith, which climaxes by his initiation into the world of literature, beautifully symbolized by the story of Cupid and Psyche. The tentative love of Marius for Flavian is precisely the awakening of the literary sense under the awareness of death that Pater traces in the "Conclusion" to *The Renaissance*, and the premature death of Flavian, his one masterpiece left imperfect, inaugurates the first crisis Marius must suffer.

Resolving this crisis is the "conversion," by himself, of Marius to Epicureanism, the doctrine of Aristippus. Though Epicureanism (and its Stoic rival, as represented by Aurelius and Fronto) is supposedly the dominant element of only the second part of the novel, its presence in the book's title is no accident, as in the broad sense Marius, like Pater, lives and dies an Epicurean. For the Epicureanism involved is simply the inevitable religion of the Paterian version of sensibility, or the "aesthetic philosophy" proper. "Not pleasure, but fullness of life, and 'insight' as conducing to that fullness—energy, variety, and choice of experience," is Pater's best summary of the doctrine, with his added warning that "its mistaken tendency would lie in the direction of a kind of idolatry of mere life, or natural gift."

The first crisis of this Epicureanism comes at the close of Part II, with Marius's recoil from the sadistic games of the arena, a recoil fascinating for everything that it suggests of the repressed masochism of both Marius and his creator. Like Flaubert, that other high priest of the religion of art, Pater has a way of wandering near the abyss, but *Marius* is no *Salammbô*, and finds no place in the litany of the Romantic agony. But the cruelty of the world, the pain and evil that border so near to Marius's exquisite realm of sensation and reverie, awaken in him a first movement of skepticism toward his own Epicureanism.

Part III develops this sense of limitation with regard to the fruits of sensibility, but by exploiting a more fundamental flaw in the Paterian vision. The self-criticism here is illuminating, not just for this book but for the whole of Pater, and explains indeed the justification for the elaborately hesitant style that Pater perfected. Isolation has expanded the self, but now threatens it with the repletion of solipsism. The Stoic position of Aurelius and Fronto is invoked to contrast its vision of human brotherhood with the more selfish and inward cultivation of Aristippus. But the limits of Stoicism are rapidly indicated also, even as exemplified in its noblest exponent, the philosophic emperor. The climax of Part III comes with marvelous appropriateness, in the quasi-Wordsworthian epiphany experienced by Marius, alone in the Sabine Hills. Moved by the unnamed Presence encountered in this privileged hour, Marius is prepared for the supernatural revelation that never quite appropriates him in the fourth and final part of the novel.

Here, in the closing portion, Pater's skill in construction is most evident. Part IV builds through a series of contrasts to its melancholy but inevitable conclusion. We pass from the literary Neoplatonism of Apuleius with its fanciful daemons aiding men to reach God, on to the aesthetically more powerful vision of the Eucharist, as Marius is drawn gradually into the Christian world of Cornelius and Cecilia. This approach to grace through moral sympathy is punctuated beautifully by a triad of interventions. The first is the dialogue in which the great satirist Lucian discomfits a young philosophic enthusiast, teaching the Paterian lesson that temperament alone determines our supposed choice of belief. Next comes a review of a diary of observed sufferings by Marius, coupled with an account of recent Christian martyrdoms. Finally there is the deeply moving last return home by Marius. Reverently, he rearranges the resting-places of his ancestors, in full consciousness that he is to be the last of his house. He goes out to his fate with the Christian knight, Cornelius, offering up his life in sacrifice for his friend, and dies anonymously among unknown Christians, his own quest still unfulfilled. "He must still hold by what his eyes really saw," and at the last Marius still longs to see, and suffers from a deep sense of wasted power. He is a poet who dies before his poems are written, and even the great poem that is his life is scarcely begun. The attentive reader, confronted by Marius's death, is saddened by the loss, not of a person, but of a major sensibility. And for such losses, such yieldings of a fine sensibility to the abyss, there are no recompenses.

We return always, in reading Pater, to the "Conclusion" of *The Renaissance*, where he spoke his word most freely. The lasting power of *Marius the Epicurean* stays with us not as an image, or series of images, but as a memory of receptivity, the vivid sense of a doomed consciousness universal enough to encompass all men who live and die by a faith in art:

> . . . we have an interval, and then our place knows us no more. Some spend this interval in listlessness, some in high passions, the wisest, at least among "the children of this world," in art and song. For our one chance lies in expanding that interval, in getting as many pulsations as possible into the given time. Great passions may give us this quickened sense of life, ecstasy and sorrow of love, the various forms of enthusiastic activity, disinterested or otherwise, which come naturally to many of us. Only be sure it is passion—that it does yield you this fruit of a quickened, multiplied consciousness. Of this wisdom, the poetic passion, the desire of beauty, the love of art for art's sake, has most; for art comes to you professing frankly to give nothing but the highest quality to your moments as they pass, and simply for those moments' sake.

Hardy's Tess:
The Making of a Pure Woman

Mary Jacobus

PURITY AND CENSORSHIP

Havelock Ellis, while proclaiming the modernity of Hardy's treatment of sexual questions in *Jude the Obscure,* had an important reservation about *Tess of the D'Urbervilles* (1891):

> I was repelled at the outset by the sub-title. It so happens that I have always regarded the conception of *purity*, when used in moral discussions, as a conception sadly in need of analysis. . . . It seems to me doubtful whether anyone is entitled to use the word "pure" without first defining precisely what he means, and still more doubtful whether an artist is called upon to define it at all, even in several hundred pages. I can quite conceive that the artist should take pleasure in the fact that his own creative revelation of life poured contempt on many old prejudices. But such an effect is neither powerful nor legitimate unless it is engrained in the texture of the narrative; it cannot be stuck on by a label. To me that glaring sub-title meant nothing, and I could not see what it should mean to Mr Hardy.

The label, Hardy tells us, was added at the last moment, as "the estimate left in a candid mind of the heroine's character" (1912 Preface). It caused trouble from the start. To those who accept a Christian definition of purity, it's preposterous; and to those who don't, irrelevant. The difficulty in both cases is the same—that of regarding Tess as somehow immune to the experience she undergoes. To invoke purity in connection with a career

From *Tearing the Veil: Essays on Femininity,* edited by Susan Lipshitz. © 1978 by Routledge & Kegan Paul, Ltd.

that includes not simply seduction, but collapse into kept woman and murderess, taxes the linguistic resources of the most permissive conventional moralist; as the formidable Mrs. Oliphant put it, in a review which epitomises the moral opposition aroused by *Tess*, "here the elaborate and indignant plea for Vice, that it is really Virtue, breaks down altogether." On the other hand, to regard Tess as unimplicated is to deny her the right of participation in her own life. Robbed of responsibility, she is deprived of tragic status—reduced throughout to the victim she does indeed become. Worst of all, she is stripped of the sexual autonomy and the capacity for independent being and doing which are among the most striking features of Hardy's conception.

Hardy himself makes things worse by seeming to adopt the argument for a split between act and intention—Angel Clare comes to realise that "The beauty of a character lay not in its achievements, but in its aims and impulses; the true record lay not among things done, but among things conceived." Yet Angel's response to Tess at the end of the novel is remarkable precisely because he no longer makes this distinction but—knowing her a murderess—accepts her as she is. Alternatively, it could be argued that the terminology of conventional Christian morality is ironically misapplied in order to reveal its inadequacy and challenge the narrow Pauline definition of purity-as-abstinence originally held by Angel. But however one interprets the label, the real problem—as Havelock Ellis points out—is Hardy's failure to "engrain" its implications in the texture of the narrative. In the circumstances, it is illuminating to discover that Tess's purity is a literary construct, "struck on" in retrospect like the sub-title to meet objections which the novel had encountered even before its publication in 1891. In "Candour in English Fiction," a symposium on the censorship question published in the *New Review* for January 1890, Hardy had protested at the tyranny exercised over the novelist by the conditions of magazine publication. Designed for household reading, the family magazines necessarily failed (in Hardy's words) to "foster the growth of the novel which reflects and reveals life." In particular, a rigid set of taboos—designed to protect "the Young Person" (i.e., the young girl)—governed the fictional treatment of sexual questions. Hardy's experience during the previous months in trying to publish *Tess* lies behind his protest, and the compromises he was about to make must already have been in his mind. Faced with the dilemma of "bring[ing] down the thunders of respectability upon his head" or of "whip[ing] and scourg[ing his] characters into doing something contrary to their natures," he writes of seeing no alternative but to

> do despite to his best imaginative instincts by arranging a *dénouement* which he knows to be indescribably unreal and meretricious, but dear to the Grundyist and subscriber. If the true artist ever weeps it probably is then, when he first discovers the fearful price that he has to pay for the privilege of writing in the English language—no less a price than the complete extinction, in the mind

of every mature and penetrating reader, of sympathetic belief in his personages.

In the autumn of 1889, three successive rejections of the half-completed *Tess* had shown Hardy the price he had to pay, if not for writing in the English language, at any rate for serial publication. Ironically, the very changes he made to placate "the Grundyist and subscriber" produced anomalies which the conventional moralists were quick to seize on when the novel finally appeared.

The form of Hardy's compromise is implicit in his defiant sub-title. But its effects were much more far-reaching. Hardy's own account misleadingly suggests that his solution was cynical and temporary bowdlerisation for the purposes of serial publication only. In reality he also made lasting modifications to his original conception in an attempt to argue a case whose terms were dictated by the conventional moralists themselves. The attempt profoundly shaped the novel we read today, producing alterations in structure, plot, and characterisation which undermined his fictional argument as well as strengthening it—or rather, since Hardy himself said of *Tess* that "a novel is an impression, not an argument" (1892 Preface), substantially distorted its final impression. As the novel first stood, it was not only simpler in outline, but different in emphasis. A letter to Hardy's American publisher in 1889 merely states that the "personal character and adventures" of his nobly descended milkmaid are "the immediate source of such interest as the tale may have," and notes that "her position is based on fact," but there is no hint of polemic. From the manuscript one can reconstruct the main features of the Ur-*Tess*—already comprising Tess's seduction, the birth and death of her child, Sorrow, and her courtship by Angel, breaking off with their marriage and Angel's wedding-night confession. All the events which make up the second half of the novel (Angel's departure, Tess's solitary ordeal, Alec's reappearance, the murder, and finally, the reunion of Tess and Angel before her death) belong to the later, post-1889 phase of composition. More baldly than the revised version, the Ur-*Tess* had dealt with the common enough situation of a country girl seduced by her employer on first going into service. Her social, economic, and sexual vulnerability are unequivocally defined. Tess's original name, "Love" (modified successively to Cis, Sue, and Rose-Mary before becoming Tess), suggests that Hardy always had in mind the crudely polarised attitudes to female sexuality embodied in Alec d'Urberville and Angel Clare (sexual possession versus idealization). But there is evidence that the oppositions were at this stage less clear-cut, more realistically blurred, and more humanely conceived, than they later became. The original novel was not only less polemical, but elegiacally explored the recurrent Hardian theme implied by its original title, "Too Late, Beloved!" This was to be a tragedy of thwarted potential in which unfulfilment expressed not only social and cultural ironies, but the irony of life itself.

Throughout his career Hardy was acutely sensitive to adverse criticism, and the grounds given for its refusal by the three magazines to which *Tess* was offered bear significantly on its reshaping. Hardy had promised the novel to Tillotson's, a newspaper syndicate, but it was only when the portion up to and including the death of Sorrow was already in proof that they read it. Their immediate demand for major changes and deletions led Hardy to try his luck elsewhere. Edward Arnold, the editor of *Murray's Magazine,* wrote a friendly, regretful, but firm refusal based on his decision not to publish what he called "stories where the plot involves frequent and detailed reference to immoral situations." Arnold explicitly takes his stand on the opposite side of a contemporary debate to which Hardy himself was to contribute in another *New Review* symposium, "The Tree of Knowledge" (1894), this time about sex education for women:

> I know well enough [writes Arnold] that these tragedies are being played out every day in our midst, but I believe the less publicity they have the better, and that it is quite possible and very desirable for women to grow up and pass through life without the knowledge of them.

In this version of the double standard, middle- and upper-class women are to be sheltered from knowing what men of the same class get up to with working-class women. But it was the third and last rejection of *Tess* that proved most decisive for its development. It must also have been most wounding, based as it was not on an objection of principle, but on specific objections to Hardy's treatment of his subject. Mowbray Morris, the editor of *Macmillan's Magazine*—later to reply to "Candour in English Fiction" with an editorial of his own—reacted sharply to the frankness with which Hardy had made Tess's seduction the central feature of his novel:

> It is obvious from the first page what is to be Tess's fate at Tran-tridge; it is apparently obvious also to the mother, who does not seem to mind, consoling herself with the somewhat cynical re-flection that she may be made a lady *after* if not *before.* All the first part therefore is a sort of prologue to the girl's seduction which is hardly ever, and can hardly ever be out of the reader's mind.

He goes on to reveal particular unease about the prominence given to Tess's sexuality, both in its own right and in its effect on others:

> Even Angel Clare [he complains] . . . has not as yet got beyond a purely sensuous admiration for her person. Tess herself does not appear to have any feelings of this sort about her; but her capacity for stirring and by implication for gratifying these feelings for others is pressed rather more frequently and elaborately than strikes me as altogether convenient. . . . You use the word *succulent* more than once to describe the general appearance and condition of the Frome Valley. Perhaps I might say that the general

impression left on me by reading your story . . . is one of rather
too much succulence.

Morris's prejudices—against women capable of sexual arousal as well as
of arousing others—are revealing in themselves; in an anonymous and
hostile review of the novel as it finally appeared, he was again to accuse
Hardy of tastelessly parading what he calls his heroine's "sensual qualifications for the part." It is in the light of such reactions that Hardy's purification of Tess must be seen. The changes he made tell us not only about
the strains which underlie one of his greatest novels, but about late Victorian
attitudes to female sexuality.

REHABILITATION

Hardy's reply to Arnold is summed up in the words of the "Explanatory
Note" to the first edition: "If an offence come out of the truth, better is it
that the offence come than that the truth be concealed." His reply to Morris
is contained in his subtitle. A sustained campaign of rehabilitation makes
Tess's so blatant a case of the double standard of sexual morality applied
to men and women, and Tess herself so blameless, that the tragedy of the
ordinary becomes the tragedy of the exceptional—blackening both man and
fate in the process. In Hardy's original scheme, Tess becomes exceptional
precisely through the experience she undergoes. She starts as a village girl
distinguished from others only by her freshness, her ancestry, and the
fecklessness of her parents. The gap between herself and her mother seems
less great and, importantly, she has known of her pedigree "ever since her
infancy." In the revised version, however, "Sir John" first learns of his
lineage in the opening scene of the book. Hardy's intention in making this
change is obviously to play down the inevitability of which Morris complained. Originally, her seduction had sprung from a realistic combination
of circumstances—her mother's simple-mindedness (seeing Alec's attentions as Tess's chance to marry a gentleman), her father's irresponsibility
(getting too drunk to drive the loaded cart to market, and hence throwing
on Tess the guilt of Prince's death), and her own inexperience. In the revised
manuscript, her entire tragedy springs from this opening encounter with
an antiquarian parson, and can now be blamed on a peculiarly malign chain
of events. With this development of the heroine's ancestry into the main-
spring of her tragedy goes the endowing of Tess herself with special qualities of dignity and refinement. Mrs Oliphant calls it "a pardonable
extravagance" in a partisan author to make her "a kind of princess" in her
village milieu. But is it? Later in the novel, Angel Clare recognises that the
consciousness on which he has intruded is Tess's single opportunity of
existence—that she is "a woman, who at her lowest estimate as an ordinary
mortal had a life which, to herself who endured or enjoyed it, possessed
as great a dimension and importance as the life of the mightiest to him."

Though we see Tess as one anonymous field-woman among others, harvesting at Marlott or turnip-hacking at Flintcombe-Ash, her inner world is unique. To make her tragedy inseparable from her distinction is to belie the humane and egalitarian impulse at the heart of the novel—its assertion of the value of any individual, however commonplace, however obscure.

To give Tess from the start a privileged sensibility—make her especially conscious of her parents' shortcomings, especially responsible, especially alert to the implications of Alec's behaviour—also works against a central motif in the Ur-*Tess:* that of growth through experience. Hardy's conception of character is an organic one. He starts with an unformed heroine, and shows us the emergence of a reflective consciousness close to his own. Tess's "corporeal blight had been her mental harvest," he observes; the seduction and its aftermath leave her with a sombre sense of personal insignificance and vulnerability. In her own language she expresses what Hardy calls "the spirit of modernism," the uncertainty of life without a benign providence or an assured future:

> you see numbers of to-morrows just all in a line, the first of them the biggest and clearest, the others getting smaller and smaller as they stand further away; but they all seem very fierce and cruel, and as if they said, "Beware o' me! Beware o' me!"

In this respect, *Tess*—like so many of Hardy's novels—concerns education. The actuality and the metaphor of journeying pervade the novel, reflecting both Tess's changing circumstances, and, most movingly, her capacity for endurance. In a particularly interesting passage Hardy extends the metaphor to embrace education through experience, drawing on a quotation from Ascham's *Schoolmaster.* " 'By experience,' says Roger Ascham, 'we find out a short way by a long wandering.' Not seldom that long wandering unfits us for further travel, and of what use is our experience to us then?" The context of Ascham's remark had been a criticism of experience as a mode of teaching:

> Learning teacheth more in one year than experience in twenty, and learning teacheth safely, when experience maketh more miserable than wise. He hazardeth sore that waxeth wise by experience . . . We know by experience itself that it is a marvelous pain to find out but a short way by long wandering.

Wise fathers, he continues, teach their children rather than committing them to the school of life—an injunction picked up when Tess turns on her mother with the lament, " 'Why didn't you tell me there was danger? Why didn't you warn me?' "

A necessary consequence of Hardy's compaign to purify Tess is the character-assassination of Alec and Angel. Hardy's remark that, "but for the world's opinion," her seduction would have been counted "rather a liberal education to her than otherwise" was always sweeping in view of its result, Sorrow. But it makes more sense in the context of the relationship with Alec as originally envisaged. At this stage Alec had been younger (21 or 22 rather than 23 or 24) and without the later element of fraud. Instead of being a spurious d'Urberville, a nouveau-riche with a stolen name, he is simply a yeoman-farmer called Hawnferne. Traces of this less hardened character live on in the episode—not present, of course, in the original version—in which Tess goes to claim kin at the Slopes and first meets Alec. We are told that "a sooty fur represented for the present the dense black moustache that was to be" (by the first edition, in 1891, it has grown to "a well-groomed black moustache with curled points"); although in training for the role, he is not yet the moustachioed seducer of Victorian melodrama. Present from the start, however, is the motif of sexual dominance expressed through mechanical power. In the opening pages of the Ur-*Tess*, Alec has seen Tess at the club-walking and called on her mother; as she drives along in the small hours of the next morning, Tess's last thoughts before dropping off and waking to find Prince impaled by the oncoming mail-coach are of the young man "whose gig was part of his body." Alec's gig—here tellingly juxtaposed with the death of Prince—is not simply the equivalent of a sports-car, his badge of machismo, wealth and social status. It is also a symbolic expression of the way in which Tess is to be deprived of control over her own body, whether by Alec himself or by the alien rhythms of the threshing machine at Flintcombe-Ash, in a scene where sexual and economic oppression are as closely identified as they had been in her seduction.

The gig motif makes the nature of Alec's power over Tess particularly explicit. But it also provides scope for the rough and tumble of a more robustly conceived situation in their two most important scenes together, the drive to the Slopes and—in the Ur-*Tess*—the night of the seduction itself. It is in these scenes that the effect of Hardy's later modifications to the character of Tess emerges most clearly. The drive to the Slopes, Tess's first real encounter with Alec, shows her confused but sturdy in the face of his sexual bullying; above all, it shows her as less conscious. After being forced to clasp his waist during one of the pell-mell downhill gallops contrived by Alec for the purpose, the original Tess exclaims " 'Safe thank God!' . . . *with a sigh of relief*"; the later, more aware Tess adds " 'in spite of your folly!' . . . *her face on fire*." In the same way, after her ruse to get out of the gig (letting her hat blow off), she refuses to get up again with " 'No Sir,' she said, *firmly and smiling*"—whereas the later, more sophisticated Tess reveals "the red and ivory of her mouth *in defiant triumph*." The original relationship is thus both more straightforward and more intimate. Just before the seduction itself, Hardy comments in the manuscript version that "a familiarity with his presence, which [Alec] had carefully cultivated in [Tess] had removed all her original shyness of him"; and we see this familiarity in the earlier version of the scene in which Alec gives her a whistling lesson. Tess purses her lips as he instructs, "laughing however" (revised to "laughing *distressfully* however"), and when she produces a note "the momentary pleasure of success got the better of her; and she involuntarily smiled in his face *like a child*"—the last phrase deleted from the revised version. This more naive and trusting Tess figures in the prelude to her seduction, the orgiastic Trantridge dance. As she looks on, waiting for company on her homeward walk, Alec appears; and we see her confiding her problem to him, declining his offer of a lift warily (" 'I am much obliged to 'ee, sir,' she answered") but without the formality of the later version—" 'I am much obliged,' she answered frigidly"—where she has become the alert repulser of his attentions. The suggestion of greater intimacy is picked up in a conversation later that night, after Alec has rescued Tess from the Amazonian sisters who pick a quarrel with her on the way home:

> "[Tess], how many times have I kissed you since you have been here?"
> "You know as well as I."
> "Not many."
> "Too many."
> "Only about four times, and never once on the lips, because you turn away so."

This is inconveniently explicit in the context of a purified Tess, and it is deleted altogether from the later version. But it reflects the greater degree of intimacy permitted by the Ur-*Tess*, which in turn makes the seduction itself credible.

"The girl who escapes from her fellow-servants in their jollity by jumping up on horseback . . . behind a master of such a character, and being carried off by him in the middle of the night, naturally leaves her reputation behind her." Mrs. Oliphant's absurd verdict is unexpectedly pertinent to the revised version. But the problem doesn't arise in the Ur-*Tess*. Once again the gig—the more prosaic but more probable means of Tess's rescue in the original version—plays an important part in this crucial scene. In the later version, Tess reacts to Alec's attempt to put his arm round her by a little push that threatens to make him lose his balance, perched sideways on his horse with her behind him. In the Ur-*Tess*, however, she reacts with an unladylike vigour which makes him fall right out of the gig and onto the ground, winding him in the process. Alec makes the most of his fall, capitalising on her genuine alarm and penitence—" 'O I am so sorry, Mr Hawnferne! Have I hurt you? Have I killed 'ee? Do speak to me!' "—to renew his complaints about being kept at arm's length. The incident puts Tess firmly in the wrong, and makes her acquiesce in driving on beside him with his arm round her (" 'because I thought I had wronged you by that push' ") until she realises that they are nowhere near home. It is at this point that Hardy introduces the motif of intoxication which printed versions omit after 1891. Earlier, the death of Prince had been the direct result of her father's drunkenness and Tess's exhaustion. Hawnferne's is specifically described as a drinking farm, and the Trantridge dance, with its stupefied couples falling to the ground, prepares for Tess's own collapse in the Chase. She too is caught up in the Trantridge ethos when she accepts Alec's offer of a warming draught of spirits before he goes off to look for the road. The logic of the scenario—confused, realistically mingling accident and design, character and situation—is entirely convincing. When Tess looks back on the events leading up to her fall, she reflects accurately enough: "She had never cared for him, she did not care for him now. She had dreaded him, winced at him, succumbed to him, and that was all." In 1892 Hardy accentuated Alec's role as seducer by adding "succumbed *to a cruel advantage he took of her helplessness.*" But it needed more than this to transform seduction into the near-rape demanded by the purification of Tess, and at the same time Hardy added the comments of the Marlott villagers as Tess suckles her child in the harvest-field:

> A little more than persuading had to do wi' the coming o't. . . . There were they that heard a sobbing one night last year in The Chase; and it mid ha' gone hard wi' a certain party if folks had come along.

Like Milton, Hardy has produced two versions of the fall—one, comprehensible in human terms, the other retrospectively imposed for the sake of his argument.

THE WAGES OF SIN

The aftermath of Tess's stay at the Slopes is explicitly postlapsarian; Tess had discovered that "the serpent hisses where the sweet birds sing," and she makes her exit from the paradise of unknowing pursued by the text-painter's flaming letters: "THE, WAGES, OF, SIN, IS, DEATH" (in the first edition, "THY, DAMNATION, SLUMBERETH, NOT"). Manuscript evidence suggests that the period of Tess's dejection at Marlott originally occupied a larger space, which encourages the idea that Hardy had wished to stress its part in bringing the mature Tess into being. Paradoxically, it is her seduction that has made here a fitting counterpart to the high-minded Angel Clare:

> At a leap almost [Tess] changed from simple girl to dignified woman. Symbols of reflectiveness passed into her face, and a note of tragedy at times into her voice. Her eyes grew larger and more eloquent. She became what would have been called a fine creature . . . a woman whom the turbulent experiences of the last year or two had quite failed to demoralize.

Angel has been reflective by thought as she has been by life—talking the language of religious disaffection where she expresses her sense of dissonance in the language of experience (" 'there are always more ladies than lords when you come to peel 'em' "). Angel's dissent from the rigid fundamental Christianity of his father, together with his harp-playing, single him out at once as a thinking and a feeling man. The congruence of their sensibilities is beautifully evoked in the overgrown garden where Tess has been listening to Angel's playing. The garden perfectly expresses the erotic potential of their relationship—potential coloured by the implications of a fallen world. As she "undulate[s] upon [Angel's] notes as upon billows," Tess is surrounded by a strange-smelling wilderness, "damp and rank with succulent grass and tall blooming weeds," in which snails climb the stems of apple trees and sticky blights make blood-red stains on Tess's skin. Melancholy and sensuousness are fused in the highly-charged atmosphere of a June evening: "The floating pollen seemed to be his notes made visible, and the dampness of the garden the tears of its sensibility." The same blend of sensibility with the "succulence" complained of by Morris (dutifully revised to "juicy") characterises their scenes of courtship in the richly fertile Frome valley—scenes to which Hardy once again made significant modifications.

Just as the purification of Tess had demanded the blackening of Alec, it also required an increase in Angel's coldness and, as before, in Tess's reticence. Like Alec, the original Angel had been a younger and more believable character—bowled over by Tess, perhaps against his better judgment, having had no thoughts of marriage before. The early scenes between them are pervaded by mutual sexual attraction which small but significant revisions attempt to play down. For instance, when Tess archly accuses Angel of ranging the cows to her advantage, her smile "lifted her upper lip gently in the middle so as to show three or four of her teeth, while the lower remained still"; "*severely* still" is the correction. Angel, burdened in one manuscript reading by a "*growing madness* of passion . . . for the *seductive* Tess" is less overwhelmed in the final version by a "waxing fervour of passion" for a chastely "soft and silent" Tess. The crystallising moment for both, their first embrace, is similarly censored. When Angel comes impulsively round behind the cow Tess is milking and takes her in his arms, the first version reads: "[Tess] yielded to Angel's embrace as unreflectingly as a child. Having seen that it was really her lover and no one else, her lips parted, she panted in her impressionability, and burst into a succession of ecstatic sobs." In the later version, Tess is more restrained: "her lips parted, and she sank upon him in her momentary joy; *with something very like an ecstatic cry.*" Angel has been on the point of "*violently* kissing" Tess's mouth, and declares himself "*passionately* devoted" to her; we lose both the violence and the passion, while Tess's emotion merely leads her to "become agitated" where before she had begun "to sob in reality." As Angel "burns" to be with her, so Tess is permitted to be fully responsive; equally disturbed by their embrace, the two of them (not just the Angel of the later version) keep apart—"palpitating bundles of nerves as both of them were." In so far as they are distinguished at this stage, it is by a love that is intellectual and imaginative on his side, and full of "impassioned warmth" on hers. Angel is conceived, in contrast to Alec, as a man in whom imagination and conscience are inseparable from love; he wins Tess's "tender respect" precisely by his restraint, and we are told that though he "could love intensely . . . his love was more specifically of the solicitous and cherishing mood" (by 1891 it is a love "inclined to the imaginative and ethereal"). Only in the post-1889 section of the novel do we hear of a love "ethereal to a fault, imaginative to impracticability," of Angel's "will to subdue his physical emotion to his ideal emotion" and "his small compressed mouth."

The Angel of the Ur-*Tess* is scrupulous rather than obsessional. Hardy has created an altogether more pitying portrait of a man who cannot cope with the implications of the sexuality to which he none the less responds— unconsciously preferring Tess spiritualised by the light of dawn. Although he warms to the instinctual, easy-going life of the dairy, he retains the morality of the vicarage. As Alec is trapped by his own code of seduction and betrayal, so Angel was to have been trapped by his puritan upbringing. We are told that "despite his heterodox opinions" (changed in 1892 to "heterodoxy, faults, and weaknesses") Angel never envisages sex outside marriage. His acceptance of the ethical code practised by his parents, despite his rejection of what he calls "the miraculous" element in Christianity, was to have been central to his tragedy. It is in Angel's confession that Hardy's falsification of his original intention can be seen most clearly. Angel's religious dissent has been crucial, not only in preventing his entering the Church like his brothers, but in preventing his going to university. No less than Tess, he is socially displaced, and, in the eyes of his family at least, damned for his views. The confession which he embarks on in the Ur-*Tess* is quite simply one of unbelief:

> "Tess, have you noticed that though I am a parson's son, I don't go to church?"
> "I have—occasionally."
> "Did you ever think why?"
> "I thought you did not like the parson of the parish."
> "It was not that, for I don't know him. Didn't it strike you as strange that being so mixed up with the church by family ties and traditions I have not entered it but have done the odd thing of learning to be a farmer?"
> "It did once or twice, dear Angel."

That the subject is clearly of more importance to Angel than Tess accentuates the intellectual gap between them. We cannot know how Angel would have continued, since at this point in the manuscript two pages have been condensed into one. A pencil draft for the final version, on the back of the surviving leaf, could suggest that Hardy had originally occupied the missing page with a much fuller statement of Angel's ethical position in the form of an extended quotation from St Paul (including an explicit denunciation of "chambering and wantonness" as well as the more general injunction preserved in the final version: " 'Be thou an example—in word, in conversation, in charity, in spirit, in faith, in purity' " [1 Timothy 4:12]). What is lacking is any indication whether Hardy had intended Angel to confess to a sexual episode in his own past paralleling Tess's. But although the Ur-*Tess* is disappointingly incomplete here, the clinching piece of evidence is provided by Hardy's earlier reference to this brief affair with an older woman, since it occurs on a new half page pasted to an old one, onto which extra material has clearly been fitted. The only reason for so substantial a revision would have been to make this earlier account of Angel's career square with a crucial change in his confession—a change motivated by Hardy's need to present a black-and-white case for Tess.

If Alec becomes an implausible villain, Angel, with his talk of purity, becomes a hypocritical proponent of the double standard. The overstatement does more than strain credibility—it falsifies Hardy's humane vision of individuals trapped by themselves and the ironies of their past. "Too Late, Beloved!" takes on new force in the light of Tess's marriage to the man least able to overlook her deviation from Pauline ethics. That the virginal milkmaid of Angel's imagination is no longer "pure" is as tragic for him as for her in the Ur-*Tess*. Significantly, it is only on their wedding night in the original version that Angel learns of the decayed aristocratic descent to which he has slightingly referred on previous occasions (his unexpected pride in Tess's ancestry is an invention of the later version, where she confesses to it at an earlier stage). Theirs had been tragedy of mutual incomprehension, almost, a collision of cultures as well as morals. The gulf between them is nowhere clearer than in Tess's original preparedness, before their marriage, to accept "another kind of union with him, for his own sake, had he urged it upon her; that he might have retreated if discontented with her on learning her story." Though less easy-going than her mother, Tess had been able to envisage an alternative to Angel's scrupulous morality. But such a thought is not allowed to cross the mind of a purified Tess; instead, the later version encumbers her with the naive and exonerating belief—displayed only after the confession (i.e., in the post-1889 phase of composition)—that Angel could divorce her if he wished. This high-minded heroine is not the same as the Tess of earlier scenes, torn between her desire to be honest with Angel and an understandable longing for happiness at all costs. With purification comes inauthenticity and a new straining for effect in a novel previously marked by its realism. Angel's rigidity, Tess's humility, are equally forced; and it is surely significant that in the scenes immediately following the confession—that is, in the first scenes to be written when the novel was resumed after its successive rejections—Hardy's imagination should be seen to be labouring under precisely the adverse conditions described by "Candour in English Fiction."

AFTERMATH

It would be wrong to imply that everything belonging to the later, post-1889 phase of composition fell short of an earlier truth to life. Tess's desolate period at Flintcombe-Ash is enough to show Hardy's imagination functioning at its best, creating a universal predicament out of individuals at work in a hostile landscape which at once mirrors and dwarfs their suffering. All the same, Hardy continued to modify his narrative even beyond this stage. Traces of his original conception linger on especially in his handling of Alec, whose reappearance initiates the final movement of the novel. Predictably, Hardy superimposes the portrait of a fully-formed rake on the Alec of the Trantridge period ("the aforetimed curves of sensuousness," "the lip-shapings that had meant seductiveness," "the bold prominent eye that had flashed upon her shrinking form in the old time with such heartless and cruel grossness"). But the sincerity of Alec's conversion, and the genuine agony of his loss of faith, are not questioned in the manuscript. There is irony and factitiousness, but not hedonism or fraud. The Alec who can say of his new-found faith, " 'If you could only know, Tess, the sense of security, the certainty that you can never fall away . . . ' " is expressing a religious sense deliberately dissipated by the text of 1902: " 'If you could only know, Tess, *the pleasure of having a good slap at yourself.*' " Tess's angry outburst first meets with " 'Tess . . . don't speak so. It came to me like a shining light' "; only in 1902, again, does this become " 'It came to me *like a jolly new idea.*' " When Alec reproaches himself for " 'the whole blackness of the sin, the awful, awful iniquity' " (emended in 1902 to " '*the whole unconventional business of our time at Trantridge,*' " we may recoil from the crude language of Christian condemnation, but it does not seem cynical. The impression is of a man, however mistakenly, attempting to right an old wrong in the terms laid down by his new morality, and made wretched by the reawakening of sexual passion—coming to see Tess with a marriage license in his pocket, visiting her later when he should be preaching to the "poor sinners" (by 1902, "*poor drunken boobies*") who await him elsewhere, and leaving her with the words, " 'I'll go away—to hide—and—ah, can I!—pray' " (secularised in 1902 to " 'I'll go away—*to swear*—and—ah, can I! *mend*' "). Angel's had been an intellectual tragedy: Alec's, a tragedy of passion. Ironically, it is Angel's arguments, retailed by Tess, which lead Alec to lose the faith to which he had been converted by Angel's father and which pave the way back to Tess. Here Hardy's target is less Alec himself than the religious doctrine which once more injures Tess in its failure to encompass the heterodoxy of human experience.

Mrs Oliphant wrote indignantly of Tess's collapse, "If Tess did this, then Tess . . . was at twenty a much inferior creature to the unawakened Tess at sixteen who would not live upon the wages of iniquity." Exactly; Tess's suffering may deepen her, but it breaks her in the end. If the wages of sin is death, the wages of virtue—as we see at Flintcombe-Ash—are grinding poverty and back-breaking labour. As Tess puts it succinctly when Angel finds her living with Alec at Sandbourne, " 'He bought me' " (by 1891, more reticently, " 'He ———' "). Hardy's imaginative allegiance to Tess does not flinch from her subsequent act of murder—carried out with triumphant thoroughness in the earliest manuscript readings. The workman who finds Alec's body reports graphically " 'He has been stabbed—*the carving knife is sticking up in his heart*' " (toned down to " 'He has been hurt with the carving knife' "), and Hardy himself underlines Tess's violence with "The knife had been *driven through the heart* of the victim" (similarly toned down to "The wound was small, but the point of the knife had touched the heart of the victim"). Later, when Tess tells Angel of the murder, she does so with "a *triumphant* smile" not "a pitiful white smile"; " 'I have done it *well*,' " she claims, rather than the conventionally helpless " 'I have done it—I don't know how.' " Hardy perhaps wished to play down Tess's unbalance for the sake of propriety, but his initial response to this imagined act is surely ours—that it repays the injustice to which Tess has been subjected throughout the book. Here, as elsewhere, Hardy's intuitive commitment was incompletely suppressed by the terms of reference imposed on him. Tess is not a woman to be admired for her purity or condemned for the lack of it; simply, she is a human being whose right to be is affirmed on every page, and whose death is the culminating injustice.

Mowbray Morris—to whom *Tess* was "a coarse and disagreeable story [told] in a coarse and disagreeable manner"—summed up the proper purpose of fiction in his editorial reply to "Candour in English Fiction": "to console, to refresh, to amuse; to lighten the heavy and the weary weight, not to add to it; to distract, not to disturb." Hardy's own very different views were incorporated into the novel itself in the cancelled paragraph which originally introduced his final chapter and the hanging of Tess:

> The humble delineator of human character and human contingencies, whether his narrative deal with the actual or with the typical only, must primarily and above all things be sincere, however terrible sincerity may be. Gladly sometimes would such an one lie, for dear civility's sake, but for the ever-haunting afterthought, "This work was not honest, and may do harm." In typical history with all its liberty, there are, as in real history, features which can never be distorted with impunity and issues which should never be falsified. And perhaps in glancing at the misfortunes of such people as have or could have lived we may acquire

some art in shielding from like misfortunes those who have yet to be born. If truth requires justification, surely this is an ample one.

The question must be asked: did Hardy lie, if only "for dear civility's sake?" Surely not. Though he chose to compromise in order to make his case and gain a hearing, he never falsified the issues. For all its blackening and whitewashing, the final version of *Tess of the D'Urbervilles* is justified not only by its power to move and disturb, but by its essential truth.

Women and the New Fiction
1880–1900

Penny Boumelha

The last twenty years of the nineteenth century witnessed a quite unprecedented proliferation of women novelists—a phenomenon that did not go unnoticed in its time; a writer complains in 1894 that "the society lady, dazzled by the brilliancy of her own conversation, and the serious-minded spinster, bitten by some sociological theory, still decide . . . that fiction is the obvious medium through which to astonish or improve the world" [Hubert Crackenthorpe in *The Yellow Book*]. I do not know whether solid statistical evidence could be adduced for the contemporary sense that women dominated the novel, if only numerically; but it is undeniable that they achieved a considerably higher representation in the ranks of professional authors than in any previous period. Nor were they all unknown or unrecognised minor talents: many women writers who are now forgotten were in their time widely read and discussed. Sarah Grand's novel *The Heavenly Twins* sold forty thousand copies within a few weeks of its publication in 1893; George Egerton's first volume of short stories, *Keynotes* (1893), gave its name to a whole series of books published by John Lane, known as "Petticoat" Lane partly for that reason; and a *Punch* parody of the same book, thinly disguised as "She-Notes" by Borgia Smudgiton, follows the original in such detail as to suggest that all the magazine's potential readers could reasonably be expected to know it.

But the significance of such women writers was not restricted to their numerical strength or their commercial success. They were perceived, and to some extent regarded themselves, as constituting by virtue of their sex alone a school or class of writers. They often claim to be writing with female readers in mind, and to be making a political or moral statement on behalf

From *Thomas Hardy and Women: Sexual Ideology and Narrative Form*. © 1982 by Penny Boumelha. Barnes & Noble, 1982.

of their sex; Ella Hepworth Dixon, for example, wrote to Stead that her novel *The Story of a Modern Woman* (1894) was intended as "a plea for a kind of moral and social trades–unionism among women." The example of the trades union probably underlies the recurrent suggestion, in the "New Women" fiction, that women must and will combine, either against men or against specific abuses. The solidarity of wife and mistress, or of virgin and whore, is often recognised as a crucial element in the struggle against the double standard of sexual morality, as for example, in Lucas Malet's *The Wages of Sin* (1891) or Annie Holdsworth's *Joanna Trail, Spinster* (1894). In this situation, writing came, to a degree, to be regarded as in itself a political act of sexual solidarity. It is not surprising, then, that reviewers saw in the proliferation of women writers the marks of an organised school. W. T. Stead, reviewing a rather miscellaneous collection of novels and stories by women in 1894, unites them with this dizzying definition: "The Modern Woman novel is not merely a novel written by a woman, or a novel written about women, but it is a novel written by a woman about women from the standpoint of Woman." The last phrase isolates the factor which unifies in differentiation—the tendency for the central female characters, either individually or as a group, to be the centres of consciousness in the novel, rather than merely objects encountered by male subjectivity. In fact, this tendency is by no means confined to books by women, as the evidence of Meredith or Gissing indicates; indeed, Carolyn Heilbrun has named the whole *fin de siècle* period that of the "Women as Hero." Nevertheless, the experiencing heroine was felt by women's writing, and this sense pervades much contemporary discussion.

One manifestation of the centrality of female characters was the introduction of a whole range of hitherto marginalised or suppressed subject-matter into the novel. The exploration of the experience of female characters involved a confrontation of sexual and marital relationships which had long lain on the unspoken and unspeakable periphery of fiction. Issues such as prostitution, rape, contraception, adultery, and divorce appear with increasing frequency and some explicitness, often provoking outrage and disgust in the critics. Arthur Waugh, in the somewhat unlikely setting of that citadel of decadence, *The Yellow Book*, blames women writers for the prominence of sexual themes:

> It was said of a great poet by a little critic that he wheeled his nuptial couch into the area; but these small poets and smaller novelists bring out their sick into the thoroughfare and stop the traffic while they give us a clinical lecture upon their sufferings. We are told that this is part of the revolt of woman, and certainly our women-writers are chiefly to blame. It is out of date, no doubt, to clamour for modesty; but the woman who describes the sensations of childbirth does so, it is to be presumed—not as the writer of advice to a wife—but as an artist producing literature for art's

sake. And so one may fairly ask her: How is art served by all this? What has she told us that we did not all know, or could not learn from medical manuals? and what impression has she left us over and above the memory of her unpalatable details?

This criterion of teaching something "that we did not all know" is one which does not seem to have been applied to the works of male authors.

In a sense, all this was undoubtedly exhilarating for female writers and readers, for it allowed them to take speech for themselves; one writer comments in 1896 that "It is only during the last twenty years or so that the voice of woman has really been heard in literature." Further, it opened up a far greater play of possibilities in both narrative and form, of which many women joyously availed themselves. Ethel Voynich's Gemma Bolla, for example, is a political activist in Italy (as is Mark Rutherford's Clara Hopgood). A particularly rich instance is the eponymous heroine of Lady Florence Dixie's *Gloriana; or, The Revolution of 1900* (1890), who passes for a man in order to prove her abilities—which she undeniably does, becoming in turn headboy at Eton, champion Hunt Steeplechase jockey, Commander-in-Chief of para-military women's "volunteer companies," sponsor of a successful Woman Suffrage Bill, founder of a Hall of Liberty where women students, athletes, and brass bands live and perform, and, perhaps inevitably, Prime Minister; ultimately, revealed as a woman, she finds love and marriage, sparks off a feminist revolution and is secularly canonised by succeeding generations. (This book, incidentally, has the distinction of what must surely be one of the earliest examples of a now familiar phrase, in its disclaimer of any antagonism towards men: "The Author's best and truest friends . . . have been and are men.")

Gloriana's feminist Utopia—albeit, for much of the book, a transvestite one—is only one instance of the profusion of alternative fictional forms in this liberation of experiment. Short stories, fantasies, dream-stories, essay fiction, and impressionistic sketches are all forms largely, though not of course exclusively, developed or re-worked by women writers in the period. So, Jane Hume Clapperton's *Margaret Dunmore: or, A Socialist Home* (1888), a dreary tale of eugenic "socialism," mixes epistolary form, drama, and omniscient narration; Olive Schreiner's *The Story of an African Farm* (1883) breaks its narrative with lengthy allegories; and many novels include brief or long passages of verse. The leisurely and particularised realist narrative is displaced by the fragmentary and unparticularised short story, by fantasy, by mixed modes of prose and poetry, and so on: but the period's challenge to the dominant fictional mode of realism took only in part the form of such experimentalism in genre. More than this, the characteristic narrative voice of the realist novel, that of the omniscient commentator who circumscribes and thus ironises the consciousness of the hero, is disturbed by the appearance of other kinds of voice which throw into question this distance between author and character. The "New Woman" novel was often perceived as a work of propaganda or a disguised tract for precisely this reason: not because its ideological project is any more visible or determining than in other kinds of fiction, but because of the sporadic punctuation of the narrative by meditation, harangue or lyric, by an informing commitment which constantly threatens the circumscribing narrative voice.

Now I do not wish here to suggest—with the concomitant risk of reinforcing a sexual stereotype—that the "New Woman" fiction is marked by its adjustment to a characteristically feminine subjectivity (an interpretation sometimes made at the time, as I shall show). It is rather that the pose of the "objective" narrator—the anonymous, balanced reporter who can authoritatively interpret the behaviour and states of mind of the characters—is unsettled by the tension between this male voice (it is not an accident that so many female writers take male pseudonyms) and the periodic dissolution of the boundaries between author and character. It is as if at moments there is no mediating narrator; the writing of the fiction becomes for a time its own action, its own plot, enacting as well as articulating the protest of the text. *The Story of an African Farm* holds in tension the dispassionate Emersonian pose of the objective narrator, that "Ralph Iron" who intervenes between author and text, and the commitment to a passionate vision—Lyndall's and Schreiner's—which is allowed only one articulate eruption into the narrative, but which informs and troubles the structure both before and after the chapter that bears Lyndall's name. In works by male writers, too, the realist narrative mode is frequently unsettled. The example of Hardy comes to mind: the abrupt and disturbing shifts in point of view in *Tess of the D'Urbervilles* enact the threatened dominance of the distanced narrator. In this respect, the "New Woman" fiction is at the opposite pole from the naturalist novel, which preserves a scrupulously "scientific" distance from the particularities of its text; the difference between *Tess* and George Moore's *Esther Waters* (1894) resides partly in this question of the maintenance and manipulation of points of view.

The formal experimentation of the New Fiction, together with its openly sexual character, posed a significant challenge to the power of the editors of periodicals and the proprietors of the circulating libraries; so it is that this period sees the demise of the previously dominant mode of publication, the family serial and the three-decker. As early as 1885, Gissing was able to announce this change, and also to declare his enthusiasm for the modifications in narrative mode and voice which accompanied it:

> It is fine to see how the old three volume tradition is being broken through. One volume is becoming commonest of all. It is the new school, due to continental influence. Thackeray and Dickens wrote at enormous length, and with precision of detail; their plan is to tell everything, and leave nothing to be divined. Far more artistic, I think, is the later method, of merely suggesting; of dealing with episodes, instead of writing biographies. The old novelist is om-

niscient; I think it is better to tell a story precisely as one does in real life, surmising, telling in detail what can so be told and no more. In fact, it approximates to the dramatic mode of presentment.

It is interesting to note that Gissing welcomes the new forms primarily as a new and more thoroughgoing kind of realism. New journals, such as *The Yellow Book* and its imitator *The Savoy*, sprang up to accommodate poems, short stories, and even fragments—Victoria Cross's "Theodora: A Fragment" was one of the more notorious examples of the New Woman in action. Publishing houses were quick to open their lists to new writers whose work (sometimes enormously successful on the market) dealt with women or sex, as John Lane's "Keynotes" series and Heinemann's "Pioneer" series testify. The New Fiction had an enormous impact, not only on publishers, but on readers and critics too. Reviewers, especially those who wrote in the more long-established periodicals, reacted on the whole with shocked incomprehension. The vocabulary of realism, itself seen comparatively recently as outrageous, was rapidly pressed into service to accuse these new writers of disproportion in their emphasis on the sexual:

> The new fiction of sexuality presents to us a series of pictures painted from reflections in convex mirrors, the colossal nose which dominates the face being represented by one colossal appetite which dominates life . . . everywhere it is a flagrant violation of the obvious proportion of life.

After the initial modified praise of the novelty and freshness of the New Fiction, the figure of the New Woman exploring her own womanhood came fairly rapidly to be perceived as a tired cliché, fit matter for parody. In fact, satire or parody of the New Woman became for a time a sub-genre of its own, taking in such works as Sydney Grundy's play *The New Woman* (1894) and Kenneth Grahame's role-reversal satire *The Headswoman* (1898). The opponents or reformers of marriage were particularly popular targets; this passage is from William Barry's novel *The Two Standards* (1898):

> Some, as, for instance, Miss Vane Vere, the well-known professor of Rational Dress and Dancing, spoke of "terminable annuities," by which it is suspected that they meant engagements lasting for a year and a day, but then to be dissolved at the pleasure—or, more likely, the displeasure—of either contracting party. Others— and among these Mrs. Oneida Leyden was far the most advanced—talked of "perfection." . . . Thus to be perfect and to be married—at least always to the same partner—did not seem in accordance with the Higher Law. Mrs. Leyden was thought to have obeyed the Higher Law. Into this remarkable scheme a lady from the Turkish frontier, speaking many languages, and known by her eloquent books on the subject of woman's freedom, had

brought fresh complications by recommending the Oriental household as a pattern for progressive people. But . . . this very Frau
von Engelmacher had boldly announced that superfluous babies
should be handed over to the chemist, and was known to take a
strong view in favour of vivisection.

Nordau's tireless and massively influential castigation of degeneracy
in his *Entartung* (1892; translated into English from the second edition in
1895) gave the critical hostility to the New Fiction a fresh impetus. Diagnosed in a reassuringly medical way as "erotomania" or "sex-mania," it
was variously condemned for squalor, morbidity, pessimism, and decadence, attributed with varying degrees of accuracy to the influence of
French poetry, Scandinavian problem-literature, Thomas Hardy, and Oscar
Wilde. (Shaw, in the 1905 Preface to his previously unpublished 1880 novel
The Irrational Knot, was to ridicule such attributions and argue that "the
revolt of the Life Force against readymade morality in the nineteenth century was not the work of a Norwegian microbe, but would have worked
itself into expression in English literature had Norway never existed.") The
rhetoric of attacks on the New Fiction becomes highly physical, reflecting
perhaps the "physiological realism" it condemns:

> Instead of walking on the mountain tops, breathing the pure high
> atmosphere of imagination freely playing around the truths of life
> and of love, they force us down into the stifling charnel-house,
> where animal decay, with its swarms of loathsome activities, meets
> us at every turn.

But even in the censuring of decadence, the difference in sex comes
into play. A distinction was sometimes drawn between the varieties of
degeneracy practised by male and female writers. As well as those books
by men which openly took up the "woman question"—such as the
pro- or anti-free union novels of Grant Allen, William Barry and Frank Frankfort Moore—there were within the New Fiction a number of formally
experimental works which dealt with sexual themes from a male point of
view. William Platt's *Women, Love, and Life* (1895) mixes poetry, short stories,
allegory and essays, and makes use of subject-matter including necrophilia
and masochism. In his story "A Passion," a woman experiences the greatest
happiness she has ever known through dying during a caesarean, refusing
anaesthetics; she makes her husband swear always to wear a girdle made
of her flesh. "The Child of Love and Death" is yet more extraordinary in
synopsis: a woman conceives a child while giving her virginity to her newly-
killed lover, in a vain attempt to revive him; after a fifteen-month pregnancy, she opens herself with a knife to release the child; she survives until
the child is weaned; he devotes his life to preaching purity (carefully distinguished from chastity), and is beheaded by the king, who then orders
a prostitute to have sex with his dead body; she, recognising the dead
man's holiness, kills the king instead, addresses words of love to the head-

less corpse, and commits suicide. The sexual grotesquerie of Platt's volume (described by Hardy as "mere sexuality without any counterpoise"), and the rapturously breathless style of his prose, can both be seen in this description by a woman of the consummation of a love affair:

> "He staggered up to me and the veins on his forehead stood big—he took me in his arms with no word but kissed me with red hot lips till the crisped skin of them crumbled on to my chin. No word passed—but—I would say it proudly and without shame were I standing now at the judgment seat of God!—the act of love passed between us."

Less extravagantly, Henry Murray's *A Man of Genius* (1895) and Francis Adams's *A Child of the Age* (1894; a reworking of his 1884 *Leicester: An Autobiography*) both exploit the same central situation: a struggling "decadent" artist with a strong sense of his own abilities, living unmarried with a working-class girl whom he feels to be holding him back from the fame and fortune rightfully his. Both novels offer in passing somewhat cold-blooded reflections upon the nature of these relationships. Adams's curiously modern novel, a fragmentary dream-like first-person narrative, has the artist meditating upon his Rosy:

> Then, when I was in bed, I considered what was the real condition of my feelings towards her. Without doubt, they were those of complete callousness and, perhaps, something more. . . .It seemed to me to be something little short of folly to stay here and be troubled with her. I ought to go out into the world and see its ways, so as to prepare myself for my work.

In Murray's more conventional work, a prominent motif is women's attraction towards force and glamour: "Women are like nations, they admire and love most deeply the tyrant who most completely dominates them." Again, George Street's stories in *Episodes* (1895) and his novel *The Wise and the Wayward* (1896) adopt a man-of-the-worldly tone of aristocratic boredom in incidents such as a wife's revealing to her sister-in-law that her feeling for her husband is " 'merely sensual. . . . It is simply because he is handsome and big and strong,' " or a husband's laconic reaction to his wife's adultery with his best friend:

> "You see," he continued, "you place me in a very tiresome dilemma. I must either divorce you and quarrel with a man with whom I am not in the least angry—he's one of my oldest friends and has only acted as I have acted many times—or I must put myself in the ridiculous position of the forgiving husband and allow him to laugh at me. Think! I must either quarrel with a man who was my chum at school, or appear absurd to him. See what you women do!"
>
> (*Episodes*)

Ignoring "decadent" books by women like Ella Darcy's *Monochromes* (1895) or Mabel Wotton's *Day-Books* (1896), and "high-minded" books by men like Grant Allen's *The Woman Who Did* (1895) or William Barry's *The New Antigone* (1887), pre-determined notions of sexual difference allowed the New Fiction to be split along the fault-line of the author's sex. Arthur Waugh sees "want of restraint" and "the language of the courtesan" resulting from the "ennervated sensation" of women's writing, while "coarse familiarity" and the language of "the bargee" follow "a certain brutal virility" in men's. A pamphlet, *The New Fiction*, published in 1885, distinguishes a "revolting woman" novel and a "defiant man" novel:

> On the man's side it is cynical as well as nasty; it assumes that there is no world except Piccadilly after dark, or perhaps the coulisses of some disreputable music-hall . . . On the woman's side it seems at least to be in deadly earnest, but many of the assumptions are the same, *mutatis mutandis*, and the expression of them is even less veiled.

Still more disturbing to the sensibilities of this truculently self-proclaimed "Philistine," it should be noted, is that fiction of the "morbid and lurid classes" which does not at once reveal the sex of its writer.

Not only tone and language, but also the form of the fiction, could be derived from the sex of the author through the idea of a distinct and inherent female temperament. The German critic Laura Marholm Hansson writes in 1896 that:

> Woman is the most subjective of all creatures; she can only write about her own feelings, and her expression of them is her most valuable contribution to literature. Formerly women's writings were, for the most part, either directly or indirectly, the expression of a great falsehood. They were so overpoweringly impersonal, it was quite comic to see the way in which they imitated men's models, both in form and contents. Now that woman is conscious of her individuality as a woman, she needs an artistic mode of expression, she flings aside the old forms, and seeks for new.

But if the woman writer's mind was ceaselessly returned to her sex, her body was often denied it. In the general attacks on the New Fiction, women writers above all were subjected to a great deal of personal abuse and innuendo about their sexual inclinations. Stead—a relatively sympathetic reviewer—concludes from *Keynotes* that its author is a hermaphrodite, and generalises that the Novel of the Modern Woman is often written by "creatures who have been unkindly denied by nature the instincts of their sex," who have not "had the advantage of personal experience of marriage and of motherhood." Again, C. E. Raimond's novel *George Mandeville's Husband* (1894) takes as what is clearly meant to be a representative case a woman novelist (the "George" of the title), whose ruthless devotion to her own mediocre talent demands the sacrifice of her first husband's artistic career, and then of her only child's life. There can be no mistake about the kind of novelist George Mandeville is:

> His wife was not long in realising that she had found her mission. Yes, she had "oracles to deliver." She would be not only a novelist, but a teacher and leader of men. She would champion the cause of Progress, she would hold high the banner of Woman's Emancipation. She would not consent, however, to be criticised by the narrow standards applied in these evil days to woman's work. She was assured she had a powerful and original mind—she would not allow the soft veil of her sex to hide her merit from the public eye. She would call herself "George Mandeville."

Mocked as a "large, uncorseted woman" whose size and coarseness make her sexual demands repellent, she moves in a circle composed entirely of "effeminate" actors and ugly, fanatical, 'advanced' women. Her husband is devoted to their daughter, from whom he extracts a promise that she will never write or paint, because women's artistic productions are tainted with the vices of amateurism and mediocrity which corrupt taste and lower standards. This is the height of his paternal ambition for her: "Rosina should never struggle and toil; she should be no more than a dignified looker-on at this new Dance of Death. . . . Rosina should *be*; the less she 'did,' the better." Rosina, neglected by her mother, dies of brain-fever. It would be naive, and worse, to be surprised that this novel is the work of a woman; but it is perhaps allowable to be surprised that the pseudonym "C. E. Raimond" conceals Elizabeth Robins, friend of Wilde, pioneer actress in Ibsen's plays, and later author of the suffragist play *Votes for Women* (1905). (Nor, it must be said, does the novel lend itself to an interpretation as parody, as a brilliant and strategic adoption of the male narrative voice, skillfully undermined by the manipulation of point of view.) Stead's "phallic criticism," to borrow Mary Ellmann's phrase, and Raimond's account of the woman novelist, lead to the heart of the double-bind: the trouble with women writers is that they are women—or else that they are writers.

The representative role of the woman writers, and the frequency with which such terms as "the woman question," "the problem novel," and "tract" or "propaganda" recur in contemporary discussion of the New Fiction, draw attention to the form taken by this irruption of the feminine into the novel. Women, as writers or as characters, are identified as at once the source and the focus of a "problem," the precise terms of which may vary between, say, the fate of the "surplus" women when men are outnumbered in the population, and the levelling out of the double standard. The woman writer and the New Woman alike are invariably called upon as spokeswomen: they represent, and are represented by, their sex—or, more accurately, their sex as it is bounded by their class-situation. The symbolic names of many such heroines reveal this—names like "Ideala,"

"Speranza," "Angelica," "Newman," and "Eve." Despite the historical component implicit in the name "*New* Woman," it is the typicality of sex which is dominant. The woman is continually returned to her sex, identified, analysed, and made to explain herself on the basis of her difference, her divergence from the male norm (there is, after all, no "Man Question"). This determining typicality of sex marks a shift in the ideological project of novels about women during the *fin de siècle* period, away from the immediately preceding concern with womanliness, and toward the elaboration of a concept of womanhood—a distinction which I shall try to make clear.

"Womanliness," as John Goode has shown, signifies that which is womanly, or like a woman: it is womanly to be like a woman, and a woman is one who behaves in a womanly fashion—the evident circularity of the definition makes more or less overt its reference to a socially-constructed concept. Womanliness is in this sense recognisably a political concept, proposing an external standard of judgement—it is possible, and indeed common, for a woman to be unwomanly—rather than an inherent disposition. It may (especially in the hands of women writers) hold out a promise of satisfaction to the womanly woman, but its aim is clearly the imposition and maintenance of sharply differentiated sexual roles. Dinah Craik's *The Woman's Kingdom*, first published in 1869, but evidently still popular enough to be reprinting in the 1890s, is structurally paradigmatic for the novel of womanliness: the contrasted fatherless or orphaned sisters can be traced back to Jane Austen. The novel's Ruskinian title, and its epigraph from "Of Queen's Gardens," betray its frame of reference, that all-powerful but indirect "influence" which every woman must choose to exert, but which she must never wield. The two sisters here are a teacher, plain, but intelligent and generous, and a convalescent, beautiful, but selfish and petty. They meet two precisely complementary brothers—a doctor, not handsome, but full of character and strength, and a sickly artist, handsome and charming, but weak and unstable. The exact symmetry of character, profession, age and appearance is striking. The frivolous couple drift into equivocal relations, almost marry, but do not; he wastes his talents and becomes a vagabond, while she makes a wealthy but empty marriage and has only a single daughter to show for it. The good pair, however, form a strong and stable relationship—this is the quality of it:

> She watched him coming, a tall figure, strong and active, walking firmly, without pauses or hesitation . . . There he was, the ruler of her life, her friend, her lover, some day to be her husband. He was coming to assume his rights, to assert his sovereignty. A momentary vague terror smote her, a fear as to the unknown future, a tender regret for the peaceful maidenly, solitary days left behind, and then her heart recognised its master and went forth to meet him; not gleefully, with timbrels and dances, but veiled

and gentle, grave and meek; contented and ready to obey him, "even as Sara obeyed Abraham, calling him lord."

He comes, she waits; he asserts, she assents. The two marry, live on a small income but in great happiness and mutual respect, the doctor's integrity sustained by his wife's influence. Her womanly virtues are rewarded with a family of sons. The connection between the acceptance of the womanly role and the successful marriage is so overt that the novel's religious rhetoric barely conceals the underlying economism.

But perhaps the major exponent of the fiction of womanliness is Eliza Lynn Linton, who reinforced her essays on *The Girl of the Period* (collected in 1883) with a helpfully schematic exposition of the concept in novels such as *The Rebel of the Family* (1880). Here there are three sisters, all of marriageable age and slender financial resources, to be contrasted. The eldest has every appearance of being an exemplary woman: quietly elegant, unassuming, she seemingly aims only to please:

> When she heard a new-comer say in a loud whisper to his neighbour: "What a charming smile Miss Winstanley has!" or: "What wonderful style there is about her!" or: "What a graceful person she is, and how delightfully well-mannered!" then her soul was satisfied because her existence was justified. She had done her duty to herself, her mother, her future and the family fortunes. She had therefore earned her her right to be well-dressed and taken out into society, as fairly as a workman, who has laid his tale of bricks, has earned his pint of beer and his stipulated week's wages.

But the incongruously clear-sighted economic metaphor should alert the reader to the trap, for Thomasin's exemplary behaviour is vitiated by her excessive awareness of its value as a commodity. Her motivation is too self-consciously directing her behaviour, and so her discretion and modesty are transmuted into "this quiet immorality, this cynical good sense, this apotheosis of worldly wisdom." The figure of Thomasin, with her "masculine" name, reveals something of the contradiction inherent in Linton's situation as a woman writer serving the ideology of womanliness: the novel's project is to show that womanliness is the only guarantee of success on the marriage-market, and yet to propose as a naturally womanly quality a selflessness which would necessitate ignorance of that fact. The womanliness of the project is undercut by Linton's unwomanly awareness of its fictionality, and this, as I shall argue, necessitates a certain dexterity in the manipulation of point of view.

If Thomasin is one of the figures from Linton's essays, the self-seeking girl of the period, then the youngest sister is another—the pleasure seeker. She is a kind of early Dickens heroine—blonde, blue-eyed, flower-like, lisping. But her sweetness and charm are undermined by her frivolity and lack of solid moral principle. Here again, though, that principle shows itself to be largely a matter of making the best use of her commodity-status. She fails the womanly ideal in the opposite direction, by failing to realise the full marketability of her charms: she is, literally and metaphorically, cheap. Her sisters only narrowly save her from "falling"—a possibility telegraphed from the first in her name, Eva.

The middle sister, Perdita, represents the middle way—a way which, again as the name suggests, is temporarily lost. Her combination of an intelligent mind and a generous heart causes her to be ruthlessly sacrificed by her sisters, but also gives rise to a certain questioning rebelliousness in her. She realises that her abilities are stifled by her narrow life, and longs for the change of sex which alone seems to offer a way out of the problem:

> The heart and soul of all poor Perdita's lamentations and day-dreams was always this wish—that she had been born a boy and could go out into the world to make a name for herself and a fortune for her family! . . . The *Sturm and Drang* period with her was severe; and, seeing how the current of modern thought goes, it was an even chance whether it would end in some fatal absurdity or work through its present turbulence into clearness of purpose and reasonableness of action.

The "fatal absurdity" which threatens Perdita takes the form of a third of Linton's Girl of the Period cast of characters: one of the "Shrieking Sister-hood," the New Woman Bell Blount, who, "hardened," "unsexed," "un-graceful," "mannish" and "monstrous," lectures on women's suffrage to an audience of "mannish" women and "weedy" men. She also poses a more direct sexual threat to Perdita's womanliness, for she lives as the "male" partner in a lesbian relationship which exactly reproduces the structures of power and dependence of a heterosexual marriage. (This relation of feminism to lesbianism also appears in other contemporary novels, such as James's *The Bostonians* and George Moore's *A Drama in Muslin* [both 1886].) Perdita, though repelled by the coarse talk and advanced manners, finds herself fascinated by the purposefulness of Blount's life. Her moral worthlessness is finally exposed, however, in her betrayal of Perdita's secret love for a local chemist—a betrayal which, although motivated exclusively by sexual jealousy, also serves to discredit her public role as a suffragist. Thus delivered from the dual threat of suffragism and lesbianism, Perdita finds the way that was lost in the prospect of a marriage which is given a certain spuriously radical air by its social "unsuitability." But, though her "rebellion" (stressed in the novel's title) consists in marrying for love rather than for money, the true reward for her womanliness comes in her acquiring both: her chemist makes good and rescues her family from financial ruin. Her accession to womanliness is dependent upon her at once knowing that it will serve her well (in contrast to Eva) and not knowing it (in contrast to Thomasin); the difficulty of effecting a coherent reconciliation between the two means that the narrative voice must, at a certain point, abandon its privileged insight into Perdita's consciousness, and distance her by interposing a mediating interpreter. And so it is that, by the end of the novel, she has resigned the right to speech, and it is her husband who gives the final placing of her experience for the reader—that she has found " 'a woman's duties higher than her rights; the quiet restrictions of home more precious than the excitement of liberty, the blare of publicity.' " *The Rebel of the Family* is a parable of the woman's voluntary subjection of herself to a standard of womanliness which, though it is perceived as personally restrictive and unjust, nevertheless constitutes her only means of survival.

Many of the New Woman novels rebel against the limitations and uniformity imposed by this concept. The novels of liberal feminism have as their project, to quote John Goode, "the possible freedom of woman conceived as a rational application of the social contract"; they tend either to be programmatic, embodying a future resolution of the woman question—and hence to take non-realist forms like fantasy—or to concentrate on the symptoms of the contemporary oppression of women, and so to take the form of a realist novel revolving upon the woman in society rather than in a single love-relationship. The characteristic structuring device of the novel of womanliness, the contrasting sisters, gives way to that of the brother and sister: the disparity between their respective abilities and fates gives focus to the liberal feminist programme of "equality" with men in education, professional opportunities, sexual morality, and marital rights and responsibilities. (The precursor in this case is rather George Eliot than Jane Austen.) So, for example, Gertrude Dix's *The Girl from the Farm* (1895) shows a classics graduate forced to postpone her career in order to look after her father, while her weak and selfish brother passes his time in the seduction of local servants; Lady Florence Dixie's *Redeemed in Blood* (1889) is concerned with equal rights of primogeniture for its sibling aristocrats; and Sarah Grand's *The Heavenly Twins* (1893) are a boy and a girl, inseparable in childhood, but subsequently forced apart by the differing expectations of their parents and teachers. Waldo and Lyndall, in Schreiner's *The Story of an African Farm*, are quite different, however, in part because Waldo is not in any degree complicit in the sexual oppression of Lyndall, but is rather her male counterpart, outcast and misunderstood; the submerged parallel between woman as bearer of children and male artist surfaces in the fact that Waldo's two major projects, his sheep-shearing machine and his carved stick, each take him nine months to bring to fruition. Nevertheless, Lyndall's long speech draws an explicit contrast between the lives marked out for them by their difference of sex:

> "We all enter the world little plastic beings, with so much natural
> force perhaps, but for the rest—blank; and the world tells us what
> we are to be, and shapes us by the ends it sets before us. To you
> it says—*Work*; and to us it says—*Seem* . . . To us it says—Strength

shall not help you, nor knowledge, nor labour. You shall gain what men gain, but by other means.

"Then the curse begins to act on us. It finishes its work when we are grown women, who no more look out wistfully at a more healthy life; we are contented. We fit our sphere as a Chinese woman's foot fits her shoe exactly, as though God had made both—and yet He knows nothing of either. In some of us the shaping to our end has been quite completed. The parts we are not to use have been quite atrophied, and have even dropped off; but in others, and we are not less to be pitied, they have been weakened and left. We wear the bandages, but our limbs have not grown to them; we know that we are compressed, and chafe against them."

This intensely physicalised sense of chafing against cramping limitation pervades the feminist novels; the analogy between the Chinese practice of footbinding and the constraints upon the growing middle-class girl recurs. But Lyndall's perception that she is actually *shaped* by what is inscribed upon the "blank" infant is unusual; more common is the image of a compression that, released, will allow the "natural" form to reassert itself. Correspondingly, the women of these novels *undergo* their experience, restlessly rubbing against its restrictions. Interestingly, a considerable bitterness is often directed toward the figure of the mother, bearer of the vestiges of womanliness. The womanly woman is a kind of impending threat, to be killed or maimed in self defence, rather as Virginia Woolf talks of needing to murder the hovering Angel of the House before she could write her fiction. The experiencing heroine is polarised: she is all certainty, aspiration, desire, while her doubts and contradictions are split off and embodied in the Mother who binds her about with prejudice and custom. Tant' Sannie, the mother-figure in Schreiner's novel, is a grotesque caricature of the womanly woman, hugely fat and endlessly receptive, consuming dried apricots and dessicated husbands with the same indifferent rapacity:

"Marriage is the finest thing in the world. I've been at it three times, and if it pleased God to take this husband from me I should have another."

"Some men are fat, and some men are thin; some men drink brandy, and some men drink gin; but it all comes to the same thing in the end; it's all one. A man's a man, you know."

Perhaps the clearest case of such a polarisation occurs in Mona Caird's two novels, *The Wing of Azrael* (1889) and *The Daughters of Danaus* (1894); in both, the mother is the focus of a curious mixture of guilt, resentment and pity. Every mother, for Caird, is one more link in a long chain binding women to renunciation and sacrifice, and every mother demands vicarious restitution. The mother in both books is at once disabling and disabled, a tyrannical invalid whose very helplessness adds force to her demands:

> She realized now, with agonising vividness, the sadness of her mother's life, the long stagnation, the slow decay of disused faculties, and the ache that accompanies all processes of decay, physical or moral. Not only the strong appeal of old affection, entwined with the earliest associations, was at work, but the appeal of womanhood itself—the grey, sad story of a woman's life, bare and dumb and pathetic in its irony and pain: the injury from without, and then the self-injury, its direct offspring; unnecessary, yet inevitable; the unconscious thirst for the sacrifice of others, the hungry claims of a nature unfulfilled, the groping instinct to bring the balance of renunciation to the level, and indemnify oneself for the loss suffered and the spirit offered up. And that propitiation had to be made.
>
> (The Daughters of Danaus)

The resignation of that final sentence finds an echo in many of the feminist novels of failed rebellion. Netta Syrett's *Nobody's Fault* (1896) ends rather similarly, with the woman's renunciation of her lover for the sake of her widowed mother: " 'It isn't a question of duty, inclination, religion, or *anything*, but just the one overwhelming necessity of not breaking the tie of blood.' " It is the "tie of blood" that binds fastest of all in the attempted revolt, and often plays a crucial role in defeating or subverting the woman's protest. The defeat from without, or the collapse from within, usually follows the same cycle: anger and resentment finding expression in violence, suppressed or actual; then a total, self-imposed submissiveness of behaviour combined with the attempt to preserve some inner space of protest; rebellion, sparked off by the prospect of a desired lover, marriage, or career; and a grim final result. Caird's *The Wing of Azrael* (1889)—a novel which, she claims in her Preface, aims "not to contest or to argue, but to represent"—is paradigmatic: Viola Sedley, child of a self-martyring mother and a domineering father, is tormented by the cynically clever Philip Dendraith. She pushes him over a cliff, and, although he is not seriously hurt, is so horrified and frightened by her own anger that she falls into a submissive and numbing religious fatalism. Later they marry, and he is exasperated by her passivity:

> If she had been a haughty, rebellious woman, giving him insult for insult, sneer for sneer, he might have understood it; but she professed the most complete wifely submission, obeyed him in every detail, and when he reviled her she answered not again; yet behind all this apparent yielding he knew that there was something he could not touch—the real woman who withdrew herself from him inexorably and for ever.

Viola endures his humiliating and sadistic treatment out of a sense of duty towards her mother, even when she realises that she loves someone else. Her mother's death offers a glimmer of hope, and Viola arranges to elope with her lover. Trapped at the last by her husband, whose sexual interest in her is re-aroused by this sign of rebellion, she stabs him, flees from the momentary horror in her lover's eyes, and jumps over the cliff to her death. (The combination of desperate resignation and anger erupting into violence prefigures Hardy's Tess.) Other equally bleak resolutions occur—death, breakdown into convention, or the renunciation of personal desire and the acceptance of a joyless future.

"Happy endings" are usually to be found only in works which permit of a clearly-defined programme for the liberation of women—works which eschew realism for fantasy or prophesy. I have already mentioned the feminist Utopia of *Gloriana*; into the same category falls Jane Hume Clapperton's *Margaret Dunmore; or, A Socialist Home* (1888), which shows the trials and tribulations of "a Provincial Communistic group—ladies and gentlemen who intend to live, rather than preach, Socialism; and who hope to rear children of a purely Socialistic type." After both practical and emotional vicissitudes—chapped hands from large-scale potato-peeling, and a potentially adulterous affection—a satisfactory régime is established on the basis of communal domestic labour for the women, meetings of self- and group-criticism, and a eugenic meliorism derived from the works of Patrick Geddes. A lecture hall is then set up to pass on the benefits of the community's experience to the working class.

The programmatic fantasy is a form taken up by several of the male feminist-sympathisers. George Noyes Miller's novel *The Strike of a Sex* (1895) is a dream-vision, in which women successfully withdraw their labour—the pun, intentional or not, provides the novel's structuring metaphor—in order to get an unconditional guarantee from the male "management" that " 'no woman from this time forth and forever, shall be subjected to the woes of maternity without her free and specific consent in all cases.' " This is to be effected by the implementation of "Zugassent's Discovery." The novel's form rather curiously mimics its subject in that it constantly approaches the point of defining this discovery, but repeatedly breaks off before the climactic revelation is made. Readers of Miller's pamphlet *After the Strike of a Sex* (1896)—or those who understood the significance of the phrase "Member of the Oneida Community" that appears on the title page below the author's name—were to find out that it is *coitus reservatus*.

Without doubt the oddest of the fantasy solutions to the "problem" of women can be found in Henry Dalton's *Lesbia Newman* (1889), a work whose chief distinction lies in its containing characters named The Rev Spinosa Bristley and Fidgfumblasquidiot Grewel. A politico-religious prophecy, it moves somewhat bewilderingly from the mild unconventionalities of Lesbia's membership in a bicycle club and a Reformed Dress Society, to events of rather wider significance: the Tsar is assassinated by

" 'two Nihilists, ladies in the Empress' suite,' " Ireland throws off the yoke of the English only to put itself under the voluntary tutelage of the United States, world revolution breaks out in Cork harbour, the twenty-four-hour clock is introduced (a matter of equal importance, it appears), the Catholic church returns to the true faith as the Church of our Divine Lady and appoints women priests and vestals, and women—disdaining the intermediary of the morally inferior male—acquire the ability to secrete the "zoosperm" and procreate by parthogenesis.

Most liberal feminist novels, however, content themselves with seeking rather humbler reforms; paramount amongst them is the reform of the concept and practice of marriage. The "Anti-Marriage League," of which Margaret Oliphant writes in her review of *Jude the Obscure* and of works by Grant Allen, begins rather earlier, with the female *Bildungsroman* of the 1880s in which marriage and sex are the crucial educational structures. The difficulty of establishing a satisfactory relationship between an anti-stereotype heroine, capable and independent, and a situation for her adequate to her sense of oppression often leads to the punctuation of realism by melodrama. Few marriages, for instance, are simply boring, or mutually irksome; "bad" husbands and wives must be alcoholic, syphilitic, cruelly selfish or monstrously violent. Shaw remarks humorously on this tendency in his Preface to *The Irrational Knot:* "I had made a morally original study of a marriage myself, and made it, too, without any melodramatic forgeries, spinal diseases, and suicides, though I had to confess to a study of dipsomania." The melodrama is intensified by the desire to make representative the experience of the female characters, and the shift away from a single focal heroine to a number of female characters sometimes lends a note of extravegence to the marital abuses evoked. Sensitive and intelligent women are almost invariably married to violent, boorish, or venereally-diseased husbands with a string of past or present mistresses and illegitimate children in tow. *The Heavenly Twins* offers two complementary cases of the spectre of hereditary syphilis and the possibilities of eugenic feminism, one an example, and the other a warning. Evadne refuses to live with her "moral leper" of a husband until prevailed upon by parental pressure and the threat of the law. Even then they live, at her insistence and at some cost to her health, on terms of celibacy, despite his attempts to seduce her by leaving "salacious" advanced literature—Zola, Sand, Daudet, Spencer—where he hopes she will find and read it. The saintly Edith, on the other hand, marries the depraved Sir Mosely Menteith in ignorance, bears a sickly child, and dies of syphilitic brain-fever.

Some other novels explore, not the experience of marriage, but its institutionalised status, vindicating or challenging conventional legalised marriage through alternative forms of relationship: sexless marriage, parthenogenesis, lesbianism, or celibacy, by choice or necessity. But the fiction of marital reform is unquestionably dominated by the "free union," which, on its own valuation, differs from common-law marriage in that it is contracted as a matter of principle, for the sake of humanity or of moral evolution, and not on the grounds of inclination or pragmatism. It is based on the notion of substituting the sanction of personal feeling for the degrading economic basis of legal marriage: the exchange of financial support by the man for exclusive contractual rights to the woman's sexual activity is redefined as, in Stead's phrase, "monogamic prostitution." A character of Shaw's puts the case:

> "Somebody said openly in Parliament the other day that marriage was the true profession of women. So it is a profession; and except that it is a harder bargain for both parties, and that society countenances it, I don't [sic] see how it differs from what we—bless our virtuous indignation—stigmatize as prostitution."

If marriage is to be re-interpreted as prostitution, then non-marriage is often carefully distinguished from it by the scrupulous avoidance of any taint of sensuality; the heroine is protected from confusion with the pathetic victim of a plausible seducer by being herself the initiator, while the man is reluctant. Here is one such high-minded offer:

> "Were I to do as you bid me, to go with you before priest or registrar, I should degrade myself beyond redemption. This, Rupert, is the woman's protest against the old bad order, her martyrdom if you will. It is for man to renounce honours, wealth, glory, the power which involves dominion over the weak, and is founded on their weakness. What can a maiden renounce? I will tell you. Do not shrink if I say it, conscious of the unsullied life I have led and the innocent love that is beating in my heart. Rupert, she can renounce respectability."

> (Barry, *The New Antigone*)

This woman, incidentally, backs up her plea in a rather less self-congratulatorily idealistic fashion by threatening to kill herself if Rupert rejects her. But the tone—the pre-ordained martyrdom, the stress upon the "unsullied" and "innocent" nature of the woman's life, and the preservation of the female role of loving self-sacrifice—is characteristic, and makes clear the free union's exact reproduction of the ideology of marriage (loving, lasting, monogamous). This "union" undermines the "freedom."

The novel of free union has only two possibilities: for or against, martyrdom or marriage. Of the first kind, the best known example (though neither the earliest nor the best) is Grant Allen's *The Woman Who Did* (1895). The novel's project is from the first the martyrdom of Herminia, in the "feminine" heroism of suffering. All doubt or contradiction is marginalised, as Herminia's boredom in Italy, where Alan has brought her, is rapidly resolved by his death. Herminia's experience leaves her wholly untouched, and her consciousness is so utterly and unironically circumscribed by the narrative voice that the novel can simply ride over the increasingly obvious and necessary compromises of her principles which suggest how little of an "alternative" the free union is, how futile the martyrdom she has elected. This sub-text was at once visible to its conservative reviewers:

> Those who do not know the author, but who take what I must regard as the saner view of the relations of the sexes, will rejoice that what might have been a potent force for evil has been so strangely over-ruled as to become a reinforcement of the garrison defending the citadel its author desires so ardently to overthrow. For there is no mistaking the fact. From the point of view of the fervent apostle of Free Love, this is a Boomerang of a Book.

For the "pro-marriage league," these contradictions form the substance of the narrative, allowing of a contrast between "theory" and the "reality" of living which is invariably resolved in favour of the latter. There are sacramental defences of marriage, but it is more common to see the free union confronted with, and undermined by, social ostracism, self-doubt, and jealousy. In H. Sidney Warwick's *Dust o' Glamour* (1897), the woman's increasing sense of shame, her insecurity and the social restrictions upon their life together which cause her lover to become bored and cold towards her, are all redeemed by the final marriage. In Frank Frankfort Moore's *I Forbid the Banns* (1893), the relationship deteriorates as a result of sexual jealousies and anxieties that are given frankly economic expression:

> He felt, when looking at her, as a man might feel who is in possession of a certain charming property, but who knows that he has no title-deeds, and that, consequently, he may be turned adrift at any moment. What is the noblest property in the world to anyone, so long as the title-deeds are in the possession of someone else?

It was probably this self-mocking urbanity of tone that modified the enthusiasm of the reviewers for its argument:

> On the whole the book is a blow on the right side in the discussion, though it could be wished that the author's standpoint had been rather less that of expediency and more that of principle.

Here again, the relationship is saved by legal marriage, which, dissolving all the contradictions of the preceding narrative, is represented as an unproblematic resolution. In almost every case, "for" or "against," the fiction of the free union represents the relationship in a vacuum, unrelated, for the woman at least, to any other area of activity. The concentration upon the woman's role in the relationship, and upon the double standard which presses upon her experience of that role, imparts an air of liberalism which is belied by the unchallenged reproduction of the "feminine sphere" of home and family.

But under the increasing pressure of those biologistic accounts of sexual difference which I have already outlined, the feminist revolt against the womanly took on a new impetus. Writers like George Egerton, rebelling against the womanly ideal, sought to tear aside the veil of convention and hypocrisy in order to reveal the real woman beneath; but precisely this notion of a "real" woman marks a falling back onto biological or mystical essentialism. Womanhood, in contrast to womanliness, is not an ideal or an aspiration, but an immanent natural disposition, originating in a pre-determining physiological sexual differentiation. The ideology of woman-hood necessarily predicates certain kinds of experience as female, and in doing so it privileges the interiority of the female writer and, in turn, of the female narrative voice. It draws much of its strength from its protest against the existing social oppression of women, but it subverts that protest by an appeal to the "natural" which reinforces the enclosure of women's experience by their physiological organisation. The political content of the ideology is hidden beneath its elevation of anatomically-specific female skills and abilities, which does not allow for deviation except in the sense of a far more literal "unsexing" than that implied by the failure of womanliness.

"Womanhood" can be invoked both by those who perceive themselves as feminists—as the mystico-physiological feminism of Ellis Ethelmer witnesses—and by avowed anti-feminists like Iota. Her novel *A Yellow Aster* (1894) concerns a young woman, distinctively "modern" in that she has been cheated out of her womanhood by the rationalistic and scientific up-bringing that her well-intentioned parents have given her. The title is also the novel's central symbol: Gwen Waring is the "yellow aster," a hybrid result of human experiment upon nature. The difficulty occasioned by her education is that the spontaneity of instinct and emotion is dammed up by her constant introspection and self-analysis; the unspoken postulate of a hostile duality of body and mind finds an echo in many contemporary "woman question" novels. Receiving a proposal of marriage, she is moved to accept by the dim promptings of a so far unidentified " 'something outside me,' " despite her lack of emotion and a positive aversion to the sexual side of marriage.

> She turned away to hide the crimson in her cheeks.
> "Then this one-flesh business, this is a horrid thing."
> She squeezed her hands into her eyes.
> "This is maddening!" she cried, and sprang up and stood look-
> ing out of the window.
> "One flesh!" she murmured breathlessly, "One flesh!"

The honeymoon leaves Gwen feeling degraded, possessed, irrevocably al-tered, and her subsequent pregnancy leads her to send her husband away in revulsion. The " 'something outside me' " now comes to the fore, in the form of the something inside her—the baby, agent and embodiment of the impersonal force of the maternal instinct. Only after a kind of rebirth (she almost dies during a long and difficult labour) does her impeded womanhood assert its supremacy. She bursts into a grateful rhapsody over wife- and motherhood:

> "I am a woman at last, a full, complete, proper woman, and it is magnificent. No other living woman can feel as I do; other women absorb these feelings as they do their daily bread and butter, and they have to them the same placid everyday taste, they slip into their womanhood; mine has rushed into me with a great torrent—I love my husband, I worship him, I adore him—do you hear, my dear?"

This conclusion is successfully reached, however, only through the repression of Gwen's feminist protest; her earlier half-contemptuous envy of the "full, complete, proper woman" has been given powerful expression in terms that cast an unsettling ambivalence over her final surrender:

> "A very strong woman is docked of half the privileges of her sex. . . . Helplessness is such supreme flattery. . . .
>
> The parasitical, gracious, leaning ways, the touch of pathos and pleading,—those are the things I should look for if I were a man, they charm me infinitely. Then that lovely craving for sympathy, and that delicious feeling of insecurity they float in, which makes the touch of strong hands a Heaven-sent boon to them—those women, you see, strew incense in your path and they get it back in service."

And further, the final mark of Gwen's triumph is that she has come to resemble exactly the idealised portrait of her which she has earlier dismissed as " 'pre-ordained to the *rôle* of bride,' " and which has been the occasion of an odd distinction between the "cold living abstraction" and the "warm, big-hearted, divinely-natural creature, alive there on the canvas." In order to be "alive," to become "divinely-natural"—the phrase conferring upon physiology the power of divinity—Gwen must, paradoxically, become static, fixed, a cultural object. Throughout the novel she has been the centre of consciousness, but at the end she is abruptly presented as a portrait, framed by the window, and perceived through the consciousness of her returning husband. Her accession to womanhood is also the resignation of her right (fully exercised in the rest of the novel) to speech: "she just sat dumbly on the floor." The trajectory of the novel's project is deflected by the ambivalences that threaten its uncertain grasp of point of view.

The most prominent and able of the writers concerned with womanhood, however, is George Egerton. Her stories—especially those in her first volume, *Keynotes*—unsettle the expectations and responses of the reader in their innovatory alternation of abrupt and enigmatic narrative compression with overflowing linguistic excess, and in the unprecedented candour of their reference to sexual themes. It was probably the combination of this last with a male pseudonym—though "George" had by now acquired from Eliot and Sand a certain tradition as a woman writer's name—that led the first reader of the stories, T. P. Gill, to express his views on them to the author in a swaggeringly "one of the boys" tone:

> To put it brutally you would not (however Scandinavian your ideas may be) invite your coachman, or even your bosom friend, to "assist" while you and your wife were engaged in the sacred mysteries. Why the deuce should you write it all out for them and give it them to read about! . . . For example, take the effect on a young fellow in his student period . . . of a particularly warm description of rounded limbs and the rest. It puts him in a state that he either goes off and has a woman or it is bad for his health (and possibly worse for his morals) if he doesn't.

A second, highly embarrassed letter followed when the author was revealed to be one Mary Clairmonte.

Egerton clearly conceived of herself very much in terms of writing *as* a woman *for* women; her subject-matter ("the *terra incognita* of herself") and her manner of writing are alike felt to be determined—or rather, her own phrase implies, restricted—by her sex alone: "one is bound to look at life through the eyes of one's sex, to toe the limitations imposed on one by its individual physiological functions." "The eyes of one's sex": the phrase is ambivalent, evoking at once a personalised sense of gender-identity, and a sense of what is shared with all other women. It recalls the lack of particularity with which Egerton's stories are invested by the avoidance of names and absence of personal histories for characters identified only by their sex: each woman serves to represent the immanence of her womanhood. The breaking of stereotype reveals a further ideological structure within, for the project of the stories is the nature of woman as essential and universal. The stress on physiology in the quotation above is characteristic and important, for it is by virtue of physiology that woman is bound to her "nature." The stories foreground the exclusion of women in society, but in a way that allows the protest to be recuperated into the ideology of womanhood. For what is repressed in male-dominated society is represented as something disruptive of the very terms of that society: the "natural"—woman, instinctive, intuitive, enigmatic, wild:

> [Men] have all overlooked the eternal wildness, the untamed primitive savage temperament that lurks in the mildest, best woman. Deep in through ages of convention this primeval trait burns, an untameable quality that may be concealed but is never eradicated by culture—the keynote of woman's witchcraft and woman's strength.

(Keynotes)

In this terminology, with its implied analogy between sexual difference and the polarisation of nature and culture, there dwells an unexpected echo of

Ruskin. Certainly, Egerton's glorying in the subversive amorality of her women is wholly foreign to Ruskin, but the shared analogy serves to draw out the implications of such a representation. The insistence, in Egerton's stories, upon certain common qualities in women and upon certain images of them—witch, elf, gypsy, sphinx—locate them, as if constitutionally, outside the social framework, and shift the site of their oppression into the realm of nature.

Nor does Egerton's noble female savage mark the irruption of repressed female desire into the male order, for it is the distinctive feature of the ideology of womanhood that it recuperates desire into instinct—here, " 'the deep, underlying generic instinct, the "mutterdrang," that lifts her above and beyond all animalism, and fosters the sublimest qualities of unselfishness and devotion.' " The unresolved contradiction between the "instinct" and the transcendence of "animalism" marks the spiritualising of the woman's sexuality through reproduction; motherhood is made not merely an anatomical potentiality common to most women, but, to take up Egerton's own word, the "keynote" of womanhood. Physiology becomes at once the ground and the expression of women's moral qualities:

> "the *only divine* fibre in a woman is her maternal instinct. Every good quality she has is consequent or co-existent with that. Suppress it, and it turns to a fibroid, sapping all that is healthful and good in her nature."
>
> (*Discords*)

The equipoise of "healthful" and "good," and the only half-figurative "fibroid," reveal a moral organicism invoking nature as the ratification of that morality of vicariousness prescribed for women by womanliness and womanhood alike.

A strength of Egerton's writing is the space it makes for female anger and protest. But, as Elaine Showalter has remarked, the anger and violence are constantly directed towards other women or towards children: the woman in "Wedlock" murders her stepchildren to avenge her husband's callous rejection of her own illegitimate child; and the wife in "Virgin Soil" holds her mother responsible for the abhorrence she feels for sex with her husband. Showalter argues that the anger is deflected from its true, justified target—the husband in each case—and that the "real" struggle between husbands and wives is thus concealed. It is true that there is an absence of confrontation, but that absence is necessitated by the primacy of enigma in Egerton's account of the nature of woman; her women are incomprehensible, inexplicable, to men, and so confrontation gives way to juxtaposition. The typical Egerton woman—small, slight, pale, full of quivering nervous strength and neurotic changes of mood—attracts male characters and narrator by her eroticised difference from the male. In this feminist ideology of womanhood, that difference confers a strength which the men try to wrest from her by a mixture of threat and cajolement:

"You wait on me, ay, no slave better, and yet—I can't get at you, near you; that little soul of yours is as free as if I hadn't bought you, as if I didn't own you, as if you were not my chattel, my thing to do what I please with; do you hear" (with fury) "to degrade, to—to treat as *I please? . . .* [Yet] you pity me with all that great heart of yours because I am just a great, weak, helpless, drunken beast, a poor wreck."

(*Keynotes*)

Husbands are brutal, drunken, and weakly dependent (as in "A Shadow's Slant") or else well meaning, but coarse, simple, and limited in understanding (as in "An Empty Frame"). In neither case can they satisfy the complex needs of their wives. The women are bound by " 'that crowning disability of my sex,' " affection (*Keynotes*), or by the emotional dependence of the man, or by their children; they treat the bullying child-man they have married with a vaguely contemptuous pitying affection:

"There, it's all right, boy! Don't mind me, I have a bit of a complex nature; you couldn't understand me if you tried to; you'd better not try!"

She has slipped, whilst speaking, her warm bare foot out of her slipper, and is rubbing it gently over his chilled ones.

"You are cold, better go back to bed, I shall go too!"

The recurrent imagery of hunting—traps, cages, fishing, wounded birds—powerfully conveys the sense of inturned violence in these claustrophobic marriages.

Enigma, dominant "keynote" of womanhood, structures many of the stories. In her retrospective note on *Keynotes,* Egerton describes the task of the woman writer as "to give herself away." Something of this idea of self-surrender is caught in the frequency with which her stories take the form of a woman telling her story for herself, in direct speech, to a listener who is most often also a woman, though sometimes a man. But this woman's story is not co-extensive with the text; rather, it is framed and delineated by an "objective" or first-person narrator who represents the woman to the reader as enigma, erotic or otherwise. The embedded narrative does not carry all the immediacy and authority of the framing narrative which situates it as partial; narrator and teller of the woman's story never coincide. The woman appears to the narrator from the first as the embodiment of a question (often, when the narrator is implied to be male, an erotic question) or a mystery. The sense of something tantalisingly withheld colours the objectivity of the external description of her actions:

Free to follow the beck of one's spirit, a-ah to dream of it, and the red light glows in her eyes again; they have an inward look; what visions do they see? The small thin face is transformed, the lips are softer, one quick emotion chases the other across it, the eyes glisten and darken deeply, and the copper threads shine on her swart hair. What is she going to do, what resolve is she making? . . . Again her eyes wander out with an appealing look (to whom do they appear, to part of herself, to some God of convention?) towards the camp.

Into this erotic tension established between woman and narrator (and, by extension, reader) breaks the moment of the woman's story, the moment when she "gives herself away," promising at once the explication of the enigma and the dissipation of the "woman's strength" which it gives her. Yet, because it is a narrative of direct speech, given by her in response to, and confirmation of, the narrator's question, her self-sufficient inaccessibility is preserved; just as the woman desired is never possessed by the male narrator, her consciousness is never possessed by the narrative voice. The embedded narrative, far from dissolving the enigma, implies a logic and a motivation which remain inaccessible. Even when the narrator has privileged access to the woman's consciousness, that access is partial and abridged. In "A Cross Line," the narrator makes a very intimate entry into the woman's mind, in the fantasy which dominates the story; but precisely because it is her fantasy, it offers itself only as the possibility of interpretation through a psychoanalytic interrogation which the text will not sustain. It illumines, but it does not explain or circumscribe, the consciousness of the woman. When the woman "gives herself away," the self-revelation confirms the narrator's erotic gaze.

Against the restriction of the claustrophobic marriages in the majority of the stories is set the notion of the expansion of womanhood—sometimes literally, as when a significant part of the "freeing" of the woman in the fantasy of liberation "The Regeneration of Two" is the abjuring of corsets. In that story, the restitution of womanhood, the freeing of nature from the grip of history, is effected by the attacks on contemporary sex-role degeneration of a vagabond poet:

> "I lay my heart on the brown lap of earth, and close my eyes in delicious restfulness. I can feel her respond to me; she gives me peace without taxing me for a return. I sought that in woman, for I thought to find her nature's best product, of all things closest in touch with our common mother. I hoped to find rest on her great mother heart; to return home to her for strength and wise counsel; for it is the primitive, the generic, that makes her sacred, mystic, to the best men. I found her half-man or half-doll."
>
> (*Discords*)

His spiritual "rescue" of her is counterpointed by her physical rescue of him, when she nurses him back to health after a near-fatal illness in repayment of his debt: " 'You stung me to analyse myself . . . To see what significance the physical changes in my body had from where the contradictions of my nature sprang—to find myself' '' (*Discords*). By now she has become the "sacred, mystic" woman he had sought: infinitely restful, endlessly receptive, the "great mother." The expansion of womanhood ends in a confinement. The woman's restless dissatisfaction is recuperated by a sanctified nature and its demiurge, physiology, into the maternal role of "restfulness . . . peace . . . home," bringing the ideology of womanhood full circle back to the womanly ideal against which it had defined itself.

"Different from Writing": Dracula in 1897

Geoffrey Wall

For the aristocracy had asserted the specificity of its body; but it was in the form of blood, *in terms of ancestral antiquity and prestigious alliances . . . The "blood" of the bourgeoisie was its sex. And this is not just a play on words; many of the themes proper to the caste behaviour of the nobility re-emerge in the nineteenth century bourgeoisie, but in the guise of biological, medical or eugenic notions; the concern for genealogy turned into a preoccupation with heredity.*
— MICHEL FOUCAULT, *Histoire de la sexualité: La Volonté de savoir,*
my trans.

Published in 1897, the year designated by Lenin as the zenith of imperialism, Bram Stoker's *Dracula* repeats the themes of an ideological crisis, the crisis of the bourgeois family. But read symptomatically, against the grain of its manifest argument for sexual repression, this text allows us to recover not only the content of that crisis, but the forms of its representation in discourses on the family, sexuality, race and empire. *Dracula* repeats this imaginary biology of the 1890s, all those "scientific" phantasies which took wing in the ideological twilight of an economy which was "becoming parasitic rather than competitive . . . living off the remains of world monopoly" (E. J. Hobsbawm, *Industry and Empire*).

Dracula is, persistently, an anxious text. Innocently, unironically, it contemplates its materials and methods, fascinated by the evident contradiction between the archaic stuff of its narrative and the contemporary techniques which allow that narrative to emerge. It is a folklore whose improvisations and immediacies have been eroded and reified by being passed through all the most modern means of communication: "We were struck with the fact that, in all the mass of material of which the record is composed, there is hardly one authentic document; nothing but a mass of typewriting." This final typewritten archive includes transcriptions of diverse other kinds of text: a journal written in shorthand, a psychiatric case-history recorded phonographically, telegrams, a polyglot dictionary, title-deeds, a railway timetable, a ship's log translated from the Russian, a newspaper article, the inscription on a tombstone, phonetic renderings of dialect speech, and "a workman's dogeared notebook which had hieroglyphical entries in thick half-obliterated pencil." All these materials have been scrupulously compiled so that "a history almost at variance with the

From *Literature and History* 10, no. 1 (Spring 1984). © 1984 by Thames Polytechnic, London.

possibilities of latter-day belief may stand forth as simple fact" (preface). On the one hand, we are left with the dust into which Dracula himself crumbles, on the other "nothing but a mass of typewriting": on the one hand the spectral desire which invades the bedrooms of the imperial metropolis, on the other hand, its banally material residues, that "mass of typewriting," empty nets of language which try to capture the history of that desire.

That general anxiety is elaborated as a psychological theme: it afflicts each individual narrator in the activity of their writing. *Dracula*, taking over the multiple subjectivities of the epistolary novel, gives a psychopathological twist to this theme of writing. The writers recognise in their writing a compulsive, obsessional effort to transcribe the uncanny, to establish indications of reality. "I must," confides Jonathan Harker to himself, "keep writing at every chance, for I dare not stop to think. All, big and little, must go down; perhaps at the end the little things may teach us most." Or, "I am anxious, and it soothes me to express myself here; it is like whispering to oneself and listening at the same time. And there is also something about the shorthand symbols which makes it different from writing."

The narrative movement of *Dracula* is towards a social synthesis of these private writings, towards a knowledge which can only be constituted as the relation between diverging phantasies. For there are two distinct moments in the process of the narrative. In the first moment, a self-duplication, "like whispering to oneself and listening at the same time," a self-displacement effected by "something in the shorthand symbols," a passage from the terrible fluidity of phantasy to the soothing fixity of text. In the second moment, the valorising circulation of what is written, the gift of that text: most conspicuously, the supplementary ritual at the marriage of Jonathan Harker, when he appoints his new wife as the keeper of his memories, the repository of the journal he kept during his visit to Dracula's castle—"He had his hand over the notebook, and he said to me very solemnly:—'the secret is here and I do not want to know it. I want to take up my life here with our marriage . . . Here is the book. Take it and keep it, read it if you will but never let me know . . . ' I took the book . . . and wrapped it up in white paper, and tied it with a little bit of pale blue ribbon which was round my neck, and sealed it over the knot with sealing wax and for my seal I used my wedding-ring."

It is the wife, Mina, with her "man's brain" and her "woman's heart," who is the agent of this process of the circulation of the text. She is the rewriter, the transcriber, the secretary who arranges all the documents in chronological order and composes the case (legal and medical) of Dracula. She acquires an enormous structural importance as the-woman-who-writes. But she also serves to articulate the contradictions posed by the feminism of the 1890s. Before her marriage she has been a schoolteacher, but now she will dedicate her cultural skills to the service of the masculine realm of socially productive thought. "When we are married," she confides to her friend, "I shall be able to be useful to Jonathan, and if I can stenograph well enough I can take down what he wants to say in this way and write it out for him on the typewriter." Mina represents a certain historical transition. She is dimly aware of the contemporary debates on women and marriage, but resolutely traditional in her conception of the duties of a wife and the virtues of subordination. References to the "New Woman" significantly precede Dracula's first attack on her friend Lucy: "I believe we should have shocked the New Woman with our appetites." The appetites in question are innocent, their object is merely an afternoon tea. But they recall Lucy's protest at the prospect of monogamous marriage: "Why can't they let a girl marry three men, or as many as want her . . . ? But this is heresy and I must not say it." Mina, seeing her friend asleep, briefly imagines herself as a man, as her suitor: "If Mr Holmwood fell in love with her seeing her only in the drawing room, I wonder what he would say if he saw her now?" But this phantasy is then safely projected onto the New Women, rejected as a self-evidently unnatural masculine identification: "the New Women writers will some day start an idea that men and women should be allowed to see each other asleep before proposing or accepting. But I suppose the New Woman won't condescend in future to accept; she will do the proposing herself. And a nice job she will make of it too!" As we shall see later, Lucy as a vampire, as an openly desiring woman, is offered as an awful example of what will happen if female sexuality is allowed to escape from its lawful subordination within the conjugal family. Mina's writing, in the same gesture of confinement, will be used only to repeat the words of others: "I shall do what I see lady journalists do: interviewing and writing descriptions and trying to remember conversations. I am told that, with a little practice, one can remember all that goes on or that one hears said during a day."

But Mina's discursive position is not so simple as either she or others would have it. Her masculine qualities have to be suppressed if masculine discourses are to keep their sovereignty. If we examine the various articulations of gender and discourse in *Dracula*, there emerges a typology which is intriguingly close to that in Breuer and Freud's *Studies in Hysteria* (1895). Indeed, it is Van Helsing, the "brain-scientist," the hypnotist, the reader of Charcot, who proposes the rule that "good women tell all their lives, and by day and by hour and by minute, such things that angels can read; and we men who wish to know have in us something of angel's eyes." The slide in this sentence, from voice to text to image, from woman's voice to man's eye (though the gaze is ideally ungendered, that of an angel), exemplifies a regression imposed by the men upon the women. The more resolute women can, however, escape this process. Lucy's "crime," for instance is to have resisted the masculine-medical gaze of one of her suitors. She writes to Mina, "I can fancy what a wonderful power he must have over his patients. He has a curious habit of looking straight in the face, as if trying to read one's thoughts. He tries this on very much with me, but I flatter myself that he has got a very tough nut to crack. I know that from my glass. Do you ever try to read your own face? *I do.*" Mina, subject to Dracula's power, and warning the men that she will try to deceive them, can be positioned as a "good woman" by the "angel eyes" of her husband: "God saw the look that she turned on me as she spoke, and if there be indeed a Recording Angel that look is noted to her everlasting honour."

Good women tell all their lives . . . first axiom of patriarchal ideology, motto of psychoanalysis. But *Dracula* reaches beyond this simple prescription in its investigation of masculine and feminine. There are so many other patterns of discourse and gender which deviate. Women, for example, will talk to other women behind the backs of men. The early exchange of letters between Mina and Lucy is under the sign of phantasy and the pleasure principle: "we can talk together freely and build our castles in the air." It is shaped to a specifically feminine idiom of the erotic and the confidential: "we have told all our secrets to each other since we were *children* . . . I wish I were with you dear, sitting by the fire, undressing, as we used to sit; and I would try to tell you what I feel. I do not know how I am writing this even to you. I am afraid to stop or I should tear up the letter." This feminine discourse does not produce knowledge until it has been relayed, submitted to the masculine, deciphered by it. Otherwise it remains enigmatic, shadowy, uncanny. Lucy, for example, on the night of her death, is in bed with her mother when Dracula breaks into the bedroom, heralded by "the head of a great gaunt grey wolf in the aperture of the broken windowpane." When the pre-Oedipal domain of mother and daughter is invaded by the phallus the mother dies from the shock, returning, briefly metamorphosed, a modern Philomel: "the sound of the nightingale seemed like the voice of my dead mother returned to comfort me."

But this division within discourse, whereby the feminine must be re-addressed, completed, put into circulation, this division is repeated on the other side. The masculine must relapse and regress, must find again the Mother in order to find its lost feelings. Lucy's mourning lover, Lord Godalming, the very type of aristocratic manhood, "breaks down" to a woman, to Lucy's friend Mina. She observes, "there is something in a woman's nature that makes a man free to break down before her and express his feelings on the tender or emotional side without feeling it derogatory to his manhood . . . We women have something of the mother in us." The masculine pattern of intimacy involves "yarns by the campfire," but also an asexual physical contact: "that time," as Van Helsing puts it, "you suck from my wound so swiftly the poison of the gangrene." Any display of intense feeling between men is diagnosed as hysterical, as feminine: "then he cried till he laughed again; and cried and laughed together just as a woman does. I tried to be stern with him, just as one is with a woman under the circumstances." This is contrasted with the behaviour of the exemplary Texan who "bore himself through it like a moral Viking." Empires, evidently, are founded on a certain masculinity: "If America can go on breeding men like that, she will be a power in the world indeed."

Mina, the woman who writes, with her man's brain and her woman's heart, is deliberately excluded, at a crucial moment, from the counsels of the five men who are allied against Dracula: "now that her work is done, and that it is due to her energy and brains and foresight that the whole story is put together in such a way that every point tells, she may well feel that her part is finished, and that she can henceforth leave the rest to us." The men have formed themselves into a "sort of board or committee" for the "serious work" of destroying that sexuality, aristocratic and perverse, which has insinuated itself into the bourgeois family, fastening adulterously upon its women. "The girls that you all love," taunts Dracula, "are mine already; and through them you and others shall yet be mine." But it is precisely by excluding Mina from the man's work of science that the men condemn her to the enclosed world of phantasy and desire. Left alone, while they are out hunting Dracula, she becomes his victim at the moment when she is resolving to become, precisely, the good woman who tells all her life: "I still keep my journal as usual. Then if he [her husband] has feared of my trust I shall show it to him, with every thought of my heart put down for his dear eyes to read." This section of the text enacts, as it were, a fable of repression, a repression that follows the line of sexual difference and the social relations that are constructed upon it. That which is excluded, the woman and her desire, returns, embodied in the secret language of the hysterical symptom, or in the theatricality of the perversion. Mina, like the hysterics treated by Breuer and Freud in the 1880s, "forms conclusions of her own . . . but she will not or she cannot give them utterance . . . in some mysterious way Mrs Harker's tongue is tied." And, like Anna O., Mina proposes the form of her treatment, hypnosis, the talking cure. This secret language released from the hysterical body is both speech and writing: "The answer came dreamily, but with intention. I have heard her using the same tone when reading her short-hand notes."

The desire which is transcribed in the conjugal journal, or confided, between women, undressing by the fireside, regulated, ordered and put to work within the conjugal family, deciphered under hypnosis, codified under the masculine and the feminine, this desire is never to be arrested or fixed by its conscious representations. There is, in *Dracula*, that "other scene," that theatre of the Imaginary where is enacted, corporeally, all that has been banished from the conversations in the drawing room, from the "small world of happiness." These erotic *tableaux*, scenes of sexual discovery, follow the codes of a specific theatricality which is not that of Freud's classical Athens, but that of the Victorian theatre, the theatre in which Bram Stoker himself worked for thirty years as secretary to Henry Irving. It was a theatre of spectacle, of melodrama, of clear moral symbolism, a lavish ethical-sentimental picture-book; it was a theatre, in Stoker's own definition, "whose mechanism of exploiting thoughts is by means of the human body." The bodies in question, those of Stoker and Irving, spectator and actor, both underwent a profound, reciprocal, erotic crisis in their first encounter. Irving was reciting a poem to a student audience in a Dublin hotel drawing room after dinner. Stoker recalls, in his memoir of Irving, that at the end of the recitation, "after a few seconds of stony silence, I burst out into something like a violent fit of hysterics . . . so profound was the sense of his dominance . . . I was as men go a strong man, physically immensely strong . . . I was no hysterical subject . . . no weak individual yielding to a superior emotional force . . . my capacity for receptive emotion was something akin in forcefulness to his power of creating it." The obvious psychobiographical relation between Irving and Dracula, between Stoker and Harker, is—it seems to me—of less interest than that theatricalisation of the sexual which informs the text. The "scientific, sceptical, matter-of-fact nineteenth century" equips its world-historical representatives, three Englishmen, a Texan and a Dutchman, its present, its future and its past, equips them with phonograph, typewriter and railway timetable in the struggle to defend a woman, family and empire against the archaic remnant of a feudal aristocracy. They enter that "other scene" to find themselves at a performance in Henry Irving's *Lyceum*.

Mina, for example, looking for the sleepwalking Lucy on the cliffs of Whitby, relishes the excellence of the lighting:

> There was a bright full moon, with heavy black driving clouds, which threw the whole scene into a fleeting diorama of light and shade as they sailed across . . . as the edge of a narrow band of light . . . moved across, the church and the churchyard gradually became visible . . . there on our favourite seat, the silver light of the moon struck a half-reclining figure, snowy white. The coming of the cloud was too quick for me to see much, for shadow shut down on light almost immediately . . . something dark stood behind the seat where the white figure shone, and bent over it . . . something raised a head, and from where I was I could see a white face and gleaming red eyes.

Or, more intimately, more elaborately, the scene disclosed when the men break into Mina's bedroom:

> The moonlight was so bright that through the thick yellow blind the room was light enough to see. On the bed beside the window lay the form of Jonathan Harker, his face flushed and breathing heavily as though in a stupor. Kneeling on the near edge of the bed facing outwards was the white clad figure of his wife. By her side stood a tall, thin man clad in black . . . With his left hand he held both Mrs Harker's hands, keeping them away with her arms at full tension; his right hand gripped her by the back of the neck, forcing her face down on his bosom. Her white nightdress was

smeared with blood, and a thin stream trickled down the man's bare breast which was shown by his torn-open dress. The attitude of the two had a terrible resemblance to a child forcing a kitten's nose into a saucer of milk to compel it to drink.

What, we might ask, is being enacted in this scene? What anxious phantasy has been given body on this brightly-lit marriage bed? To answer such a question, we need to look at the forms of the family, the social relations which *Dracula* proposes. Dracula himself offers the pleasures of perversion in place of the repressions of hysteria. He is the predatory libertine who will conquer the world by means of an Unholy Family of which he is the incestuous father. He propogates by a sterile metamorphosis, fastening upon the already living, bestowing his grotesque immortality, an eternity of sadistic pleasures emancipated from the imperatives of biology. Dracula's theft of blood defiles the patrimony, disrupts the ordered exchange of women, property and names, dissolves the serene continuity of the imperial Anglo-Saxon race. His object of attack is London itself, the metropolis from which capital sets sail on its world voyages; there, in Jonathan Harker's words, "for centuries to come he might, amongst its teeming millions, satiate his lust for blood, and create a new and ever-widening circle of semi-demons to batten on the helpless." A Transylvanian Empire to supplant the British. Dracula, it is important to add, is a richly detailed historical type, the representative of the archaic neo-feudal social formations of Eastern Europe which had survived well into the "scientific, sceptical, matter-of-fact nineteenth century." "Here," he boasts to Harker, "I am noble; I am *boyar:* the common people know me and I am master." In the psychic geography of the continent, this Transylvania is Europe's unconscious:

> There are no maps of this country as yet to compare with our own Ordnance Survey . . . one of the wildest and least-known portions of Europe.

> Every known superstition in the world is gathered into the horseshoe of the Carpathians, as if it were the centre of some sort of imaginative whirlpool.

> There are deep caverns and fissures that reach none know whither.

> Every speck of dust that whirls in the wind a devouring monster in embryo.

Horseshoe, whirlpool, cavern, fissure, every speck of dust, a monster in embryo: as well as the historical-political threat of a counter-empire, Dracula carries a biological phantasy, a masculine nightmare of femininity, of the female body, out of control, ingesting and spawning indiscriminately, violating the territories of the body, the home and the state. It is Lucy, on the eve of her marriage, whose heretically polygamous wish—"Why can't they let a girl marry three men?"—initiates this process, this dissolution of the body politic, which ends only with the birth, on the last page, of Mina's son, the son whose "bundle of names links all our little band of men together." Between these two moments, reproduction and circulation of every kind is under threat. All secrecies, all privacies, all territories and rules for contact between bodies are unravelling. Much masculine ingenuity is devoted to the creation of sealed and impregnable spaces, where what is in stays in, where what is out stays out. Bedrooms with charmed windows, asylums with locked doors, coffins with lids screwed down, graves properly inhabited and accurately inscribed, diaries tied in blue ribbon: all in vain. Windows are broken, locks are picked, lunatics escape, coffins open, tombstones tell lies and graves are empty, women walk in their sleep and talk under hypnosis, men have wickedly voluptuous dreams and hysterical attacks, blood is sucked from the neck and transfused from the veins in the arm. "And so," laments Van Helsing, "the circle goes on ever-widening." The centre of this circle ever-widening is, explicitly, female sexuality. Lucy, in her vampire incarnation, exemplifies that "sweetness turned to adamantine, heartless cruelty, purity to voluptuous wantonness."

> The eyes seemed to throw out sparks of hell-fire, her brows were wrinkled as though the folds of flesh were the coils of Medusa's snakes, and the lovely blood-stained mouth grew to an open square.

Recalling Freud's interpretation of the Medusa, it comes as no surprise that Lucy's punishment-salvation is to be effected by means of a monstrous phallus:

> a round wooden stake some two and a half or three inches thick and about three feet long . . . one end hardened in the fire and sharpened to a fine point.

to be wielded by her cheated lover. "Brave lad!" says Van Helsing, paternally. "A moment's courage and it is done." This ritual penetration is enacted on the day after the cancelled wedding:

> He struck with all his might. The Thing in the coffin writhed; and a hideous blood-curdling screech came from the opened red lips. The body shook and quivered and twisted in wild contortions; the sharp white teeth clamped together until the lips were cut and the mouth was smeared with crimson foam. But Arthur never faltered. He looked like a figure of Thor as his untrembling arm rose and fell, driving deeper and deeper the mercy-bearing stake, whilst the blood from the pierced heart welled and spurted up round it.

To conclude, a fragment of masculine conversation:

> Then we had supper upstairs in our shirtsleeves (at the moment I am writing in a somewhat more advanced négligé), and then

came a lengthy medical conversation on moral insanity and nervous diseases and strange case-histories—your friend Bertha Pappenheim also cropped up—and then we became rather personal and very intimate and he told me a number of things about his wife and children and asked me to repeat what he had said only "after you are married to Martha." And then I opened up and said: This same Martha . . . is in reality a sweet Cordelia, and we are already on terms of the closest intimacy and can say anything to each other. Whereupon he said he too always calls his wife by that name because she is incapable of displaying affection to others, even including her own father.

Two doctors talking, professionally, speculatively, with all the intimacy and informality of being in shirt-sleeves after supper. Their conversation is that of colleagues, but also that of not-quite-equals, senior and junior, the married and the merely engaged. But professional secrets lead to family secrets, to the danger that these secrets may continue to circulate beyond the closed circle of the medical conversation. They may, through the networks of love and friendship, reach the ears of the patient in question.

The two doctors are Freud and Joseph Breuer, co-authors of the *Studies on Hysteria* (1895), an investigation of femininity and the family written from within the same ideological moment as *Dracula*. This account of their conversation is part of one of the many letters that Freud wrote to Martha Bernays during the four years of their engagement. Martha's friend Bertha Pappenheim, the subject of the "strange case-history," will be known to posterity as Anna O., the first case of hysteria to be made intelligible. Read alongside that case-history, Freud's letter to Martha exhibits, in its protestations of intimacy and its actual reticence, that same division, those same articulations of gender and discourse that we have found in *Dracula*. We know that Freud and Breuer had discussed the details of Anna O.—Bertha Pappenheim—repeatedly; that Breuer, about this time, had confided despairingly to Freud that Anna-Bertha was "quite unhinged," wishing that "she would die and so be released from her suffering"; that Breuer had "fled the house in a cold sweat" when faced with Anna-Bertha's phantom pregnancy at his hands.

None of this emerges in the letter to Martha. Instead, in place of the "unhinged" Bertha, we meet the figure of "sweet Cordelia," potent fiction of feminine virtue, one who commands herself to "love, and be silent." This Cordelia is summoned to fill the place of those three real women, Bertha Pappenheim, Frau Breuer, Martha Bernays: "incapable of displaying affection to others," a punctual conjugal desire, cleansed of anxieties, jealousies, hysteria.

Parables of Adventure:
The Debatable Novels
of Robert Louis Stevenson

Alastair Fowler

Stevenson's position in relation to the Victorian literary canon seems to be in rapid movement. The enquirer who consults *Victorian Fiction: A Guide to Research* will find something odd. That is, he will find nothing. Disraeli's and Bulwer-Lytton's inclusion implies a widely flung net. It is fine enough for Moore. And yes, it has caught Wilkie Collins and Kingsley and Gissing and Reade. But not Stevenson. Worse, as if to justify the lapse of taste, a Preface explains that "Stevenson has been omitted, in spite of his influence on romantic fiction, because his adult novels are few and of debatable rank." I am not sure that I understand how "adult" is meant here. True, Stevenson spread his efforts among several popular kinds. But *Victorian Fiction*, influential as it is, exemplifies a common silliness about these. The error of demoting Stevenson's fiction to a "debatable rank" arises from a confusion of evaluative and generic criteria. Generic hierarchies are still recognised in practice, however strenuously execrated in theory. And, because he wrote in kinds thought low, Stevenson has been fired from the canon.

But Constable's connoisseurs (who always think the art is already done) have blundered again. An increasingly educated liking for stories gathers strength with us. Jamesian critics may not all have quite learnt, yet, to rise to all of the Master's immense, really quite matchless admiration of the different art of Stevenson. But those who find high quality in Hawthorne and Melville should experience no difficulty in recognising the genius of Stevenson's romantic, un-novelistic stories. This is not an occasion to investigate differences between the novelistic genres and what James and Stevenson called the "romance." We need only recall that features admirable in the one group of kinds may be positively undesirable in the other.

From *Nineteenth-Century Scottish Fiction: Critical Essays*, edited by Ian Campbell. © 1979 by Alastair Fowler. Carcanet New Press Ltd., 1979. Notes have been omitted.

In speaking of romances and tales, questions of character development, or of authorial omniscience, will often be crassly impertinent. Who would be so generically idiotic as to question the probability of Poe's "MS. Found in a Bottle"? Yet to be less idiotic about stories that are not novels may call for critical methods of a new sort. We need a way, in short, of talking critically about effects of pure narrative. At present we only read and enjoy them, or read over and miss.

The need is nowhere greater than with Stevenson, who cultivated the forms of narration as an abstract art. What pleasures such an art can give seems to be little understood. E. M. Forster, who detested story as a tape-worm sapping a novel's life, expresses the common view of them, when he describes the storyteller keeping an audience of shock-heads (fatigued by contending against woolly rhinoceros) awake with suspense. "What would happen next?" Suspense is certainly common in the adventure. Thus, even a reader tired by life's rhinoceros-race will want to know the result of the duel between St. Ives and the giant Goguelet in their pitch-dark prison-shed. But Stevenson's art has less to do with suspense than with surprise: with surprising turns of events: what Chesterton called "zig-zag energy of action, as quick as the crooked lightning." Not the least element of surprise is verisimilitude of detail. In the present instance, we have the invention of duelling weapons (not easy in a prisoner of war camp); the grim practicality of stripping to obviate bloodstains on clothes; and the unforeseen but appropriate staunchness of Goguelet, who saves St. Ives by his soldierly silence. A defeated duellist is generally seen to his carriage and out of the plot; we have to go to Tolstoy for the partial exception of Dólokhov. But Goguelet—an authentic Stevensonian touch, this—lingers on with his castration-wound, leaching away our sympathy for St. Ives. The reader may feel suspense. (Will Goguelet talk?) But he may feel more strongly an unlooked-for respect for the hateful noble brute; together with a correspondent aesthetic surprise. In other words, suspenseful narrative serves as a medium of art, to be modulated, articulated, plastically formed. The narrative sequence, for example, may be ordered mimetically, even in so casual a work as *St. Ives*. Thus, the escape route from Edinburgh Castle is kept secret altogether, until the time comes to use it. And the first mention that St. Ives started his climb without thought falls when he is already dangling by his hands: "I had never the wit to see it till that moment." Again, St. Ives may be an unconvincing Frenchman. But would a truly French character quite have served Stevenson's purpose? He meant to lead us up the beaten path of patriotic British adventure, so as to trap us into a moralised adventure of psychology. The country of *St. Ives*, in fact, is on inward borders. It is a story taken up with the crossing and recrossing of lines of nationality, legality, and moral and sexual loyalty: a frequent theme is sympathy with the enemy, even such an enemy as the dark double Viscount de St. Yves. So fully moralised does the narrative become that the smallest practical detail may turn out to have a farther implication. St. Ives, about to descend by rope, offers himself with the gallows bravery "Here is the criminal." Boy's Own pluck? Not to the adult reader who thinks St. Ives guilty of a form of murder. He had better have hung in a noose, in more senses than one.

Most kinds of novel have a rule governing the selection of events, which might be called the constraint of the ordinary. It is often confused with the criterion of probability. But extraordinary events must occur sometimes; indeed, Aristotle even allows probable impossibilities. These would not do in novels. In romances, however, the unusual has its place and function: events, atmosphere, setting and other features compose a different world, as free as our own from the determinism of the ordinary. Yet Stevenson's romances also have their flavours of fact. He is indeed something of a specialist in unusual probabilities; a master at the admixture of likelihood beyond the ordinary. Only a Stevenson would make his duellists use authentic unscrewed scissor-halves lashed to wands with resined twine—"the twine coming I know not whence, but the resin from the green pillars of the shed, which still sweated from the axe." Defoe (an early model of Stevenson's) might have managed the resin; hardly the scissors. This is a classical art, delicately balancing and blending high tones of the unusual with a drab *repoussoir* of unmarvellous commonplaces. Only by working a long enough passage across mundane particulars—"the sun was setting with some wintry pomp"—can Stevenson persuade us to accept St. Ives's precocious balloon escape courtesy Lunardi, or the encounter with Scott (that so bold superimposition of fictional worlds, which recalls the sighting of a huge eagle *en route* to still-suffering Prometheus, in the *Argonautica*). In fine, Stevenson's freedom from the constraint of the ordinary is far from unconditioned. Besides obeying formal patterns, as when St. Ives's last ascent answers his first descent, it also responds to introspective intimations. Indeed, the liberty seems to be taken in the interest of these. Stevenson's better stories often have the implication of an inner, secondary narrative. The common notion that his work grew away from childish romances towards "adult" novels (*Weir of Hermiston* is usually cited) oversimplifies the contrasted genres, and falsifies both the chronology and the direction of the actual development.

To the last, Stevenson's artistic development was less a progression of literary kinds than a search for fuller psychological mimesis. And from the first, he had used a wide range of forms as material for an art already idiosyncratic. There was never any such thing, for him, as "mere adventure." Even *Treasure Island* (to take an adverse example, serialised in a boy's magazine) reaches out after very special narrative and descriptive effects. These Chesterton has percipiently connected with Stevenson's fondness for the abrupt angularity and contrast of woodcuts. It is an eighteenth-century clarity: "just as all the form can best be described as clean-cut, so all the colour is conspicuously clear and bright." And besides this aesthetic shaping there are firm moral patterns; to which, however, the story answers with deeper questionings, less clear, less bright.

Not that it answers by offering much fine moral texture of characterisation. The narrator, Jim Hawkins, is of an age that easily excuses amoral externality: so easily that a reader may not notice when his inadequate moral standpoint is undermined. But to call *Treasure Island* a children's book without qualification, without acknowledging its deeper expressions, would be unthinkable. At least, it would be unthinkable if Robert Kiely had not done it. Professor Kiely accepts Jim's narrative on its own opaque terms, as a tale told by a child, signifying nothing, relating "an invigorating and harmless adventure." Its whole pleasure is in the external conflict: "To try to speak seriously of good or evil in *Treasure Island* is almost as irrelevant as attempting to assign moral value in a baseball game, even though . . . enjoying the contest involves a temporary if arbitrary preference for one side or the other." Morton Zabel [in his introduction to the novel], on the other hand, has Jim gaining stature as a mature character; risking his integrity to share in Silver's cunning; and learning the reality of manhood's battle. There may be insufficient surface morality for this view, however, to carry much weight. Edwin Eigner, moreover, has questioned whether Stevenson (of all people) can have represented the goal of maturity in quite so favourable a light. May not the story's conclusion hint, chillingly, that to reject Silver is to exchange vitality for inglorious retirement? This note, of Jim's parting youth and separation from Silver, belongs not to the official theme but to a second subject, more intimate.

Every critic of *Treasure Island* has to begin by noticing the limitations of kind and Stevenson's zestful acceptance of them. But the disclaimers of "My First Book"—"a story for boys; no need for psychology or fine writing"—need to be read together with the more considered account in "A Humble Remonstrance": "The author, for the sake of circumstantiation and because he was himself more or less grown up, admitted character, within certain limits, into his design; but only within certain limits." A further limitation (which Henry James remarked) arises from our relative ignorance of the psychology of the Spanish Main. As Stevenson says in his defence, however, the boy is his own younger self, who searched for treasure, although not "in the fleshly sense." Within these limitations, the story deals with deep and nightmarish experience—the emergence into the light of day, in fact, of Jim's fearful dreams. For "the seafaring man with one leg" turns out to be smiling Long John Silver. So far as this dream narrative is concerned, criticism may be said to begin with Wallace Robson's "The Sea Cook." Professor Robson has given an admirable account of the increasingly unpleasant and progressively mutilated antifathers: Billy Bones, one sabre-cut; Black Dog, two fingers; Pew, blind. We can only be convinced by his tracing of "a line of candidate foster-fathers who constitute Jim's social relations in the story," beginning with Bones, whose death affects Jim more than that of his own father. Our single hesitation concerns the status of the analysis: is it perhaps so penetrating as to go through the canvas of the picture Stevenson meant to paint? True, only the ignorant claim to know how far man's mysterious consciousness may extend. But is it conceivable that Stevenson should have been at all aware of the oedipal content of dreams and fantasies?

This question is very nearly answered by Stevenson's remarkable essay "A Chapter on Dreams" (written at Saranac and printed in *Scribner's Magazine*, January 1888). Here he traces the genesis of his stories through dreams and half-waking fantasies. His unconscious faculties, which he calls "brownies" or lubber fiends, "do one-half my work for me while I am fast asleep, and in all human likelihood, do the rest for me as well, when I am wide awake and fondly suppose I do it for myself." To illustrate he tells a dream of almost unbroken narrative coherence. (Its accessibility to interpretation, however, is equally notable.) He dreamed that he was the son of a bad-tempered father, and "had lived much abroad, on purpose to avoid his parent." Returning home, he found his father remarried to a young wife "supposed to suffer cruelly." Because of the marriage—"as the dreamer indistinctly understood"—father and son met on a desolate shore, and the son "struck down the father dead." Most of the dream is taken up with the subsequent guilt, which works at cross purposes with the stepmother's misunderstood but at last openly declared passion for her son. Stevenson had realised, on waking, "that in this spirited tale there were unmarketable elements." Unmarketable, that is, because of taboos that would lead to suppression—the actual fate of "The Travelling Companion" (an earlier attempt on the theme of *Dr. Jekyll and Mr. Hyde*), returned by an editor as "indecent." Stevenson himself, who was no Carus or Charcot, may have thought of his fantasies in moral terms. But—and this is my point—he allowed them within the pale of responsible consciousness. Instead of banishing them censoriously, he evaded his own censor to rehearse them carefully and explore their "crafty artifice." Dreams had once taken him to "a certain doctor"; but now Stevenson could look at the "spirited tales" of his unconscious with humorous detachment— perhaps even (who knows?) with a little understanding.

But we should distinguish between a psychoanalytic approach (tempting, but not my present idea) and a heuristic use of biographical information. The latter approaches the inner narrative of a meant fiction. For example, "A Chapter on Dreams," with its case history of childhood night-hags and adolescent repeated dreams, may encourage attention to the dreams in *Treasure Island*, not least in its fine closure: "Oxen and wain-ropes would not bring me back again to that accursed island; and the worst dreams that ever I have are when I hear the surf booming about its coasts, or start upright in bed, with the sharp voice of Captain Flint still ringing in my ears: 'Pieces of eight! Pieces of eight!' " Associated with his capture at the stockade, these are to Jim words of fear—"The name of Captain Flint . . . carried a great weight of terror." Of course, fear is a generic feature of the adventure; as Stevenson himself framed its rule, "danger is the matter with which this class of novel deals; fear, the passion with which it idly trifles." But in this case the fear, which occasions a repeated dream, may be thought particularly deep and sustained. Fear of what, we may ask? Pirates, obviously; unpredictable killers; or, as Robson puts it in connection with the earlier dream of Silver, "the castrated father raging for revenge." Perhaps, with Stevenson's biography in mind, we might risk a more specific formulation: fear of an angry father and forbidden aggression against him. Of striking the father dead, in fact, as Silver strikes Tom—aggression that Jim escapes consciousness of, by fainting. Stevenson confesses an autobiographic relevance through the vestibular dream that ends the story. As Jim has told his dreams of a parrot with the voice of the murderer Flint, so the author has told the story of Jim, with a parrot voice very like his own, if not "in a fleshly sense." And as even Flint feared Long John Silver, so too Stevenson-Hawkins feared his loved father, his own aggression, and the maiming of challenged adulthood. Stevenson's "secret has been told to the parrot," Captain Smollett would say.

To open the open secret a little, one might first ask simply what *Treasure Island* is about. It would be too simple to answer, A quest for treasure. The "Treasure Hunt," after all, takes up only two chapters of thirty-four. And the comparative weakness of emotional charge in the treasure itself is quite problematic. Professor Robson asks whether Stevenson may not have avoided the theme because of inability to accommodate, at the time, representation of the possessed treasure (whose latent meaning is the mother's body). At all events, most of the story is not about a search. It recounts a series of contests for power. First comes the Admiral Benbow narrative, of struggle for a map; then the voyage under subverted authority; the mutiny and first struggle for the *Hispaniola*; the battle for the stockade; Jim's rebellious adventure and renewed struggle for the *Hispaniola*; and then (after his terrifying recapture) yet another power struggle, Silver's bid to retain the captaincy of the stockade. Throughout, the material consists of conflicts of authority, loyalty, obedience and duty. So far as these concern Jim, they could be shown to correspond to stages of growth in the scope of his volitions. To begin with, as critics have remarked, he displays little initiative, being caught up in events beyond his control. But later he achieves power of action, and becomes a sort of hero. We should not fail to notice (although children may) that this comes about through his flouting of Captain Smollett's authority: something that he is never quite forgiven for, even at the end—"You're a good boy in your line, Jim; but I don't think you and me'll go to sea again."

Outwardly, Jim achieves this independence through his "Sea Adventure," which also forms a cardinal threshold for the action as a whole. He recaptures the *Hispaniola* single-handed. Or, almost single-handed. He receives one indispensable piece of assistance: the use of Ben Gunn's boat. Professor Robson regards the wild man as a mere *ficelle*, or piece of plot machinery. But Ben Gunn's function seems to me of a different order of significance. After all, who achieves the quest for Flint's treasure? Not the pirates; not Dr. Livesey; not even Captain Smollett; but Ben Gunn the maroon. The solitary, that is to say; one who has achieved independence and survived rejection by a society tired of the quest. We recall a possible meaning of what has been named the "treasure hard to attain" archetype: selfhood, independence, identity. Treasure in this sense appears to constitute the story's goal. How significant, therefore, that Jim should achieve independence by entering Ben Gunn's dangerous coracle—by being, as it were, in the same boat with the solitary. This theme receives immediate development in Jim's brief, and very nearly disastrous, captaincy of the ship of life *Hispaniola*. Moreover, when he finally comes to possess the treasure, it takes the form of images of authority: his pleasure is to sort "the pictures of all the kings of Europe for the last hundred years."

Stevenson's disclaimer of "psychology" (that is, detailed mimesis of emotions) should not be thought to imply disregard of motive or morality. *Treasure Island*, as Chesterton remarked, is almost too consistent in implementing moral patterns. These mostly concern Jim's shifting attitudes to various codes, such as ordinary decency (the Squire) and principled duty (Captain Smollett). In a limited sense, one might speak of development in the boy's character towards maturity or ambivalence. He learns, at least, that honest gentlemen in authority may not be faultless, and that agreeable "gentlemen of fortune" may not be honest. It was in his first innocence that he "hated the captain deeply" for sternly eschewing favouritism; while finding Silver "unweariedly kind," ready always to favour Jim with a welcome to the clean, trim galley. However, the irony in Silver's characterisation—"he had a way of talking to each"—never quite becomes the narrator's. Even when villainy is unmasked at the apple barrel, Jim's artlessly remembered response is one of injured jealousy: he had felt like killing "this abominable old rogue addressing another in the very same words of flattery as he had used to myself." Contrast the episode's original, a family anecdote of how Stevenson's father "with the devilish penetration of the boy" had seen through a sycophant called Soutar and deliberately eavesdropped from the *Regent's* apple barrel. Jim may hate Silver's disloyalty; but he never quite sees through him or ceases to take favouritism for granted. Even after witnessing murder, even in the enemy's camp, Silver is still, for Jim, "the best man here."

And one must admit some truth in this. Long John is a complex figure (although not a complex character), who has justly puzzled critics. One of them dallies with the idea that Silver and Jim really might have "done a power of good together." The problem of Silver's attractive vitality is sometimes approached *via* "The Persons of the Tale," a fable in which Stevenson appears to offer a theological solution to it. This *parados* or interpolated frame or (if one may so describe it) *in persona personae* comment arises when Silver and Captain Smollett step outside *Treasure Island* after chapter 32 into a limbo of indeterminate status. Silver (of course) exults in being the maker's favourite: "If there is sich a thing as a Author, I'm his favourite chara'ter. He does me fathoms better'n he does you—fathoms, he does. And he likes doing me." Since the fable gives Smollett no effective answer, it is taken to imply the human liveliness of sin. But it may have more to do with the sinful creature's claim on God ("If there's an author . . . he's on my side."), or with the paradox of the justified sinner. But Stevenson's fear of judgment could pierce deeper than this. The limbo has its own fictive deceptions; among which is its placement before chapter 33. Silver's downfall and his worst hypocrisy lie ahead. "The Treasure Hunt" has just shown Silver turning his eyes on Jim "with a deadly look." Even Jim, then, realises something of Silver's evil—a realisation that the reader is to share: "Certainly he took no pains to hide his thoughts; and certainly I read them *like print*" (my italics). No longer neat but with "a hot and shiny countenance," Silver has at last looked like his murderous self—the clean hands were those of hypocrisy. In fact, he is anything but a likeable rogue. What sort of author could love such a creature as this?

Yet Silver has a secure place in the narrator's feelings, at least. His domination of Jim is sharply set out in one of the book's strongest visual images. Fast as the action moves, it moves from one fully realised picture to another. (We have only to think of the sabre-cut inn sign, or the attentive apple barrel, or the sloping mast of the beached schooner, to see why the tradition of *Treasure Island* illustrations should be so illuminating.) Often, the pictures take on an emblematic value (quite as much as any of Stevenson's so-called Emblems with their odd left-handed morals). The skeleton with hands "raised above his head like a diver's" came, we know, from Poe; but it might have come from Quarles. Among all the pictures, none is more memorable than this: "We made a curious figure, had any one been there to see us. . . . I had a line about my waist, and followed obediently after the sea cook, who held the loose end of the rope, now in his free hand, now between his powerful teeth. For all the world, I was led like a dancing bear." A dancing bear is made to perform, deprived of the power of independent action.

This is not to say that Silver merely symbolises what dominates Jim. He is too real, too much of a man, for that. To the end he retains convincing viability, if not as a leader then as a survivor. Think of his presence of mind, for example, when the treasure *cache* is found rifled:

> With Silver the blow passed almost instantly. Every thought of his soul had been set full-stretch, like a racer, on that money; well, he was brought up in a single second, dead; and he kept his head, found his temper, and changed his plan before the others had had time to realise the disappointment. . . . He passed me a double-barrelled pistol.

Being a leader of pirates no doubt taught a man to respond rapidly to life's challenges; but by any standard Silver's is an outstanding human performance.

The ambivalence of Silver may have to do with his function in a symbolism of character formation. He is the worst of the story's evil fathers, a father of lies; but a father none the less. At his most threatening, in the enemy's camp, he voiced this paternity: " 'It's all that you're to hear, my son' . . . 'And now I am to choose?' " If Jim had chosen as Silver wanted, he would indeed have become the son of a sea cook. On the other hand, Silver's kind treatment of his protegés as fellow-adults— "You're young, you are, but . . . I'll talk to you like a man"—seems to offer a genuine *entrée* to the insincere adult world. In a grown-up way he is tremendously knowing about his job, and full of unidealistic circumspection: "Now, the most goes for rum and a good fling, and to sea again in their shirts. But that's not the course I lay. I puts it all away, some here, some there, and none too much anywheres by reason of suspicion. I'm fifty, mark you; once back from this cruise, I set up gentleman in earnest." Shrewd calculation of the odds, in fact, is what enables Silver to assert so frequently, and with such plausible confidence, "you may lay to that." How shockingly far-sighted his cool predictions sound, to the innocent ear: " 'It were fortunate for me that I had Hawkins here. You would have let old John be cut to bits, and never given it a thought, doctor.'—'Not a thought,' replied Dr. Livesey, cheerily." Both have counted the cards; but Silver is the smoother at concealing this. He has more, so to say, maturity. If *Treasure Island* were a Renaissance work, one might speak of Long John as offering (like Autolycus) a mercurial component—a quicksilver facility in the change of roles, in persuasive eloquence, in lies. At any rate, Silver helped Jim to form his adult identity. What moral identity, then, what character can that be? We cannot look to the narrator himself for much questioning of this. But a thoughtful reader may share Captain Smollett's view of Silver, and be disturbed to imagine how far the criminal may have influenced Jim for the worse: how far he too may have become, in the end, a "gentleman in earnest."

The autobiographical echoes from all this are too clear to need amplification. Stevenson himself lived through a passionate drama of adolescent rebellions, friendships with surrogate-parents and intense reconciliations with his father. But we should avoid the genetic cul-de-sac. No doubt intimate feelings were engaged. No doubt Louis would explore, as he was apt to do, intimations of unconscious passions. But subsequently he and his brownies formed these into a fuller communication than psychoanalysis, at its present stage at least, can hope to match. Certainly Stevenson, interested though he was in psychological research, would have preferred a moral statement of the main issue of *Treasure Island*. I mean the choice that Jim was faced with in the enemy's camp—"now I am to choose?" It was a choice between hypocritical compromise, to save his skin, and loyal honesty. Jim chose to face the terrible father. In his finest hour, he even made an aggressive boast. And the reward for his boldness was not only that Silver kept him alive, but that the good father's party cut the tether of dependence and ratified the free selfhood that he had stolen.

So far, the story leads to individualism as much as individuation. But at last the achieved self is restored to society, and the individual to the fold. Outwardly, this comes about through reconciliation with Dr. Livesey and partial reconciliation with Captain Smollett. Indirectly, there are several statements of a similar idea. Perhaps the clearest is Ben Gunn's return to the human race. Another may be concealed in the treasure's final lodgement. We are told that Jim was "kept busy all day . . . packing the minted money into breadbags." The symbol of the achieved self is thus enclosed and fused with another symbol: containers of bread, the element of community.

The quest occasioned many deaths—fifteen, in fact, in the tradition of the island called The Dead Man's Chest. But the conclusion demands still more subtractions from the microcosmic community. Three mutineers were marooned to continue the harsh process of individuation. And Silver, helped by the anarchic Ben Gunn, subtracted himself, with a little Treasure-manna. His escape is variously interpreted. It may be merely to save him from the legal embarrassments of repatriation. Or it may imply doubt about civilised society's ability to arrest Silver's tendencies. Or perhaps Robson is right to see a connection with the abandonment of the bar silver. Stevenson may hint at deferred judgment and the silver of Jeremiah 6.30— "Reprobate silver shall men call them, because the Lord hath rejected them." If so, Ben Gunn was right to warn that the lives of the company "would certainly have been forfeit" had Silver remained aboard. It is sobering that Captain Smollett can think of a comparable exclusion of Jim, and proves to be right in his prediction: "I don't think you and me'll go to sea again. You're too much of the born favourite for me." But to press the point farther might be "not to enrich but to stultify [the] tale": to break a butterfly on the wheel, or make it walk the plank.

Similar existential questionings underlie the surface of all Stevenson's better adventure novels, romances, and short stories. We have to think of a continuing inner search, passages of which might be traced throughout his writing: beneath the light improbabilities of *New Arabian Nights* and *The Wrong Box*; the doubles of *Dr. Jekyll and Mr. Hyde* and *The Master of Ballantrae*; the psycho-history of *David Balfour* and *Weir of Hermiston*; and the social questions of the underestimated late works, *The Wrecker* and *The Beach of Falesá*. In *The Ebb-Tide: A Trio and Quartette*, Stevenson's last completed work, the search reached a climacteric point. Partly for this reason and partly because it would be desirable, if possible, to bring more of the Stevensonian *oeuvre* into the critical canon, I should like now to draw attention to that "most grim and gloomy tale."

To those who allow themselves the freedom of not condemning Story on principle, *The Ebb-Tide* offers a high pleasure. At the same time, it presents the problematic features of Stevenson's fiction in an acute form. (I am not thinking of its collaborative character, which is a problem only for the genetic critic.) How does it relate to his other fiction? How seriously, in a literary way, is it meant? How are we to know, even, what it means? Or to take its unpalatable moral? It seems calculated, cynically, to disgust rather than convert. "That Grimy Work," as its author called it, is at times very unpleasant; at times quite unsuccessful; at all times sharply interesting. Even its admirers must concede it to be uneven. Yet it remains a compelling work, and also one of some historical import. Within the narrow island limits of its derelict paradise, it holds, as who should say, *rationes seminales* of much of Conrad's fiction. Its weakness, but also in a way its strength, arises from excessive seriousness; which may explain why Stevenson found it so difficult to write. It was deeply involved in his quarrel with God.

The first part, "The Trio," follows the fortunes of three beachcombers on civilisation's Pacific margin. All lack the pliability, but also the firmness, to make a legal living: Davis is a former ship's captain, broken for drunkenness; Huish a hard, nasty, vulgar, indomitable Cockney clerk; and the quasi-authorial *persona*, Robert Herrick, a timid failure and skulker from life's battles. (The Virgil that Herrick uses for *sortes* surely always opens at *facilis descensus Averni*: "each had made a long apprenticeship in going downward.") We find the three starving in an old jail, which Stevenson based on the Papeete calaboose where Melville and his co-mutineers had been imprisoned. Besides starving, Huish suffers from an influenza plague that has Tahiti in its grip—the same virus, we may suspect, as Camus's *peste*. The end seems close. But Davis's good fortune brings a reprieve. He is given charge of a schooner, whose drunken captain (an *alter ego?*) has died of a worse plague, smallpox. The three adventurers sail for Australia with a native crew and a cargo of champagne, having agreed—Herrick quite reluctantly—to steal the ship. Then Davis and Huish take to drinking the cargo, while Herrick is left to run the ship. And when the converted cannibals prove morally superior to their officers—"It was a cutting reproof to compare the islanders and the whites"—the *Farallone* seems to be on a course well logged in *Typee* and *Omoo*. As for the erring ship, surely it is a microcosm of civilisation, sailing the allegorical deep waters of *Moby-Dick* or (rather) *Israel Potter?* But now the schooner comes about, for Stevenson's own form of fraud-within-fraud picaresque. The thirsty pirates discover that most of the wine is water—the *Farallone* voyage has been planned as an insurance swindle. This insight not only offers a fresh perspective on human society, but a new moral dilemma, another change of course, a deeper *bouge* of hell. The three will go along with the swindle so as to blackmail the dishonest owners. Immediately (presumably in consequence of their choice) they are lost and short of provisions; so that when they raise a mysterious island it is nothing at all short of providential.

The second part, "The Quartette," begins with arrival at the island. As often with Stevenson, the shaping imagination plays over a setting, until full realisation of place gathers. In this, his art resembles Melville's, or Hugo's. It patiently cultivates *mise-en-scène*, so discreetly that one only realises later how deeply the meditation has gone. In *The Wrecker* it dwells on the bird-obliterated *Flying Scud*; in *Weir of Hermiston* on the Covenanter-haunted moors; and in *The Ebb-Tide* on a bare atoll. When the island is first sighted, by one of the Kanakas, it appears as "a greenish, filmy iridescence . . . floating like smoke on the pale heavens." Farther in,

> The isle was like the rim of a great vessel sunken in the waters; it was like the embankment of an annular railway grown upon with wood: so slender it seemed amidst the outrageous breakers, so frail and pretty, he would scarce have wondered to see it sink and disappear without a sound, and the waves close smoothly over its descent. . . . A spur of coral sand stood forth on the one hand; on the other, a high and thick tuft of trees cut off the view; between was the mouth of the huge laver. . . . The sea turned (as with the instinct of the homing pigeon) for the vast receptacle, swept eddying through the gates, was transmuted, as it did so, into a wonder of watery and silken hues, and brimmed into the inland sea beyond. The schooner worked up, close-hauled, and was caught and carried away by the influx like a toy. She skimmed; she flew; a momentary shadow touched her decks from the shore-side trees; the bottom of the channel showed up for a moment, and was in a moment gone; the next, she floated on the bosom of the lagoon; and below, in the transparent chamber of waters, a myriad of many-coloured fishes were sporting, a myriad pale flowers of coral diversified the floor.

Simply as description, this would be well enough. But consider that it is only a correlate, or outward husk, and its achievement may seem of a high order indeed. Jacques Rivière has noted the "free, radiant curiosity" of this landfall, "the delightful unfurling of our spirit before the future, very near but still silent," with congenial sensitivity:

> During those moments when nothing is yet happening, when events are still in preparation—not a breath of wind on the deck of the ship—I feel myself quietly growing equal to everything prodigious in the universe. And my ecstasy resembles that of Herrick who, leaning over the diaphanous scarce-moving water of the lagoon, saw "a trail of rainbow fish with parrot beaks" swim by.

It is the characteristic moment, for him, of the *roman d'aventure*.

After the suspense, surprise. The island, itself not quite ordinary in its presentation, is inhabited by a distinctly extraordinary white aristocrat, Attwater, able to offer Herrick "a dry sherry that I would like your opinion of." Yet the uncertainly-charted Zacynthos is no ideal Shangri-La. It has been so ravaged by smallpox that only four inhabitants survive. True, it is wealthy. But its wealth has a mundane basis in pearl-fishing. The pearls come as welcome news to the adventurers, who scent plunder more valuable than anything from the *Farallone*. Plainly Zacynthos is another microcosm of the undeveloped native society to which Europeans "carry activity and disseminate disease." The urban similes in its description may thus be more apt than Kiely allows. Now, however, a counter-action develops: Attwater's attempt to divide the adventurers. At first he treats Herrick as a favoured elect, Davis and especially Huish as reprobate. But when the complex *entrainement* of conversion engages with the machinery of the pirates' intrigues, the plot turns and alignments change. Now Davis is with Herrick, now with Huish. And the self-righteous Attwater: is he always on the side of Stevenson's angels? We wait in suspense to know who will control the island when the pearl-fisher's private schooner, *Trinity Hall*, returns. In the end it is Attwater who wins, but with Davis as repentant sinner instead of Herrick. This edifying turn may provoke the same response that Huish made to Herrick's story: "It's like the rot there is in tracts." But cooler reflection will find that Stevenson means the *dénouement* (which went through much revision) to stimulate analytic appraisal. The four characters make up a quartette indeed, of psychological forces contending for a single mind: Herrick and Huish even share the same *nom de guerre*. All along the story has been a psychological investigation. The conclusion, therefore, should be seen as raising a question whether there may be other, deeper, religious strata underlying the psychomachic material. It remains a question that gives *The Ebb-Tide* enduring interest.

Doubt particularly attaches to the character of the failed missionary, who is central enough for the story to have been called, at one stage, *The Pearlfisher*. Attwater belongs with Stevenson's most powerful father-surrogate characters: he is in the same class, as a moral invention, with Long John Silver and Weir of Hermiston. He is clearer than the first, more felt than the second, subtler than either. As a character, however, he may be too uncertainly realised—by turns flattering and insolent; brutal and pious; evangelically sincere and unscrupulously Machiavellian; the object of satire and subject of enigma. Some will find him implausible as soon as he leans (swiftly) to Herrick and says "University man?" Too abrupt, surely, even allowing for *temps* and *moeurs*? Perhaps. But the point is a nice one: Herrick has shown himself pained by Huish's vulgarity, and Attwater may be seizing his chance. Besides, the enquiry implies—though not in terms of character—judgment of the snobbery. A similar jolt may be felt when Attwater later appeals to Herrick, with evangelical fervour, to "come to the mercy seat." The atheistical Herrick will not surely be alone in calling this "beyond bearing" in its presumptuous directness. He cannot, cannot believe. But notice the ex-missionary's response: "The rapture was all gone from Attwater's countenance; the dark apostle had disappeared, and in his place there stood an easy, sneering gentleman, who took off his hat and bowed. It was pertly done, and the blood burned in Herrick's face." This *volte face* momentarily recalls *Confessions of a Justified Sinner*; but the effect seems here more tactical. Stevenson makes Attwater so often surprising that he seems to challenge the reader to come to terms with him. Sometimes the surprises suggest Providence. Attwater is ready for the adventurers when they first arrive; sees through them immediately; acts with the inevitability of fore-knowledge; and is a fatalist. Yet he also prevents the thought of a "God figure": "I have nothing to do with the *Sea Ranger* and the people you drowned. . . . That is your account with God. . . . I do not kill on suspi-cion." Is he, then, a religious fanatic, for whom the chief end justifies any means however grimy? But his ruthlessness is too casually cruel for that, his foresight too readily that of a Winchester. It is a Braxfieldian anecdote of his, about inflicting summary justice with his two-handed engine, that precipitates Herrick's breakdown, attempted suicide and final submission. (He runs off, tries to drown himself, but elects instead to swim to the island and give himself up to Attwater and salvation.) Some have seen in Attwater the Accuser himself—"dark apostle" indeed. But if that naive machinery is present, it can only form a part of the author's own advanced conversion machine. To Herrick-Stevenson, the cruelty of the universe seemed quite evil enough to be hated—or to warrant "an insultin' letter to Gawd."

But Stevenson as Tusitala, as storyteller, presents a larger parable. And perhaps it is one with political or anthropological edge. In the end, Herrick and Davis are to leave on the *Trinity Hall*, the *Farallone* having been de-stroyed as incriminating evidence. (It is none of Attwater's affair.) Religion's main effect on them, Herrick seems to imply, has been to make a "sure thing" surer, more respectable. It has certainly been hardest on the pro-letarian reprobate Huish ("Whish," Attwater class-consciously calls him): he is not spared, like the others, to embark in the security of the Trinity, or the more secular *Trinity Hall*. Zacynthos, in short, could be represented as the image of a society quite as unacceptable, politically, as the Tahiti of the opening chapters. Only, Davis has achieved now the respectability of the Scotch Captain who earlier humiliated him; and he belongs to a com-munity too lost in self-delusion to recognise itself as satirised. It is more than a community of colonialists, for Attwater embodies every respectable believer. He locks up the pearls of his faith in a safe, hoping to make a good thing out of them. He builds his life around an efficient monopolistic business enterprise. And he is quick to defend in-groups: believers, whites, Cantabrigians, *bourgeois*. Herrick's submission to him, therefore, is cynical despair, Herrick's final cynicism enlightenment. The sequel will be to move away from the island's old, doomed, religious state.

This view might explain much. It would help, for example, with the Melvillean icon of the buried ship's figurehead, a "woman of exorbitant stature and as white as snow . . . beckoning with uplifted arm," set into the beach, "the ensign and presiding genius of that empty town." Once, the figurehead was on a ship of state moving on some great historical course. Now, it is grounded among the bones of a dead atoll. But it has enough force still for Herrick to regret that he cannot commit himself to it in the simple old way:

From the crown of the beach, the figure-head confronted him with what seemed irony, her helmeted head tossed back, her formidable arm apparently hurling something, whether shell or missile, in the direction of the anchored schooner. She seemed a defiant deity from the island, coming forth to its threshold with a rush as of one about to fly, and perpetuated in that dashing attitude. Herrick looked up at her, where she towered above him head and shoulders, with singular feelings of curiosity and romance, and suffered his mind to travel to and fro in her life-history. So long she had been the blind conductress of a ship among the waves; so long she had stood here idle in the violent sun that yet did not avail to blister her; and was even this the end of so many adventures, he wondered, or was more behind? And he could have found it in his heart to regret that she was not a goddess, nor yet he a pagan, that he might have bowed down before her in that hour of difficulty.

As it is, the image seems too ambivalent: "shell or missile" punningly directs aggression that takes simultaneous forms of trade and war. Here the thrust of European civilisation is hard to miss. We cannot be sure, however, as to whether the figure-head's gesture of hurling meets a response in Huish's attempt to throw acid. (Had he succeeded, Attwater too might have been a "blind conductor.") At least Huish is the adventurer who seems closest to honouring the figure-head. And it would be in character for Stevenson to prefer the outcast: in the fable "Faith, Half-Faith, and No Faith at All" it is the rover with his axe who goes "to die with Odin." Huish is defiant enough; although if the figure-head figures "high adventure," it is hard to see him as a worshipper, exactly. He seems to have a more social import—to embody, perhaps, the coarse yet vital energy of the European colonial volition. In any event, white civilisation's dynamic marine emblem is now run aground, bogged down, stuck. That does little to reduce the level of its aggression, however. Huish has to be violently repressed by the super-egotistical Attwater (himself a hurler of shells). Indeed, "The Quartette" brings a marked accentuation of the aggression earlier displayed towards the cockney only in threats. Obviously Stevenson does not mean us to wish that the acid-thrower had lived to inflict a power-emasculating injury on Attwater. But maybe there is relief in the final prospect of embarkation: of moving on after the episode (to put it a little crudely) of Christian Capitalism.

The various ships and *mises-en-scène* thus symbolise forms of social organisation progressively, in order of chronology. (Or of viability: The island itself, we recall, was first described as a "fragile vessel.") Turns of plot that Kiely dismisses as mechanical stimuli really function organically to exfoliate more and more radical ideas of human society. For Stevenson, indeed (as for Kipling), the whole adventure form served a revelatory or exploratory purpose, ever disclosing deeper, less suspected and more surprising insights. Its type is the gradual uncovering of the *Farallone*'s fraudulent cargo: "Deeper yet, and they came upon a layer where there was scarcely so much as the intention to deceive." In some ways the form anticipated post-modernist fabulation. But Stevenson continued to use conventional generic terms, such as *romance* and *parable*—even if he applied the latter with a new-old Aesopian ambivalent emphasis. We can almost see a self-referring sequence of kinds, in *The Ebb-Tide*, from the epic of the "tattered Virgil"; through the letters home (Huish's being pure romance); Herrick's "tract" and *graffiti*; and the "sea-romances" that provide nautical words of authenticity; to the parables of Attwater and of Stevenson.

"Fond of parables?" asked Attwater abruptly when he came upon Herrick in the diving shed. And he told him the parable of the diving suits:

> "I saw these machines . . . come up dripping and go down again, and all the while the fellow inside as dry as toast . . . and I thought we all wanted a dress to go down into the world in, and come up scatheless. What do you think the name was?" he enquired.
>
> "Self-conceit," said Herrick. . . .
>
> "And why not Grace? Why not God's Grace, Hay?" asked Attwater. "Why not the grace of your Maker and Redeemer, He who died for you, He who upholds you, He whom you daily crucify afresh? There is nothing here"—striking on his bosom—"nothing there"—smiting the wall—"and nothing there"—stamping— "nothing but God's Grace! We walk upon it, we breathe it; we live and die by it; it makes the nails and axles of the universe; and a puppy in pyjamas prefers self-conceit!"

This comes dangerously near to giving God the best tunes. Can such words have come from the same pen as "The Yellow Paint," that anti-parable of religion's worthlessness as a life-preserver? Understandably, Herrick was baffled. He still saw Attwater's iron cruelty and insensibility. But now there was something else—"to find the whole machine thus glow with the reverberation of religious zeal, surprised him beyond words"; so that he laboured (in vain) to piece together Attwater's character. Perhaps the reverberation was deeper than he recognised, deeper than even the author could quite have sounded. The episode suggests genuine puzzlement and introspective ("psychological") search; not least in its description of the diving shed. This fascinated Herrick with a "disorder of romantic things," profuse debris from "two wrecks at least," and "commonplace ghosts." Doubtless, the wonderfully inventorised detritus is emblematic (a compass, for example, "idly pointing, in the confusion and dusk of that shed, to a forgotten pole"). It was a voyage of empire that had failed: the *Asia* from whose wreck Attwater preserved relics. But there may also be less conscious tones. The episode uses the sort of material that furnishes dreams—material that may well have had a source in experiences far anterior to the Anstruther period, when Stevenson himself learnt to wear an unfigurative diving suit and come up scatheless. Similar depths seem to yield up religious images and symbolic actions throughout; in which even the unbelieving Herrick participates unawares. Even when he attempts suicide by drowning, it constitutes the "immersion" of a baptism of repentance. He is conscious, however, only that his cowardice is ignoble; and "with the authority of a revelation" that "another girds him and carries him whither he would not." Similarly, Attwater's killing of the *alter ego* Hay-Huish enacts the mortification of the body of sin. And, more obviously still, the island itself is a vessel of the Grace of repentance. ("We walk upon it, we breathe it.") It is called a "huge laver": the water that Attwater lives "at" represents the cleansing water of life. For this reason, too, Stevenson makes each description of water vibrantly alive; as when "the silence of death was only broken by the throbbing of the sea." In the most pervasive way imaginable, the story's myth is implicitly Christian. In other words, Attwater's religion makes a real challenge, however much we may dislike the man. His fatalism (to mention only one trait) has a character hard to distinguish from Stevenson's own. Both believed in a distinctly savage deity. But then, it is the coward who "loathes the iron face of God."

Attwater epitomised not so much Stevenson's missionary enemies, in fact, as his missionary heroes. The ex-missionary was even a part of himself. This he thinly disguised by chronological reversal. Attwater's romantic interest in missions declined; whereas Stevenson, at first temperamentally antipathetic to the missionaries, later revised his view. After visiting a Molokai leper colony, he defended Father Damien, and in Samoa he became very friendly with James Chalmers the New Guinea missionary. It would be presumptuous (in several ways) to assert that between *The Beach of Falesá* and *The Ebb-Tide* Stevenson experienced religious conversion. In time of composition, indeed, they overlap. In spite of the latter's epigraph from *Julius Caesar*, the eponymous tide is beyond doubt that of Arnold's sea of faith (which must ebb, for a ship to leave Zacynthos' lagoon). But at least Stevenson was swimming with Herrick, "without illusion," for Canaan's side. The Christian atheism of "If this were faith" accorded well enough with Sunday-school teaching and pious addresses. Perhaps, to use the terms of *The Ebb-Tide*'s fable, we may say that in it Stevenson perceived civilisation as a fragile vessel, more dependent than he had thought on the faith and duty and discipline that keeps ships of various kinds from being put on the rocks. Certainly his own sense of duty became quite intense. It is not impossible, after all, to see *The Ebb-Tide* as something of a tract, in its fashion: quite in line, say, with "The House of Eld."

Or does this view miss the best of the story, its finer psychological intimations? Attwater, besides being a fatalist, is also an experimentalist. And I have hardly touched on the psychology of true and false belief; of the relation of ageing to believing; and of moral reformation. The exploration is conducted allegorically, through the interactions of four personifications of internal faculties. Sometimes they compose a moral spectrum, or form a psychodynamic series—as when Huish threatens Davis in such a way as to remind him of "something he had once said to Herrick, years ago, it seemed." Herrick acts as Davis's better self, Davis as a better self to Huish. Considering, too, that Davis often initiated action—at least until Huish "carried him on to reprobation"—one thinks of psychological schemes such as the Platonic souls (with Huish as the concupiscible), or the various Renaissance triads (*mens-ratio-passio; intellectus-anima-voluntas*).

These adumbrations, however, are strongly over-printed by others. Stevenson, like many nineteenth-century writers, was fond of the motif of doubles. He used paired characters not only in *Dr. Jekyll and Mr. Hyde*, *Kidnapped* and *The Master of Ballantrae* but also in minor works such as *The Owl*. This interest in divided or multiple personality, which he pursued in correspondence with F. W. H. Myers the psychical researcher, found some of its farthest reaches in the intricacies of *The Ebb-Tide*. The story so coruscates with doubled pairs as to dazzle with their excess. As Stevenson told an interviewer in February 1893 (the same month when he returned to revising *The Ebb-Tide*): "My profound conviction is that there are many consciousnesses in a man . . . I can feel them working in many directions." The doubling of Hays is an explicit instance of something pervasive: there are doubled ships, wrecks, islands, and incidents—Attwater's laving Davis's face as Davis laved Herrick's; Davis's and Attwater's calling Herrick to Jesus; and many others. But it is no static array of diptychs. The quartette continually rearranges itself (like the Pythagorean elements) to form new pairs of pairs. Thus, the fatalistic Attwater and superstitious Davis are believers, the others sceptics. This pairing seems to be confirmed by the authoritarian roles of the first pair—the ex-missionary's stern paternalism and Davis's captaincy, natural fatherhood and respect for forceful command. Davis is fond of the expression "my son," and it is his prayer for his children that saves his life, to put him at last on Attwater's side. However, a different grouping altogether brings Attwater and Herrick together. It makes them gentlemen, university men, "respectable," but puts Davis and Huish in the same boat as grosser natures. At times this class structure can seem fundamental: Davis says to Herrick, "He's your kind, he's not ours. . . . Save him if you can!" Yet another grouping is generated by the axis of moderation and extremity. Attwater and Huish are both, in their different ways, "sinister": given, that is, to non-natural behaviour. But Davis and Herrick normally inhabit a more average middle ground of ordinary experience and half-faith. It is they who are liberals perplexed about whom to betray. So Herrick resists an "immense temptation" to warn Attwater, while agonising over the three lives that "went up and down before him like buckets in a well"; just as Davis later agonises over the ethics of vitriol. The dilemmas are not so much moral as existential—which part of experience should be eliminated: the supernatural, or the natural body of sin? Even Herrick can see that to eliminate Attwater might be to lose a living energy and purpose vital to human existence. And yet. . . .

The reader may never resolve the quartette into a settled scheme of relations. Perhaps because he is reading about change, his feelings are perpetually disturbed by some unanticipated turn, or some new valuation, which forestalls the equilibrium of mere understanding. Each characteristic he counted best turns out to have its repellent aspect; each truth to be a form of "romance." The monstrous Attwater, explicitly, makes Herrick say "I am attracted and repelled." A reader may agree that "circumstance was like a consecration of the man"; but then the dominating personality will be given unpleasantly hard, or else homosexual, overtones ("You are attractive"). Similarly with honest Captain Davis. Nothing could be more sincere than the father's love for Ada—until we learn that he has no daughter. But *after* we learn about the glass menagerie? False or doubtful emotions of this sort abound. Indeed, familial sanctities seem in this story to operate more often as means of justifying crime than as ameliorating influences. The paternal Davis could even be construed as a tempter. But how could Herrick be expected to cut the human bond he embodies? It is the dilemma of "The House of Eld" again. Davis's ambivalence culminates in the last invitation to Jesus. If a reader is capable of compassion, it may trouble him to think that Davis's weakness caused, among other things, Huish's death. Moral readers will have no time for vitriol throwers. Yet Stevenson more than once writes of the "innocence" of Huish, whose courage commands Davis's respect, and who can fairly be called "the least deserving, but surely the most pitiable." Attwater, we recall, threatened Davis: "Whatever you do to others, God shall visit it again a thousandfold upon your innocents." In this way, every value has its opposite; every absolute becomes relatively fictional. But the effect is not, in the end, quite like that of Poe's nihilistic *exposé*. With Stevenson, demystification goes farther; demythologising itself is shown to be a form of fiction. The outcome reminds one of the practicalities of Tolstoy (another harsh fabulist). For all its scepticism, *The Ebb-Tide* offers a sort of bleak faith, in a savagely rational religion that never forgets its origin in folklore. Stevenson could call the concluding chapters "the most ugly and cynical of all" (Letter to Colvin, 23 August 1893). But "was even this the end of so many adventures . . . or was more behind?" Ulysses' course, after all, led on past Zacynthos to Apollo's shrine *formidatus nautis*. We can take the parable, like Attwater's, in different ways; but each leads to our own next change of heart.

The tract-like seriousness of such a parable carries fiction to a limit. And surprisingly the limit lies on the instrumental, not the formal, border of literature. Some have regarded the fineness of Stevenson's style as an obstacle to modern readers (presumably they prefer literature to be written badly). But Stevenson's own search during his last years, an opposite endeavour to Henry James's, was always for simplicity. In particular he had come to dislike the forced "alembicated" or high-pitched style, to which the earlier beginning of *The Ebb-Tide* partly committed him. In a letter to Colvin of 23 May 1893 he writes: "I am discontented with *The Ebb-Tide*, naturally; there seems such a veil of words over it; and I like more and more naked writing; and yet sometimes one has a longing for full colour and there comes the veil again." But the veil was drawn only comparatively; *The Ebb-Tide* depended most on its "intrinsic horror and pathos"—and on its "fierce glow of colour" in another, far from rhetorical, sense. Stevenson meant it, even, anti-mechanistic as it was, to appeal to admirers of Zola's "pertinent ugliness and pessimism" (Letter to James, 17 June 1893).

Rivière wished to promote kinds of fiction that might provide models for an emergent French form of the 1920s. But in the event, ironically, it was Conrad, that drawer of many veils of words, who most immediately found inspiration in Stevenson's South Sea fiction. Critics trace the connection through narrative motifs. Thus *The Ebb-Tide* anticipates *Victory*, in its plot of three adventurers bent on another man's wealth; *Lord Jim*, in its failure recouped. Or, Donkin is modelled on Huish. And many passages give atmospheric hints of Conrad's doomed, rotting, "tenebrous land," where only stars and heroes stand out from the vile darkness: "On shore, through the colonnade of palm stems, Attwater's house was to be seen shining steadily with many lamps. And there was nothing else visible, whether in the heaven above or in the lagoon below, but the stars and their reflections." A more significant resemblance between the two *romanciers*, however, may reside in the tentative forms of meaning towards which they liked to grope. Each develops a firm setting of "formidable immobility," splendidly described and deeply considered, with its roots in memories of experience; and each recounts, within this eloquent symbolic world, a story with numerous moral facets. But neither the facets nor their sum exhaust the story's meaning. In a famous passage, Conrad says that to Marlow "the meaning of an episode was not inside like a kernel but outside, enveloping the tale which brought it out only as a glow brings out a haze, in the likeness of one of these misty halos that sometimes are made visible by the spectral illumination of moonshine." Stevenson, although he considered himself "preoccupied with moral and abstract ideas," seems to have illuminated *The Ebb-Tide*, at least, according to a poetic that Marlow would have found congenial. An encompassing yet elusive phosphorescence of moral meaning was a quality of several nineteenth-century writers—one thinks of Melville, Hawthorne, Dickens. Not the least valuable legacy to the literature of our own century, however, has been variously inherited by Conrad and Greene and Borges, and such postmodernists as Donald Barthelme, from Stevenson. For the special obliquity of moral that he taught is remarkably close to the way in which serious dreams often convey their sense; as Stevenson himself realised:

Sometimes a parabolic sense is still more undeniably present in a dream; sometimes I cannot but suppose my Brownies have been aping Bunyan, and yet in no case with what would possibly be called a moral in a tract; never with the ethical narrowness; conveying hints instead of life's larger limitations and that sort of sense which we seem to perceive in the arabesque of time and space.

Among all Stevenson's late works, *The Ebb-Tide* is not only the most interesting as a work of narrative art, but also one of the most commanding as a work of intellect. It may not stand out as *Weir of Hermiston* a massive crag from the moorland. But like its own atoll it is founded deep.

The Artist and the Critics: Advertising, *Dorian Gray*, and the Press

Regenia Gagnier

In the 1984 film *The Picture of Dorian Gray in the Yellow Newspaper*, German director Ulrike Ottinger brilliantly probes the idea of total media control: Frau Dr. Mabuse, head of an international press cartel, creates the stunner and personality Dorian Gray. A bizarre, simultaneous double ending has Dorian both the victim of the media tycoon and the image that she cannot control. Wilde's *Picture of Dorian Gray* is not German expressionist cinema about total media manipulation, but it is about the relationship between the image and the real, between art and life. Under the influence of its Mabuse, Harry Wotton, Dorian's image dominates his life and others', and life responds with a vengeance—or according to an alternate reading, with a final concession to a moralistic marketplace. But more important than the novel itself is the controversy it generated, for it recapitulated the novel's themes. Dorian attempted to divorce himself from life and history through an image impervious to experience, an attempt to live "aesthetically." The press attacked Wilde because his book and, it was feared, he were divorced from middle-class life: in *The Picture of Dorian Gray* the press could see nothing of itself. For his part, Wilde responded by perfecting an adversarial image to that of their gentleman: that of the dandy. Both received considerable publicity.

Although the controversy surrounding *Dorian Gray* couched itself in terms of art and morality, it was a product of social tensions that had been brewing for decades. These concerned the much-advertised images of dandies and gentlemen, and to a lesser extent, they also concerned the much-advertised images of women. The meaning of decadence in British literature of the 1890s is revealed in these tensions, rather than in any particular literary style. The images of the dandy, the gentleman, and the woman—comprising the relatively primitive form of the cult of personality in the 1890s—cannot be divorced from an advertising, consumerist culture. For what might have begun as the gentleman's self-reliance, the woman's self-help, or the dandy's "burning need to create for oneself a personal originality" (Baudelaire) often ended in self-promotion. If we uncover the history of these conflicts, which amount to a crisis of the male, we shall see that the dandy's rubric of "Art" counteracted an entire spectrum of perceived losses in the age of mechanical reproduction, advertising, and middle-class conformity.

Therefore we must shift our analysis from the artwork alone to encompass [two] interrelated phenomena of the time: the art of advertising in the 1890s that reflected the crisis of images, for the dandies in *Dorian Gray* could not have arisen except as rejections of, and counterparts to, the normative image of the gentleman [and] *Dorian Gray*'s very public production, from Wilde's addition of the inflammatory preface to his responses to criticism. . . .

For the researcher in Wildeiana, perhaps the most surprising data are the astonishing numbers of popular cartoons, songs, scores, dances—like "The Oscar Wilde Forget-Me-Not Waltzes" in the United States—and parodies that the public figure Wilde generated on both sides of the Atlantic. Then there are the novels, stories, essays, apologies, biographies, and tributes very different in tone that began to flood the market in 1895. When Wilde went down from Oxford to London, he entered a world in which product advertising was matched by the ability of persons to advertise themselves. Reviews of his plays are especially interesting in this context. Not only were his first successes reviewed exhaustively in the London press, but the provincial papers also duly responded to his first nights in London. Moreover, reviewers then did not criticize the drama so much as they advised the dramatist. Wilde and theater managers were instructed to delete acts, eliminate characters, revise scripts, and modify their own behaviour during curtain calls and were generally subjected to the opinions and directorial talents of writers and reviewers who today often seem barely literate. But this treatment and self-treatment of work and artist as improvable and sellable commodities partook of the same odd mixture of idealism and commerciality that product advertising exhibited.

For Wilde to employ the tactics of advertising and publicity at the very time he was expressing a socialist theory is not so contradictory as it has appeared to critics. The late-Victorian socialist propaganda and the management of advertising in the last decades of the century used similar techniques of dissemination—for example, the engaging of the lower classes—and a similar rhetoric of "free choice," "promise," and "the goal of a better life." Sidney Webb worried that as monopoly trusts came to dominate business, advertising would become, not the herald of better products and services, but rather the competitive means of various industries to gain the largest share of the consumer's income. In his introduction to G. W. Goodall's *Advertising: A Study of a Modern Business Power* in May 1914, a year in which Britain was spending as much on advertising—£10,000,000—as on its Army and Navy combined, Webb discussed the potential of advertising as well as its perversion in a capitalist state. Thomas J. Barratt's £3,000,000 on soap advertisement represented for Webb "the value of the wrecks to which the competition of this giant soap manufacturer has reduced so many old-fashioned soap boilers." Better, thought Webb, to imagine advertising in a "co-operative commonwealth," where it would serve as an educational force and a tool for freedom of choice:

> Even when all our various manufactories and stores have become public services, and when no capitalist levies a toll upon our supplies, we can easily imagine the various public health departments advertising their baths and other hygienic opportunities; the educational authorities importuning every young man and maiden to try their attractive lecture courses and organised games; the municipalities of the various pleasure resorts commending their holiday attractions; the national railway and steamship administration tempting us to enlarge our minds by travel; the State Insurance Department urging us all to insure for allowances in old age or sickness, supplementary to the common provision; in short no end of advertising intended to influence our decision as to how to spend our incomes in the ways the "general will" of the community felt to be good.

The years 1914 to 1918 brought about enormous increases in state advertising to produce a new national identity, but one very different from that imagined by Webb. Yet if Webb saw that the current practice of advertising benefited the capitalist rather more than the worker, others saw it in more democratic terms.

As early as the *Tatler*, Addison had called advertisements "instruments of ambition . . . of great Use to the Vulgar": "A man that is by no means big enough for the *Gazette* may easily creep into the advertisements; by which means we often see an Apothecary in the same paper of news with a Plenipotentiary, or a running Footman with an Ambassador" (14 September 1710). Samuel Johnson admonished that every advertiser "should remember that his name is to stand in the same paper with those of the King of Prussia and the Emperor of Germany, and endeavor to make himself worthy of such association" (*Idler*, 20 January 1759). Through the work of Bulwer Lytton, Brougham, Gladstone, and Disraeli, the advertising tax was abolished in 1853, the stamp duty on newspapers in 1855, and the last "tax upon knowledge," a duty on paper, in 1861. Macaulay was quoted with approbation by Gladstone that "advertising is to business what steam is to machinery—the great propelling power." And by 1901 the Prince of Wales spoke the sentence that was elaborated by the press and publicized by manufacturers as the "Wake up, England!" speech at the Guildhall. He encouraged manufacturers to advertise internationally: "To the distinguished representatives of the commercial interests of the Empire, whom I have had the pleasure of meeting here, I venture to allude to the impression which seems generally to prevail among their brethren across the seas, that the Old Country must wake up if she intends to maintain her old position of pre-eminence in her colonial trade against foreign competitors."

"Advertising," declaimed Churchill, "nourishes the consuming power of men. It creates wants for a better standard of living. It sets up before a man the goal of a better home, better clothing, better food for himself and his family. It spurs individual exertion and greater production. It brings together in fertile union those things which otherwise would never have met." Like the dreams of the socialists, advertising imaged infinite posibility—personal, national, global. The consumer need not be recognized by the Queen to be successful, for the arena of success was shifting; the symbols of status, industry, and comfort were as plentiful as the ads, and the ads determined the "wants." Thus in "The Soul of Man under Socialism," Wilde would regret people wasting their lives "in accumulating things, and symbols for things" and deplore the culture that encouraged it: "So completely has man's personality been absorbed by his possessions that the English law has always treated offenses against a man's property with far more severity than offenses against his person, and property is still the test of complete citizenship." (Students of British culture should recall that respect for private property was one of the Thirty-Nine Articles of Religion. Article 38 begins, "The Riches and Goods of Christians are not common.")

The 1890s in England, a time of overproduction (or underconsumption) at home, initiated modern practices of advertising, those that identified products with desired modes of living. The significance of these practices cannot be overestimated insofar as they initiated an ideology of choice dependent on the proliferation of images: the consumerist ideology of a free life-*style*.

On the other hand, Samuel Johnson (like John Berger today) had discerned that the democratic practice more often than not debased and leveled all to the status of objects. He protested the humiliation of "a famous Mohawk Indian warrior" who was advertised as on exhibition with his war-paint and scalping knife but was juxtaposed in the ads with Dublin butter. By the 1890s, the *Times*'s reports of advertising excesses had spurred enough indignation to found the S.C.A.P.A. (Society for the Checking of Abuses in Public Advertising), predominantly directed against posters and billboards; and the battle still raged at the end of the century when the moon lay fair on two monstrous signs for oats competing halfway up the cliffs of Dover. Although in *The Sorrows of Satan* (1895) Marie Corelli wrote that Millais's "Bubbles" poster, exploited by Pears soap, "[would] prevent [Millais] ever standing on the dignified height of distinction with such masters in Art as Romney, Sir Peter Lely, Gainsborough, and Reynolds," and W. P. Frith complained when his little girl with "The New Frock" was turned into a soap poster entitled "So Clean," the Royal Academy continued to be ransacked by meat extract firms for portraits of healthy cows; art and advertising were inextricably tied.

The great proliferation of the ephemeral "little" (art) magazines may have begun in the spirit and tradition of arts and crafts in the manner of Morris, but they survived only when they were commercially viable. The most successful of the little magazines, the *Yellow Book*, was successful precisely because it was directed toward an inclusive market beyond traditional coteries, individual arts, and esoterica. After its death in 1895 because of its association in the public's mind with Wilde, its successor, the *Savoy*, failed largely because its management rejected advertising. Even that marvel of craftsmanship, the Bodley Head book, dedicated to the Revival of Printing in the (simplified) mode of Blake, Rossetti, and Morris, owed its success to the very shrewd and firm business practices of John Lane, whose strategies were much scrutinized and criticized by the reading public and bookselling competitors.

Regardless of the concerns of gentlemen journalists and women novelists about the effects of advertising, the liberals had abolished the taxes on both advertising and paper. The result was not only to increase the number of newspapers in Britain form 640 to 3,000 between 1855 and 1900, to decrease the costs of advertising, and to make the papers more affordable for the masses, but also to eliminate numerous shady practices on the parts of tax collectors—for example, that of taxing favorable book reviews as advertisements. (This practice may have interesting implications for literary reception theories of the first half of the nineteenth century. As Turner writes in his history of advertising, "An author whose book was savaged by an impecunious periodical could be pardoned for harbouring base suspicions.") When Max Nordau sought the etiology of fin-de-siècle exhaustion, one of his factors was the proliferation of periodicals, and he cited the 500 percent increase between 1840 and 1890. Recent bibliographies suggest that the increase was much higher.

Wilde, who had the socialist's commitment to human possibility, had the more immediate accessibility of advertising to accomplish his personal mobility. "Advertise what you sell, not yourself, unless you are for sale," advised the American encyclopedist of advertising, the stunningly successful N. C. Fowler, Jr., in *Fowler's Publicity* (1897). By 1890 Wilde had advertised himself on two continents. Leaving Oxford as a Professor of Aesthetics and turning journalist to educate the "public"—itself a creation of modern advertising practices and as we have seen [elsewhere], a sort of objectified commodity for Wilde—he lectured on art and interior design to coal miners in Colorado.

Wilde would later write that the two great turning points of his life were when his father sent him to Oxford and when society sent him to prison; but in an acute unpublished essay A. J. A. Symons recognized the significance of Colonel Morse's sending Wilde to the United States—where the lecture, circus, Barnum's "moral" museum, and subscription publication had flourished. The precocious and romantic Oxonian, managed by a hardened publicist, came back hardened, commercial, responsible, and determined to be a dramatist. Despite the ridicule it inspired, Wilde's elaborate "aesthetic" costume was not his own choice at all, but rather a costume he had contracted to wear in his commercial dealings with Morse, and it was successful. Back in England, he peddled his—and, as Whistler said, everyone else's—views on art in the provinces. However romantic or revolutionary his theories of art, the romantic artist, as Yeats said of him, had entered a commercial area. Hence the flurry of essays, dedications to potential patrons, reviews, and letters to editors.

It was in fact journalistic hostility toward the socially mobile self-advertiser that led to the controversy over *The Picture of Dorian Gray*, and it was with the reception of the novel that Wilde paid for his attacks on journalists in his literary and political theory. But both sides in the debate were so caught up in the opaque images of advertising that both presented contradictions—contradictions clearly related to an age more materialistic than its participants could admit.

Wilde insisted on the "moral" of the story, a constant moral throughout his prose fiction: that an exclusive preoccupation with the physical and material surfaces of life would result in the attrition of human creativity. But simultaneously his prose insisted on ornate description of material conditions and an obsession with physical beauty. Indeed, to a great extent *Dorian Gray* is about *spectators*, from spectators of the beauty of others such as Basil of Dorian's or Dorian of Sybil Vane's to "spectators of life," as Wilde called Wotton. Similarly, critics of what was considered Wilde's aristocratic pose and immorality could not see the moral of the novel because of their own preoccupation with its physical and material representations. Both Wilde and his critics argued for spirit; both sides' energy was directed toward externals. Both sides were situated in the context of public images and self-advertisement: the journalists posing as the gentlemen guardians of public morality, Wilde advertising himself as the subtle dandy-artist of higher morality, thinking himself within the Symbolist ranks that Arthur Symons called the "revolt against exteriority, against rhetoric, [and] against a materialistic tradition."

The press's vicious attacks on *The Picture of Dorian Gray* in many ways duplicated *Fraser's Magazine*'s attacks on dandiacal literature a half-century earlier, but by 1891 the periodical arena was even more brutal in its competition to construct and undo public identities. Wilde coolly denied to an editor that he was indefatigable in his public appreciation of his own work, since of the 216 reviews he had read of *Dorian Gray* he had taken public notice of only three. Although his critics' ostensible concern was with the book's potentially "immoral" influence, its author's assertive familiarity with an aristocratic mode of life accounted for most of the journalistic hostility. Like the new commodities, the author's image seemed to imply a mode of living which "in reality" he did not enjoy. So once again, the gentlemen, with their self-image of sincerity and particular kinds of morals, battled with the dandy and his particular kind of manners.

According to a typical aesthetic reaction against middle-class materialism, Wilde divided the world of *Dorian Gray* between the upper and lower classes exclusively. He respectively associated these with Lord Henry Wotton and with Dorian's connections to the East End (the home of the Vanes) and quayside establishments of questionable services. Since it appeared unlikely that he had much authority for speaking of either, middle-class journalists numbered him among "simpleton poseurs . . . who know nothing of the life which they affect to have explored." Such "posing" was judged even more reprehensible because, as all of his biographers concur, by 1890 rumors had begun to surface of his participation in homosexual circles in London. Journalists like W. E. Henley, who felt responsible in the tradition of *Fraser's* for upholding "public morality," transferred their hostility from the opportunistic and mildly ill-reputed author to his book.

The best way to demonstrate the prejudice against Wilde the dandy and social butterfly is to compare the reviews of *Dorian Gray* with those of his other prose fiction, his fairy tales and short stories, which did not provoke a scandal. Although Wilde's novel and stories were consistent in both themes and style, the first was excoriated on all accounts while the second were praised for both their "morality" and their literary craft. The only explanation for the reviewers' contradictory reaction is that the novel, unlike the stories, removed art from the locales and sentiments of middle-class life. [Here] I want to consider these textual differences. In doing so, I hope to demonstrate that the decadence of *Dorian Gray* lay in what the novel *did not* include and was therefore external to the text.

Wilde wrote to the editor of the *St. James's Gazette* that the "moral" of *Dorian Gray* was that the unyielding perspectives of the three major characters reduced them to incomplete human beings, almost, we might say, to caricatures. The artist Basil Hallward worshipped physical beauty far too much; Dorian abandoned himself to sensation and pleasure; Wotton sought only to be a spectator of life. In Wilde's stories, composed during the same period as *Dorian Gray*, the same "moral" consistently surfaces. Hallward's kind of materialism is supplanted by Christian love; mysterious, unnamed sins either are treated satirically or are condemned; Wotton's epigrammatic style is treated as shallow. Wilde's critics, on the other hand, could not see Wilde's consistency because the novel presented the moral in an "aesthetic" and aristocratic environment whereas the stories presented it in bourgeois households or fairyland.

When the novel was published in the American periodical *Lippincott's Monthly Magazine* in 1890, the few favorable reviewers found the characters "abnormal." Ethical and mystical journals like the *Christian Leader*, the *Chris-*

tian World, and *Light* focused on Wilde's "psychological explorations" of these characters and were willing to discern the moral Wilde derived from them. The much greater number of negative reviewers transferred the epithets they applied to the "abnormal" characters onto the book and Wilde himself. The *Athenaeum* called the book "unmanly, sickening, vicious (although not exactly what is called 'improper'), and tedious." The *St. James's Gazette* found it "mawkish and nauseous . . . tedious and stupid," and sneered at Wilde's idle, "effeminate" characters who "fill up the intervals of talk by plucking daisies and playing with them, and sometimes by drinking 'something with strawberry in it.' " The *Daily Chronicle* discerned immorality in Wotton's (and by extension, the book's) appeal to cure the soul by the senses, and accused Wilde of self-advertisement:

> Dulness and dirt are the chief feature of *Lippincott's* this month. The element in it that is unclean, though undeniably amusing, is furnished by Mr Oscar Wilde's story of "The Picture of Dorian Gray." It is a tale spawned from the leprous literature of the French *Décadents*—a poisonous book, the atmosphere of which is heavy with the mephitic odours of moral and spiritual putrefaction—a gloating study of the mental and physical corruption of a fresh, fair and golden youth, which might be horrible and fascinating but for its effeminate frivolity, its studied insincerity, its theatrical cynicism, is tawdry mysticism, its flippant philosophising, and the contaminating trail of garish vulgarity which is over all Mr Wilde's elaborate Wardour Street aestheticism and obtrusively cheap scholarship.

The *Scots Observer,* edited by Wilde's one-time friend the moral crusader W. E. Henley, called the book "nasty" and ran a review that provoked a two-month running controversy on the relevance of moral concerns to artworks:

> Why go grubbing in muck heaps? The world is fair, and the proportion of healthy-minded men and honest women to those that are foul, fallen, or unnatural is great. Mr Oscar Wilde has again been writing stuff that were better unwritten; and while "The Picture of Dorian Gray," which he contributes to *Lippincott's,* is ingenious, interesting, full of cleverness, and plainly the work of a man of letters, it is false art—for its interest is medico-legal; it is false to human nature—for its hero is a devil; it is false to morality—for it is not made sufficiently clear that the writer does not prefer a course of unnatural iniquity to a life of cleanliness, health, and sanity. The story—which deals with matters only fitted for the Criminal Investigation Department or a hearing *in camera*—is discreditable alike to author and editor. Mr Wilde has brains, and art, and style; but if he can write for none but outlawed noblemen

and perverted telegraph-boys, the sooner he takes to tailoring (or some other decent trade) the better for his own reputation and the public morals.

One is struck by the profusion of such terms as "unclean," "effeminate frivolity," "studied insincerity," "theatrical," "Wardour Street aestheticism," "obtrusively cheap scholarship," "vulgarity," "unnatural," "false," and "perverted": an odd mixture of the rumors of Wilde's homosexuality and of the more overt criticism of Wilde as social poseur and self-advertiser. Although the suggestion was couched in terms applying to the text, the reviews seemed to say that Wilde did not know his place, or—amounting to the same thing—that he did know his place and it was not that of a middle-class gentleman. Between "outlawed noblemen and perverted telegraph boys," the upper and lower classes, the press discerned no place for itself.

It goes without saying today that the reviewers' insinuations of Wilde's homosexual practices had a basis. On the other hand, their basis was certainly not evident in the text of *Dorian Gray*, in which, with the exception of murder, the protagonist's "sins" are never named and are only briefly alluded to. Wilde had, in fact, been associated with an unabashedly homosexual and pornographic novel. In 1890 he brought the manuscript of *Teleny: A Physiological Romance of Today* to Charles Hirsch's bookshop on Coventry Street and requested that it be passed on to a friend who would call for it. The friend called, took it away, and returned it to be picked up by another friend. The process was repeated several times by several friends until Wilde retrieved the manuscript. In 1893 Leonard Smithers altered the text by transposing the setting from London to Paris "so as not to shock the national *amour propre* of his English subscribers" and published 200 copies with the subtitle "The Reverse of the Medal." Gay Sunshine Press has only recently (1984) reissued the unexpurgated English edition, and excerpts from the 1893 edition, describing what the police called homosexual "liaisons" on the quayside and luxuriously exotic rooms and suppers amid which artists and affluent men perform spectacular sexual acrobatics, are included in Brian Reade's anthology of homosexual literature, *Sexual Heretics*.

But although Wilde handled the manuscript whose consumption was so covert, and in spite of a recent Parisian foreword that attributes the work entirely to Wilde, it is fairly certain that he was neither the author nor a major collaborating author of this anonymous work. The most that can be said about its relation to *Dorian Gray* is that Dorian's haunts and pleasures, particularly in chapter 11, share an ambience with the luxurious settings of *Teleny*, and that Dorian, too, walks down by the river. In any case, whether or not readers of *Teleny* saw hints of it in *Dorian Gray*, in 1891 *Teleny* was known to only a few. And in their suspicions of immorality the reviewers cited only Dorian, whose sole explicit sins were murder and callousness; whereas the figure that homosexual readers sympathized with was probably Hallward. With his long-suffering, platonic love, the artist was much more characteristic of the period's homosexual literature. In *Teleny*, the protagonist, a pianist, ultimately commits suicide.

As Wilde said in his explication of *Dorian Gray*'s moral, the crimes in the novel were the characters' exclusive preoccupations with the physical and material aspects of life. The result of the crimes was that Hallward lost his model and his life, Wotton saw his friends and family disgraced and was left without an audience for his pratings, and Dorian's "soul" was transferred and confined to the material image, the horrible, brittle picture. The reviewers saw the wrong sins and failed altogether to see the retribution. Rather than responding to their implicit allegations concerning his own "sins," Wilde turned the tables on his critics in a feat of condescension and self-promotion.

First, he published "A Preface to *Dorian Gray*" in the *Fortnightly Review* (1 March 1891), including among his maxims on art the dicta "Those who find ugly meanings in beautiful things are corrupt without being charming"; "Those who go beneath the surface do so at their peril"; "The highest as the lowest form of criticism is a mode of autobiography"; and "It is the spectator, and not life, that art really mirrors." This and several other maxims in the Preface were consistent with *Intentions* in that they shifted the focus from the work to the spectator. The Preface said, in effect, what Wilde had written of *Dorian Gray* earlier: "What Dorian Gray's sins are no one knows. He who finds them has brought them." In a letter to the *Scots Observer* he was able to support this statement by describing the reviews: the journals concerned with ethics discerned the moral, the journal of mystics discerned its spiritual import, the journals of British hypocrisy discerned its sinfulness.

Second, Wilde made some minor deletions in the *Lippincott's* version and added six new chapters for the book form, published in April 1891. The deletions were few, primarily individual sentences and fragments, but their force was to make Hallward more pathetically enthralled with Dorian, to make Wotton more deeply sad in the silences between his epigrams, and to make Dorian's ostracism only slightly more complete. Third, Wilde formulated the laissez-faire policy toward artists included in "The Soul of Man," and continued to advertise himself in his archly arrogant letters to editors—in which he repeated the "moral" of *Dorian Gray* and lamented that "the prurient" could not see it.

Thus the novel did double duty in that it conceded to two distinct audiences. . . . Members of the homosexual community could read *Dorian Gray* sympathetically, for characters like Hallward were a staple of their literature. (Writers like Marc-André Raffalovich, intimate friend of the visual inspiration of Dorian, John Gray, tirelessly proposed a connection between artistic genius and homosexuality. Even the name "Dorian" bore its significance for some as the classical term by which polemicists for the amendment of homosexual laws designated their noble ancestors in ancient Greece.) On the other hand, because of the story's obliqueness regarding Dorian's sins and, especially, its entirely moralistic conclusions, journalists could only hint at their suspicions concerning Wilde.

However, Wilde's suspected homosexuality was but secondarily related to the general disapprobation of *Dorian Gray*. The short stories were well received although they included similar innuendos, particularly *A House of Pomegranates*. The reviewers' tone reflected not Wilde's innuendos but whether his settings were aristocratic and aesthetic or bourgeois, idyllic, and pastoral.

Up to our present day, critics have been unable to reconcile the stories' Christian, socialist, and pastoral themes with the themes they discerned in the novel. When the first collected edition of Wilde's works was published in 1908, reviewers began to contrast the stories and *Dorian Gray* as if the latter marked a sort of demise on Wilde's part. The *Times*'s review, attributed to Arthur Symons, stated: "Only three years after ['Lord Arthur Savile's Crime'] came 'The Picture of Dorian Gray'—a withering comment on the lack of conviction and of a standard in art and life in one who would teach, or even amuse, his fellows. In that horrible book all the imagination, the power, the ingenuity of the short stories, are perverted to deplorable uses." F. G. Bettany wrote in the *Sunday Times:* "Compared with ['The Happy Prince,' 'The Birthday of the Infanta,' and 'The Young King'], 'Dorian Grey' [sic] is but a *tour de force* in morbidity, interesting mainly because it gave a forecast to some extent of Oscar Wilde's own eclipse." Yet although *The Happy Prince and Other Tales* (1888) was published before *Dorian Gray*, the other two collections, *Lord Arthur Savile's Crime and Other Stories* (1891) and *A House of Pomegranates* (1891), were published later. Therefore, Wilde's "lack of conviction and of a standard" or "forecast" of his "eclipse" cannot be so easily dated according to divisions in his work.

In fact, when the prose collections were first published, the reviews were overwhelmingly favorable. The *Athenaeum* and the *Saturday Review* praised *The Happy Prince* as comparable to Hans Andersen's fairy tales, with the added attraction of contemporary satire. The *Universal Review* praised the stories' morals, poetic feeling, and literary craft. Even after *Dorian Gray*, the *Athenaeum* recommended *Lord Arthur Savile's Crime* for reading aloud— whose title story is but a satiric version of the novel—and the American journal the *Nation* approved of its "agreeable satire" on the British upper classes. *A House of Pomegranates* suffered some criticism for its "wordy descriptions," "fleshly style," and "glut of description and epithet," but the same reviewers nonetheless commended the tales' "beauty," "force," and "poetry." Although they had received Wilde's extravagant descriptions of the stunner Dorian with disapproval, reviewers were noticeably appreciative of his descriptions of a red-haired witch in a green cap and of a mermaid with a pearl-and-silver tail. In the *New Review*, George Saintsbury commends "The Fisherman and His Soul" as "what seems to me the best thing

Mr. Wilde has yet done." This was regarding a story with more purple prose and unnamed sins than even *Dorian Gray*.

The only difference between the stories and the novel is the novel's aristocratic setting, its removal of art from middle-class life. The stories, on the other hand, reek of middle-class virtue and sentimentality. The swallow in "The Happy Prince" launches into luscious descriptions of Egypt, comparable to chapter 11 of *Dorian Gray*, but here the Happy Prince cuts him off and tells him to take the Prince's jewels to the poor of the city. In "The Nightingale and the Rose," the student of philosophy quips aesthetic maxims while the bird dies of love, much like Harry Wotton and Basil Hallward. The Miller in "The Devoted Friend" bestows his *sententiae* on amicability to the kind friend he is exploiting. "Lots of people act well," he says, "but very few people talk well, which shows that talking is much the more difficult thing of the two, and much the finer thing also"—a claim very like Wotton's position that "I never quarrel with actions. My one quarrel is with words. . . . The man who could call a spade a spade should be compelled to use one." The views of the "Remarkable Rocket" parody Wotton's egotism and aestheticism.

In *Lord Arthur Savile's Crime*, Wilde demystifies the suspenseful air of crime surrounding Dorian by satirically inverting the themes of the novel, reinserting art into life. In "The Sphinx without a Secret," the mysteriousness of Dorian's sins becomes a harmless, bored woman's desire for excitement. In "Lord Arthur Savile's Crime," a cheiromantist (palm reader) is to Savile what Wotton is to Dorian: he foresees for him a future of illicit actions. Yet unlike Dorian, who cannot just act but refers himself to a work of art as conscience, Savile simply commits the murder and marries the girl (named, in fact, Sybil Merton: Sybil Vane plus Hettie Merton, the two women Dorian sacrificed). That is, Savile is a practical man of action and common sense, so he kills the cheiromantist and puts an end to his crisis of conscience. The effete, aristocratic Dorian, on the other hand, permits Wotton to dominate him. Similarly, in "The Canterville Ghost," the specter of a sixteenth-century uxoricide, obsessed with his aristocratic roles of shame and sin, is frustrated by the pragmatism of a modern American family.

In *A House of Pomegranates*, the worship of materialism is described in a style as overblown as that chapter 11 in *Dorian Gray*; and, as in the novel, the worship of physical beauty is moralized. Like Dorian, the young king is the object of rumors due to his obsessive love of exotic materials. Bithynia, known during the time of the Roman empire for its homosexual practices, is significant as the homeland of the beloveds of Julius Caesar, Hadrian, and Elagabalus (all names which surface in *Dorian Gray*):

Many curious stories were related about him at this period. . . .
He had been seen, so the tale ran, pressing his warm lips to the
marble brow of an antique statue that had been discovered in the

bed of the river on the occasion of the building of the stone bridge, and was inscribed with the name of the Bithynian slave of Hadrian. He had passed a whole night in noting the effect of the moonlight on a silver image of Endymion.

All rare and costly materials had certainly a great fascination for him, and in his eagerness to procure them he had sent away many merchants, some to traffic for amber with the rough fisher-folk of the north seas, some to Egypt to look for that curious green turquoise which is found only in the tombs of kings, and is said to possess magical properties, some to Persia for silken carpets and painted pottery, and others to India to buy gauze and stained ivory, moonstones and bracelets of jade, sandal-wood and blue enamel and shawls of fine wool.

But the young king gives up such treasures and is finally crowned in the church by God's sunlight.

In "The Birthday of the Infanta," all those who are physically beautiful are cruel, like Dorian, and the reader's sympathies are with the dwarf, who looks into the mirror and hates his image as much as Dorian loved his portrait. In "The Fisherman and His Soul," the fisherman sells his soul for love. Like Dorian's soul in the portrait, the banished spirit wanders through exotic backgrounds committing unnamed sins. Like Dorian and his portrait, the story concludes with the fisherman's soul and body reunited in death. The "Star-Child," like Dorian, is so enamored of his own beauty that he utters an irrevocable wish to distance himself from ugliness. He says to his plain mother: "Thou art too foul to look at, and rather would I kiss the adder or the toad than thee." Like Dorian's portrait, the Star-Child's physical aspect is condemned to bear the burden of his wish: he takes on the appearance of the toad as to his face, and the scales of the adder as to his body. The Star-Child learns generosity through extreme acts of penance and reverts to his original comeliness before he dies, just as Dorian's portrait regains its youthful aspect when he dies.

Thus in the stories Wilde represents the same themes as in the novel, but in *Dorian Gray* these are dictated as elements of aristocratic and artistic or bohemian life. In the stories, either conflicts are resolved by men of action, rather than idle lovers of beauty, or they involve only harmless water rats and rockets. When a young, pastoral king languishes amidst tapestries and repents, his story bears a "pretty morality"; when the same lush prose describes a contemporary aristocrat in a setting reminiscent of French *décadence*, his story is "poisonous."

With *Dorian Gray*, which seemed to smack too much of art for art's sake, the reviewers felt that Wilde violated the social function of art—that is, to present the normative values of society, to present the middle class. In exclusively representing the part of society that he did—idle aristocrats and romantic artists—Wilde offended an ethic of industry and productivity.

He seemed to expose himself as a presumptuous social climber who penetrated aristocratic circles with offensive ease. In addition, his indefatigable self-advertisement was simply not acceptable behavior for a gentleman, much in the same way that his and Harry Wotton's lounging on sofas was not the acceptable carriage of gentlemen. The author's decadence lay in his unwillingness to capitulate to the image of the gentleman. *Dorian Gray's* decadence lay in its distance from and rejection of middle-class life. This, not stylistics, is how decadence in British literature should be understood.

Yet there is one other related aspect of the novel that is decadent: it was not only dandiacal, it was "feminine" in a sense not intended by the press's use of that term. Here is a brief excerpt from a long passage in the most notoriously decadent chapter of the novel. In chapter 11, Dorian reads "a fascinating book"—generally accepted as Huysmans's *A Rebours* although Wilde's typewritten copy for *Lippincott's* originally named the text "*Le Secret de Raoul* par Catulle Sarrazin." In a passage modeled on the *ubi sunt* formula, Dorian contrasts his face, now a timeless work of art, with the ephemerality of material things, in this case legendary works of embroidery:

> Where was the great crocus-coloured robe, on which the gods fought against the giants, that had been worked by brown girls for the pleasure of Athena? Where the huge velarium that Nero had stretched across the Colosseum at Rome, that Titan sail of purple on which was represented the starry sky, and Apollo driving a chariot drawn by white gilt-reined steeds? He longed to see the curious table-napkins wrought for the Priest of the Sun, on which were displayed all the dainties and viands that could be wanted for a feast; the mortuary cloth of King Chilperic, with its three hundred golden bees; the fantastic robes that excited the indignation of the Bishop of Pontus, and were figured with "lions, panthers, bears, dogs, forests, rocks, hunters—all, in fact, that a painter can copy from nature.". . . Catherine de' Medici had a mourning-bed made for her of black velvet powdered with crescents and suns.

Wilde lifted this passage almost verbatim from his review of Alan Cole's translation of Lefébure's *History of Embroidery and Lace* in the *Woman's World* of November 1888. The title of the review, 21 pages in length, is "A Fascinating Book." In addition to its "decadent" descriptions of lace as sensational history opposed to Dorian's modern (that is, historyless) face, the review includes most of Wilde's opinions about art.

During his brief editorship of the *Woman's World* (November 1887 to July 1889) Wilde reviewed, favorably, dozens of examples of what he called after George Trevelyan the "art-literature" of the day—novels narrating "the workings of the artist soul . . . in which the creation of a picture forms the dominant motif"—all written by women. He also reviewed dozens of "psychological" novels by women, all concerned with the effects of "sin" on personality. And contributors supplied the magazine with numerous poems and plays on sin, as well as many articles on tapestry, lace, embroidery, and jewelry, all bearing the rich "decadent" style of chapter 11 in *Dorian Gray*. Indeed, such works, and lighter works reminiscent of the society and wit of Harry Wotton, appear to have made up a consistent diet for the readers of the *Woman's World*, readers whom Wilde cultivated as women of "culture and position."

Just as Wilde had dedicated his stories and tales to women of Society who would thereby ensure his reputation, he constructed the narrative of *Dorian Gray* from the standard elements of a certain genre of upper-class women's literature: art, psychology, sin, and luxury. These elements often combined to form a particularly modern problem: the relation of influence and history to present action. This was certainly the Modern Woman's problem, and in this as well as in its thematic components, the novel was indeed "effeminate." The outcry against Wildean decadence on the part of gentlemen journalists was in part an outcry against the male author who won the support of Society—an institution managed by women—by writing a book that would appeal to women. Through his experience of advertising women's books, Wilde learned the tricks that would make his own book, and himself, such a dear commodity. After Harry Wotton's dialogues, he was barraged with invitations to dinner parties.

Novelist of the Modern City: George Gissing's Early Fiction

John Goode

What is important about *Demos* in the development of Gissing is something that is continued and extended from *A Life's Morning*, the foreshortened awakening of the oppressed woman, Adela, into the trammels of social actuality. It is extended importantly because Adela's sense of oppression is linked with the oppression of the working-class girl Emma Vine, and the spokesman for both is, as it were, the mother of the oppressor, Mrs. Mutimer. A group of women, coming from different classes but equally displaced from those classes—Stella Westlake, Adela, Emma, Mrs. Mutimer—hover questioningly on the edge of the novel's polemical narrative.

But through this connection, the novel achieves something else which is to be the center of Gissing's effectivity. Emma and Mrs. Mutimer live out the contradictions voiced by Adela and Stella in a specific area of London. I have shown [elsewhere] how this is beginning to happen in *The Unclassed*. Working-class London, however, is treated differently in that novel. Litany Lane is a slum enclave, a contaminated spot very similar to Dickens's Tom-All-Alone's—it has neither specific location nor inner differentials. It is not a containing zone, a function of the network of boundaries that constitute the modern city. Hoxton, however, has these features. It is realised as an area just as St. Marylebone is in *The Unclassed*, and because it is also realised as an area with a demographic identity more sharply focussed than the mixture of *The Unclassed*, it becomes also, if only fragmentarily, the site of the exploration of a group with a specific problematic. Hoxton is the best thing about *Demos*, and it is in the end on the margins of the novel. But it is very important, and very different from what has gone before. It launches Gissing into the next stage of his evolution, the achievement of his London through the realisation of the London of

From *George Gissing: Ideology and Fiction*. © 1978 by John Goode. Vision Press, 1978.

the urban poor. Not the slum so much as the ghetto, and from the ghetto he will emerge as the first novelist of the modern city, the forerunner, if never consciously acknowledged, of Dreiser and Joyce, and the line of writers who have made fictions of the urban revolution. We must now attend to this development in the two finest of Gissing's early novels, *Thyrza* and *The Nether World*.

"He taught people a certain way of regarding the huge city"—Gissing's tribute to Dickens's value as the novelist of London has the more weight precisely because he has spent much of his own career portraying aspects of London life, and because he has portrayed them so differently from Dickens. For if Dickens is vivid it is partly because he is picturesque, and Gissing is clearly not. However, it would be naïve to assume that because he himself portrays London with no sense of its imaginative propensities, that he therefore portrays it more accurately. On the contrary, there is a sense in which the photographic reproduction of the ordinary is achieved in language only by a certain verbal distance, most flagrantly evident in, say, the classical allusions ironically used in the description of bank holiday in *The Nether World*, but present also in more routine linguistic strategies. For example, at the very opposite of the ironic rhetoric is the very bald and detailed naming of streets and buildings. You can trace the movements of Gissing's characters on a map of London and this seems to constitute a kind of objectivity, an unmediated mimesis by which the story is placed in an actual terrain, as though he doesn't want to fictionalise the context. But the effect of this, as with much naturalistic description, is to make that terrain "exotic" rather than representative. You won't recognise anything about it unless you know it, and the rhetorical relationship between the author and the reader assumes that you won't know it. One way of describing the difference between Dickens's London and Gissing's is to say that Dickens establishes a world the reader can enter, so much so that Gissing himself first saw London through Dickens's eyes, while Gissing makes a report back.

Certain features of Dickens's London make it into an imaginative world. First, the organisation of space in Dickens is based on a tension between obscurity and proximity. The city is specifically an agglomeration, so much so that its crowdedness creates areas of darkness which are stressed by the hierarchical distances of the social structure. Thus its capacity for suspense, drama, the sheltering of evil, derives from unknown contingencies which only the author with his synoptic vision, as the scribe of a whole social world, can uncover and manipulate. Secondly, the city is a palimpsest, an overlapping multiplicity of functions—rule, commerce, manufacture, or simply the redistribution of surplus (which is served primarily by crime at one end of society, and expropriation at the other)—and overwritten histories which inscribe themselves on archaic institutions and pursued lives. So that if space is full of unknown contingencies, time is loaded with obstruction and catastrophe only grasped by the author's right to make plots and establish denouements. Finally, the city is located in pastoral values. Urban as he is, Dickens, as Gissing realised, is always looking at the city in terms of his contrast with the country, with a rural past which always beckons back. These are crude generalisations, but they form the basis of "imagination" in any meaningful sense: for "imagination" entails the esemplastic power—the constituting of the disparate fragments of the seen as an organic whole—and this is only possible in a space whose lacunae can be leapt by vision, in a time whose disjunctions are under-written with continuities, and above all in a world whose complexity can be held in a frame of value.

Gissing has none of this. His London, though it might be unfamiliar, is not unknown—it is charted, literally mapped out, and that mapping creates distances which have no contingency. The distances have to be travelled, the districts lie next to one another, not stacked like squares of wheat as in Philip Larkin's deliberately idealised image, but as zones func-tioning as class and economic differentials. And although historic London is evoked, it is usually only to remind us that the history is forgotten. There is no Court of Chancery, no Circumlocation Office, no centre whose ob-structiveness folds in the passage of time like the coil of a spring. Characters are caught in daily lives, as they are enclosed in zoned spaces. The novels, especially in the 'eighties, are full of plots that come to nothing, as though the organic time of the novelist is defeated by the mechanical time of eco-nomic exigency, just as the effective space of the palimpsest is replaced by the created space of productive and consumptive functions. Clerkenwell and Lambeth, or for that matter Camberwell, are not thrown up by the tangle of history, they are made because industry needs workers, and capitalism needs markets. This is why there is so little sense of class relations in Gissing—for such relations cannot be located in human contacts, how-ever rigidly controlled. They are embodied rather in the mediated demands and accommodations of streets, factories and trades. Chancery may be inhuman, but to be inhuman requires its negation, the human. Gissing's city is rather non-human, an indifferent terrain which acts like a fate. For all its overcrowding, it is as it is imaged, a curiously empty city. You take the crowds for granted—what you are conscious of is the manipulation of physical geography. It is not in any sense an imaginative city.

The most succinct summary of the differences between Gissing and Dickens from this point of view is Adrian Poole's: "The city has been drained of its epistemological excitement; the blank streets, the gritty light, the coarse sounds, seem to provoke sullen resignation rather than vigilant expectancy." He links this with an ideological transformation, the increas-ing isolation of the observing self which with Gissing, as with many of his contemporaries, emerges as a failure of language of the kind just noted (ironic aloofness, or exotic reportage) that consolidates rather than over-comes distances. Gissing's value, for Poole, is that, unlike some of his contemporaries, he stares across the lines of separation with enough clarity and intensity for us to be conscious of the desire to uncover the "human reality" beneath class differences, but still we lack an "extension of perception and feeling." Gissing tends, in this argument (which is certainly important and convincing), to become a second-best Dickens—faced with an intensifying alienation, he is unable to combat it, but at least he realises its dangers. I have been arguing, however, that it is precisely what makes Gissing unlike Dickens that constitutes his effectiveness, and I want to try to establish that although we are faced with a very different London in Gissing, that this is because his London is not mid-Victorian London, and because he has a very different fictional task from Dickens, a task which cannot be identified as the assimilation of knowledge into a "human reality."

The difference between Dickens and Gissing can be related to the differences between the two great sociologists of London with whose work their novels are roughly contemporary. In fact, Eileen Yeo's criticism of [Charles] Booth (*The Unknown Mayhew*) resembles, in a number of ways, Poole's criticism of Dickens. Essentially both argue that the two later writers are characterised by an apparent objectivity which merely covers an ideologically controlled distance from their observed material. We must try to understand the way in which this distance works in Booth in order to have a precise sense of the ideological formation of Gissing and what possibilities it releases, for although Gissing's most important writings on working-class London precede the first appearance of Booth, he shares the same intellectual climate and confronts the same city. More than this, Booth makes very clear the ideological shaping of his knowledge in his concern for methodology. Thus, for example, he is explicit about the way in which his conception of knowledge actually excludes certain kinds of evidence:

> At the outset we shut our eyes, fearing lest any prejudice of our own should colour the information we received. It was not till the books were finished that I or my secretaries ourselves visited the streets amongst which we had been living in imagination. But later we gained confidence, and made it a rule to see each street ourselves at the time we received the visitors' account of it. With the insides of houses and their inmates there was no attempt to meddle. To have done so would have been an unwarrantable impertinence; and, besides, a contravention of our understanding with the School Board, who object, very rightly, to any abuse of the delicate machinery with which they work. Nor for the same reason, did we ask the visitors to obtain information specially for us. We dealt solely with that which comes to them in a natural way in the discharge of their duties.
>
> (*Labour and Life of the People*, 3rd ed., 1891)

The vocabulary reveals an extreme scientificity—shutting one's eyes for fear that they will colour the truth, remaining outside the lives of the people, as though the observer is necessarily kept at a photographic distance, not seeking information but only taking what comes in a "natural" way. It denotes an epistemology of extreme empiricism, and at the same time a kind of idealism which only trusts knowledge which is mediated; an epistemology of the resolutely detached observer. Booth openly acknowledges the limits of this knowledge. At the end of the first volume, he says that the survey is confined to "how things are" and does not concern itself with how they got there or where they are going. But if there is no history, neither is there any depth: "to interpret the life of either (individual or class), we need to lay open its memories and understand its hopes," but the facts presented do not attempt that. Indeed, the empirical evidence itself is doctored to produce an impression of averageness:

> The materials for sensational stories lie plentifully in every book of our notes; but, even if I had the skill to use my material in this way—that gift of imagination which is called "realistic"—I should not wish to use it here. . . . My object has been to attempt to show the numerical relation which poverty, misery, and depravity bear to regular earnings and comparative comfort, and to describe the general conditions under which each class lives.

That linking of realism and sensationalism, the commitment to the numerical relation and general conditions show how determined Booth is that the survey should not be ruffled by an actual sense of what it means to be poor.

Not surprisingly, this epistemology is related to a tacit social doctrine, despite denials that the evidence is approached without theory. The rather crude, pre-experimental scientism is backed up, as Yeo says, by a biologistic and moralistic ethic which amounts effectively to a political commitment. At the basis of the survey is an entirely static concept of class. Booth's classes are in fact categories which lie on top of one another and which consist of spaces through which the individual passes by virtue of his fitness to survive. There is no real sense of classes having a functional relationship to a mode of production. The dividing line in society thus becomes the boundary between two zones—poverty on one side and sufficiency on the other. What emerges from this is that although the percentage of people living in poverty is much higher than expected (30 percent), it constitutes no major threat to the social structure, not certainly the kind of threat that many read into the riots of 1886 and 1887. Nevertheless, there is a muddled fear that naive charity, socialist agitation, and a social competitiveness that is too absolute, might combine to exacerbate the problems latent in the social process. Social action must be confined to encouraging temperance and thrift so that the observed difference between those "who actually suffer from poverty" and "the true working classes, whose desire for a larger share of wealth is of a different character" can be cultivated. The danger of agitation is that it elides this difference: "it is not by welding

distress and aspirations that any good can be done." Booth's specific pro-
posals reflect this faint fear of socialism. He divides the working class into
six "classes" of which two, A and B, are below the poverty line; two, C
and D, are on it; and two, E and F, above it. Most of the problems of
poverty come from the pressure on C and D (who have intermittent earnings and small regular earnings respectively) exerted by the presence of A
and B, so that if we can eliminate A (a small class of occasional labourers,
loafers and criminals) and take B out of the social process by a limited form
of social welfare, C and D will find the struggle to survive less vexed by
chance and despair:

> The poverty of the poor is mainly the result of the competition of
> the very poor. The entire removal of this very poor class out
> of the daily struggle for existence I believe to be the only solution
> of the problem.

The daily struggle for existence, however, remains the norm. Booth's scientism is a commitment to a modified capitalism.

We have to acknowledge this kind of distancing not merely as an
epistemological limitation but as a function of the demands of the higher
organisation of capitalism to naturalise its social relations of production as
"the daily struggle for existence," but I think that ideology is not merely
a limitation, it is also a way of seeing. And Booth, if he lacks [Henry]
Mayhew's sharp insight into the lives of the poor, if more than this he is
naïve about class relations, has another value quite different from Mayhew.
That loss of human contact, that reduction of Class to categories of space,
enables a distinctive contribution to the theory of urbanisation which is
vital for our understanding of Gissing. For Mayhew, as for Dickens, London
is an experience, and because most of our responses to literary texts are in
terms of experience, Booth seems a curiously unimaginative writer. But the
city can only be experienced as a city as long as it can be seen, and there
comes a time in the development of cities when this is very difficult because
of its expansion and its change of function. In the mid-Victorian period,
London is still primarily an administrative and redistributive city. By the
time of Gissing and Booth it is a generative city with its own productive
function and its own markets. When Mayhew looks down on London from
St. Paul's, he is seeing it as a place—it can be grasped as an experience
because it has an outside. The generative city is like a universe, however,
a self-contained system of distances and zones which interrelate not with
another world, but with one another. To put it another way, we are speaking not of an identifiable object, the city, but of a total process, urbanisation,
which begins to invade the countryside. It seems to me no accident that
Booth's survey first appears in the same year as *Tess of the D'Urbervilles*, a
novel which records the urbanisation of country life. Thus, the city itself
has to be analysed as a spatial organisation. And in a sense, it is unfair to
look to Booth for its anthropology when its distinctive value is topograph-

ical. It is very significant that the final metaphor of the introduction is that of photography, which is not naïvely conceived of as a mimetic technique:

> As in photographing a crowd, the details of the picture change continually, but the general effect is much the same, whatever moment is chosen. I have attempted to produce an instantaneous picture, fixing the facts on my negative as they appear at a given moment, and the imagination of my readers must add the movement, the constant changes, the whirl and turmoil of life.

The photograph is a piece of specifically limited evidence, the making of a stasis from the mobility of experience, a process of abstraction. And the abstraction in Booth is not the individual life, but the social space of a demographic process, the structure of an urban universe. Harold Pfautz's essay on Booth shows precisely this. Booth, he says, makes two major innovations. First, by making an enquiry into distribution patterns made by class, occupation, and "the general law of successive migration," he is able to identify the forces which determine these patterns: population increase, excess of immigration, business expansion, developing standards of living, and such special factors as transport facilities, lie of the land, constitution of the family and localisation of labour. Secondly, he establishes areal units, of which the most important are "analytic areal constructs" made possible through the understanding of boundaries, barriers, social character (population's type, physical site, type of institution) and situation (accessibility, etc.). In this way, Booth establishes the city as a spatial order: urbanisation as a process is analysed in terms of the structure it determines, the map it draws [introduction to *On the City*]. Booth could not, obviously, have seen this had he not committed himself to a specific mode of distance which is that of the natural scientist—in short, to the structuration of agglomerated human interactions. This in turn depends on seeing class relations as a dehumanised state. In the truly urbanised city, lives are fought out in zones, individual dramas in the context of a given structure which constitutes effectively an intractable universe.

Thus, in Booth, a conscious self-distancing means two things: first, an ideological distortion, a false consciousness which reifies the social order; but second, a way of seeing which, in comparison with Mayhew, takes account of the city as a spatial order reflecting a total process (urbanisation). If we are to understand Gissing's fiction we need to relate this to his way of presenting London. Gissing shares many of Booth's insights, and much of his ideology. Above all, he shares that distance which leaves city life to appear as a biological phenomenon, a structured space in which individuals survive or die caught in behaviour patterns that can no more be changed by minor contingencies than a polar bear's fur can be turned brown by being born in the London Zoo—biology is not Lamarckian in the late nineteenth century. But, because he is a novelist, and therefore entangled with the subjective experience of this biology, what tends to appear a complacency in Booth is sharply ironised recognition in Gissing. Booth states, for example, that the lives of classes C and D are "an unending struggle . . . but I do not know that they lack happiness." Most of the protagonists of Gissing's working-class novels fall within that category, and it is clear that such happiness is either a fleeting illusion or the product of an effective ruthlessness or insensitivity. Equally, some of the recommendations of the survey, such as Octavia Hill's injunction that a housing policy should "scatter rather than intensify," is realised with all its implications for the quality of living in *The Nether World* when Sidney and Clara Kirkwood are taken from the acute depression of Clerkenwell to the slow attrition of isolation in Crouch End. Many individual points like this can be made about Gissing's work in relation to Booth. Gissing's concern with the nature of slums, the ironies of luxury production, the unemployed, the ambiguities of model dwellings, the distorting eye of philanthropy, are all confirmed by Booth, as is the detailed description of specific districts and even streets. Booth paid tribute to *Demos*, and *Thyrza* and *The Nether World* especially are vindicated again and again by Booth's survey as an accurate picture of London life. At the same time, he shares the same distance without any of the ideological comforts of the sociologist.

But what is more important is that Gissing makes fictions out of the spatial order of the city as a totality. There can be no synoptic image, because what concerns him is precisely the patterns of areal distribution which hold industrial and commercial London together. His novels are based on maps, fictional terrains which are equivalents of analytic areal constructs. It is not London that constitutes the setting of his novels but Hoxton or Lambeth or Clerkenwell whose definition is made by reference outward to other areas of London, Islington or Bloomsbury or Westminster, so that what characterises the setting is what separates them within the urban universe. Even when, as in *Thyrza*, somewhere outside London like Eastbourne becomes a point of reference, it tends to be presented as another, wealthier suburb, and when, in some of the later novels, characters go away from London to a country area it is usually *on holiday*, which is merely the middle-class equivalent of the excursion, the contained time which reflects the enclosed nature of the park. So there is no city and country theme (especially after the very immature *Isabel Clarendon* and *Demos*) but only a system of mobility and fixity. And once the "regional" working-class novels give way to the middle-class novels, and the degree of mobility is increased, we still have no sense of a unified place but only distances to be traversed, locations which define an economic situation: Regent's Park to Islington, Walworth to Herne Hill, and so on. The relationship of fixity and mobility is based on the system of distances and conjunctions which organise the space of the terrain, and in the early novels particularly we have a strong sense of intramural boundaries—Regents Canal (*Demos*), the river as an object to cross (rather than to go along) in *Thyrza*, the non-residential vacuum of Bloomsbury which buffers Clerkenwell from the West End in *The*

Nether World. You cross these boundaries into new areas which mark themselves out by non-pervasion. Thus a very modest migration, from Clerkenwell to Islington, for example, entails a whole set of social mutations. This areal significance reflects the social relations of the inhabitants. Great stress is laid in Booth's survey by his researchers on the differentials in industry (Clara Collett's description of a factory girl is an important case in point) and on the hidden ironies of the contrast between the worker and his beneficiaries who people the consumer zone of the same city (Beatrice Potter makes the same point about dockers that Gissing makes about the jewellery trade—that the contiguity and connection of supplier and user only emphasises the distance in life-style and environment). This is not Dickens's kind of proximity—there is no sense that the underworld might suddenly erupt into the complacency of the dominant classes, merely that it is close and apart, at a distance inexorably governed by a mode of production. That is the precise significance of the structure of the generative city, the city of Booth and Gissing. Space is structured to guarantee the divisions on which it rests.

But this is to talk about the London Gissing is to arrive at, and it is not there ready-made. On the contrary, it only emerges as a fictional solution to the problems that pose themselves throughout the novels of the 'eighties. From very early on, Gissing is, as we have seen, very conscious of the determinant role of class, and to begin with, he attempts to realise this in the manner of the mid-Victorian novel in terms of a dramatic confrontation—Arthur and Helen, Waymark and Ida, Mutimer and Adela, and so on. Equally, however, London proves intractable because the relationships which it makes possible are not cognate with class relationships. The characters of *The Unclassed* are both bound by their roles in society—teacher, prostitute, rent-collector, and so on—but also form an unclassed community through the casual contiguity of the London streets. Thus they tend to wander about London without much rhyme or reason. After the startling opening with its sense of streets which represent the social structure, and journeys which confirm the distance between the social categories, the physical structure of London has little to do with the lives of the protagonists. *Demos* focusses more narrowly on an area, and on class relationships, but Gissing cannot hold the two together. The reason is not difficult to see. I pointed out earlier that class relationships as functions of a mode of production were just what Booth doesn't photograph. The social space of the city, insofar as it is created space (which is more and more true as the city stops serving the country and becomes an end in itself, enclosing its own production and consumption), is partly organised to keep class relationships to an abstraction—suburbs, ghettoes, thoroughfares are all ways of keeping the possibilities of direct confrontation at bay. So that if Booth is going to reflect the social space of the city, it must be by the repression of relationships, the whirl of life, and class must be but the personification of zoning. Gissing's solution is ultimately not to combat the physical structure of the city in order to personalise class relations, but to use that structure precisely to fictionalise the reification of those relations.

The working out of this is most evident in *Thyrza*. Gissing's fifth novel, it is set in Lambeth, or more precisely the area bordered by the river, Westminster Bridge Road, Kennington Road and Broad Street, and is the story of Walter Egremont, guilt-ridden heir of his father's oilcloth works who tries to start evening classes for his workmen, but instead falls in love with the betrothed of his best pupil and librarian, Gilbert Grail. He decides to break off the romance which more or less destroys both heroine and lover. Thyrza is rescued by a benevolent friend of Egremont and returns to Grail, but only to die. The plot thus has all the makings of a drama of class relationships, but it is also a very thin and sentimental story which in fact is little more than a pretext for the portrayal of life in Lambeth. "I am living at present in Lambeth," Gissing wrote in 1886, "doing my best to get at the meaning of that strange world so remote from our civilisation." Egremont in fact has to play a double role—agent of the middle-class, he is also the displaced consciousness abroad in a remote zone (though it is only just across the river). The class relationships have to be personalised within this assumption of distance.

It is a great advance on *Demos,* because it makes the confrontation take place between the industrial capitalist and the worker, rather than between the aristocrat and the worker-become-capitalist, and it takes place in the area of its origin rather than in a distant rural world. Moreover, if Egremont is an unusual capitalist, he has a context in the whole intellectual imperialism of the philanthropic and education movements which dominated the 1880s—Toynbee Hall, the People's Palace, and so on. For such movements take working-class London as a *problem* (the 1880s is the decade of dramatic metaphors—"darkest London," "the maiden tribute to modern Babylon"), and this in itself is an index of social distance. "What if his life were to be a struggle between inherited sympathies and the affinities of his intellect? All the better, perchance, for his prospect of usefulness; he stood as a mediator between two sections of society. But for his private happiness, how?" (chap. 7). Egremont is truly the son of an industrial capitalist, involved in and yet intellectually and financially removed from the processes of production. Part of the novel's strength is that it establishes this paradox with unusual irony. Egremont is trying to bring Culture to the working class, but they already have a culture as the "friendly lead" shows. It is true, as Poole shows, that Gissing's observation of working-class life, which is rich and informed in this novel, is enclosed in an idiom of "a generalized and distancing compassion" ("if they lacked refinement it was not their fault . . . " the narrator comments). But the whole established reality of working-class life also measures the ambiguity of Egremont's concern—his philanthropy, as Mrs. Ormonde tells him, is not heroic. It is significant that what draws Egremont to Thyrza is her voice, and that, in the end, his passion for her is limited, an aesthetic ideal ultimately which doesn't become any more heroic than his social conscience: "You were tried, Mr. Egremont, and found wanting" (chap. 41).

Thus the double role of Egremont, agent of knowledge, agent of reform, is up to a certain point fictionally very fruitful, because it precisely reflects the problematic of the class relationship in a zoned city. The contradictory desire in Egremont, to emancipate the working-class world, and to possess it through love, builds up an intolerable tension in the first twenty-four chapters of the novel. Furthermore, unlike *Demos,* the working-class world is not limited to an ideological function. Grail and Thyrza are not merely sports, because they live their lives among characters who have their own distinctive vitality: Lydia, Totty Nancarrow, Luke Ackroyd, Mrs. Poole, even Bunce, are not externally portrayed—they have a psychology as well as a biology and this makes the personalisation of class relationships possible. The contact is broken, in fact, by the middle-class world. The inhumanity of Dalmaine, the scheming of Mrs. Ormonde and, above all, the passivity of Egremont himself conspire to make Lambeth a separate and obscure world. If the novel becomes broken-backed once the crisis in Egremont's relationship with Thyrza has been reached, it is because at that point the novel can only logically go one of two ways—towards romance or towards cruelty. Through intrigue, Dalmaine's exposure of the truth and Mrs. Ormonde's complex stratagem to get Thyrza out of the way, the denouement is taken out of Lambeth, to the Caledonian Road, to Eastbourne. Lambeth is sealed off. Any vitality the novel has after this point is in the tissue of minor stories which take place in this sealed-off Lambeth—Lyddy and Ackroyd, Totty and Bunce, and so on. Meanwhile Thyrza's death, which is effectively an apotheosis, is the price paid on behalf of Egremont's vacillity. The plot foreshadows Tess and Angel, and indeed much of the novel is implicitly asking questions about the nature of woman. But, of course, in Hardy's novel, that sexual conflict is deeply embedded in the economic structure. In *Thyrza,* it is taken out of the domain of class confrontation at precisely the point where it threatens to open up the class conflict.

And yet if this is the novel's failure, it is a failure which is instructive. For the sealing off of Lambeth is not merely a backing away, it is also the basis of a recognition. The sign of this recognition is a physical location—Lambeth Bridge. Grail is our first register after he has heard from Egremont that he is made librarian in Egremont's scheme and thus taken out of the rut of factory work. The passage in chapter 9 begins with Grail in Lambeth walk stopping to listen to a street organ, "that music of the obscure ways" which speaks for "all that is purely human in these darkened multitudes" (which is not some kind of transcendent passion, but is the expression of desire, revolt and striving for enjoyment before the darkness of the future). It is the "secret of hidden London," you can only know it if you make yourself at one with "those who dwell around . . . in the unmapped haunts of the semi-human." Later, of course, Egremont hears Thyrza singing, and this too is the music of obscurity. But it is Grail, no outsider, who listens to the organ, a privileged moment for the reader who will watch Egremont destroying what he wants to emancipate and love. After this, Grail reaches the bridge to the music of the parish church bells, "a harsh peal of four notes, endlessly repeated." The bridge itself is ugly, its iron superstructure, mean by day, invested at night with a grim severity. If the organ suggests a human continuity, the bells and the bridge, the created symbols of the city, are hostile—harsh and severe. Grail walks out to the middle of the bridge and looks down river, along the other shore to Parliament ("obscure magnitude") and the "dim grey shape" of the Abbey, resting place of poets, which fills his heart with worship. Then the eye travels back along the south shore to the hospital (block after block) and the Archbishop's Palace, dark, lifeless. The shores are thus the sites of institutions, but what strikes us is their obscurity. In Westminster Dalmaine lives; a little further away, Egremont has his pied-à-terre. But Grail is not to cross—only to walk to the middle and contemplate the distant worlds of politics and culture. Finally there is only the eddying water and the piercing wind. He has gone out to "realise" the great joy which has befallen him, but he is drawn by an unknown power to this severe reminder that the other side is obscure, unreachable, and that there are other times when he could have wished that the water could take his life. An inexorability of structures frames a changeable tide. Later in the novel, it is the bridge that is the scene of Egremont's farewell to Thyrza. This time they almost cross to the other side, because Thyrza is confused by the jangle of bells. What they see on the other side is not Westminster but Millbank Penitentiary. When Egremont has indirectly broken off with Thyrza, he wishes that they had stayed on the Lambeth side where the bells allow "no delicacies of tone" (chap. 24). After this, she hides in the parapet, so that he can't pursue her to the Lambeth side. And when he arrives there he meets Grail. Soon he stops worrying abut Thyrza in his hurry to get away from Lambeth where his conscience is so exposed. But alone, he crosses the river via Westminster Bridge.

These are perhaps self-consciously symbolic passages. Gissing might seem to be using an equivalent of the great unifying images of Dickens's London. What is crucial, however, is that the bridge is a sign of distance, a distance which is natural, but which forms the basis of the social space of the city. The imagery which surrounds the bridge is counter to any sense that it might function as a means of communication: not the overcoming of space but the structuring of space. The road on it is narrow, as though to indicate that crossing is minimal. And this structuring is implacable. The sealing off of Lambeth, which is the failure of the plot of the novel, is also a response to something more important—the constituent factor of Gissing's London, the physical shaping of social relationships by the created space of the industrial and generative city. It would be a more human place if the secret of hidden London was truly discoverable in a musical sound. But it is rather the mapping of the unmapped streets that opens it up, and maps designate a world structured by its physical institutions, streets, buildings, bridges. Gissing's final solution to the problem of portraying class relations is in the novel which follows *Thyrza*, where the zoning off is accepted as a site of the fiction. The other world enters here only as an abstraction, money, motivating the greed and the suffering of an enclosed hell. I have discussed this novel at length in other essays, and there is no point in repeating what I have already said. Its importance here is that it represents the final evolution of Gissing's London, a world of sealed-off zones which replace the dramatic confrontations of Dickens's London with named streets, contrived distances. It is true that this reflects the ideology of Booth, of the late capitalist sociology. But there is this major difference, that Booth is almost exclusively concerned with a world that is other— darkest London. For Gissing, *The Nether World* is only a phase. It establishes the bases of a geography whose major feature is the distribution of the necessary but incommodious working-class. But it is a geography which has meaning too for the whole social structure, and the inexorability of the working-class zone is only a narrowly focussed prototype for the more complex inexorability of the unclassed. They share a common geography, though they have apparent freedom of movement. And in this respect, the ideological distance is to be differentiated from the distance necessary for the novelist. What is finally significant about Gissing is not that he can't reach beyond a certain point in his presentation of working-class life, but that he comes to the world of his own class knowing how the physical space of an urbanised world is what holds his characters finally in their places. The named streets of London map the fate of his protagonists.

A motif and a domain, then, separate Gissing from the realistic novels of the mid-century. The motif can be defined as the condition of being unclassed, as distinguished from being declassed, and this has several consequences. [The declassed protagonist is displaced from a given world and sent on a journey to another; the unclassed protagonist is in a place that has no bearing on a potential function, he has no privilege.] First, it means that Gissing's characters do not possess the middle of the social road—they are mobile but not travelling, and they occupy a marginal en- clave which is both a determinant condition (in fact, superfluity) and a determinant psychology (polemical egotism). Second, the unclassed par- adoxically constitute a kind of class—because it is not a privileged condition (as declassment is), the protagonist can only become an exposing agent, a register of a social world because he is part of a group. Class in Gissing cannot be defined in terms of consciousness, because class relations cannot be dramatised: class is therefore present as an unconsciously shared re- sponse to material conditions. The group in Gissing is evident in a shared function, or disfunction, which to the individual is only an abstract struggle against circumstances. The best example of this is *The Nether World* in which the working class operates in a sequence of internal rivalries and oppressions motivated by a single external form of oppression—poverty—which is common to everybody and derives from the relationship of the nether world to the upper. But it is equally true of the middle-class novels: Harriet and Ida, Isabel and Kingcote, Emily and Dagworthy, act out conflicts which are internalised versions of a common condition. The third consequence of the motif of the unclassed is one that is only resolved very slowly in the 'eighties, and that is that the specific identity given to the industrial working class by their role in production has to be matched in the group of the unclassed by a specific role which is generated as the "theme" of the novel. The early novels, *The Unclassed, A Life's Morning* and *Isabel Clarendon,* all have unclassment as a theme in itself, which is why they tend to have become more and more abstract rehearsals of ideas. But in the fully evolved Gissing novel it is transformed into a structuring principle which attaches itself to either a topic or the concept of a career (or both together). This is partly present already insofar as these three novels begin to use the theme to dramatise the problems of women in society—the prostitute, the governess, the protected wife—but the break really comes with *The Emancipated,* in which Gissing is experimenting with the idea of a group placed by their social position in the confrontation between Hebraic and Hellenic cultural values.

But in another sense, *The Emancipated* is a parenthetical novel, written, one feels, as a relief from the intensity of *The Nether World*. A group of tourists vaguely trying to adapt to the challenge of classical, pagan art is not Gissing's *métier*. Significantly the only time at which the novel begins to have any life is when the heroine returns from abroad and lives in London. For Gissing's kind of London is an essential constituent of his fiction, because without that sense of zoning, of restricted mobility, of being placed by the names of streets, the unclassed are necessarily in a vacuum. What makes them reflective agents is marginality, but this marginality can only have meaning if it is enclosed within the urban world which produces it and accommodates it. Most of Gissing's major novels are special studies— the writer, the unmarried woman, the suburban family. But this specialisation is the key to Gissing's London. The zoned city fosters the zoned life, and although the very specific zoning of *The Nether World* is never repeated, his marginal people always have their lives mapped out by their very uncertainty of place. Is the nether world Clerkenwell or Hell?—is poverty a historical phenomenon or a metaphysical conditon? The novel hinges on precisely that question. It does so because the city is no longer the meeting-place of the classes; on the contrary, it is the structured space of a separation and an abstraction. Because of this, it is those who are entangled in the interstices of that structure who light it up most graphically. Gissing wrote what is probably the best novel about working-class London in the late nineteenth century when he wrote *The Nether World*. But that is not what constitutes his importance as a novelist. It is rather that he is able to go on to make fictions which expose the determinants of the oppression so hopelessly given voice in that novel, not by personalising the class structure or by humanising its urban symbolism, but by inserting into it his own class of the unclassed and making them struggle to survive in the streets. Only London could create the unclassed, but only the unclassed can see London. A motif which is a point of view, the point of view of a specific ideology, but which is also a structure (the group, as opposed to the protagonist or the panorama), and which is also a plot (the story of a career, the story of a topical phenomenon), and a domain which is at once the location of these constituents and the object of their exposure—these are the elements of a Gissing novel.

By defining these elements, I hope I will have countered one very commonplace attitude to Gissing, and that is that he is a novelist whose interest is entirely thematic: formally, he writes slavishly within the conventions of the mid-Victorian novel. It is true that, in very superficial terms, Gissing's novels have plots and characters and that they present themselves to us as representations rather than artefacts. But no writer can be really interesting if what he has to realise is realisable within the forms available to him from writers of a previous generation. Gissing's novels are no more conventional than James's or Hardy's in this sense. On the contrary, it is precisely because of that "thematic" interest to which he has access, that Gissing is compelled to evolve a method of writing which violates the given forms in specific ways (most notably, the decentering of the protagonist, the demystification of landscape, and the thwarting of plots) and takes on its own identity. The presence in that identity of the most obvious features of "low mimetic" fiction is not because of Gissing's formal anonymity—it is precisely because those features constitute a fictive world that has to be overturned.

Ideas of Dialogue
and Conrad's Forced Dialogue

Aaron Fogel

In 1912, in two scalding and irritated essays about the *Titanic*, Conrad voiced some unusually direct public anger. The shipwreck gave him the chance to comment as a sailor on the bad architecture of large modern ships, and more generally to criticize technological grandiosity. But though they are nautical polemics, the essays also read like prose poems: they deploy, with casual force, some of the key words and images of his fiction. A reader following changes in the fiction to this year has to notice that some of Conrad's terms reapply almost too easily—almost as in a parody of his typical scenes—to his account of the *Titanic*. He emphasizes, among other things, disproportion, stupidity, and "detonation." In its totality the sinking is to him not a tragedy but a "stupid catastrophe" of misunderstood navigational scale. He treats it partly in the style of Augustan satire, as if *Peri Bathous: The Art of Sinking in Poetry*, Pope's guide to writing bad poetry by abandoning any sense of proportion, could now be translated back again into a modern anti-handbook of navigation, in which the new first principle would be technological madness. He writes, for example, that since side-swiping while trying to avoid the iceberg had probably caused the sinking, "the new seamanship" will require great ships, on sighting icebergs, to ram them head on. The *Titanic*, like the big Russian novels Conrad tried to despise, had been a technical "elephantiasis," the result of a naive equation between size and progress. Modern failures of scale cause stupid disasters in both navigation and writing.

But for all this nautical conservatism, or even reaction, the two essays are at the same time, and as usual, politically hard to locate, because of their protest for the working people destroyed by the stupidity. The *Titanic*

From *Coercion to Speak: Conrad's Poetics of Dialogue.* © 1985 by the President and Fellows of Harvard College. Harvard University Press, 1985.

figures as a class disproportion, a grand hotel with too great a gap between its leisure-class tourists and its sailors, with unnecessary luxuries abroad—French cafés and smoking-rooms nearly in the "style of the Pharaohs or . . . Louis Quinze"—and with the sailors degraded not by hard labor, but by its trivialization, including the final demand that they die for a commercial extravagance. Any elegy is for the sailors, not the passengers. From the failure of what Conrad presents as the older value of handling at sea, both in physics and in social relations, there follows the scene of oblique, unlikely collision, between the ship, now relatively small, and the iceberg, immense. "All the violence of that collision," the narrator had told us about a similar collision in *Nostromo*, "was, as usual, felt only on board the smaller craft." This is commonsensical physics used to illustrate the most ordinary moral fact of power: the smaller unit always suffers, as the engineers trapped below on the *Titanic* die the worst death, and as Poland, a smaller large nation, has suffered in relation to Russia.

In this poetics of social and physical disproportion leading to disaster, one result of the collision is a mystifying "detonation"—a muffled explosion as the ship goes down—a sound, a "report," caused, Conrad insists, simply by the underwater collapse of decks, but now misunderstood by some landlubber inquirers as a mysterious hint that there may have been foul play. The disproportionate collision with its resulting "detonation" recalls similar moments elsewhere—Gould's threatened detonation of his mine in *Nostromo*, the Professor's pocket detonator in *The Secret Agent*, the final explosion of the ship *Emma* (which is being used as a magazine) in *The Rescue*, and the most impressive and understated, the two "detonations" of Razumov's eardrums toward the end of *Under Western Eyes*. "Detonations" are, in Conrad's poetic glossary, oxymoronic: loud explosions which are at the same time silencings, muffled events: "de-tonings," or final losses of any clear tonality, and of the conventional expressive difference between loudness and silence. Detonation is probably his strongest and most typical closure: the loud silence which absorbs, without completely resolving or explaining, all the conflicted political noises and silences that have accumulated in the course of the action.

"There is reason in things," Conrad insists here, appealing to the idea that instrumental reason and moral reason are allied. This "reason in things" can only be understood in and through active labor. Responsibility involves a grasp of kinetic reason, a recognition of physical limits and working ratios; moral awareness grows partly out of the experience of physical obstacles during real work. Instruments represent fixed uses rather than new possibilities. By comparison to Conrad's characters, Thomas Hardy's people, though caught in even more fatal personal patterns, show much more incidental "ingenuity," or physical wit in converting old instruments to new uses. In *Jude the Obscure*, for instance, the farmer takes a thwacker meant to scare birds and beats young Jude with it; Jude converts his baker's wagon into a reading stand; Arabella uses what she says is the folk custom of incubating birds' eggs between her breasts to tempt Jude; little Jude, in a final act of ingenuity, uses nails meant for hanging clothes to kill himself. Acts like this make Hardy's people seem, though certainly not free, at least tragically witty with old things, able to reuse agencies at will, and so to express personal humors. But it is hard to think of a Conrad character who revises an instrument in this way, whom we come to know and like for "ingenuity." Things—both natural givens and old instruments— have permanent, inherent uses, scale, and rules of handling; and the carefully chosen verb of motion is at the center of his style. But there are tragically ingenious reuses in Conrad as in Hardy, only they are more obviously political: the treatment of persons as reusable instruments. Living subjects are reused inventively, as Razumov is converted into a spy, Stevie into a bomb carrier, or the skulls of natives into warning signs around Kurtz's house. Persons, not things, are the typical reusables. Storytelling itself is apprehended as a forced, disproportioning reuse of the person represented. Even the most tactful narrator, when describing a life, forces it into disproportion. Marlow is angelically self-conscious about the ways in which he forces Kurtz or Jim into narrative realization. As the story goes on, this moral narrator is also seen, as if to confirm the guilt of telling, to have participated unwillingly in the destruction, rather than the rescue, of the subject. Readers are repeatedly shown by Conrad's methods that "communication" and "information," far from being good or neutral or innocent, can be given only in and through conditions of participatory disproportion and force that resemble those of the physical world. Narration occurs not as a complex of freely various "points of view," but within a political force field of disproportions, hearsays, pressures, and overhearings. This is not new: what is original is Conrad's imagery of "reports" and "detonations"— which take place as strange composites of silence and explosive exaggeration. The modern tale has to represent and include the danger that tone is being removed by a steady onslaught of exaggerations and silences, not unrelated to the commonplace and banal complaint we hear now about the news as so much numbing hyperbole, disinformation, and censorship. Hardy begins *Jude the Obscure* with the image of a pianoforte stored in a tool shed—the expressive romantic instrument put away so that he can write a more flatly adaptive prose. Conrad repeatedly and variously dramatizes the ways in which a social and political world of plural "intonations" end in forced resolutions of "detonation."

One job of prose imagery in this context is to remind readers forcibly and sometimes crudely of the necessary disproportion in all information and in the methods of reason itself. To illustrate the structural weakness of the *Titanic*, Conrad compares its construction unfavorably to that of "a Huntley and Palmer biscuit-tin"—a comparison possibly lifted from Stephen Crane—and writes a little rudely that this sort of tin is "probably known to all my audience." This audience, distant from sea life, not knowing about proverbial "biscuit-tins" like Marlow's boat in *Heart of Darkness*, has figured in the writing at least since the Preface to *The Nigger of the "Narcissus"*: an audience that must be "impressed" by sharp disproportions and crudely "made to see" the facts of working life it doesn't know. To understand the *Titanic*, first understand a tin can. Heyst's glowing cigar resembles a distant volcano. Deliberately stupid, funny, or childish comparisons like these are aimed at the assumed naive disproportion in the reader's mind, and so are comically wise: "In my varied and adventurous career I have been thrilled by the sight of a Huntley and Palmer biscuit-tin kicked by a mule sky-high, as the saying is. It came back to earth smiling, with only a sort of dimple on one of its cheeks." Subtlety isn't the purpose here. The illustration, a sort of elementary physics textbook analogy—and a little in the kindergarten voice—suggests that the average biscuit-tin is more soundly built than the *Titanic*, and can take a kick from the Ass of circumstance better. The tone is Menippean, vulgarly commonsensical, against grandeur and titanism, mock-sublime. We're not supposed to wonder, mainly, where or whether Conrad saw some mule kick a tin but to see a popular iconography in all of it, mules in Conrad emblematizing labor, practical work, everyday physics, and the "asinine" as in some respects the stubbornly intelligent. When MacWhirr's father says of him, "Tom's an ass," it's to be understood as part praise. Though a social fool, Tom has a sort of Menippean virtue in contrast to philosophers and other abstract thinkers—a physical grasp of work and things.

All these motifs—"handling" as analogous to moral reason; physical and informational disproportions; "detonation" as loud silence; the simple division of humanity into the two classes of the idle and the laboring; animality or *bêtise* as a fundamental perspective on existence; the ironies of "overhearing"; and the reader's need to be impressed by hyperbole—are interrelated, and contribute to the feeling that the essays on the *Titanic* are exemplary Conradian prose-poetic sketches. They deserve a little more attention than they have received, because they repeat in compact and acerbic form his dramatic idea of the route to disaster. But in listing these typical features of the two essays I have so far left out the one major motif which is for this study of Conrad the most important. The specific occasion of the two essays is not, to be exact, the sinking itself, which is too large and potentially pseudosymbolic an event to tackle. Instead, Conrad begins to write out of a specific practical annoyance at the United States Senate for setting up an instant inquiry. The second of the two essays pretends to apologize for, but actually reinforces, the first essay's contempt for this senatorial meddling (a protest letter had come from a friend in America defending the good will of the senators), and carries the nearly Swiftian title "Certain Aspects of the Admirable Inquiry into the Loss of the *Titanic*." Conrad denies a satiric intention like Swift's, and tries to compare his tone to W. S. Gilbert's. But in fact, he is closer to Swift, and for all his angry disgust about the physical mishandling, what gets him writing, what he efficiently makes the occasion of these essays, is the image he has of a dialogical practice, the "bullying and badgering" interrogation of the second officer and of the "Yamsi" (businessmen and planners involved in the ship)—the "lot of questions" thrown at them by a group of politicians who, though perhaps under the guise of a "praiseworthy desire for information," do not even understand the work-reality about which they inquire. Conrad obviously has a picture of this other disproportion—dialogical but virtually physical in its misapplied force—a useless scene of disproportionate coercion to speak which has become representative for him of a general condition. Even though he sees its inevitability, it annoys him no end and starts him writing with unusually direct and fluent belligerence, in contrast to his more usual posture in England of taut politeness. He seems to feel that inquiry must by nature be disproportionate and forced, but at the same time to resent the fact.

These minor essays on the *Titanic* serve as a suggestive model for the organizing principle of Conrad's prose craft, or prose poetic: events that are physically and socially too big, intractably disproportionate, are given shape through a focus on a picturable imbalance or disproportion in the dialogue of inquiry. The "idea" of disproportionate forced dialogue ironically gives beginning, occasion, coherence, and shape to events which in themselves might be uncontrollable by representation. Disproportions and coercions in dialogue are among the main Conradian prose instruments for handling the modern event. Here, by their mishandling of the dialogue of inquiry, the senators unconsciously mimic, and therefore reenact, the prior mishandling of the ship's construction, and the mishandling of class relations aboard. The mistaken dialogue technique is linked, as a practice, to the mistaken physical technology which produced the *Titanic*. They are at the very least analogous, and at the most, twin expressions of the same relational ignorance. Dialogue and physical labor are not two different spheres of imagination.

Dialogue as an instrumental practice, conceived on a model of physical events, involves the application of force between persons, which like force in work can be creative or annihilating. As in physical events, disproportion and force create movement. There is, further, a sense of "measure" in dialogue, which makes the *relative amount spoken* by the persons (very visible on the page and highly formalized, especially from the period 1902–1912, roughly Conrad's "middle period") one of the most important features of many of his scenes of speech—more important, say, than the more usual features of dialect and idiolect, interference, mannerism, or even sympathetic understanding and intimacy. Though these other dialogue motives appear to one degree or another, the primary "keys" to his dialogue are much more often what he calls "force" (most dramatically coercion to speak itself) and the relative amount spoken—notions we will see played out with extraordinary scope of representational and formal vision and profound understanding of the history of dialogue forms. No other novelist makes the abstract proportional model (the relative amount spoken) a figure on the page to be *seen* so consistently, so forcibly, or with such cumulative effect as Conrad does in his "political" works. It is most obvious, probably, to the new reader either in the famous last dialogue between the Verlocs leading to her murder of him, where he wants her to speak and she remains largely silent for about twenty pages; or in Marlow's lengthy talk contrasted to the occasional grunts of his listeners, itself ambiguously parallel to Kurtz's reported verbosity. Undoubtedly, Conrad might be said to have instituted these principles of radical dissymmetry and coercion to speak in dialogue just because he could not institute the more conventional conversational ones with any success, for the obvious reason that he was not a native speaker of English, and perhaps for the less obvious reason (familiar to readers of memoirs about him) that he was probably uneasy in most polite conversational settings, and might himself have had some of the "taste for silence" that he gives to Axel Heyst in *Victory* and to many other characters. But these are not really good reasons. The "lack"—the negation of "conversation," with its substitution of a view of dialogue as labor and force—whatever its source, turns out to be a great gain. Though it makes Conrad's work weak just where the other novelists in Leavis's "great tradition" (Austen, Eliot, James, Lawrence) are strong—in rendering conversational contact—it introduces the question of dialogue as proportion and production, which had not been seen enough in serious English novels, to displace the more intrasocial questions of conversational intimacy, irony, sympathy, and repartee. This new measure of dialogue yields a whole set of insights into the history of dialogue itself, in many different literary genres and social settings; it allows Conrad also to cut across the usual categories separating "political," "metaphysical," "aesthetic," and "psychological" ideas of dialogue from each other, to give an interpretation of human relations in dialogue as primarily nonconversational and relatively unfree. In other words, Conrad for his own tragic and political purposes often undoes the conversational idea of speech in the high English novel. His work invites instead a cumulative contemplation of disproportional and coercive dialogue scenes—as in filibuster; yarning; extorted speech (from inquisition to selling); remaining abnormally silent (a well-known and early observed feature of many strong Conrad characters); overhearing (as coercion to hear and in the sense of overreacting to what is heard); and operatic high-pitched duets. Comparison of such scenes with each other often generates much of the formal power of his stories and novels.

Dialogue form as a visual image—and therefore as a kind of "idea"—may be possible only to printed fiction, or to the dialogue as a written genre, and not to drama or to spoken social practice. Or it may be that even unwritten social practices, like Athenian eristic debate, the Quaker meeting, the talk show, playing the dozens, or the classroom, which are repeatedly performed, are in effect pictured and enjoyed for their dialogue rules "written," or spatialized, in the minds of participants and spectators. To begin with, however, I would like to put aside the many theoretical tensions about spoken versus formal, aural (for example, I and Thou) versus visual, and spiritual versus structural models of dialogue, along with the whole current controversy about logocentricity versus writing, and along with the very complicated and various discussions of the "dialogical" to be found in the works of Buber, Bakhtin, Gadamer, Burke, Freire, Habermas, Ong, Goodman, Rorty and others. These variously dialogical theorists are all, of course, important to any contemporary discussion of dialogue forms or ideas, and have not been studied enough in relation to each other. They will return later as this study continues to describe Conrad's own "dialogic." But Conrad himself ought to be considered first a dialogue craftsman, a worker in dialogue as he once called himself a "worker in prose," concerned with practical rather than metaphysical issues of represented speech; and most perplexed in any case by tough obstacles for him as a nonnative speaker trying to build good dialogue scenes—scenes that would interest or even "arrest" readers—in the absence of easy colloquialism and dialect and other standard means of entertainment.

"The rendering of speeches gave Conrad and the writer more trouble than any department of the novel whatever," Ford Madox Ford writes in his account of their collaboration. With mock solemnity he goes on to describe an "unalterable rule" that they founded for dialogue: "no speech of one character should ever answer the speech that goes before." Ford insists, with heavy irony, that "this is almost invariably the case in real life where few people listen, because they are always preparing their own next speeches." Finally, Ford professes to see in these mock-realistic dialogues of mutual disregard "a profoundly significant lesson as to the self-engrossment of humanity." This little scene of collaboration on a dialogue "rule" is itself an irony of production: where we might want to think that the act of collaboration itself would lead naturally to an idea of dialogue as mutual and sympathetic, their collaborative work led them to found a dialogue rule of nonconversation and noncooperation. But Ford's comments are most important for giving us major hints, if not anything like a complete story, about the ways in which Conrad himself thought about novelistic dialogue as rules and form rather than as the rendering of spontaneous or "natural" conversation governed by a principle of freedom.

Ford's unalterable rule of non sequitur, taken no further, leads to an idea of dialogue suited to pessimistic ego psychology, or to the farce of manners and unassailable egotism. Swift's *Polite Conversation*, the Shandy household, Lewis Carroll's mad tea party, as well as some of Conrad's scenes of egoistic self-engagement where each one talks to himself, are examples. Clearly this ironic "rule" could be helpful to a learning novelist if it boldly got rid of the restrictive, abstract notion that dialogue must always be thematically centered to hold the reader: energetic dialogue in individualistic fiction, on the contrary, often shows general egotism, with each character pursuing his own themes through a general nonconversation. An eloquent statement of this negative rule for the world's dialogue can be found in Leopardi's *Pensieri XXI*, which argues that since "in speaking, we feel no real or lasting pleasure unless we are allowed to speak of ourselves," it follows that the best company is that which "we have most bored," and that there are, in the universal disproportional dialogue (though this "idea of dialogue" does not shape his lyric poems), only two types of speaker, "the amiable man" who listens and the "egotistical man" who talks. The satisfaction in such comic definitions of "all dialogue" is their defense against pious and humorless articulations of rules for "meaningful dialogue" that we hear too much about—not to indulge in any cheap dismissal of all those efforts. This witty, pessimistic, psychological mode, where the egotist talks a great deal and the other is silent, can often be found in Conrad, of course, as when Elliot bores Whalley, or Gould listens to Holroyd, or each anarchist talks to himself at the Verlocs. But if Conrad's dialogue rested at this formal ironic rule of disproportion, one-sidedness, contactlessness, and non sequitur, we would have a Conradian dialogic which is only psychological, pessimistic, and ironic. Such a dialogic would leave us with a "model of mind" and of dialogue, which, as in Bruce Johnson's version of Conrad, makes the ego psychology of Schopenhauerian pessimism his primary concern, with politics being only a screen to reveal this mood, even in works like *Nostromo* and *Under Western Eyes*.

Even in Ford's account of their craft, however, the rigid rule of total anarchic egoism—"never answer the other"—dissolves. Ford continues with mock resignation: "Here again, compromise must necessarily come in: there must come a point in the dramatic working up of every scene in which the characters do directly answer each other, for a speech or two or for three speeches. It was in this department, as has already been pointed out, that Conrad was matchless and the writer very deficient." The funny double meaning of "compromise"—does he mean the compromise of the writers, committed to portraying absolutely disconnected characters, or that of the characters themselves, forced to speak to each other?—is entirely conscious for Ford, and gives us a hint of the irony about "speech acts" which has a place in the writing of both authors. But the main point is Ford's honest emphasis on the difference between himself and Conrad. Earlier in the memoir, Ford has said that while he himself knew more about "words" (presumably English diction), Conrad knew "infinitely" more about "architectonics." Thus, in Ford's account of their collaboration, Conrad becomes the one skillful at forcing otherwise isolated characters into speech with each other. Accurately or not, Ford represents himself as contributing the anarchy, while Conrad contributes the dramatic, unlikely contacts. But in regard to Conrad this alters the "unalterable" rule to such an extent that the emphasis falls on something entirely different. If Ford is correct about the difference in their powers, what he laughingly calls the "compromise" would be for a writer like Conrad the real interest of the scene, the architectonic goal of making the characters meet and speak in spite of obstacles. And, to make a final point, the radical difference here is that Ford's idea of dialogue as egocentric anarchy or chaotic freedom becomes in Conrad the nearly opposite idea of dialogue as involuntary, forceful, and productive bondage of speakers to each other.

Ford's entertaining description gives us a valuable glimpse (accurate, I think, in spite of disparagement of Ford by some Conrad scholars) into the prehistory of the dialogue form I will here call "forced dialogue." During the composition of "The End of the Tether," or perhaps one step earlier, in the closing scene of *Heart of Darkness*, where the Intended compels Marlow to say the oxymoronic detonated phrase "your name" (since "your name" is not her name), Conrad makes a transition from preoccupation with the egotistical speakers whose desire is *to make the other listen* to a preoccupation with figures who desire *to make the other speak*. This shift is not absolute or exclusive, but it is highly marked, and helps us to locate a difference between early Conrad and middle (roughly, political) Conrad. The structural format of the "forced dialogue," at its simplest, runs as follows: there are two speakers, and one repeatedly tries to make the other speak. For a series of exchanges (in its most ritual form, three), we have, in quotation marks, the speeches of the person demanding speech from the other. These are counterpointed—or to use a visual metaphor, "striped"—to narrative prose passages which describe mainly the silence and gestures of that other. The prose may also describe the surrounding scene. The effect of this is a highly stylized and ritual feeling. The reader cannot help noticing the "striping," apparently more formal than naturalistic, between direct speech and narrative prose, as if the two were themselves in a kind of struggle. This dynamic ends, however, with some speech or action of the heretofore silent character which amounts to an answer and yet is at the same time a "detonation," or a loud silencing, a final non-answer. The silent person is at last driven by combined motives and circumstances—which Conrad tries with very exact artistry to make clear as including the provocation by the other, the specific personalities, the background of the scene, and some inner forces—to respond in one way or another. The answering non-answer, when Conrad is writing at his best, amounts to a great, concise "sentence upon" their relation. The whole scene works toward the production of a single sentence, or of an action which has the status of a *sentence* in both meanings—that of a statement and that of a punishment, often mutual. Note here that Ford's statement of the rule for dialogue—characters must "never answer the speech that goes before"—has been converted from a psychological irony about selfish manners to an image of dramatic struggle which can have pronounced political implications without losing its psychological cast. The action of not answering, instead of showing static, universal egotism, self-involvement alone, has become a violent and conscious conflict between characters over the production of speech. A character who consciously refuses to answer another who is demanding speech openly is very different from the figure who talks to himself because he is unaware of the other. Ford's merry recipe undergoes a radical conversion. The demand for speech might now generate scenes in the spirit of Cassandra's refusal to answer Clytaemnestra, Teiresias's resistance to Oedipus and his final outburst of punitive prediction, Bartleby's one-line responses under pressure to speak and participate, and so on: scenes which in their reverberations go beyond ego psychology to deal with the politics of the production of language. These scenes in Conrad's middle novels, further, usually have a marked "frame," or appear as set pieces, or "centerpieces," or even as ideas of dialogue, with their own cumulative rhythms.

Though there are many scenes of pressure to speak amid disproportion throughout the work, a set of major scenes might be mentioned in this introduction, so that the reader familiar with Conrad will note both that they are major points within their respective works and that they are strikingly various: (1) the dialogue with the Intended in *Heart of Darkness*; (2) the central encounter between Whalley and Massy in "The End of the Tether"; (3) the plurality of inquisitorial scenes in *Nostromo*, but particularly Sotillo's torture of Hirsch and Hirsch's own earlier attempt to make Gould speak in order to sell him hides or dynamite; (4) the recurrent dialogue rhythm of the Verloc marriage, a marriage built up almost entirely of variations on the "forced dialogue" with increasingly grim closures, until she at last murders him, in Conrad's most protracted forced dialogue; (5) the confrontation between Bunter and Johns in the minor, extremely interesting problem story "The Black Mate"; (6) the great scene between Mikulin and Razumov in *Under Western Eyes*, with its complex background of allusions to other coercions to speak, both within the novel itself and within history; (7) "A Familiar Preface" to *A Personal Record*, where Conrad describes the pressure Ford put on him to write his autobiography, and makes it parallel to the scene of Conrad's master mariner's examination in that same book, in which coercion to speak seems to be presented, in contradiction to most of Conrad's work, fondly, as a wholesome educative method. These are by no means the only scenes in Conrad where there is "pumping," or where a demand for speech meets resistance to establish the dominant mood; but they are I think exemplary ones, in which we can reasonably say that Conrad makes it clear to the ordinary reader that coercion to speak is itself a main theme, not just an instrument for forwarding the action, and has its own increasingly visible, nonconversational forms. It would be nonsense, of course, to write about Conrad discussing only such scenes, and the following chapters [of *Coercion to Speak*] will take up many other issues and discuss several novels in detail. But these scenes do work as extraordinary dialogical "centerpieces"—indications of Conrad's idea of dialogue—and therefore have a great deal to tell us about his fiction as a whole and about his sense of social existence.

"Forced dialogue" has to be understood in at least three larger contexts: (1) coercion to speak as a scene both in literature and in social practice; (2) recurrent dialogue form in the novel as leading to the sense that each novel has a distinctive "idea" of dialogue; (3) the development of dialogue forms over the course of Conrad's own work. Without these contexts, this scene would seem falsely isolated here, as Conrad's single, static "meaning." Before approaching Conrad's interpretation of the complex literary and social history of the scene of coercion to speak, which is the larger theme of this book, let us look first at the simplest and most formal of these issues—that of recurrent dialogue form in the novel—and then at the dialogue forms in Conrad's early work, before he concentrated on the specific problems of forced dialogue.

Robert Louis Stevenson, in "A Humble Remonstrance," quietly rejected the idea that fiction can mimic life's density, or achieve a full realism, and argued instead that the novelist as a conscious craftsman looks for formal limits, for instance the "invention (yes, invention) and preservation of a certain key in dialogue." He was in this essay dissenting (humbly) from Henry James's ambitious sense of the scope of fiction, but was at the same time to a great degree sharing James's own formalism, since James himself tended to see actual social dialogue as a kind of formless chaos, passively mirrored in the "deluge of dialogue" in popular novels. James wanted to make dialogue a steady vehicle of the action. To Stevenson's musical "key" and James's controlling forms, we could add that most nineteenth-century novelists, such as Austen, Balzac, Tolstoy, and Dostoevsky, have recognizable ideas of dialogue, founded on particular assumptions about what generally happens when people meet to talk. To make very quick reductions: Defoe pictures contractual negotiation, mutual exploitation that can profit both sides; this is not the same as Balzac's idea of encounter, most vividly that of elitist power struggle, often among more than two persons; this in turn differs somewhat from Dostoevsky's comic vision of gatherings as struggles to include the excluded, and of talking to oneself as fallen prayer; which in turn is different from Tolstoy's emphasis on emotive sympathy; which in turn differs from Austen's emphasis on a kind of rational sympathy. There are, that is, common themes, but also ideas specific to each about what holds one speech to the next, and what forces—erotic and eristic—combine speeches. The "idea of dialogue" must be taken, in this sense, as a clue to the author's entire notion of what links any one sentence to any following sentence: and obviously the causal connection between characters' sentences may itself be very close to the essence of a writer's social vision. The reader who learns to read the ironies and causalities of a Balzac or Austen dialogue is learning (like Rastignac in Mme de Beauseant's drawing room) a specific social contract, and in a much more ironic sense than was meant by most political theorists. Dialogues display a kind of miniaturized, static social constitution. When repeated they become ironic (not necessarily simply representational, but rather more "liturgical") models of the novel's implicit "social contract." My readings of Conrad here will try to show that he belongs roughly with those novelists (Scott being the most facile and impressive and also the most enjoyably lacking in portentous implications) who emphasize the action of coercion to speak over the various kinds of "sympathy" in the social coherence of dialogue. This is what makes his dialogue scenes alien to the high English novelistic tradition (Leavis's "great tradition"), with its vision of conversational liberation. But this major question—sympathy versus force as the main cohesive principle in dialogue—must also be put aside for now in a return to the simple technical point. In the novel, powerful and pleasurable dialogues come about not only through naturalness of speech but also through formal predictability and repetition—not only in the representation of idiolects and dialects, speech tics, characteristic habits and mannerisms of spontaneity, and digression, but also in the patent repetition of whole, strict forms of dialogue into which the characters repeatedly fall together.

The novelist, that is, often has a distinctive "idea of dialogue," made available to the reader through formal repetition, sometimes subtle, and sometimes deliberately highly outlined and visible. The reader watches for and enjoys the repetition of the strict pattern, which is in its own way analogous to socially instituted repetitions of dialogue forms, like those in religious meetings, or those in entertainment (for example the talk show) or pedagogy (Athenian eristic or the American classroom), or street play ("playing the dozens"). The novel first of all does not represent but actually shares in the cultural passion for and pleasure in formal dialogical repetition. "Conversation" itself, though we like to think of it as freedom, may be a complex form, as Austen and James knew, learnable only by an elite, and implicit set of rules of freedom, devices for appearing free. But putting aside the difficult question of whether there is a human universal of conversation or instead only a set of class and cultural devices for appearing free and intimate, at which the most skillful and accomplished conversationalists win, there is certainly a group of works that might seem at once extremely "novel," and at the same time borderline as novels by the more conservative definition, which exaggerate this formulaic quality. This is true, for instance, of *Don Quixote*, Lewis Carroll's *Alice* books, *Bouvard and Pécuchet*, *The Confidence-Man*, and *Catch-22*, each of which could be said in its own way to have a fixed "idea of dialogue" that recurs, that centers the pleasure of the book, and that is far from a simple spontaneous naturalism; and it is likewise true, no less fiercely though in a more subtle sense, of conversational novels like Goethe's *Elective Affinities*, Austen's *Emma*, Turgenev's *Smoke*, and James's *Awkward Age*.

In these works, against the standard wisdom that dialogue is most mimetic or enjoyable when "free" and "natural," the reader is successfully let in on dialogue as form, even as ritual, and the result is neither simply formal-aesthetic nor simply representational and historical. A sharp and pleasurable awareness of dialogue as socially repetitious formal action is closely bound up with the genre of the novel. The dramatist often fills out a unified action with as full a range of dialogue types as possible; many novels, by contrast, have a various or anarchic and wandering action which returns "home" repeatedly to a unified idea of dialogue. Such novels do not, however, exactly represent some specific socially practiced form, but instead the quality of mutual dialogical obsessiveness itself, the desire to return together to one format of relation. This return is often comic, comforting. For example, one way to define the repeated dialogue between Don Quixote and Sancho Panza: Quixote asserts absolute faith in a hallucination by citing his romances, and Sancho, less certain, objects by citing his senses. We have a dialogue—of course this only one statement of the form—with someone who derives more certainty from his books than his servant does from his senses. Whether this image of their dialogue is acceptable or not, the point is that the audience—not entirely unlike Quixote himself in his reliance on texts—comes to rely on the way in which Quixote and Sancho (like Melville's confidence man and his rubes, or Huck and his adults, or Socrates and his students, or Bouvard and Pécuchet in their curriculum, or Emma and Mr. Knightley in their mutual teaching) will square off and return to their "home" in dialogues of interpretation of the world together. If the world of the novel is, as Lukács echoing Novalis said, "homesick," impossibly large, plural, and adventurous, nevertheless recurrent dialogue form may be its "home." To give one preliminary reading of this effect tragically reversed in Conrad: while dialogue repetition in Conrad has not received much attention, John Hagan, Jr., has argued that the unity of *The Secret Agent* comes not from the plot, which at least on a first reading is exploded and retarded like Stevie himself, but from the "recurrent interview structure." Yet since the strongest of these recurrences is the formal repetition of forced dialogues in the Verloc marriage, the irony is that their "home" together in dialogue, their repeated married dialogue, sounds rather like the "forced" interviews that take place in the external, political world. And while in the drama, as among Shakespeare's lower classes or between some of his battling lovers, there is often a kind of predictability in dialogue marked as pleasure for the audience, the novel tends to objectify this repetition in a way that leads us to think of it by itself: to see something akin to a contract of dialogue in the particular social milieu being described. This in turn gives the novel a very complex representational and imaginative relation to the existence of dialogue contracts, or recurrent dialogue practices, in social groups—Quaker meetings and so on—those forms that are the subject matter of the "ethnography of dialogue." To such an ethnography, the term *dialogue* itself is not universal but refers to a Greek idea of the logical division of speakers; friendly or intimate "conversation" has different rules in different places. The twentieth-century habit among thinkers of identifying oneself by one's "dialogic"—I and Thou, or deconstruction, or speech-act theory, or Harold Bloom's "agon," or Erving Goffman's "interaction," or Richard Rorty's "conversation," and so on—might itself be an ethnographic fact related to earlier religious liturgical emblems or self-identifications. If the only home in a novelistic world is a dialogue idea, such "novelistic" thinkers also make themselves known by particular dialogue signs.

For reasons particular to each, no theorist of the novel has been centrally interested in recurrent dialogue form. Bakhtin, who steers outside the usual dilemmas (formalism versus antiformalism, invention versus representation, structuralism versus historicism) for a socially vital definition of the novel, though he points to Lucianic dialogue as a major source of the novel and implies that the "dialogic" of true novelistic prose subverts the hierarchical "dialectic" of philosophy, is out to emphasize the unresolvable wildness of ideological and marketplace speech, the interference of plural consciousness and plural glossaries. It would not be in accord with this stance to spend too much time on the contractuality of dialogue in great novels like *Don Quixote* or *Moll Flanders*. Lukács, of course, would find this feature of dialogical recurrence, even where there is a "progress of dialogue" as in Bunyan or Austen, too static, marginal—perhaps a symptom of the bourgeois will to static constitution and resistance to dialectical change. In *The Rise of the Novel*, Ian Watt, discussing Richardson's epistolary form, describes just such a resistance in a class fixation on one kind of discourse, but does not in his account of the novel as "formal realism" discuss dialogue form itself as repetition. He also alludes only briefly and dismissively to the connection between the novel and the Platonic dialogue. James, though he called "the question of our speech" central, and filled his late novels with a dictated, spoken syntax that returns to the American tradition of spontaneous Protestant witness bearing—the talk show—referred, as already noted, to real speech as "deluge" and as first chaos. The essence of the world's actual dialogue is for him an almost terrifying lack of form, which the novelist works to direct, moving over the face of the waters. (Stevenson, recall, when citing the "key" of dialogue, called it invention, as *against* representation.) Mark Lambert, in an excellent book on dialogue technique in Dickens, also associates dialogue emphatically with the "fun" and "free" part of the novel, indulgence, white space. Such readers as Stanley Rosen in *The Symposium*, Kenneth Burke in *A Rhetoric of Motives*, and Gilbert Ryle in *Plato's Progress* probably come closest to mediation on recurring dialogue form as the shape of a work, but they deal with what are generally considered philosophical dialogues. Strong critics and theorists of the novel, then, whether antiformalist or formalist in final perspective, have generally associated "speech" and "dialogue" as they occur in the world with freedom: the spontaneous, uncontrolled, plastic, idiomatic, digressive part of life that, to the formalists, has to be reined in, made part of the action, and to a genius of pluralism like Bakhtin represents the ultimate potential of the novel as an open genre.

Of course in practice not all dialogue is free, natural, spontaneous, informal, or lively. On the contrary, it may be true that most real dialogue is variously constrained and forced. But for some reason we usually say that the best novelistic dialogue has those qualities: the unforced movement of common, popular, or natural talk; vivid displays of low (dialect, idiolect, oaths) and high (mutually liberating) free speech. It would be shabby to dismiss all images of free dialogue as nothing but ideology, or I-Thou philosophy as just a utopian myth. But revelatory and intimate I-Thou conversation, of the kind that the greatest characters in Austen, Eliot, Lawrence, and Forster reach toward, does usually occur between those who belong to a high, even an ideal, spiritual class, who can master difficult rules; the conversational idealism of the "great tradition," with its images of autonomous but energetic intellectual intimacy, describes heroes and heroines who transcend dialogical constraints that they are alert, witty, and sensitive enough to understand. They are the "winners" in the conversational scene: an elite of sympathetic imagination, who can even overcome the flaws and limits in conventional ideas of "sympathy"; slightly below them in this world picture is a class of common people whose talk is "natural." Novelistic dialogue, however, obviously doesn't begin and end with free, natural lower-class speech and freely achieved upper-class mutual sympathy. Most real speech between classes is probably not conversational. And there is a set of great nineteenth-century *anti*-conversational, yet extremely dialogical, novels which fix on a more coercive and authoritarian dialogue regime to return it incessantly upon the reader. Scott's meditation on the varieties of dramatic forced speaking in *The Heart of Mid-Lothian* is probably the first great example. Alice's recurrent encounters with illogical, self-absorbed, and insane pedagogues is another. Melville's *The Confidence-Man* may be the most furious. Its barrage of scenes of forced selling amounts not only to a formal burden but to an attempted ethnography of American dialogue. In this American Menippean satire, dialogue formalism and cultural representation meet: extreme dialogue repetition represents the scene of selling. Possibly dialogue between the classes, as opposed to "conversation" which takes place within a class, will involve more "drama," more actions like coercive inquiry, detection, selling, negotiating, blackmailing, and so on. If we can define Leavis's unstated principle in choosing most of the works of the "great tradition" as a high-conversational bias, in which moral insight and the worth of life appear through developing conversational struggle, it may be a kind of contrary, somber, critical realism, rather than an obsessive formal impulse alone, that overformalizes and even stagnates dialogue in the novel, to indicate, with necessary repetition, the rule-governed, hierarchical, fatal fixation of social and political dialogue, as Conrad oppositionally does. Here, "form" and "key" in dialogue are not just compositional or aesthetic requirements, as for Stevenson; they are, on the contrary, at the heart of the novel's critical realism.

The Conradian novel, then, as defined here—along with a small group of novels since Scott to which it belongs—has a very strong will to objectify and contemplate dialogue as constrained form, and the plurality of such dialogue forms in their social distribution. In this light, consider *Heart of Darkness* as a story about the progressive objectification of its own disproportionate and forced dialogue forms. It is, of course, easy to take Conrad's most famous story as an instance of free-spoken "oral literature," in which Marlow is the skaz, yarn spinner, or ancient mariner. But the story itself has to be seen as having for one of its main actions the increasing objectification of the speaking narrator himself, so that as it proceeds, the reader has an increasingly uncanny—partly comic, partly disappointed—feeling that Marlow's long-winded yarn is proportionally and therefore somehow morally linked to the more obviously imperial and abject forms of excessive talk like Kurtz's. That is, Marlow and Kurtz, as speakers, are progressively identified with each other through a covert appeal to the reader's sense of "normal" prose masses, and of the ordinary length of a talk. We increasingly see that each does "almost all" the talking in his own dialogical context: Marlow to his audience, Kurtz to the natives and to his clownish Russian disciple.

Here is a typical short passage from *Heart of Darkness* which in its onrush might go unnoticed but which is meant to make us contemplate and "equate" three or four dialogue scenes formally. Marlow has come ashore and is listening to the young Russian, exploding with a need to talk, tell about Kurtz:

> In the next breath he advised me to keep enough steam on the boiler to blow the whistle in case of any trouble. "One good screech will do more for you than all your rifles. They are simple people," he repeated. He rattled away at such a rate he quite overwhelmed me. He seemed to be trying to make up for lots of silence, and actually hinted, laughing, that such was the case. "Don't you talk with Mr. Kurtz?" I said. "You don't talk with that man—you listen to him," he exclaimed with severe exaltation.

These sentences set up a hierarchy of dialogue scenes—which the reader is invited to tear down. Lowest, apparently, are the simple natives, overwhelmed by a boat's whistle. On the next level, the Russian's talk itself, a kind of social chatter, here ironically overwhelms Marlow. At the presumed highest level is philosophical discourse like Kurtz's, aweing disciples into pious silence. Implicitly, on the fourth level, framing all this, and making its own claim to truth, is Marlow's narration to his audience, who object and grunt a few times. We might, that is, easily organize these scenes of forceful speech and disproportionate dialogue, combined so rapidly and formally that they seem to make a "dialogue fugue," into a self-congratulatory heirarchy similar to the Russian's, but with the last—ours—fiction or art, at the top, as transcendent consciousness: Marlow's ironic contemplative art, the truest frame. But just as clearly, Conrad stands behind the analogous disproportionate dialogues to suggest that all the scenes, including Marlow's art, and his writing to us, are alike: imperial assertions of "overwhelming" force. In each scene, the speaker impresses the listener by the force of sound. If the jungle's "darkness" and civilization's "light" will nearly be "welded together without a joint" by the story, the same fusion applies to our preconceived images of some dialogues as civilized and some as uncivilized. The natives overwhelmed by the ship's whistle resemble the Russian himself (their narrator and explainer) being overwhelmed by the force of Kurtz's altruistic oratory. Less clear, but most important, Marlow's silent audience (representing ourselves) falls—at least potentially—into this field. But whether we accept or refuse this last irony, this passage shows *how* Conrad asks the reader to think about dialogue as formal and proportional rather than simply expressive: by seeing and hearing the parallel ratios so as to find startling affinities among apparently discrete dialogue scenes.

Note, in terms of the history of readings of *Heart of Darkness*, that Marlow's portentous, forceful repetition of adjectives can be understood somewhat differently. Leavis's conversational idealism rejects some of Marlow's incessant rhetoric as hot air—which of course it is. But in this reading, Marlow's relentless insistences, his own excess of verbal steam (even the mist that pervades the landscape is an image of rhetoric), is part of the conscious imagery of the story, and of the dialogical mood of imperialism, of "overwhelming the other" by misty imperial words. The scene of "overwhelming" noise is the common denominator of the story's main theme—imperialism—and what Conrad called its "secondary" theme, Marlow's obsession with the image of Kurtz speaking. The "dialogic" here welds together the two themes "without a joint." The proportional resemblance of all dialogue scenes is both tragic and comic, even oddly hilarious, and appears as an irrationally temporal, rather than simply atemporal, simultaneity: Marlow the young man, we could say—if we break with rational time sequence—became obsessed with his image of Kurtz talking "because" Kurtz talks to his disciples in the same disproportion which Marlow the older man and narrator *now* has vis-à-vis his audience. Young Marlow was obsessed by the image of Kurtz speaking, which was itself the metaphoric and predictive image of older Marlow narrating. The "cause" of Marlow's inexplicable obsession with Kurtz's talk is his own "later" identity with its proportions during the time of the story's actual telling. From a perspective of speech production, of course, this is all rational, because the older Marlow's production of the story for his audience *is* the "origin" of the story. There is, then, a simple repetition of dialogue form in time (Kurtz's overwhelming verbosity generates Marlow's overwhelming verbosity about him), but also a simultaneity or "knot" of dialogue scenes, which has to do with the production of the story itself. Marlow's original obsession with Kurtz—which Conrad has to impose on the reader partly by fiat or pure of insistence—has its strongest but most irrational explanation in his predestined identity with Kurtz as the current talkative narrator before us (almost in the way that Oedipus' rational power to conduct judicial inquiries and force speech from his witnesses is inherited from the Sphinx's earlier grosser power—which he dissolved and inherited—to demand the answer to the riddle, to force replies).

The fusion of categories such as "psychological" and "political" in and by dialogue form can be seen clearly here. While Marlow's resemblance to

Kurtz can be read psychologically, so that each is the other's son and father in speech disproportion, and the two are "insanely" identified as willful speakers (Marlow of course trying but failing to eradicate this will to power in himself), there should be no question that this resemblance presents itself to us first as a historical and political idea. Disproportion and coercion in the speech scene become the constants because, as Conrad writes in one essay, "man is a conquering animal," and history is imperialist. The famous "horror" at the end of the story is partly a joke, said twice, narcissistically, by self-echoing Kurtz, and partly a non-answer, punch line, or "detonation" coming at the close of what we could call a "shaggy dog story" (the entire action of *Heart of Darkness* is more defiantly funny than most critics have argued); but it is lastly the identification of art and politics as imperial speech. The first sentence of the story describes how the ship "swings to" (describes a forced circle about) its anchor until it rests. The secondary action of the story is the "swing to" that Marlow's own freer telling makes toward Kurtz's compulsive talk, becoming slowly and inevitably linked to it in moral and political status. In this gradual parallelism, a universal "dialogic" is being contemplated and objectified: by the end of the story the "swing to" has implicitly united philosophical dialogue (Kurtz as mock Socrates), fictive narration (or the dialogue between writer and audience), and imperialist cant into a single scene of dialogue, and Conrad has assigned himself and the reader to the same unvoidable intention of conquest and the same imperial scene. Artistic force, the desire to make the reader see, hear, or feel, is a sublimation at most of the other desires to conquer. It "must" participate in the general dialogue form.

In *Don Quixote* the repeated dialogue, in addition to its comedy, mimicked a typical debate of the age, between biblical authority and sense experience; it was then also used in the second part for baroque paradoxes, in which the *Quixote* became a new profane Bible, a book determining reality. Conrad constructs *Heart of Darkness* on similar lines, to make a baroque "knot," a "mirror" of dialogues reflecting each other out onto the audience, so as to define the typical dialogue scene of his time. As *Quixote* mimics a typical dialogue of the age, Conrad brings contemporary imperialism home in his forced dialogues. The point is that the proportions of imperialism are everywhere in an imperial age—even in stories told on yawls on the Thames, or in our reading of the novella. What bothered Leavis—Marlow's incessant, insistent, domineering, adjectival style—was meant to bother. The story could not exist without an excess of fiat. The disproportions in Kurtz's speech, in Marlow's telling, and in Conrad's representation of Marlow's telling, resemble each other; from different angles each could be said to come first and "cause" the others. Conrad "repeats" the scene of dialogue abstractly, not merely in the story of the characters but from level to level of the story's production, until we finally see Conrad, or the author, in a dialogical relation to us that resembles, in its desire for conquest, all the others. What Conrad called the "secondary" plot of *Heart of Darkness,* in this reading, is this gradual identification of all dialogue relations as disproportionate and imperial.

Parenthetically, it is worth adding that this process is not primarily "deconstructive" despite some apparent resemblances. "Deconstruction," from the standpoint being developed here, is another philosophical sublimation of the Oedipal drama of forced inquiry: text, language, writing oversees its own intentional disintegration. The "text" plays the role of Oedipus, undoing itself for a general sacrificial peace; though it can be argued in reverse that Oedipus' inquisitorial self-eradication is a dramatic version of what in fact writing does. But in any case all deconstructions, as Derrida writing about force half-indicates, have eristic elements, and, though "playful," are shaded by inquisition. To "make" the other's text decenter by a reading of disjunctive metaphors reenacts Socrates' forcing of the other into logical self-contradiction—elenchus. But when Kurtz scribbles "exterminate the brutes" at the bottom of his enlightening canticle, or when Marlow closes with the evasive lie "your name," or when Conrad himself uses various methods to call attention to the forced conditions of his own writing, there is certainly a drama *like* that of deconstruction, a change of intonation violent enough to be a "detonation," but the stress falls not on self-contradiction, or on endless linguistic difference and reinterpretation, but on the idea that all dialogue, even dialogue with the self, involves coercive disproportion. Kurtz's relation to himself, when he repudiates himself, remains imperial. Implicitly, nobody quarrels even with himself as an equal. Conrad is not as interested, then, in the tropes and actions we call deconstruction—which make the text itself the sublime Oedipal actor—as in outlining the inescapably disproportionate forces at work in any dialogue, including storytelling, lyrical quarrel with the self, and philosophical critique.

The power to abstract and objectify dialogue forms, then, gives fiction the force of "comparative dialogic." The novel can make startling juxtapositions of dialogues in broadly different scenes. Comparative dialogic makes it possible to move among discrete institutions of dialogue—social, religious, literary, pedagogical—to compare them formally. For example, let us isolate a dialogue pattern found in the *Oedipus Tyrannus,* that of the punishment of the speech-forcer, the discovery of the guilt of the coercive interrogator himself. We might then put aside, at least temporarily, distinctions between literary genres, between psychology and politics, or between literature and reality, and ask if we find this dialogue form anywhere else. It could be posited that this form is inscribed in the unconscious as "Oedipal"—in a sense of the term which combines Sophoclean and Freudian insights to supplement each other. It is the scene in which the father figure initiates a coercive dialogue and is surprisingly and "thrillingly" annihilated by the answers he forces from those he interrogates. In this scene the father is punished by the examination or catechism he appears to institute, but of which he is in fact the predestined victim. This dream of vengeance upon the father by the surprising but inevitable "boomerang" of catechism could be regarded either psychoanalytically or politically. And it would not be surprising to find variants of this scene both in literature and in ongoing public ritual: in the opening of *Lear*, in Dostoevsky's "Grand Inquistor," in the resolution of the McCarthy hearings, in a popular television show of journalistic inquisition like *60 Minutes*, or in Foucault's vision (an unconsciously Oedipal vision by this account) of the world as all examination without real subjects. Wherever the democratic punishment of the speech-forcer, or the idea that inquiring power might be undone, or undo itself, by its own inquiry, is attended by feelings of fear and gratification, we might see an Oedipal dialogue process.

Likewise, a simpler idea of dialogue, the notion of necessary disproportion between speakers which I have been exploring here—the picture of one speaking a great deal and one very little—can itself be applied expressively to diverse worldviews. For Leopardi, dissymmetry is the expression of a pessimistic psychology; for Valéry, dissymmetry is the essence of all dialogue, an aesthetic-mathematical universal; for Richard Ohmann, disproportion is a sign of class domination in sociological interviews. My thesis is that Conrad was, if anything, a dialogist conscious of these plural possibilities, and that he used the stark universal of dialogue disproportion, sometimes adding to it the more complex Oedipal dynamic of the punishment of the speech-forcer, to "fuse" categories like the psychological, the poetic, and the political. Teaching this idea to a class, one might draw a long line and a short line on the blackboard, representing the speaker who speaks a great deal and the speaker who speaks very little, and then show how this simple, radical disproportion ironically covers diverse dialogue scenes in Conrad's works (marriage, inquisition, storytelling, selling, hiring, courtship, séance), and might incidentally be applied to other well-known scenes such as psychoanalytic dialogue. In each case the one doing most of the speaking, or the one doing very little, may be the forcer, and there are many other specific variables. The power of this formal objectification is precisely that it allows him to cut across conventional categories, putting aside any one rational standpoint—psychology, aesthetics, politics—to merge all of these into a deeply disturbing dialogical constant. Just as the interrogation of Joan of Arc in Carl Dreyer's film can't be said to be singly political, religious, or sexual but all of these fused, so strategies of reading Conrad which make him out as primarily a psychologist, a metaphysician, or political thinker have tended to ignore his dialogical understanding. He is the novelist who most consciously understands the classical action of coercion to speak as a sometimes explicit and sometimes sublimated unifying motif. The implicit ground of poetics itself becomes the scene of coercion to speak, and genre and tone become responses to this ground.

Theories about dialogue are relatively common, but theories about the historical development and change of dialogue forms are scarce. There have been many practical comments on the uses of philosophical dialogue for pluralistic exposition by Hume, Herder, Diderot, Landor, and others; and many theories, for instance in Plato criticism from Schleiermacher to Gadamer, or in the modern line of dialogical polemics that runs from Buber to Bakhtin, give the term *dialogue* a very high place. Rudolf Hirzel's *Der Dialog* is the one major scholarly study of the development of the dialogue as a genre; but it does not really apply to the novel. It is Gilbert Ryle who has in a searching and jovial way written the one modern study of Plato, skeptical and formal, which takes changes in dialogue form not as the transcendental sign of the interpersonal as the true but as an indication of someone's actual changing social milieu. It is of course daring and ironic to apply this strategy to Plato. Looking at changes in the dialogue forms, Ryle argues—iconoclastically, entertainingly, not very believably—that Plato in the end was moving away from the theory of Ideas toward a sort of Aristotelian naturalism. He hints at an ironic novel—the book is called *Plato's Progress*—in which the hero finally forsakes Ideal Forms. Plato is (by the present definition) novelized—that is, made into a dialogical progress in a historical setting. We see him first practicing eristic dialogue forms in Athens, then moving toward his Forms when politically cut off from real educational encounter, and then finally coming back to a different, less transcendental notion of form itself. Recognizing Ryle's joking allusion to Bunyan in the title word *progress* (Ryle seems to see the connection between English Protestanism and the search for new liturgical dialogue forms), we might take Ryle's hint, and for a moment, consider . . . Conrad's own early "progress" in dialogue.

There is no question that Conrad before the middle period which will be the main concern of [*Coercion to Speak*] was already a conscious formalist in dialogue. Each of the major early works has its own dialogue craft, partly distinct from that of the others, and selectively matched to its themes. There is time here only to sketch the development. In *An Outcast of the Islands*, Willems, allegorically named, is a crude early version of the parallel talkatives Kurtz and Marlow; Willems bullies his wife by making her the audience of his egotistical monologues. The Malays, by contrast, have a capacity for inexhaustible and free *collective* speech. They are viewed, romantically enough, as a primitive people "to whom talk is poetry and painting and music, all art, all history; their only accomplishment, their only superiority, their only amusement." In this early novel there is a stark contrast between the civilized man's egocentric, one-sided, disproportional talk and the native's unforced, communal, totally "immersed" collective talk, never exhausted or decayed, and beyond representation. The phrase "their only superiority" seems purposely duplicit—this talk with its continuity and force (it is not represented as dialogue, because the Greek word now implies formal division of the speakers) gives them their only superiority to animals, or nature, but likewise their only superiority to civilization. The idea of a purely continuous and generative speech is probably high romantic, as expressed most convincingly in Wordsworth or Hölderlin. With *The Nigger of the "Narcissus,"* certainly a technical breakthrough for Conrad in many ways, this idea undergoes plastic revision and modernization. Perhaps taking a hint from Stephen Crane, Conrad amasses forecastle talk into paragraphs containing many short speeches, many of which are oaths, more "force of sound" than "meaning." He abandons the convention of speeches individuated into separate paragraphs (rejecting the image of talk as an individual act, or "dialogue") in order to suggest that forecastle "we" speech is immersed in its collectivity. The talk clusters, partly because he doesn't discard quotation marks, look radically different from the earlier idealized image of Malay talk as pure collective genius: pointillistic, lonely, isolated, the forecastle's amassed speeches are at once orchestral and anomic. This conscious break with the conventions of dialogue paragraphing to represent forecastle speech as pointillistic solidarity is one of the clearest instances in early Conrad of the association of speech and labor; it could be seen as patronizing. In a very different formal mode, *Lord Jim* collects a sort of international symposium of responses or commentaries—French, German, English—around the hero. The philosophical symposium, with its verdict of uncertainty, is reemployed here, with strong traces of Menippean satire, or attack on the presumptions of intellectual understanding.

After this, we have the highly conscious temporal arrangement of dialogue forms in *Heart of Darkness,* just discussed. It criticizes the romantic ideal of a historically prophetic speech that itself has continuity and force but is innocent of evil. Tentatively, the story decides that the modern storyteller cannot get back to Malay ideal talk but rather has to be only another imperial speaker, conscious at best, "immersed" in coercion to speak rather than in a community of free speakers. The story's closure, the dialogue with the Intended, predicts Conrad's increasing turn toward dialogues of force: the turn away from romantic ideas of lyrical speech toward an objectification of tragic forced dialogue. The heart of darkness reached at the end of the story is partly the realization that fiction cannot be lyrically and narratively produced as an "only superiority," a pure lyrical freedom outside historical force, but is itself the product of coercion. The fact is that the Intended, however "horrible" and grotesquely melodramatic the scene, rescues Marlow from the idea of a sublime internal compulsion to speak out by showing him external compulsion. Partly liberated by this scene from the romantic idea that his own writing should be inner compulsion, Conrad himself can go on to become a more "objective" dramatist (whether it is a loss or gain is not the point), who makes the scene of forced speech take place between the characters rather than inside a character. This is precisely what "The End of the Tether" begins to study. In that story there is a rich distribution of dialogue forms, intended to be seen and compared by the reader, but the forced dialogue . . . now occupies the central place, rather than the place of ironic closure. That is, with "The End of the Tether" we come to the middle period of Conrad's work, in which the forced dialogue now gives the central organization to Conrad's dialogues; and this will remain the case until the completion of *Under Western Eyes* in 1911, the book in which Conrad raises to its highest pitch, analyzes, and perhaps also has done with, his interest in coercion to speak, after which he will go on to write a series of romances of "interference," *Chance, Victory,* and *The Rescue.*

"The Great Mirage":
Conrad and *Nostromo*

Robert Penn Warren

Conrad, in one sense, had little concern for character independently considered. He is no Dickens or Shakespeare, with relish for the mere variety and richness of personality. Rather, for him a character lives in terms of its typical involvement with situation and theme: the fable, the fable as symbol for exfoliating theme, is his central fact. . . .

Conrad writes in *A Personal Record:* "Those who read me know my conviction that the world, the temporal world, rests on a few very simple ideas, so simple that they must be as old as the hills. It rests notably, among others, on the idea of Fidelity." Or again in his tribute to the Merchant Service in 1918, an essay called "Well Done": "For the great mass of mankind the only saving grace that is needed is steady fidelity to what is nearest to hand and heart in the short moment of each human effort." Fidelity and the sense of the job, the discipline of occupation which becomes a moral discipline with its own objective laws, this, for example, is what saves Marlow in *Heart of Darkness* as it had saved the Roman legionaries, those "handy men," when they had ventured into the dark heart of Britain.

Fidelity and the job sense make for the human community, the solidarity in which Conrad finds his final values, "the solidarity of all mankind in simple ideas and sincere emotions." It is through the realization of this community that man cures himself of that "feeling of life-emptiness" which had afflicted the young hero of *The Shadow-Line* before he came to his great test.

The characteristic story for Conrad becomes, then, the relation of man to the human communion. The story may be one of three types: the story of the MacWhirr or the Don Pépé or the Captain Mitchell, the man who

From *Selected Essays*. © 1951 by Random House, Inc., © 1958 by Robert Penn Warren. Random House, 1958.

lacks imagination and cannot see the "true horror behind the appalling face of things," and who can cling to fidelity and the job; the story of the Kurtz or Decoud, the sinner against human solidarity and the human mission; the story of the redemption, of Lord Jim, Heyst, Dr. Monygham, Flora de Barral, Captain Anthony, Razumov.

The first type of story scarcely engages Conrad. He admires the men of natural virtue, their simplicity, their dogged extroverted sense of obligation and self-respect. But his attitude toward them is ambivalent: they are men "thus fortunate—or thus disdained by destiny or by the sea." They live in a moral limbo of unawareness. They may not be dammed like Kurtz or Decoud and achieve that strange, perverse exultation of horror or grim satisfaction by recognizing their own doom, or be saved like Dr. Monygham or Flora de Barral. We may almost say that their significance is in their being, not in their doing, that they have, properly speaking, no "story"; they are the static image of the condition which men who are real and who have real "stories" may achieve by accepting the logic of experience, but which, when earned, has a dynamic value the innocent never know. The man who has been saved may reach the moment of fulfillment when he can spontaneously meet the demands of fidelity, but his spontaneity must have been earned, and only by the fact of its having been earned is it, at last, significant. Therefore, it is the last type of story that engages Conrad most fully, the effort of the alienated, whatever the cause of his alienation, crime or weakness or accident or the "mystic wound," to enter again the human communion. And the crisis of this story comes when the hero recognizes the terms on which he may be saved, the moment, to take Morton Zabel's phrase, of the "terror of the awakening."

In this general connection some critics have been troubled by, or at least have commented on, the fact that Conrad's prefaces and essays, and even his autobiographical writings and letters, seem ambiguous, contradictory, false, or blandly misleading in relation to the fiction. His comments on Fidelity, such as that above from *A Personal Record,* and his remarks on human solidarity seem so far away from the dark inwardness of his work, this inwardness taken either as the story of his heroes or as the nature of his creative process. When we read parts of *A Personal Record,* for example, we see the image of the false Conrad conjured up by reviewers long ago, the image that William McFee complained about: "a two-fisted shipmaster" telling us simply how brave men behave. And we realize how far this image is from the Conrad who suffered from gout, malaria, rheumatism, neuralgia, dyspepsia, insomnia, and nerves; who, after the Congo experience and its moral shock, says of himself, "I lay on my back in dismal lodgings and expected to go out like a burnt-out candle any moment. That was nerves". . . ; who suffered "moments of cruel blankness"; who on one occasion, years later, had two doctors attending him, each unaware of the other, and who at the same time emptied all medicine into the slop; who advised an aspiring writer that "you must search the darkest corners of your heart," and told the successful and simple-souled Galsworthy, a sort of MacWhirr of literature, "the fact is you want more scepticism at the very fountain of your work. Scepticism, the tonic of minds, the tonic life, the agent of truth—the way of art and salvation"; and who said of his own work, "For me, writing—the only possibly writing—is just simply the conversion of nervous force into phrases."

But should we be troubled by this discrepancy between the two Conrads, the Conrad who praised the simple ideas and sincere emotions and the Conrad of the neurotic illnesses and the dark inwardness? No, we should not, but in saying that we should not I mean a little more than what has been offered elsewhere as a resolution of the discrepancy, the notion that the introverted and lonely Conrad, with a sizable baggage of guilts and fears, yearned, even as he mixed some contempt with his yearning, for the simplicity and certainty of the extroverted MacWhirrs of the world. I mean, in addition to this, a corollary of what has been said above about the story of awakening and redemption being the story that engaged Conrad most fully.

Perhaps the corollary can be stated in this fashion: If the central process that engaged Conrad is the process of the earned redemption, that process can only be rendered as "story," and any generalization about it would falsify the process. Instinctively or consciously, Conrad was willing to give the terms of the process, the poles of the situation, as it were, but not an abstract summary. The abstract summary would give no sense of the truth found within, in what, according to the Preface to *The Nigger of the "Narcissus,"* is "that lonely region of stress and strife."

There is another discrepancy, or apparent discrepancy, that we must confront in any serious consideration of Conrad—that between his professions of skepticism and his professions of faith. Already I have quoted his corrosive remark to Galsworthy, but that remark is not as radical as what he says in a letter to R. B. Cunninghame Graham:

> The attitude of cold unconcern is the only reasonable one. Of course, reason is hateful—but why? Because it demonstrates (to those who have courage) that we, living, are out of life—utterly out of it. The mysteries of a universe made of drops of fire and clods of mud do not concern us in the least. The fate of humanity condemned ultimately to perish from cold is not worth troubling about. . . .

Here, clearly enough, we see the trauma inflicted by nineteenth-century science, a "mystic wound" that Conrad suffered from in company with Hardy, Tennyson, Housman, Stevenson, and most men since their date.

Cold unconcern, an "attitude of perfect indifference" is, as he says in the letter to Galsworthy, "the part of creative power." But this is the same Conrad who speaks of Fidelity and the human communion, and who makes Kurtz cry out in the last horror and Heyst come to his vision of meaning in life. And this is the same Conrad who makes Marlow of *Heart of Darkness* say that what redeems is the "idea only," and makes the devoted Miss Haldin of *Under Western Eyes* say of her dead heroic brother, "Our dear one once told me to remember that men serve always something greater than themselves—the idea."

It is not some, but all, men who must serve the "idea." The lowest and the most vile creature must, in some way, idealize his existence in order to exist, and must find sanctions outside himself. This notion appears over and over in Conrad's fiction. For instance, there is the villainous Ricardo of *Victory*, one of the three almost allegorical manifestations of evil. "As is often the case with lawless natures, Ricardo's faith in any given individual was of a simple, unquestioning character. For a man must have some support in life." Or when Ricardo thinks of the tale of how Heyst had supposedly betrayed Morrison:

> For Ricardo was sincere in his indignation before the elementary principle of loyalty to a chum violated in cold blood, slowly, in a patient duplicity of years. There are standards in villainy as in virtue, and the act as he pictured it to himself acquired an additional horror from the slow pace of that treachery so atrocious and so tame.

Then there is the villain Brown of *Lord Jim*. When, after Jim as allowed him to escape, he falls upon the unsuspecting men of Dain Waris, the act is not a "vulgar massacre":

> Notice that even in this awful outbreak there is a superiority as of a man who carries right—the abstract thing—within the envelope of his common desires. It was not a vulgar and treacherous massacre; it was a lesson, a retribution. . . .

Even bloodthirstiness or villainy must appeal beyond itself to the "idea." The central passage of *Lord Jim*, Stein's speech about the "destructive element," is the basic text for this theme of Conrad:

> A man that is born falls into a dream like a man who falls into the sea. If he tries to climb out into the air as inexperienced people endeavor to do, he drowns—*nicht wahr?* . . . No! I tell you! The way is to the destructive element submit yourself, and with the exertions of your hands and feet in the water make the deep, deep sea keep you up.

I take this, in the context of the action, to read as follows: It is man's fate to be born into the "dream"—the fate of all men. By the dream Conrad here means nothing more or less than man's necessity to justify himself by the "idea," to idealize himself and his actions into moral significance of some order, to find sanctions. But why is the dream like the sea, a "destructive element"? Because man, in one sense, is purely a creature of nature, an animal of black egotism and savage impulses. He should, to follow the metaphor, walk on the dry land of "nature," the real, naturalistic world, and not be dropped into the waters he is so ill equipped to survive in. Those men who take the purely "natural" view, who try to climb out of the sea, who deny the dream and man's necessity to submit to the idea, who refuse to create values that are, quite literally, "super-natural" and therefore human, are destroyed by the dream. They drown in it, and their agony is the agony of their frustrated humanity. Their failure is the failure to understand what is specifically human. They are the Kurtzes, the Browns, in so far as they are villains, but they are also all those isolated ones who are isolated because they have feared to take the full risk of humanity. To conclude the reading of the passage, man, as a natural creature, is not born to swim in the dream, with gills and fins, but if he submits in his own imperfect, "natural" way he can learn to swim and keep himself up, however painfully, in the destructive element. To surrender to the incorrigible and ironical necessity of the "idea," that is man's fate and his only triumph.

Conrad's skepticism is ultimately but a "reasonable" recognition of the fact that man is a natural creature who can rest on no revealed values and can look forward to neither individual immortality nor racial survival. But reason, in this sense, is the denial of life and energy, for against all reason man insists, as man, on creating and trying to live by certain values. These values are, to use Conrad's word, "illusions," but the last wisdom is for man to realize that though his values are illusions, the illusion is necessary, is infinitely precious, is the mark of his human achievement, and is, in the end, his only truth.

From this notion springs the motif of the "true lie," as we may term it, which appears several times in Conrad's fiction. For a first example, we may think of the end of *Heart of Darkness*, when Marlow returns from the Congo to his interview with Kurtz's Intended, whose forehead, in the darkening room, "remained illuminated by the unextinguishable light of belief and love." She demands to know her beloved's last words, and Marlow, confronted by her belief and love, manages to say: "The last word he pronounced was—your name." He is not able to tell her the literal truth, the words, "The horror! The horror!" that Kurtz had uttered with his failing breath. If he had done so, "it would have been too dark—too dark altogether . . ." He has, literally, lied, but his lie is a true lie in that it affirms the "idea," the "illusion," belief and love.

Again, in *Under Western Eyes*, Miss Haldin speaks of bringing Razumov, supposedly the friend of her dead brother, to speak to the bereaved mother: "It would be a mercy if mamma could be soothed. You know what she imagines. Some explanation perhaps may be found, or—or even made up, perhaps. It would be sin."

And even in *Nostromo* the lie that is true, that is no sin, reappears. The incorruptible capataz, dying, is on the verge of telling Mrs. Gould the secret of the stolen treasure, but she will not hear him. When she issues from the room, Dr. Monygham, with the "light of his temperamental enmity to Nostromo" shining in his eyes, demands to know if his long-nourished suspicion of the "incorruptible" Nostromo is correct. He longs to know, to soothe the old wound of his own corruptibility. "He told me nothing," Mrs. Gould says, steadily, and with her charitable lie affirms forever the ideal image of the dead capataz.

Skepticism is the reasonable view of the illusion, but skepticism, the attitude of the intelligence that would be self-sufficient, cannot survive, ironically enough, except by the presence of illusion. The fate of the skeptic Decoud, the "imaginative materialist," who had undertaken to be the natural man in that he had erected passions into duties, is the key parable, among many parables in Conrad, of the meaning of skepticism. Decoud had thought himself outside the human commitments, outside the influence of the "idea," the worshiper of reason, who told him that the only reality is sensation. In so far as his skepticism is "natural," he recognizes the skepticism of Nostromo, the natural man who, "like me, has come casually here to be drawn into the events for which his scepticism as well as mine seems to entertain a sort of passive contempt."

But Decoud's worship of nature and reason is not enough. As soon as he finds himself outside the human orbit, alone with sea and sky, he cannot live. Even skepticism demands belief to feed on; the opposite pole of the essential situation must be present for skepticism to survive.

> Solitude from mere outward condition of existence becomes very swiftly a state of soul in which the affectation of irony and scepticism have no place. . . . After three days of waiting for the sight of some human face, Decoud caught himself entertaining a doubt of his own individuality. It had merged into the world of cloud and water, of natural forces and forms of nature. In our activity alone do we find the sustaining illusion of an independent existence as against the whole scheme of things of which we form a helpless part.

Decoud has reached the ultimate stage of skepticism: his skepticism has dissolved his identity into nature. But even at this moment of his spiritual, and physical, death, he experiences the "first moral sentiment of his manhood," the vague awareness of a "misdirected life." Now both intelligence and passion are "swallowed up easily in this great unbroken solitude of waiting without faith." In this "sadness of a sceptical mind," he beholds "the universe as a succession of incomprehensible images." His act of shooting himself and letting his body fall into the sea is merely the literal repetition of an already accomplished fate: he is "swallowed up in the immense indifference of things."

How are we to reconcile the moral of the story of Decoud, or of Heyst, with Conrad's statements of a radical skepticism—or with even a radical pessimism, the notion of man as a savage animal driven by a black ego? Can we say, as F. R. Leavis says, that "*Nostromo* was written by a Decoud who wasn't a complacent dilettante, but was positively drawn towards those capable of 'investing their activities with spiritual value'—Monygham, Giorgio Viola, Señor Avellanos, Charles Gould"? Or can we say, as Albert Guĕrard, Jr., says, that against man's heart of darkness we can "throw up only the barrier of semi-military ethics; courage, order, tradition and unquestioned discipline; and as a last resort, the stoic's human awareness of his own plight, a pessimism '*plus sombre que la nuit*' "? Both these statements are, in one sense, true. They do describe the bias of Conrad's temperament as I read it, but they do not describe, to my satisfaction at least, the work that Conrad produced out of that temperament. We must sometimes force ourselves to remember that the act of creation is not simply a projection of temperament, but a criticism and purging of temperament.

If Conrad repudiates the Decouds of the world, even as they speak with, as Leavis says, his "personal *timbre*," he also has for the MacWhirrs of the world, the creatures of "semi-military ethics," a very ambivalent attitude, and some of the scorn of a man who knows at least a little of the cost of awareness and the difficulty of virtue. In other words, his work itself is at center dramatic: it is about the cost of awareness and the difficulty of virtue, and his characteristic story is the story of struggle and, sometimes, of redemption. Skepticism, he wrote to Galsworthy, is "the tonic of minds, the tonic of life, the agent of truth—the way of art and salvation." This is, I suppose, a parallel to Hardy's famous statement: . . . "if way to the Better there be, it exacts a full look at the Worst. . . ." It is a way of saying that truth is not easy, but it is also a way of saying that truth, and even salvation, may be possible. Must we choose between the Decouds and the MacWhirrs? There is also Stein; and Emilia Gould, who thought: "Our daily work must be done to the glory of the dead, and for the good of those who come after."

Let us turn, at long last, to *Nostromo*, the novel. In this book Conrad endeavored to create a great, massive, multiphase symbol that would render his total vision of the world, his sense of individual destiny, his sense of man's place in nature, his sense of history and society.

First, *Nostromo* is a complex of personal stories, intimately interfused, a chromatic scale of attitudes, a study in the definition and necessity of "illusion" as Conrad freighted that word. Each character lives by his necessary idealization, up the scale from the "natural" man Nostromo, whose only idealization is that primitive one of his vanity, to Emilia Gould, who, more than any other, has purged the self and entered the human community.

The personal stories are related not only in the contact of person and person in plot and as carriers of variations of the theme of illusion, but also in reference to the social and historical theme. That is, each character is also a carrier of an attitude toward, a point of view about, society; and each is an actor in a crucial historical moment. This historical moment is presumably intended to embody the main issues of Conrad's time: capitalism, imperialism, revolution, social justice. Many of the personal illusions bear quite directly on these topics: Viola's libertarianism, with its dignity and leonine self-sufficiency and, even, contempt for the mob; Charles Gould's obsession in his mission; Avellanos's liberalism and Antonia's patriotic piety; Holroyd's concern with a "pure form of Christianity" which serves as a mask and justification for his imperialistic thirst for power; even the posturing and strutting "Caesarism" of Pedrito Montero, whose imagination had been inflamed by reading third-rate historical novels.

All readers of Conrad know the classic picture of imperialism at its brutal worst in *Heart of Darkness*, the degradation and insanity of the process, and remember the passage spoken by Marlow:

> "The conquest of the earth, which mostly means the taking it away from those who have a different complexion or slightly flatter noses than ourselves, is not a pretty thing when you look into it too much. What redeems it is the idea only."

In *Heart of Darkness* we see the process absolutely devoid of "idea," with lust, sadism, and greed rampant. In *Nostromo* we see the imperialistic process in another perspective, as the bringer of order and law to a lawless land, of prosperity to a land of grinding poverty. At least, that is the perspective in which Charles Gould see himself and his mine:

> "What is wanted here is law, good faith, order, security. Anyone can declaim about these things, but I pin my faith to material interests. Only let the material interests once get a firm footing, and they are bound to impose the conditions on which alone they can continue to exist. That's how your money-making is justified here in the face of lawlessness and disorder. It is justified because the security which it demands must be shared with an oppressed people."

This passage and Gould's conception of his own role may be taken as the central fact of the social and historical theme of *Nostromo*. But how does Conrad intend us to regard this passage? Albert Guérard, Jr., in his careful and brilliant study of Conrad, says that the mine "corrupts Sulaco, bringing civil war rather than progress." That strikes me as far too simple. There has been a civil war but the forces of "progress"—i.e., the San Tomé mine and the capitalistic order—have won. And we must admit that the society at the end of the book is preferable to that at the beginning.

Charles Gould's statement, and his victory, are, however, hedged about with all sorts of ironies. For one thing—and how cunning is this stroke!—there is Decoud's narrative, the letter written to his sister in the midst of the violence, that appears at the very center of the book; and the voice of the skeptic tells us how history is fulfilled. For another thing—

and this stroke is even more cunning—old Captain Mitchell, faithful-hearted and stupid, the courageous dolt, is the narrator of what he pleases to call the "historical events." His is the first human voice we have heard, in Chapter II of Part I, after the mists part to exhibit the great panorama of the mountains, campo, city, and gulf; and in Chapter X of Part III, just after Nostromo has made his decision to ride to Cayta and save the Concession and the new state, the voice of Captain Mitchell resumes. He is speaking long afterward, to some nameless distinguished visitor, and now all the violence and passion and the great anonymous forces of history come under the unconscious irony of his droning anecdotes. We can say of Captain Mitchell what Conrad says of Pedrito Montero, inflamed by his bad novels read in a Parisian garret: his mind is "wrapped . . . in the futilities of historical anecdote." Captain Mitchell's view is, we may say, the "official view": "Progress" has triumphed, the world has achieved itself, there is nothing left but to enjoy the fruits of the famous victory. Thus the very personalities of the narrators function as commentary (in a triumph of technical virtuosity) as their voices are interpolated into Conrad's high and impersonal discourse.

But we do not have to depend merely on this subtle commentary. Toward the end of the book, at a moment of pause when all seems to be achieved on a sort of Fiddler's Green at the end of history, a party has gathered in the garden of the Casa Gould. They discuss in a desultory way the possibility of a new revolution, and the existence of secret societies in which Nostromo, despite his secret treasure and growing wealth, is a great force. Emilia Gould demands: "Will there never be any peace?" And Dr. Monygham replies:

> "There is no peace and no rest in the development of material interests. They have their law and their justice. But it is founded on expediency, and is inhuman; it is without rectitude, and without the continuity and force that can be found only in a moral principle. Mrs. Gould, the time approaches when all that the Gould Concession stands for shall weigh as heavily upon the people as the barbarism, cruelty, and misrule of a few years back."

The material interests have fulfilled their historical mission, or are in the process of fulfilling it. Even Charles Gould, long before, in defining his mission to bring order through the capitalistic development, had not seen that order as the end, only as a phase. He had said: "A better justice will come afterwards. That's our ray of hope." And in this connection we may recall in *Under Western Eyes* how, after hearing the old teacher of languages give his disillusioned view of revolution, Miss Haldin can still say: "I would take liberty from any hand as a hungry man would snatch at a piece of bread. The true progress must begin after." In other words, the empire-builder and hard-bitten realist Gould and the idealistic girl join to see beyond the era of material interests and the era of revolution the time of "true progress" and the "better justice." Somewhere, beyond, there will be, according to Miss Haldin's version, the period of concord:

> I believe that the future will be merciful to us all. Revolutionist and reactionary, victim and executioner, betrayer and betrayed, they shall all be pitied together when the light breaks on our black sky at last. Pitied and forgotten; for without that there can be no union and no love.

Emilia Gould, trapped in her "merciless nightmare" in the "Treasure House of the World," leans over the dying capataz and hears him say, "But there is something accursed in wealth." Then he begins to tell her where the treasure is hidden. But she bursts out: "Let it be lost for ever."

If in this moment of vision, Emilia Gould and (in a sense that we shall come to) Conrad himself repudiate the material interests as merely a step toward justice, what are we to make of revolution? We may remember that Conrad most anxiously meditated the epigraphs of his various books, and that the epigraph of *Nostromo* is the line from Shakespeare: "So foul a sky clears not without a storm." It is innocent to think that this refers merely to the "storm" which is the action of the novel, the revolution that has established the order of material interests in Sulaco. If the sky has cleared at the end of that episode, even now in the new peace we see, as Dr. Monygham sees, the blacker and more terrible thunderheads piling up on the far horizon.

Heart of Darkness and *Nostromo* are, in one sense, an analysis and unmasking of capitalism as it manifested itself in the imperialistic adventure. Necessarily this involves the topic of revolution. The end of *Nostromo* leaves the sky again foul, and in the years immediately after finishing that novel Conrad turns to two studies of revolution, *The Secret Agent*, begun in 1905 and published in 1907, and *Under Western Eyes*, begun in 1908 and published in 1911. These books are in their way an analysis and unmasking of revolution to correspond to the already accomplished analysis and unmasking of capitalism and imperialism. In the world of revolution we find the same complex of egotism, vanity, violence, and even noble illusion. As the old teacher of languages in *Under Western Eyes* puts it:

> A violent revolution falls into the hands of the narrow-minded fanatics and of tyrannical hypocrites at first. Afterwards comes the turn of all the pretentious intellectual failures of the time. Such are the chiefs and the leaders. You will notice that I have left out the mere rogues. The scrupulous and the just, the noble, humane, and devoted natures; the unselfish and the intelligent may begin a movement—but it passes away from them. They are not the leaders of a revolution. They are its victims: the victims of disgust, of disenchantment—often of remorse. Hopes grotesquely betrayed, ideal caricatured—that is the definition of revolutionary

success. There have been in every revolution hearts broken by such successes.

We could take this, in appropriate paraphrase, as a summary of the situation at the end of *Nostromo*. There is the same irony of success. There has been the same contamination of the vision in the very effort to realize the vision. As Emilia Gould reflects: "There was something inherent in the necessities of successful action which carried with it the moral degradation of the idea."

Man, however, is committed to action. The Heysts, who repudiate action, find their own kind of damnation. Wisdom, then, is the recognition of man's condition, the condition of the creature made without gills or fins but dropped into the sea, the necessity of living with the ever renewing dilemma of idea as opposed to nature, morality to action, "utopianism" to "secular logic" (to take Razumov's terms from *Under Western Eyes*), justice to material interests. Man must make his life somehow in the dialectical process of these terms, and in so far as he is to achieve redemption he must do so through an awareness of his condition that identifies him with the general human communion, not in abstraction, not in mere doctrine, but immediately. The victory is never won, the redemption must be continually re-earned. And as for history, there is no Fiddler's Green, at least not near and soon. History is a process fraught with risks, and the moral regeneration of society depends not upon shifts in mechanism but upon the moral regeneration of men. But nothing is to be hoped for, even in the most modest way, if men lose the vision of the time of concord, when "the light breaks on our black sky at last." The Platonic vision is what makes life possible in its ruck and confusion, if we are to take Conrad's word from the essay called "Books":

> I would require from him [the artist] many acts of faith of which the first would be the cherishing of an undying hope; and hope, it will not be contested, implies all the piety of effort and renunciation. It is the God-sent form of trust in the magic force and inspiration belonging to the life of this earth. We are inclined to forget that the way of excellence is in the intellectual, as distinguished from emotional, humility. What one feels so hopelessly barren in declared pessimism is just its arrogance. It seems as if the discovery made by many men at various times that there is much evil in the world were a source of proud and unholy joy unto some of the modern writers. That frame of mind is not the proper one in which to approach seriously the art of fiction. It gives an author—goodness only knows why—an elated sense of his own superiority. And there is nothing more dangerous than such an elation to that absolute loyalty towards his own feelings and sensations an author should keep hold of in his most exalted moments of creation.

To be hopeful in an artistic sense it is not necessary to think that the world is good. It is enough to believe that there is no impossibility of its being made so.

Nothing, however, is easy or certain. Man is precariously balanced in his humanity between the black inward abyss of himself and the black outward abyss of nature. What Conrad meant by and felt about man's perilous balance must already be clear, if I can make it clear at all. But now I shall speak of *Nostromo* as an image of this.

The setting of the story, the isolation of Sulaco, is in itself significant. The serrated wall of the Cordillera, hieratic and snow-capped, behind the Campo, the Azuera and the Golfo Placido define a little world that comes to us as complete—as a microcosm, we may say, of the greater world and its history. Man is lost in this overwhelming scene. The story of the two gringos, spectral and alive, on the peninsula of Azuera is, of course, a fable of greed and of the terrifying logic of material interests unredeemed. But it is also a fable, here at the threshold of *Nostromo*, of man lost in the blankness of nature. At the center of the book, to resume the same theme, we find the story of Decoud, who loses his identity into the "world of cloud and water, of natural forces and forms of nature." When he commits suicide, he falls into the "immense indifference of things." Then at the very end of the novel, in the last paragraph, Dr. Monygham, in the police-gallery, hears the wild, faithful cry uttered by Linda, the name of Nostromo: "Never! Gian' Battista!"

> It was another of Nostromo's successes, the greatest, the most enviable, the most sinister of all. In that true cry of love and grief that seemed to ring aloud from Punta Mala to Azuera and away to the bright line of the horizon, overhung by a big white cloud shining like a mass of solid silver, the genius of the magnificent capataz de cargadores dominated the dark gulf containing his conquests of treasure and love.

This, too, is a fable: the passionate cry in the night that is a kind of triumph in the face of the immense indifference of things. It is a fable with a moral not unlike that of the second of Yeats's "Two Songs from a Play":

> Whatever flames upon the night
> Man's own resinous heart has fed.

Or to take another fable, one from Conrad's essay on Henry James:

> When the last aqueduct shall have crumbled to pieces, the last airship fallen to the ground, the last blade of grass have died upon a dying earth, man, indomitable by his training in resistance to misery and pain, shall set this undiminished light of his eyes against the feeble glow of the sun. . . .

For my own part, from a short and cursory acquaintance with

my kind, I am inclined to think that the last utterance will formulate, strange as it may appear, some hope now to us utterly
inconceivable.

I have tried to define my reading of Conrad's work in general and of
Nostromo in particular. In these matters there is not, and should not be, an
ultimate "reading," a final word and orthodoxy of interpretation. In so far
as a work is vital, there will continually be a development, an extrapolation
of significance. But at any one moment each of us must take the risk of his
sensibility and his logic in making a reading. I have taken this risk, and
part of this risk is the repudiation, or at least criticism, of competing
interpretations.

There is one view, not uncommonly encountered, that Conrad did not
intend his fiction to have "meaning." We encounter, for example, the comment of Edward Crankshaw: "Bothering about what Conrad meant in *Heart
of Darkness* is as irrelevant as bothering about what Mozart meant in the
Haffner Symphony." Conrad himself gives some support to this view in
his skeptical bias, in his emphasis on the merely spectacular value of life,
and in not a few of his remarks on his literary intentions, particularly in
the famous one: "My task which I am trying to achieve is, by the power
of the written word, to make you hear, to make you feel—it is, before all,
to make you *see*."

All of this seems to me, however, to mean nothing more than that
Conrad was an artist, that he wanted, in other words, to arrive at his
meanings immediately, through the sensuous renderings of passionate experience, and not merely to define meanings in abstraction, as didacticism
or moralizing. Conrad made no split between literature and life. If anything,
he insisted on the deepest inward relationship. As he put it about the writer
in the essay "Books": "It is in the impartial practice of life, if anywhere,
that the promise of perfection for his art can be found, rather than in the
absurd formulas trying to prescribe this or that particular method of technique or conception."

Over and over again, Conrad implies what he says in the Author's
Note to *Chance:* "But every subject in the region of intellect and emotion
must have a morality of its own if it is treated at all sincerely; and even the
most artful writer will give himself (and his morality) away in about every
third sentence." And even to the famous sentence about his intention being,
before all, to make us "*see*," we find an addition: "That—and no more,
and it is everything." To seeing in its fullest sense, to "our sympathetic
imagination," as Conrad says in "Autocracy and War," we must look "for
the ultimate triumph of concord and justice."

If in *A Personal Record* Conrad declares himself an "imperfect Esthete,"
in the same sentence he admits that he is "no better philosopher." Leavis
goes so far as to affirm that Conrad cannot be said to have a philosophy:
"He is not one of those writers who clear up their fundamental attitudes

for themselves in such a way that we may reasonably, in talking of them, use that portentous term." In discussing this remark, as I am about to do, I run the risk of making Conrad's work seem too schematic and of implying that he somehow sat down and worked out a philosophy which he then projected, with allegorical precision, into fiction. I mean nothing of the sort, but I do mean to say that in my judgment Leavis takes Conrad's work as too much a casual matter of temperament. For I think that even if Conrad is as "imperfect" philosopher as aesthete, he is still, in the fullest sense of the term, a philosophical novelist.

The philosophical novelist, or poet, is one for whom the documentation of the world is constantly striving to rise to the level of generalization about values, for whom the image strives to rise to symbol, for whom images always fall into a dialectical configuration, for whom the urgency of experience, no matter how vividly and strongly experience may enchant, is the urgency to know the meaning of experience. This is not to say that the philosophical novelist is schematic and deductive. It is to say quite the contrary, that he is willing to go naked into the pit, again and again, to make the same old struggle for his truth. But we cannot better Conrad's own statement for the philosophical novelist, the kind of novelist he undertook, quite consciously, to be: "Even before the most seductive reveries I have remained mindful of that sobriety of interior life, that asceticism of sentiment, in which alone the naked form of truth, such as one conceives it, can be rendered without shame."

For him the very act of composition was a way of knowing, a way of exploration. In one sense this is bound to be true of all composition, but the matter of degree and self-consciousness is important in our present distinction, even crucial. We know a little of how *Nostromo* came to be, how it rose out of a feeling of blankness, how its composition was, in sober fact, an exploration and a growth, how the "great mirage," as Edward Garnett called it, took shape until it could float before us, vivid and severe, one of the few mastering visions of our historical moment and our human lot.

The Form of Content: *Lord Jim*

Fredric Jameson

First impressions [of *Lord Jim*] raise interpretive temptations: in particular the idea, encouraged by the text itself, that the novel is fundamentally "about" the problem of heroism, and indeed, even before we get as far as that, that the novel "has" a hero and is "about" Jim himself. These temptations our earlier chapter [of *The Political Unconscious*] on the ideological nature of the category of a narrative "character" has perhaps supplied us with the means to withstand. Indeed, we there wondered whether it would not be desirable to consider the possibility that the literary "character" is no more substantive than the Lacanian ego, and that it is to be seen rather as an "effect of system" than as a full representational identity in its own right. The idea was to explore the systems, the network of preconscious *pensée sauvage*, in terms of which a given "character" had meaning, whether that meaning took on the form of an antinomy, as will be found to be the case here in Conrad, or on the other hand was the bearer, as in Balzac, of a more stable quasi-allegorical content: the hypothesis of a character system presupposes another one, namely that the subject, in the immediacy of his or her consciousness, has no meaning, but that when a given subject is endowed with meaning (as, for example, when it becomes a representation for another subject or when another subject becomes part of the cast of characters of our own private fantasies), then that particular meaning can be traced back to the system that generates it, and of which we have taken Greimas's semantic or semiotic rectangle as one of the most useful emblems.

In the present instance, it is certain that to dissolve the verisimilitude of the character of Jim into the mere effect or pole of some larger signifying system would at once discredit and dispatch into critical dilettantism the

From *The Political Unconscious: Narrative as a Socially Symbolic Act.* © 1981 by Cornell University Press.

whole thematics of heroism and individual guilt and expiation about which we have already complained. On the other hand, it would seem that a book so completely organised around the investigation of a single individual destiny, a single unique yet also more largely consequent and socially significant life experience ("he was one of us"), risks being shattered by such a refusal to take it on its own organizational terms.

How does one go about rewriting and rereading this narrative in such a way that "Jim" comes to be the name for an empty slot in a system which then, far more than the "lifelike" character, proves to have been the absent center of the narrative? Such a process can often conveniently begin in typology, provided it gets out of it at the appropriate moment. The reiterated but enigmatic "one of us" suggests that the binary terms of Jim's system are probably not to be sought for in the direction of Marlow and his listeners, but rather elsewhere: for example, in Jim's own reflections on types of people and types of vocation during his enforced idleness in port after his accident:

> While waiting, he associated naturally with the men of his calling in the port. These were of two kinds. Some, very few and seen there but seldom, led mysterious lives, had preserved an undefaced energy with the temper of buccaneers and the eyes of dreamers. They appeared to live in a crazy maze of plans, hopes, dangers, enterprises, ahead of civilization, in the dark places of the sea; and their death was the only event of their fantastic existence that seemed to have a reasonable certitude of achievement. The majority were men who, like himself, thrown there by some accident, had remained as officers of country ships. They had now a horror of the home service, with its harder conditions, severer view of duty, and the hazard of stormy oceans. They were attuned to the eternal peace of Eastern sky and sea. They loved short passages, good deck-chairs, large native crews, and the distinction of being white. . . . In all they said—in their actions, in their looks, in their persons—could be detected the soft spot, the place of decay, the determination to lounge safely through existence.

That Jim must initially test himself against these two categories, that neither is adequate to house him, suggests that the character system, if one is at work here, is far from complete and lacks certain key features or semes. Jim is presumably not one of the deck-chair captains, who from another point of view, are the non-narrative terms, the "characters" who have no story and no destiny; but though he may well, like the first group, have the eyes of a dreamer, the characterization of these Europeans is still, at least at this stage, too comic-satiric to suit him either, and ultimately finds a first generic fulfillment in the episode of the guano empire ("all at once, on the blank page, under the very point of the pen, the two figures of Chester and his antique partner, very distinct and complete, would dodge into view with stride and gestures, as if reproduced in the field of some optical toy. I would watch them for a while. No! They were too phantasmal and extravagant to enter into anyone's fate"): such dreamers will, however, return in a more baleful guise in the second half of the novel.

But in half a paragraph, Jim has a new berth (chief mate on the *Patna*) and in another half a page, in its passengers-to-be, confronts a new type of human being and a new category of human existence:

> They streamed aboard over three gangways, they streamed in urged by faith and the hope of paradise, they streamed in with a continuous tramp and shuffle of bare feet, without a word, a murmur, or a look back; and when clear of confining rails spread on all sides over the deck, flowed forward and aft, overflowed down the yawning hatchways, filled the inner recesses of the ship—like water filling a cistern, like water flowing into crevices and crannies, like water rising silently even with the rim. Eight hundred men and women with faith and hopes, with affections and memories, they had collected there, coming from north and south and from the outskirts of the East, after treading the jungle paths, descending the rivers, coasting in praus along the shallows, crossing in small canoes from island to island, passing through suffering, meeting strange sights, beset by strange fears, upheld by one desire. They came from solitary huts in the wilderness, from populous campongs, from villages by the sea. At the call of an idea they had left their forests, their clearings, the protection of their rulers, their prosperity, their poverty, the surroundings of their youth, and the graves of their fathers. . . .
>
> "Look at dese catttle," said the German skipper to his new chief mate.

The crude irony underscores the most obvious feature that distinguishes the pilgrims from the Europeans anatomized on the preceding page: their lack of "individualism." Yet even on this most superficial level, the initial stirrings of a differential system are at work; we return from these anonymous masses to the equally faceless "deck-chair captains" of the previous page, themselves each utterly lacking in individuality, yet living their indistinction one by one, in the isolation of their bourgeois comfort, rather than, as here, collectively.

Meanwhile, telltale expressions like "the call of an idea" not only warn of semic echoes with the other category of European seamen, those of the mysterious lives and "the eyes of dreamers," but also suggest that from our now distant vantage point in late twentieth-century consumer society we need a semantic reconstruction of these terms themselves—terms such as "idea," and later, in *Nostromo*, "sentimentalism"—which are too charged not to carry with them a whole historical ideology that must be drawn, massy and dripping, up into the light before the text can be considered to have been read. Conrad's discourse—an overlay of psychoanalytically charged terms and ideological, public slogans—must be regarded as a foreign language that we have to learn in the absence of any dictionary or grammar, ourselves reconstructing its syntax and assembling hypotheses about the meanings of this or that item of vocabulary for which we ourselves have no contemporary equivalent.

Before trying to reconstruct the semantics of this key passage, however, we must also argue something else: namely, that what is merely a narrative device or pretext (Jim's crisis requires him to have put lives in danger, but it can scarcely matter which ones; these Mecca-bound pilgrims might just as easily have been replaced by Indian emigrants to South Africa, say, or by a group of families of overseas Chinese) has a substantive meaning in its own right, which is constitutive for the text. This is, it seems to me, the kind of situation in which the Althusserian notion of "overdetermination" is useful: we cannot argue the importance of this particular evocation of the pilgrims from its necessity in the mechanism of the plot, yet we can propose a secondary line of determination such that, even as narrative pretext, this content imposes itself and becomes unavoidable. Its necessity is, in other words, not to be found on the level of narrative construction, but outside, in the objective logic of the content, in the unavailability of any other "illustration" to fill this particular empty slot. So it is significant that from our enumeration of other possibilities passengers of European stock were excluded (for one thing, the Europeans would not have remained calm while the officers abandoned ship); the other Asian possibilities are also inappropriate, since both would represent commerce and business motives rather than the religious pilgrimage here described, and itself reinforced (or once again, "overdetermined," if you like) by the attitude of the nonpilgrim Malay pilots, who keep their stations and continue to guide the abandoned ship for no reason other than sheer *faith* ("It never came into his mind then that the white men were about to leave the ship through fear of death. He did not believe it now. There might have been secret reasons"). (Obviously, the thematic selection of Islam is no historical accident; it is ironic that this mirage of plenitude attributed to the historical and cultural Other should also be the instrument—"Orientalism"—by which that same Other is systematically marginalized.) Here too, in this secondary loop of the plot, equally necessary for the construction of Jim's central ordeal—but was it not Valéry who observed that what is merely necessary in art is the place of the flaw and the soft pockct of bad writing?—the apparently secondary content of blind faith comes as a "motivation of the device" and a reappropriation of the plot mechanism in the service of some quite different thematic and semantic system.

So at length we find ourselves interrogating, as though it were the fundamental concern of this sea story and adventure tale, the clearly secondary and marginal phenomenon of religion and religious belief. We do not generally associate Conrad with the nineteenth-century ideologeme of aesthetic religion. The key moments in its development might be quickly sketched in as those of Chateaubriand, its inventor, in *Le Génie du christianisme* (1802), Flaubert's archeological passion for dead religions, his appropriation of that whole ideology of perception, sense-data, and hallucination mentioned [elsewhere] for the evocation of religious visions, as in *La Tentation de Saint Antoine* (1874) or *Trois Contes* (1877)—not to speak of the contemporaneous fascination with belief of the positivists, most notably Renan—and finally such late variants as Malraux's books on painting and sculpture after World War II, books in which the retreat from Marxism to a Gaullist nationalism seems to impose an intellectual detour through a meditation on all the dead religions, all the divers embodiments of the Absolute, in the human past. Into this genealogy of an ideological fascination now relatively foreign to us (and it should be noted that the religious revival of the late nineteenth century and, in particular, phenomena like neo-Catholicism are quite different from this aestheticizing contemplation of religion from without), we must assuredly insert its most intellectually illustrious and productive monument: the studies undertaken by Conrad's virtual contemporary, Max Weber, of the dynamics and function of religion, not only in *The Protestant Ethic,* but above all in the elaborate, posthumously published *Sociology of Religion.* Indeed, Weber's wry characterization of himself as "religiously unmusical" may serve as the motto for the curious intellectual stance of all of these non-believers, who combine the allure of a religiously fellow-traveling agnosticism with the secret longings of the impotent in matters of belief. In the British tradition, the institutional position of Anglicanism and the historical shock of Darwinism's implicit challenge to it lend the thematics of religious belief a somewhat different symbolic and political meaning than they held in the flood-tide of bourgeois city life on the continent; still, Conrad was not really British, and it may be a useful estrangement to place him for a moment in a different context than those (English intellectuals of the Ford/Garnett type, a romantic Polish intelligentsia, the world of the merchant marine) in which he is normally grasped.

The name of Weber makes it clear that we cannot begin to sense the real ideological function of religious aestheticism unless we place it within that larger intellectual and ideological preoccupation which is the study and interrogation of value, and which, even more than with Weber, is associated with the name of the latter's master, Nietzsche. From this standpoint, Nietzsche's "transvaluation of all values" and Weber's misnamed and misunderstood ideal of a "value-free science" must both be seen as attempts to project an intellectual space from which one can study innerworldly value as such, the whole chaotic variety of reasons and motives the citizens of a secular society have for pursuing the activities they set themselves. These ideals are implicit or explicit attempts to parry the powerful Marxian position, which sees intellectual activity as being historically situated and class-based: the Marxian objection makes it clear that the vocation to study value cannot simply embody one more inner-worldly value (the passion for knowledge? the pursuit of sheer disinterested science?) without at once itself becoming ideological, or, in the Nietzschean formula, one more embodiment of the will to power. Framed in these terms, then, the problem (it will later, with Max Scheler and Karl Mannheim, flatten itself out into that "subdiscipline" conventionally labeled the "sociology of knowledge") is insoluble; but what is interesting about it for us are its preconditions, namely, the objective historical developments without which such a "problem" could never have been articulated in the first place.

These are clearly, first and foremost, the secularization of life under capitalism and the breaking up (or, in the current euphemism, the "modernization") of the older tradition-oriented systems of castes and inherited professions, as the combined result of the French Revolution and the spread of the market system. Now indeed, for the first time in any general and irreversible way, the realm of values becomes problematical, with the result that it can, for the first time, be isolated as a realm in itself and contemplated as a separate object of study. To say that value becomes a semi-autonomous object is to observe the way in which, in the new middle-class culture, for the first time people (but mainly men) must weigh the various activities against each other and choose their professions. What we call private life or the new subjectivity of individualism is objectively simply this distance which permits them to hold their professional activites at arm's length; hence the originality, in the realm of the novel, of the "Quel métier prendre?" of a Stendhal, whose works explore, as it were, the atomic weights of the various professions and political regimes as alternate life forms.

In Weber's scheme of things, all social institutions describe a fatal trajectory from the traditional to the rationalized, passing through a crucial transitional stage which is the moment—the vanishing mediation—of so-called charisma. The activities of older societies are for the most part inherited (the blacksmith's father and grandfather were blacksmiths), and the question about value—about the reason for pursuing this or that life task, in this or that fashion—is short-circuited by the classic reply of all traditional societies: Because it was always done that way, because that is the way we have always lived. The problem of value cannot therefore arise in this environment; or, to put it another way, in the world of the traditional village, or even of tribal culture, each activity is symbolically unique, so that the level of abstraction upon which they could be compared with one another is never attained: there is no least-common-denominator available to compare iron-welding or the preparation of curare with basket-weaving or the making of bread or pots. To use the Marxian terminology, in such societies we can only contemplate an incomparable variety of qualitatively different forms of concrete work or productive activity, because the common denominator of all of these forms of activity—equivalent labor-power—has not yet been made visible by the objective process of abstraction at work within society.

For Weber, the charismatic moment amounts to a kind of myth of meaning, a myth of the value of this or that activity, which is briefly sustained by the personal power and authority of the charismatic figure, generally a prophet. But this moment tends to give way at once to a system in which all activities are ruthlessly rationalized and restructured in forms we have already described. The moment of rationalization, then, is Weber's equivalent of Marx's notion of the universalization of equivalent labor-power, or the commodification of all labor; yet if we see the latter subterranean infrastructural process as the objective precondition for the former developments in the relations of production and throughout the superstructure there need be no particular inconsistency between the two accounts.

What we are here concerned to stress is the paradox of the very notion of value itself, which becomes visible as abstraction and as a strange afterimage on the retina, only at the moment in which it has ceased to exist as such. The characteristic form of rationalization is indeed the reorganization of operations in terms of the binary system of means and ends; indeed, the means/ends opposition, although it seems to retain the term and to make a specific place for value, has the objective result of abolishing value as such, bracketing the "end" or drawing it back into the system of pure means in such a way that the end is merely the empty aim of realizing these particular means. This secret one-dimensionality of the apparent means/ends opposition is usefully brought out by the Frankfurt School's alternate formulation, namely the concept of instrumentalization, which makes it clear that rationalization involves the transformation of everything into sheer means (hence the traditional formula of a Marxist humanism, that capitalism is a wholly rationalized and indeed rational system of means in the service of irrational ends).

Thus, the study of value, the very idea of value, comes into being at the moment of its own disappearance and of the virtual obliteration of all value by a universal process of instrumentalization: which is to say that—as again in the emblematic case of Nietzsche—the study of value is at one with nihilism, or the experience of its absence. What is paradoxical about such an experience is obviously that it is contemporaneous with one of the most active periods in human history, with all the mechanical animation of late Victorian city life, with all the smoke and conveyance inherent in new living conditions and in the rapid development of business and industry, with the experimental triumphs of positivistic science and its conquest of the university system, with all the bustling parliamentary and bureaucratic activity of the new middle-class regimes, the spread of the press, the diffusion of literacy and the rise of mass culture, the ready accessibility of the newly mass-produced commodities of an increasingly consumer-oriented civilization. We must ponder the anomaly that it is only in the most completely humanized environment, the one most fully and obviously the end product of human labor, production, and transformation, that life becomes meaningless, and that existential despair first appears as such in direct proportion to the elimination of nature, the non- or anti-human, to the increasing rollback of everything that threatens human life and the prospect of a well-nigh limitless control over the external universe. The most interesting artists and thinkers of such a period are those who cling to the experience of meaninglessness itself as to some ultimate reality, some ultimate bedrock of existence of which they do not wish to be cheated by illusions or "philosophies of as-if": "Lieber will noch der Mensch *das Nichts* wollen," cried Nietzsche, "als *nicht* wollen." Rather nihilism than ennui, rather an orchestral pessimism and a metaphysical vision of cosmic entropy than too stark and unpleasant a sense of the systematic exclusion of "value" by the new logic of capitalist social organization.

These are clearly the absolutes with which Conrad's own private pessimism has its "family resemblance" (although in the next section we will find it necessary to distinguish proto-existentialism as a metaphysic—pessimism, nihilism, the meaninglessness of existence, the absurd—from the rigorous analytical dissolution of acts and events by existentialism as a technical philosophy). It is also the perspective in which to grasp the ideological meaning of aesthetic religion: the melancholy of disbelief, the nostalgia of the nineteenth-century intellectual for the "wholeness" of a faith that is no longer possible, is itself a kind of ideological fable designed to transform into a matter of individual existence what is in reality a relationship between collective systems and social forms. Religion has the symbolic value of wholeness, no doubt: but it is the wholeness of the older organic society or *Gesellschaft* that it conveys, and not that—in any case surely a mirage—of some fully unified monad. Religion, to the henceforth "religiously unmusical" subjects of the market system, is the unity of older social life perceived from the outside: hence its structural affinity with the image as such and hallucination. Religion is the superstructural projection of a mode of production, the latter's only surviving trace in the form of linguistic and visual artifacts, thought systems, myths and narratives, which look as though they had something to do with the forms in which our own consciousness is at home, and yet which remain rigorously closed to it. Because we can no longer think the figures of the sacred from within, we transform their external forms into aesthetic objects, but also monuments, pyramids, altars, presumed to have an inside, yet housing powers that will forever remain a mystery to us.

So religion, in this particular sense, takes its place in that complex of ideological themes and terms with which the nineteenth century sought to explore the new world of universal instrumentalization and to express its bewilderment at what that world excluded as much as at what it contained: other motifs, some of which appear in the evocation of the pilgrims quoted above, are the "idea" or the "ideal" (generally art or love) as that which allows one to transcend the intolerable double bind of means and ends; the somewhat lower but also more overtly social concept of the "philan-thropic," as we observed it at work [elsewhere]—a conception of a form of social action which would not be that of mere "interest," or would, in other words, transcend the antivalue of the purely instrumental; Conrad's term "sentimentalism," finally, which comes to designate activities that cannot be reduced to interested motives and must therefore be credited to the account of some unbusinesslike and whimsically nonserious caprice (the Gidean *acte gratuit* will be a final, more heroic avatar of this still fairly leisure-class attribute).

Now we may reinvest the language of *Lord Jim* with something like its original ideological and semantic content, and make an effort to disengage the "system" that generates the typology of characters we have begun to articulate, and beyond that, assigns the narrative its ultimate terminus and dynamics. I believe that this system may best be grasped in terms of the major themes of the dilemma just outlined, and in particular of the op-position between activity and value. It is an opposition not unlike that which underlies Lukács's *Theory of the Novel*, where it takes the form of a dissociation between *Leben*, life, sheer contingent, inner-worldly experi-ence, and *Wesen*, essence, meaning, immanent wholeness. The inner dy-namism of such oppositions springs from their incommensurability, their ec-centricity as a weighing of two incomparable phenomena: on the one hand, genuine degraded but existent inner-worldy experience, and on the other, sheer ideal, nostalgia, an imagined wholeness that is part of the existent real only insofar as it is dreamed there and projected by this par-ticular real world, but has no other substance. In Conrad, however, as we have seen, owing to the coexistence of capitalism and precapitalist social forms on the imperialist periphery, the term value is still able to have genuine social and historical substance; it marks communities and ways of life which still, for another moment yet, exist, and have not been reduced to the icons and melancholy images of the mainstream of religious aestheticism.

The point about this binary opposition, however, is not its logical accuracy as a thought concerned to compare only comparable entities and oppose only terms of the appropriate category, but, on the contrary, its existence as a symptom; the opposition between activity and value is not so much a logical contradiction, as rather an antinomy for the mind, a dilemma, an aporia, which itself expresses—in the form of an ideological closure—a concrete social contradiction. Its existence as skewed thought, then, as a double bind and a conceptual scandal, is what accounts for the restless life of the system, its desperate attempts to square its own circles and to produce new terms out of itself which ultimately "solve" the di-lemma at hand. Thus, in an initial move which Greimas's semantic rectangle allows us to register, each term generates its logical negation or "contradictory"; the nucleus of our ideological system thus contains the four terms of activity and value, and not-activity and not-value, articulated as in the diagram.

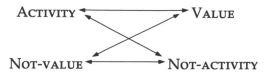

So far, clearly, these are semes or conceptual features, and not in any sense the slots of narrative characters or indeed other narrative categories. The place of characters and of a character system is opened up only at the point at which the mind seeks further release from its ideological closure by projecting combinations of these various semes: to work through the various possible combinations is then concretely to imagine the life forms, or the characterological types, that can embody and manifest such contradictions, which otherwise remain abstract and repressed. Thus, to follow our rectangle around clockwise beginning on the righthand side, it does not seem particularly farfetched to suggest that the synthesis of value and not-activity can be embodied only by the pilgrims, who are a breathing and living presence which does not exteriorize itself in any particular activity, in acts, struggles, "goal-oriented behavior": even the pilgrimage is simply the emanation of their being, as of an element, water draining the great watertables of Malaysia, "rising silently even with the rim."

Moving to the lower horizontal opposition, between not-activity and not-value—a synthesis suggestively designated as the neutral term in Greimas's version of this model—we see that the very terms of the judgment are virtually explicit in Conrad's contemptuous account of the "deck-chair sailors" who have no ideal but that of their own comfort, and whose energies, insofar as they have any, are wholly dedicated to avoiding activity as much as possible. These are indeed the "neuters" of Conrad's universe, the faceless anonymity against which passions become identifiable in all their own specificity.

As for the next possible synthesis, which would unite activity with not-value, the evocation of Nietzsche has perhaps made it more familiar to us than Conrad's text, at this stage in our reading of it, would authorize: "There are people who would rather will *nothingness* than want nothing at all." What is meant here is clearly not the merely eccentric figures of South Sea port "originals" (of which Jim himself for a moment becomes one), so much as nihilism itself, that formidable combinaton of energy and, more than utter lack of scruple, a passion for nothingness. To test our hypothesis would be to expect the text at length to generate such a figure, which, indeed, it does in Jim's Nemesis, the character of Gentleman Brown (about whom we will have more to say in a later section).

Finally, we come to what Greimas calls the "complex term," the ideal synthesis of the two major terms of the contradiction and thus the latter's unimaginable and impossible resolution and *Aufhebung*; the union of activity and value, of the energies of Western capitalism and the organic immanence of the religion of pre-capitalist societies, can only block out the place of Jim himself. But not the existential Jim, the antihero, of the first part of the novel: rather, the ideal Jim, the "Lord Jim" of the second half, the wish-fulfilling romance, which is marked as a degraded narrative precisely by its claim to have "resolved" the contradiction and generated the impossible hero, who, remaining problematical in the *Patna* section of the book as the Lukács of *The Theory of the Novel* told us the hero of a genuine novel must do, now solicits that lowering of our reality principle necessary to accredit this final burst of legend. (There has been considerable debate as to the "meaning" of the ending of *Lord Jim*, and in particular as to whether Jim can be said, by his death, to have "redeemed" himself; the exalted tone of the ending suggests a positive response which a sober reading of the narrative makes it rather difficult to accept. Surely this "undecidability" of the ending confirms the present analysis, and offers a virtual textbook illustration of an "imaginary resolution of a real contradiction," it being understood that an imaginary resolution is no resolution at all. All of Conrad's artfulness is in this concluding section mustered for a kind of prestidigitation designed to prevent the embarrassing question from being posed in the first place.)

The completed character system may therefore be schematically presented as follows:

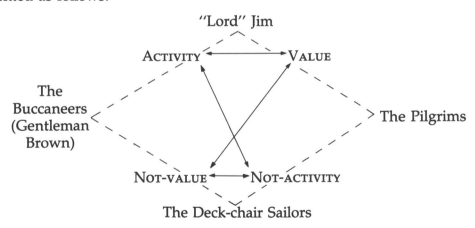

Such a schema not only articulates the generation of the characters, insofar as it represents a contradiction to be "solved," or an antinomy to be effaced or overcome; it also suggests the ideological service which the production of this narrative is ultimately intended to perform—in other words, the resolution of this particular determinate contradiction—or, more precisely, following Lévi-Strauss's seminal characterization of mythic narrative, the imaginary resolution of this particular determinate real contradiction. Such models—sometimes loosely formulated in terms of analogies with the "deep structures" and surface manifestations of linguistics—find their proper use in the staging of the fundamental problems of the narrative text—the antinomies or ideological closure it is called upon to imagine away—and in the evaluation of the narrative solution, or sequence of provisional solutions, invoked for this purpose. They are, however, less able to bridge the gap between an ideological deep structure and the sentence-by-sentence life of the narrative text, as a perpetual generation and dissolution of events, a process for which we must now propose a rather different kind of lens.

Lord Jim is, however, a privileged text in this respect—a kind of reflexive or meta-text—in that its narrative construes the "event" as the analysis and dissolution of events in some more common everyday naive sense. The "event" in *Lord Jim* is the analysis and dissolution of the event. The originality of the text goes well beyond the conventional redoubling of plot and fable (Aristotle), *discours* and *histoire* (Benveniste), the conventional distinction between the exposition and "rendering" of narrative events and those events as sheer data, raw material, anecdotal precondition. Certainly, the slow unfolding of the "real story" of the *Patna* has all the excitement of a detective story and not a little of that form's peculiarly specialized and redoubled structure: but we have understood very little about this narrative unless we have come to realize that even that "real story" itself is for Conrad hollow and empty, and that there is a void at the heart of events and acts in this work which goes well beyond simple anecdotal mystification.

Consider for instance the following moment of crisis in the Patusan narrative: on arrival, Jim finds himself virtually but unofficially imprisoned by an old adversary of Stein and his allies. He passes his time in a closed courtyard, amusing himself by repairing the Rajah's broken clock. Suddenly, in panic, for the first time conceiving his plight and imminent danger, he climbs the stockade and makes his way across the mud flats to freedom. What interests us is the inner structure of this event, which is indubitably an act on Jim's part:

> The higher firm ground was about six feet in front of him. . . . He reached and grabbed desperately with his hands, and only succeeded in gathering a horrible cold shiny heap of slime against his breast—up to his very chin. It seemed to him he was burying himself alive, and then he struck out madly, scattering the mud with his fists. It fell on his head, on his face, over his eyes, into his mouth. He told me that he remembered suddenly the courtyard, as you remember a place where you had been very happy years ago. He longed—so he said—to be back there again, mending the clock. Mending the clock—that was the idea. He made efforts, tremendous sobbing, gasping efforts, efforts that seemed to burst his eyeballs in their sockets and make him blind, and

culminating in one mighty supreme effort in the darkness to crack the earth asunder, to throw it off his limbs—and he felt himself creeping feebly up the bank. He lay full length on the firm ground and saw the light, the sky. Then as a sort of happy thought the notion came to him that he would go to sleep. He will have it that he *did* actually go to sleep; that he slept—perhaps for a minute, perhaps for twenty seconds, or only for one second, but he recollects distinctly the violent convulsive start of awakening. [At which point, then, Jim leaps to his feet again and continues his escape, racing through the village to safety.]

Now a passage of this kind can be taken, as its contemporaries surely would have taken it, as a psychological curiosity; we can almost hear them admiring this knowledge of the "human heart," this exploration of the intricacies of human reactions. We have already mentioned [elsewhere] the "psychological" framework which limits Jamesian point of view. Now we must go even further and grasp "psychology" as a particular episteme that includes within itself, alongside the appropriate blueprints of normal mental machinery, a fascination with the data of the abnormal and psychopathological as well, one that envelops Dostoyevsky and Krafft-Ebing, and for which this particular "notation" of Conrad—extreme stress under crisis coupled with sleepiness—becomes an "insight" and a valuable note for the file.

But such a passage can also be read quite differently, and this is the moment to register the peculiar affinities of Conrad's work with certain of the themes of Sartrean existentialism, of which the obsession with treason and betrayal and the fascination with torture (compare the Monygham sections of *Nostromo* with analogous sequences in *Morts sans sépulture*) are only the most superficial. Such themes evidently find their source in the common patrimony of Nietzschean nihilism and may in both cases be seen as a rather more consequent effort to imagine what kind of things are really possible if God is dead. The structural affinities between these two otherwise very different bodies of work must be ultimately sought in the nature of the concrete social situation they address. The juxtaposition of Conrad's work with existentialism, however, needs a further initial clarification: I have indeed already implied the need to distinguish between a properly existential "metaphysic"—in other words, a set of propositions about the "meaning of life," even where the latter is declared in fact to be "the absurd"—and that more properly existential analytic, found principally in Heidegger and Sartre, which, an offshoot and a development of certain phenomenological explorations, lays out a whole anatomy of lived time, action, choice, emotion, and the like. The former, the metaphysic, is an ideology; the latter can be used ideologically, but is not necessarily in itself ideological. The distinction is one between showing that there is never any irreducible temporal present or presence at the heart of a project, and concluding, from the demonstration that action is itself hollow and unreal. Both "existentialisms" are present in Conrad's work; but it is the latter, the existential analytic, that we will be concerned with in the present section.

It should be clear that I am neither suggesting an influence of Conrad on Sartre, nor, inversely, making a case for Conrad as Sartre's precursor in this or that area. What we can argue at most is that there are objective preconditions for working out a particular thought system or thematics, and that the superficial similarity of two quite different works from different moments and spaces of the recent European past ought to direct our attention first to the similarity of the social situations and historical conditions in which, as symbolic gestures, they are meaningful. We ought therefore to make a first step by trying to understand the historical conditions of possibility of the existential analytic—a project that, whatever it tells us about Conrad, would be the start of a more concrete historical regrounding of Sartre's work than has been done so far (see Lukács's book on existentialism, with its clumsy mediations, for an object lesson in how not to do this particular job). But the methodological resistance to a symptomal or sociological regrounding of technical philosophy is far greater than to similar operations in the areas of culture and ideology; that technical philosophy has historical preconditions is a view of the history of philosophy which has never adequately been worked out, indeed which the cruder Marxian efforts (like that of Lukács just mentioned) have tended to discredit.

Yet it seems clear that we are already in a position to construct a historical and social subtext able to naturalize or make more plausible the otherwise peculiar experience of moments of action like Jim's escape from the courtyard, in which the act itself suddenly yawns and discloses at its heart a void which is at one with the temporary extinction of the subject. (Compare, in *Nostromo*, Mrs. Gould's brief loss of consciousness in the proposal scene, and Decoud's unconsciousness after writing the letter: "he swayed over the table as if struck by a bullet"; not to speak of his suicide: "the stiffness of the fingers relaxes, and the lover of Antonia Avellanos rolled overboard without having heard the cord of silence snap in the solitude of the Placid Gulf, whose glittering surface remained untroubled by the fall of his body."

What we are witnessing in such passages is essentially the emergence of the once hegemonic but now antiquated modernist experience of temporality: to interrogate the objective conditions of possibility of representations like these is to ask what the social and historical preconditions are for an experience of time "as a still cord stretched to the breaking point," an experience in which "natural" or *naturwüchsige* temporality, at first bracketed as a purely formal "unity of apperception" (Kant), then as though by way of some inexplicable muscular relaxation in the prospective and retrospective projections that bind future and past to this present of time, is suddenly seen to shatter like glass into random instants. To construct the subtext of that technical Sartrean and Heideggerian interrogation of time (the former essentially considering its active form in the project and the choice, the latter its passive dimension as the suffering of mortal finitude), we must identify and reestablish the mediation of a concrete experience of temporal activity which—the specific precondition required for the development of this or that technical philosophical investigation—may then itself be studied as a social and historical phenomenon in its own right. The point is thus less the "truth" of the philosophical description—our condemnation to be free, the discontinuity of time, ultimately even, if one likes, the absurdity of natural or organic life and of being itself—which every modern individual is surely prepared to accept as such: it is rather the situation which suddenly allows the veil to be ripped away from this intolerable ontological bedrock, and imposes it on consciousness as the ultimate lucidity ("I want to see how much I can bear," Weber wrote of a similarly unpleasant vocation for truth). As for the relationship of Marxism to such descriptions, it would surely be preferable not to substitute edifying sermons for them: that life is meaningless is not a proposition that need be inconsistent with Marxism, whose affirmation is the quite different one that History is meaningful, however absurd organic life may happen to be. The real issue is not the propositions of existentialism, but rather their charge of affect: in future societies people will still grow old and die, but the Pascalian wager of Marxism lies elsewhere, namely in the idea that death in a fragmented and individualized society is far more frightening and anxiety-laden than in a genuine community, in which dying is something that happens to the group more intensely than it happens to the individual subject. The hypothesis is that time will be no less structurally empty, or to use a current version, presence will be no less of a structural and ontological illusion, in a future communal social life, but rather that this particular "fundamental revelation of the nothingness of existence" will have lost its sharpness and pain and be of less consequence.

At any rate, this abstract structure of temporality clearly cannot emerge until the older traditional activities, projects, rituals through which time was experienced, and from which it was indistinguishable, have broken down. We are discussing a process of abstraction whereby, among many other things, a supreme abstract form slowly appears which is called that of Time itself, and which then holds out the mirage of some pure and immediate experience of itself. But as Kant showed (and in a different sense Hume before him), such temporality is not an object of experience but only a pure form, so that the failure to replace its nature as an abstraction—the reality of Bergson's physical or clock time—with some plenitude of experience—the mirage of Bergson's full or lived time—is scarcely surprising, even though it may have disastrous consequences for the individual subject.

My argument is, then, that the questions raised in Jim's apparent quest for self-knowledge—whether he was a coward and why, and the related Sartrean problem of whether cowardice is thus something that characterizes his very being, or whether it would be possible in some analogous situation, to choose otherwise—these ethical questions which turn around the nature of freedom are in fact (as in *Being and Nothingness*) something like a structural pretext for the quite different examination of what an act and what a temporal instant really are: when does the act happen, how much preparation is necessary, how far do you have to go in it before it suddenly "takes" and becomes irrevocable, is it then infinitely divisible like the sprint-lengths of the hare, or of Zeno's arrow, and if not, then (the other face of Zeno's paradox) how could that single hard ultimate indivisible atom which is the instant of action ever come into being in the first place?

It has not been sufficiently observed that the very situation which will become symbolically invested and privileged for Jim—jumping into a lifeboat, fleeing the doomed *Patna*—is one to which, in its empty form, he has already been sensitized. The episode is not, therefore, an example of a moral illustration, that "simple form" or molecular genre which Jolles calls the *casum*, a vehicle for the debate and exercise of all of those ethical questions which we have here regarded as diversionary rather than irrelevant. Jim's trauma is, on the contrary, quite literally that and is constructed on the basis of an initial *repetition*. There was indeed an earlier scene that contained the elements of this one: lifeboat, people in distress, hesitation at the abyss of the instant and on the brink of the leap to freedom. The point is that in that earlier scene Jim *failed* to jump:

> Jim felt his shoulder gripped firmly. "Too late, youngster." The captain of the ship laid a restraining hand on that boy, who seemed on the point of leaping overboard, and Jim looked up with the pain of conscious defeat in his eyes. The captain smiled sympathetically. "Better luck next time. This will teach you to be smart."

So the cutter returns without Jim with its rescued survivors, and an alter ego wins the glory and the satisfaction of celebrating his own heroism ("Jim thought it a pitiful display of vanity"). No wonder, then, that at the climactic moment of decision in the *Patna* crisis—the cutter dancing ready below, people in imminent danger, Jim poised "as if I had been on the top of a tower"—"instinctively" Jim corrects his earlier mistake and this time "does the right thing." The longing for the second chance, for the return of a situation in which you can prove yourself, this time triumphantly, is, when it declares itself in Jim's agony after the *Patna* episode and his trial, merely the repetition of a repetition: the real second chance, in the event the only one, is the *Patna* crisis itself, in which Jim is now given the unexpected opportunity to complete his long-suspended act, and to land in the cutter over which he was poised so many years before.

It is of course now exactly the wrong decision; my point is, however, that this "irony," if we must call it that, is incommensurable either with the various "stable ironies" of satire and comedy, or with those other more disturbingly "unstable" ones of Jamesian or Flaubertian point of view. If irony is the right word, then we must distinguish between those ironies, which remain locked in the categories of the individual subject (either more objective ethical judgments, or more solipsistic "psychological" experiences within the monad) and this one, which is transindividual and more properly historical in character, but by some ideological misunderstanding projected back onto individual experience. This kind of irony is that of the "lessons of history," from which one is said to learn, for example, that they teach no lessons; it is the irony of reequipping oneself better to wage the previous war, for which one was so grievously unprepared, with the result that one is equally unprepared, but in a new way, to fight the following one. Such irony is, if you like, a negative version of the Hegelian "ruse of reason," and one which in this form is relatively cyclical and has no content (the latter would begin to emerge only when in a determinate historical situation we ask why the French general staff learned the lessons of 1870 so well that they had to unlearn them in 1914, and so on). The value of *Nostromo*, however, will lie for us in its attempt to pose this question all over again, yet this time with concrete content, a remarkable and form-transfiguring effort at lifting this entire problematic of the empty act up to the level of collective experience. For, as we shall see [elsewhere], *Nostromo* is, like *Lord Jim*, the interrogation of a hole in time, an act whose innermost instant falls away—proving thus at once irrevocable and impossible, a source of scandal and an aporia for contemplation. But the contemplation of *Nostromo* is a meditation on History.

That of *Lord Jim* remains stubbornly deflected onto the problematic of the individual act, and puts over and over again to itself questions that cannot be answered. The analytical interrogation of Jim's climactic moment indeed shows that nothing was there: " 'I had jumped . . . ' he checked himself, averted his gaze. . . . 'It seems,' he added.'' There is no present tense of the act, we are forever always before or after it, in past or future tenses, at the stage of the project or those of the consequences. The existential investigation has been rigorously prosecuted, but ends up in neither truth nor metaphysics, but in philosophical paradox.

At least for Jim himself. For however impossible the problem of the act may be at the level of the individual subject, it is evident that the social at once washes back across it, to transform it utterly. Here the focus on the existential problematic alters, or rather it becomes clear that there were always two problematics: the technical philosophical one, what we have called the existential analytic—Roquentin's "discovery" of being in *La Nausée*, with all the unavoidable results for himself as an individual subject— and that quite different matter which is the relationship of the social institution—the bourgeoisie of Bouville—and its structures of legitimation to this shattering discovery, and to the scandal of the asocial individual. Conrad pretends to tell us the story of an individual's struggle with his own fear and courage; but he knows very well that the real issues are elsewhere, in the social example Jim cannot but set, and the demoralizing effect of

Jim's discovery of Sartrean freedom on the ideological myths that allow a governing class to function and to assert its unity and legitimacy: thus Brierly, Jim's judge, whose own suicide thereby becomes a social gesture and a class abdication rather than that existential discovery of nothingness that it has so often been interpreted to be:

> "We aren't an organized body of men, and the only thing that holds us together is just the name for that kind of decency. Such an affair destroys one's confidence. A man may go pretty near through his whole sea-life without any call to show a stiff upper lip. But when the call comes.

Nor is Marlow's reading any different, when at the inconspicuous turn of some elaborate sentence he blurts out his astonishment at his own interest in "an occurrence which, after all, concerned me no more than as a member of an obscure body of men held together by a community of inglorious toil and by fidelity to a certain standard of conduct." But the body of men thus held together in the ideological cohesion of class values which cannot without peril be called into question is not merely the confraternity of the sea; it is the ruling class of the British Empire, the heroic bureaucracy of imperial capitalism which takes that lesser, but sometimes even more heroic, bureaucracy of the officers of the merchant fleet as a figure for itself. Here, more even than in the practice of a Flaubertian verbal aesthetic, Conrad's work finally becomes contiguous to the elaborate presentation and self-questioning of the British aristocratic bureaucracy in Ford's *Parade's End*, and uses much the same anecdotal form of social *scandal* to deconceal social institutions otherwise imperceptible to the naked eye. In both works, therefore, the existential "extreme situation" (the *Patna's* bulkhead, World War I) is less a laboratory experiment designed to expose the inner articulation of the act and of the instant than the precondition for the revelation of the texture of ideology.

But if this is what *Lord Jim* is really all about, then it only remains to ask why nobody thinks so, least of all Conrad himself; it remains to raise the last but exceedingly troublesome formality of the reality of the appearance, the structural origins of a misreading which is at once error and objective reality. Our reading of this novel had been based on—and has perhaps tended to confirm—a model of modernism according to which the latter is grasped as canceled realism, as a negation of "realistic content" which, like a Hegelian *Aufhebung*, continues to bear that content, crossed out and lifted up all at once, within itself. In short, it is evidently wrong to imagine, as Lukács sometimes seems to do, that modernism is some mere ideological distraction, a way of systematically displacing the reader's attention from history and society to pure form, metaphysics, and experiences of the individual monad; it is all those things, but they are not so easy to achieve as one might think. The modernist project is more adequately understood as the intent, following Norman Holland's convenient expression, to "manage" historical and social, deeply political impulses, that is to say, to defuse them, to prepare substitute gratifications for them, and the like. But we must add that such impulses cannot be managed until they are aroused; this is the delicate part of the modernist project, the place at which it must be realistic in order in another moment to recontain that realism which it has awakened.

The burden of our reading of *Lord Jim* has been to restore the whole socially concrete subtext of late nineteenth-century rationalization and reification of which this novel is so powerfully, and on so many different formal levels, the expression and the Utopian compensation alike. Now we must turn to the mechanisms that ensure a structural displacement of such content, and that provide for a built-in substitute interpretive system whereby readers may, if they so desire—and we do all so desire, to avoid knowing about history!—rewrite the text in more inoffensive ways. The two strategies of containment which are constructed for this purpose are clearly both on some level ideologies, and they might well be examined as such. In the present instance, however, they are narrative projections of ideology, narrative strategies that have as their common aim the rewriting of a narrative whose dynamics might otherwise elude categories of the ethical and of the individual subject. Yet, as we have seen, the contents of *Lord Jim* are themselves heterogeneous, and are drawn from the seemingly unrelated dimensions of the microscopic (reified time, desacralized action) and the macroscopic (history and praxis). It is therefore appropriate that not one, but two distinct strategies of containment should be evolved in order to manage these two distinct sources of scandal and of ideological challenge.

The two strategies in question will therefore take forms we will characterize as metaphysical and melodramatic respectively; they aim to recontain the content of the events of Jim's narrative by locating "responsible parties" and assigning guilt. We have indeed already discussed the first of these strategies, the metaphysical, which projects a proto-existential metaphysic by singling out Nature, and in particular the sea—what crushes human life—as that ultimate villain against whom Jim must do anthropomorphic battle to prove himself. Nature in this personalized sense is fundamental if Jim's quest is to remain a matter of courage and fear, rather than that quite different thing we have shown it to be in the preceding section. This is not to say that people do not drown or that the sea is not frightening, but rather that any genuine existentialism would have to unravel itself and if nature is genuinely meaningless, would, in order to be consequent with itself, have painstakingly to undo all those anthropomorphic impressions of some "true horror behind the appalling face of things," "something invisible, a directing spirit of perdition that dwelt within, like a malevolent soul in a detestable body."

But Jim is not destroyed at sea, and to prove oneself in this sense always seems to require a human adversary (see the analogous displacements back from nature to human agency in *The End of the Tether* and *Typhoon*). Thus, if the second part of the novel is to retrieve or ideologically to "resolve" what the first part so implacably laid out in the form of a dilemma, we must have recourse to the rather different strategy of melodrama, where the malevolent agency of Nature is replaced by that of man, in the person of Gentleman Brown.

The problem is the "motivation" of this device: how to imagine and to cause readers to accredit a motive for this remorseless pursuit of Jim at the very moment of his triumph? But as we showed [elsewhere], such a motivation is available everywhere in late nineteenth-century ideology, devised initially as a psychological explanation of the revolt of mobs, but also for the revolutionary vocation of disaffected intellectuals, and then more largely applied to the presentation of daily life generally, and to the discrediting of the political impulse in particular: this is, of course, the concept of *ressentiment*, of which Conrad is by way of being the epic poet. There is not a single work of his (although here too *Nostromo* is uniquely privileged and almost an exception) in which the typical, gratuitously malevolent bearer of this diseased passion does not lie in wait for the innocent and unsuspecting. Indeed, the great political novels, *Under Western Eyes* and *The Secret Agent*—as powerful counterrevolutionary tracts in their own ways as the masterpieces of Dostoyevsky or Orwell—emit the message of *ressentiment* (and its role as the true source of all revolutionary vocation) so obsessively that they betray their own inner dynamic: the concept of *ressentiment* being, as I have observed earlier, itself the product of the feeling in question.

This is not to say that Gentleman Brown is not a powerful figure, although even his single-minded nihilistic power depends on a rather complicated character system, whereby it is the lesser *homme de ressentiment*, Cornelius, who draws off everything that is grotesque about this passion to himself, thus leaving a purer vision of evil and energy for Jim's worthier and more absolute adversary:

> The others were merely vulgar and greedy brutes, but he seemed moved by some complex intention. He would rob a man as if only to demonstrate his poor opinion of the creature.

> There was in the broken, violent speech of that man, unveiling before me his thoughts with the very hand of Death upon his throat, an undisguised ruthlessness of purpose, a strange vengeful attitude towards his own past, and a blind belief in the righteousness of his will against all mankind, something of that feeling which could induce the leader of a horde of wanderng cut-throats to call himself proudly the Scourge of God.

> I had to bear the sunken glare of his fierce crow-footed eyes, . . .
> reflecting how much certain forms of evil are akin to madness,
> derived from intense egoism, inflamed by resistance, tearing the
> soul to pieces, and giving factitious vigor to the body.

In such powerful rhetoric, we can sense something of the violent displacement that must be done to narrative and to its *actants* to produce what we may call the effect of melodrama, and to conjure up the mythic feeling of the villain—so archaic and historically ugly a feeling, which has its genealogy deep in immemorial lynchings and pogroms, in the expulsion of the scapegoat and the ritual curse. It is mind-cleansing to juxtapose with this self-perpetuating vision of evil the great Brechtian lines on the mask of the Japanese demon, with its swollen veins and hideous grimace

> all betokening
> What an exhausting effort it takes
> To be evil.

". . . A Great Blue Triumphant Cloud"—*The Adventures of Sherlock Holmes*

Stephen Knight

No literary figure has a stronger hold on the public imagination than Sherlock Holmes. The name is a synonym for a detective; he has been parodied, imitated and recreated in all media with great success. The triumph of the figure made Conan Doyle wealthy, but forced him to keep writing Holmes's adventures and discuss him in public when he much preferred other topics. These pressures are irresistible proof of real social meaning in the stories. The embarrassing success depended on the hero's power to assuage the anxieties of a respectable, London-based, middle-class audience. The captivated readers had faith in modern systems of scientific and rational enquiry to order an uncertain and troubling world, but feeling they lacked these powers themselves they, like many audiences before them, needed a suitably equipped hero to mediate psychic protection.

When Doyle was trying to make a living as a doctor he took up freelance writing to earn more—the artistic activities of his male relatives were a stimulus and a model. He had some success with short stories and as a writer in search of sales he naturally enough came upon the detective story. In *Memories and Adventures* he recalls:

> At this time I first thought of a detective—it was about 1886. I had been reading some detective stories and it struck me what nonsense they were, to put it mildly, because for getting the solution of the mystery, the authors always depended on some coincidence. This struck me as not a fair way of playing the game, because the detective ought really to depend for his successes on something in his own mind and not on merely adventitious circumstances which do not, by any means, always occur in real life.

From *Form and Ideology in Crime Fiction.* © 1980 by Stephen Knight. Indiana University Press, 1980.

Doyle has two premises: the rational scientific idea that events are really linked in an unaccidental chain, and the individualistic notion that a single inquirer can—and should—establish the links. He domesticates these ideas by his nerveless style and familiar asides—"to put it mildly," "by any means"; and he uses game language to make an ethical faith in this ideology seem both pleasant and natural. Doyle's ability to popularise and naturalise rational individualism runs through the stories and is central to their success.

When he fashioned a figure to carry his meaning he turned, like many others who have drifted out of religion, to an academic intellectual model. He thought of his own outstanding teacher, Dr Joseph Bell, who gave demonstrations of "deduction," diagnosing from mere observation his patients' characteristics as well as their illnesses. Even the physique of Holmes owes something to Bell. There may have been a stage when Doyle thought of making his inquirer a doctor. In his diary he records his reading of Emile Gaboriau's *M. Lecoa*, obviously one of the novels he hoped to surpass. On the same page he sketches the history of an army doctor, much like that given to Watson in the opening of *A Study in Scarlet*. It would have been odd for Doyle to conceive of his narrator before his hero; the implication that a doctor detective preceded Holmes fits Adrian Conan Doyle's statement that he had seen a draft of *A Study in Scarlet* which did not contain Holmes. It may also explain the curiously forceful name, Ormond Sacker, given to the Watson figure in a surviving note which sketches in the first details of the emerging figure of Holmes—who was then christened "Sherrinford."

When Doyle did decide on a detective hero, the medical link remained. Holmes is neither a languid amateur like Dupin nor a professional policeman like Lecoq; his position as a consulting detective is parallel to that of a medical specialist—and this is what Doyle then aspired to be. By the time he started the short stories he had set up as an eye specialist in Devonshire Place, round the corner from Baker Street. Holmes was a heightened version of Doyle's own ambitions; a man of science, acting independently, serving the community. Watson was a deliberately lowered version of Doyle himself, humourless and plodding but full of sound virtues. Between them Doyle would realise the virtues he, like many of his class and time, had most faith in—those of middle-class morality and individualised rationality.

Another model is Robert Louis Stevenson. His influence has not been noticed very often; unlike Poe and Gaboriau, Doyle does not make Holmes refer to him, presumably because Stevenson wrote no specifically detective stories. *The Rajah's Diamond* and *The Dynamiter* were published with success in 1882 and 1885 respectively and a good deal of plot material for the first two long stories came from them. More generally, Doyle borrowed their mood and setting: they showed young professional men encountering crime, surprises and love in modern London under the overall protection and guidance of the aristocratic, all-knowing and deeply ethical Prince Florizel of *The Suicide Club*, now made more accessible as the *patron* of a

Soho cigar-divan. Such stories had obvious appeal to the young men who had, as economists now put it, disposable personal income. The first Holmes adventures, *A Study in Scarlet* and *The Sign of Four,* convey a less whimsical version of Stevenson's pattern. In them Watson discovers London, a wife and the amazing and comforting authority of Holmes. These publications did not have Stevenson's success, but then they did not appear in London periodicals; when Doyle had a major magazine outlet his less excitable, better controlled and more plainly ethical fables of adventure against disorder in London were to eclipse what Stevenson had achieved.

In the two novellas Doyle developed the characters of Holmes and Watson, the "deductive" method, and the blend of a material and exciting presentation that was to be important to his success. In structure these first two works differ from the short stories which fully created the Holmes phenomenon. With their length and their retrospective elements they are slower and less organically united, less swiftly converging on a climax of revelation than the later adventures. The retrospective pattern derives from Gaboriau, and like him the novellas present the crime as being a largely justified punishment for past immorality. As a result they tend, like Stevenson's tales, to be a sensationalist inspection of crime from the outside, not the internalised realisation of aberrance that will appear later. The novellas are lively and original developments on the earlier patterns, but they do not fully dramatise the ideology so pervasive and so important in Doyle's great success. A grasp of the meaning of the Holmes phenomenon must come from a study of the material that first gripped a mass audience, and this chapter will concentrate on *The Adventures of Sherlock Holmes,* the collected reprint of the first twelve short stories.

By early 1891 Doyle had moved on from the Holmes novellas to historical novels. *Micah Clarke* had been well received and *The White Company,* then appearing in *The Cornhill Magazine,* satisfied him deeply. Historical moralism was to be his mode. But these novels demanded slow research and to supplement his meagre income as an eye consultant Doyle turned back to Sherlock Holmes and submitted two short stories to the new and successful magazine *The Strand.* Greenhough Smith, the editor, was very impressed; he later recalled that he ran to the office of George Newnes, the proprietor, and told him excitedly this was the work of the best short-story writer since Poe.

Newnes had established himself with *Tit-Bits,* a weekly paper which culled the world of news and literature for small interesting items. It aimed at the growing audience of literate but hurried readers who sought diversion and a sense of contact with a world that seemed increasingly complex. Then he moved on to *The Review of Reviews* which offered guidance through the world of serious periodical literature for those without the time and probably the expertise to master it. Newnes's strength already was to compress and popularise material for an urban audience aware of modern forces but unable to handle them adequately.

He struck his goldmine when, aiming between his earlier efforts, he designed a new magazine that had a bourgeois, middle-brow content and a satisfyingly modern format. *The Strand* started in 1890 and the first issue sold 300,000 copies. It cost sixpence (quite a small sum compared with other journals), was widely distributed through railway bookstalls to catch the commuting white-collar market, and was strikingly up-to-date in form. Newnes imitated the rising American magazines by having an illustration on every opening, using newly developed photographic and photo-etching techniques to lighten and dramatise the text.

The contents of early copies define the magazine's ideology: prominent are the biographies of successful men, stories about courage and adventure, features about new machines. But there are also stories that realise bourgeois sentimental morality, and sections for housewives and children regularly occur. The magazine was to be read and taken home by the white-collar man who worked in London. It was a central piece of middle-class ideological literature, oriented towards the family and respectable success in life. The cover of the magazine brought form and content into a masterly union: an etching from a photograph of The Strand itself, taken just where the head office was located. The busy and then fashionable street had rich symbolic meaning: it stretched from the city where the purchasers mostly worked to the West End where they might one day aspire to live. The anxious, alienated, upwards-looking white-collar workers of the capital were caricatured in the Grossmith's tellingly titled *The Diary of a Nobody;* in *The Strand Magazine* they could find a validation of their morality and a prospect of all they could look forward to, in dreams at least.

There are many relations between the meaning of the Holmes stories and the world-view of *The Strand* and its purchasers. It is best to assess first how the form of the stories worked, how Doyle affectively created patterns that supported, even developed, the attitudes of his audience. With these formations in view, it will be easy to understand how the nature of the plot and detail shapes a problematic responding to the concerns of the audience and resolvable in comforting terms.

The titles of the short stories have the crisp materialism, the briskly objective, unemotive quality that Doyle first encapsulated in the title of *The Sign of Four*. This final version was itself just a little firmer and more mysterious than "The Sign of the Four," the title of the original American publication, commissioned by *Lippincott's Magazine*. Most of the short story titles are briskly specified: "The Beryl Coronet," "The Noble Bachelor," "The Blue Carbuncle." Some titles use a material but unexpected qualifier to create an enigma: "The Engineer's Thumb," "The Five Orange Pips," "The Speckled Band." The early titles "A Scandal in Bohemia," "A Case of Identity" and "The Boscombe Valley Mystery" include a less material term that suggests the genre of the stories. But they too have an objective aura, clearly abandoning the manipulative rhetoric Doyle sought in his first title "A Study in Scarlet." That was originally "A Tangled Skein," a weakly emotive title, and the final choice is reminiscent of Gaboriau's melodramas, especially *L'Affaire Lerouge* (although Lerouge is the murdered woman's surname). The rejection of this emotive element is quite conscious: in *The Sign of Four* Watson refers to the "somewhat fantastic title" of the previous adventure.

The early stories show a brisk attack from the beginning. Like *The Sign of Four* the first three adventures all use Sherlock Holmes's name in the opening sentence. The initial paragraphs are increasingly crisp and briefly suggestive. One of the motives is Doyle's conscious production of a series, encouraging regular purchase of the magazine; he assumed that readers of the later stories would know the established patterns and characters. But at the same time he wanted to grip the audience, plunge them into the matter with less of the narrator's comment than opens "A Scandal in Bohemia." The direct openings bring the hero into active involvement with problems, reducing his earlier aloof distance from the reader and his world. This effect is also created by the greater simplicity of the endings. In the two novellas and in "The Red-Headed League" Doyle continues Poe's pattern, giving his detective a final comment, separated from the action both by its lofty, judging tone and its foreign language. In "A Case of Identity" the comment is translated, and from then on they disappear; the final disengaging remarks, when they occur, are English and moralistic, not isolated pieces of intellectualism.

These features all tend to involve the hero in action, not isolate him in cerebration like Dupin. This model responds to the world-view of a basically uncerebral audience, and it is most fully created by the varied and dramatic action. The pace accelerates as Holmes comes to grips with his problem: the paragraph where he studies the King of Bohemia's notepaper is a fine example of a vigorous and object-dominated presentation which enacts the worldly involvement of the hero. Watson examines the paper and sees some letters in its watermark:

> "What do you make of that?" asked Holmes.
> "The name of the maker, no doubt; or his monogram, rather."
> "Not at all. The *G* with the small *t* stands for 'Gesellschaft,' which is the German for 'Company.' It is a customary contraction like our 'Co.' *P*, of course, stands for 'Papier.' Now for the *Eg*. Let us glance at our Continental Gazeteer."
> He took down a heavy brown volume from his shelves.
> "Eglow, Eglonitz—here we are, Egria. It is in a German-speaking country—in Bohemia, not far from Carlsbad. 'Remarkable as being the scene of the death of Wallenstein, and for its numerous glass factories and paper mills.' Ha, ha, my boy, what do you make of that?" His eyes sparkled, and he sent up a great blue triumphant cloud from his cigarette.

Details flow out, under the control of Holmes's supreme knowledge—did he know all the time, and just gave Watson a lesson in method? Or was he really looking something up? The passage does not make it clear: the method is a little clouded in mystery. Built into the passage are Holmes's special and amazing powers, and also information perfectly comprehensible to anyone with common sense. But the vitality of the passage, the expressive dynamism of the created personality, make us believe he has brought off a triumph. Where Poe expressed an almost prophetic mystery in the smoke that wreathed Dupin, Holmes's signal is of victory over a material enigma—and one located in notepaper, an object straight from the everyday experience of the white-collar worker.

The speed of the stories derives not only from a vigorous style. The fast-moving and interlocked plot has its own meanings. First, since nothing is accidental, and cause and effect control the relationship of events, the incidents converge with rapidity and increasing sureness on the climax of the story. This convergence brings all the satisfaction of organic unity, and true to the attitudes that lie behind the development of that structural pattern, discussed [elsewhere], the convergence is only made possible by the power of a single intelligence. The hero—and behind him the author—is the individual understanding and resolving contemporary problems, so realising in shapely and persuasive fictions the motives that led Doyle to deplore Gaboriau.

Doyle's plots are not only organic and rapid; they also present many puzzling incidents in a short space for hero and form to resolve. They are dense enough to seem valid representations of the packed experience of everyday life. Doyle knew well that full and tightly connected plot was essential to his success, saying accurately: "every story really needed as clear-cut and original a plot as a longish book would do." Many later crime novels use less actual puzzle-plotting than Doyle puts into six or seven thousand words. His action and dialogue are rarely extraneous to the mystery; the long sequences of description, comedy or emotion that fill out a novel by, for example, Dorothy Sayers are absent here. The brief sequences of characterisation or setting operate in close connection to the central mystery and this strict sense of relevance etches deeply the effect of the stories. Doyle recognised the importance of a tight, stylised manner when he wrote of "the compact handling of the plots" and said that Holmes's character "admits of no light or shade."

With a vigorous material style and a compressed, rapidly linked structure, the emphasis of the presentation falls all the more sharply on events and objects. These tend to be less exotic and essentially melodramatic than the phenomena of the novellas; even the royal romance of the first story centres on nothing more recherché than a cabinet photograph, and the objects used for deduction—a watch, a typist's sleeve, a letter—make the superior powers of the detective operate in a very familiar and real world. It is not only the evidence of the detail itself that establishes this; Doyle presses the point through Holmes himself. "It has long been an axiom of mine that the little things are infinitely the most important" he tells Watson when discussing nothing further from the ordinary business world than a typewriter, in "A Case of Identity." The set of the stories towards enigmas of the ordinary world, materially presented, is given specific and authoritative expression by Holmes in the opening of the same story:

> We would not dare to conceive the things which are really mere commonplaces of existence. If we could fly out of that window hand in hand, hover over this great city, gently remove the roofs, and peep in at the queer things which are going on, the strange coincidences, the plannings, the cross purposes, the wonderful chains of events, working through generations, and leading to the most *outré* results, it would make all fiction with its conventionalities and foreseen conclusions most stale and unprofitable.

The passage is fascinatingly double in its tone. The image of flying and the notion of peering into other people's lives reveals an alienated intelligence dramatising its own isolated power; the romantic artistic consciousness is created, and ratifies itself not only in the image but also in the final reference to Shakespeare—and that to Hamlet himself, prince of alienated intelligence. Yet the interest is real, and the subtle mind elevates the everyday. The power of Holmes is not only to resolve the problems of ordinary life, but to make that life seem rich in itself, and therefore emotionally fulfilling.

A world is created where people enmeshed and to some extent daunted by the puzzling and the mundane nature of their experience can find comfort both in the Holmesian resolutions and in the aura of grandeur, the sheer heroism and enrichment he brings with him. In terms of epistemology we have a materialistic model, which can read off from physical data what has happened and what will happen. The succession of incidents in explained and necessary relationship to each other expresses the ideas of material causation and linear history so important to the Victorian worldview. The perception of these patterns by the heroic individual manages to balance those essentially deterministic attitudes with the basically contradictory idea of the individual as noble and free, untrammelled by the laws of material causation. A deeply satisfying and heavily ideological view of the world is made in the stories by concealing the fissure between heroism and materialism; this illusory resolution will be discussed further in terms of content but it is brought to life in the crisp and compressed creation of those two forces by Doyle's mastery of lively and suggestive writing.

The structuring of the narrative units within an organic, convergent model is in some ways simple, in others quite complex; here too the effect is dual. At its barest, analysis of the Holmes story would have three parts: relation, investigation and resolution of mysterious events. This reveals an unchanging basic structure, but, like a lot of structural analysis, tells us little about what the stories mean as they are communicated. In the early Holmes stories there is surprising flexibility in presenting relation, investigation and resolution. Not until later stories does a fixed pattern emerge, the structural system so well remembered. In that formula, the story opens with Holmes and Watson at Baker Street; a client arrives; Holmes deduces from the client's appearance; the problem is outlined; Holmes discusses the case with Watson after the client leaves; investigation follows—usually some is conducted by Holmes alone, but most occurs at the scene of the crime with Watson and the police looking on; Holmes identifies what has happened, normally in action of some kind; Holmes explains all to Watson, back at Baker Street. This formula is used in the skilful pastiches by Adrian Conan Doyle and John Dickson Carr, but it is by no means a constant pattern in *The Adventures*, nor even in the second book of stories, *The Memoirs of Sherlock Holmes*.

As you read through *The Adventures*, the elements often seem familiar but there is no sense of formulaic repetition; each story has something different in its structure or in the context of some of the structural units. The effect is much more lively, varied and interesting than the usual re-membered model which is established in the later collections. Two of *The Adventures* never go to Baker Street at all—"The Boscombe Valley Mystery" and "The Man with the Twisted Lip." These variations are outside the basic pattern of relation, investigation, resolution and include them, but within those bare categories there is also much variety.

The dominant pattern in relation is for the client to explain what has happened, but in three cases Holmes himself outlines the problem—"The Boscombe Valley Mystery," "The Blue Carbuncle" and "The Man with the Twisted Lip." Investigation has a whole set of variable features. It can be very sketchy, when Holmes thinks about events taking their own course, as in "The Five Orange Pips," "The Man with the Twisted Lip" and "The Copper Beeches." Or he may just put himself in the right place to find the answer, as in "A Scandal in Bohemia" and "The Blue Carbuncle." Other stories present detailed investigation and so approach the later "clue-puz-zle" where a great amount of detected data is put before us, but only the detective can see the pattern that gives the answer—"The Red-Headed League," "The Boscombe Valley Mystery" and "The Speckled Band" are of this sort, and "A Case of Identity" as well, though in it most of the data comes out of the relation.

If the intensity of investigation varies, its methods also have consid-erable flexibility. There are three types: armchair analysis at Baker Street, often with the use of reference books; Holmes goes alone to make inquiries, sometimes in disguise; Holmes and Watson go together to the scene of the crime. No story in *The Adventures* has all three of these methods; most have two, a few rely entirely on a joint field investigation. You gain a sense of a common pool of methods, of familiar patterns being re-enacted, but the reader of *The Strand* would not have found this month's story quite like the previous one. This commercial skill has wider meaning. Holmes's abil-ities are flexible enough to make him a convincing respondent to the variety and difficulty of the problems he tackles; the varying form creates an aura of spontaneity, of resourceful vigour that strengthens the hero's authority.

The resolutions of the stories are formally more similar than the investigations, but two differences can be seen, one of context, one of content. As to the first, five of the stories are resolved at Baker Street and the dénouement of the others occurs in the field. This is merely a non-significant varying of pattern, but the second, contentual variation has considerable impact on meaning. In some stories Holmes is not fully triumphant: he understands the crime but has not brought the criminal to justice. At the end of "The Five Orange Pips" comes a report that the ship carrying the criminals has sunk; justice has been done, but not through Holmes's hands, and the story also show his failure when John Openshaw is murdered after consulting him. This reduced control by the hero appears in "A Scandal in Bohemia" and "The Engineer's Thumb" where the perpetrators escape. This does not necessarily weaken the hero's authority: an analysis of the content-meaning of these endings will be offered later, but here it should be noted that Holmes's relative uncertainty can itself be an element of variety in the narrative.

The overall structural pattern is one of fairly intense variation within an unchanging order; in no story do the three basic units, relation, investigation and resolution, change position. Even in "The Man with the Twisted Lip," where Holmes has worked on the case off-stage for days before explaining the problem to Watson, his successful investigation occurs in the story, as he sits up all night and smokes his way to the resolution. Overriding order and intrinsic variation are common enough features of popular story, of course. V. I. Propp has shown in his well-known analysis of Russian folk tales that "functions" (the controlling actions) come in the same order, and while some may be omitted, the normal series will continue in order from where the story picks it up. In this way Holmes's solitary investigation, if it occurs, will come before the climactic field investigation with Watson. The compulsive order causes some slightly odd plotting in "The Boscombe Valley Mystery," where Holmes has to visit a prison at night because fieldwork is scheduled for the next morning. This order creates the ideologically important meaning of a hero whose individual, isolated action in response to problems is always a means towards a social end; his lonely researches must be realised in the setting of a public inquiry, shared with Watson who represents the public, and with the ineffectual police authorities looking on. This rigid order emphasises the active movement of the story and hero from knowledge of a problem towards its resolution. A dynamic model of applied intelligence is created in the structure, quite different in its vigorous, engaged effect from the retrospective explanatory structures that Poe and Freeman (especially in his "reverse" stories) were led to create by their valuing of the quite isolated intelligence.

And if the permanence of structural order is meaningful, so is the consistent absence of a feature ever-present in fairy tale. The stories Propp discusses and most of those that have come down to us from the past have an essential "Provider" function. That is, as the hero is about to undertake his quest or has just started on it, a "Provider" gives him a magical object which will help him in a crisis. This is obviously present in the James Bond stories where the armourer gives the hero items of technological magic to rescue him from danger. The "Provider" helps heroes who need supernatural aid to bring order to a troubled world. But Holmes is his own provider: self-help, that great Victorian virtue, is embodied in his power to succeed with no more than his own abilities.

Skilful variation within the structural order itself emphasises that resourceful independent power. The emphasis may arise affectively, as from changes of location and from the variety in presenting the relation and the resolution; or it may be directly created by the varied ways of investigating. In both cases the strength and ideological force of the figure come together with the inventive variety to please the audience.

A modern audience's pleasure in innovation is not a free-floating phenomenon. The idea that originality in art is a virtue is itself modern, rising from the concept that the individual artist communicates something of a special, private and inventive nature. It also relates to the market-place situation of the artist, needing to distinguish one product from another to sell his wares for cash. The copyright act which recognised originality in law was passed to cover the situation of emerging market-artists like Hogarth: uniqueness was not sought or even much approved in earlier work, just as the idea that a human individual could triumph alone was not then entertained. Repetition formulae and supernatural assistance together are actively pursued and applauded in art outside the consciousness of bourgeois individualism, like the stories of Gaelic shanachies or the narratives of medieval chroniclers.

In its varied, original-seeming construction, in its materialist presentation and in its stylistic vitality Doyle's art found formal patterns that were valid fables about a problem-solving hero who works in a recognisable world with essentially graspable and credible rational methods. The linked plotting, the driving pace and the dominance of the hero over the action (patterns which were fully developed in *The Sign of Four*) have been compressed in a short story form to combine richness with speed into a mixture both ideologically satisfying and easily readable for people who bought *The Strand* and who subscribed to the values the stories ultimately dramatise and support. These values are specifically realised, the formal energies are channelled, by the selection and the details of content, and it is now appropriate to examine this process, starting with the characterisation of the hero himself.

The notes Doyle first jotted down about his detective establish some crucial features. Holmes has a private income of £400 a year—a decent, but not enormous sum, enabling him to live in reasonable comfort without relying on his chosen profession for support. He is in, but not enclosed by, the world of bourgeois professionalism. The notes also imply Holmes's arrogance and commanding nature: a brief piece of dialogue is given: " 'What rot is this,' I cried—throwing the volume petulantly aside." This forceful, quasiprofessional hero is qualified for success by his mastery of science. The opening pages of *A Study in Scarlet* made the point at length, but in the first short story Doyle works more subtly, realising these qualities in images rather than action. Watson describes Holmes as "the most perfect reasoning and observing machine that the world has seen." This power involves a certain distance from human normality; in particular, feeling would damage the scientific force: "Grit in a sensitive instrument, or a crack in one of his own high-power lenses, would not be more disturbing than a strong emotion in a nature such as his."

The importance of science—more exactly, of the aura of science—in Holmes's methods is well-known; it mobilises for the audience's fictional protection the contemporary idea that dispassionate science was steadily comprehending and so controlling the world. But Holmes's power does not only reside in his well-known romantic scientific insights. The steady collection and analysis of data was in itself the basis of nineteenth-century science and a strong feature of other areas of thought—such as Doyle's own beloved history. And Holmes, it is less well-known, is also a master of the data of his subject. He has collected thousands of cases, can remember them and see the patterns of similarity in new problems: this power is in itself part of the Victorian romance of knowledge. Holmes does not "deduce" in a vacuum; he understands through his materialist, association-based science the probable meanings of physical data and through the patterns of criminal action. This latter part of his armoury is, like his science, expressed in detail in *A Study in Scarlet* and touched on more lightly, but insistently, in the short stories.

The dispassionate isolation arising from Holmes's scientific powers meshes with his aloof, sometimes arrogant personal qualities. His drug-taking was, at that time, seen as an excitingly dangerous means of elevating and isolating the consciousness, closely bound up with the romantic artistic persona. His moody reveries, strangely atonal violin-playing, arrogant, dismissive tone to Watson are all other parts of the model for a superior being, a superman whose world differs from that of limited and often baffled people like Watson. The trenchant style Doyle gives to Holmes realises this aspect of his personality well, as does his occasional sarcasm, threatening Watson, and the audience, that he might cut himself adrift from their mundane realm. But he does not; Holmes is never the self-indulgent dandy American and French presentations of his figure have made of him, he is that familiar figure in English fable, the stern, distant yet ultimately helpful patronising hero.

The importance of this figure in nineteenth-century culture has been documented in W. E. Houghton's chapter on "Hero Worship" in *The Victorian Frame of Mind*. Great emotional value was found in an individual who seemed to stand against the growing collective forces of mass politics, social determinism and scientific, superindividual explanation of the world, all of which appeared as mechanistic threats to the free individual. A figure like Holmes, who treated all problems individualistically and who founded his power on the very rational systems which had inhumane implications was a particularly welcome reversal of disturbing currents. Aloofness, self-assertion, irritation with everyday mediocrity were not merely forgivable—they were necessary parts of a credible comforting hero.

The crucial device by which Doyle makes this figure so effective is the limit he sets to Holmes's distance. The passage quoted above, where Watson tells how this machine-like scientist avoids emotion, ends by almost reconciling him with ordinary human feeling: "And yet there was but one woman to him." The story tells how Irene Adler can not only match his skill, but inspire something suspiciously like affectionate admiration in the hero. The whole characterisation of Holmes contains many dualities of this sort, that assert both his isolation and his contact with normality. He chooses to be a lone agent, but he takes cases, neither a mundane policeman nor a self-gratifying amateur. He is a self-confessed Bohemian, yet he lives in busy professional London, not in a Dupin-like romantic hermitage. He shares his lodgings with Watson, being neither a solitary nor matched by a partner. For all their eccentricity his rooms are cosy, filled with masculine gadgets for comfort. He will not eat when the hunt is up, but good meals are available, with a decent English housekeeper to provide them. He travels in normal conveyances, not some special heroic vehicle, yet his movements are sudden and dramatic. His atonal violin playing can give way to amusing Watson with favourite sentimental pieces, and he is a keen concert-goer—for him music is both private incommunicable reverie and social activity. His chemistry is smelly and dangerous, but can be practical and applied. His explanatory language, for all its learned aura, remains materialist, never withdrawing into the idealist intellectualism of Dupin. He works alone, often in disguise, but will use agents and the street arabs of the Baker Street Irregulars, so revealing his demotic touch. His world is modern, real London, not some imagined or mistily foreign city.

These details make the critical link across the fissure between the special hero and the "dull routine of existence" that at his most isolative he claims to abhor. The action of the stories sets this dualism in motion. In "A Scandal in Bohemia" Holmes's reasoning is interwoven with active investigation, disguise, play-acting and the dramatic activity of smoke bombs and mock blood. The thoroughness with which Doyle makes Holmes a dual figure is clear when he examines his client in "A Case of Identity": "he looked her over in the minute and yet abstracted fashion which was peculiar to him." It is his special power to embrace both detail and analysis. The mixture of modes is constant and intimate: Doyle's hero is never bogged in mundanity or lost in etherealness. Doyle never lets the audience forget either aspect of the hero.

The special, distant features of Holmes's personality are threaded through the stories. He has a copy of Petrarch on the train in "The Boscombe Valley Mystery," he quotes Cuvier in "The Five Orange Pips." Yet neither writer is so abstruse to be unknown to the average reading man; the spread of science and the medieval tendency of much Victorian art made both figures known generally as the sort of thing knowledgeable people comprehended. The physical aloofness that authorises Holmes's greatest efforts is also touched on. He does not eat all day in "The Five Orange Pips," he thinks with his eyes firmly closed in "The Red-Headed League," he smokes all night in "The Man with the Twisted Lip."

Holmes's heroic quality is exerted in a professional direction. He accepts fees for his work, though only unusual rewards tend to be mentioned. But this mystification of his income does not mean he will not work for the public. Where Dupin's heroic action made him strangely, passively transformed, Holmes is enlivened when he engages with human problems. His eyes glitter on the chase in "The Boscombe Valley Mystery," they sparkle through the smoke when he cracks the enigma of the notepaper in "A Scandal in Bohemia." Activity is often quite hectic, even when he is following, rather than elucidating events. Withdrawal is the state in which he activates his special resources of knowledge and insight, but these episodes are only the inspiration and impetus for busy, involved implementation of that almost oracular knowledge.

Apart form Holmes's involvement in ordinary life there are many occasions when he openly shares the values of his clients. To the lady typist in "A Case of Identity" he shows "the easy courtesy for which he was remarkable." He often belittles his own ability with a proper English modesty and feels the threat of failure in a very native way. In "The Man with the Twisted Lip" he says "I think, Watson, that you are now standing in the presence of one of the most absolute fools in Europe. I deserve to be kicked fom here to Charing Cross." It is a demotic, physical, London-based self-deprecation. Holmes can feel restrained chagrin at a degree of failure; in "The Five Orange Pips" when he hears of John Openshaw's death " 'That hurts my pride, Watson,' he said at last. 'It is a petty feeling, no doubt, but it hurts my pride.' "

This human side of Holmes is shown in his deference to Irene Adler, and he often has attitudes like a normal man about London. As the King of Bohemia arrives at Baker Street, he says "A nice little brougham and a pair of beauties. A hundred and fifty guineas apiece. There's money in this case, Watson, if nothing else." And as he reads the biography of Irene Adler from his files he deduces her status as a retired mistress with a slightly prurient amusement: " 'Contralto hum. La Scala, hum. Prima Donna Imperial Opera of Warsaw, yes. Retires from operatic stage—ha. Living in London—quite so.' " We find in Holmes many signs of the "knowledge of the world" that he praises at the end of "A Case of Identity," and we also find disenchantment with aristocrats—a feature shared by many middle-class people, who felt both attraction and jealousy towards those of the undeniably upper-class. He is drily sharp to Lord St Simon in "The Noble Bachelor":

"I understand you have already managed several delicate cases of this sort, sir, though I presume that they were hardly from the same class of society."

"No, I am descending."

"I beg pardon?"

"My last client of the sort was a king."

But as the story develops we find this is not just an instinctive dislike of a lord; St Simon has dismissed a mistress with the inhumanity of the King of Bohemia. Holmes's rudeness turns out to be a moral evaluation, just as his ironic shaft at the King of Bohemia has a critical basis. The king asks of Irene Adler " 'Would she not have made an admirable queen? Is it not a pity she was not on my level?' " Holmes's reply has fine irony: " 'From what I have seen of the lady, she seems, indeed, to be on a very different level to your Majesty,' said Holmes coldly." It is highly likely that this royal figure, like that in "The Beryl Coronet" is a transparent disguise for the Prince of Wales. Holmes is the agent of middle-class feeling against the manipulative, immoral hedonism of aristocrats. Sir George Burnwell in "The Beryl Coronet" is another; he leads both son and daughter astray and, according to his suggestive name, is headed for the everlasting bonfire.

Holmes's power to evaluate is ratified by his wide experience as well as his personal authority. He is in touch with all levels of society. In "The Noble Bachelor" a letter from St Simon, the son of a duke, reminds Watson that the morning's letters came from a fishmonger and a tide-waiter, that is a beachcomber in the tidal mud of the Thames. The extraordinary breadth of his experience, the story suggests, is one of the sources for Holmes's insight, just as he can turn street urchins into an effective force of detectives.

This contact with the lower reaches of London life is really a rhetorical flourish on Doyle's part, not crucial to the plotting; it is an extension of the complex by which Holmes is partly an ordinary man, partly a very superior figure. A similar piece of rhetoric, taken effectively from Poe, is the simple-subtle paradox, as when Holmes speaks of "those simple cases which are so extremely difficult." These are finishing touches to the solidly created dual figure, aloof and yet available, who is constantly recreated and was clearly in Doyle's mind from the opening of the first story. The situation is put lucidly in "The Red-Headed League," when Holmes says " 'My life is spent in one long effort to escape the commonplaces of existence' " but he is reassured by Watson, high priest of the commonplace, " 'And you are a benefactor of the race.' " Doyle himself has sent up a cloud of triumphant characterisation, a smoky illusion concealing the real nature of detecting crime and the difficulty of controlling contemporary threats to order. To read further into the appropriateness of Doyle's image of Holmes, his cigarette smoke was blue, and the whole creation fulfils the implications of that colour in the period. The aura of chivalry, of patronising autocracy and essential conservatism is a pervasive feature of the heroic personality and its function.

The effect is not only Doyle's work. Sidney Paget's dramatic illustrations of the hero did much to create the incisive and consoling image. He provided the legendary deerstalker hat that naturalised Holmes's hunter-protector element, and by the time of "The Boscombe Valley Mystery" Doyle had altered his earlier description of Holmes's features to fit Paget's authoritative version. Paget's flair linked Doyle's imaginative creation to the exciting new force of the illustrated medium, and he caught exactly the aloof nobility and material bourgeois setting so important to the duality that is central to the power of Holmes as a figure. Paget used as his model his elder brother, in itself a relevant image of authoritative familial guidance. His brother was the man Newnes had meant to commission for the illustrations, but by a most irrational error the job went to Sidney instead. It is a fine revealing irony; inside the all explaining image are fragments of human chaos: beneath the production of the text lie the strains the text is dedicated to resolving.

The creation of Watson does not have the weight that the more overt feeling and greater length of the story gave him in "The Sign of Four." In the early stories Watson is married, but by various plot devices is with Holmes through most of the action. From "The Speckled Band" on Doyle goes back in time before Watson's wedding. This does not diminish him as the representative of family solidity and bourgeois morality: Doyle has settled down for a long series of stories and presumably did not want to explain each time how Holmes and his narrator came together.

Watson personifies the virtues of middle-class manhood: loyal, honest and brave—these features come out especially in "The Red-Headed League," "The Speckled Band" and "The Copper Beeches." Holmes explains all to him, and so to the audience, but Doyle avoids letting Watson stand as the presence of the audience in the story. His characterisation enables the reader to see him as a little foolish, and so to bypass him and construct the one-to-one relation with Holmes that the underlying individualist epistemology requires. Doyle achieves this delicate and important effect largely through a careful modelling of Watson's voice. At times it is a hopeful imitation of Holmes's decisiveness, a deferential recognition of his mastery; but he can also be sharp enough to remind Holmes of the values of common humanity. But between these two tones that indicate the limits of Holmes's dual personality lies the tone that is Doyle's triumph, the one that Watson adopts to comment at a story's beginning. It is the voice of a mildly self-satisfied bourgeois who feels he has a mastery of things: a slightly wordy style, a little too much insertion of the first person pronoun and his own self-conscious opinions, along with a delicately banal rhythm. The opening of "The Beryl Coronet" is a good example: " 'Holmes,' said I, as I stood one morning in our bow-window looking down the street, 'here is a madman coming along. It seems rather sad that his relatives should allow him out alone.' " The fussy inversion of "said I," the flat prepositional phrases that follow, the carefully limited "rather sad," all sketch the figure with almost subliminal effect. The reader can like him, admire his virtues, but also can suspect the situation is more complex and threatening that Watson can really handle. The hero's greater incisiveness is needed to control anxieties. The closeness Watson has to Holmes links the detective firmly to the actual bourgeois world; the crucial difference between them, the definite diminishing of Watson through his own mouth are the features which make the hero distant from and also immediately, personally accessible to an anxious, individualist bourgeois audience.

The major effect of Doyle's characterisation is a duality of the familiar and the exotic: this exists between Watson and Holmes and within Holmes himself, as has just been demonstrated. It is no surprise, then, to see that the methods by which Holmes solves problems are themselves dual in effect, a set of fairly simple procedures within an aura of elaboration. In the novellas Doyle carefully described "The Science of Deduction"—a chapter heading in each book—and established Holmes's credibility as a master of scientific and criminological knowledge. Then he went on to show him making fairly straightforward, commonsense deductions. In the short stories a similar illusion is at work, but the higher qualifications are not clearly realised. There are general statements like "He was still, as ever, deeply attracted by the study of crime, and occupied his immense faculties and extraordinary powers of observation in following out those clues, and clearing up those mysteries, which had been abandoned as hopeless by the official police." This appears in the opening of "A Scandal in Bohemia" and sets the tone for the series in *The Strand*. Later on, in "The Five Orange Pips," Watson mentions "those peculiar qualities which my friend possessed in so high a degree." Less stress is laid on science and information, more on "those deductive methods of reasoning by which he achieved such remarkable results" (in "The Engineer's Thumb") or "severe reasoning from cause to effect" (in "The Copper Beeches").

Doyle gives this process the elevated name of "deduction" and claims it is both highly scientific and also a means of ordering the confusing data of experience. Both of these claims are illusory. Firstly, if Holmes really were finding patterns in facts he would be practising "induction": in reality he has a knowledge of what certain phenomena *will* mean, and is practising deduction, that is drawing from a set of existent theories to explain new events. Doyle's wish to protect old values, ideas and their social setting is innate to his hero's methodology; the weakness of his own reason is clear in misnaming his hero's methodology. The dress of modern materialist science is used for conservative thinking, for a failure to face the real, disorderly experience of data: Doyle's own process and the needs of the bourgeois audience faced with threats of disorder are quite the same.

But, secondly, even the genuine, conservatively based deduction that Holmes does practise is not carried out at the abstruse level that Doyle asserts; an effective illusion allows the average reader contact with the hero's method. The contexts of medical science, the chemistry and the exhaustive knowledge of crime are only gestured at, and we are actually shown no more than a special rational process. This is, of course, closer to the powers of the mass audience, and so makes the detective more accessible in his heroism. It is a corollary of the less melodramatic plotting we find in the short stories, and the new direction of the crimes and criminals, as will be discussed later. In *The Adventures* the scientism of the early Holmes is contained, and deduction alone offered as his method in action.

Yet there is still an illusion present, because the resolution of the mysteries often does not depend on the deduction itself, or not very much on it. Doyle was aware of this sleight of hand. He spoke in his memoirs about "clever little deductions which often have nothing to do with the matter in hand, but impress the reader with a general sense of power." In "A Scandal in Bohemia" the "deductions" about Watson's watch merely validate Holmes's power; the only "deduction" involved in the plot itself is that a woman will fetch her most treasured object in a fire. Other early stories are less illusionary. In "A Case of Identity" there is a good deal of reasoning from the details of the case after an initial smokescreen of irrelevant "deduction" about the client. "The Red-Headed League" also involves sharp analysis, and Watson himself realises he has all the data but can make nothing of it.

But this thorough analysis is not always basic to resolutions. In "The Blue Carbuncle" the elaborate interpretation of Mr Baker's hat has nothing to do with tracing the stone itself—Baker answers an advertisement for the hat, and in any case he knows nothing of the carbuncle. Holmes finds James Ryder, the thief, by something suspiciously like a coincidence when he visits the poultry-stall just as Ryder returns in search of his goose. In a story like this the reader is asked to believe—and does so readily enough—that the skill Holmes demonstrates with the hat ratifies the luck that leads him to the solution. Similarly, the penetrating and confident analysis Holmes gives Watson of what has so far happened in "The Man with the Twisted Lip" validates the fact that he can just sit down, smoke a lot and resolve the whole puzzle. The stories only rarely provide all the details, as in "The Red-Headed League" and "The Speckled Band."

The reduction in *The Adventures* of Holmes's sheer scientific expertise might make ordinary people think they could imitate the master. Doyle forecloses this possibility, and makes sure that accessibility does not become identity when Jabez Wilson, whose head seems as thick as it is red, reacts unfavourably to the explained deductions: " 'Well I never!' said he. 'I thought at first you had done something clever, but I see that there was nothing in it after all.' " The trace of foolishness in Watson also helps to keep Holmes, close as he is to commonsense reasoning, a crucial distance away from normality. The proximity to the thinking powers and the epistemological grasp of the man in the street that develops in *The Strand* stories is very important to their success: the hero is less distant than he once was, though he still trails clouds of powerful cerebration and withdrawn intellectual force.

This development is parallel with a change in the central ideological aspect of the stories, their treatment of crimes and criminals. Disturbing events are not now caused by past and foreign-based immorality, but represent dangers present in contemporary London and so both credible and fearful. The threats and their perpetrators are now conceived within the limits of bourgeois ideology.

The crimes that underlie the mysteries in the first twelve short stories are not in general as melodramatic or exotic as those in the two novellas. In only two stories is a murder actually committed, and they both resemble the previous pattern. In "The Boscombe Valley Mystery" and "The Five Orange Pips" the disorders stem from past misdeeds, and in neither case is the villain punished by law—the Ku Klux Klan murderers drown in a storm and Mr Turner, who kills his old blackmailer at Boscombe Valley, dies a natural death like Jefferson Hope in *A Study in Scarlet*. These two stories do not follow directly on from the novellas, and their plots may well have arisen because Doyle was short of invention. Before they were written he had produced three stories where not a blow is struck, not a drop of blood is spilt (apart from Holmes's simulated blood and blows in "A Scandal in Bohemia"). Indeed, in two of the first short stories no crime at all has been committed; of the later stories "The Man with the Twisted Lip" and "The Noble Bachelor" are simply misunderstandings, and there may not be any specific crime in imprisoning a stepdaughter in "The Copper Beeches."

From a modern distance it may seem odd that the greatest detective of all established himself so successfully with so little contact with violence, and even relatively little with crime itself. But the unexotic nature of these problems is crucial to the stories' success; Doyle, aware as usual of the essential elements of his work, lets Holmes and Watson present the issue. At the beginning of "The Blue Carbuncle" Holmes is looking at the hat that has turned up, and Watson naively suggests "this thing has some deadly story linked to it."

> "No, no. No crime," said Sherlock Holmes, laughing. "Only one of those whimsical little incidents which will happen when you have four million human beings all jostling each other within the space of a few square miles. Amid the action and reaction of so dense a swarm of humanity, every possible combination of events may be expected to take place, and many a little problem will be presented which may be striking and bizarre without being criminal. We have already had experience of such."
>
> "So much so," I remarked, "that of the last six cases which I have added to my notes, three have been entirely free of any legal crime."

The problems are little, city-bred—but also whimsical and bizarre; in some the lack of any criminal action makes the issue inevitably one of moral and family disorder rather than any external criminal threat. A daughter's freedom and property are under attack in "A Case of Identity," the fragility of a respectable man's grasp on his professional role is examined in "The Man with the Twisted Lip" and both the sensuality and arrogance of the upper-classes are dramatised in "A Scandal in Bohemia." "The Noble Bachelor" and "The Copper Beeches" are modified reprises of the themes of "A Scandal in Bohemia" and "A Case of Identity" respectively. These five stories deal expressly with family irregularities, and something of the same effect is found in the two stories where Doyle uses the "past crime" plot of the novellas. In "The Boscombe Valley Mystery" and "The Five Orange Pips" the evil done in the past not only destroys its perpetrators but disturbs their innocent families in the present. The natural logic of a marriage between James MacCarthy and Alice Turner is upset by the past of their parents (though it should be noted that James MacCarthy, like Thaddeus Sholto in *The Sign of Four*, has some of his father's irresponsibility). In "The Five Orange Pips" John Openshaw is completely innocent, and what was in the novellas a distant, almost symbolic treatment of evil, insulated from being a pressing concern by its very pastness, has become a vividly realised threat to family life in the present.

In the seven stories just mentioned, allowing for the different emphasis in those based on the older plot pattern, it seems fair to say that the dynamic meaning of the plot is disorder threatening the normative morality of bourgeois, respectable England. Breaches of fidelity are central; these may involve interfering with another's property—that of women in particular—but financial greed itself is not a major motive. The disturbance arises from selfishness and a failure to respect the rights of others.

The five remaining stories specifically involve a crime for greed in the present. Two of them also concern undervaluing of respectable family order. In "The Speckled Band" Dr Grimesby Roylott interferes with his stepdaughters' right to life and property, so the story has links with the group already discussed. (His own colonial origin and the off-stage murder of the elder girl also give it some resonances of the two "past-crime" stories.) "The Beryl Coronet" shows an aristocrat subverting a family—the son is distrusted by his father and the daughter loses her sense of family and self-respect. In a rather savage ending Holmes expresses the Victorian distaste, not without a touch of prurient sadism, for the fallen woman—"whatever her sins are, they will soon receive a more than sufficient punishment." Neither of these stories concerns everyday crime; in each of them a disorderly, selfish influence disturbs the order based in one case on rightful inheritance, in the other on expertise—those twin pillars of augmenting and protecting income and property in the middle-class Victorian world.

The three other crime-based stories deal with types of professional villainy; a bank robbery in "The Red-Headed League," a jewel theft in "The Blue Carbuncle" and coining in "The Engineer's Thumb." There was a great deal of organised crime in nineteenth-century England, especially in and around London; records show, perhaps surprisingly, baby farming and forgery as the most common detected offences and robbery with assault—mugging—the most commonly known in ordinary experience. But Doyle selects his crimes, aims the threats at bank deposits, jewels and coins, the tangible forms of property, the totems of an acquisitive and money-conscious society.

The presentation of the criminals is even more ideologically selective than their crimes. They are not unregenerate members of a professional gang, or part of those "dangerous classes" who genuinely did threaten bourgeois London. They are respectable people gone wrong, turned aside from their proper roles. The fact that these are "real" crimes, not family disturbances, places most of the criminals outside the ring-fence of middle-class family structure, but in one way or another they are marginal members of that society, and should have respected its values. James Ryder in "The Blue Carbuncle" is a superior servant who succumbed to "the temptation of sudden wealth so easily acquired" Holmes judges, and feels able to let him go, sure that "This fellow will not go wrong again." The coiners of "The Engineer's Thumb" are an English doctor and foreigners who mislead him and seem themselves to be middle-class renegades. They all get away, and though "from that day to this no word has ever been heard" of them, this does not suggest that they were reformed—there are other reasons for the equivocal ending to this story that will be discussed below. The remaining criminal, John Clay of "The Red-Headed League" is a professional who has been in jail and is arrested. Yet even he has an oddity that conflicts with criminal reality. He is the grandson of a royal duke, and he has been to Eton and Oxford, so partly represents the weak aristocrat figure. Even in him the mundane reality of crime is avoided.

The economic or psychological origins of crime are not recognised: the stories assert that if decent people pulled together, did their duty and fulfilled their moral roles these disorders would not occur. The ideas are not unlike those basic to *The Newgate Calendar*, but here a secular and fragmented view of the world makes a heroic agent of order necessary, and also causes the mystery to be presented in terms of one person's experience. Holmes can only expose the errant and restore order through the channel of a normal, innocent person who is involved in and damaged by the crime, so symbolising the personal threat felt by the individuated audience. Jabez Wilson in "The Red-Headed League," Henry Baker in "The Blue Carbuncle" and Victor Hatherly in "The Engineer's Thumb" are innocent bystanders drawn into disorder by accidental contact with the criminal process. Of the three, only Hatherly is physically damaged, and his is a rather special case, to be discussed below. The other two, though ruffled by their experience, continue ordinary life, but it is interesting that both are presented in a critical light: Wilson is rather stupid and Baker has fallen into bad habits. It seems as if the very fact of being involved in such a business must cast doubt on the individual—and so shelter the self-consciously upright bourgeois from the threat of such contact.

Pierre Nordon is one of the few critics to have discussed Doyle's work along socio-cultural lines; he has pointed out the special selection of the crimes involved, but his analysis of the situation seems over-simple. He suggests a line is drawn between the rich and the poor, and that villains in the stories before 1910 tend to be "the calculating enemies of order." There are figures who emerge in the second collection of stories who fit such a description, notably Charles Augustus Milverton and Professor Moriarty himself. But these ogres simplify Doyle's meaning by naturalising evil, giving it an incorrigible presence in dedicated villains, and in the opening volume of stories that first gripped the reading world things are not so simplistic. The evil that arises from selfishness in *The Adventures* is often expressed in calculating terms and does usually seek money; it is also certainly a threat to order as well as property. But Nordon's summary wrongly identifies an embattled class seeing and facing enemies outside itself. Doyle is more self-conscious, more attuned to middle-class worries about the ability to protect and reproduce itself. His stories do not present the foreign, loathsome enemies encountered by Sexton Blake, Bulldog Drummond or, in the modern period, by James Bond. Doyle offers fables in which the class whose language, epistemology and values are enacted can examine the dangers that arise if its members are untrue to its codes.

It is important to recognise that doubt and fear are firmly directed at other members of the class, their potential failure to remain faithful to the shared morality. Yet none of the stories imply a sense that the individual might himself fail to maintain these standards; this is achieved through the absolute trustworthiness of Watson and the clients who bring the problems to Holmes. Watson never fails in morality, however inadequate his intellect might be. Through him the stories express self-confidence in bourgeois ethics and by recognising his limitations they clarify the need to know more, to improve the educational skills of the audience to defend their personal moral fortresses. The clients who invoke Holmes's special intellectual force are always puzzled, but never dishonest or immoral. Agatha Christie will develop a sense of disquiet about the self by using unreliable or criminal narrators, and Raymond Chandler will isolate the hero by making his clients untrustworthy. But here a series of respectable people experience disorder, and an unfailingly honest narrator and a comforting reliable hero close ranks with them. At the same time, the stories never invoke intelligence in the clients, never suggest the reader can match the hero's intellectual power: he is acccessible, but not imitatable. Later writers allow the reader to doubt the existence of a shared and automatically restorative morality and also suggest the reader can match the intellectual skill of the hero. . . .

The only enemy clearly identified outside the class is the aristocrat who does not subscribe to middle-class values—an interesting corroboration of the fact that through the nineteenth century the upper-class had steadily become more bourgeois in outlook. Here too Doyle could sense and realise the forces of his period. This fear of a distinct aristocratic class and its different values is a part of the uncertainty that arose from the middle-class awareness that it had "made itself," and that its successful position depended on vigilance, on a sustained defence and propagation of the virtues that seemed central to its continued security. The fact that they "seemed" central is important. Doyle's stories are concerned with property and money, but they do not show acquisitiveness and protection of money as virtues in themselves. Money and property are considered the natural result of correct ethics, and failure in morality causes the attack on property and even on life. Dr Roylott, the memorable villain of "The Speckled Band," is an eccentric irascible man as well as greedy for his stepdaughters' property; John Clay is a renegade gentleman and a thief; James Ryder is weak and so tempted by the great carbuncle; Sir George Burnwell is a profligate first and a thief second—and the nobleman who puts the beryl coronet in pawn and triggers the whole crime has himself acted badly to come to this state.

Weber argued that protestant ethics were a substantive cause of bourgeois financial success; others have agreed with Marx that the pervasive bourgeois morality was an ideological screen for the acquisitive and self-defensive instincts of a newly self-conscious class. Whatever the truth of the dispute, Doyle's stories dramatise the dialectic effect of that morality: it both justifies the possession of property and is shown protecting the possessors in their comfort.

The nature of the resolutions themselves is an important part of the ideology of the stories. Only rarely does the legal system operate at the end of a case. An arrest is made in "The Red-Headed League" but we hear no more of the criminals; they are out of sight and out of interest. Comprehension of their attempt has been enough to dissolve their threat. In "The Blue Carbuncle" and "The Boscombe Valley Mystery" for Holmes to know all is for him to pardon: one criminal dies naturally, the other is set on what we are asked to believe will be a life of reform. In several stories punishment is autonomous, rising from the machinations of the criminal. The grisly fates of Dr Roylott and Jephro Rucastle, attacked by their own savage animals, are satisfying self-created judgements, and in "The Five Orange Pips" the stormy weather that broods over the whole story is the indiscriminate agent of fate, sinking the ship *Lone Star*—apparently with all hands, innocent as well as guilty. In "A Scandal in Bohemia" and "The Noble Bachelor" no actual penalty falls on those who have directly caused the disorder; Holmes's scorn punishes the aristocrats judged to have been most at fault—and this kind of resolution operates in "The Beryl Coronet" as Sir George Burnwell gets away with a mere £600 for his boldy immoral crime and feels Holmes's contempt. Doyle, like many middle-class people, cherished ideas of his family's past grandeur—his mother was obsessed with heraldry, especially that of her family. His scorn for aristocrats who failed in their moral duty was strong and expresses both the middle-class dislike of and impotence towards the classes they admired and sought to join. Such class values cause Holmes's contempt for James Windibank in "A Case of Identity." He has shown improper greed and broken familial ties; the threatened beating is the traditional punishment for a man who betrays a woman. The only criminals who escape unscathed are the coiners of "The Engineer's Thumb"; the destruction of their press is certainly a handicap to them, and it may be the real purpose of the story, as will be discussed below.

Selection of setting is a crucial ideological feature in crime fiction, and the physical world in which Holmes operates is basically that of the natural audience of *The Strand Magazine*. The vivid pieces of London life in "The Blue Carbuncle" and "The Red-Headed League" move around the fringes of the City of London itself; though there is no "Saxe-Coburg Square," the Jabez Wilson country is familiar enough and many streets are those the readers would walk through to catch their trains. A few precise details set each story in the world of contemporary experience, however much they may now seem to be charming pieces of nostalgia. But much of real London is omitted; there are ideological absences in the treatment of the setting. Watson's perception of the gloomy menaces of London and its darker areas, strong in the novellas, is not now usually present. Watson himself does not go into these areas, with the exception of "The Man with the Twisted Lip," which has a special significance, to be discussed below. The real threat to respectable life posed by the grim areas where the working-class and the "dangerous classes" lived is thoroughly subdued. Just as the stories have mastered a problematic which locates disorder in the failure of middle-class people—and some aristocrats—to be faithful to their moral roles, so the story omits that more real criminal pressure from dispossessed, outcast London in a period of economic depression. When the plot needs to recognise such people and such areas, which is not often, Holmes goes among them, frequently in disguise, but the story does not go with him. He returns with his messages of comprehension and comfort and the actual contemporary threats are omitted from the story. Here, as in the treatment of crimes and criminals, selection and omission build up the ideological pattern of the story.

The grim London weather seems in the novellas to be an emotive displacement of the potential disorder of London life, but here this element is much reduced. Only one story deals to any extent with bleak weather; this is "The Five Orange Pips," already shown to be harking back in structure and theme to the earlier patterns. It has developed a new, consoling element though: the bad weather may express affectively a displaced sense of fear, but it has become the agent which punishes criminals that even Holmes cannot reach.

The treatment of the setting in the short stories expresses a greater sense of illusion, a firmer grasp on imaginary ideological comfort of the stories. To describe Holmes's problems as "whimsical little incidents"—a motif repeated in several stories—itself implies that all disorders can readily enough be mastered. In one striking passage Doyle suggests to his audience that life in London is not really as bad as it may seem. Holmes and Watson take the train down to Winchester to sort out the mystery at The Copper Beeches, and when Watson admires the country houses Holmes retorts:

> "You look at these scattered houses, and you are impressed by their beauty. I look at them, and the only thought which comes to me is a feeling of their isolation, and of the impunity with which crime may be committed there."
>
> "Good heavens!" I cried. "Who would associate crime with these dear old homesteads?"
>
> "They always fill me with a certain horror. It is my belief, Watson, founded upon my experience, that the lowest and vilest alleys in London do not present a more dreadful record of sin than does the smiling and beautiful countryside."

Perhaps the passage engages the anxieties of Doyle's prosperous country readers and the increasing number of city men who commuted a good way into London—many of the later stories are set in the country, where Doyle lived in prosperity. But the main point of Holmes's claim is to draw the sting of the threats of city living, and it demonstrates how far Doyle is from presenting a realistic account of the sources and patterns of real crime in late nineteenth-century England.

The emphasis here has been to establish the social meaning of the patterns of form and content in Doyle's stories. This crucial aspect has been too little observed. But as with Poe's stories, the ideology, however much a shared one, is essentially that of personal achievement and personal morality threatened in a subjectively perceived way—and ultimately defended by an individualistic hero to whom the audience relates on a one-to-one basis. It would be surprising, then, if there were not some resonances in the stories of Doyle's own anxieties. One obvious channel for these, so clearly present in Poe, lies in the hints that respond to Freudian analysis. Neither the space nor the expertise is available here to identify these features in any satisfactorily full way, but two aspects of male anxiety seem to thread their way through the stories.

Loss of masculinity is the fear behind some details. For all his vigour the King of Bohemia is crucially weakened because Irene Adler (her name in his own language means that rapacious bird, the eagle) has locked away a power totem in her most secret compartment. Jabez Wilson, whose head is aflame with virility, is suborned in his own house, and his betrayers penetrate the bank, that fastness of security, by a suggestive back passage. The vigorous, phallic-necked animal that would make James Ryder as powerful as his surname implies, is found to be empty of its stone. Victor Hatherley loses his thumb, a prime phallic symbol; Neville St Clair becomes hideous and deformed in the quest for money; Lord St Simon finds his wife has disappeared and belonged all the time to someone else.

This last case perhaps moves away from sheer loss of masculinity to the other main anxiety, the fear of supplanting that is most firmly felt by the father for the daughter; several stories act out this family drama. James Windibank not only desires his stepdaughter to stay at home and allow him to control her person and property, he actually provides a suitably weak-voiced and unthreatening rival to himself. Dr Roylott goes so far as to attack his stepdaughter with a snake, forced through a hole he has pierced in her wall. Alexander Holder (a tenacious man?) finds his daughter's virtue is stolen along with the jewelled coronet that symbolises it as well as wealth and honour; the tug of war between the supplanter and the son who, though suspected by the father is still his own image, shatters the perfect circle. "The Copper Beeches" also presents a possessive father whose neck, well-known phallic object, is savaged by the beast kept in his own home as his daughter is finally lost. There may well be many more such details, and a close analysis would chart the meaning more fully. But the presence of such material can hardly be denied; here too Doyle has the power to realise the fears and urges that seethed in the respectable personality and that needed to be contained by normative influences like the unperturbable yet comprehending hero Sherlock Holmes. If there were any doubt of Doyle's artistic sense of these topics, they would be dispelled by a glance at his novella *The Parasite*. Written in 1894, this vivid case-study of a man possessed by the id only achieves the triumph of the superego by the foreclosing coincidental incursion of Victorian moralism. The vicar arrives just before the hero is about to destroy his proper, respectable lady friend for the sake of the ugly but powerful and sensual woman who has possessed him.

There was a very strong response to the stories that appeared in *The Strand* in 1891 and 1892 and Doyle found himself committed to a hero and a story-type he had intended as an occasional potboiler. "It was still the Sherlock Holmes stories for which the public clamoured, and these from time to time I endeavoured to supply," he remarks in his memoirs. His attempts to disengage himself from Holmes are well known. He asked more for a second set of stories, but Newnes paid up happily. Then Doyle killed Holmes off; the firmly entitled story "The Final Problem," where Holmes and Moriarty plunged together down the Reichenbach Falls was published in 1893, made even more vivid by a particularly fine full page illustration by Paget. After great pressure Doyle wrote *The Hound of the Baskervilles* in 1901, but set it back in time, before the liberating death, and the story is notable for the absence of Holmes for six of its fifteen chapters. Finally he resurrected Holmes for the stunning sum of £100 a thousand words, but reluctance persevered. After the *Return* stories were published he called the next series *His Last Bow*, but another volume, *The Case-Book of Sherlock Holmes* was forced out of him in 1927, not long before he died. In the last of the novellas, *The Valley of Fear*, written in 1915, he used a long Gaboriau-like retrospective section, found before only in *A Study in Scarlet*, and so limited Holmes's place in the narrative. This all shows how the wide acceptance and need of the figure of Holmes operated against the very wishes of his creator; the facts press a social meaning upon the success of the stories. But Doyle's distaste for Holmes developed surprisingly early, and there are signs of its operation within the first series.

When *The Adventures* had been running for only six months Doyle wrote in his diary "Holmes keeps my mind from better things." But even before this his interest in Holmes was limited. After completing "The Boscombe Valley Mystery" Doyle had a bad attack of influenza, and on recovering decided to be a full-time writer. It was not the Holmes stories he saw as his métier—his mind was on another historical novel, to be *The Refugees*. But he did complete the promised half-dozen Holmes stories. The next was "The Five Orange Pips" where the strong resonance of the past-crime plot of the novellas suggests the barrel is being audibly scraped and where Holmes comes close to failure. The sixth story was "The Man with the Twisted Lip." In this and "The Engineer's Thumb" Doyle appears to be dramatising his dislike of the Holmes phenomenon, his sense that it weighs him down and interferes with his real work and his self-respect.

The two stories are linked by unusual structural features—which first drew my attention to them as a pair. In both stories Watson controls the opening action, pushing Holmes into the background in a surprising way and when he appears his powers are considerably reduced, as they were in the preceding adventure. He is mistaken for most of "The Man with the Twisted Lip," saving himself by a quite unexplained piece of overnight deduction, and in "The Engineer's Thumb" he makes only one simple piece of analysis (that the villains drove round in a circle). Holmes's limitations and Watson's added weight suggest a doubt in Doyle's mind about the validity of the hero. The symbolic meaning of the stories' content makes it clear that this arises from Doyle's unusual element of self-expression.

"The Man with the Twisted Lip" tells the story of a respectable reporter who, in the course of a special commission, finds he can earn more disguised as a deformed, sharp-tongued beggar in the city than in his real employment. When he is short of money he takes up the role again and begging becomes his livelihood. Ultimately his wife sees him in circumstances that will reveal his shameful state. He is unable to reappear as himself, and so is accused of his own murder.

The parallels with what Doyle felt he was doing are obvious. A respectable writer, for the sake of gaining large sums of money in a way he has accidentally discovered, degrades himself and takes profits made in the street from City workers. Doyle, *The Strand* and the Holmes phenomenon are effectively symbolised. The beggar reveals Doyle's projected fear. A handsome body is distorted and a mouth that should produce decent speech is twisted into a sneer to bring in more cash; this shameful practice amounts to a murder of the real self, a betrayal of the family. "It was a long fight between my pride and my money, but the dollars won at last," says the disgraced man. When Holmes finally sifts the matter he wipes clean the soiled face, restoring honour and clean upright life to the money-dazzled reporter.

It is a fascinating allegory, revealing Doyle's growing dislike of what he saw as vulgar potboilers which kept him from the scholarly and overtly moralising work of his historical novels. Watson's introduction itself offers an even more alarming model, a respectable well-connected man who, becoming a drug-addict was "an object of mingled horror and pity to his friends" and was no more than "the wreck and ruin of a noble man."

Apart from these patent traces of meaning and the reduced power of Holmes himself, there is a quite unusual intensity of feeling in the writing. Doyle rarely works with imagery, but this story is rich with motifs of light and dark more intense even than those of *The Sign of Four*. Holmes and Watson drive through "sombre and deserted streets" across "the murky river" through "a wilderness of bricks and mortar" and the reporter's wife stands "with her figure outlined against the flood of light" from her warm respectable house. When he begins to grasp the case Holmes says "the clouds lighten" and when he has cracked the problem he and Watson go out into "the bright morning sunshine." This sort of emotional landscape has been used generally in the novellas, but here it is locked into the meaning of the man defined by his own situation, by his own filth that is washed away and, above all, by being called Neville St Clair. The aristocratic Christian name and the holy light of the surname have been besmirched in shameful money-grubbing—the fact that it came as a sudden, unexpected and eventually troubling gift may well be subconsciously expressed in his beggar's name, Hugh Boon.

The problem is still resolved by Holmes, limited though his powers might be. This clarifies Doyle's ambiguous relationship with his hero. Though he is still writing stories he dislikes, he actually uses the distasteful hero to resolve the problem that, symbolically at least, has been set by that figure. In his own anxiety Doyle employs the absolving force of the hero who combines isolated intellectualism and social service: in the story Holmes does for Doyle just what he did for Doyle's kin among his audience.

Having worked out his feelings in this manner Doyle refused to provide more stories. But as the public and Newnes clamoured for more he weakened, demanding £50 a story in the hope of a refusal. Newnes agreed gladly and Doyle had to set to work again. His professionalism and the relief found in the previous story set the next two, "The Blue Carbuncle" and "The Speckled Band," among his most brilliant efforts, vigorously written and inventively plotted. Yet the shadow of Holmes was not so easily dispersed, as the later events reveal, and as is plain in "The Engineer's Thumb," a more deeply troubled story than "The Man with the Twisted Lip."

Here Holmes is distanced further from events at the start of the story, as Watson actually brings the case to him. Watson is himself consulted and acts with Holmesian decisiveness. This reduction of Holmes's force in the action leaves an emotive gap filled by Doyle himself: the figure of Victor Hatherley, the client, is very much like the author. Hatherley is a consulting scientific specialist with few clients, seduced by a lucrative offer that turns out to be disabling. The Doyle who has just decided to give up his specialist's role for writing, but who has Newnes's money to weigh him down is clearly enough presented. More sharply still Hatherley has shown the link between his own engineering knowledge and medicine in his ability to treat his wound; his "suit of heather tweed with a soft cloth cap" and "strong masculine face" could come straight from a surviving photograph of the young Doyle. The client's disturbing involvement is not, as was Neville St Clair's, a matter of impersonation and losing self-respect. The threat is deeper and more damaging; Hatherley has been seduced into dealing with people who, for all their vigour and apparent respectability, are criminals, and their crime is literally to make money with a press—of all things. The covert reference in the villains to the respectable Greenhough Smith and the Newnes who brought foreign know-how into his press operations to coin money is quite irresistible. The physique of Colonel Lysander Stark is remarkably like Greenhough Smith's, and Dr Becher has a general resemblance to Newnes in his portly, comfortable English appearance.

The plot tells how the press closes in on the young idealist just as he discovers the false villainy of the whole operation. The light he has, literally, brought in burns down the press but though he escapes with his life he leaves behind his thumb—a clear sign that he has lost his masculinity in the process. The story has the wish-fulfilling power to illuminate and destroy the whole of Newnes's establishment, but the villains themselves are untouched. They do vanish: they are exorcised from consciousness at least, but not destroyed. True to the legends of Victorian manhood, a good woman has saved the hero; but the crippling wound remains. Holmes has watched all this happening without any real act of analysis, but the authority of his final words gives comfort to the client as if he really were an author: "you have only to put it into words to gain the reputation of being excellent company for the remainder of your existence."

This final comment shows Doyle's anxiety to avoid being the shameful outcast pictured twice in the earlier story, and his desire to gain and hold respect through his chosen profession of author. The greater disturbance of this story, compared with "The Man with the Twisted Lip," is shown by the increased obscurity and distancing of the symbolism, by the client's career being that of the Doyle who was not a writer, and in the failure of Holmes or any other agency to find the villains. There is no renewal here, just a wished for destruction of the press, and a remaining sense of emasculation. The debilitation that gave rise to the story seems to have lasted; the next, "The Noble Bachelor," continues the theme of impotence though it is distanced further from Doyle because the client is a feeble aristocrat.

In spite of this partial recovery, the story shows how Doyle was exhausted by his exegesis of anxiety: it is one of the weakest of all the Holmes stories, as Doyle later admitted.

The pattern covertly present in these two stories is fascinating. Firmly in the grip of contemporary moralistic ideas about what was good art, Doyle could not see the ideological function for a particular audience (including himself) of his work. Critics can be as blind as authors; Charles Higham, in his recent book *The Adventures of Conan Doyle*, can do no more than trace these two stories to fairly similar events in contemporary news reports. This approach, itself reifying and fragmenting the force of fiction, belittles both the imaginative power Doyle possessed and the neurotically urgent pressure of the stories.

Doyle's financial commitments and the comparative failure of his other work in critical and market terms kept him returning to the figure he had created better than he knew or wished. But as time went by Holmes and the stories changed a good deal. Like so many of his readers, the young Doyle lived close to relative poverty and to class disgrace as a result. The dialectic force of respectability as both perilous state and a power for its own defence is strongly felt in the early stories—and beneath their surface there bubbles the muted force of a vigorous man's sexuality and the accompanying anxieties, channelled into family strains by the period's taboo on acknowledging extra-marital sex. The conflict between money and morality is another of the realised tensions that invigorate the early stories.

The older Doyle was a much more prosperous and prestigious man, and the later Sherlock Holmes becomes more respectable, more certain—less expressive of the strains that the younger Doyle and his readers felt. Holmes gives up cocaine, goes for healthy walks, gets on better with the police and is much less barbed towards Watson. A reduced individuality is structurally reified as the story-patterns become formulaic and Holmes even narrates some of his own stories: previously Watson had been essential to mediate his quicksilver aloofness.

The later stories are more concerned with murder and crimes directed against property, without the mystifying concealment of property-ownership behind morality, so important in the early stories, as has been discussed. This development is visible in *The Memoirs*, even before Doyle killed off his hero. The emergence of master criminals as threats which are naturally evil also steers the stories away from the anxious enactment of a class's suspicions of its own kind into a world where right and wrong are clearly defined, enemies easily identified and confronted by the unfragmented force of bourgeois morality and law. The settings, the characters themselves and the large sums involved tend to move the stories into the environment of upper-middle-class prosperity where Doyle now moved. The loosening grip on a problematic of moral anxiety and this movement towards one based on a simple aggressive defence of prosperity causes Doyle, as Nordon has well shown, to replace the earlier self-conscious tensions with grotesque detail and sensational crimes. Excitement is manipulated into the stories, rather than rising from innate patterns of plot and from Holmes's delicately balanced duality.

A similar artificiality comes from Doyle's habit of giving comic titles to Holmes's unreported cases. This is an ironic revenge on the hero that deliberately trivialises his meaning, where originally listing of other, serious cases made his power seem denser and more all-embracing. The structural form also becomes less varied, more formulaic and perfunctory. The restless dramatisation of the "whimsical little incidents" of the average Londoner's life is much less in evidence; stylisation hardens into caricature as the earlier realised moral dialectic tends to become a clear-cut fight between right and wrong, between the immutable good characters and the naturally evil agents of disorder. It is interesting to notice the same development in the Brigadier Gerard stories; the first volume, published in 1893, has a double dialectic based on the forbidding yet fascinating power of Napoleon and the admirable yet foolish chivalry of Gerard. In the second volume, published ten years later, Gerard has become much more a buffoon, Napoleon a more clearly admired man of strength.

In spite of these changes, the brand-name qualities that Holmes had gained through the early period survived to the present. There is, for all the weakened force in the later stores, more vigour and concern with bourgeois morality in them than in most of his competitors. Chesterton and Freeman today seem cold and clever ratifications of very narrow approaches to reality, while even the last Holmes adventures have a mobile and inventive application of the power of materialist, moralising thought that still gives them convincing ideological force to many.

The Holmes stories, especially in the period when Doyle's success and Holmes's nature were formed, are a contemporary analogue to a series of folk-tales, or a set of epic lays in which a figure fitted to be a culture-hero of his period was presented in a medium and form technologically and epistemologically valid for a contemporary class. The function of epic and folk-tale has been well described by anthropologists and folklorists; a most succinct account of their social meaning, along with other human behaviour, has been given by Clifford Geertz (who describes himself as an anthropologist of culture). Man, he says, is an uncompleted animal who completes himself through culture. Through his habits, rituals and fictions he explains the world to himself and justifies his place and his actions in that world. Month by month in *The Strand Magazine* readers could see, through the plots, the crimes and the criminals of the Holmes stories, an account of what they felt might go wrong in a world that was recognisably theirs and which was, through the force of omissions and the formation of its problematic, one where their own sets of values would work. The consolations were great, and the wit and verve of Doyle's writing give those comforts the illusory vitality of a living system. The essential functions of folk-tale are to explain the world, to protect the folk against psychic and physical threats, to offer escapist entertainment and to be socially norma-tive—to urge that these values will keep society on an even keel, resist discommoding change. All of these functions are manifest in the Holmes stories: we find scientist and rational explanation of a materially known world; the psychic protection of a powerful hero and the exclusion of real physical threats from the plots; lively dialogue, wry jokes and sensually sharp presentation of admired objects and valued feelings; and above all central bourgeois values which operate through Holmes as the tools of maintaining order, and through the victims as the qualities that earn Holmes's care and deserve the correction of disorder about them.

Holmes was a hero shaped for a particular class in a particular time and place, but like many other heroes he has survived out of context as a figure of heroism. Such characters, equipped with memorable details that symbolise their methods and the setting of their greatness, retain a central core of meaning made newly valid in other periods. Arthur with sword and round table meaning martial fraternity, Robin Hood with bow and greenwood setting to symbolise the force of anti-authoritarian morality are two major British examples. Holmes with magnifying glass and London fog has attained the same status, epitomising the rational hero who resolves urban disorder. A fine irony is that by killing Holmes off and then resur-recting him, Doyle gave his hero one of the constant features of the heroic pattern. Lord Raglan was the first to identify the fact that mythic heroes tend to exhibit a group of identical features; the descent into apparent death and miraculous return is a crucial stage. But it may not be just an accident; Joseph Campbell has traced the recurring patterns of the hero's career to archetypal patterns of human need, and the final struggle where Holmes gave his life to defeat mankind's foe is, as in the case of Beowulf and Roland, mythic whether the hero returns or not. The patterns of human imagination and story were there, working in the author's imagination at the time; made dynamic by Paget's stirring illustrations and Doyle's vivid realisation they can retain their force.

As time and socio-cultural patterns change the Holmes myth may itself be demoted by a new force, as in Nicholas Meyer's pastiche *The Seven Per Cent Solution* where the hero of a different culture, Sigmund Freud, is "the greatest detective of them all." Holmes may survive as a symbol of rational enquiry and rational superiority as in many an English advertisement, or as a standard totem of detection in passing references or jokes. The quality of the realisation and the far-reaching nature of the print medium made the detective's name a household one—and that domestic metaphor is perfect for a hero whose name emerges from Doyle's imagination to imply that we can, in fiction at least, have a sure lock on our homes.

One particular formation of the Holmes myth is of more than passing interest for a writer and academic. Intellectuals and professionals have cultivated the myth in clubs and quasi-scholarly journals, and in particular have tried to fill in the background of the life of Holmes, to explain the many inconsistencies that Doyle carelessly and uncaringly created. Completion is a common process in mythical development—the life of Christ attracted commentary and clarification from an early date; the vulgate Arthuriad on which Malory partly based his work was a scholarly attempt to bring inconsistent stories into a corpus that replicated the encyclopedic, knowledge-ordering instinct of the thirteenth-century cleric. The academic professional mind tries to tidy Holmes up as if he were the subject of a Ph.D. thesis or a formal biography, and so finds in its own reworking of the myth a realisation and a validation of its own values—especially those of trivial research and tidy unitarian structures that organically justify the narrow concern with a single subject. Even Doyle's interest in rationalism and organic structures was not so obsessive, so opposed to the tumultuous confusion of real life; he made his stories a bridge between the disorderly experience of life and a dream of order, by containing both aspects in a graspable, contained and controlled form.

Kipling in the Light of Failure

Robert L. Caserio

> *"The weakness . . . the wickedness . . . and the fat-headedness of
> deliberately trying to do work that will live, as they call it."*
> —The Light That Failed

We no sooner rediscover Kipling than we lose him once more. In every
attempt at revaluation he is made to appear as a peculiar psychological or
political case, to which his work is only subordinate. As a result he keeps
escaping us, since we have yet to find terms in which to read not him but
his writings, and we have yet to "place" his writings sensibly in a relevant
literary tradition. Edmund Wilson and T. S. Eliot are responsible for this
focus on the case rather than on the work; in spite of their sympathies,
they make attention to Kipling's life or his "ideas" a necessary priority for
reading him. Fortunately, the last quarter-century has provided good disinterested commentary on the writing itself by J. M. S. Tompkins and Elliot
L. Gilbert, although only W. W. Robson's "Kipling's Later Stories" (1963)
and David Bromwich's "Kipling's Jest" (*Grand Street*, Winter 1985) can stand
as first-rate examples of scrutiny. If critics had read Andrew Rutherford's
1971 Penguin selection of the later stories with Robson in mind, we at last
might have had an adequate revaluation of what Kipling wrote. But this
did not happen. In the new Viking *Portable*, Irving Howe's comparison of
Kipling's ideas about authority with Freud's is stirring, but it is too loose
an assignment of Kipling to our intellectual traditions, and Howe's conventional selections for the anthology may be a sign of the critic's greater
interest in the psychoanalyst than in the writer. In spite of Howe, it remains
as easy and acceptable as ever for criticism to use Freud against "the Kipling
case." Reviewing Alec McCowen's *Kipling*, a theatrical reading, John Simon
insists that Kipling has no Freudian awareness of his own conflicts and
contradictions—and that this is "a major cause of his not becoming a major
writer." Simon insists on Kipling's "political and artistic reactionariness."

From *Grand Street* 5, no. 4 (Summer 1986). © 1986 by Robert L. Caserio and Grand Street
Publications, Inc.

And so it goes. It looks like the Kipling nobody read will always be Kipling whom nobody reads. Yet in the ironically perduring loss of Kipling there is an appositeness to his work. Critical insistence on Kipling's failure blinds criticism to the way its evaluations adhere to ideas about "success" that Kipling—and a significant Victorian literary tradition to which he belongs—calls into question.

Kipling's social thought or his ideas about art cannot be understood without an analysis of his treatment of failure, especially as it appears in 1891 in his first novel, *The Light That Failed*. Now it happens that criticism has always judged the novel itself to be a failure. This judgment, I propose, has been based on unreliable, inadequately thought out critical evaluation. As a result, the orthodox judgment has overlooked the power of the novel's thematic meditation on the meaning of success and failure in modern art and life. Kipling wrote the novel at a point in his career when a rigorous meditation on success may virtually have imposed itself on him. Although in 1890, the year of the novel's composition, Kipling was only twenty-five, he had already produced two books of poems and three books of short stories. This work had grown out of his experience as a journalist in India since 1882; and the work's fame had preceded his arrival in 1889 in London, where throughout the next year he was lionized, with what seems to have been unprecedented adulatory attention. As if to attest to the merit of his celebrity, Kipling worked incessantly in 1890—worked so hard in fact that he brought himself to the point of emotional collapse. As it turned out, the novel that promised to crown his labors brought his reputation as well to the point of collapse. Now that in 1890 Kipling had chosen—for the first time, and at full length—to write about a world not foreign to his English contemporaries, about modern painters and English life, the critical tide turned. Having hailed him first as the Balzac of Anglo-Indian life, criticism said now that Kipling was more callow and self-indulgent than not, was brutal in thought and emotional quality, misogynistic, and on the whole ignorant of life. These epithets have stuck to the novel. In this way the critical tradition from the start obscured Kipling's treatment of success as an important subject throughout his writing; and it did so by an assertive, apparently infallible evaluative stance. And at the same time, the first evaluation of *The Light That Failed* got itself transferred to Kipling personally. What the short-sighted reviewers helped to establish as a fixed tradition was the image of Kipling as a person whose flaws were identical with those assertively assigned to *The Light That Failed*.

One possible reason for the short-sighted critical misreading of Kipling's novel is the lack of attention paid by the first reviewers to the literary tradition with which the novel seems to want connection. Swinburne and Swinburne's mid-Victorian reading of Blake, the entire pre-Raphaelite legacy in fact—a legacy that for Kipling was a family matter, because of his close relation with his uncle, Edward Burne-Jones—influence *The Light That Failed*. But before I open the case for this influence—or for at the very least the appositeness of the connection—it will be well to set out the novel's story of success and failure, and their modern motives. The novel's hero, Dick Heldar, is the 1880s equivalent of a photojournalist. During the British attempt to annex the Sudan, he is employed by a newspaper syndicate to draw pictures of scenes at the front. His pictures are good enough to gain the attention of London's art world, so that when he returns from the war he finds himself famous as an artist. Although he immediately sets up to practice art for art's sake, it is clear that Dick's success pleases him for reasons that are not aesthetic. We are shown that his choice of art as a vocation is the reflex of rancor from his orphaned childhood, when he was victimized by a sadistic legal guardian. His art and his success are indistinguishable from his need to take revenge for his early misery. Now Dick is in love with a childhood sweetheart, Maisie, another orphan and victim who is also an aspiring painter. Maisie too wants not just art but success and fame, and she believes that intimacy with Dick—let alone marriage— is too heavy a burden for her career. In courting Maisie, Dick derogates careerism and success, but even as he does so he is breaking up an affair between his journalist friend Torpenhow and a prostitute, Bessie, because he thinks the affair is damaging to Torpenhow's successful career. To revenge herself for Dick's interference in her attempt to "make it" by escaping the streets, Bessie destroys what may be Dick's masterpiece—a work he is painting as part of his virtually sadistic drive to succeed as Maisie's lover. But all these wars for success are doomed. Dick's career is coming to an abrupt end, because a head wound he suffered in the Sudan begins to make him go blind. Desperate to save themselves from the failure of their separate aims, the enemies Dick and Bessie briefly consider marrying each other; but by this point in the story Kipling has made it clear that success has an irreparably destructive dynamic. In the 1880s the British failed to conquer the Sudan, and at the end of the novel Dick returns to the scene of the imperialist failure. He finishes off his career by getting himself shot in a skirmish. In this suicide he exemplifies how, as the novel comes to suggest, the experience of loss of worldy ambition, and even death itself, are for the novel's characters more needful than anything else.

In its presentation of this story, *The Light That Failed* is sensationally vivid and realistic. The immediacy and directness that is the effect of the writing is what we might expect only from the generation of writers after Kipling—from Lawrence or Hemingway. But the novel uses this effect not just for its own sake, but as an uncanny means to foreshorten (so to speak) an abstract, visionary analysis of an historical situation—of which its artist hero and heroine are representative. The novel presents its characters and their era as rooted in a terror of failure; and the motive for the terror is dramatized as an inordinately defensive response to loss—of love, of identity, of society, of life. All these losses are felt by Kipling's men and women to be in need of compensation; and since any form of success seems to deny vulnerability to loss and death, his characters make success a compensatory protective fetish. In the absence of any coherent religious or institutional address to death, Kipling suggests, modern failure—especially in love and in work—is a personal death, as if it were a likeness of the ultimate loss and vulnerablility that are to be shunned and denied. Kipling's novel records a world and an era in which failure and death alike have become, as it were, unacceptable.

The typical psyches of the English world are thus exhibited in the novel as forms of counter-violence that use success to master failure, loss and death. Perhaps surprisingly, Kipling points out both artistic creativity and psychosexual differentiation as two symptoms of the attempt at mastery. His artists, Dick and Maisie, make art and make love as enraged strategies in a battle for control over failure. Because each thinks the other has this control, both Dick's and Maisie's war and their artistic creativity are rooted in jealousy, which appears in *The Light That Failed* in every human phenomenon and which further produces or creates a spectrum of defenses against vulnerability. For Kipling the worldy struggle to dominate loss has overtaken biology. Human sexual differentiation has become one of the defensive products of each sex's jealousy over the other's imaginary domination of death. The struggle between Dick and Maisie is a culturally determined combative difference of male and female, which creates an illusion of something jealously to struggle *for*, something jealously *to* dominate. But this struggle between the sexes which has come to define the sexes is only a diversion of their undifferentiated vulnerability to death. The counter-violence intended to master death makes impossible any love that is not a power struggle, not a secondary form of aggressive defense against loss. Love that may arise out of this struggle Kipling sees as only a mask for sadistic pity, for kindness or care felt by aggressors for their vicitms.

The historical world out of which Kipling writes is thus a totalized order of fruitless creative jealousy, which the novel exhibits in order to criticize. But it does more than criticize; it gestures towards a possible though grim road toward liberation: radical submission of "creative" human affairs to death. In making this gesture, the novel criticizes all its agents, not just Dick and Maisie but Kipling too. As a form attempting to portray the world, the novel must exhibit itself, its writer, and writing in general as modes of failing light. As we shall see, Kipling even includes in the ending of the novel a self-reflexive moment that humbles the representational vividness from which his style derives its strength. Because the novel's and the novelist's own ambitions to ease the burden of mortality or to be enlightening about what lies beyond creative jealousy must avoid indulging the impulse to master failure and death, the visionary content of *The Light That Failed* suggests an ultimate, necessary rubbing out of its own power to act as a world-portraying canvas.

Perhaps only a twenty-five-year-old youth could assume and argue so abstract and comprehensive a pessimism about the world and about the

place of creativity—whether aesthetic or sexual—in it. I think that a revaluation and recovery of this pessimism and the Victorian imaginations that
are behind it might have a special current value. The thought is certainly
in contrast to John Simon's gnashing of teeth over Alec McCowen's Kipling:
"What purpose does it serve?" he asks—especially in America; what purpose will any revaluation of Kipling and his tradition serve, one might add,
if the revaluation is not to be just academic? The question deserves an
immediate response. Recovering Kipling and his tradition may justify itself
to begin with if I briefly consider a kind of literary and political writing
about failure that is closer to home and that indeed is, although without
any acknowledgment, influenced by Kipling.

The Light That Failed, because it is about English war correspondents
in the Sudan a century ago, gave writers from Stephen Crane on—Hemingway, Orwell and Norman Mailer among them—the possibility of an
alliance between war journalism and literary art. In its development this
alliance has produced a body of work that has continued to focus on versions of Dick Heldar, versions of a failing or failed hero at odds with the
battle for success being waged around him and within him. The most recent
American product of this alliance grows out of American combat in Vietnam; and the acclaim in 1977 given to Michael Herr's *Dispatches*, a book
about special correspondents in the war, might have been more cogent had
it mentioned Kipling. The interest of Herr's book lies in a direction predicted
by *The Light That Failed*. *Dispatches* suggests a need to live on the brink of
personal and public failure and loss, without defensive denial of them. Yet
this need for a radical lapse from—or liberation from—success can scarcely
be admitted by American traditions, although the denial is costly. As
C. Vann Woodward long ago pointed out, the South had an advantage in
suffering defeat in the Civil War: it experienced the failure which every
historical people has suffered, but which the United States has made unacceptable even to admit as a national experience. Herr's attachment to
Vietnam is probably due to its having freed him from "success," to its
having enabled him to breathe the un-American air of mortal vulnerability.
In contrast to the soldiers, Herr and his fellow correspondents chose to live
in death's shadow—a choice both full of fear and fearless, both vulnerable
and defenselessly careless about life. This liberation from the fear of loss
without any shirking of the fact of loss is what Kipling moves Dick Heldar
towards, and what seems to have moved Herr to write *Dispatches*. But
whereas Kipling shows the subversion of his hero's attachments to the
social and sexual order and to art's place in both, in a way that analyzes
the historical order as the reflex of culture-wide terror of loss and death,
Herr is cut off from such analysis. As a result his book seems merely
confused about the role failure and death play in his experience. Herr says
"the press . . . never found a way to report meaningfully about death,
which of course is what it was all about," but he goes on to say that he
finally had to stop his observation of the war for reasons he can only cloud

over. "We came to fear something more complicated than death, an annihilation less final but more complete, and we got out. . . . If you stayed too long you became one of those poor bastards who had to have a war on all the time"—presumably because the "something more complicated than death" *insists* on generating war "all the time." In Kipling's light Herr might have seen that it is the modern state's order of jealousy which has become the thing more complicated than death, that this order relentlessly and ironically generates war as the way to succeed against death, indeed against any vulnerability. Instead of making an analysis, Herr refuses explanation and suddenly turns his narrative into a success story. "All right, yes, it had been a groove being a war correspondent, hanging out with the grunts and getting close to the war, touching it, losing yourself in it, and trying yourself against it. I had always wanted that, never mind why . . . I'd done it. [There] had always been marines or soldiers who would tell me . . . *You're all right man . . . you got balls.*" The courage to be "all right" connotes the surmounting of death, and the success story turns out to be vulgarly male and vulgarly American. America lost, but the special correspondents did not. Nevertheless, against the success of rigorous male "fearlessness" in *Dispatches* one might set—more clearly than Herr finally does—the attractiveness his book assigns even if incoherently to a vulnerability that no "balls" can succeed against. It seems to have been *The Light That Failed*'s intention to make the case for such vulnerability, as the only escape from the historical and social state's way of having become the thing that must have a war on all the time.

The immediate purpose a revaluation of Kipling might serve, then, has to do with the historical relevance for an American context of the "moral" of failure suggested by *The Light That Failed*. This "moral" is that no ideology, no public purposes or wars, and no private "success" can negate mortality in any but a factitious and injurious way—though the way may be the path of shining worldly accomplishment, even of accomplishment in art. Artistic creativity, *The Light That Failed* asserts, can not be separated out from the worldy aggressions that are produced by the attempt to master all loss. But this assertion is not merely young Kipling's. Having sketched an immediate American purpose to be served by thinking again about Kipling, I turn to the way Kipling's early vision must be tied to Blake's and Swinburne's role in Kipling's environment. It will be easier to contradict and to move beyond the traditional complaints about the novel once the literary sources that influence or at least coincide with Kipling's drama have been suggested.

To those who cherish the received ideas about Kipling, Blake and Swinburne—Blake especially—will seem too removed from Kipling for serious connection with him. Yet Eliot persistently couples Kipling and Swinburne, since Kipling's poems are full of Swinburne's rhythms and diction; and Dick Heldar's sketchbook—which belongs to the days before Yeats's edition of Blake, when the latter was virtually a pre-Raphaelite possession, interpreted by Swinburne's pioneering *William Blake* (1868)—contains drawings of a model to whom Dick exclaims, "What a fortune you would have been to Blake!" Of course I am hypothesizing influence, not documenting it; but environing influences of this kind, or at the very least the possible coinciding of these strong poetic imaginations produced by romanticism, must be allowed a major place in any speculative biography of Kipling's work. Kipling's immediate personal relations have been fair game for his interpreters; but for any author the writings and the writers he admires are no less live or personal than the author's parents, siblings, or children. The biographical treatment of *The Light That Failed* has analyzed the novel as a merely personal, literal family matter. Kipling was born in Bombay of Anglo-Indian parents, and he experienced the disturbing but customary fate of Anglo-Indian children: just before he was six, he and his young sister Trix were sent back to England and separated from their parents, so as to receive an English education at home. Ironically, "home" meant boarding in the house of strangers, with a retired naval officer and his wife in Southsea. Kipling's parents made a poor choice of guardians: the officer's wife was viciously repressive, and the house's educational order of the day was caning. Hence Dick Heldar's victimized childhood in *The Light That Failed* is autobiographical; and Maisie turns out to be a composite of Trix and another young woman, Flo Garrard, who came later to live in the same boarding establishment. In the analysis of Kipling's response to this experience, it has become conventional to say that it explains his alleged bent for coarseness and bullying, which he adopted as a defensive imitation of the canings; and that it made him hate women. His misogyny resulted from feeling betrayed and abandoned by his mother; and because Trix was treated better by the foster family than Kipling was, he felt enviously inferior to the sex that betrayed him. Now there is no reason to reject this biographical hypothesis; but since it is a hypothesis, it is at least questionable, and not a fact. My alternative hypothesis is that in the Burne-Jones household—during what Kipling himself called paradiselike vacations from Southsea—he early on became exposed to a literary culture which provided his precocious mind with a way to make sense of his misery that is as good as if not better than our psychologistic way to make sense of it. Burne-Jones was Swinburne's intimate, to whom the poet dedicated the notorious *Poems and Ballads* of 1866; his family was continually together with the Robert Brownings and the William Morrises; the Burne-Jones, Morris and Kipling children published a family literary magazine. Kipling left Southsea in 1876 for school at the United Services College in Cornwall, where the headmaster who devotedly stimulated the boy's literary ambition was Cormell Price. Price was a schoolmate of Burne-Jones, a close friend of D. G. Rossetti, and had been one of the painters of the famous pre-Raphaelite frescoes at the Oxford Union. So it is surely arguable that Kipling grew up saturated in pre-Raphaelite culture, whose greatest poet was Swinburne and one of whose saints of art had been Blake. The biography of Kipling by Lord

Birkenhead describes Kipling's celebrity in London in 1890 in terms that starkly contrast Kipling with Wilde, Beardsley and the aesthetes, themselves the cultural offspring of pre-Raphaelitism. But C. E. Carrington's biography keeps closer to the truth. At school, he tells us, Kipling "was a rebel and a progressive which is to say, in 1882—paradoxically—that he was a decadent. His friends, his teachers, were liberals, his tastes were 'aesthetic.' " It is scarcely credible that the young man who returned to London—and to the Burne-Joneses—in 1889 had cut himself away from his literary origins.

So it is arguable that at the end of *The Light That Failed*, when Dick Heldar divests himself of his identity and his art, in a blind surrender to the hazard and obscurity of death, Kipling's portrait of the artist as a young man follows the events central to Blake's portrait of the blind artist Milton. It is also arguable that Kipling insists on Dick's submission of his creativity to death's dominion because Swinburne's reading of Blake presents Blake as in fact a critic of artistic creation or generativity—as indeed a proponent of the failure of creation. Surprising though it may be, Swinburne enlists Blake in the cause of art for art's sake just because Swinburne sees Blake as an antagonist of creative power. For Swinburne, Blake is a consummate aesthete because he failed at worldly success, because he failed to attach art to any ulterior worldy purpose. He did so, according to Swinburne, because Blake cared not for creation but for salvation—and for Blake salvation was liberty, even liberty from the world. This radical freedom meant liberty from "the Creator's power" and from "the creative daemon," both of which rule the world as an order of creative jealousy. "The creative daemon," Swinburne says in one of his summaries of Blake's ideas, has "power . . . which began with birth" and "must end with death; upon the perfect and eternal man he had not power till he had created the earthly life to bring man into subjection, and shall not have power upon him again any more when he is once resumed by death." So death is the way of release: "where the Creator's power ends there begins the Saviour's power"; and Swinburne goes on to note that "confusion of the Creator with the Saviour was to Blake the main rock of offense in all religious systems less mystic than his own." Now the creative daemon in Swinburne and to some extent in Blake is both the Judaeo-Christian God and the poet-god, the creator Milton for example, whose salvation will come in the yielding of his pride of life and art to a resumption by death. Not identifying his own work with such daemonism, Blake is said by Swinburne to believe "all form and all instinct is sacred; but no invention or device of man's"; and for the same reason Blake is said to have assigned his books to "inspiration" and to "no invention"—because Blake believed, Swinburne says, that the "inlets and channels of communication [are] now destroyed by the creative demon." But although the fabrications of this demon-daemon have become the order of things, Blake is far from passive in response. Swinburne emphasizes Blake's destructive "ardour of rebellion and strenuous battle" against the Creator, against His inhibitings of liberty. "The God of nature . . . must have the organ of destruction and division, by which alone he lives and has ability to beget, cut off from him with the sharpest edge of flint that rebellious hands can whet."

This castration of the Creator practiced by the artist suggests the artist's self-violation in turn, insofar as he too is a generative god, whose creation of words and worlds by articulation's divisions must fall victim to his own war of liberation from articulation itself. No wonder Blake became what Swinburne—in a way surely attractive to Kipling—describes as "full of the vast proportion andd formless fervour of Hindoo legends." It is by becoming formless and inarticulate, by destroying the rational divisions and articulations of the Creator, that Blake practices art for art's sake—and for failure's sake. As Swinburne represents Blake's art, it is a mode of obscurity and darkness because it deliberately cultivates the loss of the world. The loss has no compensation. Accordingly, when Swinburne summarizes *Milton*, he neither mentions nor quotes the ecstatic hymning of imagination that in the poem follows Milton's liberation from selfhood. If the selfhood articulated by the creative daemon must fail, Swinburne thereby suggests, that failure must be the sole object of our attention and our advocacy. In Dick Heldar's career Kipling writes another version of Swinburne's suggestion, inspired by Blake.

The source of Blake's animus against the Creator-figure is the dynamics of the human terror of loss, with its consequent ironically destructive psychic and sexual defenses against that terror. What Kipling draws in Dick and Maisie was earlier drawn by Blake in Los and Enitharmon, especially in the initial sections of *Vala; or, The Four Zoas*. A few points in those sections will be seen to bear on *The Light That Failed*. In *Vala* "Tharmas, Parent pow'r" identifies his and Enion's daughter, "the infant joy" Enitharmon, with "Everlasting brooding Melancholy" because the child breeds fear in the parent that the love of the parents for each other will be lost to the child. This fear of loss gives birth to just the loss that is feared, so that a new infant, Los, is engendered. The infant's name keeps in play the idea of creative generation as a diminution of being, as itself a fall. Moreover Los's name stands for the loss that produces creative daemonism if loss is defended against rather than submitted to. Yet the children of the parent powers will not submit any more than their parents do. Reproducing in themselves their parent's terror of loss, the children compensate for their fears by regenerating themselves as agents of deceit, jealousy and aggression. "If we grateful prove," Enitharmon tells Los, "they [the parents] will withhold sweet love, whose food is thorns and bitter roots." Thus the children seek to coerce love by bringing bitterness to their parents and then to each other. "Strong vibrations of fierce jealousy" make the children struggle to dominate each other, as a way to master the vulnerability in their mutual need. When Enitharmon smites the "sphery harp" to sing "a song of Death / It is a Song of Vala!"—Blake's very own poem—she is perpetuating a "rapturous delusive trance" whereby she can dominate Los. Blake here identifies his own art-song with a delusive, defensive strike against loss, with a beating or hammering that is a defense against vulnerability. But the exertion of the hammer is always the very loss it tries to drive away. Recognizing Enitharmon's coercive design, Los retaliates by striking her down, literally hammering his sister. Then he feels pity and contrite repentance for his jealous rage and fear—and calls it love. The result is a wedding of the two young artists, but they sit down to the wedding feast "in discontent and scorn." The desire to dominate vulnerability, to succeed against every weakness and dependency, creates an institution of love that is only the veil of a struggle. As Blake tells us in *Jerusalem*, in another attack on creativity, "Vala would never have sought and loved Albion / If she had not sought to destroy Jerusalem; such is that false / And generating love, a pretense of love to destroy love." It comes to seem as if the pretense of love to destroy love is the origin of sexual differentiation, a point Swinburne emphasizes when he speaks—concerning *The Gates of Paradise*—of Blake's idea that humanity was "neither good nor evil in the eternal life before this generated existence; male and female, who from of old was neither female nor male, but perfect . . . without division of flesh." So, Swinburne comments, from "the separation of the sexes come jealous love and personal desire, that set itself [*sic*] against the mystical frankness of fraternity."

Now Kipling may not have known *Vala; or, The Four Zoas* because Swinburne himself did not tackle the poem when he was in his twenties; Swinburne seems not to have read it even in 1906, when he comments on Yeats's edition. And after *Vala*, Blake softens his picture of Los and Enitharmon, to make them out as figures of mercy more than as harsh representatives of the order of creative jealousy. Yet there is an uncanny way in which Swinburne after all did "read" the *Vala* and did hand on to Kipling an accurate version of Blake's unsoftened picture of the brother-sister daemons. With penetrating ability to complete—in the form of his own work—whatever aspect of Blake's mythology was not available to him, in *Atalanta in Calydon* and in *Poems and Ballads* Swinburne imagines psychosexual fables that reproduce the struggles of Enitharmon and Los to dominate loss by "creative" jealousy. In *Atalanta* (which Kipling in his schooldays knew by heart) Althaea's fear of the loss of her son becomes a defensive, death-dealing aggression; her parent power, maternally jealous of Atalanta, comes to abet the paternal God whom the chorus curses as "the supreme evil" because he has created humanity as slaves to his jealousy. In *The Triumph of Time* in *Poems and Ballads* Swinburne turns away from the generative mother to a different maternal power, the sea—a liberator from the order of creative jealousy in which Eros too is trapped: "Death is the worst that comes of thee: / Thou are fed with our dead, O mother, O sea / But when hast thou fed on our hearts?" The sea promises a redemptive resumption by death, a liberating careless violence, that makes even suicide appear better than the human order instigated by fear of mortality.

Los and Enitharmon, and Swinburne's muse of liberating suicide—the mothering sea—reappear in the opening chapters of *The Light That Failed*. We might try now to see what specific help Blake and Swinburne contribute to a reevaluative reading of *The Light That Failed*. The standard reading, which needs to be set aside if we read Kipling's work on its own merit and yet with the antecedent poets in mind, is recirculated in Angus Wilson's opinions of 1978: the novel is "a farrago . . . of misogyny and false heroics and self pity"; the misogyny shows itself as male "wounds received in contact with the deadly other sex"; and "to balance all this misogyny," Wilson says, "we have the idealized world of men's men." It takes only ordinarily prejudiced inattention to make the facts of Kipling's plot fit this evaluation. We can say that Dick Heldar is destroyed by two women; by Maisie, who is frigid; and by Bessie Broke, who is a whore: the former breaks his heart, the latter destroys his last and greatest painting. In this misogynistic light the blindness Dick suffers can be read as Kipling's barely disguised fantasy of castration by women. Presenting its hero as a victim of this castration, the novel arguably rebukes women for trying to share the male's creative prerogatives. To support this standard reading what has been enlisted along with the facts of Kipling's childhood is the content of the novel's first, second, and fourth chapters, and their style—a striking, peculiar style that experiments with prose exposition as a form of rhyme. The first two chapters put back to back a first love-scene between the young adolescents Dick and Maisie—a scene in which they exchange kisses during a seaside pistol-shooting practice—and a war scene, much later in time, in which Dick suffers the head injury that will cause his eventual blindness. It is especially the rhyme of elements in both scenes that has led to the interpreter's connection of Maisie with aggression against Dick. In the first chapter Maisie misfires the revolver and sends gunpowder into Dick's eyes; when she then kisses Dick, the kiss on his cheek "stung more than gunpowder"; and after the kiss Dick's own aim with the gun is spoiled when Maisie's hair blows across his face. In the next chapter, as Dick in the Sudan is caught in literal gunfire, the momentary blindings of the episode with Maisie are echoed, in phrases that virtually quote the first chapter. Then in the fourth chapter once again the same phrases accompany the first reunion of Maisie and Dick since chapter 1. Moreover, in each moment of blindness Dick hears something like "Get away, you beast"—this command in the first chapter is from the children to their pet goat; in the second, from a wounded soldier to an attacker; in the third from a woman passerby on London Bridge to her lover. This "rhyme" has been taken by critics as Kipling's clinching equation of sexuality with bestiality—an equation necessary for any reading of the novel that identifies the female with the ultimate brutality, that sees her as a double (in the novel) for the most brutal aggressor, death.

But if we allow the possibility that Kipling, in the tradition of Swinburne and Swinburne's Blake, is not prosecuting one of the sexes, but is dramatizing a human order in which "jealous love and personal desire" have created the frightened separation of male and female and have set them both against each other, then the novel's opening, in all of its aspects, is not open to the customary dismissive reading. Like *Vala* or *Atalanta in Calydon* the first chapter of *The Light That Failed* presents a compact vision of a world in which order is the creation of jealous agents, whose aim is to master the terrifying loss of love and life by successfully striking at or beating vulnerability whenever it is manifested. In this world the orphans Dick and Maisie are a fledgling Los and Enitharmon who respond to the threat of loss by becoming creator-sadists. This development makes them mimics of the parent powers whose own defensive response to loss is tragically regenerated by the children. In the novel's first chapter Dick and Maisie have secretly purchased a revolver as a recourse against the beatings they receive from Mrs. Jennett, "the guardian who was incorrectly supposed to stand in the place of a mother to these two." Yet the beatings come from the mother only because, like Althaea in relation to the Supreme Evil, the female's sadism copies the male's. Dick receives the "average canings of a public school—about three times a month" and this "filled him with contempt for [Mrs. Jennett's] powers" to cane him. It fills him with contempt as well for the supreme caner, the male God. Dick's "home-training," as Mrs. Jennett calls her punishments, are inspired by her "religion manufactured in the main by her own intelligence and a keen study of the Scriptures. At such times as she herself was not personally displeased with Dick, she left him to understand that he had a heavy account to settle with his Creator; wherefore Dick learned to loathe his God as intensely as he loathed Mrs. Jennett." But although this loathing promises a revolutionary attack on the punitive Creator, Kipling shows how the attack is not executed because the movement towards liberation is overwhelmed by the fear of loss. Revolution is thereby diverted and the revolutionist becomes a copy of the oppressor. Mrs. Jennett herself, "anxious to remarry" because widowhood has made her an orphan of sorts, has turned the fear of what she has lost in life or will continue to lose into thorns and bitter roots, into the mastering of her dependents by beating them. And at the very moment in which the children play at killing Mrs. Jennett and her Creator they are frightened into continuing the order of beatings rather than liberating themselves from them. Realizing that they are about to lose each other (because Maisie just now announces that she is of age to leave her guardian), Dick's first and only recourse is to think of worldly vocation. His life's work will be a substitute for her—but it can be so only if it will also be a success. But what can Dick succeed at? " 'I don't seem to be able to pass any exams; but I can make awful caricatures of the masters.' 'Be an artist, then,' said Maisie," who has decided to become an artist herself. Art is the perfect calling for resentment: it caricatures the masters, and yet also reproduces them. Kipling's idea is that in a world ordered by offensive and defensive aggressions, art is no alternative to them. The imperialist caning of the Sudanese will be the arena in which appropriately Dick's art comes into its own. The violence Dick and Maisie are rehearsing in the first chapter thus passes into creativity itself; and their terror of the loss of love and power seals them into an aggression that becomes fatal competition with each other.

Although *The Light That Failed*, as we shall see, will go on to endorse a form of violence that is not terrified and defensive, Kipling is not endorsing the violence that the children use the revolver—and their choice of life's work—to implement. The signal to the reader not to endorse Dick closes the first chapter in the form of a dream that condenses the Blakeian and Swinburnian vision of loss-inspired creative aggression and psychosexual division. On the night of the shooting practice, Dick dreams he "had won all the world and brought it to Maisie in a cartridge box, but she turned it over with her foot, and, instead of saying, 'Thank you,' cried—'Where is the grass collar you promised for Amomma? Oh, how selfish you are!' " The cartridge box enclosing the world makes the world ammunition for the revolver. This detail is accurately analytic and foretells the truth. Dick's creativity will be a resentful stockpiling of aggressions; the success he will achieve will not be a matter of artistic "quality" but of his power of menace. Of course Kipling's point here is not concerned just with Dick; in the world he portrays, all the talk about art's achievement will be a mask for the competitive buildup of jealous power. Blake the visionary escaped the practice of art as ballistics because he was blind to the world and so to "success." Dick's dream tells us that he is not yet blind enough—he is too much of a worldling. The dream masks his own recognition of the terror of loss that motivates his world-beating. In *this* blindness he scapegoats Maisie: supposedly *she* is selfish, because she thinks Amomma, her pet goat, is worth more than the world Dick wins for her. But of course the blame attached here to Maisie keeps Dick from seeing anything clearly about himself.

What the reader can see clearly about both Dick and Maisie is concentrated in Kipling's use of Amomma in the dream and in the pistol practice. The goat has eaten some of the cartridges, and the children become terrified that the goat will explode. Trying to drive the animal away "because he might blow up at any time," Maisie exclaims to Amomma, "Horrid little beast!" But the goat is the children's totem, and they themselves have become containers for bullets—as Dick's dream shows. Terrified of their losses and about to feed on the thorns and roots of the war for success, the children are becoming themselves the beast. The goat who substitutes as a momma for them is also the explosive God-father. Kipling's way of giving the he-goat a female sounding name forecasts the novel's questioning of male and female alike as culturally determined components of the war against failure. Later in the text Dick will utter an apparently unmotivated exclamation against "hermaphroditic futilities." Both this exclamation and the hermaphrodite goat-totem find their appropriate comment in Swinburne on sexual division in Blake: "Contradictory as it may seem . . . the hermaphroditic emblem is always used [by Blake] as a symbol seemingly of duplicity and division, perplexity and restraint. The two sexes should not combine and contend; they must finally amalgamate and be annihilated." In swallowing the world as ammunition, the children are incorporating the duplicity and division that has already beaten them and that will devote them in turn to administering beatings. And although by means of the pastoral grass collar the dream suggests a world outside creative jealousy's modes of order, for Kipling this *is* only a dream, and every worldly, loss-terrified alternative is beastly.

Thus when Kipling repeats or varies "Horrid little beast!" in the second and fourth chapters, the variation harks back to what the goatlike bullet-swallowing children dramatize at the novel's start about the creative jealousy they are not able to escape. To see the "beast" motif or rhyme as an attack on women or as prudery about sex is to read with prejudice, and inflexibly. And like the "beast" motif, the opening chapters' other significant rhymes—all of which use momentary blindness to forecast Dick's loss of sight—repay disinterested attention. Before each of the moments of temporary blindness, Kipling presents Dick focusing on reflections in water or on metal of the setting sun. The sun is always associated with aggressive wrath: "a wrathful red disk" is varied as a "savage red disk" on a spearpoint that is "a red splash in the distance," which in the fourth chapter becomes "a blood-red wafer." There is reason to read these repeated suns as figures for the explosive resentment against loss that Dick sees everything in the light of; it is this wrathful light, which is a figure of the creative order of jealousy Dick wants to succeed in, that the novel claims is the light that fails. Like Amomma, the red disk is used by Kipling to compound vivid immediacy with abstract analysis. In the case of the sun-figure the analysis comes from Kipling's view of imperialism (in this novel)—a view covered up by critical insistence that the wrathful light is only a sign of Maisie's aggression against Dick. When during the second chapter's sunset Dick receives his ultimately blinding injury from a Mahdi attacker, he is also dealing out wounds, and his best friend Torpenhow is using a thumb to put out an Arab's eye. What we might well understand here is that even where the usually noncombatant correspondents are concerned, there is a correspondence between violent imperialist wrath inflicted on native populations and secret, internal wounds these inflictions wreak in turn on the imperialists. During the scene of Dick's desert skirmish, Gordon's death at Khartoum—the failure in the 1880s of British imperialism against the Mahdi—is occurring. But this wounding failure is not represented by Kipling as the pity of an imperialist defeat. In fact Kipling's "moral" is that the infliction of victimhood on the victor (unlike Gordon, Dick's cohorts win their skirmish) is a first opening towards blindness to the world dominated by the jealous order of British success. Eventually, the novel says, the wound of failure opens one to freedom from the creative daemon. If like the Mahdieh Maisie wounds Dick, then the imperialist's native victims are a likeness of Maisie—of woman; she then is the native force whose rebellion has the potential to open the hero to liberation from success—and from the terror of loss.

Once worldly life—figured by the blood-red disk of wrath—fails, what there is to see, and to see in the light of, is what we might call visionary, even though it is an obscurity or darkness from the worldly point of view in which failure is feared and is not acceptable. This obscurity of vision, a twin to the obscurities of failure and of death, is the genuine counter-violence that contrasts with Dick's defensive aggression. Maisie has been criticized for being an agent of this saving counter-violence—though Kipling's rhymes on Maisie's association with Dick's growing darkness even predict this salvation. When Maisie's hair blows across Dick's face in the first chapter and thereby spoils his aim, Kipling makes the spoiling agent not Maisie but a "thrashing" night wind—an extension of Mrs. Jennett's Creator and his jealous wrath. The aim that is being spoiled needs to be spoiled since it is an aiming at resentful anger as a vocation. Within two pages of the description of the blinding darkness of Maisie's hair, as the children assert the comfort of belonging to each other, the evening becomes "the kindly darkness [that] hid them both"; and then, when in the fourth chapter, Dick rediscovers Maisie just after the black smoke of a Thames river steamer has obscured his vision, we are reminded—or should be—of the kindly obscurity that has enveloped hero and heroine within mutual belonging. The failure of light, the "rhymes" on darkness suggest, is a loving and saving obscurity.

So, in conjunction with the thematic influence of Blake and Swinburne, the "rhymes" that organize the exposition of Kipling's novel work—when they are read closely—in a way that undoes the customary evaluation and its grounds. And the "rhymes" are an essential part of a formal aspect of *The Light That Failed* that has a bearing on Kipling's work in general. One of Kipling's failures, it has been said repeatedly, is his inability to write extended works, novels rather than tales. The possibility that Kipling intended to reform "the novel" in the direction of radical condensation and brevity, that he wanted the customary extent of fiction to fail, and that this intention is the result of his thematic visions and obsessions, is not broached; yet it ought to be. In *The Light That Failed*, Kipling describes one of Dick's best paintings as the result of the artist's "going out of my way to foreshorten for sheer delight of doing it." This is a tip to the reader about the method of the novel's composition, and about the delight even the reader might take in the technique.

Kipling's fiction is the development of an art of foreshortening. Although Dick's painting illustrates Poe, a practitioner of the same art, here too Blake and Swinburne are inspirations. Blake foreshortened by his habit of condensing extended psychic and narrative sequences into one simultaneous moment, and Swinburne by his habit of forcing antitheses to become oxymorons. But above all Kipling's thoughts about failure set the pattern of formal foreshortening for *The Light That Failed*, and they make use of the rhymes as an essential part of the pattern. The rhymes impact Dick's rising career and the novel's rising action upon moments of sunset and decline. By seeming to repeat the novel's start three or four times over via the same details, Kipling produces in the reader a discomfort with the novel's mode of succession. With his initial and initiatory aspects set in a constant glow of sunset, the writer makes the reader sense succession of a linear and temporal sort as blocked, as steps forward that are a mere walking in place. This sense of blocked narrative succession transfers itself back and forth, in a kind of formal pun, between the novel's structure and its theme of success: the latter is from the start not a progress but a stasis, is an ascension in a frozen state of decline. By the third chapter, in fact, before Dick's reunion with Maisie, the hero already has begun to decline. Torpenhow kicks in one of Dick's canvases in protest against the way success is spoiling Dick's aim. Success is spoiling just because it seems to surmount vulnerability to discontinuity, to loss of effort and life. The unperceived blinding Dick receives in the second chapter shows the omnipresence of the loss that success may appear to overcome, but never will. The succession of achievements called a career is thus an illusory flight from the obscurity environing light and life. What rises at the start of the novel is the setting sun, the intrusiveness of ending, the violence done to moments that succeed each other. Kipling's rhymes surprisingly and paradoxically disjoin the novel's initial and sequential elements, in a way predicting not just the hero's breakup but the text's.

But before we see how Kipling attempts to make the text itself witness its own demise as a vivid and visual picture of things, Kipling's presentation of Maisie and Bessie needs to be reclaimed as much as his novel's beginning. In their own pursuits of success, Maisie and Bessie share the male's terrified reaction to loss; all three compose an hermaphroditic emblem of "duplicity and division," of futiley "jealous love and personal desire." The three characters must be read as emanations of each other; what combines and contends in each are aspects of the other two. Yet even when we do read the characters so, we see that Kipling has furnished Maisie with an aura of integrity of character superior to Dick's. Like Dick, Maisie is terrified by loss and mortality into choosing art as a defense, but she maintains this choice in a less incoherent way than the man. Dick represents for Kipling the incoherence of the male attachment to success, like his knowing male friends, Dick insists he is liberated from success, and harangues Maisie to free herself from its pursuit; but his emotional attachment to what his mind opposes persists, and as a result of his self-contradiction he appears to be more enslaved to success than Maisie. At least Maisie knows what she wants and does not compromise her desire; Dick is all compromise, cannot practice what he preaches and exhibits even his vaunted liberation as yet another way of beating the world—and Maisie. Having admitted in chapter 5 that "there is too much Ego in my Cosmos," and having made that into a sermon to Maisie on the superiority of craft to worldly success, in chapter

7 (the novel's midpoint) Dick confesses that he still believes the world owes him money and recognition: he cannot get over the rancor of having once been down and out in London and of having been cheated then of three-pence he never got for carrying a man's bags. Maisie teases Dick into confessing his stubborn resentment of failure, hence his persisting worship of success; and then she playfully restores the lost threepence out of her own pocket. "The very human apostle of fair craft" takes the coin though it is not "befitting the man who had preached the sanctity of work." Kipling sets this confession at exactly the seaside scene of the early pistol shooting, to remind us of the origins of Dick's career in anger fixated on loss. And then when Dick takes the "restored" coin and throws it into the Thames, we learn that the coin's drowning "seemed to cut him free from thought of Maisie for the moment." So Maisie is for Dick the coin he has not gotten out of the world; thereby his solicitations of her in the name of love remain the token of his war for success, against vulnerability. His "love"—which he usually feels as pity for her bad habits and lack of talent—seems a self-deceiving compunction for a kind of secret violence he keeps doing her. Although grown-up Maisie has told Dick forthrightly that she neither loves him nor wants to, he refuses to take her honesty to heart—refuses, that is, to take her loss to heart. "The end was only a question of time now," he thinks, "and the prize well worth the waiting." And while he waits, he proposes a competition: they will each paint a figure of Melancolia as it appears in "The City of Dreadful Night," and they will see who better succeeds at the portrayal. We find Dick swearing—in a way that is funny at his own expense—"I'll make her understand that I can beat her on her own Melancolia." It's just this order of beatings that produces the melancholy order of things Kipling portrays.

Maisie seems stronger than Dick, less liable to beat others (*and* less liable to succeed) just because she is able not to confuse her fear of loss, her desire for success, or her pity, with love. Maisie's last appearance in the novel is when Torpenhow brings Maisie back from France to England, in a rather callous attempt to palm blind Dick off on her. While she has been abroad, Maisie has begun to suspect that Dick is helping someone else to paint, so she has grown jealous to the point of thinking that she is after all "in love with him." Faced with Dick's invalidism, she is on the verge of feeling the love Los and Enitharmon feel whenever one sees the other wounded. This is just the kind of "love" Dick's male friends are feeling for him—a fact curiously not faced by those who claim the novel idealizes male friendship. Since the men consider Dick a failure now—"out of the race,—down,—*gastados*, expended, finished, done for"—they must get rid of him, so that their own work will not be hampered. They assume that woman's place is to "love" pitiful dropouts from the all-important success they pursue—even though, like Dick, the friends preach craft for craft's sake while they practice craft for unhampered success's sake. But, in spite of the friends' considerable pressure on her to take a "selfless" place in the world of male success, Maisie resists. She is horrified by Dick's blindness, but we are told she does not confuse things as the men do: "she was only filled with pity most startlingly distinct from love." Maisie's ability to keep love and pity distinct gives her a clear-sighted integrity that no man in the novel possesses—and that the hero will not possess until he has got used to being blind.

Bessie Broke, like Maisie, is another of the aspects that combine and contend in Dick. This other member of the hermaphrodite trinity also has a coherence superior to the male's. Following what he has done with Maisie, Kipling uses Bessie as a touchstone for the reader's view of Dick's confusions. In painting the Melancolia, Dick makes the face of the portrait a composite of Maisie's and Bessie's faces. This detail has aptness when we think of the origin of the picture in Dick's "pique"—as he calls it—against Maisie. The prostitute's role in the composite face asks to be read as a likeness for Dick's attempt to prostitute Maisie to his will to succeed as her lover. Kipling in his foreshortening way is also showing that the prostitute's role in the picture is a sign of Dick's own continuing prostitution to the public success which Dick says he despises even as he makes Maisie a stand-in for it. Choosing to make Bessie destroy the Melancolia, Kipling is picturing the way the prostitution and the coercion that produce art ruin it. Of course, Bessie spoils the painting since Dick has spoiled her masterpiece, the housekeeping she had aimed to set up with Torpenhow. Dick insists on packing off Torpenhow because he claims the latter's affair with Bessie will spoil for good the foreign correspondence; but Dick has recently been preaching the fatheadedness of believing in lasting work, and he already has asked Maisie to run off to the tropics on the assumption that domesticity anywhere will not impair art. As the victim of this incoherence, Bessie, who fully knows what *she* wants, has a right to avenge herself. The Bessie-part of his own self is racking Dick here, and his ultimate freedom from his contradictions is actually helped along by Bessie's justifiable adversity.

But while the novel shows the women in a better light than it shows the man, *The Light That Failed* does not endorse the success either the man or the women pursue. And whether the pursuit is aesthetically or domestically oriented, whether unconventionally or conventionally, the novel's claim is that all pursuits of success grind at the same terror-driven mill. Out of the desire for compensation for loss and out of pity, Dick in his blindness proposes marriage to Bessie, but this would be a way of sitting down to the marriage feast in "secret discontent and scorn." And in contrast to Maisie, Bessie confuses pity for Dick with love; her domestic ambitions are her rancorous way of collecting threepence from the world. When Dick breaks off the marriage, he is no longer acting incoherently—he would be continuing to act incoherently only if he pursued the marriage. We are to understand that his blindness and the destruction of his work have brought him to believe that even marriage abets the structure of self-contradiction that is the order of creative jealousy. Neither the work of art nor the work of marriage can succeed against darkness, because aesthetic and domestic order remain within the pale of displaced defensive rage against loss. We perhaps can see Kipling himself coming more definitely to his novel's ideas about marriage by means of a striking fact in the publication history of *The Light That Failed*. Within five months Kipling published two versions of the book, the second of which he declared was the story "as it was originally conceived." The second is the version we have; the first appeared in America in *Lippincott's* magazine, is shorter, and ends happily, with Maisie marrying the blind hero. It is possible the magazine asked for changes in the "original" harsh story; it is also said that Kipling's mother asked him for a more pleasant finale. Yet, in line with the criticism of success, the marriage in the "happy" version is presented as a liberating escape from the success Dick's fellow-journalists pursue, with what is shown to be coarse self-confidence. But in the months before the English appearance of the novel, what may have come clear to Kipling was that the privacy of marriage—any domestic arrangements, in fact—could not escape the social order's devotion to beating loss.

As a way of demonstrating the logic of his vision and hence of the inescapable link between domestic order and a society founded on beating failure, Kipling entwines Dick's last phase with Bessie with a sudden focus on the family of Dick's landlord, the Beetons. Beeton and his wife steal from Dick things they insist are useless to a blind man; in exchange they send their boy Alf to minister to Dick. The Beetons pin their hopes for worldy success on Alf, a talented mimic whose receptivity to education and whose sentimentality about domestic order are highly promising of worldly achievement. "He do read beautiful, seeing he's only nine" and "only to 'ear Alf sing 'A Boy's Best Friend is 'is Mother'! Ah!" the parents exclaim. The Beetons are a version of what Dick has been, and what London relies on for stability while Britain attempts to succeed in mastering the world. And Kipling suggests that Alf is what he himself is or has been—and what Dick and Kipling together must leave behind. The novel's publication in its original form begins with dedicatory verses, apparently to Kipling's mother, that might as well carry the title of Alf's song. If Mrs. Kipling urged the bowdlerized version of the novel in *Lippincott's*, presumably this ending gave the novel a better chance at worldly success. But in publishing the novel's unhappy ending Kipling makes it obvious that he does not want to underwrite the dictates of success. The dedicatory poem both asserts and subverts the novelist's possible identification with Alf by a sly equivocation: the "mother o'mine" in the verse's refrain could be *Swinburne's* sea, the sea that brings liberty and destruction together and that Dick talks about in Swinburnian terms in the novel's eighth chapter, which also was not published in *Lippincott's*. Bessie Broke, the Beetons, and Mrs. Kipling too, want to defeat loss with a form of domestic success that for Kipling is already broken and failed by its dependence on beatings, both at home and abroad. Because we are asked to see this order as inescapable, Dick does not take up the opportunity of marriage with Maisie's friend, a jealous yet admiring impressionist painter. In his final trip to Africa, the novel's hero steps out altogether from the order of creative jealousy.

The surrender to loss means for the artist Kipling—and not just for the artist Dick—an insistence on the failure and mortality of all picturings of the world. To insist on any surmounting of failure by the success of creative articulation would endorse the order of things the novel criticizes. *The Light That Failed* does not evade facing its own consequent paradox: it offers its readers an urgent abstract vision of the world in a vivid verbal mode of picturing things, at the same time as it calls into question the accuracy and trustworthiness of its very mode of envisioning. The novel—and the novelist—must enact their own self-blinding, in order to point beyond that order of creative jealousy in which even the delineations of art are defensively imbedded. Whatever the psychoanalytical dimensions and motivations of this may be, the historical dimensions and motivations are fully set out by Kipling. To the surprise of our prejudices about him, he suggests that art must undergo and face its own blinding in order to be saved from, above all, alliance with the imperialist aspect of creative jealousy. Kipling ties his Blakeian and Swinburnian vision to concrete history in order to resist the ties his own work has with the Beetons. They intend to command the future by a surprising alliance with art, because for them art clarifies obscurity, and its picturings enlighten, in a way that serves their self-aggrandizing power. In the world of the Beetons, that is, the Beetons together with artists like Maisie and Dick want art to succeed against obscurity, want art's contemplations to invent the world as an intelligible place, not as a place of violence done to clarity and articulation. In such invention there is a defense against loss; success then is picturing (especially in Kipling's own vivid mode), success is articulation itself. "Whether Gordon lived or died, or half the British army went to pieces in the sand" does not matter, as the special correspondents know; what matters is that "The Soudan Campaign was a picturesque one, and lent itself to vivid word-painting. . . . All [the masses] demanded was picturesqueness and abundance of detail." "Amused and thrilled and interested" by the success of portrayal, "England at breakfast" (identified as "Lover of Justice, Constant Reader, Paterfamilias, and all that lot") can withstand the loss of Gordon, because at least the special correspondents have beaten the darkness. They have brought to the eyes of England, in the form of thrilling delineations, the Mahdi natives themselves. Like the artists with whom they remain in close alliance, the special correspondents in Kipling's novel testify to the way in which confidently articulated mediation of the world is expected to be an ally against loss.

To oppose this alliance against loss makes Kipling not want to identify his art with such special correspondence. The confidence in what the artist can see or can make visible is a blind for the artist's situation in the imperialist order of creative jealousy. Kipling's analysis of the artist's tie to imperialist success pervades his youthful work. We see it in the same year as *The Light That Failed* in a story called "A Conference of the Powers," where the celebrated novelist Eustace Cleever discovers that his clever art fails to articulate or even suggest the experience in India of a young soldier called the Infant. Yet for Cleever to succeed here would amount to a treacherous domination of the Infant who is an indomitable object of wonder because he has not been and cannot be articulated. And when the Infant tells a story about a Burmese native, Boh Na-ghee, we see that the Boh is to the Infant what the latter is to the novelist: an impenetrable but awesome obscurity. The Infant can only lisp about the Boh, but just this saves the Boh from being mastered by the imperializing success of portrayal. Even in the Stalky series, "The Flag of Their Country" (1899) presents another version of Cleever in the figure of the M.P. whose confident clarity about the Empire's servants and its governed peoples is reprehensible to Kipling.

It is clarity itself that the creative order of jealousy has made reprehensible, so that Kipling must play Bessie Broke to his own work, rubbing out his own canvases. The way to rub out melancholia rooted in the fear of loss, Kipling seems to think, is to join with loss to exhibit articulation's failures. This violent self-impairment of the artist and his work is the counter-violence that must be done to the Creator-daemon, to his defensive aggression. There is only one moment in *The Light That Failed* which sharply contradicts Kipling's identification with violence committed against creative jealousy. When Dick hears that Bessie has destroyed his work, the narrative asserts that a man, unlike a woman, "will never forgive the destruction of his work." The statement is perhaps a sign of Kipling's resistance to the bowdlerizing of his novel, but it is also perhaps a sign of his joining with his aggressors in the name of success. Whatever its motive, the assertion is both artistically and sexually offensive because the rest of the novel belies it. Neither Maisie nor Bessie forgives the destruction of her work, considered either as art or as domesticity; but it is just this lack of forgiveness for such destruction, rather than destruction itself, which the novel refuses to countenance in women and men alike. Perhaps it would be more accurate to say that Kipling must play not Bessie but the female Impressionist to his work, for Maisie's friend provides a model of accepting destruction of one's art. Dick has long felt guilty for the way he has mastered his human subjects—"all the people in the past whom he had laid open for the purpose of his own craft." One day he is "laid open" in turn by Maisie's friend, whose accuracy of portrayal is a way of mocking and beating Dick. Yet the Impressionist deliberately destroys her sketch of Dick, both to save him pain and to surrender her own defensive aggression—for she is bitterly jealous (another hermaphroditic futility) of Dick and Maisie.

Again, then, a woman is the model for what Kipling must do to his own art—make it surrender its ambition to master the world by submitting to the vulnerability and mortality that are feared by mastery. Art must be brought to view the place where it fails, the borderline site where it cannot even articulate an object. At this borderline, art's ventures are sunsets; they are exposed as thresholds of loss. Yet this thresholding is not to be lamented; the violence of loss and failure art undergoes in *The Light That Failed* is the only possible counter to jealousy. So not just the Impressionist, but Dick and Torpenhow actively destroy their work, and suffer and forgive the destruction. In the eighth chapter Dick tells without regret the story of the loss of what had been his best work: a fantasy of Poe's "Annabel Lee" done on the walls of a hold of a ship long since sunk and hence triumphed over by that "mother o'mine," the sea. In the same chapter we are told of Dick's sketchbook in which satiric cartoons portray the life of a special correspondent called by the name of a Sudanese tribe, the Nilghai. Although the sketchbook is copiously and wildly inventive, we are told that Dick cannot—and will not—portray the most important event in the life of the Nilghai; like the Boh's, the heart of the Nilghai can't be penetrated by portrayal. Even the artist's power of conviction about what he cannot articulate or about the vulnerable dignity of his craft cannot secure for his work any forgoing of the violence of loss it must accept. The talk in the novel about the importance to art of convictions is a red herring; neither convictions, nor will, nor hard work guarantees any surmounting of failure and death.

Summarizing the "moral" of Blake's portrait of the blind artist Milton, Swinburne writes, "Only by vision or by death shall we be brought safe past the watch guarded by the sentinels of material form and bodily life, the crude tributary 'Afrites' (as in the Aeschylean myth) of the governing power which fashions and fetters life." For *The Light That Failed*, "the sentinels of material form and bodily life" are the thresholds art must designate as such, to show the obscurity of what lies beyond the sentinels, even though the demonstration costs the "governing power" not just of art but of historical life, even of psychosexual life. If art is to have justification, *The Light That Failed* suggests that its defense can lie in its vulnerable attempt to point out the contradictions in which the empire's art and experience together are trapped by their terror of loss. Interestingly, it is the "Afrites" whom the British want to make tributary who lead Dick out of the fabrications and fetters of material life and Western success; it is the Mahdieh, whose leader is a mystic visionary, impenetrable by Western eyes, and the Mahdieh's violence done to the Empire's light and power that bring Dick "past the watch." The last strikingly vivid picture of *The Light That Failed*, the last one Kipling delineates and also rubs out in order to end his text, conveys a powerfully darkened Blakeian vision—something like an assertion that "only by obscurity of vision and by death can we be safe." The picture epitomizes the careless violence Kipling suggests must be done to vivid aesthetic picturings, to free them from the world's jealous fetters, and to make them faithful to an obscure but trustworthy alternative to the world.

In the novel's finale, blind Dick has made his way back to the Sudan, and rides an armored troop train, looking like "one long coffin," out to Suakin; from there he commandeers a camel and a camel-driver to take him to an outpost where he hopes to find Torpenhow. So as not to be tricked, he must ride the camel with a gun in the driver's back. Half-asleep atop the camel, revolver in hand, he hallucinates he is learning "a punishment hymn" at Mrs. Jennett's. But the only lines in the hymn he can learn are about deliverance, because he is being delivered from the order of creative jealousy. The image of this deliverance is marked by a shift in his hallucination: he thinks he is back in London, picturing on canvas the desert scene that is blindly before him:

> The last hour before the light lengthens itself into many eternities. It seemed to Dick that he had never since the beginning of original darkness done anything at all save jolt through the air. Once in a thousand years he would finger the nailheads on the saddle-front and count them all carefully. Centuries later he would shift his revolver from his right hand to his left and allow the eased arm to drop down at his side. From the safe distance of London he was watching himself thus employed,—watching critically. Yet whenever he put out his hand to the canvas that he might paint the tawny yellow desert under the glare of the sinking moon, the black shadow of the camel and the two bowed figures atop, that hand held a revolver and the arm was numbed from wrist to collarbone. Moreover, he was in the dark, and could see no canvas of any kind whatever.

There is great summary power here for Kipling's thematic and formal intentions. At the moment when the writer is picturing for us the blind man's ride in the desert, he reminds us of how difficult it is to see once one has traveled beyond the place where picturing has its capital in the world of success. Yet this traveling into the eternities of darkness is necessary just because it remains out of the reach of the artist's eye, arm and aim. The attempt to delineate or articulate the darkness that lies on the other side of creative jealousy can only do defensive violence to that darkness; commanded by such enlightening intention, the artist's art is a form of imperialism, a gun in the back of what is beyond the empire's sentinels and front lines. Dick has harassed Maisie to "go on with your line-work," but neither color nor line has any capability of correspondence with the obscurity that must spoil all lines. Like the brush or the pen, the "creative" weapons that succeed in the worldly London distance, the revolver here is what it was in the novel's first chapter: the aggressive instrument, using terror as a defense against terror. But the rhyme of the revolver here with the earlier pistol practice also bears a different meaning. The gun is rendered impotent because the numbness of the wrist holding it is the sign of vulnerability—of the mind's and the body's vulnerability to failure and loss, which no creative act can overcome. The revolver memorializes the defensiveness that for Dick is past. And now that the worldly canvas cannot be seen in any light whatsoever, now that it is no longer the scene to which Dick's ambition is attached, the revolver also figures the nondefensive, careless violence with which Dick is joined. It is a violence that enacts loss, that actively takes the side of mortality by abetting death's work. His mortality gives Dick the energy to carry through this last adventure in the desert. The death that succeeds the adventure is, of course, a suicide, which under Western eyes has long been held to be unacceptable as a sane, voluntary and not shameful act. For the young visionary Kipling, it seems that salvific human possibilities other than the acceptable ones needed to be pursued, at no matter what violent cost to history, to selves and to creative art.

Like Dick Heldar, in *Dispatches* Errol Flynn's son Sean, one of Michael Herr's most admired fellow "specials," disappears into the darkness, never to be seen again. Was he a "victim" to "something more complicated than death" or merely free from the fear of death? In contrast to Flynn, Herr retreats from loss to America and "success," even at the expense of what he seems on the verge of seeing as an identity between success and the war that is on, all the time. The sadly notable thing about Kipling, of course, is that he too may have retreated from his vision of failure after *The Light That Failed*. Perhaps the subsequent events of Kipling's life—the deaths of two of his three children especially—tested the novel's implications with so unremitting a pressure that Kipling could no longer face what young strength had given him the pessimism to see. In his subsequent worldly politics he may have capitulated to a resistance to all the darkness of failure. Nevertheless, the later work does not put aside and cancel the thematics and poetics of *The Light That Failed*, no matter what Kipling's life put aside. And Kipling's life does not matter to his work or to his literary tradition. Loss without compensation and failure as a redress to the world of creative beatings continue to show themselves in Kipling's writing. And just as more needs to be said about the writing, so more needs to be said about Kipling's literary roots (I have not even mentioned Browning); and much more about the tradition Kipling made rather than the tradition he was made by. How long, for example, will it be still possible to ignore Kipling's influence on Conrad? We have celebrated *Heart of Darkness*'s venture into the blinding of vision without a thought of Kipling; yet Conrad published an unsigned article on him in *Outlook* in April 1898; and the curious detail that turns up a painting by Kurtz at the Congo Central Station may owe itself to the Melancolia. Kurtz's painting is of an allegorical blindfolded woman carrying a lighted torch, a picture that forecasts Marlow's adventure as a study of a light that has failed and as an enactment of sight's replacement by impenetrable obscurity. Before he writes *Heart of Darkness*, Conrad proclaims the artist's duty as "before all, to make you see," in apparent contrast to Kipling's assertion that the artist's task, before all, is to darken sight, to make your sight fail. Yet when Conrad comes to his Congo story, it is as if he has changed his mind about the artist's task and is following Kipling. We keep ourselves from seeing this sort of influence by dismissing *The Light That Failed* as a failure. But it is with an ironic appropriateness to his work that we continue to maintain our loss of Kipling.

World within Worlds:
Kipling and Nesbit

Stephen Prickett

> *In his earliest time I though he perhaps contained the seeds of an English Balzac; but I have given that up in proportion as he has come down steadily from the simple in subject to the more simple—from the Anglo-Indians to the natives, from the natives to the Tommies, from the Tommies to the quadrupeds, from the quadrupeds to the fish, and from the fish to the engines and screws.*
>
> —HENRY JAMES

One of the reasons why Kipling's reputation has always been so controversial is the difficulty of classifying him. Was his the voice of the arch-imperialist? or the cool-headed and pessimistic critic of imperialism? or simply that of the hooligan? Was he a natural short-story writer, or a novelist manqué? Was he primarily a "realist" or a creator of "fables"? Was there, as James implies in his letter of 1897 quoted above, a progressive and alarming dehumanising in his writing? Into such discussions, sometimes almost by accident, we find still more elusive "hints of yet another Kipling," as C. S. Lewis puts it:

> There are moments of an almost quivering tenderness—he himself had been badly hurt—when he writes of children or for them. And there are the "queer" or "rum" stories—"At the End of the Passage," "The Mark of the Beast," "They," "Wireless." These may be his best work, but they are not his most characteristic.

It is the last throwaway sentence that gives us pause: "his best work, but . . . not his most characteristic." Even Lewis, who is one of Kipling's most perceptive critics, has a clear preconception of his characteristics that, somehow, excludes his best work—which is simply if quaintly described as "queer" or"rum."

Another formidable critic, Bonamy Dobrée, sees much of Kipling's work in terms of "fables"—but has some difficulty in defining what, in Kipling's case, the word means.

> All stories worthy of the name are partly fables, in that they contain an idea—otherwise they are no more than anecdotes. The "point"

From *Victorian Fantasy.* © 1979 by Stephen Prickett. The Harvester Press, 1979.

of a story is its revelation of, or singling out of, some characteristic of human nature or behaviour; its moral is applicable to our daily doings. The "idea" of a fable goes beyond the local or immediate; its theme is universal. But it is impossible to draw a clear line between the two. In any event, the word "fable" is very vague, more so than "parable" or "allegory," in themselves constituting elements in a fable, which, according to common usage, is an impossible, or at least highly unlikely story, though improbability is not in itself a criterion.

Kipling himself offers us a definition in a somewhat different key. It is clear enough, up to a point.

> When all the world would keep a matter hid,
>   Since truth is seldom friend to any crowd,
> Men write in fable, as old Aesop did,
>   Jesting at that which none will name aloud.
> And this they needs must do, or it will fall
> Unless they please they are not heard at all.
>   ("The Fabulists," 1917)

Fables are for the "inner ring" of those few who can understand. As Kipling tells us, *Puck of Pook's Hill* was intended to come into this category of stories with a secret meaning, but this, I suspect, has little to do with the qualities that Lewis valued in his children's books, nor does it entirely satisfy Dobrée's meaning of a "fable." For almost all his readers, what is best about *Puck* or the other fables is not a hidden allegorical meaning—though that may contribute to it—but a sense of *extra* meaning in the events because they suggest a universe that is richer and fuller of possibilities than had hitherto been dreamed of. For those of us familiar with the tradition of Victorian fantasy that lay behind him, this difficulty of exact definition is a familiar one. Kipling is a natural fantasist, in the sense that he is always trying, in even his most realistic stories, to cram more into "reality" than it can possibly hold. The reasons that led him in middle life to turn increasingly away from the realism of his early Indian stories towards the world of Mowgli, Puck, and the *Just-So Stories,* were in essence the same as those which had made George MacDonald before him repudiate the charge of being an "allegorist" and insist that he was a writer of "fairy stories." The turning to fantasy was neither a degeneration "from the simple to the still more simple" as James had supposed, nor a psychic retreat from the complexities of the adult world, as others have suggested, but the logical next step in Kipling's development as a writer. The fact that they were "children's fantasies" was irrelevant. Of *Rewards and Fairies*, he commented, "the tales had to be read by children, before people realized that they were meant for grown-ups." From the first, Kipling was a man haunted by other worlds, and as his art developed he became progressively more skilful in sggesting the intersection of different plains of reality.

At its simplest we can see this in his fascination with the world of work. The mysteries of a man's profession make one kind of "inner ring" of knowledge about people, and what they are. In his autobiographical sketch, *Something of Myself,* he describes how at the age of seventeen he became a member of the "Punjab Club" at Lahore.

> And in that Club and elsewhere I met none except picked men at their definite work—Civilians, Army, Education, Canals, Forestry, Engineering, Irrigation, Railways, Doctors, and Lawyers—samples of each branch and each talking his own shop. It follows then that that "show of technical knowledge" for which I was blamed later came to me from the horse's mouth, even to boredom.

Other more esoteric worlds were opened for him by the Freemasons, which he was able to join under age "because the Lodge hoped for a good secretary." "Here I met Muslims, Hindus, Sikhs, members of the Arya and Brahmo Samaj, and a Jew tyler, who was priest and butcher to his little community in the city. So yet another world opened to me which I needed." Lewis, like other critics since, has observed how "Kipling is first and foremost the poet of work," showing in detail men in their professional skills almost for the first time in fiction. But even he does not see how this delight of Kipling's with the closed worlds of particular professions is only a part of a still wider fascination with the possibilities of yet other closed worlds lost to us through time, or the limitations of sense and mortality. For Lewis it is only an extension of the thrills of the secret society:

> In the last resort I do not think he loves professional brotherhood for the sake of the work; I think he loves work for the sake of professional brotherhood . . . To belong, to be inside, to be in the know, to be snugly together against the outsiders—that is what really matters.

But Kipling wants to be in the know about things at a much more profound level than either the professionals of the Punjab Club or the Freemasons could offer. He wants to be in the know about the universe.

In "The Bridge Builders," one of the best of his early fantasies, the dazzling display of intricate technical knowledge of bridge construction is set within a story of Hindu gods that is only incidentally a "fable." The bridge in question is an enormous railway bridge across the Ganges.

> With its approaches, his work was one mile and three-quarters in length; a lattice-girder bridge, trussed with the Findlayson truss, standing on seven-and-twenty brick piers. Each of those piers was twenty-four feet in diameter, capped with red Agra stone and sunk eighty feet below the shifting sand of the Ganges' bed. Above them ran the railway-line fifteen feet broad; above that, again, a cart-road of eighteen feet, flanked with footpaths. At either end

rose towers of red brick, loopholed for musketry and pierced for big guns, and the ramp of the road was being pushed forward in their haunches. The raw earth-ends were crawling and alive with hundreds upon hundreds of tiny asses climbing out of the yawning borrow-pit below with sackfuls of stuff; and the hot afternoon air was filled with the noise of hooves, the rattle of the driver's sticks, and the swish and roll-down of the dirt. The river was very low, and on the dazzling white sand between the three centre piers stood squat cribs of railway-sleepers, filled within and daubed without with mud, to support the last of the girders as these were riveted up. In the little deep water left by the drought, an over-head-crane travelled to and fro along its spile-pier, jerking sections of iron into place, snorting and backing and grunting as an elephant grunts in the timber-yard. Riveters by the hundred swarmed about the lattice side-work and the iron roof of the railway-line, hung from invisible staging under the bellies of the girders, clustered round the throats of the piers, and rode on the overhang of the footpath-stanchions; their firepots and the spurts of flame that answered each hammer-stroke showing no more than pale yellow in the sun's glare. East and west and north and south the construction-trains rattled and shrieked up and down the embankments, the piled trucks of brown and white stone banging behind them till the side-boards were unpinned, and with a roar and a grumble a few thousand tons more material were thrown out to hold the river in place.

In charge of the works are two British engineers, Findlayson and his assistant Hitchcock, and their lascar foreman, Peroo. the first part of the story is entirely taken up with the excitement of watching the bridge grow: the skill and patience required of the engineers, and their hopes and frustrations: "the months of office work destroyed at a blow when the Government of India, at the last moment, added two feet to the width of the bridge, under the impression that bridges were cut out of paper, and so brought ruin to at least half an acre of caluclations—and Hitchcock, new to disappointment, buried his head in his arms and wept." As the bridge nears completion, there is a sudden flood, and the exhausted Findlayson, partly under the influence of opium pep-pills taken to keep himself going, is swept away down river in a small boat with Peroo. Uncertain whether the bridge is holding in the floodwaters, or already collapsing, they are washed up on a tiny island in the river. On it is a tiny Hindu shrine surrounded by animals which have also apparently fled there to escape the rising waters. The animals however can speak. They are witnessing a council of the gods: Kali, Shiv, Hanuman, Ganesh, Krishna, and the rest. The river, in the form of a crocodile, complains bitterly of the bridge by which men have tried to bind her, and still more bitterly of her failure to destroy it with the flood.

There follows a debate among the gods on the bridge's significance. At first the implication seems to be that it is of no importance at all in the vast time-scale of India. People are only "dirt" after all. "It is but the shifting of a little dirt. Let the dirt dig in the dirt if it pleases the dirt," says Ganesh, the elephant. But, it is then hinted, even the gods themselves are fated to fade and decay before this immense time span. The bridge is meaningless in itself—yet it is also a portent of changes that are more than meaningless cycles of events.

There is much in the story that smacks of fable, yet an account of it purely in those terms is inadequate. It seems to have not one, but many morals, according to the point of view. Is the white man's engineering no more "than scratching the surface of the dirt, or does it portend the beginning of enormous changes that will affect the whole sub-continent, including, eventually, the worship of the old gods themselves? Are men before the gods no more than "flies to wanton boys," or are they, in spite of appearances, masters of their fate? The story looks at the act of bridge-building at a number of simultaneous levels: at what it means in terms of the sheer technology (the "Findlayson truss" is a new invention); what it means for the men who have given years of their lives on the project; what it means for India, materially and spiritually; and, finally, at what is the ultimate meaning of such a vast undertaking? The worlds can be seen separately, yet they interconnect. In order to be "realistic" in the widest sense Kipling has, as it were, been forced into fantasy for a technique that will encompass his theme.

Yet it would be a mistake to regard Kipling's growing use of fantasy merly as an extension of the techniques of the short story. What links him with the other writers we have been looking at [in *Victorian Fantasy*] is his fascination with the way in which fantasy allows him to write of the fringe areas of human consciousness inaccessible to "realism." In "The Brush-wood Boy," for instance, we have what could be taken as a fable about the nature of fantasy itself as an artistic medium. The hero, George Cottar, is a man of almost mechanical perfection. His name even suggests the "cotter pin" in a machine: the pin or wedge which fits into a hole to fasten an object in place. As the son of a wealthy landowner, the head boy of his public school, at Sandhurst, and as an officer in India he is a model of all that is expected of him. Yet beneath the totally conventional and correct exterior he is possessed by dreams of a strange country beyond a pile of brushwood on a mysterious sea shore. The total exclusion of fantasy from his waking life is matched by the peculiar vividness and richness of his dream-world. Eventually, and by accident, he meets in "real life" the girl who has shared his dreams. As a story it is not wholly successful: though the dream-world is vivid and convincing, the waking reality is much less so. George is just *too* perfect. As a symbol of the fantasy-writer, however, whose dreams offer another parallel inner world which he both wants and fears to share, the story has a power which overrides the weakness of characterization. More successful is " 'The Finest Story in the World' " (1893) about a young bank clerk with literary aspirations. What he wants to write is "high art"—which, unfortunately in his case, means bad pastiches of popular poets. He has little or no originality or real literary talent. Yet there is another side to Charlie Mears. He tells the author (who, it is implied, is Kipling himself) of a story he wants to write about a galley-slave. As he describes his "story" it is clear that he is not inventing so much as remembering what he has once seen.

> The long oars on the upper deck are managed by four men to each bench, the lower ones by three, and the lowest of all by two. Remember it's quite dark on the lowest deck and all the men there go mad. When a man dies at his oar on that deck he isn't thrown overboard, but cut up in his chains and stuffed through the oar-hole in little pieces.
> "Why?" I demanded amazed, not to much at the information as the tone of command in which it was flung out.
> "To save trouble and to frighten the others. It needs two overseers to drag a man's body up to the top deck; and if the men at the lower deck oars were left alone, of course they'd stop rowing and try to pull up the benches by all standing up together in their chains.

Charlie is, it seems, able to recall fleetingly and fragmentedly episodes from previous existences with a wealth of detail unknown even to scholars of the period. The raw material of what would be the "finest story in the world" is dangled temptingly before the author—if only he can draw it out from Charlie without leading him to suspect that he is recalling previous incarnations. "The Lords of Life and Death would never allow Charlie Mears to speak with full knowledge of his pasts," as an Indian friend, Grish Chunder, explains when the author consults him. His prophecies come tragically true, as Charlie Mears falls in love and his "memories" are erased for ever.

> I understood why the Lords of Life and Death shut the doors so carefully behind us. It is that we may not remember our first and most beautiful wooings.

At its simplest, " 'The Finest Story in the World' " is an excellent short story—but it also introduces us to another much more odd and disturbing characteristic of Kipling's fantasy: its habit of coming true. The recently published "Bloxham Tapes" are the accounts of what purport to be previous existences of various people who, under hypnosis, can recall vivid details of the past of which their conscious minds knew nothing. One man has recalled a naval battle from the Napoleonic Wars including circumstantial details unknown to naval historians in a weird parallel to Charlie Mears's story. Nor is this an isolated example. It is difficult to know how to phrase it without implying an explanation, but the fact remains that Kipling frequently appears to be in possession of information that he has no business to have. In *Puck of Pook's Hill*, for instance, he brings in a well in the wall of Pevensey Castle that was not in fact discovered until the year 1935. Other examples are even more dramatic.

> I quartered the Seventh Cohort of the Thirtieth (Ulpia Victrix) Legion on the Wall, and asserted that there Roman troops used arrows against the Picts. . . . Years after the tale was told, a digging-party on the Wall sent me some heavy four-sided, Roman-made, "killing" arrows found *in situ* and—most marvellously—a rubbing of a memorial-tablet to the Seventh Cohort of the Thirtieth Legion!
>
> *(Something of Myself)*

Such uncanny prescience makes one wonder if other stories of an apparently fanciful or speculative nature may not turn out similarly to be based on "inside knowledge." In "Proofs of Holy Writ" certain passages of the King James Bible of 1611 are attributed to Shakespeare. "Unprofessional" is a story about a doctor who cures a dying woman by the discovery that there are tidal actions in the body related to astrological influences. A critic of the 1960s objected that "There is surely something inartistic in the triumph within the fable of a therapy we know to have no existence outside it." More recent research has suggested that the planets do indeed have a measurable effect on living tissue, and modern medical opinion would be much more cautious about dismissing Kipling's idea.

Other stories, including some of Kipling's best fantasies such as "Wireless," "They," and "The Wish House," show a similar psychic streak, although they do not depend on ideas or facts not generally known. Yet it would be wrong to assume that Kipling believed in the occult. Through his sister, Trix, who was a medium of sorts and practised such phenomena as automatic writing, producing "messages" from the dead, he knew a good deal about spiritualism, and resolutely set his face against it, even after the death of his only son during the First World War. His best comment on it is in his poem "Endor":

> The road to En-dor is easy to tread
>   For Mother or yearning Wife.
> There, it is sure, we shall meet our Dead
>   As they were even in life.
> Earth has not dreamed of the blessing in store
> For desolate hearts on the road to En-dor.
>
> Whispers shall comfort us out of the dark—
>   Hands—ah God!—that we knew!
> Visions and voices—look and hark!—
>   Shall prove that the tale is true,

And that those who have passed to the farther shore
May be hailed—at a price—on the road to En-dor.

. . . .

Oh the road to En-dor is the oldest road
    And the craziest road of all!
Straight it runs to the Witch's abode,
    As it did in the days of Saul,
And nothing has changed of the sorrow in store
For such as go down the road to En-dor!

In *Something of Myself* he observes that "there is a kind of mind that dives after what it calls "psychical experiences." And I am in no way "psychic". . . . I have seen too much evil and sorrow and wreck of good minds on the road to Endor to take one step along that perilous road." Though at least once in his life he seems to have had a clairvoyant experience, he suspected and feared the obsessional triviality of "Spiritualism" as a system, and saw clearly enough how the misery of many of the people who resorted to mediums made them blind to the manipulation and fraud that so often goes along with psychical experience. But the interest in psychic phenomena was genuine, and clearly to some degree personal, providing much of the raw material of the other worlds on which his fantasy depends.

We have already seen in " 'The Finest Story in the World' " how Charlie Mears's mind contained layer upon layer of previous "memories." Such an idea, used in a quite different way, was to form the basis of one of his most sustained and complex works: the "Puck" books. Here the "mind" in question is not that of the individual children, Dan and Una, but of the English as a whole—made to come alive in the stories of the people of Sussex where Kipling had come to live. "England," he wrote in delight from his house at Burwash, "is a wonderful land. It is the most marvellous of all foreign countries I have ever been in." To be English (and here he means "English" rather than "British") means to have assimilated and grown up with the experiences of Parnesius, Sir Richard Dalyngridge, De Aquila and Hugh the Saxon, Hal Dane and the rest. They have become part of a collective unconscious, part racial, part cultural. The familiar hills and woods of the Weald are simultaneously parts of Merlin's Isle of Gramarye, where every name and landmark is charged with historical meaning. Puck's song sets the theme:

See you the dimpled track that runs,
    All hollow through the wheat?
O that was where they hauled the guns
    That smote King Philip's fleet.

See you our little mill that clacks,
    So busy by the brook?

> She has ground her corn and paid her tax
>   Ever since Doomsday Book.
>
> See you our stilly woods of oak,
>   And the dread ditch beside?
> O that was where the Saxons broke,
>   On the day that Harold died.
>
> . . . .
>
> She is not any common Earth,
>   Water or wood or air,
> But Merlin's Isle of Gramarye,
>   Where you and I will fare.

Kipling wrote here of what he knew. In digging a well on his land his workmen found "a Jacobean tobacco-pipe, a worn Cromwellian latten spoon and, at the bottom of all, the bronze cheek of a Roman horse-bit."

> In cleaning out an old pond which might have been an ancient marl-pit or mine-head, we dredged two intact Elizabethan "sealed quarts" that Christopher Sly affected, all pearly with the patina of centuries. Its deepest mud yielded us a perfectly polished Neolithic axe-head with but one chip on its still venomous edge.

With the Puck stories, Kipling could truly be said, as he claimed, to be playing his cards as he had been dealt them. The stories wrote themselves.

But if these objects and their stories are part of what it means to be English, it does not follow that one must be conscious of that heritage. Stories in which children are taught their history by magic trips into the past are not a new idea: *The Story of the Amulet* was published the same year as *Puck of Pook's Hill*, but the two stories are entirely different in technique. In *Puck* the children *stay* in their own time, and the people they meet come to them, under Puck's aegis, from out of their own. In a rather poignant story from *Rewards and Fairies*, the girl from the eighteenth century who tells her tale to the children is clearly (to an adult reader) dying of T. B., but she is unaware of the fact—in other words, she is *still* living in her own time, and has been conjured from it, not from any place after death. The magic of the story, made by the children acting scenes from *A Midsummer Night's Dream* three times on Midsummer Eve in the middle of a fairy ring under Pook's hill, brings all history to a timeless point—the present. Even more interesting, by Puck's magic of "oak, and ash, and thorn" the children are made to forget each story almost as soon as they have heard it. There are no doubt deliberate echoes here of " 'The Finest Story in the World,' " where the "Lords of Life and Death" shut the doors so carefully on our memories of other ages that we shall not go mad, but there is no suggestion here that the children's knowledge is dangerous; simply that one does not need to be conscious of what one knows in order to know it. Puck is in himself a kind of collective unconscious. His stories do not need to be recalled, but recognized when they are met with—just as the children recognize and remember Puck, Parnesius, or Sir Richard when they meet them in the woods. Dan and Una are England's future, and they inherit the past as they grow up within the common culture. Though they originated in Kipling's own children—who, incidentally, did act a version of *A Midsummer Night's Dream* at the very spot near Batemans in Burwash—Dan and Una are also very obvious symbolic children. Their very names suggest the masculine and feminine virtues of courage and unity England needs.

The second story of the group, "Young Men at the Manor," shows how the two are connected. There is no suggestion that the Norman Sir Richard's vow never to enter the Hall of his newly won Manor until he is invited by the bitter and resentful Saxon Lady Aelueva is anything but exceptional and extraordinary. De Aquila's attitude to Richard is like that of Maximus to Parnesius: impressed by his sense of honour, but contemptuous of someone so politically naïve that he cannot see his own advantage:

> "You'll never be an Emperor," he said. "Not even a General will you be."
> I was silent, but my father seemed pleased.
> "I came here to see the last of you," he said.
> "You have seen it," said Maximus. "I shall never need your son any more. He will live and he will die an officer of a Legion—and he might have been Prefect of one of my Provinces."

Maximus, like De Aquila, is apparently taken at his own valuation, and it is only slowly in the course of the stories that we discover how utterly wrong they both were about their young subordinates. Maximus has to depend on Parnesius' loyalty to hold the Wall under conditions that a more politically-minded officer would have refused or evaded. Richard gains the friendship of Hugh, the loyalty of the Saxons—who would otherwise have murdered them all (including probably De Aquila)—and finally marries Aelueva. The moral courage to resist short-term expediency eventually brings much bigger rewards. Such courage is not typical, but it is of exceptional deeds that history is composed. "In God's good time," says De Aquila, "which because of my sins I shall not live to see, there will be neither Saxon nor Norman in England." In *Rewards and Fairies* this theme is extended in stories like "Brother Square Toes" to include the Americans, whom Kipling sees as sharing a common history and destiny. It is left to Puck to point the final moral: "Weland gave the Sword! The Sword gave the Treasure, and the Treasure gave the Law. It's as natural as an oak growing." We are almost convinced, and yet . . . Puck's confident political wisdom seems to echo the voices of Maximus and De Aquila, not of Parnesius and Richard. Not for the first time we are aware of two voices in Kipling that seem to be saying very different things.

Perhaps because of their moral complexity, the Puck stories held a special place in Kipling's affections. In *Something of Myself* he tells us more about their creation than he does about any of the rest of his work.

> . . . since the tales had to be read by children, before people realized that they were meant for grown-ups; and since they had to be a sort of balance to, as well as seal upon, some aspects of my "Imperialistic" output in the past, I worked the material in three or four overlaid tints and textures, which might or might not reveal themselves according to the shifting light of sex, youth, and experience . . . So I loaded the book up with allegories and allusions, and verified references . . . put in three or four really good sets of verses; the bones of one entire historical novel for any to clothe who cared; and even slipped in a cryptogram, whose key I regret I must have utterly forgotten.

The combination of particular events, like the finding of the Roman horse-bit or the neolithic axe, and the allegorical framework of the whole gives us a clear lead as to the way Kipling constructs his fantasy. Alternative worlds are built upon each other like the layers of a cake: the worlds of child and adult, fairy and familiar each enrich and provide comment on the others.

Though the style is unique to Kipling, it is not difficult to see how this method of construction has been evolved from his earlier Victorian fore-runners. He was brought up in a world of myth, poetry, and fantasy. Staying with his cousins, the Burne-Joneses, during his brief holidays from the dreadful "house of Desolation" where his parents had left him in South-sea when they went back to India, the young Kipling was exposed to a world in which the exotic was normal. In addition to his uncle, Sir Edward Burne-Jones the painter, who would play elaborate games of make-believe with the children, there was "the beloved Aunt herself reading us *The Pirate* or *The Arabian Nights* of evenings, when one lay out on the big sofa sucking toffee, and calling our cousins 'Ho Son', or 'Daughter of my Uncle' or 'O True Believer.' " Among the visitors to the house were "an elderly person called 'Browning' who took no proper interest in the skirmishes which happened to be raging on his entry," and William Morris, who did. On one occasion he recalled Morris, or "Uncle Topsy" as he was known, sitting on the rocking-horse in the nursery "slowly surging back and forth while the poor beast creaked" telling "a tale full of fascinating horrors, about a man who was condemned to bad dreams." Much later he was to recognize this story in *The Saga of Burnt Njal*. The child Kipling's own secret reading of adventure and poetry at Southsea, and later at the United Services College at Westward Ho!, where he was allowed the run of the Head's private library, reinforced this delight in mystery and romance.

His fantasy is the culmination of one strand in the Victorian sensibility. The problems of an extended plot always inherent in the Gothic tradition are solved by the medium of the short story—where Kipling's greatest skills lay. His one full-length novel, *The Light That Failed*, was itself a failure. The brilliant and haunting images that give the fantasies of Dickens, Kingsley, MacDonald or Morris their power are made even more striking by the concentration and compression of Kipling's plots, which work precisely through such images. One revealing use of reference illustrates the point. In *At the Back of the North Wind* MacDonald tells us of two people who had returned before little Diamond to give accounts of what it was like "at the back of the North Wind." One was Dante; the other was Kilmeny, the peasant girl from the Thirteenth Bard's Song in James Hogg's *The Queen's Wake* (1813). According to the legend she went up the glen to listen to the birds and pick berries, and when she did not come back, she was given up for dead. Eventually she returned with the story that she had been carried away to the land of spirits, of glory and light, from where she had had a vision of the world below, with its war and sin. She had asked to be allowed to return and tell her friends, and she came both transformed and sanctified. After a month she returned from whence she had come, and was never seen again. MacDonald quotes some fourteen lines of Hogg, which clearly for him sum up the essence of visionary fantasy:

> "Kilmeny had been she knew not where,
> And Kilmeny had seen what she could not declare;
> Kilmeny had been where the cock never crew,
> Where the rain never fell, and the wind never blew;
> But it seemed as the harp of the sky had rung,
> And the airs of heaven played round her tongue,
> When she spoke of the lovely forms she had seen,
> And a land where sin had never been;
> A land of love and a land of light,
> Withouten sun, or moon, or night;
> Where the river swayed a living stream,
> And the light a pure and cloudless beam:
> The land of vision it would seem,
> And still an everlasting dream."

The parallels with Novalis and his emphasis on the greater reality of the "dream world" are striking enough to account for MacDonald's interest in Hogg's poem. Kipling's use of this, however, is even more interesting. As Dan and Una return after their first meeting with Puck their father asks them how their play had gone, and it turns out that neither can remember what had happened afterwards. Apparently amused, Father echoes MacDonald's quotation:

> "Late—late in the evening Kilmeny came home,
> For Kilmeny had been she could not tell where,
> And Kilmeny had seen what she could not declare."

It is not until we remember that the children's father is, of course, Kipling himself that we begin to realize with what economy he has packed the brief reference. By the magic of "oak, and ash, and thorn" the children cannot declare where they have been or what they have seen in their timeless vision of history. Kipling, however, the creator, can do, and has done so—in the process establishing Puck's link with the visionary worlds of Hogg and MacDonald. For those privileged to see, the magic world is all around us, in every mark in the corn or name of a hill. The initiation of Dan and Una, so far from being a unique event, is part of a tradition of visionary experiences—and it is essentially a *literary* tradition. What Dante, Hogg, MacDonald, and Kipling are all doing is describing publicly, to you, the reader, secret and private experiences in such a way that you can continue to feel their privacy. It is a paradox at the heart of literature.

But not all the influences on Kipling's fantasy were from the past. Among the most immediate stimuli for the Puck stories had been Edith Nesbit's *The Phoenix and the Carpet*, published in 1904. As was her habit with authors she admired, Nesbit had sent Kipling a copy on publication and it had been received with delight by the children at Bateman's. His influence is no less marked on her. As early as *The Wouldbegoods* in 1901 she had made the Bastable children act out stories from *The Jungle Books* and even try to talk in the language of Kipling's characters. The parallels and contrasts between the two writers show us the final flowering of the Victorian tradition of fantasy—even though the best work of both falls strictly into the Edwardian period. In spite of the fact that she was seven years older than Kipling, Nesbit had shown none of his precocious development, and she did not begin to write any of the books she is now remembered by until the early years of the twentieth century, when she was over forty. Like Kipling, she was a natural fantasy writer, and her late start was due as much as anything to her difficulty in discovering her true bent in face of the overwhelmingly "realistic" conventions of the Victorian novel. Her now-forgotten novels for adults failed partly because of their tendency towards the fantastic.

Like Kipling, Nesbit had had a disturbed and somewhat insecure childhood. Her mother was widowed when she was four, and thereafter they moved frequently, and seemingly at random. She was sent to a variety of more or less unsatisfactory schools in England and France. Her career as a professional writer was more or less forced upon her by circumstances. A hurried marrage at the age of twenty-one when she was seven months pregnant had left her as the bread-winner for a family when, within a few months, her husband, Hubert Bland, contracted smallpox. While he was ill his partner in business made off with the funds. This shaky start to the marriage set the pattern that was to continue. In contrast with the order and stability of the Kipling household under the beneficent dictatorship of Mrs. Kipling (who held the purse-strings and even gave Rudyard his "pocket money"), the Nesbit/Bland household, even in its later years of prosperity, was disorganized, unstable and bohemian. Hubert Bland's two great hobbies were socialism and womanizing. To H. G. Wells, whose tastes were much too similar for friendship, he boasted that he was "a student, and experimentalist . . . in illicit love." Like many compulsive seducers, he combined promiscuity with a strong sense of the conventions he defied. He was a staunch, if not strict Roman Catholic, and relations within the Fabian society were severely strained when he found Wells making advances to his daughter Rosamund while she was still a teenager. All Shaw's acid but calculated tact was needed to heal the breach. The quarrel was the more ironic since Rosamund was not Nesbit's child at all, but one of Bland's by Alice Hoatson, her companion-cum-housekeeper—and Bland's mistress. It says much for Edith Nesbit's character that she adopted both the illegitimate children of this union, and brought them up with her own. It was many years before they found out the truth. Commenting on this often strained *ménage-à-trois*, Wells observed "all this E. Nesbit not only detested and mitigated and tolerated, but presided over and I think found exceedingly interesting." [Nesbit's biographer Doris Langley] Moore agrees, but adds that "It had taken her many years to reach that comparative detachment." In the meantime, Nesbit herself indulged in a number of love affairs, perhaps partly compensatory, with (among others) Shaw, Richard le Galienne, and even Dr. Wallis Budge of the Egyptian section of the British Museum. Yet the marriage endured, and in a strange way Nesbit and Bland were deeply dependent on each other. When he died in 1914, she was heartbroken.

If the nonsense fantasies of the mid-Victorians, Lear and Carroll, had been the product of inhibition, it would scarcely be possible to argue the same of Nesbit, who made a point of matching the unconventional state of her private life with equally unconventional public behaviour. Noël Coward described her as "the most genuine Bohemian I ever met." She dressed in long loose-fitting flowing dresses, very far removed from the elaborate tightly-corseted costumes of late Victorian and Edwardian fashions, and smoked heavily, even in public—a habit which almost certainly contributed to her death of lung and heart disease in 1924. Moreover, she had begun her scandalous ways early—long before she met Bland. When she was removed from a French convent school at the age of eleven, she left behind her, for the nuns to discover, two empty wine-bottles of which she had presumably drunk the contents, and in middle age she persuaded officials at the Paris Opera to open all the windows (an unheard-of thing) by pretending to faint and gasping for air at various strategic points in the building. As she herself seems to have recognized by her frequent references to him, if she had an affinity with any of the early fantasy-writers it would be with Kingsley. To some child fans she wrote:

> I am very pleased to have your letters, and to know that you like my books. You are quite right to like Kingsley and Dickens and George MacDonald better than you like me.

The modesty was not assumed. Nesbit always thought of herself primarily as a poet, even after the great financial success of her children's books.

While her serious poetry is scarcely remembered, it is the poetic sensibility in her prose that links her with Kipling, and makes her, with him, one of the fantasists.

It is this quality too that marks unmistakably the great writers like Nesbit and Kipling from other late Victorian fantasists, such as F. Anstey, probably best known today as the author of *Vice Versa* (1882). Anstey's novel *The Brass Bottle* was published in 1900, and several critics have noted the similarities between it and *The Phoenix and the Carpet*. The brass bottle of the title contains an Arabian Jinn which had been imprisoned there thousands of years before by Solomon for various misdeeds. His effusive gratitude to his rescuer in modern London is, of course, a menace, and provides the setting for a series of comic magical disasters. As do so many of the nineteenth-century fantasies, the story draws heavily and in some detail on *The Arabian Nights*. Nevertheless, clever as much of it is, it remains at the level of situation-comedy, lacking the sharpness or depth of character to be found in either Nesbit or Kipling, or any of the wider social and philosophical concerns. As in most light comedy, Anstey's world is a thinner simpler place than the one we all know.

The sense of an extra poetic richness and depth in the worlds of both Nesbit and Kipling was helped by a common illustrator of remarkable talent, H. R. Millar. He worked closely with both authors, and with Nesbit in particular he became adept at translating her slightest hints into substantial visual images—sometimes a matter of necessity when she was so late with her copy that he had to work from scrawled chapter précis rather than the finished text. Nevertheless his results so delighted her that she used to insist there was telepathy between them. His picture of the Psammead, was, she declared, "exactly like the creature she had in her own imagination." Certainly it was Millar who gave form to so many of her most dramatic images. We have already seen [elsewhere] what he did with her prehistoric monsters, the Great Sloth and the "Dinosaurus." He captures no less successfully the table-top architecture of the Magic City, at once grandiose and exotic in design, yet familiar and domestic in detail and materials. As with all the great illustrators of fantasy, Cruikshank, Doyle, Lear, or Tenniel, it is the meticulous attention to details where every article tells a story that brings the pictures to life. Behind that ability to add "something more" to a scene than we might perceive in real life lay a visual tradition stretching back to Hogarth, and beyond. Millar was to Nesbit's fantasy what Tenniel was to Carroll's.

As both Nesbit and Kipling developed as writers it is clear that it is this "poetic" element, the desire always for something *more*, that made the confines of conventional realism increasingly unsatisfactory. Dobrée writes of how Kipling's "broodings on life," his family disasters, and his own ill-health led him more and more towards "adding a fourth dimension to the pictures he presented of human beings, their actions and reactions." Nesbit's work in the early 1900s shows a remarkably similar tendency. The world of *The Wouldbegoods* and *The Treasure Seekers* gives way to that of the

Phoenix and the Psammead and the Three Mouldiwarps, and the more complex supernatural of *The Magic City* and *The Enchanted Castle*. Like Kipling, Nesbit came to need a larger stage for her "realism" than reality permitted. Just as Dan and Una, growing up in a Sussex village, could only come to understand the complex tapestry of their cultural inheritance through the "magic" of Puck, so Nesbit's children needed "magic" to see their suburban London society in perspective.

The Story of the Amulet, for instance, is built around a series of visits to the remote past, or, in one dramatic case, the future. But given the superficial framework, the resemblance to *Puck* is slight. As has been pointed out, Kipling's children themselves stay in the present. As a result their view of history is personal: it is essentially series of deeds, great or small, performed by unsung heroes. There is cumulative progress, but it is made up of the actions of brave individuals who played their cards as they had been dealt them. "What else could I have done?" is the refrain of *Rewards and Fairies*. Nesbit, the socialist, is less concerned with individuals than with societies. She wants to show not the similarities with our own time, but the enormous differences betrween the outlook of other ages and our own. C. S. Lewis records how, as a child, it was his favourite Nesbit novel for this reason. "It first opened my eyes to antiquity, the dark backward and abysm of time." But the resulting picture, as it is slowly built up, incident by incident, is a devastating critique of her own society. We have already had hints of this from the Phoenix, but his open disapproval of the drab dreariness of Edwardian London might well be dismissed as the natural nostalgia of a creature more accustomed to an Egyptian temple of its own than the modern Fire Assurance Office. But *The Amulet*'s message is more insistent. The children find a dirty little girl crying in St. James's Park. Her parents are dead, and she is about to be taken into the Workhouse. With an ironic echo of Shakespeare's *Cymbeline*—shortly to be explained— she is called Imogen. The children take her to see their lodger, the "learned gentleman" from the British Museum, who wishes sadly that they "could find a home where they would be glad to have her"—and the Psammead, being present, is at once forced to grant his request. They find themselves in ancient Britain. The children are amazed. "But why *here?*" says Anthea in astonishment, "Why *now?*"

> "You don't suppose anyone would want a child like that in *your* times—in *your* towns?" said the Psammead in irritated tones. "You've got your country into such a mess that there's no room for half your children—and no one to want them."

Then the little girl meets a woman who resembles her mother, and who has lost a child just like her—and there is a joyful reunion. As in Kipling, there are hints here either of reincarnation, or of the recurrence of certain types in every generation—but the Psammead refuses to be drawn. "Who knows? but each one fills the empty place in the other's heart. It is enough."

Twentieth-century progress is such that it no longer has a place in anyone's heart for the unwanted child. But this is in turn symptomatic of a much wider inhumanity. By means of another unguarded wish in the Psammead's presence, the Queen of Babylon is enabled to visit London. The children proudly show her the sights.

> And now from the window of a four-wheeled cab the Queen of Babylon beheld the wonders of London. Buckingham Palace she thought uninteresting; Westminster Abbey and the Houses of Parliament little better. But she liked the Tower, and the River, and the ships filled her with wonder and delight.
>
> "But how badly you keep your slaves. How wretched and poor and neglected they seem," she said, as the cab rattled along the Mile End Road.
>
> "They aren't slaves; they're working-people," said Jane.
>
> "Of course they're working. That's what slaves are. Don't you tell me. Do you suppose I don't know a slave's face when I see it? Why don't their masters see they're better fed and better clothed? Tell me in three words."
>
> No one answered. The wage-system of modern England is a little difficult to explain in three words even if you understand it—which the children didn't.
>
> "You'll have a revolt of your slaves if you're not careful," said the Queen.
>
> "Oh, no," said Cyril; "you see they have votes—that makes them safe not to revolt. It makes all the difference. Father told me so."
>
> "What is this vote?" asked the Queen. "Is it a charm? What do they do with it?"
>
> "I don't know," said the harassed Cyril. "It's just a vote, that's all! they don't do anything particular with it."
>
> "I see," said the Queen; "a sort of plaything."

In a society brought up on the Bible, Babylon has always had a bad press. To compare twentieth-century London, with all its tourist attractions, unfavourably with Babylon, not merely in terms of architecture, but even in morals and general humanity was a final calculated insult. The condemnation of the present is rounded off by a visit to the future. The first thing they notice in comparison with the "sorry-present" is the cleanliness and lack of pollution.

> As they came through the doors of the (British) Museum they blinked at the sudden glory of sunlight and blue sky. The houses opposite the Museum were gone. Instead there was a big garden, with trees and flowers and smooth green lawns, and not a single notice to tell you not to walk on the grass and not to destroy the

trees and shrubs and not to pick the flowers. There were comfortable seats all about, and arbours covered with roses, and long
trellised walks, also rose-covered.

In view of the recent fight by conservationists to preserve the buildings
opposite the British Museum, the passage has an unintentionally ironic
ring today. The general picture of a clean London with gardens and flowers
everywhere inhabited by people with long flowing clothes and happy faces
is an amalgam of the vague Fabian day-dreams of the time about the coming
socialist paradise. Though there are sharper typical Nesbit touches, such
as men being in charge of babies, and playing with them, the overall picture
is similar to the sort of optimistic view of the future being painted by H. G.
Wells. The similarity is deliberate: the children meet a small boy named
Wells, after the "great reformer." The real parallel, however, is with Imogen. This boy too is crying in the park, but, it turns out, this is because
he has been punished for the dreadful crime of dropping litter by being
expelled from school for the day—"for a whole day!" Having explained the
joys of his project-centred curriculum to the children, he takes them home.
His house has no need of ornaments because every single thing in it is
beautiful. For safety, it is centrally-heated, and the furniture in the nursery
is padded to prevent children hurting themselves. To show their gratitude
for the hospitality they have received, the children offer to take his mother
with them through the amulet to see *their* London.

> The lady went, laughing. But she did not laugh when she found
> herself, suddenly, in the dining-room at Fitzroy Street.
> "Oh, what a *horrible* trick!" she cried. "What a hateful, dark,
> ugly place!"
> She ran to the window and looked out. The sky was grey, the
> street was foggy, a dismal organ-grinder was standing opposite
> the door, a beggar and a man who sold matches were quarrelling
> at the edge of the pavement on whose greasy black surface people
> hurried along, hastening to get to the shelter of their houses.
> "Oh, look at their faces, their horrible faces!" she cried. "What's
> the matter with them all?"
> "They're poor people, that's all," said Robert.
> "But it's *not* all! They're ill, they're unhappy, they're wicked."

The parallel with the Queen of Babylon is complete.

Nesbit's hatred of the sorry-present is taken to its logical conclusion
in one of her last books, *Harding's Luck* (1909). Dickie Harding, a little lame
orphan boy from the slums of Deptford, acquires by magic another "self"
as his own ancestor, Richard Arden, in James I's reign. No longer a cripple,
in this other life he lives in a great house with servants and friends among
the green fields and orchards of Deptford. As always, Nesbit is not above
loading the dice: just as it was sunny in the future and wet in the present

(not *all* fog and rain is due to pollution!), so it helps to be rich and an aristocrat if you are to live happily in the early seventeenth century. Nevertheless, the comparison is a serious one. The "welfare state" of the great Jacobean house, where everyone has his place but all are looked after, is contrasted with the misery of *laissez-faire* Edwardian England with its ugliness and unemployment and neglect of its children. The men of the twentieth century seem to be all manipulators of people or money: con-men or pawnbrokers; the men of the seventeenth century (who closely resemble some of the twentieth-century characters in looks) are craftsmen of skill and integrity.

The possibilities of time-travel are exploited for their own dramatic value, however, and not merely for social comment. One of the most effective scenes is where Dickie's cousins, Edred and Elfrida, who are the central characters in an earlier Nesbit story, *The House of Arden*, nearly get the whole family executed for High Treason by singing "Please to remember the Fifth of November / Gunpowder treason and plot," *before* the Gunpowder Plot has happened. But even here the opportunities for social comment are not altogether wasted. Dickie's nurse, who mysteriously seems to understand about time-travel, warns him to be very careful what he says, or she will be "burned as a witch." He urges her to come back with him to the twentieth century—for "they don't burn people for witches there."

> "No," said the nurse, "but they let them live such lives in their
> ugly towns tht my life here with all its risks is far better worth
> living. Thou knowest how folk live in Deptford in thy time—how
> all the green trees are gone, and good work is gone, and people
> do bad work for just so much as will keep together their worn
> bodies and desolate souls. And sometimes they starve to death."

Eventually Dickie makes the choice to return for ever to the seventeenth century, where he is not crippled (both literally and, we presume, metaphorically) and can be happier than he ever will in the present. Though it is done partly as a sacrifice, to allow the other Arden children to inherit, it is the most complete rejection of the present in any fantasy of the period.

In an argument with Edred and Elfrida in *The House of Arden*, Richard makes use of the nurse's argument himself for rejecting the twentieth century.

> "Why don't you want to come with us to our times?"
> "I hate your times. They're ugly, they're cruel," said Richard.
> "They don't cut your head off for nothing anyhow in our times,"
> said Edred, "and shut you up in the Tower."
> "They do worse things," Richard said. "*I* know. They make
> people work fourteen hours a day for nine shillings a week, so
> that they never have enough to eat or wear, and no time to sleep
> or be happy in. They won't give people food or clothes, or let

them work to get them; and then they put the people in prison if they take enough to keep them alive. They let people get horrid diseases, till their jaws drop off, so as to have a particular kind of china. Women have to go out to work instead of looking after their babies, and the little girl that's left in charge drops the baby and it's crippled for life. Oh! I know. I won't go back with you. You might keep me there for ever." He shuddered.

As a book *Harding's Luck* is uneven. With its companion volume, *The House of Arden*, it forms a separate group from either Nesbit's earlier fantasies, which, like *The Phoenix* or the Psammead books, centre on Edwardian London and are fairly episodic in structure, or the late ones which involve totally "other" worlds. They are in some ways her most ambitious experiment in that they tell essentially the same story from two points of view, and involve some of the basic problems of science-fiction: time-travel, for instance.

This was one of the questions that always puzzled the children—and they used to talk it over together till their heads seemed to be spinning round. The question of course was: Did their being in past times make any difference to the other people in past times? In other words, when you were taking part in historical scenes, did it matter what you said or did? Of course it seemed to matter extremely—at the time.

They are told by the nurse that they can, in fact, leave no trace on times past—from which we, if not the children, may be intended to glean some theory (Hegelian or Marxist?) of the inevitability of history. But the difference between Dickie's journeys into the past and those of the children in *The Amulet* is that they always remained physically *themselves*—visibly visitors to another time or place—whereas Dickie *is* somebody else. In Jacobean England he is not lame, for example. He is a different physical person, Richard Arden. This raises an even more puzzling problem—which Nesbit herself is aware of—that if Dickie has "become" young Richard Arden of 1606, what has happened to the boy who was previously "Richard Arden"? Indeed, if we read the text closely it is not clear that the "Richard" who refuses to come to the twentieth century with Edred and Elfrida is in fact Dickie. His comment that "in *your* time nobody cares" is, to say the least, ambiguous. The nurse in *Harding's Luck* suggests that the "missing" Edred and Elfrida from 1606 are "somewhere else—in Julius Caesar's time, to be exact—but they don't know it, and never will know it. They haven't the charm. To them it will be like a dream that they have forgotten." But this system of interchanging personalities has to be endless, if it is to work at all. Moreover, the more people that are doing it, the less remarkable it becomes—unless we are to assume that, as in " 'The Finest Story in the World,' " we all carry within us the memories of every life that we have "lived." The very strengths of fantasy are in danger of becoming weak-nesses—the "rules" are in danger of being lost.

Nevertheless *Harding's Luck* has some of the best descriptions to be found anywhere in Nesbit, such as the opening passages which set the tone of the whole book.

> Dickie lived at New Cross. At least the address was New Cross, but really the house where he lived was one of a row of horrid little houses built on the slope where once green fields ran down the hill to the river, and the old houses of the Deptford merchants stood stately in their pleasant gardens and fruitful orchards. All those good fields and happy gardens are built over now. It is as though some wicked giant had taken a big brush full of yellow ochre paint, and another full of mud-colour, and had painted out the green in streaks of dull yellow and filthy brown; and the brown is the roads and the yellow is the houses. Miles and miles and miles of them, and not a green thing to be seen except the cabbages in the greengrocers' shops, and here and there some poor trails of creeping-jenny drooping from a dirty window-sill. There is a little yard at the back of each house; this is called "the garden," and some of these show green—but they only show it to the houses' back windows. You cannot see it from the street. . . . There were no green things growing in the garden at the back of the house where Dickie lived with his aunt. There were stones and bones, and bits of brick, and dirty old dish-cloths matted together with grease and mud, worn-out broom-heads and broken shovels, a bottomless pail, and the mouldy remains of a hutch where once rabbits had lived. But that was a very long time ago, and Dickie had never seen the rabbits. A boy had brought a brown rabbit to school once, buttoned up inside his jacket. . . . So Dickie knew what rabbits were like. And he was fond of the hutch for the sake of what had once lived there.
>
> And when his aunt sold the poor remains of the hutch to a man with a barrow who was ready to buy anything, and who took also the pail and the shovels, giving threepence for the lot, Dickie was almost as unhappy as though the hutch has really held a furry friend. And he hated the man who took the hutch away, all the more because there were empty rabbit-skins hanging sadly from the back of the barrow.

As a child's view of the world, this movement from the general to the particular, with its trains of association about the rabbits, is among the best things she ever wrote. But alongside this kind of acute observation are passages of slack writing and hackneyed themes. The nurse wavers be-tween "Odds Bodikins!" and modern English—not wholly to be accounted for by her time changes! For many modern readers the discovery that little lame Dickie of Deptford is really the rightful Lord Arden in the twentieth century does not give quite the thrill that this unwearied theme, with its echoes of Curdie's hidden royalty and *Little Lord Fauntleroy*, clearly gave Nesbit's contemporaries. Yet, this said, *Harding's Luck* does display at its best a quality that gave Nesbit's fantasy its enduring greatness, and sets her beside Kipling as one of the giants of the genre.

This is the underlying sense of a stable and ordered moral world. Her magic is often mysterious, and occasionally perfunctory, but it never gives the impression of being arbitrary or meaningless. In part, this is achieved by a network of literary cross-references to other writers—particularly, as we have seen, to fellow writers of fantasy. Just as Kipling's Puck knows his *Midsummer Night's Dream* and is steeped in English literature, so we get the impression from Nesbit that her magic is not her creation, but belongs to a much deeper and older world than can be conjured up by any single writer alone. Her work is studded with allusions of this kind. Dickie Harding reads Kingsley when he gets the chance. The children in *Wet Magic* are reading from *The Water-Babies* at the beginning, and when the mermaid wishes to convince them that they really will be able to come under the water with her, she too makes reference to it.

> "Someone once told me a story about Water Babies. Did you never hear of that?"
> "Yes, but that was a made-up story," said Bernard stolidly.
> "Yes, of course," she agreed, "but a great deal of it's quite true, all the same."

On the page before there had been casual references both to Heine and Matthew Arnold. Even the invocation that summons up the mermaids is a quotation from a master of fantasy on a cosmic scale: Milton himself.

> Sabrina fair,
> Listen where thou art sitting,
> Under the glassy green, translucent wave.
> (*Comus*, ll. 859–61)

More delightfully zany is the parrot in *The Magic City* who is disinclined to "ordinary conversation" and will only quote from Dryden's translation of *The Aeneid*—which sends everyone to sleep. In both *The Magic City* and *Wet Magic* buildings or caves are actually made of books, and characters, both pleasant and unpleasant, are constantly leaking out of them into the respective magic worlds. The symbolism of literature as itself constituting a "magic world" is obvious. All literature is a way of enriching our reality and enabling us to discover in it more than we knew. Fantasy is the extreme example by which we understand how the rest works.

Yet mere references alone are not sufficient to establish continuity with the tradition. As MacDonald had clearly seen, an invented world may have any set of rules the writer chooses, provided they are consistent with each other, but the moral law "remains everywhere the same." There is no hint of Nesbit's own unconventional life-style in her writings: indeed, her stories may be seen as a tribute to the order that she personally so much lacked. But, if so, the "order" is not that of the Victorian conventions. Like her predecessors, and like Kipling, she lays stress on the permanent values of honour, truthfulness, fair-mindedness, loyalty, love, and self-sacrifice. At their most limited these need be no more than the virtues of the tribe or in-group against the rest, but, as with Kipling at his best, Nesbit is also aware of the limitations of the tribal code. Beyond what Kipling called "the Law," but not superseding it, are other qualities of reconciliation and forgiveness whose roots are religious. This is a fact that it is easy to overlook. It is only when we meet their contemporaries like Ballentyne or Rider Haggard who lack this other dimension that we begin to see what differentiates the fantasy of a Kipling or a Nesbit from mere adventure stories or excursions into the exotic. In the twentieth century it marks the difference between the great fantasy writers, such as Tolkien or Lewis, and a host of science-fiction writers who, however good they may be as story-tellers, seem in the end to inhabit an arbitrary and simplified world rather than one richer and more complex than our own. Writers will often show more of themselves in their books than to their friends, and it would have come to less of a surprise to many of her readers than to her circle of Fabian friends when, in 1906, just after she had begun her great series of magical fantasies, she was received into the Roman Catholic Church. It was a quest of a different kind for another world that would enrich her own. Though she later became sceptical about the exclusive claims of Catholicism, Nesbit never lost her religious faith. From her letters, and from accounts of close friends it seems clear that towards the end of her life it grew increasingly important to her.

From her books we have a surprising amount of evidence of a philosophical kind. It has often been noticed tht Plato and the Bible are the two greatest philosophical influences on English literature; it has less often been observed how great their influence has been specifically in the direction of fantasy. Nevertheless, their pull is obvious. Both suggest the existence of "other worlds" impinging on this, but of a greater reality, as part of a greater metaphysical and moral whole that is ultimately beyond man's understanding. We have already seen [elsewhere] something of the Biblical influence. The writers Nesbit seems to mention most often, Kingsley, MacDonald, and among her contemporaries, Kipling, all owe much to the Christian Platonic tradition, but in many ways Nesbit was possibly the greatest Platonist of them all. It is the side of her work most frequently misunderstood even now. Ever since her biographer, Doris Langley Moore, placed *The Magic City* and *The Enchanted Castle* among her least successful books, they have been largely ignored or dismissed by critics. She herself finds the construction of the former "loose and rambling," and another writer on children's books, Anthea Bell, is even more forthright. "Not much need be said of *The Magic City*, she declares, "For once, she had an excellent idea and never rose to it; she develops it in rather a prosaic, plodding manner foreign to the other fantasies." Nor has *The Enchanted Castle* fared any better, being "not quite in the same rank with the works which preceded it." The problem with any writer who worked as quickly and, often, as carelessly as Nesbit did is that peculiarities in her work can be plausibly dismissed as bad workmanship. In fact, Nesbit is very rarely a bad workman in her children's books. *The Magic City* and *The Enchanted Castle* present us with a very different kind of fantasy from stories like the *Phoenix* and the *Amulet* which, for all their serious social awareness, are essentially humorous and episodic. Both have quite a complicated cumulative philosophical structure. They involve the discovery not so much of magic creatures in this world, as of the existence of other worlds alongside this one.

The Magic City is in a world of art—in its widest sense. It is only entered by an act of creativity of some kind. Not merely is Philip's table-top city there and all his other models, but so is Mr. Perrin, the carpenter who made his first set of bricks—"true to the thousandth of an inch"— and so is every other person who helped to make any part of the materials. "D'you see," asks Perrin, "*Making's* the thing. If it was no more than the lad that turned the handle of the grindstone to sharp the knife that carved a bit of a cabinet or what not, or a child that picked a teazle to finish a bit of the cloth that's glued on to the bottom of a chessman—they're all here." Even the evil "Pretenderette," the steely-eyed nurse, is there, who absent-mindedly rebuilt a few bricks of Philip's city she had knocked over with her sleeve. Through Mr. Noah Nesbit goes to unusual trouble to explain the rules of her universe.

> You see, you built those cities in two worlds. It's pulled down in *this* world. But in the other world it's still going on. . . . Everything people make in that world goes on forever.

If we had met this in a serious adult novel we would most probably recognize it at once. The underlying Platonism is obvious. Moreover, the idea that our created works of art have a timeless existence in an ideal order is a common twentieth-century critical notion with roots in the nineteenth century as far back as Coleridge. And Nesbit goes out of her way specifically to include literature in the artistic forms of her magic world. People and animals are constantly escaping from books. We have already mentioned the Great Sloth. . . . Others include the Hippogriff, or flying horse, and even finally Barbarians and a Roman army under Julius Caesar. Though Plato, of course, denied works of art a place in his world of ideal forms, the appeal of his ideas has, paradoxically, always been greatest among artists—who have traditionally emphasized that his was primarily a mystical vision rather than a carefully worked-out system.

As always, Nesbit is inclined to present her beliefs in the form of parody—often, even, as self-mockery. Her obsessional and quite irrational belief that Bacon wrote Shakespeare's plays makes its appearance in the form of the gaoler, Mr. Bacon-Shakespeare, who has written twenty-seven volumes all in cypher on the subject of a crocheted mat that no one can unravel, but unfortunately forgotten the key. The structure of her ideas, however, is significant: though the construction of the book is complicated, it is the very antithesis of "loose and rambling." Philip's *official* task is to perform a series of heroic deeds to prove himself the "Deliverer" and not the "Destroyer" (the only two options open to him). Each is presented as a further stage of initiation and is marked by an ascending order of chivalry. When the Pretenderette, mounted on the winged Hippogriff, kidnaps Philip and flies away with him Lucy protests that Mr. Noah had told her that "the Hippogriff could only carry one." "One ordinary human being," said Mr. Noah gently, "you forget that dear Philip is now an earl." In fact, of course, Philip's *real* task is to learn to love Lucy, the daughter of the man his sister has just married, and whom he deeply resents. The tasks are an opportunity for them to work together. In the first, Philip has to rescue Lucy from a dragon. In the second they have to unravel a carpet which is not woven, but crocheted— a fact which Philip cannot see until Lucy points it out to him. As they proceed, the tasks become progressively more psychologically "unravelling" as they deal with personal renunciation, self-sacrifice, and finally the Great Sloth and the Pretenderette herself—who had become unlovable from being unloved. By a device faintly reminiscent of "The Brushwood Boy," Philip's sister Helen, who has created with him as a game a secret and forbidden island, is found to be on the island—because it is part of her dream as well as his. In giving the island away, Philip has to renounce her, since that is her only route into the magic world. Again, the symbolism of their changing relationship is obvious. Later in real life when she has returned from her honeymoon she admits to remembering dimly her "dream."

In both *The Magic City* and *The Enchanted Castle* there are repeated hints that all knowledge is but a recognition of what we have known all along. This Platonic "recognition" theme is central to the growing maturity of the children. Many of Philip's deeds are in fact performed first, as the thing which needed to be done, and then discovered to be the next stage afterwards. The giving of the forbidden island to the homeless islanders is done simply because they *are* homeless, and must be found somewhere to live. It is immediately after this act that the reconciliaton of Philip and Lucy takes place. Similarly, in *Harding's Luck*, long before Dickie has first been into the past, he finds that he recognizes the interior layout of Arden Castle when he helps to burgle it, although he has never been there before. Being a burglar in what is, unknown to you, your own "home" is a typical Nesbit twist of irony—but as a symbol it can be seen at a number of levels. Much of the story can in fact be taken as an experiment in *déjà vu:* the feeling of having "been here before." Sometimes, as in Kipling, this is specifically linked with notions of reincarnation. Dickie, for instance, meets people in Jacobean England who are apparently "the same" as people he knew in the slums of Deptford, but the way in which the device is used suggests that Nesbit is more interested in the way the same people will behave under different circumstances, than she is in actual reincarnation—although this, too, of course is a Platonic theme. Much more specifically Platonic is the nurse's question to Dickie, when she has been trying to explain what has been happening: "Dids't never hear that all life is dream?"

Nesbit certainly had, and it is in her treatment of this central notion of so much Victorian fantasy that she stands most clearly in the Platonic Christian tradition of James Hogg, Novalis, MacDonald, and Kingsley. The unreal or illusory nature of time, which comes in almost every one of these later fantasies, is part of a wider feeling that life itself is but a dream into which we bring reports, like the poor shepherd girl Kilmeny, of a greater reality beyond. In *The Enchanted Castle* there is a magic ring that—disconcertingly—is just what its possessor *says* it is. Much of the story is taken up with a series of comic misadventures similar in kind to those with the Psammead in *Five Children and It*. The ring can be used to create things, to become rich, to become invisible, and even to grow—all with equally confusing and disastrous consequences. At the same time, however, the ring also initiates its wearers into another world where statues become alive and monsters roam the grounds of Yalding Castle. The statues of Greek gods scattered around the grounds become the real Greek pantheon, and the children join them in a feast—a literal symposium. In the final chapter the children with Lord Yalding and his fiancée are present at a vast mystical vision of the great dance of creation:

> The moonbeam slants more and more; now it touches the far end of the stone, now it draws nearer and nearer the middle of it, now at last it touches the very heart and centre of that central stone. And then it is as though a spring were touched, a fountain of light released. Everything changes. Or, rather, everything is revealed. There are no more secrets. The plan of the world seems plain, like an easy sum that one writes in big figures on a child's slate. One wonders how one can ever have wondered about anything. Space is not; every place that one has seen or dreamed of is here. Time is not; into this instant is crowded all that one has ever done or dreamed of doing. It is a moment, and it is eternity. It is the centre of the universe and it is the universe itself. The eternal light rests on and illuminates the eternal heart of things.
>
> . . . Afterwards none of them could ever remember at all what had happened. But they never forgot that they had been somewhere where everything was easy and beautiful. And people who can remember even that much are never quite the same again. And when they came to talk of it next day they found that to each some little part of that night's great enlightenment was left.

. . . Then a wave of intention swept over the mighty crowd. All
the faces, bird, beast, Greek statue, Babylonian monsters, human
child and human lover, turned upward, the radiant light illumined
them and one word broke from all.

"The light!" they cried, and the sound of their voice was like
the sound of a great wave; "the light! the light—"

There is an extraordinary, yet significant, parallel to this scene in a
minor key at the end of *The Magic City*. To rid the city of Barbarians who
have escaped from Caesar's *Gallic War*, Caesar himself is summoned from
the same book. He and his legions are clearly meant to stand for order and
civilization against chaos and barbarism. After a night of fighting the barbarians are safely driven back between hard covers, and as dawn breaks
Caesar passes judgement on the Pretenderette. Though he had been called
up originally for a limited military objective, he now seems to have taken
over the role of lawgiver. But the "Law" is that of love. In a "Last Judgment"
scene the loveless Pretenderette is condemned to serve the people of Brisk-
ford, newly released from the Great Sloth, until they love her so much they
cannot bear to part with her—at which point, of course, her "punishment"
ceases to be one. Any possible theological implications of this judgement
of Caesar are rapidly passed over because as he speaks both children now
see an extraordinary resemblance between him and Lucy's father (now to
be Philip's also). At the same moment the sun rises and they are dazzled
by the light on his armour. When they open their eyes he is gone. The
justice transmuted into love, the glimpse of a father in this (for Philip a
new discovery), and the dazzling light are all familiar images. The whole
incident is important in that it is not necessary in any way to the plot, but
presents a sudden, and slightly incomprehensible twist to the story.
Though we can recognize in the "light" echoes of Plato's Sun myth in *The
Republic*, there are also nearer and more immediate references here to the
European mystical tradition. As Kingsley did at the end of *The Water-Babies*,
Nesbit is harking back here (and even more in the passage from *The Enchanted Castle*) to the consummation of space and time in the contemplation
of the "Light Eternal" at the end of Dante's *Paradiso*.

Finally, in such scenes as these there is the hint (it is no more) of that
odd metaphysical *frisson* that links Dante with this minority tradition of
Victorian children's writers, and that transforms fantasy from simple es-
capism into something much more enduringly rooted in the human psyche.
It is present in Canto III of the *Paradiso* when Dante suddenly discovers
that the faces he thought were either reflections or figments of his own
mind were, in fact, more real and alive than he could easily comprehend.
It is present (as Keats saw) in Adam's dream in *Paradise Lost*, where he
awakens and finds his dream is truth. It is present . . . tantalizingly and
fleetingly in Carroll, Kingsley, MacDonald and Kipling—and again here
with Nesbit as Philip discovers that what he has glimpsed for a moment,
after so much moral struggle, within the "magic city" has become part of

the reality of his everyday life. The uncompromising Platonism of Anselm's ontological proof of God owes something of its curious magnificence to this same basic human desire for the dream that comes true. Keats had boldly attributed this power to the "Imagination," but by mid-century the all-important shock of this transformational view of the imagination had been lost—and largely replaced by theories of aesthetics. In "Art" the mystery and urgency of other worlds had largely faded or become dissipated. It was left to children's writers such as Nesbit to create anew, and at a different level of experience, the "high fantasy" of a world too rich and complex to be contained by the conventions of Victorian naturalism.

Evolutionary Fables:
The Time Machine

Frank McConnell

In the last chapter [of *The Science Fictiion of H. G. Wells*] we examined some of the dominant currents of thought that shaped the mental landscape of Wells's youth. But, in the ten years of transition from the nineteenth to the twentieth century, Wells shaped the landscape into a new visionary order. In his essays, his realistic novels, and above all in his scientific romances of these years he both summarized and recast into a distinctively modern form the intellectual and emotional concerns he had inherited.

The very idea of the "modern," of course, is a modern idea. Not until the calendar began to approach the magical number of two thousand years since the birth of Christ did people—philosophers and poets and charlatans alike—begin to think obsessively in terms of what might happen rather than what had always been. The nineteenth century is the great age of the discovery of *History:* that is, of the present as not just a repetition of an immutable social and political structure, but rather as the link between a dynamically changing past and a looming, challenging, and dangerous future. The idea of the "modern," then, is mainly a particular way of thinking about the possibility and the limits of change. As with hypochondria and some kinds of religious conversion, wishing (or fearing) makes it so. You are "modern" the moment you begin to *regard* yourself as modern. And in this respect it is just to regard Wells as one of the founders of the modern sensibility. His fiction, to be sure, was never experimental in its techniques, and his ideas, even at their most evolutionary, never aimed at a total break with the great traditions of social and political thought. But few men of his age thought as much or wrote as much about what it felt like to live in an era of change, an era coursing headlong toward an uncertain and perhaps terrible fate.

From *The Science Fiction of H. G. Wells.* © 1981 by Oxford University Press.

I have mentioned [elsewhere] that P. N. Furbank defines the central effort of Edwardian writers as that of redeeming the suburban. This is not a contemptible, nor is it an easy, task to set oneself. It is also not a new one in the history of English letters: and thereby hangs much of our understanding of Wells and his early fiction. Since the emergence, in the middle of the eighteenth century, of Dr. Samuel Johnson as the most distinguished man of letters of his time, there had existed in England the tradition of the middle-class prophet. This is the man of extraordinary intelligence and ordinary sympathies whose energies are devoted not toward the formation of a school or the establishment of a doctrine, but toward just the *interpretation* of modern schools and doctrines for the embattled and distraught, reasonably intelligent and literate common reader. The discipline of explainer may not, finally, be as exalted as that of prophet or originating heresiarch. But it is one that, from Johnson's essays through Arnold's poetry and criticism and Wells's best fiction, has accounted for much of what is most lasting and most humanizing in the history of English prose.

This is the best context in which to view both the original intent and the original success of Wells's first major novels, *The Time Machine* and *The Island of Doctor Moreau*. In both, strains of current confusion are evident—about the nature of society, about the purpose of art, and most of all about that still-threatening concept, "evolution." But both tales, besides merely articulating contemporary fears, transcend those fears in providing fictions that *reconcile* the comfortable sense of the ordinary with the terrifying sense of "what might be." This is not to say that either *The Time Machine* or *The Island of Doctor Moreau* is an optimistic or "uplifting" fiction: both stories end in shattering and, for their time, shockingly original visions of disaster and loss. Nevertheless, even in the imagination of disaster, Wells manages to give a name and a shape to forces and tendencies that threaten his—and our—age. And by naming them he helps render them visible and controllable.

THE TIME MACHINE

Whatever else it is—and it is many things—*The Time Machine* is certainly an exercise in that curious literary subtype called utopian fiction. As such it belongs to a very old tradition, indeed. Sir Thomas More's tale *Utopia* (1516) gave a name to the genre: *ou topos* in Greek means "nowhere," and More's story is about the totally rational, sane, subordinated, and peaceful society men have developed in an ideal state which lies—Nowhere.

Even as early as More's book, the fictional description of an ideal, "utopian" society has always involved an irreducible element of satire of society as it really exists. But though More may have given a permanent name to the form, he was not its first exponent. The visions of the Hebrew prophets, especially Isaiah and Jeremiah, the description of the New

Jerusalem by the author of the Book of Revelations, the Republic of Plato, and even the idealized Christian kingdoms hinted at by some medieval allegorists—all these and many more examples may be taken as "utopias" before the invention of the term. It is safe to say that as long as people have lived in society (which means as long as there have been people), they have had the tendency to imagine what such society might be like at its best—or its worst. And those extremes, once put in the form of narratives, represent the whole range of utopian fiction.

There is an important difference between earlier utopias and their nineteenth-century heirs, however, in the concept of time. The word means "*nowhere*," and even in biblical presentations of an ideal society to come, that society is always imagined as occupying more a special place (the land of milk and honey, the New Jerusalem) than a special time. It is a distinctively nineteenth-century—and therefore modern—habit of mind to imagine that the perfect "place" for an ideally good or allegorically evil human society may be literally no place at all except in time, in history itself.

As we said [elsewhere] . . . the beginnings of this phenomenon can be traced to the Romantic movement and its emphasis upon the creative, sometimes mystical, force of historical process. Two of the greatest English Romantics, William Blake and Percy Shelley—both of whom Wells read and admired as a young man—created utopian visions that we can call "futuristic" in the sense we are discussing. Blake's *Jerusalem* and Shelley's *Prometheus Unbound* both imagine history as an immense series of cycles which, at their completion, will liberate man into a new perception of his own godhead. For both writers, of course—as for Marx in his myth of the revolution of the proletariat—the idea of the "fulness of time" also carries strong associations of much more ancient myths of liberation through history, i.e., Messianic hopes or the Christian expectation of the Second Coming. But between Blake and Shelley and Marx, the work of Darwin intervenes. And Darwinian theory . . . forever altered the European perception of history and its crucial, inexorable pressure on human events.

Darwin's importance for utopian visions in the late nineteenth century is as great as for other, more "serious" areas of thought. One of the first, and richest, literary responses to the theory of evolution by means of natural selection is Robert Browning's poem of 1864, "Caliban upon Setebos." This complex satire is, at least in part, an ironic commentary on the pretensions of theological speculation in the face of man's newfound, bestial heritage. The poem may be regarded as the first evidence of that new sensitivity to evolutionary change, to the slow, subtle, but all-important grinding away of the geological, ecological clock that later came to inform even the "realistic" fiction of authors such as Thomas Hardy, Joseph Conrad, and D. H. Lawrence. And "Caliban upon Setebos" is also important as part of the background of Wells's grimmest and most deliberately shocking evolutionary parable, *The Island of Doctor Moreau*.

More to the point of *The Time Machine*, however, is the array of more explicitly utopian, sociological fictions that follows in Darwin's wake and takes account of the implications of natural selection for the human community. Edward Bulwer-Lytton's *The Coming Race* (1871) describes an ideal community of gigantic, further-evolved humans existing in the present time in a subterranean world into which the narrator stumbles. Their nobility and their altogether proper-Victorian acceptance of natural dynamism are a comforting assertion that "evolution," whatever its direction, will not lead us astray. Samuel Butler's *Erewhon* (1872), on the other hand, entertains some darker notions about the implications of natural selection for the future of the human race. "Erewhon" is a dystopia of sorts—literally, it is "Nowhere" spelled (almost) backwards—where machines have evolved an intelligence of their own, and where man is the servant of his superior, more efficient tools. The idea that man might eventually create a "race" of artificial beings who supplant his lordship over the planet has, of course, always been one of the most fecund themes for science fiction, from *The War of the Worlds* to *2001: A Space Odyssey* and beyond. And Butler gets credit for being the first writer to understand that such a theme underlies many of the assertions of evolutionary theory.

Two other utopias, though, are even more central to the background of *The Time Machine*, for in both of them the idea of the *future* as the real "place" of utopia is much more explicit. They are Edward Bellamy's *Looking Backward (2000–1887)* and William Morris's *News from Nowhere; or, An Epoch of Unrest*. Both books appeared in 1888—the same year in which Wells wrote the first, very amateurish draft of what was to become *The Time Machine*.

Bellamy was an American socialist, with a great faith in the benevolence of technological development. In *Looking Backward* the hero, Julian West, through a strained series of circumstances, falls asleep in Boston in 1887 to awaken in the Boston of the year 2000. It is a Boston miraculously transformed, like the rest of the world, into an orderly, hygienic, mechanically run, and absolutely self-satisfied socialist paradise. Everyone has exactly as much as he or she needs for a modest yet comfortable existence, and everyone contributes to the common fund of labor exactly as much as society and the individual feel is just. Massive networks of producing and calculating machines keep the world supply of goods balanced, and citizens are "paid" for their contributions not in coin or cash, but by tiny cards that register their productivity and their appropriately calculated purchasing power. And all this wonderful change has come about simply through the inevitable but kindly ministrations of history, without bloodshed or revolution. As Dr. Leete, West's host (and the father of the girl West eventually marries), explains:

> "It was not necessary for society to solve the riddle at all. It may be said to have solved itself. The solution came as the result of a process of industrial evolution which could not have terminated

otherwise. All that society had to do was to recognize and cooperate with that evolution, when its tendency had become unmistakable."

The distance from the threatening technology of Butler's *Erewhon* is vast. And *Looking Backward*, though clumsily written and often mawkishly sentimental, exercised a profound influence over speculation on society and technology for many years. Of all modern utopias, it is perhaps the most unabashedly optimistic. Present trends are toward the increasing mechanization of society, Bellamy acutely observes; and, he insists, those trends can only work to our good, since the bigger and better machines we keep building will turn the world into one giant, intricately organized, and brightly lit city. It is an unfair distortion of Bellamy's passion and earnestness to say that, for him, the vision of the future resolves itself into a global, climate-controlled shopping center. But it *is* a distortion: not, that is, entirely a misrepresentation.

William Morris, if he had known about shopping centers, would doubtless have used the image as a weapon against Bellamy and all Bellamy stood for. In *News from Nowhere*, written explicitly as a refutation of *Looking Backward*, Morris's narrator tells how he falls asleep and dreams that he has awakened in a future civilization where benevolent socialism has transformed the world according to anti-industrial, anti-technological principles. If Bellamy's future can, at its worst, look suspiciously like a shopping center, Morris's, at its worst, can look like a romanticized, nineteenth-century painting of a medieval fair. One of the dreamer's informants explains to him how the world of cities and machines was changed:

> "The town invaded the country; but the invaders, like the warlike invaders of early days, yielded to the influence of their surroundings, and became country people; and in their turn, as they became more numerous than the townsmen, influenced them also; so that the difference between town and country grew less and less; and it was indeed this world of the country vivified by the thought and briskness of town-bred folk which has produced that happy and leisurely but eager life of which you have had a first taste."

The world at its best, that is, has become a garden; but a garden inhabited by city folk who, for all their pastoralism, retain their city-bred sophistication of taste.

Between Bellamy and Morris, the terms of the modern utopian debate are firmly established. The question is no longer, "How shall we form an ideal society?" It is now, "Toward what kind of society are history and cultural evolution leading us, and how can we best control the process for our own good?" There is an important paradox in that set of questions, one that will govern later utopian thought. For according to strict Darwinian dogma, we are literally *out of control* of history. Evolution will change us into what we will become whether or not we like it—and even before we know we have been changed. But the most persistent of human illusions is that of free will; and almost from the opening of the Darwinian controversy, thinkers were suggesting ways in which *our* species, blessed and cursed with self-consciousness, might come not only to understand but to guide, to control, the evolutionary process to our own ends (this was the central belief of Wells's great disciple of the 1930s, Olaf Stapledon). The paradox of determinism and free will has always been a crucial one in Western social and religious thought, of course. But Darwin (and, in their different way, Marx and Freud) raised it to a level of particular urgency for their age and ours. Enter Wells, and *The Time Machine*.

It is a risky thing for an author to create a masterpiece in his first published book: success of that sort can be a terrible burden for the writer who then has to go on to his next book, and his next, etcetera. But that is what Wells did with *The Time Machine*. And the next fifty years of his extraordinary career can be thought of as, among other things, a heroic living-up to the promise of that great first book. As late as 1940, in one of his last fictions, *All Aboard for Ararat*, he was still acknowledging the influence and the pressure of that book in his career.

At least part of the novel's genius is the way it catches, crystallizes, clarifies so many current (and still very live) controversies. Jean-Pierre Vernier, a French critic of Wells, has observed of *The Time Machine* that, however dire its implied prophecies and however dark its central vision, it is still primarily an entertainment, a fantasy intended, and taken by its audience, less as a cautionary parable than as a diversion. And Vernier is partly right. The subtitle of *The Time Machine* is *An Invention*, a witty reference by Wells to the "invention" of the time machine within the book, and also to the book itself as a primarily aesthetic, quasi-musical "invention" or fantasia (showing here the strong influence of Wilde and the *Yellow Book* aesthetes on Wells). But in Wells, even from the beginning, the artist was never very far from the social planner and prophet. In an important early essay, "The Rediscovery of the Unique" (1891), he writes of the implications of modern science (mainly, of course, biological science) for man's understanding of himself. And the concluding paragraph of the essay perfectly catches both the popularism and the pessimism of his voice at its best:

> Science is a match that man has just got alight. He thought he was in a room—in moments of devotion, a temple—and that his light would be reflected from and display walls inscribed with wonderful secrets and pillars carved with philosophical systems wrought into harmony. It is a curious sensation, now that the preliminary splutter is over and the flame burns up clear, to see his hands lit and just a glimpse of himself and the patch he stands on visible, and around him, in place of all that human comfort and beauty he anticipated—darkness still.

It is a magnificent passage (and one that helps explain why young Wells was so eagerly sought out by newspaper editors as a feature writer). And in its tones, we get a startlingly accurate premonition of some of the images of *The Time Machine:* questing man, as a vulnerable character surrounded by darkness trying to light a puny match to illuminate his condition; humanity as imprisoned in a giant building or temple of uncertain origin and not of his own device; and above all, perhaps, darkness itself—that terminal darkness that lies at the end of all our questing and all our struggle, and which Wells, however much he dramatized or popularized it, could never take less than seriously. One way, indeed, of describing the track of his career is to say that he increasingly discovered, and made increasingly explicit, the grim implications of his early, artistically designed scientific romances and sketches.

In *The Time Machine*, he casts a cold eye upon the quarrel between Bellamy's and Morris's visions of utopia. Both versions of the future are there in the year 802,701 to which the Time Traveller journeys. The world has indeed become a massive and smoothly running complex of machines as well as a garden, an Edenic landscape where men and women share an uncomplicated and blissful, toil-free communal existence. But the smooth-running machines have reduced the men who tend them to a state of mindless cannibalistic bestiality, and the inhabitants of the garden world have become dwarfed, childish caricatures of mankind, the unprotesting and ineffectual prey of their once-brothers, the tenders of machines. The brutal Morlocks and the lovely but sickly Eloi of the year 802,701 are very grim visions, indeed, of Bellamy's hyperindustrial and Morris's postindustrial utopians. Where is evolution leading us? According to Wells in *The Time Machine*, at least, it matters little whether it is leading us toward the socialistic garden world of Morris or the socialistic technology of Bellamy: for both are terrible places, and spell the end of mankind as we now know it.

When a species overadapts to its environment, it starts to die: that is a central Darwinian tenet, and is very near the heart of *The Time Machine*. For the environment will inevitably change over the course of geological, cosmological time. And the species that has become too at home in one phase of climate and ecology will probably lose the resiliency to change and meet the demands of another phase. This is to say that, on the evolutionary scale, a certain dis-ease, a certain genetic "restlessness" ought to be built into the structure of a surviving organism. And Wells, that perennially restless man, was quick to adopt the Darwinian generalization as a kind of pledge that the universe was, after all, on the side of his own energetic permanent self-dissatisfaction. It is perhaps why he was able to write such a stunning refutation of the utopias of his Darwinian predecessors. For them, the end point of society would be the point at which the struggle for existence ceased, resolved itself into a new Eden. But for Wells, a world without struggle and tension would be, simply, uninhabitable. This is what the Time Traveller reflects upon after he has encountered the graceful, ineffectual Eloi and before he meets their brutal counterparts, the Morlocks. Man, he thinks, has finally subdued nature, has finally wrested the world to his own imagination of a Golden Age where all effort is unnecessary:

> I thought of the physical slightness of the people, their lack of intelligence and those abundant ruins, and it strengthened my belief in a perfect conquest of Nature. For after the battle comes Quiet. . . . No doubt the exquisite beauty of the buildings I saw was the outcome of the last surgings of the now purposeless energy of mankind before it settled down into perfect harmony with the conditions under which it lived—the flourish of that last triumph which began the last great peace. This has ever been the fate of energy in security; it takes to art and to eroticism, and then come langour and decay.

That "perfect harmony" with the environment is, for Wells, the inevitable and irreversible prelude to decay and death. And, of course, the Eloi with their "hectic beauty"—the delicate beauty of the fevered or the tubercular—and their life of uncomplicated art and eroticism are, among other things, a bitter parody of the aesthetes and decadents of the nineties. But, as the Time Traveller tells us at the end of these reflections, his theories are wrong: he has not yet seen the Morlocks, and not yet learned the great fear under which the Eloi live. When he first meets the Morlocks, and visits their subterranean dwelling among the great machines, he will venture another theory: that the present distinction between rich and poor has become increasingly pronounced in the process of social evolution until the capitalist and laboring class divide into two distinct species, with all the energy of the race concentrated in the antlike, uncomprehending busyness of the wretched and deformed children of the workers. Not until the end of his stay in 802,701 does he come to the full realization of that world's terror, the realization that the two distinct species into which man has evolved are now predator and prey, acting out a massive and bloody ritual of self-consumption:

> I understood now what all the beauty of the Over-world people covered. Very pleasant was their day, as pleasant as the day of the cattle in the field. Like the cattle, they knew of no enemies and provided against no needs. And their end was the same.
>   I grieved to think how brief the dream of the human intellect had been.

Three theories of society are in the end put forth by the Time Traveller, each of them cancelling out its predecessor, each of them a more complex view of the possibilities of social evolution over an immense period of time, and each of them more grim. For all the flurry of Darwinian elements or evolutionary speculation in late-nineteenth-century utopias, not until *The*

Time Machine did the real power, and the real terror, of evolutionary theory find adequate expression in fiction. I have said [elsewhere] that one of the most important shockwaves cast by *The Origin of Species* was not simply the idea of man's heritage from lower animals, but rather the disorienting discovery of the immense vistas of time upon which any definition of "man"—or of man's success—has to be imagined. "I grieved to think how brief the dream of the human intellect had been," says the Time Traveller in the year 802,701. And, on the scale of the age of the Earth, the elapsed time between 1895 and 802,701 is brief; it is terribly brief, and that is the whole point of that melancholy line. Here, again, is the Time Traveller looking up at the night sky as he and Weena, the Eloi girl who loves him, flee from the Morlocks:

> Looking at these stars suddenly dwarfed my own troubles and all the gravities of terrestrial life. I thought of their unfathomable distance, and the slow inevitable drift of their movements out of the unknown past into the unknown future. I thought of the great precessional cycle that the pole of the earth describes. Only forty times had that silent revolution occurred during all the years that I had traversed. and during these few revolutions all the activity, all the traditions, the complex organizations, the nations, languages, literatures, aspirations, even the mere memory of Man as I knew him, had been swept out of existence.

This, like so many passages in *The Time Machine*, is a passage of great lyrical power, a kind of prose poem. And its theme is time, but "time" imagined in a way that, except for the very act of imagination that calls it into being, reduces all things human to triviality. This is a very romantic sentiment, desperately lonely in its vision of man's place in the universe and desperately assertive in its faith in the power of imagination and language to make that universe habitable. Almost a century before *The Time Machine* Shelley had ended his great meditation, "Mont Blanc," with the defiant question

> And what were thou, and earth, and stars, and sea,
> If, to the human mind's imaginings,
> Silence and solitude were vacancy?

The answer to that question, of course, can be either "everything" or "nothing," and on the gamble implied rests the central romantic gamble on behalf of man's position in the universe. But note that, while Shelley asks that question in terms of man's position in *space*, i.e., in a potentially infinite universe of things, Wells asks it in terms of man's position in *time*, a potentially infinite universe of duration. In the difference between those two meditations lies much of the emotional history of the nineteenth century as well as much of our own discomfort, not knowing which answer to choose.

The invention of the Eloi and the Morlocks is finally not as central to the brilliance of *The Time Machine* as is the invention of the machine itself, and the consequent imagination of time in its fullest, longest, and most challengingly inhuman dimensions. Here is the description of the model Time Machine that the Traveller first shows to his dinner guests:

> The thing the Time Traveller held in his hand was a glittering metallic framework, scarcely larger than a small clock, and very delicately made. There was ivory in it, and some transparent crystalline substance. And now I must be explicit, for this that follows—unless his explanation is to be accepted—is an absolutely unaccountable thing.

What follows is a description of how the Traveller sends his model into the future. But notice what has happened in this brilliant, and brilliantly vague paragraph. The machine has been described, but nothing of its precise form has been given. It has, in fact, been made real without being at all realized. And in using this kind of description Wells set a precedent for most of his later science fiction. His concern was not really with technology, but with the effects, the human implications, of possible technological advances. Time travel may be (in fact, is) impossible; but Wells really does not care. What he cares about is inventing just enough convincing hardware to allow him—and us—to speculate about the possible fate of the human race as of the year 802,701.

The very date, 802,701, as numerous critics and commentators have pointed out, is a kind of hieroglyph of entropy, a numerical metaphor for a machine about to run down, a process about to play itself out. (In the 1894 serialization of the novel, the date the Time Traveller reached was the rather less portentous 12,203.) But it is not simply a matter of numbers or social prophecy. What Wells manages to do in *The Time Machine* is to articulate, for the first time and distinctively for his age, a vision of the abyss of geological time. The great passage with which the Time Traveller's story concludes, his vision of the end of the world, is one of the most powerfully imagined passages in modern English fiction. But it is powerful precisely because the whole novel has anticipated and adumbrated its dark tones.

We have been discussing *The Time Machine* so far in terms of the traditions of utopian, social-prophetic storytelling out of which it arises. But it is impossible to think about the tale for long without considering it for what it finally is, a major and brilliant work of literary art. Harold Bloom, perhaps our most perceptive critic of Romantic and modern poetry, has observed that the structure of the archetypal Romantic poem involves a visionary dialectics on the part of the speaker. Confronted by a particular problem or paradox, that is, the speaker of a Romantic poem entertains first one solution to the problem, then another (usually unrelated) one, and finally a third one that either resolves or transcends the first two. This is, indeed, the way Wordsworth's "Tintern Abbey" and Shelley's "Mont

Blanc" work; it is also the way *The Time Machine* works, once we begin to understand it as not simply a post-Darwinian utopian fiction but a lyrical meditation on the nature and the terror of time itself.

We have already seen that the Time Traveller, in his visit to the year 802,701, makes up three successive explanations of what he sees. The Time Traveller (and, of course, Wells) is quite explicit about the difference of this narrative procedure from the ordinary course of utopian fiction. Other utopias always involve excessively detailed description of the scenery and architecture of the ideal state, the Time Traveller says. "But while such details are easy enough to obtain when the whole world is contained in one's imagination, they are altogether inaccessible to a real traveller amid such realities as I found here." Wells in a single stroke lets himself out of the boring burden of describing fully the future world in which his hero finds himself, and at the same time (since indeterminacy and confusion are always the best alibis) makes that world more believable, more *notionally* real than it would otherwise have been.

Other utopias also involve, as the Time Traveller is careful to point out, conveniently informative guides or historians to explain how things came to be as they are in the great good (or the great bad) place. But the Traveller has none of these aids. The Morlocks do not talk at all, and of the Eloi, he observes, "their language was excessively simple—almost exclusively composed on concrete substantives and verbs." An ideally Edenic language, but one emptied of the powers of abstaction or a sense of history. The Traveller is confronted with the future in much the same way the Romantic poet finds himself confronted with the inhospitable rockface of nature: a mute, gigantic, threatening, and absolutely uncommunicative presence, about which one can only speculate, only entertain notions. It is one of the most brilliant devices of *The Time Machine* that no one, in the Traveller's narrative of the future, *speaks*. Weena gives the Traveller some flowers she has gathered, which he produces in the only interruption of his narrative. But that gesture, so touching and so sentimental—and so crucial to the end of the story—is also a sign that the future *is* inarticulate, that it has no names except the names we choose to give it. Silence and solitude, Shelley insists, are really not vacancy: but, in the romantic tradition, you can only insist upon that as long as you are willing to take silence and solitude in their full frightening reality. And that is what the Time Traveller does.

The central narrative device of *The Time Machine*, then, is a first-person narrator entertaining a number of alternate explanations for the phenomena he witnesses, coming to the true conclusion about the reality of things only at the end of his tale. This structure not only recapitulates the movement of a romantic meditation, but also provides the novel with a reasonable facsimile of what was being increasingly celebrated as "scientific method." Faced with the implied question, "What does the future of mankind hold in store?" the narrator, like a good scientific investigator, tries out explanation after explanation of the observed facts until he finally hits on the one explanation that suffices, that explains all the facts as observed and nothing but them.

It is a structure that was to serve Wells in good stead for the next decade. . . . Most of his major scientific romances turn on the same process of alternate and progressively accurate explanations of the impossible or the unspeakable. To be sure, there are precedents for this kind of narrative. Herman Melville in "Benito Cereno" and Nathaniel Hawthorne in *The Scarlet Letter* and *The House of the Seven Gables* both give us stories in which an object or set of objects is first presented, then perceived in various ways, and then finally revealed in the full clarity of its meaning. And behind Melville and Hawthorne lies the whole tradition of the Gothic novel in English, that curious amalgam of supernaturalism and narrative indirection that dominated the popular tastes of England and America during the late eighteenth and early nineteenth century. Wells knew this tradition of tales intimately, and in the first version of *The Time Machine* barely departed from it. "The Chronic Argonauts" is the very Poe-esque (or Hawthorne-esque) story of a mysterious man named "Dr. Nebogipfel" who arrives to take over occupancy of an old manse in an English village, seems to practice arcane and dangerous arts, and is finally revealed to be a traveler from the future, an exile out of time. This information, however, is made known only *after* the major (and unnarrated, since the tale is incomplete) action has taken place—and it is made known by the country doctor who is Nebogipfel's unwilling companion on his journey through time. So that even from its crude beginnings, *The Time Machine* incorporated its central narrative-framing device—having the story told after the voyage into time has taken place, and having the story of the adventurous, eccentric Time Traveller told *through* the mediating voice of a more conventional narrator. This is also the procedure, of course, of one of the most successful and most lasting nineteenth-century tales of horror, Robert Louis Stevenson's *The Strange Case of Dr. Jekyll and Mr. Hyde*, published in 1886, two years before Wells began "The Chronic Argonauts." And Wells, like Stevenson, was—from *The Time Machine* onward—fascinated with manifestations of dual personality, even, in his early story "The Late Mr. Elvesham," writing a Jekyll-and-Hyde tale of, if anything, more terrifying dimensions than Stevenson's.

Nevertheless, *The Time Machine* as we have it now is as distinct an advance over those early Gothic and post-Gothic frame-tale narratives as it is over previous nineteenth-century utopias. We begin in the most cordial and comfortable of surroundings, a late-nineteenth-century dinner party, where a group of talented men are exchanging serious but politely vague, conveniently mellowed after-dinner views:

The Time Traveller (for so it will be convenient to speak of him) was expounding a recondite matter to us. His grey eyes shone and twinkled, and his usually pale face was flushed and animated. The fire burned brightly, and the soft radiance of the incandescent lights in the lillies of silver caught the bubbles that flashed and passed in our glasses.

This is the beginning of the tale in its final version, and it is important to note that it is all we ever learn of the Time Traveller's physical appearance: he has grey eyes, and a usually pale, but now animated and flushed, face. He is, in other words, an abstraction: as is his vaguely described machine, and as is appropriate for this most abstract of speculations on the future of the human race. Even his last vision of the end of all life on the planet is abstract and disembodied, although it is also one of the great chilling passages in the history of the English language. This passage was added to the book on the insistence of W. E. Henley, Wells's editor. But it is nevertheless one of the finest, most unrelentingly apocalyptic things Wells wrote. Journeying past the year 802,701, past the death of the human species on the planet, the Traveller alights at a time when the Earth is dying. What follows must be quoted in full.

> The darkness grew apace; a cold wind began to blow in freshening gusts from the east, and the showering white flakes in the air increased in number. From the edge of the sea came a ripple and whisper. Beyond these lifeless sounds the world was silent. Silent? It would be hard to convey the stillness of it. All the sounds of man, the bleating of sheep, the cries of birds, the hum of insects, the stir that makes the background of our lives—all that was over. As the darkness thickened, the eddying flakes grew more abundant, dancing before my eyes; and the cold of the air more intense. At last, one by one, swiftly, one after the other, the white peaks of the distant hills vanished into blackness. The breeze rose to a moaning wind. I saw the black central shadow of the eclipse sweeping towards me. In another moment the pale stars alone were visible. All else was rayless obscurity. The sky was absolutely black.

There is little that need be said about a passage like this. Not often in the history of the language has a vision of The End, a vision of the absolute conclusion, collapse, and catastrophe of all things been so powerfully imagined. Wells here is the chosen poet of the abyss, the perfect lyricist of entropy. "All that was over," he writes of the whole range of human and animal life on the planet—and in those four words is compressed a universe of melancholy. In this passage we come very close to looking into what Wells at his most despairing could imagine—and what he refused, at all cost, to let himself imagine.

For if the Traveller and his final vision are cold and inhospitable, the dinner party is not. We know that there is a fire, champagne, and we even know into what shape the incandescent lights over the table are fashioned. We know such things for two important reasons, two related reasons: First, because they are precisely the comforting, recognizable details which the Traveller's grim vision of the future is about to upset; and second, because they are precisely the details of scene and decor that the narrator of the story would remember. This narrator—or editor—of the Time Traveller's story is an important character, and one who, during the rest of Wells's career, will engage in a fascinating and unending struggle with the despairing voice of the Time Traveller. At the next dinner party, a week after the opening scene, the Traveller appears, scarred and shaken by his voyage into and return from the distant future, and tells his awful tale of the Eloi, the Morlocks, and the final journey to the end of all things. But, at the very end of the book, after the Traveller has again departed on a voyage into time (never to return), the final word on the tale's meaning is held in a curious ambiguity between the vision of the Traveller (who sees into the cosmic meaninglessness of things) and the narrator, his friend (who remembers champagne and firelight from dinner parties). "He," says the narrator of the Traveller:

> He, I know—for the question had been discussed among us long before the Time Machine was made—thought but cheerlessly of the Advancement of Mankind, and saw in the growing pile of civilization only a foolish heaping that must inevitably fall back upon and destroy its makers in the end. If that is so, it remains for us to live as though it were not so. But to me the future is still black and blank—as a vast ignorance, lit at a few casual places by the memory of his story. And I have by me, for my comfort, two strange white flowers—shrivelled now, and brown and flat and brittle—to witness that even when mind and strength had gone, gratitude and a mutual tenderness still lived on in the heart of man.

Some readers have taken this final comment by the narrator as an exercise in fatuity, a falsely comforting conclusion to a book whose *real* conclusion is the Time Traveller's preceding vision of the end of the world in darkness and meaninglessness. But to read *The Time Machine* this way is to misread it. The narrator is given the last word for the same reason those two white flowers, which the Traveller produced in the middle of his narrative, are there at all. Wells *wants* the future to remain, however threatening or despairing aspects of it may appear, fundamentally "black and blank"—black *and* white, that is, depending on the state of mind or soul with which we behold it. The two voices of *The Time Machine*, in other words, encapsulate between them that elementary tension between cosmic determinism and freedom of the will that we have seen at the heart of all speculation about the future of mankind. Wells's achievement in *The Time Machine* is to fuse that intellectual dubiety into the very structure of his narrative so that, as with a Symbolist poem, what the story *means* (is the future unrelievedly dark? is there any hope for our species before the tribunal of history?) is absolutely indistinguishable from how the story *works* (which voice is the "real" one, that of the Traveller who has been to the future and back, or that of the narrator who stays with us to record and interpret his tale?).

Returning to Vernier's observations about *The Time Machine* as entertainment, we can say that the book works as marvelously as it does as entertainment precisely because of the seriousness and complexity of the intellectual contradictions it incorporates; and, of course, it makes those contradictions so powerfully real for us just because it is such a finely fashioned aesthetic machine for producing ambiguity (much like the Time Machine). For once in his career—and, some would say, for the only time—Wells found the perfect vehicle for his intellectual, artistic, and personal obsessions, the perfect story and method for bringing them all into an intricate, if ambiguous, harmony. And the contradictory voices of hope and despair, the narrative procedure of doubtful and successive explanations of outrageous phenomena, and above all the abiding sense of a great darkness just outside the range of human ken were to remain the major attributes of his genius during the years of his great scientific romances, and perhaps during his whole career.

"Absolute Realism": Arnold Bennett

John Lucas

In 1907 Bennett published *The Grim Smile of the Five Towns*. It was his second collection of short stories, and a considerable improvement on *Tales of the Five Towns*, which had appeared in 1905. *Tales of the Five Towns* is filled with bread-and-butter stories, teased-out anecdotes of little worth. The title is misleading, for not all the tales are of the Five Towns. But whether Bennett is writing about Hanbridge and Bursley or London and Vienna there is the same lacklustre slightness. It is not that the tales are incompetent or botched. There is simply nothing to them. They read like space-fillers. And one can see why. The period 1900–14 was the heyday of weekly and monthly magazines specializing in the short story. Bennett was a professional writer who could be relied on to meet editorial deadlines and to produce any number of words to order. No wonder, then, that he should write short stories. But it isn't his natural medium. Nearly all his stories rely far too heavily on anecdote, and while his worst faults glare out heavily from them his special virtues have very little chance to show themselves. Bennett needs elbow room to be at his best. The short story rarely allows him that. Even the most successful story in the first volume—"His Worship the Goosedriver"—is little more than an extended anecdote and is marred by a ponderous jokiness and thinness of detail. We don't really know anything much about the characters, and this weakness is even more marked in the other tales. Anyone reading through *Tales of the Five Towns* would be perfectly justified in concluding that as a short-story writer Bennett had very little talent.

But *The Grim Smile of the Five Towns* is a different matter. The same faults recur, and in abundance. The flat-footed humour of "The Nineteenth Hat" (apparently built out of an incident involving Eleanor Green), and of

---

From *Arnold Bennett: A Study of His Fiction*. © 1974 by John Lucas. Methuen & Co., 1974.

"Vera's First Christmas Adventure"; the trivial anecdotage which is all that "The Lion's Share" and "Baby's Bath" amount to; the unsatisfactory, external view of "The Silent Brothers." There are compensations, however. In the first place this collection feels much more authentically about the Five Towns than the first one had. There are deft touches of comic observation, as where the hero of "Beginning the New Year" "climbed into a second-class compartment when the train drew up, and ten other people, all with third-class tickets, followed his example." There is the perception on which "From One Generation to Another" depends, that in the Five Towns "families spring into splendour out of nothing in the course of a couple of generations, and as often as not sink back again into nothing in the course of two generations more" (a perception that has much bearing on *The Old Wives' Tale* and the *Clayhanger* trilogy). There is also the grim smile itself. Bennett's Five Townspeople are vividly evoked in that phrase. Laconic, tough, rueful, gritty, quick to seize the main chance, generous without grace, towards which, indeed, they profess indifference or scorn, and proud in a way that blends in shifting proportions the boorish and the decent. The collection as a whole is shot through with the kind of observation and incident which justifies Bennett's title. And there is one story, substantially longer than the rest, where the grim smile is seen at its fullest and in which Bennett fashions a masterpiece.

John Wain has called "The Death of Simon Fuge" the most delicate product of Bennett's art, and I would not want to disagree with that judgement. Indeed, what he has to say about the story rings so true that there is not a great deal that can be added to his account. But let me give the tale in outline. It is told us by Loring, a southerner and aesthete, whose professional work—he is an expert on ceramics—brings him to the Five Towns. On the train journey down he reads of the death of Simon Fuge. Fuge had been a painter of some genius. He had also been born in the Five Towns, though he had long ago left them for a cosmopolitan existence. Loring recalls a tale Fuge had once told of a night he had spent boating on a lake with two beautiful Five Towns girls. Will he be able to discover more about this romantic episode? The question is much in his mind when he gets out of his train to be met by his host, Brindley. So is the shock of his first encounter with the Five Towns:

> As I stood on that dirty platform, in a *milieu* of advertisements of soap, boots and aperients, I began to believe that Simon Fuge never had lived, that he was a mere illusion of his friends and his small public. All that I saw around me was a violent negation of Simon Fuge, that entity of rare, fine, exotic sensibilities, that perfectly mad gourmet of sensations, that exotic seer of beauty.

Loring's way of putting things mustn't be thought to cast doubt on his opinion of Simon Fuge. It does, however, clearly indicate why he is so shaken by his first view of Five Towns and of his host who "although an architect by profession . . . appeared anxious to be mistaken for a sporting squire."

Much of "The Death of Simon Fuge" is about Loring's gradual realization that for all the outward appearance of meanness and dirt, the Five Towns are not the haunts of barbarians. Installed at Brindley's house, he discovers that his host is a discriminating book collector. Brindley's friend Colclough drops in and the two men play Richard Strauss and Mozart. Throughout the evening there is a constant whirl of activity and drinking, and it ends with a visit to the house of a doctor friend of Brindley's, who turns out to have an even finer collection of books than Brindley's own. Loring passes from hostility through bewilderment to a reluctant admiration for Five Towns life and the sheer happiness of the people with whom he comes in contact. And Bennett, of course, manages quite effortlessly to give us the feel of this life. He packs so much in, and so casually. The bleak, dirty station, muddy, greasy streets and cobbled ways, Brindley's house with its ingenious heating arrangements and large, comfortable rooms, supper accompanied by bottles of ale, electric trams like large boxes of light on wheels, the warm, male-dominated pubs: all these are seen through Loring's innocent and wondering eyes, so that the details spring before us, fresh and alive.

But what of Fuge? And what of his tale of the night on the lake? Gradually Loring discovers that Fuge's version of the story bears little relation to the facts. He also discovers that nobody has anything much to say about the dead artist. It is not that they dislike him, merely that they have dismissed him as he dismissed them when he left them for the larger worlds of London and Paris. In the Bursley Museum Loring sees a small painting by Fuge. He knows it to be a work of genius:

> It *was* Simon Fuge, at any rate all of Simon Fuge that was worth having, masterful, imperishable. And not merely was it his challenge, it was his scorn, his aristocratic disdain, his positive assurance that in the battle between them he had annihilated the Five Towns. It hung there in the very midst thereof, calmly and contemptuously waiting for the acknowledgement of his victory.

Loring asks Brindley if the painting isn't by Fuge.

> "Which?" said Mr Brindley.
> "That one."
> "Yes, I fancy it is," he negligently agreed. "Yes, it is."
> "It's not signed," I remarked.
> "It ought to be," said Mr Brindley; then laughed. "Too late now!"
> "How did it get here?"
> "Don't know. Oh! I think Mr Perkins won it in a raffle at a bazaar, and then hung it here."

The local papers are every bit as indifferent to Fuge's death as Brindley has proved to be. It may make headlines in the national press, but the *Staffordshire Signal* devotes its headlines to the fact that Knype F. C. have signed a new centre-forward. Brindley defends the *Signal:* " 'You don't understand these things. If Knype Football Club was put into the League Second Division, ten thousand homes would go into mourning. Who the devil was Simon Fuge?' " That question hangs over the entire story. For Loring, Fuge was an artist of genius. But for Brindley and his friends Fuge was a boaster, a loudmouth and a deserter. Besides, he hasn't any relevance to their lives, he isn't materially important. We have to take this last point seriously or we will soften and sentimentalize the story. Through Loring's eyes we are allowed to see that Brindley and his circle are cultivated and sensitive people. But there are inevitable limits to their sensitivity, limits placed on them by the Five Towns, by their grim smile of acceptance of a life which is a compromise between contradictory elements. Brindley accepts the Five Towns. He is proud of his own moneymaking abilities. He is tough, abrasive, hard-headed. He likes books and is genuinely and passionately devoted to music. But if it came to a choice between them or the Five Towns—well, who the devil was Simon Fuge? Brindley is lucky, of course, for there is no need for him to choose. He can enjoy both Bursley and books. But the limitations in his own way of life are implicit in the very fact that Fuge left. Bennett does not criticize Brindley. There is no shadow of disapproval in the way he shows him to us, and the use of Loring is crucial here, because if anyone were to disapprove of Brindley it would be him, and he finds that he cannot.

And yet—who the devil was Simon Fuge? The plain answer is—an artist who left for the good of his art. Inevitably one feels that the question came from somewhere deep inside Bennett. "The Death of Simon Fuge" holds the Five Towns in perfect equivocal poise. But we know that Bennett, like Fuge, chose to leave. He is their critic and their champion. He knows what is good about the place, but its grim smile is not for him. Except, that is, as an artist who can draw on it for his art. And when he next writes about the Five Towns his view of it will be darker, gloomier than in his fine story. It will also produce his greatest novel.

II

But before I speak of *The Old Wives' Tale*, I need to say a little about *Buried Alive*. At first called *The Case of Leek*, this novel occupied Bennett during January and February of 1908. It was published in June and by July he was noting in his *Journal* that the reviews "have been simply excellent." Yet *Buried Alive* is not very good. In fact it is no more than a faintly humorous anecdote spun out to novel length. A famous English painter with the very un-English name of Priam Farll arrives back in London from foreign parts, unannounced and unaccompanied except by his valet, Leek. Leek dies suddenly and the doctor attending takes him for Farll and Farll for his own valet. The artist sees in this confusion a chance to escape into welcome anonymity. He marrys a working-class woman, Alice Challice, lives in Putney, and for a while gives up painting. But he begins again and subsequently finds himself called upon to prove his identity in court (the reason for this being that an art-dealer recognizes his new work as that of Priam Farll, buys and sells it as such, and is then accused of false dealing since Farll is officially dead, has indeed been given a burial in Westminster Abbey).

As a short story *Buried Alive* would do well enough. Stretched out to novel length it becomes tedious, at least until the court scenes, when it picks up considerably. There is also an odd wavering of tone throughout the novel which suggests that Bennett wasn't sure just how seriously he shold take his own idea. For Priam Farll to be buried alive in Putney is, I think, a reasonably knowing joke (Bennett was, after all, aware of Swinburne's semi-incarceration); and the notion of a famous artist marrying a working-class woman might seem to be a spoof on the habit, which had started up in the 1890s, of the artist seeking love and life in the music hall and pub. Even the name, Alice Challice, hints at this, just as it reminds us of the Edwardian fondness for using religious imagery in a secular context, in order to insist on the "holiness of the heart's affections" (I use the phrase which Forster borrowed from Keats and used so fervently in *A Room with a View*). Bennett wants us to see Alice as comic in herself and doubly comic because Priam thinks of her as perfection: "She had a large mind: that was sure. She understood—things, and human nature in particular. . . . She was balm to Priam Farll. She might have been equally balm to King David, Uriah the Hittite, Socrates, Rousseau, Lord Byron, Heine or Charlie Peace" (chap. 5). I don't find that particularly funny, but I think it is a bit distasteful. Oddly so, for Bennett would never adopt such a dismissively jocular tone for any character in a Five Towns novel. But it is a fact that his London novels are often marred by this leaden facetiousness. *Buried Alive* certainly is, though not consistently so. For Bennett also wants us to take Alice seriously. We are told that she gives Priam new joy in life. Because of his marriage "all life gave him joy; all life was beautiful to him." As for Alice: "She lived. She did nothing but live. She lived every hour. Priam felt truly that he had at last got down to the bed-rock of life" (chap. 6). But for this to be anything like convincing we would need to see a good deal more of Alice than Bennett is prepared to show us. Instead, he reports—and very cursorily at that.

Indeed, with the honourable exception of the court scenes, *Buried Alive* is nearly all report. As such, it becomes tiresome. We know nothing about Alice, and we know precious little about Farll. He is typical of what happens to a Bennett hero when the author isn't greatly interested in his own subject. Priam Farll is merely sketched in, and so are all the other characters. We see them in hazy outline, and such a view is woefully incomplete. It is also irritating, because both Farll and Alice are little more than clichés. Compared with *The Horse's Mouth*, a novel which flirts with clichés about the unworldy artist and "life," but which blasts through them to something altogether more convincing, *Buried Alive* is poor stuff.

The question arises, why did Bennett write it? Partly, of course, because he was Bennett, the professional craftsman, able to turn his hand to any kind of tale. And without doubt *Buried Alive* is neatly told. The very unlikely plot hasn't any loopholes in it and as a whole the novel is mechanically competent. The best one can say for it is that it is a distinct improvement on those early entertainments to which it looks a likely successor, though Bennett never classified it as one. But that is to say very little.

It is, however, important to realize that *Buried Alive* was an act of interruption. It was written while Bennett was on holiday, one might say, from the exhausting labour of *The Old Wives' Tale*. We know how long the plan for his great novel had been maturing in his mind; and it is obvious that the strain of actually writing it, of finally and irrevocably putting into print the fiction on which he was prepared to stake so much, must have been very great. Not that Bennett is prepared to give a great deal away, either in his *Journals* or in letters of the time. But the *Journals* supply hints enough:

> *Friday, May 29th:*
> I worked well at *Old Wives' Tale* yesterday, but indifferently today.

> *Tuesday, June 2nd:*
> Gradually got involved in one of my periodic crises of work, from which I emerged last night, having written the first chapter of Part III of *Old Wives' Tale*.

> *Sunday, July 19th:*
> I don't know when I wrote the last entry.
> I finished the third part of the *Old Wives' Tale* on Tuesday last. Everything else gave way before it, and I simply did nothing but that book. It meant the utter defeat of all other plans.

Writing *Buried Alive* during the opening months of 1908 must have been a welcome rest. It is true that very few people would consider that the writing of a novel, however slight, is the most satisfactory way of taking a rest. But then Bennett wasn't ordinary. If he had been we should not now be in possession of *The Old Wives' Tale*.

III

But why should *The Old Wives' Tale* have meant so much to him? Perhaps there is no way we can confidently answer that question. Yet I think it reasonable to suggest that Bennett saw the novel as a vital test of his worth as an artist. He would stand or fall by its success or failure. Reading between the lines of the *Journals* and letters, one has the strong impression that despite his show of calm certainty in himself and his career, Bennett was liable to the doubts and uncertainties that trouble all creative men. There is something close to self-parody in his presentation of himself as Artist: book collector, bon vivant, adopted Parisian, opera-goer, dandy, lover: it is as though he takes on various roles in order to convince himself, or others, or himself through others, that he is, after all, the genuine article. Speculation? Yes, indeed. But inevitably one speculates about the painfully shy, sensitive man with the protective carapace of tough stoicism and invulnerability—"I began to try to explain to Marriott the philosophy of the Stoics, the inferiority of ambition as a motive and of glory as an end, etc. But I doubt if he understood what I meant by the control of the mind and its consequences" (*Journals*, August 1907). I do not blame Marriott for his imcomprehension. How could anyone who knew Bennett at all well really believe in him as a convincing disciple of Epictetus? Apart from anything else, Bennett was an ambitious man. All through the planning of *The Old Wives' Tale* he kept vividly in mind "the example and challenge of Guy de Maupassant's *Une Vie*. . . . *Une Vie* relates the entire life history of a woman. I settled in the privacy of my own head tht my book about the development of a young girl into a stout old lady must be the English *Une Vie*" (preface to *The Old Wives' Tale*). One is reminded of another, later novelist who was determined to take on the best: "I started out very quiet and I beat Mr Turgenev. Then I trained hard and I beat Mr de Maupassant. I've fought two draws with Mr Stendhal, and I think I had an edge in the last one." But where Hemingway is boastful and absurd, Bennett is merely truthful. He *did* want to write the English *Une Vie*. Yet if he had settled for beating "Mr de Maupassant," *The Old Wives' Tale* wouldn't be the fine novel that it is. Its flaws do perhaps come from the French writer, or from something that was deep in Bennett himself and which attracted him to de Maupassant. But the novel's strengths are uniquely Bennett's. And they prove him to be a rare and genuine artist. At his truest, Bennett is not to be compared with de Maupassant but with another writer whom he much admired, and who largely replaced de Maupassant in his affections:

> As you read him you fancy that he must always have been saying to himself: "Life is good enough for me. I won't alter it. I will set it down as it is." Such is the tribute to his success which he forces from you.
>
> He seems to have achieved absolute realism. . . . His climaxes are never strained; nothing is ever idealised, sentimentalised, etherialised; no part of the truth is left out, no part is exaggerated. There is no cleverness, no startling feat of virtuosity. All appears simple, candid, almost childlike.
>
> (*Books and Persons*)

Bennett on Chekhov. The words might be applied to *The Old Wives' Tale*. Almost. One has to add the qualification because the shade of de Maupassant undoubtedly hangs over the novel; its dark influence shows itself in the pessimism which Bennett felt himself to share with the Frenchman—though in de Maupassant's case it is closer to cynicism—and which occasionally distorts the "absolute realism" at which *The Old Wives' Tale* aims.

It is a point to come back to. For the moment I need to sketch in the development of the novel, from the moment when the first idea for it lodged in Bennett's mind to its final flowering. We first hear of it in a *Journal* entry, for 18 November 1903. Bennett has gone to dine at his usual restaurant, and discovers that the seat opposite to his has been taken by a "middle-aged woman, inordinately stout and with pendant cheeks." The fat woman is annoyed that Bennett should sit opposite her, moves all her belongings to another seat, then to another and yet another, until everyone in the restaurant is secretly laughing at her odd behaviour.

> The fat woman was clearly a crotchet, a *maniaque*, a woman who lived much alone. Her cloak (she displayed on taking it off a simply awful light puce flannel dress) and her parcels were continually the object of her attention and she was always arguing with her waitress. And the whole restaurant secretly made a butt of her. She was repulsive; no one could like her or sympathise with her. But I thought—she has been young and slim once. And I immediately thought of a long 10 or 15 thousand words short story, *The History of Two Old Women*. I gave this woman a sister fat as herself. And the first chapter would be in the restaurant (both sisters) something like tonight—and written rather cruelly. Then I would go back to the infancy of these two, and sketch it all. One should have lived ordinarily, married prosaically, and become a widow. The other should have become a whore and all that; "guilty splendour." Both are overtaken by fat. And they live together again in old age, not too rich, a nuisance to themselves and to others. Neither has any imagination.

And there, in the outline of a short story, is the beginning of the 200,000-word novel. It might well be the outline for a story by de Maupassant. "She was repulsive; no one could like her or sympathise with her." The sisters are to be "a nuisance to themselves and to others." Something of this remains in the novel; something, too, of the "sketch" of their lives, from infancy to grave. But is that all? According to E. M. Forster, yes:

> Our daily life in time is exactly this business of getting old which clogs the arteries of Sophia and Constance, and the story that is a story and sounded so healthy and stood no nonsense cannot sincerely lead to any conclusion but the grave. It is an unsatisfactory conclusion. Of course we grow old. But a great book must

rest on something more than an "of course," and *The Old Wives'*
Tale is strong, sincere, sad, it misses greatness.

(Aspects of the Novel)

But *The Old Wives' Tale* does rest on something more than an "of course"
(whereas the proposed *History of Two Old Women* certainly doesn't). For
Bennett's novel isn't simply about Constance and Sophia; it is about a whole
family, its successes and eventual failure and disappearance; and because
the Baines family is in trade in Bursley, *The Old Wives' Tale* is also and
inevitably about the Five Towns. In "The Death of Simon Fuge" Brindley
tells Loring that "there's practically no such thing as class distinction here.
Both my grandfathers were working potters. Colclough's father was a joiner
who finished up as a builder." Families rise, families fall. And though of
course there *is* class distinction in the Five Towns it is maintained only by
that ceaseless movement from success to failure, failure to success which
characterizes Five Towns life.

The Old Wives' Tale opens in the 1860s and comes to a close in the 1900s.
By the time it has ended the Baines family has ceased to be the principal
haberdashers of St Luke's Square in Bursley, St Luke's has "gone down"
in the social scale, and Bursley itself has been replaced by Hanbridge as
the economic centre of the Five Towns. This is not to say that *The Old Wives'*
Tale is primarily about these matters; but they are very important to the
novel, and they explain why at least some of the many deaths which the
novel records can be set down so matter-of-factly, made into an "of course."
Mr Baines dies, Mrs Baines dies, Constance's husband, Samuel Povey, dies,
and Constance reflects that "Her career seemed to be punctuated by interments. But after a while her gentle commonsense came to insist that
most human beings lose their parents, and that every marriage must end
in either a widower or a widow, and that all careers are punctuated by
interments" (book 2, chap. 5).

Deaths occur, careers continue. Time subjects those careers to different
experiences. The young Samuel Povey is funny, grows into a splendidly
conscientious manager-proprietor of Baineses' and good husband and father, dies a bit absurdly. Cyril, his son, declines from glittering promise as
an art student to contented acceptance of his mediocrity. Dick Povey, his
cousin, rises from self-pitying ineptitude to become an energetic and successful businessman. And so on. The novel is threaded through with these
different careers, and manages effortlessly to give the feeling of a community "set down as it is," in a manner which "appears simple, candid,
almost childlike."

The Old Wives' Tale is equally successful in its feeling for place. This
isn't something that can be demonstrated by quotation, because although
there are one or two sustained descriptions—as for example, the Baineses'
kitchen—the real success comes from the way in which Bennett slowly
builds the solidity of the world he is writing about. The result is that, as

Arnold Kettle has said, "we come to *feel* every stairway and passage, to relish every piece of furniture in that stuffy house on the corner of the Square in Bursley" (*An Introduction to the English Novel*). Bennett is supreme among English novelists in his ability to communicate this sense of place, of domestic interiors, streets, squares, parks, railway stations, shops, pubs, chapels, theatres. That may seem faint praise, but I intend no damnation. It is the achievement of a very considerable novelist to be able to convince one about the texture of his characters' lives. And we are interested in and sympathetically responsive to Bennett's characters because of the dense particularity with which they are socially placed.

Nor does this mean that Bennett's view of Bursley is either myopic or uncritical. In "The Death of Simon Fuge" he had discovered a way of using a double perspective on the Five Towns; and he pushes this further in *The Old Wives' Tale* through his use of Sophia. Sophia wants to get away from Bursley. She yearns fo the world beyond the Five Towns, and Bennett makes her ache of rebellion against her family and Bursley thoroughly plausible and sympathetic. When, years after her flight, she returns to her home, we suddenly see St Luke's Square through her eyes and not those of the stay-at-home, contented Constance, for whom the square is more or less the world:

> Several establishments lacked tenants, had obviously lacked tenants for a long time; "To Let" notices hung in their stained and dirty upper windows, and clung insecurely to their closed shutters. And on the sign-boards of these establishments were names that Sophia did not know. The character of most of the shops seemed to have worsened; they had become pettifogging little holes, unkempt, shabby, poor; they had no brightness, no feeling of vitality. And the floor of the Square was littered with nondescript refuse. The whole scene, paltry, confined, and dull, reached for her the extreme provinciality.
>
> (book 4, chap. 2)

Bennett makes no attempt to arbitrate between the two views: Constance's devotion to the square is as authentic and proper as Sophia's sense of revulsion from it. And any temptation we may have to identify with Sophia's way of seeing things is prevented by Bennett's way with Constance. We find ourselves sympathizing just as much with her choice of "career" as we do with Sophia's.

It is of couse true that the sisters' lives are essentially those of middleclass women, and this might seem to undermine my suggestion that Bennett is concerned with a community. What, for example, of the servants? Well, there is Maggie, the Baineses' maid-of-all-work.

> Maggie had been at the shop since before the creation of Constance and Sophia. She lived seventeen hours of each day in an under-

ground kitchen and larder, and the other seven in an attic, never going out except to chapel on Sunday evenings, and once a month on Thursday afternoons. "Followers" were most strictly forbidden to her; but on rare occasions an aunt from Longshaw was permitted as a tremendous favour to see her in the subterranean den. Everybody, including herself, considered that she had a good "place," and was well treated.

(book 1, chap. 1)

It looks from this as though Maggie is to be treated with typical middle-class complacency, Bennett's every bit as much as the girls'. Maggie is to be a figure of fun.

But when, much later, Constance is to be married and take over the shop, Maggie hands in her notice.

Constance looked at her. Despite the special muslin of that day she had traces of the slatternliness of which Mrs Baines had never been able to cure her. She was over forty, big, gawky. She had no figure, no charms of any kind. She was what was left of a woman after twenty-two years in the cave of a philanthropic family. And in her cave she had actually been thinking things over! Constance detected for the first time, beneath the dehumanized drudge, the stirring of a separate and perhaps capricious individuality. Maggie's engagements had never been real to her employers. Within the house she had never been, in practice, anything but "Maggie"—an organism. And now she was permitting herself ideas about changes!

(book 2, chap. 1)

And later still, Constance is made to realize how deeply offended Maggie is by not having been invited to Samuel's funeral: "Constance perceived that by mere negligence she had seriously wounded the feelings of Maggie. . . . The truth was, she had never thought of Maggie. She ought to have remembered that funeral cards were almost the sole ornamentation of Maggie's abominable cottage" (book 2, chap. 6). I have traced something of Maggie's "career" in order to show that Bennett has no intention of letting us settle complacently into a single—middle-class—view of her life, and that he takes every opportunity to unsettle the "fixed" or simple view that we may think ourselves encouraged to take of her. It is true that most of what we see is through the eyes of Constance and Sophia, but Bennett refuses to endorse any one point of view. As the two sisters see St Luke's Square very differently, so they can be made to change their view about people. Bennett establishes a many-sided view of the community, not by exhaustively tracing each career, but by showing the sisters occasionally having access to views which customarily they are denied.

But here we come to a difficulty. For if Maggie represents an aspect of Bennett's sucessful way with community, it has to be admitted that other characters show where he can go wrong. Miss Insull, for example. She works in the Baineses' shop and she is, we are told, "honest, capable, and industrious." There speaks the novelist-creator. And he goes on:

> Beyond the confines of her occupation she had no curiosity, no intelligence, no ideas. Superstitions and prejudices, deep and violent, served her for ideas; but she could incomparably sell silks and bonnets, braces and oilcloths; in widths, lengths, and prices she never erred; she never annoyed a customer, nor foolishly promised what could not be performed, nor was late nor negligent, nor disrespectful. No one knew anything about her, because there was nothing to know. Subtract the shop-assistant from her, and naught remained. Benighted and spiritually dead, she existed by habit.
>
> (book 2, chap. 7)

This is not how one of the sisters sees Miss Insull, it is how Bennett himself sees her. Yet later we learn that, married to the ancient misogynist, Critchlow, who has taken over the Baineses' business after Samuel's death, the former Miss Insull has tried to kill herself and has been committed to an asylum. She is surely more interesting than that earlier account suggests? But Bennett offers no explanation for why she should at one point have been "Benighted and spiritually dead" and at another possessed of enough imagination to hate the life she leads with Critchlow. The inevitable result is that we feel cheated. Why can't we know more about her?

It is a feeling that extends to other characters. Arnold Kettle says that because Bennett

> for all his sympathy with the poor and servants, conveys across to us nothing of the other side of the coin, the beginnings to trade union organization for instance, the total effect of his picture of the Potteries is bound to lack something in vitality, is bound to give a certain sense of life running down like a worn-out spring.

This seems to me less than fair to Bennett. It is not only that his sympathy with Maggie has nothing of pathos about it; not only that he shows us younger servants cheeking and abandoning the ageing Constance; not only that Dick Povey, with his gaiety and sense of the future, hints—along with Maggie and the others—at precisely that vitality or sense of renewal which Professor Kettle thinks leaks out of the novel. No, the point is that taken together such flickerings of unguessed-at consciousness and life make it clear that Bennett is by no means writing out of a sense of historical or social catastrophe. He simply isn't that kind of an author (though as we shall see [elsewhere] he came nearer to it after 1918). I do not find Bennett's historical sense at all bothersome in *The Old Wives' Tale*. He doesn't possess the kind of middle-class consciousness that is masochistically attuned to its own feeling for defeat. What does worry me is his refusal to tell us enough about his own characters, and his occasional altering of them in the interests of a (perhaps) fixed disposition which he himself sees in metaphysical terms and which sounds out loud and clear when he remarks of Sophia that "the vast inherent melancholy of the universe did not exempt her" (book 2, chap. 2). At its truest, *The Old Wives' Tale* combats such melancholy; at its falsest it endorses it and does so through the deliberate interventions of its author. It is as though he is saying that all we need to know about Miss Insull is that she is unhappy, and will die; and that the rest is vanity. Which it clearly isn't, as his presentation of Maggie shows.

And there is Sam. When we first meet him he is suffering from toothache, and is too cowardly to go to the dentist. For Sophia and Constance he is a figure of fun. And he is a shade ridiculous, a Mr Polly. But like Mr Polly he has qualities which we come to admire because Bennett makes us see that Sam amounts to much more than his absurdities. He is certainly absurd when he asks Mrs Baines if he may marry Constance. But not *merely* absurd.

> The aspirant wound up: "I must leave if that's the case."
>
> "If what's the case?" she asked herself. "What has come over him?" And aloud: "you know you would place me in a very awkward position by leaving, and I hope you don't want to mix up two quite different things. I hope you aren't trying to threaten me."
>
> "Threaten you!" he cried. "Do you suppose I should leave here for fun? If I leave here it will be because I can't *stand* it. That's all. I can't stand it. I want Constance, and if I can't have her, then I can't *stand* it. What do you think I'm made of?"
>
> "I'm sure—" she began.
>
> "That's all very well!" he almost shouted.
>
> "But please let me speak," she said quietly.
>
> "All I say is I can't *stand* it. That's all, . . . Employers have no *right*. . . . We have our feelings like other men."
>
> He was deeply moved. He might have appeared somewhat grotesque to the strictly impartial observer of human nature. Nevertheless he was deeply and genuinely moved, and possibly human nature could have shown nothing more human than Mr Povey at the moment when, unable any longer to restrain the paroxysm which had so surprisingly overtaken him, he fled from the parlour, passionately, to the retreat of his bedroom.
>
> (book 1, chap. 7)

Bennett's authorial comments are a little clumsy but they are in no way offensive. They reveal how seriously he takes Sam, and from now on everything he shows us of him increases our respect and admiration. Sam, new-married, daring to smoke a cigar, Sam designing a new signboard for

Baineses', Sam chastising his son for stealing: the more we see of this entirely ordinary and unremarkable person the more impossible it becomes to take up a condescending attitude towards him. Sam is, quite simply, a good man. And his efforts to secure a reprieve for his cousin, condemned to death for the murder of a drunken wife, ennoble and kill him. Bennett comments:

> A casual death, scarce noticed in the reaction after the great febrile demonstration [a protest ceremony over Daniel Povey's execution]. Besides, Samuel Povey never could impose himself on the burgesses. He lacked individuality. He was little. I have often laughed at Samuel Povey. But I liked and respected him. He was a very honest man. I have always been glad to think that, at the end of his life, destiny took hold of him and displayed, to the observant, the vein of greatness which runs through every soul without exception. He embraced a cause, lost it, and died of it.
>
> (book 2, chap. 5)

I see no reason to complain about Bennett's use of the word "destiny" in this passage. True, it would have been more accurate for him to have written that Sam took hold of destiny, not destiny of him, and Bennett's way of putting it hints at the pessimism which elsewhere can be so debilitating. But not here.

One is, however, troubled by the statement that Sam "lacked individuality." He didn't. I know Bennett is thinking of the unobservant burgesses on whom Sam could hope to make no impression, but it is surely proper to note that Sam is fully individualized, and that such individuality doesn't have to be traced to the "vein of greatness which runs through every soul without exception." Bother greatness, one wants to say, Sam is unique enough as it is. You have shown us as much. We don't need the rhetoric, it demeans everyone, you, Sam, and the reader. After all, there is nothing at all implausible about the moment when we are told that Constance has gradually "constructed a chart of Sam's individuality, with the submerged rocks and perilous currents all carefully marked, so that she could now voyage unalarmed on those seas" (book 2, chap. 2).

Why, then, did Bennett feel impelled to say that Sam "lacked individuality?" The answer to that question is that somewhere very deep inside him was an habitual melancholy, and indeed he admitted as much. "Like most writers," he confessed in *The Truth about an Author*, "I was frequently the victim of an illogical, indefensible and causeless melancholy." It is this melancholy whose presence can be so disturbing in *The Old Wives' Tale*, because so misplaced. Bennett shows us how remarkable the unremarkable can be, and then denies it, as who should say: there is nothing remarkable beneath the visiting moon, nothing can be said except that I am sick, I must die. Tragedy, Lawrence said, ought to be a great kick at misery. And the remark was directed against Bennett. As Bennett's treatment of Sam shows, there is much more than misery to *The Old Wives' Tale*. But it cannot be denied that running through the novel there is a streak of something which it is perhaps more accurate to call melancholy rather than misery, often submerged but sometimes rising to gleam blackly through its study of provincial lives. So Bennett writes of Mrs Baines and Sophia:

> They sat opposite to each other, on either side of the fire—the monumental matron whose black bodice heavily overhung the table, whose large rounded face was creased and wrinkled by what seemed countless years of joy and disillusion; and the young, slim girl, so fresh, so virginal, so ignorant, with all the pathos of an unsuspecting victim about to be sacrificed to the minotaur of Time!
>
> (book 1, chap. 6)

And there is not doubt that Sophia is a victim. Bennett sees to that.

Yet it would be quite wrong to conclude that he does no more than pursue her career along labyrinthine paths that lead her unerringly to defeat and death. He also convincingly gives her a toughness and resilience, an imaginative liveliness and vitality which don't really square with an account of her as victim. Nor do I think that in any serious sense Sophia is a blurred figure. It is rather that Bennett, as commentator, interferes with his own creation in order to haul us back, preacher-fashion, to that vanity of vanities which, as melancholic, he takes life to be. And though this doesn't radically damage his study of Sophia it can be irritating. It is also liable to produce some very odd moments, as when Sophia comes to the bedside of her paralysed, dying father.

> And, with his controllable right hand, he took her hand as she stood by the bed. She was so young and fresh, such an incarnation of the spirit of health, and he was so far gone in decay and corruption, that there seemed in this contact of body with body something unnatural and repulsive. But Sophia did not so feel it.
>
> (book 1, chap. 3)

But if Sophia didn't feel it, why bother to mention it? Why draw attention to what "seemed" unnatural and repulsive in the contact of father and daughter? The answer is that here as elsewhere Bennett is determined to suck melancholy out of a scene. He is unfairly intruding into the novel. One remembers, and with a certain uneasiness, that "strictly impartial observer" to whom the impassioned Samuel Povey might have appeared "somewhat grotesque"; and reflects that too often such an observer is supposed to be one possessed of Bennett's own glum reading of life.

Yet read on a little further and you find him using the same contact between father and daughter to establish a perception of an altogether different order. Sophia wants to train as a teacher. That is why she has been sent to her father, for her father will refuse permission and she will have to abandon the idea. Or so her mother thinks. And indeed, he won't allow it. "You understand me!" he says, speaking as head of the household.

> It was her father who appeared tragically ridiculous; and, in turn, the whole movement against her grew grotesque in its absurdity. Here was this antique wreck, helpless, useless, powerless—merely pathetic—actually thinking that he had only to mumble in order to make her "understand!" He knew nothing; he perceived nothing; he was a ferocious egoist, like most bedridden invalids, out of touch with life, and he thought himself justified in making destinies, and capable of making them! Sophia could not, perhaps, define the feelings which overwhelmed her; but she was conscious of their tendency. They aged her, by years. They aged her so that, in a kind of momentary ecstasy of insight, she felt older than her father himself.
>
> "You will be a good girl," he said. "I'm sure o' that."
>
> It was too painful. The grotesqueness of her father's complacency humiliated her past bearing. She was humiliated, not for herself, but for him. Singular creature! She ran out of the room.

Compared with the previous moment quoted, that seems to me utterly authentic and really very moving. Bennett is so sensitive, tactful and imaginative in his understanding of the young girl. And although one regrets the rather lumpen facetiousness of "singular creature!" it doesn't take away from the rightness of the scene as a whole.

The whole of book 3 is a triumph of Bennett's art. Whether he is writing about Sophia's elopement with Gerald Scales, his desertion of her in Paris, her struggle to survive, her eventual triumph as owner of Frensham's, the small Paris pension, or whether he is writing about her tangles with other women and her rejection of proffered love, Bennett writes and imagines flawlessly. And how convincing it is that, after so many years of exile, Sophia should suffer a partial crack-up when confronted by a young man from the Five Towns who has links with her family—the family from which she has cut herself off. She reflects:

> She was the most solitary person on earth. She had heard no word of Gerald, no word of anybody. Nobody whatever could truly be interested in her fate. This was what she had achieved after a quarter of a century of ceaseless labour and anxiety, during which she had not once been away from the Rue Lord Byron for more than thirty hours at a stretch. It was appalling—the passage of years; and the passage of years would grow more appalling. Ten years hence, where would she be? She pictured herself dying. Horrible.
>
> (book 4, chap. 1)

She gives up Frensham's, goes home to Bursley, and she and Constance live together once more. And still Bennett follows her career with such tact and discreeet understanding that one marvels that he should ever go wrong. But then a telegram comes to inform her that Gerald, the long-lost husband, is dying in Manchester. The news shocks her. And Bennett comments:

> One might have pictured fate as a cowardly brute who had struck this ageing woman full in the face, a felling blow, which however had not felled her. It seemed a shame—one of those crude, spectacular shames which make the blood boil—that the gallant, defenceless creature should be so maltreated by the bully, destiny.
>
>   (book 4, chap. 4)

One notices with what apparent inevitability the word "seemed" has cropped up here, as it had in the scene between the young Sophia and her crippled father. And one also notices—how could one not?—the crudeness of Bennett's rhetoric when he writes of fate and destiny, and the sad sentimentalizing of Sophia as a helpless victim. *Sophia* defenceless? In view of what we have been so fully and sensitively shown throughout book 3 the word is absurdly inappropriate. It can be there only because Bennett is determined to make his "point." What point? Well, it can be understood once we attend to the title of book 4. "What Life Is," and as soon as we realize the significance of that moment when Sophia turns from Gerald's dead body and thinks that "Youth and vigour had come to that. Everything came to that."

> It was the riddle of life that was puzzling and killing her. By the corner of her eye, reflected in the mirror of a wardrobe near the bed, she glimpsed a tall, forlorn woman, who had once been young and now was old; who had once exulted in abundant strength, and trodden proudly on the neck of circumstance. He and she had once loved and burned and quarrelled in the glittering and scornful pride of youth. But time had worn them out. "Yet a little while," she thought, "and I shall be lying on a bed like that! And what shall I have lived for? What is the meaning of it?" The riddle of life itself was killing her, and she seemed to drown in a sea of inexpressible sorrow.
>
>   (book 4, chap. 4)

And there the word is, once more—"seemed." It provides the clue to what I find truly unsatisfactory about this passage (leaving aside such vague and windy phrases as the "neck of circumstance" and the "glittering and scornful pride of youth"). The fact is, that in the last analysis you cannot tell when Bennett imagines that he is transcribing Sophia's thoughts and when he is interpolating his own. Of course, all the thoughts are really his own, since he has invented Sophia. But the Sophia he has invented and so finely put before us in book 3 cannot be the one who "seems" to be drowning in a sea of inexpressible sorrow. She is simply too tough a nut to do anything of the sort. And why "seems"? Doesn't he know? Is it that she seems to herself or to him to be drowning? It isn't that I think Sophia is being imposed on. Faced with the fact of her dead hsuband it is obviously very possible that she would ask herself what she had lived for. At a pinch one might even concede that she felt inexpressibly sorrowful. But however that may be, one must surely object to Bennett's identification with her—"the riddle of life itself was killing her"—since one comes to this moment with the magnificently impressive study of Sophia's life so fully and weightily in one's mind. To put it rather differently, "What Life Is" ought to be the subtitle for *The Old Wives' Tale* as a whole, not just for the last book. If it had been, one wouldn't have needed to feel that Bennett was perilously close to Constance when, after Sophia's death, she reflects:

> What a career! A brief passion and then nearly thirty years in a boarding-house! And Sophia had never had a child; had never known either the joy or the pain of maternity. She had never even had a true house till, in all her sterile splendour, she came to Bursley. And she had ended—thus! This was the piteous, ignominious end of Sophia's wondrous gifts of body and soul. Hers had not been a life at all. And the reason? It is strange how fate persists in justifying the harsh generalisations of Puritan morals, of the morals in which Constance had been brought up by her stern parents! Sophia had sinned. It was therefore inevitable that she should suffer.
>
> (book 4, chap. 4)

A passage such as that is plainly clogged with the misery that Lawrence so despised and which he insisted should be kicked, hard. The point I think it important above all others to make is that *The Old Wives' Tale* itself provides the kick, which is why it is so considerable an achievement. It is there in book 2, in the study of Samuel Povey, it is there in book 3, where Sophia is neither a victim nor defenceless—indeed, it would be absurd to apply either word to her—and it makes itself equally felt in the account of Constance's life. It remains for me to say a little about her.

Bennett offers Constance's life as a kind of ironic counterpoint to Sophia's. Constance is the stay-at-home. She is thoroughly conventional and completely ordinary. But she is also shown to us as the sister who perhaps achieves more. Bennett very successfully employs a double perspective when he is writing about her. We both see her from the outside—through the eyes of Sophia, Cyril, her son, and Cyril's friend, Matthew Peel-Swynnerton, Dr Stirling, Dick Povey and Lily, all of whom condescend to her—and from Bennett's nearer point of view, which allows us access to her thoughts and feelings. I do not pretend that he always succeeds here. He claims more than he is able to show. As a young wife, Constance is, we are told, aware of death and sorrow, but she is also aware that any feeling of melancholy was "factitious, was less than transient foam on the deep sea of her joy" (book 2, chap. 1). Which would be all very well if Bennett could make her joy seem convincing. But in fact he shows us next to nothing of Constance as a young wife enjoying her marriage. The result is that when, after Sam's death, she is made to reflect that "she had had nearly twenty-one years of happy married life," one is bound to wish that we had seen something of its happiness. Constance goes on to think of "their naïve ignorance of life, hers and his, when they were first married, [so that it] brought tears into her eyes. How wise and experienced she was now!" What is the point of that exclamation mark? Is Bennett being ironic? Should we assume that Constance isn't really wise and experienced, or are we meant to read into it her own firm sense of these gradually acquired possessions and knowledge? And either way, where in the novel itself can we find the necessary evidence of her wisdom and experience? To be honest, I am not sure that we can find it at all, and at best it is only thinly imagined for us. Constance's career isn't nearly so richly presented to us as Sophia's is, though I do not think Bennett intends us to see her life as in any way empty. It is simply that he does not give us any sustained insight into the way she can be redeemed from unexceptionable drabness. Hence, so I suspect, that exclamation mark. He approves of Constance right enough, but he can't "see" her with the kind of intensity and verve that would allow him to do away with guarded qualifications about it.

This is not, however, to say that Constance is an imaginative failure of Bennett's. For in some respects he brings her very remarkably alive. And this is especially true in his writing about her feelings for Cyril. Here at least Bennett gives Constance a depth and reality which makes it impossible for us to speak about his "external" treatment of character, and seems to me to provide the perfect rejoinder to Virginia Woolf's complaint that he couldn't imagine what went on in his characters' minds. Constance wanting to cling to Cyril but unable to throw off the habits of restraint, Constance pained and grieving over Cyril's careless indifference to her; or Constance in an ecstasy of self-pity when Cyril goes away to London, thinking to herself "I'm a lonely old woman now. I've nothing to live for any more, and I'm no use to anybody." Again and again Bennett pierces through to the very heart of the matter in his study of Constance as mother (and he is unwaveringly exact in his treatment of the spoilt, talented, ruthless son). There can be no complaints here. Nor can there be any about his study of the ageing Constance, her devotion to her home, her keen regret that it has to be altered, her flaring out at Sophia when she suggests they should leave it: " 'Now, what do you say?' Sophia gently entreated. 'There's some of us like Bursley, black as it is!' said Constance. And Sophia was surprised to detect tears in her sister's voice" (book 4, chap. 3). This surprise, the access to a point of view of Constance which disturbs us by unsettling our fixed view of her, is one that Bennett repeatedly springs in book 4. I think, for example, of that moment when Matthew Peel-Swynnerton has returned from Paris to Bursley, having discovered Sophia's whereabouts, and meets a "short, fat, middle-aged lady dressed in black, with a black embroidered mantle, and a small bonnet tied with black ribbon and ornamented with jet fruit and crape leaves." The lady is, of course, Constance, and the description of her comes as a considerable shock, since the last glimpse we had of her was taking leave of Cyril, and for all her mournful feelings that she was to be a "lonely old woman," she was so intensely present to us that it would have been impossible to think of her as quaint and mildly ridiculous, which is how she now appears. But then we adjust to the shock because between that earlier view and this one has come the long book 3, taken up with Sophia's career, so that we feel that a considerable passage of time has passed between the last close view we had of Constance and the one we are now given, through Peel-Swynnerton's eyes. And in addition, we have by now acquired Sophia's "foreign" perspective. The positioning of book 3 is crucial. Yes, we come to agree, in the eyes of the young and of those who can now see Bursley from the outside, Constance is bound to seem quaint. The young man tells her of his meeting with Sophia: "She stopped and looked at him with a worried expression. Then he observed that the hand that carried her reticule was making strange purposeless curves in the air, and her rosy face went the colour of cream, as though it had been painted with one stroke of an unseen brush." He takes her home:

> It seemed to him that gladness shold have filled the absurd little parlour, but the spirit that presided had no name; it was certainly not joy. He himself felt very sad, desolated. . . . He knew simply that in the memory of the stout, comical, nice woman in the rocking-chair he had stirred old, old things, wakened slumbers that might have been eternal.
>
> (book 4, chap. 1)

In its unobtrusive way this is surely masterly. It so finely catches Constance's position in a shifting social process—she is outmoded, has gone down a little, just as St Luke's Square has; and it also makes perfect use of that double perspective by means of which we see her through Peel-Swynnerton's eyes as "comical" and at the same time see her as much more than that, because we know so much more about her than he does.

If Constance doesn't feel gladness, what is it that she does feel? We find out in the letter she writes to Sophia. This letter is, I think, one of the very highest achievements of Bennett's art, and a triumphant vindication of his realism. It is quite unremarkable and also very remarkable. For more than anything else in the novel it establishes how decent a person Constance is, how loving; and how being these things matters. The letter is too long to quote and if it were lifted out of context it would not seem so unerringly right and movingly true as it does when we come to it towards the end of the novel itself; but Sophia's reflections on it are perfectly accurate. "Tact? No; it was something finer than tact. Tact was conscious, skilful. Sophia was certain that the notion of tactfulness had not entered Constance's head. Constance had simply written out of her heart" (book 4, chap. 1). Anyone wanting to take the measure of Bennett's achievement would be well advised to start with Constance's letter to Sophia.

After Sophia's death, Dick Povey and his fiancée, Lily, help to solace Constance's loneliness. Bennett is again able to bring the double perspective into action, and to good effect. Constance gives Lily a fine cameo brooch.

> "I should like to see you wearing it. It was mother's. I believe they're coming into fashion again. I don't see why you shouldn't wear it while you're in mourning. They aren't half so strict now about mourning as they used to be."
>
> "Truly!" murmured Lily ecstatically. They kissed
>
> . . . .
>
> "What a magnificent old watch!" said Lily, as they delved together in the lower recesses of the box. "*And* the chain to it!"
>
> "That was father's," said Constance. "He always used to swear by it. When it didn't agree with the Town Hall, he used to say: "Then th' Town Hall's wrong." And it's curious, the Town Hall *was* wrong. You know the Town Hall clock has never been a good timekeeper. I've been thinking of giving that watch and chain to Dick."
>
> "*Have* you?" said Lily.

Later, Lily tells Dick of Constance's idea:

> "Thank you for nothing!" said Dick. "I don't want it."
>
> "Have you seen it?"
>
> "Have I seen it? I should say I had seen it. She's mentioned it once or twice before"
>
> . . . .
>
> "Poor old thing!" Lily murmured, compassionately.
>
> Then Lily put her hand silently to her neck.
>
> "What's that?"
>
> "She's just given it to me."
>
> Dick approached very near to examine the cameo brooch. "Hm!" he murmured. It was an adverse verdict. And Lily coincided with it by a life of the eyebrows.
>
> "And I suppose you'll have to wear that!" Dick said.
>
> "She values it as much as anything she's got, poor old thing!" said Lily.
>
> (book 4, chap. 5)

It seems as though Constance is now to be put firmly into perspective as a relic of the past, mocked at by the younger generation. But Bennett has not quite done. For a little later, when she is lying ill—it is to be her last illness—and musing over her life, she thinks of Dick and Lily:

Perhaps they would have been startled to know that Constance
lovingly looked down on both of them. She had unbounded admiration for their hearts; but she thought that Dick was a little too
brusque, a little too clownish, to be quite a gentleman. And though
Lily was perfectly ladylike, in Constance's opinion she lacked back-
bone, or grit, or independence of spirit.

(book 4, chap. 5)

It is, I think, an important moment just because it prevents Constance from
being merely a figure of pathos, of "running down like a worn-out spring."
Given the drift towards melancholy resignation that shows itself in *The Old
Wives' Tale*, Bennett must have been strongly tempted to let the last word
on Constance be spoken by the necessarily impercipient young. And if we
think back to the younger Bennett determinedly recording in his *Journal* in
1903 that the fat woman he had observed was "repulsive; no one could
like or sympathise with her," we are bound to recognize how far he has
travelled in order to be able to say that Constance "lovingly" looked down
on Lily and Dick; and without a shade of irony.

I do not mean that my earlier criticisms of Bennett's failures with Constance can now be withdrawn. Just above those sentences on Dick and Lily,
we read that when she "surveyed her life, and life in general, she would
think, with a sort of tart but not sour cheerfulness: *Well, that is what life is.*"
The italics are Bennett's and they provide a ready-to-hand objection. Life
in general isn't what Constance takes it to be, yet there is every indication
that at this moment Bennett totally identifies himself with her. Bennett,
that is, the disciple of de Maupassant, Bennett the man of causeless melancholy. But the truly important Bennett is the one who throughout the
pages of his novel has shown us that life is much more various, bewildering
and fulfilling than any one person can know, the Bennett who comes near
to achieving that absolute realism which he found and cherished in Chekhov, and as a result of which he created one of the finest of twentieth-
century novels.

Galsworthy's *Man of Property:*
"I Feel More Like a Sort of Chemist"

James Gindin

Initially *The Man of Property* was only a moderate success with the public; the 1906 edition in England selling 5,000 copies. Its reviews, however, were more extensive and enthusiastic than any Galsworthy had received before. Many commented on the writing as skilful and delicate, and on the effective characterizations. The figure of Irene elicited considerable sympathy. Yet a few reviewers dissented, some on the grounds of Galsworthy's cynicism, the one in the *Spectator* paying him the compliment of finding him just slightly and interestingly depraved. This reviewer described his own moral struggle, concluding that, although the book's "general tendency" was not "demoralizing," some details were so "repellent" that, despite the author's talent, the book was "unacceptable for general reading." None of the reviews mentioned any of Galsworthy's previous work or gave any sense of his career, most writing as if considering a new author's first novel. Not only did they see the novel as singular, but, as time went on, as representing a phenomemon strikingly new. The reviewer in *The Times Literary Supplement* thought Galsworthy perhaps commented too much rather than letting his characters develop and that the novel ended a "little brutally," but centrally praised the thought and determination in this "new type of novel."

Galsworthy himself was still most interested in the reactions of the literary friends he respected. When he had written to [his sister] Lilian earlier, defending *The Man of Property*, he cited the approval of Conrad, Garnett and Ford, as if their authority mattered most. He sent a copy of the book to Thomas Hardy, with whom he was later to become friendly, and received a polite thank-you note in return. He was pleased with the

From *John Galsworthy's Life and Art: An Alien's Fortress.* © 1987 by James Gindin. University of Michigan Press, 1987.

response of E. V. Lucas, who understood and appreciated his intentions concerning Bosinney, although Lucas was not entirely uncritical:

> You allow no escape. I think you are the most merciless author I know. But I believe you tell too much; there surely are occasions where a phrase ought to do the work to which you give a page? . . . On the whole I found it, I fancy, lacking in air; but perhaps you meant that. I cannot sufficiently admire your patience and tolerance; you put my rapid impressionism to shame. I know no Forsytes; they are out of my line. I wish you could have avoided the hand of God at the end.

Conrad's opinion was still pre-eminent. During those years, the two writers exchanged letters almost weekly when they did not meet. When he dedicated *Nostromo* to Galsworthy, Conrad acknowledged in his help in "correcting" the novel and wrote that it "is to be dedicated to you as life is uncertain and I am not sure of ever finishing something more worthy of your affection." In the summer of 1906, the Conrad family stayed at Addision Road for two months while the Galsworthys were on the Continent. There, on 2 August, Conrad's second son, named John Alexander Conrad Korzeniowski and called "Baby Jack" after Galsworthy, was born. And Conrad's older son, Borys, who always regarded Galsworthy as his favourite among his parents' friends, wrote his first letter to "Mr. Jack," thanking him for letting the family stay. A few months earlier Conrad had written about the soon to be published *The Man of Property:*

> The book is in part marvellously done and in its whole a piece of art—indubitably a piece of art. I've read it 3 times. My respect for you increased with every reading. I have meditated over these pages not a little. . . . But, I say, the socialists ought to present you with a piece of plate.

When the novel appeared, Conrad arranged with the editor of the *Outlook* to publish an extensive review.

Conrad's essay, published on 31 March 1906, begins with the statement that it is difficult to "get critical hold" of Galsworthy's work because he has no thesis or theory, yet the book has a "disconcerting honesty": "Light of touch, though weighty in feeling, it gives the impression of verbal austerity, of a *willed* moderation of thought." Claiming it has more "critical spirit" than the usual "fairy tales, realistic, romantic, or even epic," Conrad then digresses for most of the article's length about the popular appeal of "fairy tales," only incidentally offering Galsworthy's treatment of "middle class family," the title of the essay, made formidable by the possession of property, as an alternative, Finally, Conrad discusses Galsworthy's achievement:

> The foundation of this talent, it seems to me, lies in a remarkable power of ironic insight combined with an extremely keen and

faithful eye for all the phenomena on the surface of the life he observes. . . . It is the style of a man whose sympathy with mankind is too genuine to allow him the smallest gratification of his vanity at the cost of his fellow creatures. In its moderation it is a style sufficiently pointed to carry deep his remorseless irony and grave enough to be the dignified vehicle of his profound compassion. Its sustained harmony is never interrupted by those bursts of cymbals and fifes which some deaf people acclaim for brilliance. Before all, it is a style well under control, and therefore never betrays this tender and ironic writer into an odious cynicism of laughter or tears.

Although a just appraisal of *The Man of Property*, Conrad's essay, recalling his own earlier recommendation of "irony" to Galsworthy, as well as his comment about fidelity to "the surface" of life, is somewhat general and tepid, showing less enthusiasm for the novel than he expressed in private and praising it almost as much for the simplicities it avoids as for what it is. Conrad concludes with the slight reservation that "I myself, for instance, am not sure of Bosinney's tragedy," but this might be a "hesitation of my mind" and is minute "in the face of his considerable achievement."

Within ten days of the publication of the essay, Conrad wrote to Galsworthy with profuse apologies: "I am appalled at the bad use I've made of the opportunity; but the thing is done; it is the best thing I was capable of doing." After several paragraphs lamenting his own inability to finish any of his writing, Conrad returns to *The Man of Property*:

> Seriously, my dearest fellow, my very great regard for that piece of work has stood in my way. I could have written 10,000 words on it. But I had to consider space. I took an unnatural attitude towards the book, for if I had followed my bent I would have required lots of room to spread my elbows in. My natural attitude would have been of course literary—and perhaps I would have found something not quite commonplace to say—a critical tribute not unworthy of you. But there was the risk of being misunderstood. So I simply endeavoured to send people to the book by a sort of allusive *compe rendu*—a mere "notice" in fact. How much it cost me to keep strictly to that is a secret between me and my Maker.

Conrad then refers to the talk he is hearing of the novel's popularity in "journalistic circles":

> I confess that I felt slightly sick at that, till I reflected that the *quality* of your book was too high to be affected by false admirations. And take it from me, my dear Jack, that the *quality* of your work is very high—the sort of thing that cannot in good faith be questioned but that cannot be conveniently expressed in a letter—and

not even in talk, however intimate . . . whereas that quality is something altogether more subtle, more remote, whose excellent and faithful unity is reflected rather than expressed in the book, yet is as absolutely deeply and unavoidably present in it as the image in the mirror. And there are very few books only that have this quality. *Don Quixote,* for instance, is one of the few; and you may tell dear Ada that no book of Balzac had that; in which is perhaps the reason she has her knife into the poor man—a sentiment which (however shocking to me) does her infinite honour by its mental insight and intuitive delicacy of taste. The above, developed, made as intelligible as can be in the way of feeling and conviction, should have been the fundamental theme of the article I would have liked to write on *The Man of Property.*

Within a short time, Conrad was writing again, still unctuously, this time expressing unequivocal delight at all the discussions and reviews praising Galsworthy's work. He added: "Your consecration as a dangerous man by *The Spectator* fills me with a pure and ecstatic joy." Something of Conrad's disingenuous and elaborate ambivalence concerning *The Man of Property* may well have persisted. When, in 1921, Conrad was assembling all the material for an edition of his complete works, J. B. Pinker, since 1907 the literary agent for both Conrad and Galsworthy, asked if he hadn't once written an article on *The Man of Property.* Conrad denied he had ever done so. Shown a typescript of the article in the *Outlook,* too late for inclusion in the Complete Works, Conrad was chagrined. He wrote Galsworthy an immediate and abject apology, attributing the omission to "a lamentable decay of mental faculties which I did not suppose to be advanced so far as that." He ordered fifty copies of the essay printed privately, paid for and distributed them. The essay was included in the volume entitled *Last Essays,* edited by Richard Curle, in the edition of the Complete Works published in America in 1926, after Conrad's death.

As Conrad's letters incidentally indicate, *The Man of Property* produced an impact, as something new and interesting, on those dedicated to literature, beyond the level commensurate with its moderate sales and approbative reviews. This impact was particularly visible in young aspiring writers. Compton Mackenzie, for example, still at Oxford in 1906, thought it "a hell of a good novel," arguing with Logan Pearsall Smith who thought it "second-rate," and decided that his ambition was to "do with plays what Galsworthy had done with the novel." Mackenzie does not say what it was he thought Galsworthy was doing. Other young writers responded to *The Man of Property* as the scathing satire of a class, hearlding the end of the Victorian era. But the difficulty in seeing the novel solely as satire is that, on rereading, the satire seems to vanish, overwhelmed by something else in the novel and never attached to any perspective that would provide the ideological coherence necessary for satire. In addition, reading *The Man of*

Property as simply satire forces the view that all Galsworthy's subsequent fiction represents one long decline from the initial stroke of brilliance. Many young writers, particularly those of the next literary generation after Compton Mackenzie, responded to Galsworthy in this way, initially attracted to *The Man of Property* as satire and then, with no further descriptive account of what he was doing, gradually dismissing the work. Cyril Connolly, born in 1903, represents this attitude of progressive disappointment toward Galsworthy at its most damning:

> When we examine a page from *The Forsyte Saga* it will be found that only the satire has any sting to it: a row about money, a will, a law-suit, an old man's death agony; these live—but the love scenes, the lyrical ruminations, passages which begin with remarks like "By the cigars they smoke and the composers they love, ye shall know the texture of men's souls" (which far outnumber the others) are completely insipid. Popularity is not enough.

Connolly's attitude is an extreme consequence of seeing Galsworthy's intention and value as only the satirical dissection of a class.

Elements in the novel contribute to seeing it as satire. The famous opening paragraph, so frequently quoted, of the "family festival of the Forsytes . . . in full plumage," signals satire immediately and culminates in "a paragon of tenacity, insulation, and success, amidst the deaths of a hundred other plants less fibrous, sappy, and persistent . . . with bland, full foliage, in an almost repugnant prosperity, at the summit of its efflorescence." After these metaphors, the satire is reinforced with the statement that no Forsyte had as yet died, "death being contrary to their principles." Other, more incidental, touches of satire continue throughout the novel. A young member of the Forsyte clan comes round to Bayswater Road "to borrow the Rev. Mr Scoles's last novel, *Passion and Paregoric*, which was having such a vogue." Soames's sister Winifred, after an elegant dinner in suburban Richmond, suggests they sit on the terrace overlooking the river because "I should like to see the common people making love . . . it's such fun." Old Jolyon notices "that odour of oilcloth and herring which permeates all respectable sea-side lodging houses." And Bosinney's respectable aunt, who tries to defend him, is described as "of medium height and broad build, with a tendency to embonpoint . . . in a gown made under her own organization, of one of those half-tints, reminiscent of the distempered walls of corridors in large hotels." But such descriptions, like the metaphors that open the novel, do not really represent more than peripherally the fabric of the novel. Much more frequently and characteristically, the fabric suggests an opposition, a dichotomy stated or developed and never resolved. Early in the novel, Old Jolyon searches out his own son, whom he loves, disapproves of, and has not seen in fourteen years. Old Jolyon is described as "the figure-head of his family and class and creed, with his white head and dome-like forehead, the representative of moderation, and order, and love of property. As lonely an old man as there was in London." Sometimes these oppositions are satirical and trivial, like the architect "knighted when he built that public Museum of Art which has given so much employment to officials, and so little pleasure to the working-classes for whom it was designed," or the two Forsyte brothers who cannot travel together on the Underground because one always travels first-class and the other second, each feeling "aggrieved that the other had not modified his habits to secure his society a little longer." Other oppositions, however, are more fundamental to the novel both imagistically and structurally. On the morning after he rapes Irene, Soames reads *The Times* on the Underground, using the newspaper as a barrier behind which to take solace in the account to a grand jury the previous day "of three murders, five manslaughters, seven arsons, and as many as eleven—a surprisingly high number—rapes, in addition to many less conspicuous crimes, to be tried during a coming Sessions." Soames can obtain more money he neither needs nor wants through the law courts, but not the affection that he sought to buy or own. And, in the final scene in the novel, Irene is back in Soames's house, although more uncompromisingly silent and withdrawn than she ever was. All these oppositions, central to the drama and the texture, are far closer to what Conrad meant by "irony," unresolved dichotomies in which both sides are true, than they are to any perspective of shaped and directed satire. No theory or social point of view, for the most part, provides the kind of coherence satire demands to resolve contradictions; rather, the contradictions, as well as the aversions and sympathies they sustain, remain ironically unresolved. The method is not that of the satirist's anatomical dissection, the probing that reveals the nature or the core of the phenomenon; rather, the method is closer to a complex construction of all the phenomena of contradiction. As Galsworthy wrote to Lilian, "I feel more like a sort of chemist," a metaphor that carries the suggestions Galsworthy never developed theoretically of creating new compounds out of elements. He as less "cold," less "dissective," than he sometimes thought he was. And the compounds are coloured by his values and preferences, articulated by the voice of Young Jolyon.

Galsworthy's theoretical understanding of what he was doing in *The Man of Property* was incomplete, yet he was uncomfortable with the designations of "satire" or "social commentary." He sometimes referred to *The Man of Property* as a "semi-satire," and later, in the Manaton preface to *Villa Rubein*, talked of his series of novels depicting English society "somewhat satirically." He was no more comfortable with the designations applied by social critics, like Conrad's arch suggestion that the Socialists presents him "with a piece of plate" and in spite of his own performance in *The Island Pharisees*. By 1908, Galsworthy had become explicity averse to social labels, writing in his preface for the revised version of *The Island Pharisees*: "Each party has invented for the other the hardest names that it can think of: Philistines, Bourgeois, Mrs. Grundy—Rebels, Anarchists and Ne'er dowells. So we go on! And so, as each of us is born to go his journey, he finds himself ranged on one side or on the other, and joins the chorus of name-slingers." In one of his letters to Ralph Mottram, still the recipient of a lot of the inadvertent pontification that may have been Galsworthy's means of discovering what he himself thought, he equated the use of labels with satirists and satirists with moralists. Both the satirist and the moralist, in Galsworthy's terms, were clearly inferior to the artist that he wanted to become.

Although he questioned the applicability of the simplified terms used to describe his growing reputation, Galsworthy still did not manifest any clear and positive way of explaining what his art was. At times, as in the letter to Mottram he had written two years earlier, about "getting ourselves, our feelings, our visions, known, felt, & seen by a sort of ideal spectator created by our own instinct and our experience, and who is at once our conscience and our audience," he recognized something of the self-reflective nature of fiction. He had not yet, however, recognized fully that he was recreating himself, his dramas and his dilemmas, in terms that could be objectified. He saw the polarities he established, although he did not see that his world was polarized in terms close to those of the control and release of his own psyche. He saw that he was not really a satirist because he had no belief in social creed, but he could not have seen, as one recent critic has observed, that in his "dry refusal to commit himself 'creedally' in his novels of society, there is some of Freud's puritanical retreat from the ugly battle between instinct and 'inherited renunciation.' " Galsworthy had only begun to understand what he could explain to Garnett so crisply only four years later, when answering one of the critic's objections about *The Patrician:*

> In other words, this book, like *The M. of P., The C.H.* and *Fraternity,* is simply the criticism of one half of myself by the other, the halves being differently divided according to the subject. It is not a piece of social criticism—they none of them are. If it's anything it's a bit of spiritual examination. If you knew my mother you would admit that there's quite enough of the dried-caste authority element in me to be legitimate subjects for the attack of my other half.

The internal oppositions dramatized are just as much the genesis of *The Man of Property* as they are of *The Patrician,* although Galsworthy probably did not realize this as coherently in 1906 as he did in 1910. The crucial difference between the novels is that, whereas *The Patrician* deals with his struggles against and incorporation of "the dried-caste authority" of the mother, *The Man of Property* respects, rebels from and reconciles with the more flexible, protean dominance of the father.

Old Jolyon, the patriarch of the Forsytes, its most distinguished representative, is also the one least slavish in following the conventions he represents. Galsworthy establishes his complexity from the very beginning:

"Like most men of strong character but not too much originality, Old Jolyon set small store by the class to which he belonged. Faithfully he followed their customs, social and otherwise, and secretly he thought them 'a common lot.' " His original rupture with his son had been caused less by Young Jolyon's violation of morality or Forsyte principle than by his abandonment of his daughter, June, whom Old Jolyon loves. He never relinquishes his sagacity in commerce and trade, but his purchase of Robin Hill is impelled by his desire to defeat his more narrowly sagacious brother, James, and by defence of the dead Bosinney whom he valued little while he was alive. He loves most the amiable rebel his son, who is the Forsyte least likely to cherish his sense of family or property, just as the son most respects the father he has always needed to defy. The novel is constructed of all these oppositions co-existing, not one satirically demolishing the other, but both of them apparent to the reader at every moment. A similar complexity is visible in Soames, the most intense Forsyte. His passion to possess, Irene, Robin Hill, good paintings, is visible from the beginning, not simply as an adjunct to his prosperity or a badge of good taste, but, rather, as a raging passion to assert himself outside the narrow security of his background. And he is wedded to his background. He becomes pathetic when he sues Bosinney, not because he cares about the money, but because, sadly, money and law suits are the only ways in which he can impress himself; he rapes Irene in a combination of thwarted passion, fear and the pathetic delusion that perhaps such violent assertion will make her love him. Galsworthy makes Soames able to understand the passion Bosinney feels for Irene, to equate it with his own passion symbolized by the writhing cry of the peacocks he hears in the distance on a humid summer night. The peacock's cry, mentioned just once in the novel, becomes the theme for the later expansion into the past of Soames in *On Forsyte 'Change* in the story called "Cry of Peacock." In that retrospectively-written story, taking place in 1883 just a fortnight before he is to marry Irene, Soames, walking along the river after a ball, acknowledging to himself that Irene is marrying him only to escape an unpleasant stepmother, passes her window and, unobserved, sees her close the curtains. He hears the "lost soul's cry of the peacock," which represents both his all-consuming love and his hopeless despair. The later story reinforces the complexity with which Galsworthy always regarded the character of Soames, a human complexity visible in *The Man of Property,* even though, in so far as the novel is an ideological drama, an attack on the evils of property, Soames has the villain's role.

The novel, then, set within the multiple ironies of the commercial upper-middle-class family, is a double conflict: the conflict between generations, between Old and Young Jolyon, involving the themes of rebellion and reconciliation, of the son's need to revolt from dominance and, simultaneously, to gain his father's approval; the conflict within the younger generation of Forsytes, between Young Jolyon and Soames, each finally his father's appropriate son, engaged, in their different attitudes toward "beauty" and their contrasting temperaments, in a more contemporary version of the rivalries that had engaged their fathers for years. Both conflicts are seen from the point of view of Young Jolyon, and neither conflict, in the space of *The Man of Property*, is fully resolved. Doubtless, in 1906, Galsworthy did not see the conflicts as unresolved, not realize that a fuller resolution would require a trilogy. But he developed the issues as far as he then could, and he gained a considerable following among the young literate offspring of the middle classes because he expressed something of their kind of revolt from domination. It was a tame revolt, a safe one, always desiring reconciliation and approval as strongly as it desired independence, and its terms were never very clear or carefully worked out, the child to be rescued by the parent's indulgence and generosity even as the child is still undefined, still unsure of what he is. Vicarious participation in Galsworthy's revolt required sensitivity and compassion but no commitment or definition other than the negative, or equivocal, refusal to be exactly what the parent was. And the reconciliation is a gift, or a wish-fulfilment. In the novel, Old Jolyon reconciles himself to his errant son because he loves him, and loves his grandchildren—not because the issues of the erring are ever worked out, just as old John Galsworthy could never have worked out the issues of his favourite son's defection he apparently never knew about. Young Jolyon in the novel, like young Jack in life, finds it easier, in the most attractive ways possible, to assume the guilts of his defection and the vagaries of his lack of commitment than to acknowledge, even to himself, his own desire for Irene.

The appeal of the novel for the young generaton of 1906 also inheres in the second conflict, that dependent on different ways of apprehending "beauty." Soames wants to possess it, control it; Young Jolyon wants simply to appreciate it, understand it, help it realize itself. Again, the conflict is not fully resolved in that Galsworthy, in *The Man of Property*, never acknowledges that Young Jolyon's appreciation is also implicitly a desire for possession, although a far gentler, less imprisoning one than Soames's. While chivalry substitutes for definition of the self, Young Jolyon has to wait, through more than ten years of Galsworthy's biographical time and over a dozen of fictional time, before he can work out that acknowledgement and all its implications. Yet, in terms of temperament and appreciation of relationship, Galsworthy had resolved this conflict, had become the sort of lover Ada wanted. In all Galsworthy's fiction, the good lover is always gentle, self-denying, somewhat distant; the bad lover, no matter how complex or understandable a man otherwise, is brutal and bullying, intense, possessive and, if provoked, violent, the fictional exaggeration of what [Ada's first husband] Arthur may have been as Ada saw him. Ada always valued the gentleness, as she wrote, in 1906, in a letter giving their young and then troubled friend Ralph Mottram advice about sex:

> Letting things come naturally instead of reaching for them—it's what I understand. Whereas Jack & you want to *do* things all the time—is it the broad meaning of the sexes after all? As to the

wickedness of the male animal, we don't call it wickedness in
young dogs and bulls! They don't know any different, and no boy
does either *really* until he has learnt by living and loving, that he
is not an animal—beautiful bringing-up such as you have had, no
doubt helps you quickly through the puppy stage!

The issue is a matter of relationship, of a kind of sexuality, not the silent
spirituality or "beauty" of the novel. Galsworthy, in life, as some early
references in letters indicate, was not the sexually naive young man initiated
through his affair with Ada. He had some sexual experience in his bachelor
days around London, probably some even after his affair with Ada began.
Jessie Conrad wrote of his frequent weekend visits to her and Conrad's
first cottage at Stanford-le-Hope in Essex, which dates the following episode
between the summer of 1896 and that of 1898. On one weekend, after lunch
on Sunday, although he looked perfectly well to both Conrad and Jessie,
Galsworthy suddenly said he had a headache and retired to his room to
rest for several hours before his train left. Later, Jessie realized that a new
housemaid, whom she described as exceedingly pretty, was also missing
most of the afternoon. When Jessie later questioned the maid, the young
girl hung her head and said "Mr. Galsworthy asked me to stop and help
him pack his bag." Jessie used the story to illustrate Galsworthy's consid-
erate sense of politeness and "inherent propriety," in contrast to Ford who
flaunted his conquests. The anecdote suggests that, certainly in early years,
perhaps for some time, Galsworthy may still have polarized women into
two alternative categories. *The Man of Property* also displays echoes of the
categorization in young Jolyon's first wife, dry and conventional, whom
he leaves, and his second wife, depicted as vaguely neurotic because of
her social position, with whom he stays out of guilt and duty—both replaced as centres of interest by the spiritualized, almost disembodied figure
of Irene. It is as if Galsworthy is making strenuous efforts to complicate
the simple dichotomy of madonna and whore, adding texture, motive and
some understanding of and sympathy for the issues, but something of the
dichotomy still lingers. A fuller understanding of women and relationships,
a greater respect for their wholeness and individuality, although he was
living in such a relationship with Ada at the time, had to wait, in fiction,
for later novels. The reconstruction of experience in *The Man of Property*,
much as it consciously values and abstractly compaigns for women, had a
firmly conventional male perspective.

The novel was also, even initially, occasionally seen as a chronicle of
recent English history. Some of the early reviewers talked of the Forsytes
as a class, and Conrad praised the delineation of the English upper-class
family "if not exactly of to-day, then of only last evening" as "a reproduction
in miniature of society itself." At times, Galsworthy was attracted to the
version of himself as chronicler of England. In the midst of the controversy
over Bosinney's suicide and the ending of the novel, he inserted another
topic in one of his letters to Garnett:

At the very back of my mind, in the writing of this book (and indeed of *The Island Pharisees*, but put that aside) there has always been the feeling of the utter disharmony of the Christian religion with the English character; the cant and humbug of our professing it as a *national* religion. Not an original idea this, but a broad enough theme to carry any amount of character study. I've got it in mind now to carry on this idea for at least two more volumes. Just as the theme of the first book is the sense of property, the themes of the next (or rather the national traits dealt with) are (1) the reforming spirit, (2) the fighting spirit—done of course through story and definite character study. The theme of the third book would be the spirit of advertisement, self-glorification, and impossibility of seeing ourselves in the wrong, and it would deal with the Boer War (of course only through character, not in story). I call the second book *Danaë* and the third *The Mouth of Brass*. Six years elapse between each book, and I carry young Jolyon through all three as commentator. I have figures for the second book, but only the idea for the third.

Now what I want to ask you is this.

Is it worth while to put after the title of *The Man of Property*, etc., some such addition as this:

> National Ethics—I
> or Christian Ethics—I
> or Tales of a Christian People—I

in other words to foreshadow a series upon that central idea?

Garnett replied with interest about the yet unformulated novels, but was sceptical about the pretentious subtitles and thought that Galsworthy, on reflection, might not want to commit himself to such a scheme. Galsworthy was easily persuaded and dropped the idea. Only one of the specific themes he mentions, "the reforming spirit," seems to apply to a later novel, and only one of the titles, "Danaë," was even provisional for a subsequent work. Nevertheless, Galsworthy's idea of himself as a chronicler was more difficult to dislodge than were those subtitles. The novels following *The Man of Property* were set in different areas of English society, in the Liberal town, in the Tory country, among the aristocracy, the whole a coherent composite. And, beginning more than ten years later, the Forsytes were extended through forty more years of English history. By 1922, when he wrote the Manaton preface for *The Man of Property*, having already written the two later novels of *The Forsyte Saga*, Galsworthy accepted, with some qualification, his role as chronicler. He still insisted that the central theme of *The Man of Property* was "disturbing Beauty impinging on a possessive world":

> But though the impingement of Beauty and the claims of Freedom on a possessive world are the main prepossessions of the Forsyte

Saga, it cannot be absolved from the charge of embalming the upper-middle class. As the old Egyptians placed around their mummies the necessities of a future existence, so I have endeavoured to lay beside the figures of Aunts Ann and Juley and Hester, of Timothy and Swithin, of old Jolyon and James, and of their sons, that which will guarantee them a little life hereafter, a little balm in the hurried Gilead of a dissolving "Progress."

If the upper-middle class, with other classes, is destined to "move on" into amorphism, here, pickled in these pages, it lies under glass for strollers in the wide and ill-arranged museum of Letters.

The idea of Galsworthy as chronicler of something quintessentially English has always been more widely and persistently held outside England than it has within. Many of the English, perhaps, have been too intensely aware of classes other than the upper-middle; many have lived with designations of the upper-middle not characterized by commerce or property. In addition, from a point of view outside England, it is not always easy to see how Galsworthy projected his own experience and that of this family into the world he created. His function, like *The Man of Property*, objectified, in social detail, the emotions of his background. Those looking at him from greater distances of time or space often regarded the work as much more objective than it was, as did the French critic, André Chevrillon, who claimed that "No Great English novelist of our time has shown so little of himself in his books." Chevrillon, in his lengthy essay of 1912, sees the Forsytes as representing the upper-middle class of the nineteenth century, displaying all its attributes:

> Energy, invincible vitality, worship of health, taciturn pride, secret determination not to give oneself away, irreducible egotism, passion for property, tendency to appreciate everything in terms of money, open contempt for ideas, jealous individualism strangely combined with a superstitious respect for conventions and hospitality to all who deviate from the prescribed and recognized pattern . . . [this can] almost be classified as zoology.

Chevrillon also thinks the classification particularly English, demonstrating what Hippolyte Taine had called "hypertrophy of the *ego*," which leads the Englishman, in the tradition of Meredith and James, to chronicle his "soul" and not his senses: "Self-contained and introspective, his inner life is his main object." For Chevrillon, as for many others on the Continent, Galsworthy was both the most thorough chronicler and the most accurate representative of the English of his generation. *The Man of Property* was even noticed and reviewed in Russia in 1906. And, since that time, translated and reprinted, the novel, as a representation of England, has been extremely popular in Russia, Germany, Scandinavia and the Balkans.

Part of the response to Galsworthy as a social chronicler can be attributed to the texture of very specific and recognizable detail. He describes settings and furnishings meticulously, carefully staking out the provenance for his imagination. Galsworthy was amused when, in 1927, the manufacturers, having noticed that Soames in *The Man of Property* washed his hands with "brown Windsor soap," sent him a box of it. The social chronicle is, however, more than a matter of brand-name recognition. When, in the account of Swithin's dinner party in *The Man of Property*, Galsworthy catalogues what kind of mutton each brother preferred and where it came from, the passage both is comic and evokes a nugget of the richness of historical possibility:

> Each branch of the family tenaciously held to a particular locality—old Jolyon swearing by Dartmoor, James by Welsh, Swithin by Southdown, Nicholas maintaining that people might sneer, but there was nothing like New Zealand. As for Roger, the "original" of the brothers, he had been obliged to invent a locality of his own, and with an ingenuity worthy of a man who had devised a new profession for his sons, he had discovered a shop where they sold German; on being remonstrated with, he had proved his point by producing a butcher's bill, which showed that he paid more than any of the others.

The trivial catalogue illustrates the brothers as both distinct individuals and common members of a class. Galsworthy also attempts a few examples of a more ambitious form of the historical chronicle, the synthesis of what it was like in a particular time and place. He tries the summer of Queen Victoria's Golden Jubilee, 1887:

> It was that famous summer when extravagance was fashionable, when the very heart was extravagant, chestnut trees spread with blossom, and flowers drenched in perfume, as they had never been before; when roses blew in every garden; and for the swarming stars the nights had hardly space; when every day all day long the sun, in full armour, swung his brazen shield above the Park, and people did strange things, lunching and dining in the open air. Unprecedented was the tale of cabs and carriages that streamed across the bridges of the shining river, bearing the upper-middle class in thousands to the green glories of Bushey, Richmond, Kew, and Hampton Court. Almost every family with any pretensions to be of the carriage class paid one visit that year to the horse-chestnuts at Bushey, or took one drive amongst the Spanish chestnuts of Richmond Park. Bowling smoothly, if dustily, along, in a cloud of their own creation, they would stare fashionably at the antlered heads which the great slow deer raised out of a forest of bracken that promised to autumn lovers such cover as was never

seen before. And now and again, as the amorous perfume of chestnut flowers and fern was drifted too near, one would say to the
other: "My dear! What a peculiar scent!"

And the lime flowers that year were of rare prime, near honey-
coloured. At the corners of London squares they gave out, as the
sun went down, a perfume sweeter than the honey bees had
taken—a perfume that stirred a yearning unnamable in the hearts
of the Forsytes and their peers, taking the cool after dinner in the
precincts of those gardens to which they alone had keys.

The passage is structurally important in the novel, indicating the beginning
of the dissolution of the Victorian world and Forsyte control, both, at this
point, only diluted by the perfume of the erotic in the atmosphere. But
some of the writing is vague, too elaborate, and slightly repetitious. The
passage lacks the tightness, the historical range, and the resonance of some
of the passages of historical chronicle that Galsworthy was to do later and
that Arnold Bennett, for example, was already doing.

Unevenly and occasionally loosely written, *The Man of Property*, in its
infrequent stylistic lapses, still reveals the characteristics of Galsworthy's
literary apprenticeship. There is an inserted essay, done in the manner
much more frequent in *The Island Pharisees*, when young Jolyon at London
Zoo inveighs against the barbaric confinement of animals. In a few instances, description is vague and spongy, like the account of a spring
"running riot with the scent of sap and bursting buds, the song of birds
innumerable, a carpet of bluebells and sweet growing things." Occasionally, Galsworthy overwrites, points out the lesson too stridently or injects
a moment of melodrama. In introducing the gossip who has seen Irene
and Bosinney together at the Botanical Gardens, Galsworthy pauses to add:
"This small but remarkable woman merits attention; her all-seeing eye and
shrewd tongue were inscrutably the means of furthering the ends of Providence." The intended humorous elaboration does not quite compensate
for so much attention. Or, more portentously, when conflict begins to
develop between Old Jolyon and James on one of the crowded afternoons
in Bayswater Road:

Something of the sense of the impending, that comes over the
spectator of a Greek tragedy, had entered that upholstered room,
filled with those white-haired, frock-coated old men, and fashion-
ably attired women, who were all of the same blood, between all
of whom existed an unseizable resemblance.

Not that they were all conscious of it—the visits of such fateful,
bitter spirits are felt.

The delicate development of the ironic tone is demolished by the obvious
last sentence. In the final scene of the novel, when young Jolyon, worried
about the despairing Irene, sees her through the open door, momentarily

frightened and apparently apppealing for help, Soames must clearly enclose her again inside the house. Galsworthy, however, works the scene melodramatically, having Soames refuse young Jolyon admission and, then, writes the concluding line of the novel: "And in young Jolyon's face he slammed the door." The inversion of word order heightens the melodrama, giving the statement an unintentionally comic cast, almost as if grand opera has been, somewhat uncertainly, translated into English.

In spite of these lapses, *The Man of Property* does initiate Galsworthy's considerable achievement. The novel shows the development of an irony that adequately sustains Galsworthy's deepening sense of the complexity of his characters, of many aspects of himself and his background. The theme of property is a setting, not a final truth, a coherent way of illustrating the various strands of conflict sympathetically without resolving them. In addition, the novel, with its profusion of social detail at various different levels, its considerable specific density, recreates a whole world. That world is not necessarily late Victorian England, not even commercial upper-middle-class late Victorian England; rather, it is Galsworthy's fictional world, compounded of his emotions, his background, and his observations, the things he could change and the things he could not. Yet it is a fully populated and coherent world, not yet as dense and as finely or profoundly done as it was to become, although already a world sufficiently spacious and detailed for Galsworthy and for sympathetic readers to live within. The constructive chemist had begun.

Max Beerbohm, or The Dandy Dante:
Zuleika Dobson

Robert Viscusi

THINGS TRANSMUTABLE, OR PARALLELOGRAMMATOLOGY

Rereading has no natural conclusion. One may follow a given line into infinity. There are long treatises devoted entirely to the genitive in Cicero and a whole library of Shakespeare biographies based upon small evidence and less certainty. The reader of [*Max Beerbohm, or The Dandy Dante*] no doubt, has begun to wonder how long I will think it sensible to go on holding *Zuleika Dobson* up to the light. In truth, it is not easy to stop. Max imagined his readers fifty years later standing in the Broad arguing "with some heat" which house belonged to Mrs. Batch. Aware that I had been thus foreseen, I have nonetheless actually had this dispute, inside one of the houses, with Basil Blackwell, who asserted that his shop now included Mrs. Batch's establishment, whilst I, having spent many hours poring over old street photographs in Oxford city archives, rudely maintained that it was a building just to the west. (Sir Basil returned the compliment by showing me—"I do not mean to suggest that you should buy it"—an expensive edition of *Zuleika Dobson* that his firm had just produced, bound in the blue and white of the Bullingdon.) (Nor did I buy it.) These questions do not settle easily. I have worked at Beerbohm's hopeless crossword puzzle, all along sharply aware that he had plainly prepared a comedy of commentary for his readers.

Aware, too, that Max himself never produced such a book as this. Imagine a publisher asking him for a treatise on Platonism in Pater or a biography of Cardinal Newman. "That," one hears him murmuring, "would need a far less brilliant pen than mine."

Well, to every trope its antitrope, as Freud all but said. The less brilliant pen was Beerbohm's. The reason he, with his extraordinary attunement to the curiosities of scholarship, did not engage in it was that, to put it bluntly, he was afraid to try. Picture him in the fall of 1893, preparing to study for his final examination in classical honors ("Greats"). Grandly, he assumed that he must master "*all* history and *all* philosophy," and claimed "I am not afraid; a giant may wear other people's shoes upon his little toes." But he *was* afraid, and he did not do it. Instead, he sat in the Bodleian getting up references for "A Defense of Cosmetics." In the same term that he failed to graduate, he published this essay, and it could, but for its theme, have come from the pen of an especially brilliant First in Greats (Gladstone, say), studded as it was with an obscure range of particulars drawn from all over the wide bibliography of antiquity. A parody final examination, like Beerbohm's other parodies, this essay amounted to a reinvention from outside (seen and felt as outside) of what others had done. As he reinvented examination there and later reinvented Wilde's humiliation in "Diminuendo," in *Zuleika Dobson* he combined the two and reinvented graduation.

All the elaboration of self and Beauty and dandy haughtiness of judgment which we have been examining fill this novel precisely to be drowned, to be castrated in the river, to be transformed in a ritual that is a profound parody of exactly what it is that such an institution as Oxford does when it grants a degree. One might reread "A Defense of Cosmetics" in great detail as a parody of examination style which reveals that style as itself a parody of scholarly discourse: the sweeping thesis, the flash of erudition, the utter lack of conviction, the endless turning of the admirable phrase. Likewise, one rereads *Zuleika Dobson* at this final level as a parody of the "literary institution" which Newman, Arnold, Pater, & Co. could praise in such exquisite detail without ever, any of them, seeing it from the radical angle Beerbohm's rite of transformation offers.

He gives us the literary institution caught in the deed of graduation, its primal and final scene, its act of replicating itself. This is the act of rereading which is seen, under dandy skies, as parody—that writing which is reading, that reading which is writing, that scholarship which is insertion in the covert passing along of masks and tokens we call the "symbolic order" or "tradition" or, cynically, absolute bachelorhood, marriage with the Great Mother.

It is rereading with a clear where-to-stop. The effect of conclusion, indeed, is so great that most readers are inclined not to question it. Beerbohm's texts have not produced many copious commentaries. One senses the absoluteness of closure perhaps most vividly in *Zuleika Dobson* when the heroine suddenly tires of the whole game and gives the Duke's pearls, which have undergone such dramatic permutations, to her maid, who immediately plans to sell them in order to help her fiancé open a bar.

Rereading is a form of writing, and like other forms it must stop at the point where it turns into money. Or, as Max calls the pearls, at this stage, "things transmutable." Money, like a baccalaureate, is a credential, a thing that is to be believed in accordance with some set of rules. Diplomas, moneys, contracts, and other earnests of credit have, to be sure, a complex afterlife once they have been issued, but all of this is in accordance with stipulations of exchange which come into being as the degree is granted, the coin is minted, the contract signed, or the rereading published.

Form

Like dandy desire, rereading has four dramatic stages, and we have [elsewhere] followed three of them carefully. The creation of a textual surface that includes both reader and writer is the first. The second is the discovery of the Other that appears in the textual mirror, the allegory of Beauty or shape or "structure" of the book. The third is the critique of authority, which begins as an Oedipal contest but ends as a self-examination, both for writer and reader. Finally, there is the creation of an order subsuming all this, an order that Beerbohm calls simply "FORM." This order has a shape as compact as a coin's or a scroll's and is just as useful in its way.

Max writes to Shaw in 1921, praising *Back to Methuselah*:

> [*Man and Superman*] was, I think your first really good piece of work (outside journalism). And that might have been much better, if you hadn't been more of a publicist than an artist, and hadn't felt it a civic duty to be cursory about FORM—which is my way of writing the word; form would have been *your* way of writing it. I mean that the play itself might have been ever so much better. The intermezzo, the Hell scene (like the preface, and like the Revolutionist's Handbook) is almost as good as it can be. In getting away from representation of actual things, you got off your rickety little contemporary platform and ceased your ready improvisings and sat down on earth and thought out a genuine work of art and achieved something beautiful (for *once,* thought I, the other day; but "Back to Methuselah" is something much more beautiful—or so it seems to me). You gave to a dramatic work the FORM which you had hitherto felt compatible with your conscience only in direct ratiocinative pleading. . . . One didn't have to lap the liquid up off the pavement—hurting one's tongue, and not getting much of the flavour.

Searching Shaw's vast dramatic output, Max finds FORM nowhere except in two biblical allegories, *Man and Superman*'s act in hell, and *Back to Methuselah*, where he praises the Adam-and-Eve scene as "high imagination—cosmic imagination." What is there about allegory that suggests to his acute designer's eye a parallelogram? "There are," he writes in a review of a farce he dislikes, "four corners of a parallelogram. There is A, the unsuspicious husband. There is B, the nervous wife. There is C, the nervous lover. And there is D, the husband's sister who loves the nervous lover and thus enables the playwright to dispose of him symmetrically when the farce is done. Not one of the characters has any inward existence. They are contrived simply with a view to the making of certain situations." The parallelogram, not in itself enough to insure quality, is however the sign for Beerbohm of literary analysis. And not geometry alone but mathematics in general fills this function. Here, on an adaption of Dumas, he writes:

> The plot of the original play, *Les Demoiselles de St. Cyr*, seems to have been a purely mechanical contrivance, such as Dumas loved (quite rightly) for his artificial comedies. Two men, A and B, flirt with two girls, C and D. They are entrapped into the Bastille, where A is forced to marry C, and B, D. A and B, furious leave C and D the next morning. How to convert the formula $(C-A) + (D-B)$ into the formula $(C+A) + (D+B)$, is the problem left by the first two acts, to be solved by the last two. Needless to say, there is a masked ball; A flirts with C, B with D; makes A jealous, and D, B; and all ends happily.

Playwriting, as well as play analyzing, is a question in algebra. Elsewhere, he speaks of it as a "problem," a question in logic or a mathematical maneuver like mutual "cancellation." Best of all is what he calls "a pretty little puzzle": "A is an attractive widow. B, her brother, is married to C, a frivolous girl who is beloved by D. C has confided to A that D has in his possession a foolish letter of hers and that he is using it in order to force her into an elopement. She does not wish to elope, for the Season is just beginning. What should A do?" The answer to this is the premise of a new puzzle, and so it goes, through the entire play, Beerbohm confessing, "I myself rather like this kind of thing."

Parallelogrammatology

Just what is it he likes? He chooses the parallelogram as his analytic model for biblical (or Dantean) allegory because it implies both foresight in the writer (*"respice finem,"* he would advise) and an intersecting ingenuity in the reader, who is expected to look the text straight in the face out of the corners of his eyes. Beerbohm's literary use of this term will be clearer to us if we read it as a coinage he would have been glad to perpetrate if the missing constituent had been available to him: *parallel-ogrammatology. Parallelogram* is, first, a good name for the combination of parody and allegory he wrote. For *parody* means "song-alongside," and *allegory* means "other-speaking," but he uses no song or speech. But *parallel* simply means "alongside-the-other and *parallelogram* means "writing-alongside-the-other," which is exactly what he does. *Parallelogrammatology* means, then, "reading-alongside-the-other-writing" or even "reading-alongside-the-other-writing-alongside-the-other." It is a perfect name for the stiff neck that reading Beerbohm is meant to give us.

Writing as parallelogram is writing, like *Zuleika Dobson* or *The Happy*

Hypocrite or A *Christmas Garland*, that announces itself as not merely possessing a subtext but having the quality of an interlinear translation. Reading "Him espying, the nymph darted in his direction" in the first chapter of *Zuleika Dobson*, the veteran classical schoolboy automatically looks dully up to the next line for the Latin that this so awkwardly renders. Not finding it, the reader is in a dilemma. He clearly detects the presence of a parallel, or mirrored, text, but he can not see it. He calls into play his ingenuity. He constructs possible *parallelogrammata*, as Cleverdon did, and as we have already done as well. The text is constructed so that none of these ever can be perfectly verified. Some clues have no answers. The reader grows aware of another intersecting axis of parallel lines, which we may call the reader's ingenuity and his failure or double or scrutineer. The desire to be a cleverdon meets the well-prepared caricature and condemnation of the clever dons of Judas. This brings about the complication I felt arguing with Sir Basil, where the would-be elucidator finds himself framed in a caricature which he can see as part of the text's intent. In Beerbohm's geometry:

A □ B
C □ D

A is a text. B is its double, the illustrious Beauty or subtext. C, the reader of A, seeks B by holding it up to D, *his* reader or the mirror of his own ingenuity. The room's four walls are now all mirrors. This is the image of the University.

In a convex mirror, by contrast there is "poetry." The mirror composes, internalizes, remakes the world with oneself at the glittering vertex. It is the perfect mirror for self-creation. But at Oxford, it is other people who do the looking. The quadrangle is a stage. Scrutiny can come from any window unobserved. That is the drama in the parallelogram.

Thus is the dandy undone. No longer alone with his mirror, he walks among mobs of reflections. The university that he enters is a hall of mirrors, or speculation, where we read even the physical place as itself a text, the colleges "symbols of themselves, greatly symbolising their oneness." This universal legibility marks graduation in its fullest sense. The university or literary institution calls *Zuleika Dobson* into being both by the phenomenology of its Spirit ("the Oxford Spirit" that is the "oneness" the colleges symbolize) and by the very fabric of its operations (rereading of just the kind we are engaged in). The characters, moving through the novel on parallel tracks, enact a ritual graduation, and this itself parallels the replication built into the art of speculative philosophizing which is, on the one hand, what the University does, and on the other, what we must do in order to make or find the sense of the book. The university is text, subtext, reader, and rereader—in a word, FORM This theme is not accidental. It has the same place in the history of nineteenth-century Europe that the mystical Rose occupies for Dante's world. Beerbohm's university, it is important to remember, is not Newman's. It belongs rather to the children of Arnold and Pater, for whom the medieval colleges had become the sign of an "impossible loyalty," thanks to the arrival of the higher criticism and speculative philosophy of the German university. Max's Oxford becomes vividly English only because of this powerfully present sense that it has already followed, despite itself, the university of Hegel, Fichte, and Schleiermacher, "where there is no creative scientific capacity without the speculative spirit" (Schleiermacher). The spirit of speculation, or mirroring, has an "apparatus," according to J. F. Lyotard, which "shows that knowledge is only worthy of that name to the extent that it reduplicates itself . . . by citing its own statements in a second-level discourse that functions to legitimate them." Beerbohm—did it owe something to his father's having grown up in Romantic Germany?—dramatizes from the start the English scholar's uneasy apprehension of this "scientific" doubling that had so decisively entered the game. For from his Charterhouse parody *Carmen Becceriense* to the essays in *Works* to the first chapter of *Zuleika Dobson*, where a don who has been reading too much Mommsen steps out of Blackwell's and sees the statues of the emperors perspiring, his writing is haunted by the speculative reader, the higher critic whose face he sees in the textual mirror. He sees our reflection as clearly as we see his. His preoccupation with the mortal scrutiny of this "scientific scholar" is what keeps him always in the mode of conscious parody. He writes, as is were, archeologically, at every turn alert to those parallels and discrepancies that generate speculative knowledge. *Zuleika Dobson* is a *Commedia* because it gives us precisely the fullest image of its own moment in history, the university both as theme and as this process of mirroring—a process, like Dante's own, that is most general where it is most personal.

Parallel and Paralogy

Rereading with mirrors, or parallelogrammatology, is personal because it depends upon point of view as fully as the most ideologically individualist works imaginable. But it is general as well because it always includes the eyes of the Other. We may follow its path a little more closely now. The text A and its double, the subtext B, parallel the same axis. But to perceive this is to recognize the perpendicular axis that *sees* the doubling of A in B. This perpendicular has its parallel as well. We may call this the *paralogy*, the reminder that someone else is looking, and from a point of view the reader cannot himself attain. Every reading, every rereading, has still its putative reader and rereader. This imaginary person has enormous power. It was he who so terrified Dr. Casaubon as to paralyze his ambition to write a magnum opus. So one's actual looking about in this mirrored room must not be described by a parallelogram alone but by its transsection into triangles, a boxed Z if one imagines oneself at C looking about from text to subtext to scrutineer, a boxed X if we include that dreadful don's perceptions in the picture, where he sees all the reader sees but from a different angle and is able, as well, to look through the blind spot one always makes in any mirror with the opacity of his or her own head. Imaged either way, this square of contradictions offers an intricate panorama.

Any move one makes will produce its interminable series of doubles, each of them subtly different from the next, and each moving with one's gaze, so that the very clarity and idealist closure of the situation must cause an irreducible instability in the prospect. Reading produces parallels. But parallels make paralogies inevitable. Paralogies, which are mistakes undetectable except from someone else's coign of vantage, are that part of writing which always must belong to the reader, that part of reading which can never be taken from the writer.

That is, in this account reader and writer stand and fall as equals. They are subject to the same laws of light and are in fact doing the same thing. Thus arises one of the subtler excellences of Beerbohm's writing: it is impervious to parody. Max could not parody himself successfully. His one attempt, which we have already examined [elsewhere], is so far the inferior of his usual product that it is not surprising to discover that no one else has ever done it even as well. Indeed, scarcely anyone has tried. *Zuleika in Cambridge*, S. C. Robert's sequel to the *Oxford Love Story*, simply is not funny. What protects Beerbohm's works from the very art he practiced is that the parodist's turn is already in them. Over his texts always shimmer the searching lights of innumerable reflected gazes. This universe of inspection, though it is no less public than a town square or an Oxford quad, remains personal because one of these gazes belongs certifiably to Max himself. Consequently, he allows us to move beyond parody. Its contribution, the reader's remorseless scrutiny, is already included. Instead, he invites us to practice the arts that produce his own texts: parallel and paralogy.

Things Transmutable

We may now read, as it were, beside him, understanding how our reading is the double of Beerbohm's own. We are able here to see how what is most personal, as in Dante, may become what is also most general. Mother, father, brother, sister: these intensities, very remarkably transformed, are what he offers us as mintable, exchangeable, transmutable things.

Mother.   Dante encountered Beatrice when he was nine. Beerbohm gives us the square root of this, meeting his Muse at age three: "The very earliest recollection of my life is bound up with an Oxford and Cambridge Boat Race. I was walking with my nurse along the Board Walk in Kensington Gardens, and she stopped to talk to some other nurse, with whom, I suppose, she was acquainted. I remember that my nurse said 'What are *you*?' and that the other nurse answered, 'I am Cambridge.' 'Oh,' rejoined my nurse, 'I am Oxford.' " Parallels to Dante, clearly visible in *Zuleika Dobson* in the figure of Alma Mater (nursing mother) glimpsed on the dedication page and then seen nude ("the total body of that spirit") in a primal scene of vision. Parallels to *Zuleika Dobson* itself in the The Broad, where much of the action takes place, and the Eights Race that is the climax of the plot. The parallels are clever. The paralogy is brilliant:

> Not having yet seen more than three summers, I was too young to understand this elliptical mode of speech, and long after, whenever Oxford and Cambridge were mentioned in my presence, I thought Oxford was my nurse, and Cambridge the other one. So deeply do things root themselves in the brain of a little child that even now, after the lapse of so many years, the names of the great Universities do still vaguely suggest to me the images of these two nurses. And I attribute my early preference for Oxford to the notion I had that Oxford was *my* nurse. When the time came for me to choose the venue of my adolescence, how could I hestitate? Oxford received its sacred trust. Oxford moulded me. How petty, devious and remote are the details that inform a world's destiny!

And how precise the misconstruction of a servant's ellipsis! How elegant the obsessive force that invents a plot to take Zuleika from Oxford to Cambridge, "the other one"! This account of childhood inspiration not only tropes the *Vita Nuova* but includes in advance any possible Lectura Dantis. For the commentator's misalignment is there from the start. Further, and particularly to the point, this passage demonstrates the consummation of autopsychopseudometamorphosis, where the dandy's exaggerted individualism is transformed into a general law: here, this passage says, is the most secret treasure of my research into lost time, and look! it is in fact no less, and no more, than the fabric of human histroy. I chose Oxford because of a misconstruction, but such misconstructions are "the details that inform a world's destiny."

How seriously are we to take this? The point is that in an age of higher higher criticism, when the reader's scrutiny always informs the writer's choices, the only way to say something seriously is in a joke. Seriousness, indeed, and its fugitive possibility are part of the preoccupation of this *Commedia*.

Father.   Consider the Warden of Judas. He is a "mummy," a dead father, "an ebon pillar of tradition," and a Dante, no less, in his aspect: "Aloft, between the wide brim of his silk hat and the white extent of his shirt-front, appeared those eyes which hawks, that nose which eagles, had often envied." He is the figure of what is serious, authoritative to his bone, but he is a figure of ridicule and contumely.

Parallels: for Max, Oxford authority was exactly his dead father, who passed away while Max was an undergraduate, thus giving the most vivid Oedipal color to the prospect of entering Alma Mater. This is why Max Beerbohm could not face graduation. Oxford authority also complicated itself with the figure of Arnold, the St. Paul of the gospel of Oxford, who employed his seriousness powerfully of delegitimize exactly such a son as

Max Beerbohm, born of a Deceased Wife's Sister, and such a father as Julius Beerbohm, to whom Arnold gives the gross name and figure of Zephanaiah Diggs. Thus, in the parallels is a sharp misalignment: the father figure is denied by the father figure's reflection. What to do?

Paralogies: double difficulties require double solutions. Max invents a plot in which every undergraduate achieves encaenia (Greek: *renewal*, the Oxford name for graduation) by *not* graduating: "My dear Father. By the time you receive this I shall have taken a step which. . . ." This is his restitution to his own dead father. The second difficulty is the restoration *of* the dead father, against the testimony of the great Oxford totem, Matthew Arnold. As he trumps Dante by reporting a decisive meeting at age three, Beerbohm out-Arnolds Arnold by drastically extending, with exaggeration, not only the famous purple patch about Oxford at night but many other aspects of Arnold's whole enterprise. There is the Scholar-Gypsy, who comes to haunt the river after the mass suicide; there is also the epithet "gipsy" pointedly attached to Zuleika, daughter of a circus-rider, giving her an Arnoldian filiation. Most wonderful of all, and most to the point, is his assumption of Arnold's authority over the myth of Oxford, an achievement Beerbohm was quick to underline when Michael Sadler, at the time vice-chancellor of the university, wrote an essay comparing Arnold unfavorably with the "imp" Beerbohm. Beerbohm takes this parallel and, by parology, turns it on its head, disagreeing with Sadler and calling himself a "conservative imp":

> Your suggestion that M.A. would have been the better for being the *me* "of his generation" does move me to make a stern and spirited protest in his behalf. You regret that the imp in *him* was "untimely suppressed in his childhood." Suppose it hadn't been! Suppose his father had said to him, "Matt, my child, in you I discern the makings of what is called an humorist. Here is a cap-and-bells. Here, moreover, is a wand-and-bladder. Make good practice with these, under God's blessing." What would have happened then? The seriousness that the child had congenitally might have saved him from the horrid fate of being just a fribble and a "funny man." I myself have enough seriousness to prevent me from being just that—else you never would have honoured me by speaking my name. But oh, how much more amusing I should be if I were more serious than I am! Surely it is *because* M.A. was so genuinely solemn (and even desperate) at heart that we love his outbreaks of fun so much. Without the contrast of what underlies his writing, all the time, how much less delicious would be what suddenly now and again bubbles up! "Impertinence," as you call it. Yes. But why not? Part of the joy, for you and me, is surely that it was impertinent (in the strict sense, as also in the loose sense). "A flaw"? Oh, surely not! There you speak as Vice-

Chancellor, not as Michael Sadler; and the conservative imp applauds; but the thoughtful imp dissents. Think of Arnold's exquisite side-outbursts on Mr. Odger, on Frederic Harrison (happily no longer with us), on Sir Daniel Gooch, on all those other flies in amber!—and maintain that these were "a flaw"! And maintain that their power to delight you and me, to make us really laugh aloud over the printed page, doesn't depend on the high seriousness of the preceding and subsequent pages!

He defends Arnold's "seriousness," be it noted, entirely according to the canons of Beerbohmian seriousness. "Except in union with some form of high seriousness," he writes elsewhere, "humor does not exist for me," an assertion that actually means "except in union with some form of humour, high seriousness does not exist for me." This special insincerity amounts to a reinvention of Arnold as a "better" but nonetheless definitely an "earlier" *Beerbohm.* (The crossword puzzzler notes that Arnold appears as the initials of an Oxford degree, "M.A."; initials are never accidental in Beerbohm, and these are reversed in the acronym of the dedication "Illi Almae Matri," "I AM".) Max reinforces Sadler's identification of Arnold with Max—his complaints to the contrary being founded, in any case, on an authority stolen from Arnold by Sadler and give to Max, who does not so much repudiate the gift as treat it as an inheritance that he proves is his by protesting himself unworthy of it. And who, after all, has not laughed aloud (Max's criterion for seriousness) over more of Beerbohm's pages than Arnold's?

But how seriously am I proposing that *we* take this for a criterion? Completely, I am afraid, and for good reason. Beerbohm offers a model of philosophical authority so completely informed by its own specularity that we refuse it only at risk of losing what small purchase we retain upon any honest sense of the scholarly enterprise at all. His own place in Oxford springs, he knows or at any rate reports, from a misconstruction. Likewise Arnold's whose entire paradoxical and seductive authority springs from the implied, but well known, character of his father, the illustrious and earnest Doctor of Rugby School. Beerbohm is able to continue to love Oxford because all its authority, and his own that belongs to it, has this same accidental narrative to support it. Nothing more. Indeed, his most authoritative and authorial gesture in the novel, his lordly granting of an "hour of grace" is borrowed, like the source of the interlude itself, from Arnold, who invents in his poem "Saint Brandan" a parallel hour of grace for no less a sinner than Judas Iscariot. Beerbohm's adoption of this innovation has then the charm of being granted by implication to every Oxford man, for all of them are, by his account, "old Judasians." Even to Arnold.

Brother.   All sons of the same Alma Mater, all traitors to one another, the Oxford undergraduates form a vast field upon which Beerbohm can work out the play of his own fraternal recollections. Thus, we may use parallel and paralogy here to follow Max's strategies for dealing with his monstrously triumphant brother Herbert [Beerbohm Tree, the actor-manager]. Max's successes in striking Herbert's poses make it clear how impossible it is completely to separate an "original" from a "double" in a specular quadrangle. The Duke is Max as he appears to himself in his dreams of supplanting Herbert. This is the famous "incomparable Max." Noaks is the residue, all the backstage realities left over and seen in the mirror some rainy morning. These two look at each other through the *mal'occhio* we always suspect in Beerbohm's big baby eyes, the stare of envy in the lesser and of malice in the greater. Its workings are outlined by Max in the essay "On Speaking French." "Whenever two Englishmen are speaking French to a Frenchman you may safely diagnose in the breast of one of the two humiliation, envy, ill-will, impotent rage, and a dull yearning for vengeance; and you can take it that the degree of these emotions is in exact ratio to the superiority of the other man's performance. In the breast of this other are contempt, malicious amusement, conceit, vanity, pity, and joy in ostentation; these, also, exactly commensurable with his advantage." This defines the situation as it stands between Noaks and the Duke or between Max and Herbert, in terms of a ratio of superior performance.

Performance is a question of parallels. Max, especially during his promising youth, played the Duke (or Herbert) to his friends' Noaks. Thus, to Rothenstein he will write "Dear Sir: I take great pleasure in sending you my autograph" or to Turner, "I am suffering, my dearest Reg, from a plethora of brilliancy, so I must write to someone for relief—why not to you?" He could not take this line with Herbert. Here he played not Duke but valet. He plucked his first fiancée, Kilseen Conover, an ingénue who failed to impress the family, out of Tree's troupe; he went so far as to choose his second, Constance Collier, a great beauty who impressed everybody, out of Tree's seraglio. This bold move did not prosper. Constance soon broke it off. Max understood only too well why:

> Constance and I are not going to be married after all. . . . I had a letter from her saying she had been so wretched and had not known how to tell me that she felt it would never do, after all, for us to marry—neither of us being the sort of people for the serious responsibilities of life. It was a very sweet letter indeed, and *of course* I don't blame her in the very least. . . . It *is* a pity I was not born either rich or the sort of solid man who could be trusted and would trust himself to make his way solidly in the world. Of course I am a success in a way [Max is writing to Turner, who envied Max as Max envied Herbert], and may continue to be so for some time, but that is in virtue of certain qualities in my defects; it is in virtue of a sort of nimble fantastic irresponsibility;

for solid worldly success this is no good at all. And I now, for the first time clearly, see myself as on the whole a failure—I have never coverted the *solid* quality till now, when I find that without it I cannot get, and don't deserve, Constance.

Constance returned, by way of another entanglement, to Tree, who flaunted her, playing Nero to her Poppaea, casting his wife Maude as Nero's scorned escort Agrippina, and another time playing Antony to her Cleopatra, interpolating into Shakespeare's play a scene where Constance appeared in apotheosis as the goddess Isis. Max had the pleasure of learning that he was not "solid" enough to deserve a woman Herbert could afford to keep as an ornament.

Ratio is established in a carnival of paralogies. Superior performance is superior value. Money, which is defined most precisely as the ratio between differences of value, thus becomes the sign of a performance's worth. The Duke's wealth and his brilliance in examinations are two faces of the same coin. Noaks the plodder is also poor. Zuleika's magic is technically maladroit but spectacularly effective theater; it is appropriate that her gear is all solid gold. The Duke's value is so splendid that he dominates, by an extreme paralogy, even single other undergraduate completely; they follow his fashions in dress, in love, and in death under an unremitting Midas touch that will not allow them to deviate from his pattern even when the Duke himself implores them to do so. The Duke dies, Zuleika moves on, but their value continues to act. It does so as the very object of reading, as symbols, halves of a broken coin. These symbols are the pearls. When the Duke gives Zuleika's earrings to Katie, she accepts them as a way of balancing the ratio with Zuleika, and then gives them to Noaks who sees them "as things transmutable by sale hereafter into desks, forms, blackboards, maps, lockers, cubicles, gravel soil, diet unlimited, and special attention to backward pupils." The same thing happens when the Duke's studs are pressed by Zuleika on the unwilling Mélisande, who suddenly ceases to see the pearls "as trinkets finite and inapposite" but sees them "as things presently transmutable into little marble tables, books, dominos, absinthes au sucre, shiny black portfolios with weekly journals in them, yellow staves with daily journals flapping from them, vermouths secs, vermouths cassis." This transformation is given twice to clarify the point that the essence of money is like the essence of reading: what it is worth to you is not exactly what it is worth to me. We may use this to take a step towards resolving the inconclusiveness of rereading, a difficulty neatly put by Stanley Fish: "There is always a formal pattern, but it isn't always the same one."

Conclusion in rereading, as in contracts, diplomas, and other transactions, follows upon a decision of value. We reread just as we haggle, until we come to a fair price. The pearls illustrate how this happens. People use transmutables (money, degrees, interpretations) to establish their positions relative to one another. Everyone reads the same things—and these things include, as the kernel of that humor that is high seriousness, everyone's position relative to everyone else. This ritual of universal mutual evaluation is the ritual of Oxford life. Everything from one's manner of sitting a horse to one's performance in speaking French is part of an endless examination. It amounts to the portrait of a collective superego or economic unconscious which establishes each person's relative worth according to a nicety of inspection which not only can read the precise shade of blue in a hatband at a hundred yards but can also see plainly how this pigment, establishing its wearer as a member of the Bullingdon, places him in a specific ratio of value to any other given person, oneself included. Beerbohm's dandyism takes its particular hue from his immersion in this ritual. "It is Oxford that has made me insufferable." Oxford taught him to put into niceties of punctuation and neology and French-speaking a vigilance that dandies before him had invested only in their clothes or their china or their aphorisms. Reading his hypercorrect prose, one understands that it means to sustain the inspector's gaze as impermeably as the Duke in his bow window, and that the writer fears more than anything that he will come out looking like the contemptible Mr. Noaks. This, too, is why the only time Dante appears in Beerbohm's iconology he is standing in an Oxford quadrangle under the Proctor's piercing scope, being inspected: "Your name and college?" Our place in this comedy requires us to come, then, to a fair valuation of Beerbohm's prose. We can, for example, agree with Kingsmill who said as a sneer that *Zuleika Dobson* had certainly earned Max his honorary Oxford doctorate. We can, that is, agree to graduate him. For we are the imaginary university as it sends its reduplicated image down the imaginary prospect of time. But having done this, what have we done? What do we mean by an Oxford doctorate? How much for this pearl?

Sister. "How many charming talents have been spoiled by the desire to do 'important' work," Beerbohm writes in 1898, just as he is beginning *Zuleika Dobson*. "Some people are born to lift heavy weights. Some are born to juggle golden balls." A golden ball has importance without being heavy. What importance? A week earlier, he had written, "The idea of beauty as the root of all evil is not new, no doubt, nor very profound. But it is rather a charming idea." This is the golden ball in question, enclosed in the tale of Joseph and Potiphar's wife, the story of the tempting of a virtuous youth by a lustful woman, which, he thought, had a "stong, straightforward significance." He has given his heroine something Firdausi's Zalikha and Euripedes' Phaedra did not possess, though Jenny Mere and Sister Dora did: unstained virginity. Beatrice as the root of all evil: that is the golden ball, that is the pearl.

Very tightly wound it is, too. So tightly, in fact, that no one noticed it. When the book was reprinted in the Collected Edition, Max added the following rather irritated "Note": "I was in Italy when this book was first published. A year later (1912) I visited London, and I found that most of my friends and acquaintances spoke to me of Zu-like-a—a name which I hardly recognised and thoroughly disapproved. I had always thought of the lady as Zu-leek-a. Surely it was thus that Joseph thought of his Wife, and Selim of his Bride? And I do hope that it is thus that any reader of these pages will think of Miss Dobson." I cannot resist asserting that the pronunciation Zu-leek-a, with its toilet-training overtones echoed in the scene where the heroine embarrasses the hero, has its source in a nineties music-hall song (including the lines "And I know that Zulica awaits in her tent, / The fairest in all the sun-kissed Orient"), though only my own good fortune in unearthing the thing makes it fully plausible to me. The "Note" is meant to inspire such hunting. For its mode is double-crostic oblique. Neither Joseph nor Selim was married to the Wife or Bride in question— a point you will miss if you do not know the stories. If you do, there is a bonus. The Wife belonged to Potiphar, and is a classic Oedipal temptress. The Bride was a girl from Abydos. *The Bride of Abydos* is a poem about brother-sister incest. Beerbohm's "Note" betrays a certain frustration with not only the widespread mispronunciation (still common, by the way) but also the total failure of scrutineers to see what the book is finally about. Our solution of this riddle is in fact the pearl *Zuleika Dobson* offers us.

Not much, you say?

Beerbohm thought otherwise. His parody of Henry James, "The Mote in the Middle Distance," accepts reading as a commentary on this very matter. Its critical point is that James deals with brother-sister incest in a way that seems delicate, oblique, and repressed in a manner appropriate to the difficulty of the emotion, but that this obliqueness is only the reminiscent smirk of the practiced voyeur. In "The Mote in the Middle Distance," all the indirection lies on the surface. The actual revelations are blunt to the point of prurience. Percy Tantalus wakes up one Christmas morning to see stockings at the foot of his bed and of his sister's. He imagines that she, Eva Tantalus, has "already made the great investigation on her own." But she is still asleep. She wakes and sits bolt upright. "The gaze she fixed on her extravagant kinsman was of a kind to make him wonder how he contrived to remain, as he did, rigid." They try to decide whether to look into the stockings, when she exclaims, "Don't you see?"

> "The mote in the middle distance?" he asked. "Did you ever, my dear, know me to see anything else? I tell you it blocks out everything. It's a cathedral, it's a herd of elephants, it's the whole habitable globe. Oh, it's believe me, of an obsessiveness!"

And so they consider whether to look into the stockings, as we learn under a barrage of Jamesian double entendre. "Over and above the basis of (presumably) sweetmeats in the toes and heels, certain extrusions stood for a very plenary fulfilment of desire." The "(presumably)" illustrates to what heights of leering comedy this manner can raise such a theme; the narrator's parentheses widen and widen as one reads, seeming to take in a whole rippling roomful of sexual innuendo, from the rigid extravagant kinsman and his great investigation on his own through the features of the doll and the sword and helmet the children imagine to be hidden in the stockings. Percy wants to look. Eva stops him by saying,

> "Of course, my dear, you *do* see. There they are, and you know I know you know we wouldn't, either of us, dip a finger into them." With a vibrancy of tone that seemed to bring her voice quite close to him, "One doesn't," she added, "violate the shrine— pick the pearl from the shell."

And H*nry J*m*s does not pick the pearl. Max has Percy say, "One doesn't even peer." The Jamesian narrator himself elaborately refrains: "As to whether, in the years that have elapsed since he did this, either of our friends (now adult) has, in fact, 'peered', is a question which whenever I call at the house, I am tempted to put to one or the other of them. But any regret I may feel in my invariable failure to 'come up to the scratch' of yielding to this temptation is balanced, for me, by my practical certainty that the answer, if vouchsafed, would be in the negative." The voyeur, failing "to 'come up to scratch,' " in fact exhibits himself. This is the critical point of the parody. This is what Beerbohm learned through parody to avoid and is why he obliterates from his own novel the line "The Duke's heart throbbed like the screw of a great vessel." Such freedoms of revelation are not the clarity but the self-indulgence of a narrtor like Beerbohm's J*m*s, who would rather juggle with his suppositions than actually touch the pearl. It is, for us, a question of which performance offers a higher value.

James's obliqueness is a sort of shared joke, a complicit "knowing." Beerbohm's obliqueness, by contrast, has nothing about it of the delicate poke in the ribs. He prefers to do tricks with the things themselves, manipulating objects visibly and palpably in a literary thaumaturgy that enacts, rather than gloats over, the tragedy of incest. His fingers play among his chrestomathy of allusions in order thoroughly to draw us into the drama. Consider his play with the pearls against that of J*m*s. At the beginning of dinner at the Warden's, Zuleika wears a black and a pink pearl earring, while the Duke has two white pearl studs in his shirt. Shortly after the Oriel don has failed to interest Zuleika in the "metamorphosis of the bulls in the temple of Osiris" as an example of Egyptian magic, the Duke is startled to notice that his studs have become black and pink. During the course of the intervening conversation, both Zuleika and the Duke contemplate one another's pearls. The Duke notices the change in context of a narrative digression on his character that leads up to the statement that "the dandy must be celibate, cloistral; is, indeed, but a monk with a mirror for beads and breviary—an anchorite, mortifying his soul that his body may be perfect." As soon as the "import of the studs" has "revealed itself" to him, the Duke staggers up from the table and leaves hurriedly. Reading all this properly requires in us something different from the sophisticated eye of the Jamesian reader.

One must know, or learn, for Beerbohm does not say, that the Oriel don's remark refers to a step in Isiac initiation where the novice puts on the hide of the slaughtered bull to signify the resurrection of Osiris. The change in the Duke's pearls is, strictly speaking, a prodigy (Beerbohm specifically rejects the notion that it resulted from legerdemain by Zuleika), a part of the disturbance the gods have sent in the person of Miss Dobson, a disturbance whose climax is the Duke's drowning in ceremonial robes (the hide of the slaughtered Knight of the Garter) in the Isis. We must know, or learn, that Isis and Osiris were brother and sister, as well as man and wife. We must likewise consider that Osiris in death was mutilated, castrated, and dismembered. This collaboration requires more than a grin of recognition from us. Then, however, we see the point of the black and pink pearls dangling like trophies from Zuleika's ears, and see why the River Isis is a place for young bulls to become oxen in the fold. What is Oxford as a mating-ground? Even here, Beerbohm's indirection is so great that we do not quite get the point without actively trying: "Well," he writes, "the sisters and cousins of an undergraduate seldom seem more passable to his comrades than to himself."

Thus, incest alone is not the pearl. The pearl includes the plucking of it from the shrine—Beerbohm's prestidigitation carried out in straight face, as of *le jongleur de Notre Dame,* and then our rereaderly acceptance of it, a job for light fingers and swift glances. What is in this transaction for us? Beerbohm's offer is made in terms first specified by Pater, who lays it down that the "literary artist" appeals

> to the scholar, who has great experience in literature, and will show no favor to shortcuts, or hackneyed illustration, or an affectation of learning designed for the unlearned. Hence a contention, a sense of self-restraint and renunciation, having for the susceptible reader the effect of a challenge for minutest consideration; the attention of the writer, in every minutest detail, being a pledge that it is worth the reader's while to be attentive too, that the writer is dealing scrupulously with his instrument, and, therefore, indirectly, with the reader himself also, that he has the science of the instrument he plays on, perhaps after all, with a freedom which in such case will be the freedom of a master.
>
> ("Style")

The *he* that recurs in the last few clauses of this sentence has ambiguous reference and by the strict law of proximity refers rather to the reader than to the writer. Pater intends this. Not surprising, then, that Harold Bloom has taken up Pater as a noble precursor. For central to Pater's purpose is to elevate acts of reading (*Appreciations* is the title of the book I am citing) to the plane of mastery. Pater's "freedom of a master" is precisely what Beerbohm holds out to us with the pearls.

But differently, of course, from Pater's kind of freedom. "Mastery" for Max has the intricate character of Zuleika herself: that which appeals profoundly just because it cannot be possessed. Freud says the book is Mother. Beerbohm gives it as both Mother and Sister—desirabilities catastrophically desirable because forever beyond reach. The plot of his novel ends up being the plot of our reading. He has, as Pater prescribes, provided a "challenge for minutest consideration." He has also provided, according to his own apprehension of the act, protocols for playing the "instrument." Like his "Note" of preface, it requires oblique scrutiny, but it can be seen. On Zuleika's toilet-table, he writes, "stood a multitude of multiform glass vessels, domed, all of them, with dull gold, on which Z.D., in zianites and diamonds, was encrusted. On a small table stood a great casket of malachite, initialled in like fashion. On another small table stood Zuleika's library. Both books were in covers of dull gold. On the back of one cover BRADSHAW, in beryls, was encrusted; on the back of the other, A.B.C. GUIDE, in amethysts, beryls, chrysoprases, and garnets." One translation of this is that the library that produces *Zuleika Dobson* is a pair of railway schedules. A joke. Zuleika enters and leaves the novel by train. A good joke, full of point. . . . Beerbohm means yet more by it. A railway guide is the very type of the Book. On a stage, for example, he writes that a book that is a "masterpiece" may be "merely *Bradshaw's Guide* bound in brocade." A joke, but in high earnest, as he explains elsewhere: "Implicitly, a railway timetable is as romantic a thing as could be; and there may be people who, studying it, feel themselves whirling through space, this way and that, in a wild confusion of innumerable anxious or joyous journeys. But Mr. Bradshaw is not explicitly a romantic writer. He does but hint, drily, abruptly, at possibilities. And that is just what the modern playwright does." A railway timetable hangs its romances upon times and returns and upon— as Beerbohm has literally as a child placed his novel upon—parallel wheels and parallel tracks. Follow the numbers and the letters, reader, keep your eye on the parallels, and make of it what you can.

Let us follow these protocols in reading, as a last act, Zuleika's library. We have a long string of parallels to examine if we like. There are echoes of Revelation: amethyst, beryl, and chrysoprase are stones that garnish, respectively, the eighth, tenth, and twelfth walls of the New Jerusalem, a city that is "pure gold, like unto clear glass" (Rev. 21:18–20); the gold-domed micropolis on Zuleika's toilet-table gleams against a background of such other echoes of Revelation as the emphasis upon the number twelve in the novel (twelve emperors, twelve apostles, Joseph and his eleven brothers, midnight as the "hour of grace," twenty-four chapters where the first twelve are echoed in the second), the importance to Life of the sacred river in the sacred city, and the fact that the Duke's Christian name is John, and that he actually says to Zuleika "I, John," repeating the most famous phrase in the Apocalypse. Another echo: the notorious jewelry of *A Rebours* stolen for *The Picture of Dorian Gray*. Parallels within the novel: in chapter X, Zuleika thinks of leaving Oxford and consults the *A.B.C. Guide* for a train; in the last chapter, planning her actual departure, she and Mélisande employ *Bradshaw* before deciding instead to order a special train. An important point about these books is that Zuleika never herself gets so far as to decode either of them. There is an intriguing parallel in Beerbohm's reading: Max kept in his library at Rapallo a copy of Baroness Tautphoeus's Victorian best seller *The Initials*, a novel whose title refers to its one original feature; "A. Hamilton," a younger brother whose older brother has the same initials, receives through inadvertence a letter sent to that brother from a mysterious lady who signs herself "A.Z.," and his confusion leads through a maze of further misapprehensions to the younger A. Hamilton's happy marriage, an event whose cause is emphatically ascribed to the signature "A.Z." The *A.B.C. Guide* inscribed Z.D. (Zed) in zianites and diamonds parallels this happy trope, which clearly for Max transformed an otherwise per-sample potboiler into a reflection upon the relationship between the iconic alphabet and the desires of the reader to use it in making sense.

Now we have a double set of parallels to work with. Which is to say, given the physics of mirrors, an infinite regress. Look at what is possible. *A.B.C. Guide* is parallel not only to *The Initials*, which dramatizes the distance between the inscrutability of a hieroglyph and the force of desire to make a happy ending of decoded messages, but also to *Bradshaw*, which it doubles with a kind of magnificent redundancy. Its own acronym, emphasized in jewels, doubles the very alphabet, for A-B-C is 1-2-3 in Latin, but in Greek 1-2-3 is A-B-G. Two railway time-tables, two sets of alphabetic tracks, two dry hints at possibilities, hung up in a parallelogram of intersection but also moving forever along their own axes. A-B-C suggests FORM—a term, by the way, that Pater associates particularly with music and its place in building Plato's "Perfect City": both the parallels with Revelation and Zuleika's tag line about music, the equivalent here of a Homeric epithet, suggest the force of the Apocalyptic parody. Out of that crossroads run, in one direction, Homer, and in the other, Dante. Z.D. in Greek reads as 6 times 4: not only the didodeconomy of the Alexandrian Homer and the chapters of *Zuleika Dobson* but also an indication of the breaking of the work into groups of four chapters, which was necessary to outlining the cross-word-parody *Commedia*. A to Z, complete closure, or complete railway pilgrimage, leads us towards the conclusion that Zuleika is a paralogic Beata Mater, apocalyptically transfigured, just as Beatrice is an allegorical one.

One might go on for a long time annotating possibilities and probabilities, like the famous Dean Liddell in the lifelong act of producing his famous Greek dictionary. The dean's daughter, yet more famous in literature than himself, is the heroine of two comic prose epics built upon the number twelve (itself a hieroglyphic parallelogram produced by multiplying $A \times B \times C \times D$, or $1 \times 2 \times 3 \times 4$), and about Oxford, about the looking glass, about Homer, about the return of the repressed feminine, and about incest. Zuleika has a place in a line that begins with Alice. I follow the number twelve back to the first chapter, where the paralogic twelve apostles, the emperors of Suetonius, sweat when they see Zuleika, their dissevered heads suffering the fates combined of Wilde's Iokanaan, the Cheshire Cat, and Dante's Judas in the icy mouth of Satan. They are the twelve totemic "members of Judas" who remind persistently through the novel of the real character of the Oxford Beatrice. She is more terrible than the full-grown Alice. She is rather the daughter of Pater and his consort Alma Mater, as we see her about to do a magic show in the hope that she will encourage to suicide a great crowd of the undergraduates standing about, insubstantial as leaves or playing cards, in the quadrangle of Judas: "Zuleika babbled like a child going to a juvenile party. This was the great night, as yet, in her life. Illustrious enough already it had seemed to her, as the eve of that ultimate flattery vowed her by the Duke. So fine a thing had his doom seemed to her—his doom alone—that it had sufficed to flood her pink pearl with the right hue. And now not on him alone need she ponder. Now he was but the centre of a group—a group that might grow and grow—a group that might with a little encouragement be a multitude. . . . With such hopes dimly whirling in the recesses of her soul, her beautiful red lips babbled." Pater described the contents of this good cheer as "the animalism of Greece, the lust of Rome, the mysticism of the late middle ages with its spiritual ambitions and imaginative loves, the return of the Pagan world, the sins of the Borgias."

So the paralogic conclusion is that this monstress is the Beatrice of our century, its rising Oxford nightmare of the suppressed and irresistible feminine. The woman enters the male seminary in an iron Trojan horse, with the same epochal consequence of the West defeating "steep Wilusa," as we are only now learning to call Ilion in its own tongue. Beerbohm's achievement is no mere burlesque of Dante or Homer. It is, as his best parodies always are, a devastating critique by the light of a polished glass. A usurpation, as well, in which, by specular dialectic, the usurper himself is usurped. The victory of Woman in *Zuleika Dobson* is the victory of the mirror, as it is the victory of Woman over Max Beerbohm. For it is certain, it is demonstrable, that Zuleika, whose fame is made absolute by the same guttural princely compliments that Marie Corelli used in her advetisements, took her first textual shape in the pages superscribed with that same feminist signature that Max so hated and feared. Not only the avatars of Millicent Coral stand behind Zuleika but also a certain Judith Iscariot, sister of the namesake of the Duke's college, who figures as the heroine of [Corelli's] *Barabbas*, a novel that appeared during Max's last year at Oxford:

> Nothing more beautiful in the shape of woman could be imagined than she,—her fairness was of that rare and subtle type which in all ages has overwhelmed reason, blinded judgment, and played havoc with the passions of men. Well did she know her own surpassing charm,—and thoroughly did she estimate the value of

her fatal power to lure and rouse and torture all whom she made the victims of her almost resistless attraction. She was Judith Iscariot,—only daughter of one of the strictest and most respected members of the Pharasaical sect in Jerusalem,—and by birth and breeding she should have been the most sanctimonious and reserved of maidens,—but in her case, nature had outstepped education. Nature, in a picturesque mood, had done wondrous things for her,—things that in the ordinary opinion of humankind, generally outweigh virtue and the cleanness of the soul in the sight of Heaven. To Nature therefore the blame was due for having cast the red glow of a stormy sunset into the bronze gold of her hair, . . .—for having bruised the crimson heart of the pomegranate-buds and made her lips the colour of the perfect flower,—and for having taken the delicate cream and pink of early almond blossoms and fixed this soft flushing of the Spring's lifeblood in the colouring of her radiant face.

"No apple-tree, no wall of peaches, had not been robbed, nor any Tyrian rose-garden, for the glory of Miss Dobson's cheeks." These standard nosegays of hyperbole equally suit the radiant faces of Zuleika and Judith. They also share "fatal power" over those who feel their "resistless attraction"; both are descended from respectable Pharisees, and both have a magical association with jewelry that they share with Millicent Coral, at whose feet stones and pebbles turned to diamonds and rubies. Here is Judith, choosing jewels that treachery has won her from Caiaphas and Barabbas:

> "How well they go together thus!" she said. . . . —"They should be worn in company,—the high priest's rubies and the stolen pearls of Barabbas!"
>
> Her lips parted in a little mocking smile, and for a moment or two she held the gems in her hand, absorbed in thought. Then, slowly fastening the pearls round her throat, she put back the ruby pendant into the jewel-coffer, and again peered at herself in the silver mirror, and as she silently absorbed the glowing radiance of her own matchless beauty, she raised her arms with a gesture of irrepressible triumph.
>
> "For such as I am the world is made!" she exclaimed—"For such as I am, emperors and kings madden themselves and die! For such as I am proud heroes abase themselves as slaves. No woman lives who can be fairer than I,—and what shall I do with my fairness when I am weary of sporting with lovers and fools?—I will wed some mightly conqueror and be the queen and mistress of many nations!"

It must be some coherence in the nature of such a heroine that led Max later to imagine Zuleika finally arriving at the altar with Lord Kitchener, but we can see similarities that look more delibrate. Zuleika, after the races, stands in the rain "draining the lees of such homage as had come to no woman in history recorded." In the last chapter, while Mélisande combs Zuleika's hair, the heroine sits worrying that the world will not give her credit for what she has done; but then she consoles herself: " 'We know, you and I,' Zuleika whispered to the adorable creature in the mirror; and the adorable creature gave back her nod and smile. *They* knew, these two." Beerbohm transforms what he takes from Corelli with concision, wit, and the formal elegance of a writer who fully understands what mirrors can do; and yet more fully fears what Corelli may accomplish. A crucial theme in *Barabbas* is Corelli's notion that Judas was betrayed through love. His sister Judith ensorcelled him into the belief that by betraying Jesus to the high priest he would give Jesus the chance to display true divine powers and so convert everyone. This notion appealed to Judas's self-importance but was scarely the sin Christians have always supposed. Thus, Peter can defend the suicide's memory: "Therefore I say, report my story faithfully— and if thou wilt be just say this of the dead Judas,—that out of vainglorious pride and love he did betray his Master,—yes, out of love was born the sin,—love and not treachery!" Love, stumbling on the weakness of vain- glory, falls into self-betrayal, and so Judas kills himself. "Love," terrified love, "as Death's decoy."

Parallelogrammatology reads through the uncertainly of men who uneasily acknowledge that the eyes across the gender line are seeing some- thing different, vital, and hopelessly out of reach. Thus paralogy, which enables us to call the witty serious and the trivial deadly and the small magnificent, allows us to name this our *Commedia,* our replacement of the "hopes whirling in the recesses of her [or Dante's or Beatrice's] soul" with an image, lucid and even glittering, of our own aspirations—a nervous uncertainly, a martial air accompanied by its own retrograde inversion and the sound of a train whistle rapidly approaching, a dismantling and dis- membering of the pomp of courtly love and the bones on the bank, among rats, of a festering and never-satisfied finger, scanning the lines of his lady the Book.

One must not end too grandly. We read Proust to become Proustian, as we read Shakespeare to become imperial and Dante to justify our pa- triarchal twist. We read Beerbohm for the understanding of this phenom- enon, which is no more nor less than FORM. One looks in the textual mirror as a dandy does, to elaborate one's own mastery. And one comes away as the dandy has, rewritten on the lines of the Other. His greatness, such as it is, is that he makes himself small and shows us ourselves, similarly in proportion.

COMPLETING HIS ANTITHESIS AND LEAVING THE ROOM

Parallel: Beerbohm resembles Dante in the manner of a crossword parody. Paralogic: therefore he is the dandy Dante, the exquisite's rereading and rewriting of the *Commedia.*

In the long run, there is no establishing a paralogy by reasoning. Either it declares itself or it does not. It may live a submerged life without convincing anybody, like Samuel Butler's Huckleberry Finn notion that *The Odyssey* was written by a woman. Paralogics can survive on charm. Or it may turn out to be an interesting (or uninteresting) chapter in the history of a particular problem. By now, Shakespeare biography is the paradise of paralogy: Sh*k*sp**r*'s plays have so many authors that only persons professionally interested in the matter can even find out, much less recall, who they are. Some paralogics thrive mightily, however. Blake's diabolical Milton has, in many quarters, emerged as the Standard Revised Version. Dante's Virgil is more real a character than the author of *The Aeneid*. T. S. Eliot's Donne and Northrop Frye's Blake, implausible as they seemed at first, have replaced their predecessors utterly and for good, it appears. It is no longer the fashion to regard Donne as pedantic and Blake as crazy. The force of the newer readings, which has proved resilient to several subsequent revolutions in taste and theory, depends upon their utility for the understanding of many other things. Eliot's Donne occupied the center of a whole new literary history. Frye's Blake turns out to have been a prophet of Nietzsche and Freud and a great deal beside. As I have spun out my unlikely argument in this book, I have immodestly allowed myself to take heart from these glorious examples, adding to the pioneering arguments of Riewald and Felstiner a yet more ambitious thesis of *bouleversement:* it says that Beerbohm, where he appears trivial and trifling—as Donne where he seems tiresome and Blake where he seems lunatic—is in fact in dead earnest, is for the most part far in advance of the way readers have been construing him, and is indeed to be found at the center of the twentieth-century literary enterprise.

Beerbohm creates a Beatrice who belongs to us upon the ruins of whatever sense Dante's sweet new style may once have made. His parody of the *Commedia* is more than a compliment. It is a headstone. Dante's Rose, it says, is for us an object of praise, of analysis, of historiography; but Beerbohm's university is still the one that prints our books. Dante's vision of beatitude, whatever Chesterton and Belloc and Eliot and Yeats may have wished to make of it, has for us, if we are candid, the sedate allure of a chapter in the history of language; but Beerbohm's game of mastery, with its built-in assurances of failure, is the game we play. His apprehension of the duplicity of mirrors and the double duplicity of reading makes him the prophet not only of Stanley Fish and Jacques Derrida but of the entire tradition of modernist obscurantism and postmodernist indeterminacy. He dismantles, not Dante precisely, but our persistent desire to raise Dante from the dead. The crossword-puzzle structure of *Zuleika Dobson* offers us a modest eminence from which we may look down, with a little of a dandy's paradoxical elevation, at the garden path that meanders out of the gate in the cloister wall of Lewis Carroll's Christ Church and later passes near the footnotes to *The Waste Land* and sinks under the putative archeological

Dublin that supports the thick fabric of *Ulysses,* wandering at last, like Odysseus in Atlantis, among the commentaries upon *The Cantos* and *Finnegans Wake.* The "susceptible reader" whose face we see in Beerbohm's mirror might be the author of "Borges and I" or *Ada* or, for that matter, *Ecrits.* To say as much is not merely to make the claim, sooner or later advanced for every writer of consequence since Blake, that here is a modernist or a post-structuralist or some other fashionable thing *avant la lettre.* Rather, I am crediting Beerbohm with superior insight, craft, and candor. I am saying that, against the theological and Romantic and economic nostalgias that so qualify for us the charms and excellences of Eliot and Yeats and Pound, Beerbohm's text offers the refreshment one associates with the power to see and tell the plain truth. His specular quadrangle is the first, and in many ways the most thorough, construction of the epistemological *huit clos* that has turned out to be the obsessive scene of twentieth-century literature. It is not Paradise. But then, beyond their authors, who is convinced by the ones we find in *A Vision* or *Four Quartets?* However attractive, however useful to their poets, these are shams; their power is the force of sentimental insistence. "What I tell you three times is true" cannot make Paradise in this century.

Beerbohm's remarkable clarity arose from his sharp break with the Victorian fathers, particularly Arnold and Pater, whom he reread as vainly attempting to stave off what, in the event, was to be exactly his arrival. The dandy, from the first day that George Brummell terrified the Regent with a brass button, was the avatar of the acid semiotician, the man who had learned to read everything as if it were a printed book. It was only a question of when time would produce a Beerbohm, who learned, and taught, how to read a printed book as if it were a brass button.

His eye devastates. Once one has looked with him, the landscape alters permanently. There can be no slipping into an elegant study, as Wilde would have had us do, to fly with Dante among the angels or to converse with Shakespeare among the kings. Disbelief will no longer so readily hold to the hook, male ambition will no longer so easily imprison the female in a bellied glass.

These claims have but one test. The reader of this book must not stop with going back to *Zuleika Dobson.* There lies waiting a whole corpus we have scarely touched here. There are *Seven Men, The Mirror of the Past, Rossetti and His Circle;* there is a vast iconography of important persons and revealing moments set down in a universe of caricature few have explored with care, but certainly no less comprehensive than Dante's own; one may follow a long bibliography of critiques and essays and parodies and letters (collected and uncollected) upon which I have drawn freely without treating systematically: all of these I have left for the reader who, intrigued perhaps as I was when I began by the remarkable and subtle excellence of this writer's writer, would test whether the title of my book actually promises anything more than an ingenious or farfetched hermeneutic exercise.

Parallel and paralogy—the reader will do well to remember this simple toolkit when venturing into Beerbohm's universe. Half the charm of *Seven Men* springs from the hints it offers for a speculative literary history of the *fin de siècle*. Yeats, Dowson, Shaw, Chesterton, Wilde, Hichens, Stephen Phillips, the aging Robert Browning, Henry Irving, Herbert Tree, Thomas Hardy, George Meredith, and hundreds of others peep coyly out at us from the turns of phrases and the hitches in the prosody. What is the actual story of this book? No one has really attempted to tell it yet. The other half of the charm of *Seven Men* is what it teaches us about how to read. As an essay on the impossibility of finding, much less telling, the truth about a text or a writer, *Seven Men* has no apologies to offer to deconstruction. As an essay on the necessity of mastery in reading, on the surprising powers a critic must accept over the object of the scrutiny, *Seven Men* still has boldnesses to teach to admirers of *A Map of Misreading* and *Of Grammatology*. And when the reader has mastered its instructions, she or he may turn to the yet subtler comedy of *Rossetti and His Circle*. This work is more than Beerbohm's final paradoxical compliment, by way of Rossetti and Wilde, to Dante Alighieri: it is, rather, the introduction to a hieroglyphic epic vision that merits sustained attention even as our current critical agenda will demand it. This done, one may return with perhaps adequately opened eyes to Beerbohm's Otherworld, that succession of distorted and trans-muted figures of captains and poet, kings and goddesses, which gathers in power of revelation as one turns over the leaves of his thousands of brilliant caricatures. Lord Spencer swallowed by his own collar and the Queen of England buried in her own crepe, Wilde as silky and vegetable as the lily in his hand, Rossetti adrift in a cloud of opium, and the large unblinking eye looking out at us from the infant-serious face of an impos-sibly well-groomed Oxford under-graduate—these are indelible images. Immortal images, one might write, if anything were immortal in writing. And then, all of this seen, the reader might be ready for the real work that remains to be done.

There is the fifth act of the parody play *Savonarola*, which Beerbohm leaves us to write at the end of *Seven Men*. One would have to master parody as Max did in order to attempt this. But he does make the invitation, so perhaps one day someone will do it. There is *The Mirror of the Past* to be completed. This manuscript has lately been published in part, with a very prudent and modest narrative commentary to join the fragments. More is possible. The intrepid and heroic person who attempts this will need not only to be as good a parodist as Beerbohm but also as good a speculative historian and parallelogrammatologist. The time scheme, moving rapidly in opposite directions at the same time, will not be easy to manage. (One might advert to Nabokov's *Ada* to see how hopelessly entangled it is pos-sible to get in such a scheme.) The denouement will not be easy to tease out of the numerous contradictory hints Beerbohm has left. But the person who accomplishes this feat will have attained a formidable mastery, will have understood profoundly the subtle drama that begins the moment we realize that when we look at a mirror, something in the mirror, not ourselves, is looking back. This person will be able to show us, as Beerbohm promised, all the backs the mirror has seen leaving the room.

Any reader of *The Mirror of the Past*—and I expect it will, in the fullness of time, have many—will find occasionally while reading that the desire to perform this miracle begins to have an appeal. On such occasions, the reader will experience the particular pleasures I have been at such length trying to suggest in this book. They are the pleasures of challenge and of mastery, of finding and of losing again, of making a decision that must, of its very nature, expect that it cannot be quite right. There is always another parallel behind the thousand you find. There is always another paralogy to invent—more plausible, more daring, or at an angle that enables you to see out of the corners of your eyes, down some obscure defile at the far intersection of the mirrored walls, some few more images of the back, now just a little bald, of your turning head.

The Achievement of G. K. Chesterton

Stephen Medcalf

> *"I also dreamed that I had dreamed of the whole creation. I had given myself the stars for a gift; I had handed myself the sun and moon. I had been behind and at the beginning of all things; and without me nothing was made that was made. Anybody who has been in that centre of the cosmos knows that it is to be in hell."*
>
> —(The Poet and the Lunatics)

This speech of his character Gabriel Gale reflects what Chesterton says about himself in his *Autobiography* and elsewhere. He was haunted by a constant fear of discovering that there is no real link between our selves and things: or that there is no world external to our selves, that only our selves exist. The strongest case against him is the claim that knowing such a condition painfully, he simply revolts from it before understanding what it might mean. For (one might say) the feeling that nothing else may *be*— the thirst for outside things—may itself be an adolescent defence against things happening in the back of the mind. It would be significant—if this is the case—that it is precisely in adolescence that most people have gulped down Chesterton in great thirsty swallows. Significant again would be his declaration that he became a Roman Catholic "to get rid of my sins" and even the actual innocence which makes the remark surprising. For the innocence itself is suspect as a defence against the shadowland of one's mind and against representing oneself accurately to oneself: while the danger of sacramental confession is precisely that one acknowledges the darkness without understanding it, fitting one's complicatedly guilty self into a too easy and too public objective framework. This kind of shrinking might explain why so many of the characters in his novels are not three-dimensional but flat: why the love-affairs and the women happen at the edges of his stories: why his style is so recurrently verbal and rhetorical (the manic quality of Joyce's wit without the point about consciousness which Joyce is making): and why he spoilt his style further by pugnacity and compulsively extravert activity in journalism, as if in a kind of escape.

From *G. K. Chesterton: A Centenary Appraisal,* edited by John Sullivan. © 1974 by Stephen Medcalf. Elek Books, 1974.

399

It is important to see the exact nature of the charge. It is not of lack of awareness of the back of the mind, nor even of lack of interest in it. Chesterton was remarkable in his willingness to consider such things in his theology and his ethics. Visiting the Dead Sea in which Sodom and Gomorrah are drowned, he reflects that "in all our brains, certainly in mine, were buried things as bad as any buried under that bitter sea, and if He did not come to do battle with them, even in the darkness of the brain of man, I know not why He came." And of *Dr Jekyll and Mr Hyde* he observes that people "think the book means that man can be cloven into two creatures, good and evil. The whole stab of the story is that man *can't*: because while evil does not care for good, good must care for evil. Or, in other words, man cannot escape from God, because good is the God in man; and insists on omniscience."

The case against him is that he knew his shadow side if anything too well, adopted an arbitrary set of explanations to avoid going too deep into it, and wrote therefore in a kind of bad faith. Borges for example praises him for the monstrous nature of his fantasy, for the kind of terror which he spends so much of his best writing rejecting, like the terror experienced by Syme in the Council of Days:

> He could only fancy, as in some old-world fable, that if a man went westward to the end of the world he would find something— say a tree—that was more or less than a tree, a tree possessed by a spirit; and that if he went east to the end of the world he would find something else that was not wholly itself—a tower, perhaps, of which the very shape was wicked. . . . The ends of the earth were closing in.
>
> *(The Man Who Was Thursday)*

But to praise him for this is to praise him for failing in what he intended to do—for letting in the nightmares which he thought it his vocation to dispel. Borges observes that "Each story in the Father Brown Saga [as also in *The Poet and the Lunatics*] presents a mystery, proposes explanations of a demoniacal or magical sort, and then replaces them at the end with solutions of this world. . . . Each . . . undertakes to explain an inexplicable event by reason alone." And this, he thinks, is a symbol of Chesterton's life and beliefs. Father Brown himself would retort that the Unknown God's name is Satan: "the true God was made flesh and dwelt among us. . . . Wherever you find men ruled merely by mystery, it is the mystery of iniquity. . . . If you think some truth unbearable, bear it." All the same, perhaps it is true that—not Father Brown but Chesterton—sometimes dispels his mysteries too easily to account for their initial horror.

A similarly laudatory condemnation may be made of Chesterton's language. He is acute in observing; but (it may be said) he does not attempt to convey in his style the quality of what he observes. Thus he begins a story:

A thing can sometimes be too extraordinary to be remembered. If it is clean out of the course of things, and has apparently no causes and no consequences, subsequent events do not recall it; and it remains only a subsconscious thing, to be stirred by some accident long after. It drifts apart like a forgotten dream. . . . The thing [Harold March] saw . . . simply slipped past his mind and was lost in later and utterly different events; nor did he even recover the memory, till he had long afterwards discovered the meaning.

(The Man Who Knew Too Much)

The part played by this extraordinary thing in the story (it may be remarked without betraying the plot) supports Borges's formula. But there is a further point. T. S. Eliot, perhaps remembering this passage, has something very like it in ''The Dry Salvages'':

We had the experience but missed the meaning,
And approach to the meaning restores the experience
In a different form, beyond any meaning
We can assign to happiness.

The contrast makes very clear the difference between a style like Eliot's, which by obliqueness and omission conveys the very quality of an elusive mental experience, and Chesterton's univocal style, which confines itself to statement or at most to rhetoric.

Chesterton himself defends such a style. Once more, it is not that he is insufficiently aware of the deficiencies of univocal language, but that he is too thoroughly sceptical of the capacities of any kind of language to attempt to refine it. In his first full-length book, he says that any man who believes in the perfection of language ''knows that there are in the soul tints more bewildering, more numberless, and more nameless than the colours of an autumn forest . . . . Yet he seriously believes that these things can every one of them, in all their tones and semi-tones, in all their blends and unions, be accurately represented by an arbitrary system of grunts and squeals.''

This passage in its context—it is part of an argument that pictorial allegory, such as Watts's pictures labelled Hope or Mammon, are not to be explained by such *words* as Hope and Mammon, since the pictures are symbols equally expressive of the things the words represent—may explain a great deal of the vivid visual and oral symbols expressed in slovenly language which recur in Chesterton's prose and poetry. But the slovenliness remains slovenly.

Against the charge of bad faith in style he says:

We cannot understand the eighteenth century so long as we suppose that rhetoric is artificial because it is artistic. We do not fall into this folly about any of the other arts. We talk of a man picking out notes arranged in ivory on a wooden piano ''with much

feeling," or of his pouring out his soul by scraping on cat-gut after
a training as careful as an acrobat's. But we are still haunted with
a prejudice that verbal form and verbal effect must somehow be
hypocritical when they are the link between things so living as a
man and a mob. . . . As with any other artist, the care the eighteenth-century man expended on oratory is a proof of his sincerity,
not a disproof of it. An enthusiastic eulogium by Burke is as rich
and elaborate as a lover's sonnet, but it is because Burke is really
enthusiastic, like the lover.

(A Short History of England)

This does very well as an account of the kind of writing in which Chesterton
can be impeccable. Wherever he is using langauge like a musical instrument,
wherever there is no question of that odder use of language in which there
seems to be no gap between what one says and the words in which one
says it, he can approach perfection. He can convey collective emotion in a
great hymn: in his satirical verse every word hits the target: he was a
perpetual fount of aphorisms; and a most brilliant parodist. Of one of his
translations George Steiner observes appositely: "In the no-man's land between du Bellay's *Heureux qui comme Ulysse* and Chesterton's English sonnet, so nearly exhaustive of the original, we seem to hear '*encore l'immortelle
parole*,' Mallarmé's expression for the notion of a universal, immediate
tongue from which English and French had broken off" (*Penguin Book of
Modern Verse Translations*).

This is particularly apt because in this translation of du Bellay Chesterton strikes one as being aware both of what du Bellay might have wanted
to say in English and of the gap between what one can do with French
and what one can do with English. It is poignancy that he finds in du
Bellay: but he feels that the austere classicism of

Plus que le marbre dur me plaist l'ardoise fine

may sound only frigid in English: so he gives it

More than immortal marbles undecayed,
The thin sad slates that cover up my home.

Chesterton was much embarrassed by the disjunction between his
public self and his real person: but the disjunction is presumably connected
with his ability to impersonate. And it is this ability to impersonate, modified by his awareness of a strong system of values to judge what he is
impersonating, that makes his literary criticism and his biographies so good.
Robert Browning, Charles Dickens and *The Victorian Age in Literature* (especially
the descriptions of Rossetti and Swinburne in this last) are all in some
degree combinations of impersonation of and judgment on the authors
who had done most to form Chesterton's own art and personality, and on
the Victorian compromise which he loved and attacked. After the war and

his conversion to Rome, the studies—*St Francis of Assisi, Cobbett, Robert Louis Stevenson, Chaucer* and *St Thomas Aquinas*—are less biographical and literary, are less about the authors who had formed Chesterton and more about the Church and its ideals towards which he hoped to be transformed. But they are still impersonations. In all he balances between giving us the books of these people as they would have been if he had written them, or the actions as they would have been if he had done them, on the one hand, and on the other, giving us himself as he would have been if he had written those books or done those things. In all he holds the balance by reference to the scheme of values which he called Orthodoxy. In *Heretics* and in *George Bernard Shaw*, the element of impersonation vanishes, to be replaced by a sense of conversation between personal friends. But the sense of balance remains.

Chesterton does not, however, remain so steady when he is writing immediately from himself. The trouble is, not that he writes a perfect rhetoric to which it is indifferent whether he intended what he says, but that the rhetoric itself goes astray. In his less good verse and even in his best (*The Ballad of the White Horse*, in particular) marvellous writing will suddenly become too knotted for any clear meaning to be discovered at all, or lapse into an unconvincing frenzy. Or he will spoil a fine description with a lame joke.

The description of a horse which gives the keynote of *The Everlasting Man* is a clear example:

> Out of some dark forest under some ancient dawn there must come towards us, with lumbering yet dancing motions, one of the very queerest of the prehistoric creatures. We must see for the first time the strangely small head set on a neck not only longer but thicker than itself, as the face of a gargoyle is thrust out upon a gutter-spout, the one disproportionate crest of hair running along the ridge of that heavy neck like a beard in the wrong place; the feet, each like a solid club of horn, alone amid the feet of so many cattle; so that the true fear is to be found in showing not the cloven but the uncloven hoof.

Most of this gives the horse as one might see it freshly and for the first time, as a man with no concept of a horse might see it. The prose is as good as that of William Golding's tour de force *The Inheritors* in giving us the world of a man who does not conceptualize, and promises a style as generally revelatory as Golding's or William Mayne's. But halfway through a sentence Chesterton spoils the description with a joke about the cloven hoof—entirely conceptual and verbal, in quite a different mode from the passage up till then, and not a very good joke anyway. Imagination in Coleridge's sense has been abruptly replaced by fancy. The passage suggests two faults: first, an inability to leave well alone, a compulsive need for verbal wit, and secondly an uncertainty in Chesterton about what he is doing. Is the description mere verbal fancy, a trick to alter your picture of the horse, or is it real recognition?

For both the uncertainty and the compulsive resort to wordplay there are two possible explanations: first, that Chesterton has really felt a remote tremor of fear at the monster he has seen, and secondly that he felt a fear, or at least an unwillingness to contemplate that in himself which has enabled him to see it. For this ability raises the one question which haunted him: "Is there a world of clearly distinguished external objects apart from someone's consciousness of it, or not?"

Perhaps there is no great distinction between the two explanations, the one about Chesterton's subjectivity, and the other about a queerness in objects which his subjectivity revealed to him. He regarded with horror the abandonment of clear outlines; twice he renders this fear by the image of a fog—in *Manalive* and at the opening of *The Ball and the Cross*, where he comments that "the world of science and evolution is far more nameless and elusive and like a dream than the world of poetry and religion; since in the latter images and ideas remain themselves eternally, while it is the whole idea of evolution that identities melt into each other as they do in a nightmare."

Chesterton in fact calls his primitive picture of the horse "something very like a mad vision," and is inclined to say that "the traditional grasp of the truth" about horses—or about anything—is better. But because, as he often points out, in our present stage of civilization we seem to be in a condition "of mere fatigue and forgetfulness of tradition," he offers a technique of shock for beginning to grasp again the sane vision. And when he evolves a similar primitive picture of primitive man, he suggests that what we find is a being who saw in a way surprisingly similar to the way in which we see now.

The contrast with Golding's *Inheritors* is instructive here. Both authors are in reaction against the Whiggish view which they find in H. G. Wells's *Outline of History*: the view that the further we look back at the past of man the more simply crude and violent we see him, until he becomes indistinguishable from the animals. Both agree that there was from the beginning some radical strangeness about *Homo sapiens*. "Alone among the animals," says Chesterton, "he is shaken with the beautiful madness called laughter; as if he had caught sight of some secret in the very shape of the universe hidden from the universe itself. Alone among the animals he feels the need of averting his thoughts from the root realities of his own bodily being; of hiding them as in the presence of some higher possibility which creates the mystery of shame." Both seem to think that this quality should be described as if man were at once fallen and a new creation.

But Golding imagines a man before *Homo sapiens*, man unfallen and innocent in his instincts, without guilt because without self-consciousness: a man who, not being self-conscious, would conceptualize very little and therefore would perpetually see the world as Chesterton offers it, in the shock of newness. *The Inheritors* tries to imagine consistently what this world would be like.

Chesterton does not adventure on imagining a different kind of consciousness: it is probable that he would have thought this an impossible endeavour. He describes nothing beyond the earliest man of whose mind we have any knowledge, the man who painted the cave pictures, man already an artist, whose pictures of stag and cattle already show "that love of the long sweeping or the long wavering line which any man who has ever drawn or tried to draw will recognize." The pictures mean, he says, that already "a new thing had appeared in the cavernous night of nature; a mind that is like a mirror. . . . It is like a mirror because in it alone all the other shapes can be seen like shining shadows in a vision."

Golding, like the romantics and most of their successors, envisages consciousness as like a lamp whose projection on to the world one could imagine changed. Chesterton, as he here makes clear, thinks of it as a mirror. His scepticism about modern ambitions to represent the nature of consciousness emerges when, commenting on different kinds of obscurity, he says that Browning is so eager to get to the point that he will smash a sentence and leave only bits of it, whilst Henry James—refusing to accept on the mere authority of Euclid that the point is indivisible—tries to divide it "by a dissection for which human language (even in his exquisite hands) is hardly equal."

To divide the point—to analyse experience into constituents which lie only just within the brink of consciousness—to extend consciousness, and language with it, to a fineness of definition never before achieved—Chesterton is right in saying that this was what Henry James aimed at, and would perhaps have been right in adding that this marks the chief difference not only between Browning and James, but between most Victorian and most twentieth-century writers. Underlying this aim is a wish to divide the point in a further sense—to discover the point where our consciousness of the world begins—the point where our lines of perspective converge, at the back of our minds and in the beginning of our wills—because we know that our world is partly created from that point like a projection on a screen, and we *must* know what happens there.

About this aim in using language, and this wish about thinking, Chesterton himself is divided. It is very characteristic of him that he should choose an image, that of dividing the point, which shows both that he understood profoundly what twentieth-century writers want, and that he thought it unachievable.

One of his finest feats of historical imagination is that in which he argues that the early middle ages were ascetic towards nature, because awareness of nature in the classical world had been thoroughly defiled. The centre of a Roman garden was the statue of Priapus. "It was no good telling such people to have a natural religion full of stars and flowers; there was not a flower or even a star that had not been stained. They had to go

into the desert where they could find no flowers," before they could afford—or even have—the exultant passion for nature of St Francis Assisi.

This passage was perhaps in T. S. Eliot's mind when he wrote his own
study of purgation by abstinence in "Ash Wednesday" and may account
for the presence in "Ash Wednesday" of the garden god and the desert.
But Eliot, because he senses an unreliability in self-consciousness and its
projection on the world, tries to explore the nature of purgation, penitence
and self-consciousness in themselves. Chesterton envisages instead a
change of relation to the external world—centuries of abstinence, then
rebirth. And the nature which he envisages St Francis seeing again has its
own inherent and not projected meaning. The Franciscan birds and beasts
were like symbols, "like heraldic birds and beasts; not in the sense of being
fabulous animals, but in the sense of being treated as if they were facts,
clear and positive and unaffected by the illusions of atmosphere and perspective." Chesterton senses the unrealiability of consciousness as much
as Eliot: but his remedy was not to investigate the nature of that unreliability, to build his language out of an awareness of it, but to draw attention,
even with violence, to the external world.

A great deal of Chesterton's best writing—a second area where he can
be almost impeccable—describes the external world, but not in its primi-
tiveness. He describes (in this sort of writing) things conceptualized—as
understood by an innocent man's mind but still by a mind that concep-
tualizes—and argues that this is the way the world is. His description of
St Francis's world is developed when he says of some medieval illuminated
manuscripts in the John Rylands Library that they possess

> a quality that belongs to the simplest and the soundest human
> feeling. Plato held this view, and so does every child. Plato held,
> and the child holds, that the most important thing about a ship
> (let us say) is that it is a ship. Thus, all these pictures are designed
> to express things in their quiddity. If these old artists draw a ship,
> everything is sacrificed to expressing the "shipishness" of the
> ship. . . . If they draw a flower its whole object is to be flowering.
> Their pencils often go wrong as to how the thing looks; their
> intellects never go wrong as to what the thing is.
>
> (*Lunacy and Letters*)

In accordance with this ideal, Chesterton is at his best as a descriptive
writer when he is dealing with sharply distinguished objects which have
clear significance. Some of his lovingly-drawn light effects seem as if he is
describing not light but a painting of light.

> All the heaven seemed covered with a quite vivid and palpable
> plumage; you could only say that the sky was full of feathers, and
> of feathers that almost brushed the face. Across the great part of
> the dome they were grey, with the strangest tints of violet and

mauve and an unnatural pink or pale green; but towards the west
the whole grew past description, transparent and passionate, and
the last red-hot plumes of it covered up the sun like something
too good to be seen.

(*The Man Who Was Thursday*)

It is as if he were talking of brushwork. Indeed, when he describes either
man-made or natural objects, he often returns to his experience as painter
and draughtsman, as if asking, "What was going into this as it was made?"

He is skilful therefore in depicting anything designed by man (Jerusalem, for example, in *The New Jerusalem*), but especially paintings themselves, as when he says that Gainsborough "painted ladies like landscapes,
as great and as unconscious with repose, and . . . gives to a dress flowing
on the foreground something of the divine quality of distance." But the
empathetic quality of his writing on art extends to his descriptions of landscapes, when they can be seen as responsive to man. When he talks of the
South Downs in *A Piece of Chalk* he carries his own account of Gainsborough,
so to speak, through to describing landscapes like living beings.

The first volume of the Father Brown stories, furthermore, *The Innocence
of Father Brown*, has much of its impact, both in individual stories and in
its air of cohering as a single book, from a consistent use of symbolic
landscape (this occurs in later Father Brown stories, but less consistently
through a volume). The landscapes or interiors are nearly always convincing and familiar (seven are set in London, four in the English or Scottish
countryside and one in Paris). But they are also (very much as in Stevenson)
settings of dream, objective correlatives of something allied to or contrasted
with the inner weather of the mind which (rather than the crime itself) is
the real subject of each story—the dark hotel cloakroom where Father
Brown threatens Flambeau with hell, the Christmas party of Flambeau's
last crime, or the huge and lonely setting on Hampstead Heath where Father
Brown tells him that the universe is "only infinite physically . . . not infinite
in the sense of escaping from the laws of truth." The effect is at its height
in "The Sign of the Broken Sword," the story which most clearly escapes
Borges's charge of an inadequate shift from mystery to reason. It escapes
the charge because the moral defect at the end really outdoes in shame-
fulness the air of nameless evil at the beginning (as is made clear by Flambeau's two failures to guess the answer—a brilliant structural device): and
the nature of this defect, prepared for by the description of the frozen
woods in which the story is told, is brought home when Father Brown
suddenly points at "a puddle sealed with ice that shone in the moon." "Do
you remember whom Dante put in the last circle of ice?" he says and
Flambeau replies "The traitors." The uncompromising condemnation,
made by a reference to Dante's iron system of ethics, is expressed in a
realization of Dante's symbolic landscape.

It might be said that like his own Adam Wayne in *The Napoleon of*

Notting Hill Chesterton tends to describe all the world as if it were made by man because his childhood was spent in Kensington. His attempts to transform our vision of the world are at their most intense when he works on something urban. One might further say of him what Eliot says of Baudelaire: "It is not merely in the use of imagery of common life, not merely in the use of imagery of the sordid life of a great metropolis, but in the elevation of such imagery to the *first intensity*—presenting it as it is, and yet making it represent something much more than itself—that Baudelaire has created a mode of release and expression for other men."

Only the words will not mean exactly the same thing when used of Chesterton as of Baudelaire. For one thing, though Chesterton does describe the chaotic and sordid side of his London, he prefers a different kind of intensity: and for another he does it (following perhaps Dickens) with a kind of humour which is also poetry. Thus he observes that people "talk as if this claim of ours, that all things are poetical, were a mere literary ingenuity, a play on words. Precisely the contrary is true. It is the idea that some things are not poetical which is literary, which is a mere product of words. The word 'signal-box' is unpoetical. But the thing signal-box is not unpoetical; it is a place where men in an agony of vigilance, light blood-red and sea-green fires to keep other men from death." The wit of this appears when one's first reaction—(that this defence against verbalism is itself only a fantastic firework of words)—surrenders as word by word the sentence proves to be merely true. The only sense of excess is in the word "agony." Even that may not have seemed an exaggeration to Chesterton: it is worth remembering the advice of the doctor who towards the end of his schooldays said that Chesterton "must be preserved from mental shock or strain," since it was "even chances whether he became a genius or an imbecile." But this explanation would probably overemphasize the possibility in him of real madness.

But even in such intense passages as this, the language is still being used like a musical instrument. What is happening is less a fresh sight of a thing than a rearrangement of concepts. There is no assurance here that Chesterton has thought through and defeated the misgivings about consciousness which he certainly felt: only that he had found a refuge from them in intensfying traditional words and traditional feelings, and in recognizing and causing us to recognize their appropriateness in untraditional surroundings.

However, the passage about the signal-box comes from one of Chesterton's earliest books. At the other end of his career he knew what kind of style might achieve this assurance. He adumbrates it when he says that in reading the philosophy of Aquinas, he finds it makes

> a very peculiar and powerful impression analogous to poetry. Curiously enough, it is in some ways more analogous to painting, and reminds me very much of the effect produced by the *best* of the

modern painters, when they throw a strange and almost crude light upon stark and rectangular objects, or seem to be groping for rather than grasping the very pillars of the subconscious mind. It is probably because there is in his work a quality which is Primitive, in the best sense of a badly misused word. . . . Perhaps the impression is connected with the fact that painters deal with things without words. An artist draws quite gravely the grand curves of a pig; because he is not thinking of the *word* pig. There is no thinker who is so unmistakably thinking about things, and not being misled by the indirect influence of words, as St Thomas Aquinas.

The contrast here is very striking with his early passage relating the limits of language to the symbolic painting of G. F. Watts. Then, he thought both language and painting parallel attempts to symbolize something beyond adequate expression, and chose the genre of symbolic painting to illustrate his point. Now, he chooses a genre and a style which suggest that one can after all make a certain contact with the essences of things. The point of the analogy becomes clear when we find him saying elsewhere that the angles and jagged lines of Picasso and the Cubists suggest something that "seems to happen and not merely to exist."

For the primitive quality in Aquinas's style is due, Chesterton says, to "the intense rightfulness of his sense of the relation between the mind and the real thing outside the mind. That *strangeness* of things, which is the light in all poetry, and indeed in all art, is really connected with their otherness, or what is called their objectivity. . . . They are strange because they are solid." The object becomes a part of the mind, or the mind becomes the object, according to Aquinas; but because the object exists in itself "it enlarges the mind of which it becomes a part." The mind responds to objects, eats the meat of reality because "this feeding upon fact *is* itself." "The external fact," according to the Thomist Maritain,' "*fertilizes* the internal intelligence, as the bee fertilizes the flower."

Something like this does appear to be true of Aquinas's style and its queer movement from an intense abstraction to a brilliant concrete realization. Something like it is also true of Chesterton's own style at its best, as for example in the description of the horse and elsewhere in *The Everlasting Man.* "Look," these styles say, "this is the way things are: look how they stand out." They depart strangely from the ideal of langauge as symbolizing, towards that of language as pointing out.

In the depictions of landscape and sunset already mentioned, Chesterton could plausibly be accused of describing the world as if it were created by an allegorical painter, and perhaps even of carrying his technique of impersonation into the very mind of God. This is not just a trope, but the very thing which he regarded as his greatest temptation and most dreadful nightmare, Gabriel Gale's fear of finding oneself to be the centre of creation. But in other, and on the whole later descriptions, his style, as he says in his essay on the Book of Job of the speech of God, insists "that if there is one fine thing about the world, as far as men are concerned, it is that it cannot be explained." It is a style whose main object is wonder: a world whose maker, if one *could* imagine him, would appear "astonished at the things He has Himself made."

Thomism, although it embodied Chesterton's sense that the world is utterly other than anything he could have imagined, insists on the intelligibility of things. Chesterton's exposition allows this, but with a peculiar stress. For although he speaks with admiration of a language that deals with things, he makes clear that what he is primarily interested in is not the things distinct among themselves but their otherness from the self perceiving them. He says of a child looking at grass: "Long before he knows that grass is grass, or self is self, he knows that something is something."

This emphasis, this interest in the simple being or even happening of things, may go with, but is not the same as, an interest in their essential singularities. The latter interest, which Aquinas perhaps reveals more in his style than Chesterton does, will go with comparing and contrasting things with things, and will issue in a style like Aquinas's in which things, ideas, and things analysed by ideas, stand out stark and primitive. The former, which Chesterton tends towards, goes with expression, not necessarily of any particular detail of the concrete thing, but of its overall weight and impact, especially its unexpectedness.

This stress may account for the worst (and sometimes inexcusable) defect in Chesterton's writing: his swashbuckling carelessness about factual accuracy. His historical and theoretical writing—for example, the discussion of primitive religion in *The Everlasting Man*—is seriously marred by a refusal to give precise accounts, together with the commission of actual inaccuracies. The paradoxical consequence is that while Chesterton professed to speak to plain men, only a man as learned as himself could safely read these parts of his work. And since Chesterton, despite his preference for being a plain man, was phenomenally well-read and in an unsystematic way profoundly learned, these writings are shut off from being useful.

His criticism too is careless of accuracy. There is no excuse for a man who makes detailed close criticism of a quotation which he prefaces (as Chesterton habitually does) "I quote from memory and probably wrong." And he quotes violently out of context when he attacks Kipling for admiring England without loving her.

In a very interesting poem he [Kipling] says that:

"If England was what England seems"

—that is weak and inefficient; if England were not what (as he believes) she is—that is, powerful and practical—

"How quick we'd chuck 'er! But she ain't!"

Even the full version of the refrain

> If England was what England seems
> An' not the England of our dreams
> But only putty, brass an' paint
> 'Ow quick we'd drop'er! *But she ain't!*

shows what the rest of the poem bears out: Kipling means "If England were only powerful and efficient, and all the other things that go with putty, brass and paint, we could not love her; but we find an almost inexplicable love of her, bound up with our dreams, has grown up as we have fought and watched our friends die for her."

Chesterton did not verify his references. And yet with all this, how sensitive he is to the use of language. His discussions of Othello's

> I know not where is that Promethean heat

and of how it differs from saying "I do not know how I am to bring her to life again"—of Milton's

> Dying put on the weeds of Dominic

and its "certain unexpected order and arrangement of words . . . like the perfect manners of an eccentric gentleman"—or of the "earthquake ellipsis" in Blake's

> How the Chimney-sweeper's cry
> Every black'ning Church appals—

are both good in themselves, and parts of excellent studies of the nature of poetry. Here Chesterton is saying "Look! notice!" with wisdom and effect. And he does this even with what few critics can disentangle enough from prejudice to touch at all: the Bible. His remarks on the Book of Job and the Gospels make one read those books, perhaps for the first time, as books.

One must give similar praise, in spite of all their inaccuracies, to his treatments of anthropology. The anthropology popular in his own day he accuses of "a trick of making things seem distant and dehumanised merely by pretending not to understand things that we do understand." In contrast, his own approach anticipates in many ways that since particularly associated with Professor Evans-Pritchard. As we have already seen, he insists that the most primitive men of whom we know have had an inner life essentially like our own. He not only points out how like sophisticated man primitive man may be, but how primitive sophisticated man remains. "Creative expression like art and religion" was distinct from the beginning from natural experiences and natural excitements: folklore does not deal with "stupid and static superstition" but, like the metaphors of poets, with something that "stirs in the subconscious," and was created and believed in with the same shades "of sincerity—and insincerity"—as daydreams. A sacrifice to Pallas Athene might have the same seriousness as Dr Johnson's touching all the posts in the street, or a deeper and more religious sentiment, though perhaps never the seriousness with which Dr Johnson reached towards the Cross.

This insistence on the uniformity of human awareness, which suffered under the charge of externality when we considered Chesterton's analysis and expression of his own consciousness, works like his impersonations of Browning and Dickens towards interiority when he deals with the consciousness of other men. He insists on looking at myths "from the inside," asking how one would tell the story oneself, and on knowing what totems, or loyalties, or religion "meant in the mind of a man, especially an ordinary man."

When he deals with the external world, the predominance in his concern of thereness over quiddity allows lapses into verbal wit and a thousand unnecessary hyperboles. But all the same he is interested in pointing out the nature of things, and specially the inward nature of things. At times his methods work together towards a real uncovering: for example—

> When fishes flew and forests walked
>   And figs grew upon thorn,
> Some moment when the moon was blood
>   Then surely I was born.
>
> With monstrous head and sickening cry
>   And ears like errant wings,
> The devil's walking parody
>   On all four-footed things.
>
> The tattered outlaw of the earth,
>   Of ancient crooked will;
> Starve, scourge, deride me: I am dumb,
>   I keep my secret still.
>
> Fools! For I also had my hour;
>   One far fierce hour and sweet:
> There was a shout about my ears,
>   And palms before my feet.
>
>   ("The Donkey")

The first verse is well-devised rhetoric: a piece in the tradition of the *impossibilia* which goes back through Horace and Virgil to Archilochus: not used here (as normally in earlier writing) to feed in fancy a delight in the grotesque, but, as Chesterton says of the grotesque in *Robert Browning*, "to touch the nerve of surprise and thus to draw attention to the intrinsically miraculous character of the object itself."

The fourth verse is equally good in a quite different way: it reads like pure feeling: as if a chink opens in the donkey's memory (he remembers only what a donkey might, the immediate physical sensations seen in front

and heard on all sides, with a vague sense only of something important)—
a window on something which gives sense to the world. The allusiveness
has a further meaning: what gives sense to a creature's world cannot itself
be given a further sense, and therefore must lie, half-expressed, at the edge
of that creature's world. But the palms and the shout are concrete and real
too: the connection of value with detail and concreteness is very characteristic of Chesterton. "The personal is not a mere figure for the impersonal;
rather the impersonal is a clumsy term for something more personal than
common personality. God is not a symbol of goodness. Goodness is a
symbol of God," he says.

But the intermediate verses are more puzzling. The structure is clear
and neat: the third verse leading from the donkey's tattered insignificance
to his possession of a secret, and suggesting his pains that need some
atonement, and the second verse describing a real thing, the donkey himself, in the light of the fantasy of the first verse. But it is possible to feel
that under the influence of the what-might-have-been of the first verse,
the poem has turned slightly loose from the donkey. If one is supposed to
be looking freshly at the actual, a donkey's bray may be sickening but is
his head really monstrous, his ears really like errant wings? And did the
devil really create him as a parody on, among other beasts, the hippopot-
amus? In fact, has the devil much place in this verse, even if we allow him
his presence as the cause of the donkey's outlawing in the third verse
(although the notion that the donkey looks like a creation of the devil is
important still in that verse, and still hyperbolic)? And even if one allows
the poem to remain grotesquerie, and ignore the real donkey, is it quite
consistent with itself? Is the loud diabolic monster of the second verse the
same as the maltreated meditative animal of the end? The pathos and
sublimity of the end depend on one's mind shifting to the small beast one
sees in fields—the patient ass with mild eyes, "a companion and not a
monstrosity" whose ears, admittedly "unduly developed," Dorian Wimpole scratches in *The Flying Inn*—the animal which is the first he loves
because it is "like a man."

The charge is the general one against Chesterton: able at grotesquerie,
inspired with religion, he is too irresponsible to deal with fact, will beat it
any way he likes, so that finally doubt is cast on his religion also. One
could defend the poem against internal inconsistency by saying that it is
about redemption—one's mind should shift from a diabolic creature to a
sweet and meditative one because that is the effect of Christ's riding on it.
But one cannot thus defend Chesterton against the charge of remoteness
from real donkeys, or against rhetorical inconsistency in making donkeys
whatever suits his context.

Another reading would carry the clangour and grotesquerie through
to the end; perhaps Chesterton means one to think of Christ riding on the
devil's parody with its wing-like ears and monstrous head. The grotesquerie
then would not be the device used, as we suggested earlier, to stand the

world "on its head that people may look at it," but would be what Chesterton distinguishes from it in *Robert Browning*, "the element of the grotesque [which] in nature means, in the main, energy, the energy which takes its own forms and goes its own way." He might even have in mind in "The Donkey" the passage which he quotes from *Mr Sludge, the Medium* in which God is revealed "close behind a stomach-cyst."

But, although this may be the right reading of the second verse, it strains the last verse. The word "Fools!" introducing the last verse seems to reflect back on the whole poem hitherto; and the poem seems then to shift indeed in sense from verse to verse. We begin by seeing the donkey at its most grotesque as part of a fantastic background; then for a moment the donkey described in more detail seems to fit the violence of the background. But it will not do: donkeys are not quite like that, and as in the third verse we focus more accurately on the derided beast we find its dumb donkeyness pointing beyond itself to something transcendent.

This fourfold motion—from fantasy (imagined transcendency) through a fact whose primitive essence is realized by being set in fantasy, and then, after a new attitude of the mind has been set up, to a transcendence found in the fact—is the essence of Chesterton's thought. Its expression in a movement of style from discordant imagery and clangour to something subtle and still recurs in both his poetry and prose. The second and third terms of the motion seem to correspond to Hopkins's *inscape* and *instress*. In the imagery that expresses these ideas—the vivid colours, the detailed patterning, the storm and violence—Chesterton and Hopkins have much in common. The huge difference in syntax and rhythm corresponds, as one would expect, to Chesterton's contrast of Browning and James. Chesterton cares less than Hopkins about the motion of his mind in relation to the fact, more about pointing to the fact itself. He is altogether more careless, more public, forensic, and argumentative. Yet he reaches at times a stillness while Hopkins remains in the storm. It is not too far-fetched to say that Chesterton uses the late Victorian and Edwardian violence and grotesquerie which he shares with Kipling, Swinburne and even Hopkins, as Herbert used the metaphysical conceit: to reach simplicity.

But though we may allow that Chesterton does persuade us of his capacity, and mankind's, to reach the objective, the comparison with Hopkins only emphasizes the charge that in doing this the public nature of his style is covering up something in the subjective world, and that therefore his religion and his treatment of psychology are external and uncomprehending. The earliest of his books in which these charges are seriously at issue is *The Napoleon of Notting Hill*. The theme of this book seems at first sight to be the poetry of cities, and in particular the survival of heroism and love of locality in the deadest megalopolis. It begins with a polemic against prophets of the future which suggests that what we are to have is an attack on scientific Utopianism like Forster's *The Machine Stops*, but in a comic mode.

If this were all, it would be enough to say that after the brilliant de-bunking of the preliminary essay, the book soundly thrashes the futurology of its time by giving a prophecy—remarkably funny throughout—that London in 1984 will be first concerned (under a government of civil servants and business men) with the solution of traffic problems by driving roads through unwilling communities, and then with antagonism to "the vast machinery of modern life" breaking out in violence. As a prediction, this is impressive: but if the book were only that, it probably would support the charge of externality.

But in fact Chesterton, realizing that this first theme is both comic and tragic, transforms his subject into the antagonism of humour and tragedy themselves. It is as if Blake, having written

> The fields from Islington to Marybone,
> To Primrose Hill and St John's Wood,
> Were builded over with pillars of gold,
> And there Jerusalem's pillars stood.
> (*Jerusalem*, plate 27)

had known that this was capable of being comic as well as of being sublime. Humour at the beginning of *The Napoleon* undercuts everything else (per-haps the genesis of Auberon Quin, who was partly a portrait of Beerbohm, is in Chesterton's remark on Victorianism in *George Frederic Watts*: "Mr Max Beerbohm waves a wand and a whole generation of great men and great achievement suddenly looks mildewed and unmeaning"): "I have never been to St John's Wood. I dare not," says Quin. "I should be afraid of the innumerable night of fir trees, afraid to come upon a blood-red cup and the beating of the wings of the Eagle. But all these things can be imagined by remaining reverently in the Harrow train." And it is only a joke.

But humour itself is undercut when Adam Wayne says flatly: "Notting Hill is a rise or high ground of the common earth, on which men have built houses to live, in which they are born, fall in love, pray, marry and die. Why should I think it absurd?"—at which Auberon feels as he makes his friend Barker feel by saying "Why trouble about politics?"—"as if the floor of his mind had given way."

But Wayne is not thereby proved right. He is undoubtedly slightly mad, in precisely the ways in which Chesterton usually defines madness: he is obsessively logical and "only laughed once or twice in his life." His whole tragic enterprise remains threatened for the reader, until the last dialogue, by the sheer comedy of the book, and by the sense that Quin—through whose eyes we mostly see—watches it with "a sense of detach-ment, of responsibility, of irony, of agony"—knowing that it is all a joke. There is a threat of total nihilism.

But in the last dialogue, when the division between Wayne and Quin becomes overtly an image of human life, Wayne answers the notion that a derisive omnipotence might look at the world in Quin's way with an argument not unlike that of Bertrand Russell's "A Free Man's Worship":

> "Suppose I am God, and having made things, laugh at them."
> "And suppose I am man," answered the other, "And suppose that I give the answer that shatters even a laugh. Suppose I do not laugh back at you, do not blaspheme you, do not curse you. But suppose, standing up straight under the sky, with every power of my being, I thank you for the fools' paradise you have made. . . . If we have taken the child's games and given them the seriousness of a Crusade, if we have drenched your grotesque Dutch garden with the blood of martyrs, we have turned a nursery into a temple. I ask you, in the name of Heaven, who wins?"

Satisfying as this is as a note on values in a universe of chance, it is not the book's final answer. When Wayne is persuaded that his life has been in fact Quin's joke, he realizes and makes Quin realize that they are both mad. The final appeal is beyond both their mad worlds, to the being who can both laugh and love: ordinary common man.

The book is as purely agnostic as it can be: the last dialogue is wholly humanist. Remaining on that ground it successfully challenges and defeats nihilism. It is a philosophical ballet rather than a novel: but it is a very good philosophical ballet.

Chesterton's next novel *The Man Who Was Thursday* moves on from the ground which *The Napoleon of Notting Hill* captured. The seriousness of man's life is taken for granted: the question is raised "Does that give us any guarantee that the world in which man lives makes sense?" The book's subtitle is *A Nightmare,* and its most remarkable passages embody the terror of being trapped in a dream from which one cannot escape: Syme in the presence of the Council of Days, the pursuit in snow by Professor de Wurms, the blank faces of the Professor and Dr Bull next day, the duel with the Marquis de St Eustache who cannot be wounded, and the moment on the pier when the world seems to be ending. In most of these, as in *The Napoleon of Notting Hill,* the thing to hold on to is the thought of "common and kindly people"; especially the girl Rosamund whom Syme met before the nightmare began. Once there is something else: the snowy cross on St Paul's against a sickly sky suggests that "The devils might have captured heaven, but they had not yet captured the cross." But there is neither of these supports during the passage in which nightmare extends to the physical world, Chesterton's most intense statement of the fear of solipsism. Even the story's recurrent device, that apparent evil is shown to be good, adds to the insecurity:

> The inside of the wood was full of shattered sunlight and shaken shadows. . . . Now a man's head was lit as with a light of Rembrandt, leaving all else obliterated; now again he had strong and

staring white hands with the face of a negro. . . . This wood of witchery, in which men's faces turned black and white by turns, in which their figures first swelled into sunlight and then faded into formless night . . . seemed to Syme a perfect symbol of the world in which he had ben moving for three days, this world where men took off their beards and their spectacles and their noses, and turned into other people. That tragic self-confidence which he had felt when he believed that the Marquis was a devil had strangely disappeared now that he knew that the Marquis was a friend. He felt almost inclined to ask after all these bewilderments what was a friend and what an enemy. Was there anything that was apart from what it seemed? The Marquis had taken off his nose and turned out to be a detective. Might he not just as well take of' his head and turn out to be a hobgoblin? Was not everything, after all, like this bewildering woodland, this dance of dark and light? Everything only a glimpse, the glimpse always unforeseen, and always forgotten. For Gabriel Syme had found in the heart of that sun-splashed wood what many modern painters had found there. He had found the thing which the modern people call Impressionism, which is another name for that final scepticism which can find no floor to the universe.

The sight of a peasant in a forest clearing, the common man again, rather unsatisfyingly enables Syme to recover from this mood, but it recurs in the chase of Sunday, and the goonish or even Beckettian humour of the notes he hurls back at his pursuers, as he begins to appear to be incomprehensible Nature itself. (He is incidentally the most medieval of Chesterton's creations, of a middle ages less stable and stylized than Chesterton thought them: his nearest relation is the Green Knight of *Gawain and the Green Knight*.) At the end and suddenly nature turns round and shows its face. The six friends have argued about Sunday in a way confined, like the last dialogue of *The Napoleon*, to human experience. But this book adds revelation: "I am the Sabbath," says Sunday, "I am the peace of God."

The movement of the dream persuades us that this is true: he is "contentment, optimism . . . an ultimate reconciliation." But this discovery does nothing to remove the nightmare. "We wept, we fled in terror, the iron entered into our souls—and you are the peace of God," says the Secretary, "Oh, I can forgive God His anger, though it destroyed nations; but I cannot forgive Him His peace."

As in the Book of Job, a possible answer is given by the irruption of an accuser who denounces Syme and the rest (as Syme at the comic beginning of the book denounced a policeman) for being safe. Their isolation and heroism in face of nighmare has earned them the right to answer "You lie." But though this may give a reason for their fate, it does not answer the Secretary's denunciation of God's peace. The dream ends as Sunday's face fills the universe and a voice picks up what was implied by the snowy cross on St Paul's: "Can ye drink of the cup that I drink of?" But this is a moment of nightmare, as if the pain of God answering the accusation against His peace merely surrounds us with horror. There is a further twist and a further answer: a particular physical detail, the red hair of the accuser's sister, the girl Rosamund. It several times breaks like reality into the trapped world of the dream, and the ending of the book after the dream is a still scene in which Syme sees "the sister of Gregory, the girl with the gold-red hair, cutting lilac before breakfast, with the great unconscious gravity of a girl."

There is a sense in which the whole book is about Syme's realizing that he is in love with Rosamund. The agony of aloneness in the dream, the pursuit of reality, is perhaps the reluctance of commitment to someone one loves: and the reconciliation in the book with the fact of being and the nature of the universe is grounded in the physical detail of the beauty and strangeness of her hair. Since the hair may be Frances Chesterton's, it may be thought that the book provides a very good answer to the accusation that Chesterton ignores some reluctance or defect in himself in his fear of the non-existence of the external world. The only defect about *The Man Who Was Thursday* is Chesterton's suggestion in his *Autobiography* that it was *only* a nightmare. That is precisely to treat cheaply the fear that the world is nightmare which it was the book's business to challenge and defeat. Chesterton's fiction (especially, except for *The Poet and the Lunatics*, the post-war fiction) does seem to wane in force in proportion as he fails to do justice to nightmare.

His remaining major novel, however, *The Ball and the Cross*, again challenges a kind of nightmare: not this time that the world is chaotic, but simply that it is hollow: the enemy is still a kind of relativism. In the story, so to speak, Quin and Wayne go on the wanderings begun on the last page of *The Napoleon of Notting Hill*. Wayne, as Ewan MacIan, is little changed, still heroic, still a little mad: only he is now a Catholic and wishes to fight not for his birthplace but for the Virgin Mary. James Turnbull differs more from Quin: he is an atheist of the Victorian tradition, and although the book is again in a sense about the breakdown of what Chesterton called the Victorian compromise, the breakdown comes about not because humour challenges its greatness, but because the two parties to it, common-sense ethics and Christian dogma, can no longer be held back from fighting. The book is vitiated by slightly too many dialogues in which too often MacIan as a Catholic tends to get the better of Turnbull. But he is unable to convince Turnbull, and the *story* makes it clear once again that both are wrong. Turnbull has no reason for his ethics: but MacIan is a man of superstition, who identifies a universal religion with a particular society and particular phenomena. He sees a world in which everything is transparent, such as is "figured in the coloured windows of Christian architecture": a red cloud seems to him the bloody hand of Heaven pointing at

Turnbull's death. His religion is bound up with the feuds of the highlands and with respect for the chieftain, even with the return of the Stuarts. Chesterton has been accused (wrongly, in terms of this story) of the defects of MacIan: with confusing the church militant with the church triumphant, symbol with reality. MacIan believes only in the Cross, in Christianity as religion: there is no point of contact between him and Turnbull who believes only in the Ball, in the secular world, except that they both take their beliefs and their conflict seriously, and are therefore totally isolated in the modern world. They rouse against themselves a series of representatives of the modern world's determined indifference to their quarrel and find themselves in the end in the lunatic asylum provided by complete relativism, docketed as suffering from (respectively) religious mania and Eleuthero-mania.

They are not wrong in relation to relativism, but they are wrong. In visions in the asylum, when they see respectively the King come back and the Revolution accomplished, they reject their own dreams because both find them inconsistent with justice for real and individual human beings. Still helpless to escape or to convince one another, they find everyone they have ever met confined in the asylum with them for various psychic disorders which cause the belief that one has met Turnbull and MacIan. Their combat has merely persuaded the nation into believing that insanity is present in everybody. The story almost ends in mere destruction like the conflict of Naphta and Settembrini in Thomas Mann's *The Magic Mountain:* there is no other escape from the deadlock. In fact the end is more like the outbreak of the 1914 war in that book. Turnbull and MacIan have decided that physical combat will not settle their differences: but one of their fellow madmen, a French bourgeois, having decided that the asylum represents an intolerable society, burns it down "in accordance with the strict principles of the social contract." It is the only possible escape.

But this is not the whole story. It is framed in a story with a slightly different theme, whose first episode is perhaps the heart of everything Chesterton ever wrote. It is a kind of war in heaven between Michael (a Bulgarian monk) and Lucifer (inventor of a flying machine). As they fly through a London fog which images chaos, in a diabolic heaven like that behind St Paul's in *The Man Who Was Thursday,* Lucifer assures Michael of the truth of what MacIan and Turnbull are to find in the asylum: "Since our science has spoken the bottom has fallen out of the universe." During the controversy that follows, Lucifer pushes Michael out to swing from the Cross of St Paul's.

In a magnificent description of what it would be like to climb down the dome of St Paul's, Michael after a spasm of clarity and a spasm of terror experiences some state which is not hope, nor faith, nor knowledge, but complete and of the present, positive, a satisfaction: "It seems almost as if there were some equality among things, some balance in all possible contingencies which we are not permitted to know lest we should learn indifference to good and evil, but which is sometimes shown to us for an instant as a last aid in our last agony."

When he steps out of the infinity in which he experiences this on to Ludgate Hill, Michael sees a new universe, because in that one moment there has been for him a new creation. "Everything his eye fell on it feasted on, not aesthetically, but with a plain, jolly appetite as of a boy eating buns. He relished the squareness of the houses; he liked their clean angles as if he had just cut them with a knife." This impression—this solid world—is repeated at the end when Turnbull and MacIan find Michael in a sealed cell at the asylum whose master is Lucifer: a cell of porcelain tiles such as they have been confined in, with one spike sticking out in a way which they have found they loathe. Michael tells them he is in a good place, with tiles to count. " 'But that's not the best . . . Spike is the best, said the old man, opening his blue eyes blazing; it sticks out.' "

It is Michael before whom, as he comes miraculously out of the blazing asylum, Turnbull kneels as before a saint. Michael's experience can be appealed to beyond the duel of the Ball and the Cross, and is a resting place beyond relativism. The spike sticking out and the clean-cut corners are exact symbols for a universe that is not hollow: which is satisfying because it is and has characteristics. They are like the Donkey, or Rosamund's hair or the world of *St Thomas Aquinas* or even of Picasso and the Cubists. But in *The Ball and the Cross* there is something added: this glory of finitude is the obverse of the infinite, still moment outside ordinary experience which preceded it. As Chesterton said later of St Francis's love for finite things, "the mystic who passes through the moment when there is nothing but God" sees both everything and "the nothing of which everything was made." He sees, like Michael, the act of creation.

Michael's experience (not perhaps quite one of God) is the same as that which is the centre of *The Ballad of the White Horse.* That is a poem of extraordinary heights and depths, from an inevitability like that of the sayings of Christ in

> I tell you naught for your comfort

to the appalling self-parody of

> the hands of the happy howling men
> Fling wide the gates of war

It is partly about despair, and partly about battle. But its centre is a confrontation with despair: first the despair of Alfred at circumstances, at unceasing defeat, and secondly the radical despairs which he confronts in the Danish leaders. Of the four barbarian leaders, one is a straightforward thief, a consumer of civilization: but the other three are given speeches accorded a kind of convincingness which Chesterton does not accord, for example, to the arguments of Turnbull. They seem to be feelings that he recognized in himself: Elf's song of the fallenness of the world:

> There is always a thing forgotten
> When all the world goes well
>
> . . . .
>
> The thing on the blind side of the heart,
> On the wrong side of the door.

Ogier's choking, destructive rage (a rage which, justified or not, almost kills the man who feels it, and which one might be surprised at Chesterton's knowing, if it were not for some of his political writings) and Guthrum's proclamation that death is everywhere:

> And a man hopes, being ignorant,
> Till in white woods apart
> He finds at last the lost bird dead

but most distant in battle, when "we seem to tread it down." And that does seem to be part of the point about Chesterton's own frenetic activity, and in particular about his imaginative obsession with violence and the dreadful lapses of aesthetic and moral judgment which he commits in writing about it: he fights to forget misgiving. One thinks of the "happy howling men" already quoted, or of the curiously disgusting as well as implausible description in *The Napoleon of Notting Hill* of blood, "running, in great red serpents, that curl out into the main thoroughfare and shine in the moon." The very worst example comes in *The Ballad of St Barbara*, in which Chesterton attempts to rewrite the *White Horse* in terms of the Battle of the Marne and comes out with the line

Blast of the beauty of sudden death, St Barbara of the batteries!

That is a most significant line, because rhetorically it is a good one: Chesterton's penchant for noise transmitted into poetry, both sense and sound. And it is one of his most univocal lines: first because it is so wicked a line, with its saint made into a goddess of destruction, that one can only believe that Chesterton had lost all contact with the reality of which he is talking, the bloodied flesh. It is like the blood he speaks of in *Treasure Island*, which he can bear in quantities (and he is not sure whether this is because the blood is only crimson lake or because "a child is not wicked enough to disapprove of war") but is terrified by when it is the few drops of blood drawn from the apoplectic Billy Bones's arm. But secondly the mention of "sudden death" is univocal in the sense that it deliberately excludes an overtone: St Barbara, as the poem's subtitle declares, is "the patron saint of artillery and of those in danger of sudden death." The line therefore ought to have the overtone, "Barbara, protectress of those killed by the batteries." But it does not: in the poem Barbara protects only Frenchmen, not Germans ("*They* are burst asunder in the midst") and here "sudden death" means only that she kills. The poem is like that section of the *Aeneid* which deals with the battle of Actium, in which Virgil forgets what in almost every other line is the very quality of his poetry: that both sides in a conflict have feelings. Chesterton picks on this passage as demonstrating Virgil's "moral sanity." "Nobody can doubt his feelings when the demons were driven in flight before the household gods." Chesterton's pugnacity, which took very moving form in his dying words in 1936 ("The issue is now quite clear. It is between light and darkness and everyone must choose his side.") at other times in his life so possesses him with the meaning of a conflict that he both forgets the complexity of issues and transmutes the physical reality of wounding which he never saw, into a hard, bright allegory.

Nevertheless mere pugnacity (as opposed to definiteness of choice) is only peripheral in him. When battle is joined, Alfred's captains go down in succession before the three evils: every quality in which Chesterton ordinarily trusted, first English common kindliness before Elf's eerie misgiving, then law, thought and Rome, which defeat Elf, before mere rage, and finally romantic paradoxical Irish heroism before the full rush of the Danes. Against these despairs stands "the ultimate moment of despair and its transmutation." In the stillness which follows, Alfred finds like Michael a point altogether outside ordinary feeling, and, like a child rebuilding a sandcastle, determines to fight again. It recalls the first quietness in Athelney in which his memory gave him a small image of his childhood; and in it, smaller again, a manuscript illumination of the Virgin and Child: and then suddenly the world became solid:

> All things sprang at him, sun and weed,
> Till the grass grew to be grass indeed

and the picture existed in front of him. As with "The Donkey" the essence of a thing reveals a transcendent presence: Mary's, who gives a message again beyond ordinary feeling.

As with Michael the infinite moment is the obverse of thanksgiving for finitude. And Chesterton's rhetoric is employed at its best in the defiance which Alfred gives Elf, Ogier and Guthrum:

> For our God hath blessed creation
> Calling it good. I know
> What spirit with whom you blindly band
> Hath blessed destruction with his hand;
> Yet by God's death the stars shall stand
> And the small apples grow.

The words, which normally move quickly at the speed appropriate to a narrative poem, become still and slow, so that the effects of each word can be noticed—the opposite senses of *blessed*, the surprising justice of *death* after *destruction*, and the startling stop on a detail.

It is this combination of emotions in Alfred (a plausible guess at the historic Alfred who wrote in the words quoted on the original title-page of the *Ballad:* "I say, as do all Christian men, that it is a divine purpose that rules, and not Fate") which justifies Chesterton's lines on the White Horse itself, left to fade and darken by the Danes:

> it is only Christian men
> Guard even heathen things.

The enemy is the forgotten growth, like that in Elf's song, which quietly devours the Horse.

> the little sorrel, while all men slept,
> Unwrought the work of man.

In this evil stillness the poem almost ends except that in one last verse Alfred properly ends it, defiant.

Chesterton tried to repeat the effects of the *White Horse* not only in the disastrous *St Barbara* but also in "Lepanto." That is one of Chesterton's impeccable poems: the noise, and the contrast between gallant and sick colours, work perfectly, and the rhetoric is so perfect that anyone paying due attention to the lines while reading aloud has difficulty with tears at the sudden shift

> And he finds his God forgotten, and he seeks no more a
>   sign—
> (But Don John of Austria has burst the battle-line!).

The defiance of fate is there too, and two moments of stillness against the noise—Cervantes's ironic stillness at the end, and the Pope's in

> The hidden room in a man's house where God sits all the year.

All the same, it is less lovable than the immensely flawed *White Horse:* too univocal, too forgetful that the Turks may have had human beings among them, and that the Christians certainly used galley-slaves.

The image of the hidden room, too, seems better used in the prose of *The Everlasting Man*, when Chesterton says that the story of Bethlehem "surprises us from behind, from the hidden and personal part of our being . . . as if a man had found an inner room in the very heart of his own house which he had never suspected; and seen a light from within . . . it is the broken speech and the lost word that are made positive and suspended unbroken."

Once again, one cannot help suspecting that something of this went into "Ash Wednesday," in the lines immediately following those quoted earlier about the garden:

> The token of the word unheard, unspoken

and the first lines of the next section:

> If the lost word is lost, if the spent word is spent
> If the unheard, unspoken
> Word is unspoken, unheard,

But this time, Chesterton's effect does compare with Eliot's, not univocal but evocative, and subtly moving.

There is in fact in Chesterton's writing a centre which escapes the criticisms gathered under the head of externality. It is apparent again and again in the three major novels and in *The White Horse*, although, except in *The Man Who Was Thursday*; not without being muffled up in defects.

The doctrine at this centre he exposed in the comparably good apologetic books, *Orthodoxy* and *The Everlasting Man*. *Orthodoxy* in particular succeeds in the difficult feat of expounding a total and objective philosophy while always preserving the pressure and involvement of one man's concern. Christanity in the twentieth century is normally presented as claiming the whole of experience and yet as being explicitly about only a part of experience—the religious and the more difficult parts of the ethical. In that part however it presents doctrines which transcend experience. Christians have tried to reconcile this paradox in three principal ways: by reducing the transcendent element to the secular, by reducing the totality of experience to the religious, and by claiming that there are implicit elements in Christianity and the secular which make them coincide without reduction of either. The third, the only one which escapes the charge of dishonesty, is also the most difficult: it is always liable therefore to collapse into one of the other two. Chesterton (whose temptation is to the second course) in *Orthodoxy* keeps substantially to the third. "Things," he said, "can be irrelevant to the proposition that Christianity is false, but nothing can be irrelevant to the proposition that Christianity is true."

The centre of this relevance is "the fact that one must somehow find a way of loving the world without trusting it": Chesterton's way is the belief that "God was personal and had made a world separate from Himself." The most moving passage in the book is that in which Chesterton asserts the extremity of this relation of God to the world, in Gethsemane and in Christ's cry of dereliction. He tells us that if the atheists should wish to choose a god "They will find only one divinity who ever uttered their isolation: only one religion in which God seemed for an instant to be an atheist."

This is clearly the same as the final assertion of *The Man Who Was Thursday* and involves the same theodicy: that omnipotence makes God incomplete, that God to be wholly God must know what to be a rebel is like, and what courage is—that the soul passes a breaking-point—and does not break. Paradoxically, here and throughout *Orthodoxy* Chesterton's appeal is, as in the novels, to the idea of a complete man. He develops first the idea of obsessive madness as a limitation, and points the likeness to it of various philosophies alternative to Christianity. Then, asking for an idea which does justice to the opposite good qualities in man, he develops a notion of sanity and a generous ethic which find their fulfilment in the magnificence and meekness of Christ.

Behind the particular demands which Chesterton makes of a philosophy that is to fit the universe, he says, lie fairy-tales. His defiance of fairy-tales is an important part of the tradition which runs from George MacDonald (and ultimately Coleridge) through himself to C. S. Lewis and J. R. R. Tolkien: and undoubtedly the peculiar quality of fairy-tale is important to the queerly magical quality of some of his best writing, and to the question whether one likes or even understands his work as a whole. His critical writing anyone can admire; but of his more personal works Auden is right in saying "There are, I know, because I have met them, persons to whom Grimm and Andersen mean nothing: Chesterton will not be for them."

The quality in question is not what is ordinarily associated with fairy-tale: it does not involve belief in magic, and has nothing to do with superstition, fancifulness or unreality. It is not anarchistic nor irrational. It is a vision of something perpetually fresh: always a new heaven and a new earth, which are quite certainly the old ones. "All the fire of the fairy-tales" is derived from a primal vision of the world, perhaps the first vision of childhood, "an almost prenatal leap of interest and amazement." It is a vision that we have forgotten, in which the common world was as wonderful as a fairy-tale. "All that we call common sense . . . and positivism only means that for certain dead levels of our life we forget that we have forgotten." But fairy-tales, Chesterton says in the same phrase that he used to describe Browning's grotesquerie, "Touch the nerve of the ancient instinct of astonishment," and for the same reason—"to draw attention to the intrinsically miraculous character of the object itself." "These tales say that apples were golden only to refresh the forgotten moment when we found that they were green." The arbitrariness of physical fact in fairy-tales partly reflects this. The only satisfactory words for describing nature are "charm," "spell," "enchantment": all physical fact is contingent, everything is fresh because it might have been something else.

But there is a further consequence of this arbitrariness. Seen against this background, what remains constant (in fairy tales and in the world as seen in their light) are the laws of logic and morality. Chesterton's most vivid statement of these beliefs is in the first of the Father Brown stories, already quoted for the appropriateness of the symbolic landscape in which Father Brown tells Flambeau that the universe is not infinite in the sense of escaping from the laws of truth. "Look at those stars," he goes on, "Don't they look as if they were single diamonds and sapphires? Well, you can imagine any mad botany or geology you please. . . . On plains of opal, under cliffs cut out of pearl, you will still find a notice-board 'Thou shalt not steal.' "

This pattern of a fairy setting which sheerly emphasizes the essential truth of daily experience is the pattern of a great deal of Chesterton's poems and stories: that of "The Donkey," for example, is a special form of it. The Father Brown stories, in particular, though their apparent genre is detective fiction, have much more the quality of fairy-tales. The early ones, as we saw earlier, concentrate their effect on a landscape and an atmosphere at once symbolic and real. The later ones seem often to be deliberate attacks on the conventions of realistic fiction, defences such as Iris Murdoch and John Bayley have written since of the openness of human character. But they always have some clue to a stable interpretation in the human power of imaginative sympathy, "The Secret of Father Brown."

Of all Chesterton's best fiction, what he says of George MacDonald's novels holds true.

> The commonplace allegory takes what it regards as the common-places or conventions necessary to ordinary men and women, and tries to make them pleasant or picturesque by dressing them up as princesses or goblins or good fairies. But George MacDonald did really believe that people were princesses and goblins and good fairies, and he dressed them up as ordinary men and women. The fairy-tale was the inside of the ordinary story and not the outside. One result of this is that all the inanimate objects that are the stage properties of the story retain that nameless glamour which they have in a literal fairy-tale.

The fairy-tale pattern seems to be the inward reason for Borges's formula for Chesterton's stories. Seen in this light they do not "undertake to explain an inexplicable event by reason alone": rather they surround "solutions of this world" with mystery. This attempt of course is compounded with the other attempt to combat nightmare. Partly because of this mixed aim, and partly because (as Arthur Machen observes of his own similar stories), it is too easy to translate "awe . . . into evil," (*Far Off Things*, 1922), Chesterton's stories sometimes fail. But they succeed often enough to give the lie to the criticism of Chesterton's beliefs which underlies Borges's formula. They bear witness to a religion which is not fundamentally a rationalizing escape from nightmare: it is wonder and worship.

Although, then, the charge of externality, and even of a flight from the inner, holds against a great deal of Chesterton's work, anyone who makes it against his major writings is almost certainly missing their real inner quality. Charles Williams observes that poetry does not communicate emotions or belief, but knowledge of our capacity for an emotion or a belief. Chesterton's inner quality is to communicate knowledge of our capacity for believing in God as creator and of enjoying our position as creatures. Ultimately this knowledge is based on the still, infinite moment, the experience of which he perhaps rather points to than communicates. Ultimately, that is, what he says is based on a faith or experience not of art but about the universe. But what he communicates could be understood and enjoyed short of accepting this experience.

It is possible to hate God as understood by Judaism and Christianity; to hate Him not because of any aberrations of theologians about Hell or the Atonement, but because of something essential to the idea of a God who is at once creator of the world and fountain of moral demand. We have seen something of Chesterton's dealing with the problem of the existence of external evil in a world created by the Good. We have seen that his belief in a personal Creator is actually the direct result of his apprehension of a world that is at once overwhelmingly good—whose very existence demands a loyalty and love that outweighs any particular defect— yet desperately horrible. Particularly in the chapter of *Orthodoxy* called "The Flag of the World" we find his demand for "a fiercer delight and a fiercer discontent" with the world satisfied *only* by belief in a Creator who makes moral demands of His creation.

But there is a more radical hatred of God, for which the issue is not about any removable defect of the world, but about any possible state of being of an intelligent creature who is constrained by his own identity and laid under demand by moral law. Chesterton, in an attack on Milton's treatment of the Fall, argues that Adam fell by "that profoundly inartistic anarchy that objects to a limit as such. It is not indicated [in the Bible] that the fruit was of attractive hue or taste: its attraction was that it was forbidden . . . . The finest thing about a free meadow is the hedge at the end of it. The moment the hedge is abolished it is no longer a meadow, but a waste, as Eden was after its one limitation was lost."

As this would suggest, Chesterton's strongest philosophical antipathy is to the Nietzschean tradition which denies God, constraint of identity and moral law at once. He represents the position not unfairly with another analogy from painting, in the conversation between Dorian Wimpole, Joan Brett and Lord Ivywood at a gallery of "Post-futurist" abstract art:

> "If you wake up tomorrow and you simply *are* Mrs. Dope, an old woman who lets lodgings at Broadstairs . . . in what way have *you* progressed? . . . Don't you see this prime fact of identity is the limit set on all living things?"
>
> "No! . . . I deny that any limit is set upon living things. . . . I would walk where no man has walked; and find something beyond tears and laughter. . . . And my adventures shall not be in the hedges and the gutters; but in the borders of the ever-advancing brain. . . . I will be as lonely as the first man. . . . He discovered good and evil. So are these artists trying to discover some distinction that is still dark to us."
>
> "Oh . . . then you don't *see* anything in the pictures yourself?"
>
> "I see the breaking of the barriers . . . beyond that I see nothing."

Very interestingly, it is in this novel (*The Flying Inn*) that Chesterton displays great skill in analysing radical changes of character: Dorian Wimpole's seven moods when he is left alone in a wood with a donkey, Joan Brett's decision between Patrick Dalroy and Lord Ivywood, and Ivywood's transition from gentleman to fanatic—of which the last is most impressive. It is as if he were trying to satisfy himself of what are the limits of change in human personality before the culminating event of the book—when Lord Ivywood, declaring himself "above the silly Supermen," goes mad.

About Chesterton's insistence on accepting identity as a limit, two things must be said. First, in conscious contrast with the decadents, he makes a demand for commitment at the heart of man's shifting unpredictable openness, which corresponds to his preference for clear outlines and enduring essences in the external world. In his exploration of the conditions for having an enduring self he closely resembles Kierkegaard. *Orthodoxy* insists on the necessity to living of real commitment with a real risk: and in one light essay—"A Defence of Rash Vows"—he says most of what Kierkegaard says in *Either/Or* of the difference between the "ethical" and the "aesthetic." "The man who makes a vow makes an appointment with himself at some distant time or place." But in modern times the "terror of one's self, of the weakness and mutability of one's self, has perilously increased, and is the real basis of the objection to vows of any kind. . . . And the end of all this is that maddening horror of unreality which descends upon the decadents." Throughout *The Everlasting Man* he argues that this difference of commitment exists between Christianity and paganism: polytheists do not believe in their gods in the same way as Christians believe in God, but as one believes in daydreams. Christians believe in God, on the other hand, with the same seriousness as both they and polytheists believe in ethics. The demand is again for the commitment, the seriousness which makes the difference between the aesthetic and ethical, and imposes on one the kind of limitation of identity which Adam and Lord Ivywood refuse.

But secondly, when he comes to consider despair, Chesterton recognizes that mere commitment is not enough: that human personality must pass into very strange regions indeed before it can continue its commitment to ethics or even to living. There is after all something of the idea of the Superman which is common to Chesterton's two ultimate men, Michael and King Alfred, and to his picture of St Francis as well. Like Lord Ivywood they are alone, and find something beyond tears and laughter. Their difference is that after having made the movements of infinity, they make those of finiteness. The phrases are Kierkegaard's, from his description of the knight of faith. It is probable that Kierkegaard is the thinker nearest to Chesterton: the most Chestertonian passage in literature is this same description of the man who delights in watching the new omnibuses on his Sunday afternoon walk, is interested in everything that goes on, in a rat which slips under the curb, in the children's play, who looks like, indeed is, a bourgeois Philistine or the grocer over the way smoking in the twilight—yet who makes at every instant the movements of infinity. "He knows the bliss of the infinite, he senses the pain of renouncing everything—and yet finiteness tastes to him just as good as to one who never knew anything higher."

Parabolically, when Innocent Smith throws away his house and marriage and walks round the world to find them again—to find a house with a green lamp post and a red pillar-box—he is acting out the secret Kierkegaard agonized to know—the secret by which he could marry Regine Olsen while still doing justice to his own frightful vocation and solitary temperament. He reconciles flinging the world away with taking it up again, and challenges besides the classical and Enlightenment incredulity that an infinite God could be interested in particular individuals and events. Smith believes both that we are all in exile, and that God has bidden us love one spot to defend us from worshipping infinity. "Paradise is somewhere and not anywhere, is something and not anything." Even "God is not infinite; He is the synthesis of infinity and boundary." Smith's gesture is repeated by others of Chesterton's lunatic heroes, as they sever themselves from their lives to find them again—by Gabriel Syme, Gabriel Gale, Patrick Dalroy, Ewan MacIan and by the Wild Knight. And he models his picture of the mysticism of St. Francis on the same experience.

> Sunder me from my bones, O sword of God,
> Till they stand stark and strange as do the trees

writes Chesterton, and the quotation from Hebrews—"the word of God is . . . sharper than any two edged sword, piercing even to the dividing asunder of soul and spirit, and of the joints and marrow"—is not just a trope: the sense of pain is intended, the pain of being separated from oneself in order to wonder at, know and save oneself—"I know there's a fellow called Smith, living in one of the tall houses in this terrace," says Innocent Smith. "I know he is really happy, and yet I can never catch him at it."

The outcome of this is always wonder, and the end is the peculiar simplicity—"costing not less than everything"—of Alfred, Michael and St Francis. They have believed, have despaired, and have picked up the world again through something infinite which lies on the other side of despair. Grounded in infinity, loving the finite, Man's whole happiness consists in being a creature, in receiving the world as a child receives a present, as "a surprise." "But surprise implies that a thing came from outside ourselves; and gratitude that it comes from someone other than ourselves. . . . Those limits are the lines of the very plan of human pleasure." This is the answer, and the right answer, which Gabriel Gale gives to the terror of solipsism in the story with which we began.

Kierkegaard has at the end of *Fear and Trembling* another Chestertonian passage, in which he compares the discontent of his generation, who have not reached faith, yet "assume the place which belongs by right only to the Spirit which governs the world and has patience enough not to grow weary," to children who always want a new game because they lack "the lovable seriousness which belongs essentially to play." Chesterton likewise says that in considering the perpetual repetition of the universe it is possible to feel that "we have sinned and grown old, and our Father is younger than we." Alfred is compared to a child playing and a child playing to God. A healthy man, again, is known from a lunatic because his minor acts are "careless and causeless": the final secret of God, Christ and Christianity is joy.

Perhaps the most convincing proof of Chesterton's own wisdom and even sanctity is his capacity for sheer humour. One must list among his triumphs *The Club of Queer Trades*, the conversation of Humphrey Pump in *The Flying Inn*, "The Rolling English Road," and even such a remark as Misysra Ammon's that "the Arabic article 'Al' as in Alhambra, as in Algebra [has many appearances in connection with English] festive institutions, as in your Alsop's beer, your Ally Sloper, and your partly joyous institution of the Albert Memorial."

Kafka said apropos of *Orthodoxy* and *The Man Who Was Thursday*, "He is so gay, that one might almost believe he had found God." In spite of darkness, what one primarily remembers of Chesterton is that he was a happy man: and that he looked forward to the end of the world, when God's *delight* shall be with the sons of men.

The Postponement of England's Decline: *Howards End*

Barbara Rosecrance

It is time to reinterpret *Howards End,* that strange, ambitious, uneven work, which seems to mark a final affirmation of Forster's humanism and the end of his youth. Forster's fourth novel in six years and his last major piece of fiction before the appearance of *A Passage to India* fourteen years later, *Howards End* is in important respects unique. Alone among the novels it grapples head-on with the claims of the "outer" world, confronting problems of economics and social class in a society transformed by industrial growth and shadowed by approaching war. The fantasy world of *A Room with a View* yields in *Howards End* to the realities of power, money, and class as they impinge on the values of self-realization and personal relations; Forster's critique of industrialism suggests the failures alike of the business mind and the liberalism of upper-middle-class intellectuals.

The religious impulse that in all the earlier novels takes the form of a search for individual fulfillment is here directed to the social arena: the "unseen" is to be sought in right relations of the "seen." The exhortation to "connect" encapsulates an ideal of proportion and compromise that will reconcile the "inner" values of imagination, sensitivity, and personal relations with the "outer" energies of power, practicality, and action. Concurrently with its social application of spiritual values, *Howards End* is the novel most explicitly devoted to the ideal of personal relations. Forster chooses, as his approved missionary of connection, a sensitive and articulate woman, a decision that appears to have freed him from the ambivalence he showed to earlier male heroes, for he gives Margaret Schlegel almost absolute moral authority. She and Henry Wilcox, the energetic imperialist whom she marries, are terms in the hypothesis that the action

From *Forster's Narrative Vision.* © 1982 by Cornell University Press.

tests: can the values of personal relations and connection be made to operate within the context of social reality?

As in *The Longest Journey*, the central issue becomes the question of England's inheritance, envisioned in the values of rural tradition. But England's salvation, which the earlier novel seemed to promised, has become a lost cause. The encroaching city is a dominant menace: in the dwindling countryside Howards End itself is a brave survival. In *The Longest Journey* a shepherd moved to London to embark on inexorable decline. *Howards End* presents that decline in the career of Leonard Bast, a dispossessed yeoman whose urban poverty allows him to reach the life of neither body nor spirit.

Victimized both by industrial capitalism and by the well-meaning intellectual class that is one of its beneficiaries, the petit-bourgeois Leonard is lost, doomed to the failure of his impulse to knowledge, condemned to early death by severance from his rural heritage. Howards End and its shadowy guardian, the first Mrs. Wilcox, symbolize this heritage: bequest of the farm to Margaret is intended to signify the alliance of rural virtue with the humanistic ideal. After vicissitudes, the novel ends with Schlegels and Wilcoxes living in harmony at Howards End, where Margaret presides as regent for the infant heir, who synthesizes earth and intellect and embodies what hope remains for England's survival. The diverse characters who dramatize these ideas function in a plot that must be admired for the degree to which we accept its outrageous premises and far-fetched events: the marriage of Margaret and Henry, the mating of Helen and Leonard Bast, Helen's pregnancy, Leonard's death, and the shattering and reformulation of alignments and inheritance.

Finally, the multiple themes and the action that exists to further them are interpreted by a uniquely intrusive narrative voice. The narrator of *Howards End* retains the familiar techniques of his predecessors. But *Howards End* presents more than an acceleration of earlier modes. For we encounter in this novel the most intensely personal of all Forster's narrators, of all his fictional voices the most self-conscious and dramatic. Critics have never adequately addressed the issues raised by this voice and its alterations as these define and reveal the relations in *Howards End* between Forster's narrative technique and his changing world view. They have instead focused on the novel's engagement with social issues and have accepted as Forster's intention the purpose stated in his epigraph, "only connect." Trilling, whose engaging but limited study of Forster has once again been reissued, regarded *Howards End* as "Forster's masterpiece," praising its "maturity and responsibility" and contemplating with approval its timely concern with England's fate. Wilfred Stone regards the novel as "a test of the ability of Bloomsbury liberalism to survive a marriage with the great world." Frederick Crews sees it as the projection of "a reasonable hope for the survival of liberalism."

Most critics express a common awareness of disjunction between Forster's avowed purpose of reconciliation and its accomplishment in the action. Crews sees the problem as an incompatibility between themes: "Despite [Forster's] effort to give the Wilcoxes their due, the real point of *Howards End* is the familiar individualistic one." Alan Wilde formulates the issue as a "defective articulation of the symbolic and realistic levels." In this view, plot, symbolism, and motif project Forster's longing for purpose and direction in life as it should be; the psychological dramatization of Magaret and Helen Schlegel's search for meaning comes closer to his vision of life as it is. This split also appears in discrepancies between ideology and dramatization in the portrayals of Henry and Ruth Wilcox. Critics additionally have expressed dissatisfaction with the novel's resolution because, despite the plot's assertion of connection accomplished, the ending seems rather a victory for the Schlegels than a reconciliation between values.

However accurate, such readings are incomplete. Although they recognize that *Howards End* is more complex than its predecessors, they omit an important dimension of the novel's meaning. Critics have rightly noted the strain and failures of Forster's asserted synthesis but have wrongly regarded as causes what are really symptoms of a more fundamental difficulty. Nor do such readings explain the unusual narrator of *Howards End*. Finally, *Howards End* has been seen largely as the climax of Forster's aims in the earlier novels, dramatically separate in content and implication from its successor, *A Passage to India*. Thus, for Trilling, *Howards End* is Forster's greatest work because "it develops to their full the themes and attitudes of the early books and throws back upon them a new and enhancing light." Wilde is explicit about the schism: "The gulf that separates *A Passage to India* from Forster's earlier novels is far more profound than that which exists between any two others of his books." Time and history define the gulf: the Great War appears to most critics an unbridgeable chasm between Georgian meliorism and modern alienation.

Important differences in content and technique do separate the prewar novels and *A Passage to India*. But we may more accurately assess *Howards End* if we recognize the degree to which it already formulates the attitudes and conceptions of the final novel. The substantial passage of time between the two books enabled Forster to structure and refine his issue: his experiences in India in 1912–13 and 1921 gave him the context for its embodiment in fiction. But the essential subject of *A Passage to India* is already present in *Howards End* as a growing sense of existential impasse, as the linguistic and thematic expression of negation. The essence of this view pervades the novel, as does a concurrent impulse toward a transcendent unity. Surely these are the ingredients that come together in the brilliantly coherent images of *A Passage to India*, in which Forster has taken the logical next and last step.

To understand the centrality in *Howards End* of preliminary versions of the vision of *A Passage to India* enables us better to locate and explain the unique qualities of this penultimate novel. It also allows us, while recognizing that *Howards End* brings to culmination important themes of the earlier novels, to define it as more than the climax of one phase in Forster's thought and art. Seen rather as part of a continuum in which it closely anticipates its successor, *Howards End* reveals the progression of Forster's thought toward the metaphysic of *A Passage to India*. Finally, comprehending the relation between Forster's expressions of cosmic apprehension in *Howards End* and his strenuous attempts to prove its values enables us to identify the sources of disjunction in the novel and to understand their consequence in the narrative voice.

The conscious intent of *Howards End* is to resolve conflict and affirm possibility. Yet throughout the novel Forster undercuts his attempts at an optimistic synthesis by repeatedly projecting chaos. The real source of problems in *Howards End* is neither imbalance between "inner" and "outer" values nor contradiction between the aims of conciliation and victory, but rather a deeper tension that these difficulties mirror, between Forster's efforts to "prove" his humanistic values and to sustain Western society through reversion to rural virtues, and a countercurrent of disbelief, a deepening pessimism expressed through images and motifs that evoke, in a new and menacing world, a vision of cosmic disorder and loss of meaning. The rhetoric affirms connection, but the undercurrent describes collapse. This tension invades all aspects of the novel. It explains the disjunctions in theme and character; it pervades and determines Forster's narrative voice.

The case for personal relations and the inner life opens with the novel's first episode, as Helen Schlegel becomes briefly enmeshed in a disastrous romance. The retreating Paul Wilcox who, frightened by his impulsive declaration, "had nothing to fall back on," illustrates "panic and emptiness," a phrase later to suggest a more cosmic vacuum. Here it evokes Helen's credo: "I know that personal relations are the real life for ever and ever." "Amen," responds her sister. A Moorean good-in-itself, personal relations form the keystone of the inner life, and Forster verifies the sisters' article of faith through his endorsement of Margaret, who articulates familiar components of the humanistic ideology: "at thirteen she had grasped a dilemma that most people travel through life without perceiving. Her brain darted up and down; it grew pliant and strong. Her conclusion was that any human being lies nearer to the unseen than any organization, and from this she never varied." The inner life thus comprehends a belief in the primacy of the individual and a concern with the metaphysical implications of human action. The concept also includes, as the action will demonstrate, personal integrity, the capacity for introspection, and the ability to "connect."

Seeking to vindicate the Schlegel sisters' avowal, Forster emphasizes the vicissitudes of the important relationship between them. When Margaret has decided, against Helen's advice, to marry Henry, the sisters can still maintain their relationship because, the narrator explains, "there are moments when the inner life actually 'pays,' when years of self-scrutiny, conducted for no ulterior motive, are suddenly of practical use." Margaret lapses temporarily from her own ideal when she participates in the deception of her husband's plan to "hunt" the sister who has mysteriously withdrawn from contact: to reestablish her credentials, "she had first to purge a greater crime than any that Helen could have committed—that want of confidence that is the work of the devil."

Dramatized as faith between Margaret and Helen, the inner values are more than intrinsic goods. Forster generalizes Margaret's perception of the commercialization of Christmas as "the grotesque impact of the unseen on the seen" to locate the inner life in his metaphysic. "But in public who shall express the unseen adequately? It is private life that holds out the mirror to infinity; personal intercourse, and that alone, that ever hints at a personality beyond our daily vision." The inner life is nothing less than the sole emblem of divinity: to affirm its primacy would seem the novel's major intent.

Yet the epigraph "only connect" suggests a competing purpose. As a plea for wholeness, this ideal does operate in personal relations and may apply both to the union of Margaret and Henry and to the reconciliation of extremes within the individual psyche whose absence Henry's schism of passion and prudery demonstrates: "Only connect the prose and the passion, and both will be exalted, and human life will be seen at its highest. Live in fragments no longer. Only connect, and the beast and the monk, robbed of the isolation that is life to either, will die." Forster here restates the desire to bridge human incompleteness that the earlier novels rendered in the attempts of their flawed heroes to find meaning through contact with the qualities they lack. But in *Howards End*, connection transcends the individual, as Forster seeks a social contract between power and sensibility through the union of the capitalist mind with the imagination of the liberal intelligentsia. In this search he makes a real attempt, albeit within a limited spectrum, to connect imaginative vision with economic reality. The terms imply a pluralism whose goal is England's survival. A successful rubber merchant, Henry Wilcox guides the empire. His ventures provide jobs for a growing class of urban workers like Leonard Bast and guarantee the incomes of intellectuals like the Schlegels, who seek a moral distribution of economic gain. Henry's pragmatism has saved Howards End when its surviving yeoman owners could not, "without fine feelings or deep insight, but he had saved it"; and "Henry would save the Basts as he had saved Howards End, while Helen and her friends were discussing the ethics of salvation."

But in the businessman's relation to social equity and national survival, Forster depicts neither successful connection nor well-meant failure. Critics have observed the limitations of Henry Wilcox and decried his emasculation at the novel's end. Forster's inability to give Henry his due reflects more than his distrust of Henry: it expresses the general despair of human possibility that undercuts the novel's formulas of hope and its rhetoric of affirmation.

The business mind offers no social synthesis. The employment Henry Wilcox gives clerks is subject to the vagaries of a system in which they have no share. The clichés of nineteenth-century liberalism provide Henry's disclaimer of responsibility: "it is all in the day's work. It's part of the battle of life. . . . As civilization moves forward, the shoe is bound to pinch in places, and it's absurd to pretend that anyone is responsible personally." Businessmen destroy tradition and violate the natural order. A millionaire businessman tears down Margaret's London house to build flats. Henry Wilcox owns shares in a lock that shortens the Thames. Wilcox spoliation is both personal and symbolic: dust from the Wilcox car "had percolated through the open windows, some had whitened the roses and gooseberries of the wayside gardens, while a certain proportion had entered the lungs of the villagers"; "The Great North Road should have been bordered all its length with glebe. Henry's kind has filched most of it." Finally, despite Henry's service to Howards End, he has barred himself from relation to England: "the Wilcoxes have no part in the place, nor in any place. It is not their names that recur in the parish register. It is not their ghosts that sigh among the alders at evening. They have swept into the valley and swept out of it, leaving a little dust and a little money behind."

But Wilcoxes are not simply ephemeral. Part of "the civilization of flux," they add number without quantity. "A short-frocked edition of Charles also regards them placidly; a perambulator edition is squeaking; a third edition is expected shortly. Nature is turning out Wilcoxes in this peaceful abode, so that they may inherit the earth." Implicated thus in the issue of inheritance, Wilcoxes provide a pernicious apprehension of the future: "the Imperialist is not what he thinks or seems. He is a destroyer. He prepares the way for cosmopolitanism, and though his ambitions may be fulfilled the earth that he inherits will be gray."

Despite Forster's approval, the Schlegels' share in the national synthesis is no greater than Henry's. Margaret and her sister represent the situation of England's liberal intelligentsia in a time of economic expansion and national unease. The Schlegels and their friends comprehend the economic basis of culture. Their realism extends to concern for the consequences of capitalist exploitation and for the economic and intellectual poverty of the new class of urban workers, and they spend much time discussing ways and means of achieving a more equitable distribution of money and culture. But the modern age displaces them as inexorably as it grinds down Leonard Bast. When the Schlegels' home is destroyed to make way for urban flats, it is clear that although money can save them from want, it cannot save them from the rootlessness that Forster portrays as a modern horror. Ineffective in their attempt to help the struggling classes beneath them, the liberal intellectuals present, finally, an image of liberalism's impotence to influence social change and national survival.

It is significant that although Forster exposes the ineffectuality of the liberal dialogue, he never repudiates Margaret's position. In his endorsement of Margaret's insights and didacticism, in his lack of detachment from her manipulations, Forster identifies himself not only with the intelligentsia, but also with the alienation of the outsider and the powerlessness of women. The female predicament transcends intellectual boundaries, for Ruth Wilcox, not an intellectual but a woman, cannot save her declining farm. "Things went on until there were no men." The eclipse of Margaret and Henry by Margaret and Helen offers additional evidence of his allegiance. *Howards End* takes its impetus from the failure of a heterosexual relationship and finds vindication in the success of a single-sex one. While this countering of the "official" ideology enacts the tension between love and friendship familiar from the earlier novels, its significance here lies in Forster's allegiance to characters who are alienated from power. Margaret triumphs over the philistines: "She, who had never expected to conquer anyone, had charged straight through these Wilcoxes and broken up their lives." But although women prevail at Howards End, they have no power in the public arena. Margaret does not reform Henry's politics: she only destroys the vital energy that was his chief attraction. Henry at the end is "pitiably tired," by his own admission, "broken."

The businessman retreats from the world he sought to dominate; the intellectual withdraws from hopeless debate to vanishing rural sanctities. Whatever Forster's "outsider" status contributed to his inability to conceive Wilcoxes as part of a national synthesis, his derivation of the evils of modern society from their philistinism reflects the doubt that undercuts the novel's attempts at social reconciliation. Furthermore, his displacement of focus from the social hypothesis to the privatism of affection between Margaret and Helen presents an alliance with sterility. In their limitation and disjunction, the ideologies both of personal relations and of connection imply a darker view, even though, at the same time, they represent Forster's most strenuous assertion of social possibility and human potentiality.

Amid the apostrophes to individuality and the inner life, the reader of *Howards End* becomes aware that personal relations are no longer very important. Although the values of nature and the past are posed as complementary to the human efforts to achieve harmony, ultimately these efforts are submerged in the larger question of England's fate. Well before her marriage to Henry Wilcox, Margaret begins to move beyond a concern for personal relations. She prophesies that she will end her life caring most for a place; the realization makes her "sad," but by the novel's close, Forster will describe Margaret's remoteness as an approach to metaphysical insight. Like human life, personal relations are ephemeral; the agitations of personality have no effect on the rural serenity in which ultimate value resides. Margaret's attempts to introduce Mrs. Wilcox into her "set" and her aid with Mrs. Wilcox's Christmas shopping are activities inimical to the inarticulate virtues Mrs. Wilcox represents. The party talk is empty, the shopping futile, as Mrs. Wilcox signifies by her rejection of Margaret's choices. Margaret's attempts at connection are no more germane. Her ability to connect seems the moral prerequisite for her guardianship of Howards End, but as intellectual, social conscience, comrade, and artist of the imagination she is ultimately irrelevant. To assume the mantle of the first Mrs. Wilcox, a character conspicuously devoid of creative imagination, Margaret must withdraw. In spite of her dogged affection for Henry, when she begins to acquire the essential vision, "the sense of space, which is the basis of all earthly beauty" and which leads her to contemplate England as a rural sanctity, she must forget "the luggage and the motor-cars, the hurrying men who know so much and connect so little."

Although initially Forster presented personal relations both as intrinsic good and as the sole path to the spiritually absolute, personal intercourse depends on other values. When Mrs. Munt and Charles Wilcox quarrel, Mrs. Wilcox is able to separate the foes because "she worshipped the past . . . and let her ancestors help her." In a nomadic civilization, divorced from its past, can love alone sustain personal relations? The experience of the adepts, Margaret and Helen, is instructive. The scene of their climactic reunion is Howards End, within whose farmhouse are the Schlegel possessions, unpacked by the prescient caretaker Miss Avery against Wilcox injunctions. The Schlegel movables have accrued tradition and value by their status as objects from the past and through their reinstatement in the rural context. Significantly, Margaret and Helen come to reconcilation not by talk or effort but through the past, enshrined in the rural sanctity of Howards End:

> Explanations and appeals had failed; they had tried for a common meeting-ground, and had only made each other unhappy. And all the time their salvation was lying round them—the past sanctifying the present; the present, with wild heart-throb, declaring that there would after all be a future.

The rural values not only transcend the claims of personal relations and the inner life: Forster posits the attainment of a universal human harmony through a vital relation to the rural tradition: "In these English farms, if anywhere, one might see life steadily and see it whole, group in one vision its transitoriness and its eternal youth, connect—connect without bitterness until all men are brothers." But the novel's course suggests rather the remoteness of divine unity from earthly efforts. The inheritance theme thus contains its own contradictions: nature is at once an agent of reconciliation and a nonhuman force which dwarfs human effort and which, threatened by the encroachments of the modern world, is losing potency as its kingdom diminishes. In reference to the ideals of personal relations and connection, the values of nature and tradition are similarly ambivalent, congruent in that they work together toward the possibility of earthly harmony, disjunct in that the ideologies that assert the primacy of personality and individual effort are irrelevant to the natural environment that transcends them. In its transcendence of human concerns, the natural world is linked to a concept of divine unity briefly adumbrated near the end of the novel. Restated, this idea becomes in *A Passage to India* the search for completion.

What opposes the possibility of unity in both novels is the vision of cosmic evil, rendered in *A Passage to India* through the central symbol of the Marabar caves, which in their absence of distinction suggest the negation of meaning and the absence of divinity. In *Howards End*, the suggestions of an antivision, though pervasive, are more diffuse. But their metaphysical function parallels that of the caves, and the pressure they exert similarly impels the search for a countervailing unity that will restore meaning and order to the universe. This unity is still, in *Howards End*, implied as an agnostic Christianity allied to the romantic tradition. God is no longer anthropomorphic, but the divine existence is never in question. Nature remains the means to its apprehension, still an intermediary between man and God. In *A Passage to India*, nature is no longer visible sign or ally of man; the quest, too, has changed. In *Howards End* Forster asks whether, amid the erosion of traditional values and the emergence of new and threatening modes of existence, the Western tradition and its values can endure. In *A Passage to India* he has accepted alienation as the modern condition and asks the ultimate question. Whether *A Passage to India* affirms or denies the existence of God, it is a far more coherent novel than *Howards End* because it confronts the problem of meaning directly. *Howards End* affirms human potentiality and the existence of divinity, but the unacknowledged pressure of its prevision of apocalypse undermines even its qualified optimism.

There is clearly an affinity between the goblin image of Helen's well-known reverie on Beethoven's Fifth Symphony and the vision in the Marabar caves. The goblins are an important motif. But if *Howards End* has a structural equivalent to the caves, it is not the essay on goblins but the scene at Oniton Grange, a Wilcox country house in Wales. When Helen invades Oniton on the occasion of a Wilcox daughter's wedding, with Leonard Bast and his bedraggled wife in tow, it is discovered that Mrs. Bast was once Henry Wilcox's mistress. Like the caves episode, this scene centers on a sexual catastrophe and precipitates crisis. As in the caves episode, the rhythm of confrontation begins with an apparently trivial but significant accident. Forster's brief line anticipating the Oniton scene, "So the wasted day lumbered forward," presents a compressed version of the final novel's prelude of apprehension and ennui.

The initial note of despair sounded in Helen's cry of "panic and emptiness" as her lover retreats, becomes the series of images and associations which render the cosmic apprehension that undercuts the action's strenuous efforts at reconciliation. Much of this imagery reappears in *A Passage to India*, integrated into a purposeful symbology. In *Howards End* Forster is still groping toward its formulation, but the essence of his vision is discernible in a description of King's Cross Station that considerably precedes Helen's goblins. King's Cross suggests "Infinity," its "great arches, colourless, indifferent," are "fit portals for some eternal adventure." This language inaugurates crucial motifs. The arch figures as gateway to a metaphysical journey whose values lie both in its destination and as the means of escape from urban horror: to which, nonetheless says Forster, "Alas! we return." The arch reappears as a fragment of the "rainbow bridge" that is an image of attempted completion; in *A Passage to India*, arches function in a comparable dualism as one of the symbolic paths to religious knowledge and as part of the infinite recession that questions the existence of the divine. "Colourless," "indifferent," and "Infinity" figure centrally in both novels. The motif of indifference in *Howards End* suggests the remoteness of the infinite and the indifference of the universe to man that will become the prevailing condition of *A Passage to India*. With the closely related adjective "colourless," it describes urban life, as the squalid existence of the Basts indicates, "a life where love and hatred had both decayed." To the cosmic indifference of the arch, Forster counterpoints the comic indifference of characters like Mrs. Munt—"To history, to tragedy, to the past, to the future, Mrs. Munt remained equally indifferent"—and Jacky Bast, who is "equally indifferent" to all her husband's moods.

The colorless arches of King's Cross are linked to a pervasive gray identified with modern life and concentrated in the imagery that describes London and its residents. In *A Passage to India*, "colourless" becomes "beyond colour," and describes the Indian sky that recedes to infinity, its perspective reducing the human scale almost to nonexistence. The "colourless and indifferent" arches of *Howards End* also prefigure the indifference of the Indian environment and the culmination of cosmic indifference in the overturn of all distinctions in the Marabar caves.

Beethoven's goblins formulate the experience of meaninglessness. The mode is casual but the message is not. They "merely observed in passing that there was no such thing as splendour or heroism in the world. . . . Panic and emptiness!" To this void Forster opposes hyperbolic fantasies of romantic individualism and sensory imagination: "Gusts of splendour, gods and demigods contending with vast swords, colour and fragrance broadcast on the field of battle, magnificent victory, magnificent death!" But refuting the shallow optimism of "men like the Wilcoxes or President Roosevelt," the goblins return; this time they threaten existence itself:

> It was as if the splendour of life might boil over and waste to steam and froth. In its dissolution one heard the terrible, ominous note, and a goblin, with increased malignity, walked quietly over the universe from end to end. Panic and emptiness! Panic and emptiness! Even the flaming ramparts of the world might fall.

The goblins recede with Beethoven's closing affirmation. But their warning describes a vision that *Howards End* continues to reiterate and whose implications it struggles to avoid.

The portrayal of Mrs. Wilcox also provides an approach to the negative vision. A sketch for Mrs. Moore of the final novel, Mrs. Wilcox projects a strange air of dissolution. Her voice "suggested that pictures, concerts, and people are all of small and equal value. Only once had it quickened—when speaking of Howards End." Mrs. Wilcox's voice, which "though sweet and compelling, had little range of expression," includes humanity and its artifacts in a suggestion of meaninglessness. Life—the "quickening" in her voice—remains only in the rural heritage. Conversely, Mrs. Wilcox's indistinctness, however unsuccessful as characterization, is also intended to suggest her transcendence of personality and her approach to a completion that becomes the ideal of *A Passage to India*.

The associated images of indifference, sameness, colorlessness all delineate a destructive homogeneity that renders life meaningless. London, the diabolic symbol of modern life, is evoked throughout the novel by references to the colorless color, gray. Playing thus with ideas of the absence of distinction, Forster moves in *Howards End* toward the distillation of these ideas in the master-symbol of the Marabar caves. Forster's London, like that of Dickens, is a city of fog, its atmosphere "clots of gray," its existence a mounting violation of the natural order:

> . . . month by month the roads smelt more strongly of petrol, and were more difficult to cross, and human beings heard each other speak with greater difficulty, breathed less of the air, and saw less of the sky. Nature withdrew: the leaves were falling by midsummer; the sun shone through dirt with an admired obscurity.

The "gray tides" of London proclaim the rootlessness that is the city's essence and the inner condition of its inhabitants: "emblematic of their lives, [they] rose and fell in a continual flux," and Margaret ponders lost continuities: "Everyone moving. Is it worthwhile attempting the past when there is this continual flux even in the hearts of men?" London, further, is "a tract of quivering gray, intelligent without purpose and excitable without love," its modern conveniences the machinery of diabolic imprisonment. The lift that takes Mrs. Wilcox up to her London flat is "a vault as of hell, sooty black, from which soots descended." Described early in the novel as "Satanic," London becomes, finally, the demoniac opposite of divinity: "The mask fell off the city, and she saw it for what it really is— a caricature of infinity."

The absent Helen, who eludes Margaret and her brother, and whose strange behavior suggests to them mental illness, seen thus is identified with the city in a vision of horror: "Helen seemed one with grimy trees and the traffic and the slowly flowing slabs of mud. She had accomplished a hideous act of renunciation and returned to the One." The metaphysical semantics of *A Passage to India* are extraordinarily similar. The grimy trees have become the indifferent Indian landscape, the traffic is transposed into the dirty city of Chandrapore, and the slowly flowing slabs of mud have become the abased inhabitants of India, described as "mud moving." The "hideous act of renunciation" in which Helen has merged into nothingness becomes Mrs. Moore's collapse of distinctions, which leads to her own renunciation of life.

Gray pervades the existence of the characters. "His was a gray life," says Forster explicitly of Leonard Bast. Leonard swears "in a colourless sort of way." His wife is "descending . . . into the colourless years." Characters of different classes recognize the problem that is their common condition: thus, Leonard and the Schlegel sisters "had agreed that there was something beyond life's daily gray." And Margaret believes that "doing good to humanity was useless; the man-coloured efforts thereto spreading over the vast area like films and resulting in a universal gray."

Aspects of color, the distinctions of individuality oppose the gray. When, late in the novel, Margaret makes a curious last case for the variations of individual personality, she speaks of "differences—eternal differences; planted by God in a single family, so that there may always be colour; sorrow perhaps, but colour in the daily gray." In nature too, color opposes urban gray. At Mrs. Wilcox's funeral an observer notices "the sunset beyond, scarlet and orange." Howards End is edenic in its variegated hues: "There were the greengage trees that Helen had once described, there the tennis lawn, there the hedge that would be glorious with dog-roses in June, but the vision now was of black and palest green. Down by the dell-hole more vivid colours were awakening, and Lent Lilies stood sentinel on its margin, or advanced in battalions over the grass. Tulips were a tray of jewels." Howards End itself is illuminated by "the white radiance that poured in through the windows."

> Unnoticed, the sun occupied his sky, and the shadows of the tree stems, extraordinarily solid, fell like trenches of purple across the frosted lawn. It was a glorious winter morning. Evie's fox terrier, who had passed for white, was only a dirty grey dog now, so intense was the purity that surrounded him. He was discredited, but the blackbirds that he was chasing glowed with Arbian darkness, for all the conventional colouring of life had been altered. Inside, the clock struck ten with a rich and confident note.

The clock is in harmony with the richness that emanates from the sun. Unlike the hostile Indian sun of *A Passage to India*, the natural environment still has relationship to man.

In contrast to the city, with its increasing population and its "architecture of hurry," the country retains the sense of space that Margaret loses when she rides in her husband's motor car. But the drive to London brings another prevision of void: "once more trees, houses, people, animals, hills, merged and heaved into one dirtiness, and she was at Wickham Place." Again Forster suggests a collapse of distinctions in which the elements of life, as seen in Margaret's kaleidoscopic view from the car, achieve a negative unity—"one dirtiness." The image recurs in yet another variant as

Margaret contemplates past catastrophe and future crisis. Leonard Bast's death has set in motion legal machinery that, made in the Wilcox image, will result in imprisonment for a Wilcox:

> Events succeeded in a logical, yet senseless, train. People lost their humanity, and took values as arbitrary as those in a pack of playing-cards. . . . In this jangle of causes and effects what had become of their true selves? Here Leonard lay dead in the garden, from natural causes; yet life was a deep, deep river, death a blue sky, life was a house, death a wisp of hay, a flower, a tower, life and death were anything and everything, except this ordered insanity, where the king takes the queen, and the ace the king.

This catalogue of chaos includes elements of life, culture, and nature. It not only links such disparate categories as card games, characters, natural phenomena, and logical and phenomenological concepts, but it displaces images from their earlier contexts. Death, for example, is not elsewhere associated with flowers, hay, or the colorful sky of this novel; life is ultimately to reside not primarily in human relationships but in a house. In addition to its suggestion of cosmic negation, this passage, in some of its imagery—after her vision Mrs. Moore withdraws to her deck of "Patience" cards—and in its projection of an "ordered insanity," presages the world of *A Passage to India* at a comparable moment in its action, as Dr. Aziz's trial impends.

The chaos of Howards End resolves into a harmony of asserted reconciliation and coming harvest, but the red rust of London is already visible from the farm: "Howards End, Oniton, the Purbeck Downs, the Oderberge, were all survivals, and the melting-pot was being prepared for them. Logically, they had no right to be alive. One's hope was in the weakness of logic." Prophesying the dissolution of the variegating countryside into urban gray, Forster distills in the image of a melting pot that eradicates color and distinction the essence of this vision of negation.

Hope remains, but its object has shrunk from fulfillment to survival; its mode has changed from active effort to a passive reliance on default by the enemy. That Howards End and the civilization it represents will be the future as well as the past is unlikely: as Margaret admits, "all the signs are against it." The novel ends with Helen's call to plenty: " 'The field's cut!' Helen cried excitedly—'the big meadow! We've seen to the every end, and it'll be such a crop of hay as never!' " Temporarily safe in their diminished territory, the Schlegels prepare for siege.

The contradictory impulses of *Howards End* infuse Forster's narrative voice and have important implications for its quality and function. The voice contains the schism that the action also reflects, for throughout the novel the narrator strains to bring his disparate materials into congruence and the competing formulations of his own voice into compatibility. In an accelerating tension between the impassioned rhetoric of the authorial voice and the ambivalence it attempts to suppress lies the explanation of the peculiar narrator of *Howards End*. Ultimately the increasing pressure of the negative vision undercuts the voice that contains it and alters its very nature.

It seems appropriate that *Howards End*, the novel that seeks most directly to locate ultimate value within the context of human relationships, should reveal an intensely personal narrative voice. The narrator's techniques of omniscience and engagement are familiar, but his voice goes further in self-dramatization, in manipulation of the reader, in the frequency and length of intervention than in any other Forster novel. The tendency of the narrator to step out of the action to formulate its larger significance also reaches its height in *Howards End*. No other Forster narrator establishes so personal a hegemony. His use of Margaret is instrumental to his scope, for he enters her generalizing imagination so often that Margaret functions as an extension of his voice. The narrator's omniscience, his relationship with the reader, and his self-dramatization distinguish him from Margaret. Uniquely in this novel, Forster's narrator indicates his gender, as, speculating on the difference between male and female friendships, he notes that "when men like us, it is for our better qualities. . . . but unworthiness stimulates woman." His language defines a variety of roles. As celebrant of England's glory he is a visionary bard, his literary diction means to a precarious decorum. He emphasizes his manipulations and the centrality of his function more than he does the story itself, intervening, for example, to excoriate Wilcox's repudiation of Mrs. Wilcox's will: "the discussion moved toward its close. To follow it is unnecessary. It is rather a moment when the commentator should step forward. Ought the Wilcoxes to have offered their home to Margaret?" The long essay that follows displays the narrator's judicial wisdom. But he can also present himself as a fellow-citizen, permitting the reader a rare glimpse of domestic intimacy as he extrapolates from Henry Wilcox's failure to mention the mews behind Ducie Street when he hopes to sublet his flat: "So does my grocer stigmatize me when I complain of the quality of his sultanas, and he answers in one breath that they are the best sultanas, and how can I expect the best sultanas at that price?"

Through diction and tone, the narrator seeks control of his structure and reader. With deceptive self-effacement he casts himself as the mind behind the action: "one may as well begin with Helen's letters to her sister." As the narrator continues, his grammatical emphases imply reader agreement—"Certainly Margaret was impulsive. She did swing rapidly from one decision to another." He moves toward fuller control of the reader through frequent mediations between reader and characters, in which he often furthers intimacy by direct address. Thus, defending Leonard Bast's reticence about the adventure of his all-night walk, Forster admonishes the reader: "You may laugh at him, you who have slept nights out on the veldt, with your rifle pat beside you and all the atmosphere of adventure pat. And you may also laugh who think adventures silly. But do not be surprised if Leonard is shy whenever he meets you, and if the Schlegels rather than Jacky hear about the dawn." This passage is singular in the degree to which it defines reader as well as character and commenting voice; its hostility to the imagined reader is perhaps Forster's coy attempt to produce sympathy appropriate to his character. But the passage is also noteworthy for its erosion of the boundary between experience and fiction. The rhetorical nature of Forster's narrative technique is not new, but the frequency in *Howards End* of conflations like this is unique in his fiction.

As he intrudes into a comic scene between Margaret's Aunt Juley and Charles Wilcox, the narrator interrupts his narrative to suggest its irrelevance: "Young Wilcox was pouring in petrol, starting his engine, and performing other actions with which this story has no concern." The narrator's qualification, itself an aside, renders the action he excludes parenthetical also. Yet, in a comic anticipation of *A Passage to India*, his very exclusion includes. For his distinction implies the existence of his characters in a realm of reality that is not the story, a world in which the reader may be presumed to function also. More directly, the narrator identifies Margaret with "others who have lived long in a great capitol," a classification that implies her shared reality with potential readers. Like these city-dwellers, Margaret has "strong feelings" about railway stations, emotions that become the narrator's truth: "They are our gates to the glorious and the unknown." From Margaret the narrator moves to the implied reader who coexists with her in the world outside his fiction, with the judgement that "he is a chilly Londoner who does not endow his stations with some personality, and extend to them, however shyly, the emotions of fear and love." The use of direct address intensifies the reader's participation in the narrator's rhetoric. Hoping that Margaret's connection of King's Cross Station with infinity "will not set the reader against her," he intrudes further to insist on Margaret's insight: "If you think this is ridiculous, remember that it is not Margaret who is telling you about it; and let me hasten to add that they were in plenty of time for the train." The assumption of potential conversation between Margaret and the reader merges the double fiction of character and narrator with the reader's world of experience, for it is the narrator who, ostensibly in the character's behalf, confronts the reader. The commentary has become not only a direct conversation but an argument, in which the narrator disarms potential opposition, assumes responsibility for this characters' perceptions, and buttresses his case with apparent considerations of common sense. These techniques are significant because they reveal the intensity of Forster's need in this novel to persuade, and suggest the degree of his extremity.

For despite the narrator's brilliance, his persuasion must ultimately be regarded as unsuccessful. He does not achieve a harmonious integration of ideology and dramatic representation, of content and form. His reflections are often disconnected from the action, so that the novel appears to present an uneven alternation between essay and scene, comment and action. To a degree found in no other Forster novel, the narrator's diction is abstract, metaphorical, hyperbolical; the anxiety and inflation of his tone suggest the desperation of his attempt to harmonize and persuade. The prominence, the intimate tone, the rhetorical techniques of this narrator are evoked by the impossibility of his task. Equal intensity seems to attend each exhortation. Nowhere does he acknowledge incompatibility among contending values. It is as if Forster is trying to bridge the gap between desire and disillusion by the insistence of his presence, to cover his inconsistencies of attitude and the unlikeliness of character and action by the sheer weight of his rhetoric as narrator. Consequently he is eloquent and hysterical, strained, elaborate, evasive, intimate, familiar, powerful, and unconvincing as he attempts to impose on the world of the novel a coherence that action and voice alike belie.

The narrator's rhetoric thus embodies its own limitations, which appear in all the novel's contexts. The portrayal of Mrs. Wilcox, for example, is an attempt to establish the mythic significance of an unsubstantial character. First seen by Helen, Mrs. Wilcox wears a long dress, she "trails," she picks up a piece of hay, she smells flowers, she is tired, she is "steadily unselfish." The corroborating narrator assures that Mrs. Wilcox is "just as Helen's letter had described her, trailing noiselessly over the lawn, and there was actually a wisp of hay in her hands." But in the absence of dramatic context, Forster asserts a larger significance: "One knew that she worshipped the past, and that the instinctive wisdom the past can alone bestow had descended upon her—that wisdom to which we give the clumsy name of aristocracy." Mrs. Wilcox, described throughout as shadowy, is too shadowy to bear this weight. To the degree that her behavior is recorded, she is rather a caricature of the traditional wife and mother, naive, submissive, and insular. The preciosity of Margaret's guests at a luncheon she gives for Mrs. Wilcox is balanced by the parochiality of the lady herself. Margaret's brief experience of Mrs. Wilcox doesn't warrant her belief that she and her family "are only fragments of Mrs. Wilcox's mind," and that Mrs. Wilcox "knew everything." Nor does the characterization support the narrator's direct claim that Mrs. Wilcox is "nearer the line that divides daily life from a life that may be of greater importance." Assertion seeks unsuccessfully to bridge the gap between intention and presentation.

Forster's relation to Leonard Bast is at best uneasy, a mixture of compassion and condescension. The significance of Leonard Bast is in his origin, in his pivotal position as cause célèbre for the liberal intellectuals and victim of the capitalists, and in his sentimental apotheosis into England's future. An uncertainty of narrative tone pursues Leonard throughout. Initially Forster demythifies him: "he was inferior to most rich people, there is not a doubt of it. He was not as courteous as the average rich man, nor as intelligent, nor as healthy, nor as lovable." Leonard has a half-baked mind; his conversation is querulous and banal; he is "one of the thousands who have lost the life of the body and failed to reach the life of the spirit." Margaret's assessment contains no hint of irony, although it catches her in violation of her own individualistic credo: "She knew this type very well—the vague aspirations, the mental dishonesty, the familiarity with the outside of books." Leonards's capacity for spontaneity and his questing spirit redress the balance, but even in this Forster undercuts his praise: "Within his cramped little mind dwelt something that was greater than Jeffries' books—the spirit that led Jeffries to write them." When ultimately Forster transfigures Leonard, his invocation does not create heroic significance: "Let Squalor be turned into Tragedy, whose eyes are the stars, and whose hands hold the sunset and the dawn."

In comparable interventions the narrative voice asserts dimensions that the action cannot substantiate, as when Forster tries unsuccessfully to cover Margaret's crisis with sister and husband by a rhetoric of benediction: "For the present let the moon shine brightly and the breezes of the spring blow gently, dying away from the gale of the day, and let the earth, who brings increase, bring peace." The inflation and unease of these assertions is compounded in many of the essaylike passages that stud the novel. Forster's evocation of a rainbow bridge is replete with questionable images:

> . . . she might yet be able to help him to the building of the rainbow bridge that should connect the prose in us with passion. Without it we are meaningless fragments, half monks, half beasts, unconnected arches that have never joined into a man. With it love is born, and alights on the highest curve, glowing against the gray, sober against the fire. Happy the man who sees from either aspect the glory of these outspread wings. The roads of his soul lie clear, and he and his friends shall find easy going.

How is the reader to interpret the implied parallel between prose and passion and monk and beast, the location and meaning of fire, the literal and metaphorical discrepancy of gray, the location and condition of the man "who sees from either aspect" and to incorporate into all this the sudden appearance of roads in the man's soul? One has only to contrast this jumble with the powerful and coherent imagery of arch and echo of *A Passage to India*. Groping in *Howards End* for the way to embody his thought, Forster too often substitutes preachiness for the integrated imagery of a coherent position.

The narrator presides over the survival theme, and most of the passages that celebrate England emanate from his voice. Elegiac and passionate, sentimental and unabashed, they transcend the focus on personality even as they represent a desperate attempt to retain the civilization for which it was a primary value.

> Branksea Island lost its immense foreshores and become a sombre episode of trees. Frome was forced inwards toward Dorchester,

Stour against Wimborne, Avon towards Salisbury, and over the immense displacement the sun presided, leading it to triumph ere he sank to rest. England was alive, throbbing through all her estuaries, crying for joy through the mouths of all her gulls, and the north wind, with contrary motion, blew stronger against her rising seas. What did it mean? For what end are her fair complexities, her changes of soil, her sinuous coast? Does she belong to those who have moulded her and made her feared by other lands, or to those who had added nothing to her power, but have somehow seen her, seen the whole island at once, lying as a jewel in a silver sea, sailing as a ship of souls, with all the brave world's fleet accompanying her towards eternity?

F. R. Leavis cites this passage to note that Forster "lapses into such exaltations quite easily," and he criticizes the vagueness that Forster's use of "somehow" creates in the last sentence. But do we not react more to the inflated diction of "leading it to triumph ere he sank to rest," to the frenetic personifications of "England was alive," "throbbing," and "crying"? Besides the hyperbole, of which one can find in *Howards End* surpassing examples, the passage is noteworthy for revealing Forster's ambivalence of preoccupation and uncertainty of mode. The rhetorical question about England's fate leads not to concern with "the brave world's fleet" but to an expression of conflict between power and the creative imagination. In this it reflects the disjunction between the goals of reconciliation and victory seen in the action and implies the ascendancy of those who see life whole, who have "seen the whole island at once." These, of course, are the Schlegels, and, as the only voice capable of the rhetorical question, the narrator himself. Thus while appearing to transcend the concern with personality, Forster displays the superiority of the mind whose insight includes but discounts "those who have moulded her and made her feared by other lands." Yet Leavis's uneasiness with "somehow" ought to have extended to the literary echoes and secondhand images, which suggest limitation or, as I. A. Richards put it, a "forcing" of the creative imagination. Again to contrast the ungrounded abstraction of this language with the concrete diction and intergrated imagery of *A Passage to India* is to envision the distance Forster still has to travel.

The inner tensions that these "forcings" imply may also be seen in direct expressions of ambivalence within the narrative voice. Noteworthy here is the degree to which Forster's apprehension contains something other than concern for the civilization he loves, for underlying the exhortation to human relations is a striking sense of recoil from humanity.

Their house was in Wickham Place, and fairly quiet, for a lofty promontory of buildings separated it from the main thoroughfare. One had the sense of a backwater, or rather of an estuary, whose waters flowed in from the invisible sea, and ebbed into a profound silence while the waves without were still beating. Though the promontory consisted of flats—expensive, with cavernous entrance halls, full of concierges and palms—if fulfilled its purpose, and gained for the older houses opposite a certain measure of peace. These, too, would be swept away in time, and another promontory would rise upon their site, as humanity piled itself higher and higher on the precious soil of London.

The narrative voice discriminates between house and city and, more significantly, between human life and nature. Noise, vulgarity, meaningless aggregation cover simultaneously the flats of a burgeoning city and the ephemeral but continuous flow of humanity they enclose.

This ambivalence may also be seen in Forster's treatment of characters. It is curious that this most personal narrator should display so little sympathy for the characters of whom he claims such profound knowledge. But the intimacy of his rhetoric obscures the indifference or hostility that underlies his professions of concern. To the gap between Forster's theory and his practice with Henry Wilcox and his condescension to Leonard Bast we must add the overt repugnance he feels for Jacky Bast: "A woman entered, of whom it is simplest to say that she was not respectable. . . . Yes, Jacky was past her prime, whatever that prime may have been." Even the Schlegels, though in a more disguised manner, receive a share of this ambivalence. Helen is passionate and truthful, the only character to act on the doctrine of personal responsibility that Margaret and the narrator espouse. But Forster's disapproval of Helen's excesses and his fear of her enticements undercut his support of her perceptions. On Margaret the narrator renders little judgment, but whether from unconscious intention or inability to separate himself from her characteristics, Forster has produced a character whose stridency evokes a certain recoil. And the narrator's impulse to protect himself from the vulgar crowd and the less comfortable realities of existence is mirrored in Margaret, to whom the appearance of Leonard Bast's wife, "Mrs. Lanoline," causes an anxiety that is not solely concern for the Basts: "She feared, fantastically, that her own little flock might be moving into turmoil and squalor, into nearer contact with such episodes as these."

Thus, even as Forster describes with some compassion the consequences for Leonard Bast of his entrapment in class (Mrs. Lanoline is such a consequence), he draws back from contact with the imperfectly washed. Concerned though he is with social equity and social cost, Forster shrinks from humanity in the aggregate. His ideology may be seen partly as an expression of this ambivalence: the individual is nearer to the "unseen" than any organization, humanity as a concept is associated with isms and programs. The consequences of this position engender what has been described as Forster's critique of liberalism. But although he dramatizes the impotence of the liberal intelligentsia to solve the problems of modern society, there is little evidence of Forster's separation from liberal values.

Portrayed as inhabitants of a feminine culture and divorced from power, the intelligentsia are dilettantes. While Forster yearns for masculinity, he can conceive it only as Henry Wilcox, whom he repudiates, or as Leonard Bast, who is so disadvantaged he doesn't signify. With apprehensions about the feminization of culture, expressed in his criticism of Margaret's effeminate brother Tibby and in the sisters' awareness of the need for balance, he nevertheless places his moral weight behind the Schlegels. To women as a group he is less generous. Margaret and Helen's all-female discussion club presents something of a parallel to the Apostolic session of *The Longest Journey*. But the women discuss social questions whereas the men engaged in metaphysical speculation, a Forsterian estimate of their relative capacities, as the narrator's misogynistic comment that "the female mind, though cruelly practical in daily life, cannot bear to hear ideals belittled in conversation" suggests. One should note, however, that both discussion groups are equally ineffectual.

Although Forster treats Leonard Bast more as representative of a class than as an individual, he does not conclude that social or economic action to improve the situation of Leonard Bast is desirable. On the contrary, the members of the debating society avoid the issue by bequeathing their fictional millionaire's legacy within their own class. Margaret wishes to help only the individual, but the very values of integrity and honor that comprise the "inner" ideal nullify this possibility in the novel itself. For when Helen undertakes to realize Margaret's ideal of personal philanthropy, the near-starving Leonard Bast declines her offer. His refusal, "very civil and quiet in tone," aligns him with the gentlemanly standards of Forster's own class. One could wish that Forster had shown here the hardheaded sophistry of his contemporary Shaw, whose Mr. Doolittle is concerned only about his translation to gentility. At any rate, Leonard's "higher" instincts doom him even more effectively than the indifferent machinations of capitalism. Nice guys finish last, as the contrast of his honorable behavior to Jacky with Henry's sexual opportunism also demonstrates. But although Forster dramatizes these ironies, he clings to the old formulations of honor. For him, the only alleviation of the modern condition lies in escape from the encroaching mass and its urban hive.

Forster's authorial voice itself expresses the conflicts that character and action embody. More than in any other novel Forster directs, exhorts, emphasizes, and seeks to harmonize, as the realities he presents become increasingly intractable to his hopes. Attempting for the last time to demonstrate a hopeful synthesis, straining to bring recalcitrant materials into conformity with his ideology, Forster's voice projects an anguish that moves us but does not solve the novel's problems. The narrator's intense rhetoric is a last, desperate exercise of personality, a final attempt to celebrate the creed of individuality through the colorful tonalities of a highly personal voice.

But *Howards End* demonstrates the limits of the personal, and Forster's movement away from the values of individual fulfillment and personal relations engenders the eventual effacement and withdrawal of his narrator. A valedictory persona, the narrator spends himself in a last violent effort to sustain, through his intense relationship with the reader and through characters in whom he no longer believes, his commitment to individual effort and personality. As the action coverges upon Howards End, the narrator begins to withdraw. This is not a dramatic movement, but as his presence diminishes, the narrative voice abandons its exhortations and its intimate tone: in the final pages it appears only to validate Margaret's ominous apprehension of the end of rural civilization and to underline briefly the last revelations of plot, as Margaret discovers that Mrs. Wilcox had bequeathed her Howards End long ago. With this withdrawal the novel approaches the mode, the insights, and the austere voice of *A Passage to India*.

The movement of Forster's narrative voice in *Howards End* from the celebration of personality to a near-detachment from worldly concerns, a progression mirrored in the course of his central character, may be seen as the expression of exhaustion and defeat. But it also represents the impulse to a larger unity that has been present, though in less complex forms, from the first novel. A search for human wholeness and for the perception of cosmic unity underlies the efforts and adventures of all Forster's protagonists, except Maurice, whose depiction presents a special case. The novels that precede *Howards End* focus on the metaphysical resonances of individual self-realization, dramatized in Philip's progress to salvation, Rickie's search for the meaning of reality, and Lucy Honeychurch's acceptance of her sexuality. As we have seen [elsewhere], Philip begins as incomplete both in character and vision. The price of Philip's eventual insight, his withdrawal from participation in life, is a paradox whose implications Forster does not explore. But completion remains both as the ideal for the individual and as a metaphysical condition to be perceived in the universe. Thus Forster insists in *Where Angels Fear to Tread* on the coexistence of opposing qualities. In the world some of these are separate from Philip, but they are what, to approach wholeness, he must come to see.

Forster urges Rickie Elliot to engagement with life and reiterates the moral value of Rickie's participation. Forster's equivocal treatment of Rickie undermines his conception of wholeness in *The Longest Journey*. But Rickie's incompleteness is submerged in the greater capacity of his half-brother, Stephen, and the novel suggests a more or less complete world in the alliance of Cambridge and Wiltshire, which forms a symbolic connection of mind and body, the creativity of intellect and the spontaneity of a not-yet-lost primal paradise. Simpler than its predecessors, *A Room with a View* defines wholeness both as happy sexual union and as the spiritual comradeship of man and woman.

The formulation of an ideal of completeness is far more complex in *Howards End*, and all the novel's themes partake of its conception. In *Where Angels Fear to Tread* the suburban ethos was domestic, the issue formulated simply as a clash between convention and instinct, safely played out across the Channel. The contemporary context enters with the Pembrokes of *The Longest Journey,* whose "public" values threaten the life of imagination, and with the first depiction of a technological progress that threatens the values of nature and tradition. In *Howards End* Forster extends his examination of these issues to the whole of society, seeking an application of the humanistic values that will bring the disparate elements of the social order into harmony. Because the novel asserts harmony and presents conflict, because its efforts to vindicate personal relations and social connection collide with each other and with the increasingly dominant theme of inheritance, the movement it describes appears more impasse than development. But for all its strains, *Howards End* gropes toward what becomes in *A Passage to India* the controlling idea of completion. Personal, social, and metaphysical, the attempts to connect in *Howards End* are all expressions of a single impulse to unity, whose avenue of fulfillment alters significantly in the course of the action.

Margaret herself enacts this alteration. That she has been moving toward a new definition of value is suggested quite early. As a result of Mrs. Wilcox's death, Margaret "saw a little more clearly than hitherto what a human being is and to what he may aspire. Truer relationships gleamed. Perhaps the last word would be hope—hope even on this side of the grave." This language, which hints at ultimates, recurs in association with Howards End and its wych-elm, which, in transcending sex, transcend the personal: "to compare either to man, to woman, always dwarfed the vision. Yet they kept within limits of the human. Their message was not of eternity, but of hope on this side of the grave. As she stood in the one, gazing at the other, truer relationship had gleamed."

House and tree project a sense of man's insignificance in time:

> The present flowed by them like a stream. The tree rustled. It had made music before they were born, and would continue after their deaths, but its song was of the moment. The moment had passed. The tree rustled again. Their senses were sharpened, and they seemed to apprehend life. Life passed. The tree rustled again.

Notable here is the effacement of personality, as the narrative voice sharply distances the characters. Forster's reiterations emphasize the power, continuity, and creative expression not of man but of nature. The human characters have a moment of perception, "their senses were sharpened and they seemed to apprehend life," but its transitoriness is immediately asserted in the short, bold, declarative two-word sentence, "Life passed." The tree has the last word. The moment of apprehension is a moment of peace, both timeless and ephemeral.

> The peace of the country was entering into her. It has no commerce with memory, and little with hope. Least of all is it concerned

with the hopes of the next five minutes. It is the peace of the present, which passes understanding. Its murmur came "now," and "now" once more as they trod the gravel, and "now" as the moonlight fell upon their father's sword. They passed upstairs, kissed, and amidst the endless iterations, fell asleep.

This passage persents a significant anticipation of *A Passage to India*, in which humanity is dwarfed by the vast Indian landscape and distanced by the Marabar hills, "older than anything in the world." In the final novel, nature is no longer redemptive, but there, as here, Forster develops man's subordination to a timeless and powerful nature and fixes a visionary moment at once permanent and transitory.

Howards End retains the possibility of redemption through nature, clinging to the romantic tradition and an agnostic Christianity in which, although no longer anthropomorphic, God still exists. Margaret, although "not a Christian in the accepted sense," because "she did not believe that God had ever worked among us as a young artisan," lectures to Helen on "eternal differences, planted by God in a single family." She believes in immortality for herself: "An eternal future had always seemed natural to her." But although, in contrast to the contingency of the final novel, *Howards End* clings to belief, its conceptions of negation and harmony are closely analogous to the symbolic chaos of the caves and the precarious harmony of the Indian Krishna celebration. In a passage quoted earlier, Margaret adumbrated a catalogue of chaos, a "jangle" of arbitary values and their negation. Amid this collapse of distinctions that presages the vision of the caves, motifs associated with Mrs. Wilcox suggest an ultimate harmony:

Ah, no; there was beauty and adventure behind, such as the man at her feet had yearned for; there was hope this side of the grave; there were truer relationships beyond the limits that fetter us now. As a prisoner looks up and sees stars beckoning, so she, from the turmoil and horror of those days, caught glimpses of the diviner wheels.

As in *A Passage to India*, turned the other way out, the vision is one of inclusion in God's plan, an affirmation of cosmic unity.

In the novels before *Howards End*, the potential attainment of harmony on earth is not in doubt. Although the equivocal heroes of *Where Angels Fear to Tread* and *The Longest Journey* are permitted only a glimpse of possibility, their fertile comrades, Gino and, more directly Stephen, are candidates for fulfillment. In the triumph of Lucy Honeychurch, Forster comes closest to the depiction of earthly harmony. But although Lucy's accomplishment mirrors a cosmic wholeness, it is self-contained. Perhaps because there is no discrepancy between earthly possibility and divine unity, the latter is assumed within the terms of Lucy's struggle and victory. There is no significant context beyond her.

But in *Howards End* the search for wholeness becomes implicated in a changing world view, as an intrusion of cosmic evil threatens the entire fabric. Imaged as goblins, gray, city, melting pot, the approach of a disintegrative vision lurks beneath the action, casts in doubt human possibility, and anticipates the apocalyptic symbolism of *A Passage to India.* The pressure of this vision undercuts and nearly effaces worldly hope—in the inner life, in personal and social connection, in a last desperate embrace of nature and the past. Despite the suggestions of divine order, *Howards End* presents more forms of negation than of unity, seen in its recurring imagery of indifference and collapse, in Forster's recoil from the proliferating human scene, in the strained solutions of action, in the shaky optimism of the ending, and finally, in the loss of energy of the narrative voice.

Confronting such negation, the search for meaning acquires new urgency. Forster's insistence and desperation in *Howards End* express his reluctance to admit the insufficiency of the old values, and as we have seen, the problems of the novel arise from Forster's inability to face the issue directly, to confront the implications of his own presentation. His apprehension of cosmic disaster engenders a network of allusion to infinity, eternity, the unseen—a machinery behind the action, invoked throughout the novel by the narrative voice to suggest the discrepancy between human flux and divine stasis. This discrepancy points the way toward a resolution that only the final novel articulates fully. But Margaret's development in *Howards End* shows the direction. As crisis descends, she accepts the subordination of human effort to the forces beyond it: "No, there was nothing more to be done. They had tried not to go over the precipice, but perhaps the fall was inevitable." But to approach an intuition of ultimate harmony, Margaret must withdraw: "At such moments the soul retires within, to float upon the bosom of a deeper stream, and has communion with the dead, and sees the world's glory not diminished, but different in kind to what she has supposed. She alters her focus until trivial things are blurred."

In her detachment Margaret moves toward the vision and mode of Mrs. Wilcox, in which "daily life appeared blurred." The "trivial things" that Margaret's new insight enables her to blur are the very values she has heretofore been at pains to assert and reconcile. The condition for Margaret's enlarged vision is withdrawal. It is doubtful that Forster intended that the dramatization of this movement should render Margaret as unattractive as she appears. The visible signs of her increased insight are indifference, irritation, and a proprietary concern for Howards End that focuses on matter rather than spirit. But whatever Margaret's deficiencies, her situation is significant because it expresses a dualism inherent from the beginning in Forster's fiction and paves the way for the insights of the final novel.

As she withdraws from worldly effort, Margaret reenacts the paradox seen in Forster's removal of Philip and Rickie from participation in life at the very moment of their real or potential acquisition of crucial insight. But

Margaret's situation represents a new development. For her acceptance of limitation is itself an attempt to articulate a new synthesis, to penetrate to a new metaphysic. Paradox remains, in that withdrawal from the values she championed throughout the novel is the condition for Margaret's insight of divine harmony. But *Howards End* has begun the movement, developed fully in *A Passage to India*, beyond the paradox of action to the more complex paradox of implication: Margaret's eventual position hints at the condition of Professor Godbole of the final novel, for whom the abnegation of personality and withdrawal from action are the conditions necessary to the insight of metaphysical unity.

Forster's creation in *Howards End* of a universe that must accommodate evil as well as good suggests that the negative vision must inevitably be included in any assertion of cosmic unity. Although in much of the novel Forster has seemed primarily concerned to test his humanistic philosophy in the social arena, preoccupation with the metaphysical implications of his values underlies the action more thoroughly here than in any earlier novel. *Howards End* still presents the most comprehensive expression of Forster's liberalism. But although we may find irritating the aura of sanctity that surrounds Margaret Schlegel, Forster's message in *Howards End* is that even the saved are not safe. England's decline is not averted, only postponed. Profound and irrational forces threaten the survival alike of individual and society. In *Howards End* Forster fights the implications of the personal and social failures that his novel dramatizes. In *A Passage to India*, he accepts the consequences of human inadequacy and takes as subject the limitation he sought earlier to transcend.

The Edwardian Wodehouse:
Experiments and Transitions

Richard Voorhees

LOVE AND UKRIDGE

In 1906, with three school novels to go, Wodehouse tried his hand at writing fiction for adults in a novel called *Love among the Chickens.* The hero of this novel is in some respects rather like the heroes of the light romantic novels that Wodehouse was to write later, and in others like the heroes of the comic novels (for instance, he has an uncle who will give him an allowance as soon as he marries). He may also be a self-portrait of Wodehouse in his middle twenties. For Jeremy Garnet is a devotee of the cult of fitness, a swimmer, golfer, tennis player, and perhaps even performer of Swedish exercises. He is also a devotee of the cult of the pipe, which, by public school standards, is more manly than cigarettes. In process of establishing himself as a writer of light fiction, he is self-conscious about his profession, on the one hand proud to be a practicing "author," and on the other hand apologetic because he is not a profound one. The diffidence that he feels emerges in the form of a defensive anti-intellectualism that will be part of the point of view of all the novels to follow. "I, Jeremy Garnet," he says, "harmless, well-meaning writer of minor novels. . . ." In his period of greatest frustration, he professes to see a recompense to come in his writing: "Jerry Garnet, the man, might become a depressed, hopeless wreck, with the iron planted immovably in his soul; but Jeremy Garnet, the Author, should turn out such a novel of gloom that strong critics would weep, and the public jostle for copies."

For the first time, readers of Wodehouse are introduced to a grown girl and a love affair. On a railway journey from London to Lyme Regis (changed to Combe Regis in later editions), Garnet meets Professor Derrick

From *P. G. Wodehouse.* © 1966 by Twayne Publishers, Inc.

and his daughter Phyllis. The carriage in which they travel is the scene of some low comedy between a Gilbertian aunt and a bumptious nephew, but their goings-on are not enough to break the spell that Phyllis instantly casts on Garnet. Later, staying at the chicken farm of his friend Ukridge, he pursues a hen through a hedge and meets Phyllis again. Properly introduced, he begins to dance an extremely decorous attendance upon her. In what he imagines to be a rivalry for the love of Phyllis between himself and a young Naval officer, Garnet is guided and constrained by the public school code of honor. Though he has got in disgrace with Phyllis's father and would like to ask Lieutenant Tom Chase to intercede for him, he cannot in conscience do so. In a syntax as stiff as his rectitude, he explains why: "I felt that I must play the game. To request one's rival to give assistance in the struggle, to the end that he may be more readily cut out, can hardly be considered cricket." Fortunately, Chase loves Phyllis's sister, not Phyllis, so Garnet's suit is eventually successful.

Garnet's love affair, modeled on the popular novels of the time, is a more sentimental business than any of the love affairs in the later books. Garnet moons under the drawing-room windows of Phyllis's house every night until he is chilled and soaked with dew. He talks about her to a dog named Bob and even to a star (unnamed). But since his love is such a sacred thing, he is reticent as well as extravagant. Of the crucial love scene he says, "Somehow we had stopped, as if by agreement, and were facing each other. There was a look in her eyes I had never seen there before. The twilight hung like a curtain between us and the world. We were alone together in a world of our own." Into this world the reader is not admitted very far. Garnet declares his love in the last line of the chapter, and Phyllis accepts him between chapters. The following chapter begins with a discussion of the problem of getting the consent of Professor Derrick.

In spite of its absurd sentimentality, the book has a good deal of charm even today, and Garnet is not altogether a sentimental fool. Indeed, he sometimes speaks a bitter wisdom that might have come from the *Maxims* of La Rochefoucauld: "One can pardon any injury to oneself, unless it hurts one's vanity"; and "everyone instinctively dislikes being under an obligation which they can never wholly repay." He does not, however, speak often in this spirit, which is alien to his essential nature and to the whole atmosphere of the novel. For the world of *Love among the Chickens* is, if anything, more naive and innocent than the world of the school novels. In the first place, it is the Edwardian world. Wodehouse published the book in 1906, and though he changed the price of eggs in the 1921 edition, he did not change much less. In *Love among the Chickens*, people still take trouble to maintain good croquet lawns, and they still go to Mudie's for their books. Girls carry sketch books, and young couples sing duets after dinner. Manners are so formal that Jeremy calls Phyllis Miss Derrick and she calls him Mr. Garnet after they have known each other for a whole summer, and it takes their engagement to bring them to first names.

Aside from an opening section in London and the chapter on the train, the story takes place in an idyllic Devonshire of blue skies, lovely sunsets, and sheep bells tinkling in the quiet dusk. Everybody is on vacation. Though Garnet is working on a novel, he is at Lyme Regis on a kind of holiday. Tom Chase is on leave from the British Navy, and World War I is eight years away. Phyllis is spending her usual summer with her father, a musical-comedy academic whose discipline remains a mystery and whose duties apparently require him to spend very little time at his university. To the charm of innocence and youth, Wodehouse adds the buoyancy of irresponsibility.

Wodehouse was to become in later books a plot-maker of remarkable ingenuity, but all of the vital events in the romance between Jeremy and Phyllis are completely foreseeable. If Garnet cannot, the reader can guess that Tom Chase is no rival of Garnet's. As soon as the golf match between Garnet and the Professor is arranged, the reader surmises that Garnet will allow the Professor to win, in exchange for his consent to marry Phyllis. Garnet does not get the idea of driving such a bargain until he is driving off the eighteenth tee. Moreover, Wodehouse uses in a romantic context such devices of plot as he will later use only in a comic one. In an earlier attempt to ingratiate himself with the Professor, Garnet bribes a boatman to tip Professor Derrick into the sea, and then swims out to save him and become a hero. This moronic stratagem will become a favorite one in the circle of Bertie Wooster. Garnet knows that it is a cliché of magazine romances, and he has in fact used it himself in half a dozen stories. At this stage, however, Wodehouse allows the clichés at least a marginal validity.

As the title indicates, there is comedy in the novel as well as romance, and if comedy is not the dominant note, it is the closing one. The chapter in which Garnet tells Phyllis that he loves her is followed by three chapters largely concerned with the golf match, and these are followed by three that bring the business of the chicken farm to a conclusion. Some of the comedy is no better and no worse than the situation comedy of television. Important guests are invited to a dinner that goes from one disaster to another. Forbidden topics of conversation are introduced. A comic dog and a comic cat contribute something to the imbroglios (but much less to the comedy than the cat Augustine and Stiffy Byng's terrier Bartholomew do in subsequent books).

A comedy more characteristic of Wodehouse appears in the person and the enterprises of Stanley Featherstonehaugh Ukridge, Garnet's erratic friend. A long letter from William Townend about the sorry attempts of a friend of his to get rich quickly by raising chickens, provided Wodehouse with the beginnings of the main comic plot of the novel and the character of Ukridge. Wodehouse also used his own memories of a schoolmate addicted to borrowing clothes, and Richard Usborne shrewdly guesses that Doyle's James Cullingworth served as a third model. At all events, Ukridge is the first of Wodehouse's non-heroes. He is a false Achates, rushing in and out of others' lives, invariably bringing trouble with him. Cadging (drinks, money, or anything else that he needs at the moment) is so deeply ingrained in him that it amounts to a tropism. But he would not be so bad if he merely wanted to pick people's pockets. He also wants to run their careers, imagining, perhaps, that by involving them in his cretinish schemes he is repaying them for whatever he has mooched from them. Thus he drags Garnet down to the chicken farm. (A note from a mutual friend, warning Garnet that Ukridge was in London, arrives too late for Garnet to flee.) His efforts to help Garnet in his love affair with Phyllis consist of infuriating Professor Derrick by talking of the Irish question and Edward Carson (subjects of which Ukridge is completely ignorant) and nearly drowning the Professor by swimming after him to badger him.

One need not be a friend of Ukridge to suffer for Ukridge's sins, for he is a menace not only to a small circle of acquaintances, but also to the whole of respectable society. The merchants who sell him the chickens and the tradesmen at Lyme Regis who provide him with food, pictures, a gramophone, a piano, and so on, are only a few in a long series of victims. Since they ultimately get their money, they are at least more fortunate than a tailor with whom Ukridge deals earlier in his career. Ukridge buys two suits from the tailor on the installment plan, paying a small sum in advance. He pawns one of the suits to pay the first few installments, and then he disappears. Following his usual custom, he has given a false name "as an ordinary business precaution." As for the address, the tailor eventually finds that it is a deserted house, empty except for the series of bills that he has mailed there.

Ukridge is Wodehouse's first essay in the picaresque. Besides setting up as a chicken farmer, he has taught in prep schools and sailed on tramp steamers. (At one point a friend tells Garnet that the last he heard of Ukridge, was that the lout had gone to Buenos Aires on a cattle ship, his luggage consisting of a borrowed pipe.) For the most part, he lives by his wits, such as they are, by a succession of diverse theories, each as dogmatically held as the one that preceded it, and by his spirit, which is indomitable. No other man has been so fertile in schemes for making money, and no other man has such a consistent record of failure. But from the ruins of each scheme Ukridge looks brightly out to the next one, plans his simple-minded strategy, and (if possible) ropes in a friend.

Ukridge is no more of a nitwit than many another character in Wodehouse, but he is a good deal more of a scoundrel. Garnet says that the proceedings on the chicken farm would be amusing if it were not for the fact that Ukridge's wife Millie has to be distressed by them. Millie's Aunt Elizabeth hates Ukridge (he returns her hate and names the most troublesome hen on the farm after her.) For once, an aunt in Wodehouse appears to be in the right, and a nephew in the wrong. Wodehouse himself evidently regards the Ukridge of *Love among the Chickens* as too much of a good thing, at least too much to be inflicted on Millie. In the later stories about Ukridge, Wodehouse goes backward in time to bachelor days, so that Millie is excluded from the list of casualties.

But Wodehouse early recognized Ukridge's major comic value. In the first edition of *Love among the Chickens*, Ukridge's affairs at the chicken farm are settled, and then there is an epilogue, a little play that recounts the wedding of Jeremy and Phyllis. In the 1921 revision, however, there is no epilogue, and Ukridge has the last word. First he makes an eloquent speech denouncing and dismissing his creditors. When they have gone, he turns to Garnet and begins to tell him of his newest brainstorm: a duck farm on which the ducks have no access to bodies of water. His theory is that ducks gain weight slowly because they swim around all the time. It follows, then, that ducks without ponds will fatten with great rapidity. In the final lines of the novel, Ukridge is estimating the profits to be got from such an enterprise, so much the first year, so much the second, and so on.

With the successful conclusion of their romance, Jeremy Garnet and Phyllis Derrick pass out of the Wodehouse world, but Ukridge remains to become one of the most important comic characters in it. Between 1924 and 1950 Wodehouse published seventeen stories about him. Ukridge was good for a succession of stories, since, never learning anything from an experience, he could always go on to another of a similar sort. The costumes that Wodehouse ran up for him in the early years were so successful that they have remained unchanged. Perhaps the most conspicuous article of Ukridge's dress is his dirty mackintosh, which he wears in all weathers, sometimes over dirty flannels, sometimes over pyjamas. His tennis shoes are absolutely filthy, and falling off his feet. A literal as well as a figurative myope, he wears a pince-nez, but the spring that should keep the spectacles on by gripping the bridge of his nose is defective. He therefore fastens them to his ears with ginger-beer wire (though ginger-beer had long ago ceased to be sold in stone bottles which have wire to keep in the corks).

In *Love among the Chickens*, Wodehouse also established Ukridge's speech, the basis of which is standard Wodehouse. In common with Garnet, for instance, Ukridge paraphrases Tennyson. (From the basement of the house in Lyme Regis, Garnet hears the "murmur of innumerable fowls." Ukridge complains that the tradesmen of the area are "as deficient in Simple Faith as they are in Norman blood.") Ukridge also speaks in the vigorously incongruous idiom of other Wodehouse characters. When one of the chicken merchants asks him if he would like some Minorcas, Ukridge, to whom a chicken is a chicken, replies impatiently: "Very well, unleash the Minorcas." But Wodehouse also gives Ukridge sole title to certain expressions like "old horse," which he applies to old friends, strangers in the street, and (once) to a bishop, and "upon my Sam," earlier a favorite of the boys in Kipling's *Stalky and Co.*

ENTER PSMITH

In 1909 Wodehouse published *Mike,* the last, longest, and best of the school novels. The first half of *Mike,* later published as *Mike at Wrykyn,* has already been discussed. The second half, [elsewhere] later published as *Enter Psmith* and as *Mike and Psmith,* is in many respects much like all of the other school fiction, but is in others significantly different. Sports are still a major occupation of the boys, and cricket games constitute the crucial spots halfway through and at the close of the action. Though Mike's resentment at being transferred from Wrykyn to Sedleigh keeps him out of all important school matches until the very last, he plays regularly for the village team. In common with most of the other boys, Mike cannot imagine a better life than that of his brother Joe, an estate agent to a sporting baronet who considers that Joe's chief duty is playing cricket for his country. (Mike, indeed, is later sent to Cambridge by Psmith's father, is then hired as his agent, and presumably plays cricket on every possible occasion.) The other occupations also remain much the same. There are mild rags, pranks, and breakings-out. Mike is suspected not only of ringing the school fire-alarm bell (correctly), but also of painting the school dog (incorrectly, since no good schoolboy would do such a thing, though a bad old boy would and did). There is trouble with a tyrannical housemaster who is properly frustrated and ultimately defeated.

Mike and Psmith differs from the other school novels because Psmith enters the school and becomes Mike's friend. The friendship of Mike and Psmith is an attraction of opposites and a study in contrasts, a bond between the boy who is the most sophisticated in the school novels and the boy who is perhaps the least. Mike is the schoolboy ideal of the athlete, a spectacular figure on the cricket field, already in some ways a greater delight to watch than his older brothers. Off the field, however, he is a pretty dim figure, if not the type of the dumb athlete, at least a shy and diffident one, as awkward in social life as he is agile in sports. He does not know what to say to people of a different age and class from himself unless they are cricketers. Not that he is any more snobbish than the next boy. He intuitively understands the people whom he likes, and he can be made miserable by the sight of anybody's suffering. But he is simply tongue-tied. (He continues to be inarticulate in the following book, *Psmith in the City,* even with his great friend Psmith. When, at the end of the book, Psmith has arranged Mike's future for him, Mike can get no nearer to expressing his gratitude than saying, "I say, Psmith.") Mike is still mentally and emotionally young enough to be perfectly comfortable in a school, perfectly contented with its licit and its forbidden fruits. For example, he thinks that it is a great adventure to sneak into the housemaster's dining room in the middle of the night, steal the biscuits, and turn on the gramophone.

Psmith, on the contrary, has already gone beyond the school world and his schoolboy self when he arrives at Sedleigh. He talks of his youth and even of his riper years as if they were long past. Instead of shouting and rushing about like his fellows, he speaks in a tired voice (like Aldous Huxley's Mrs. Viveash) and moves languidly. He would not get up in the middle of the night to steal biscuits or break out, nor would he get up early to practice fielding, since both sorts of enterprise would interfere with his sleep. He likes to breakfast as late as possible and, no doubt, would prefer to breakfast in bed as Bertie Wooster does. An eccentric, Psmith likes all kinds of people, takes an interest in their problems, and (unlike the clumsy Ukridge) helps them instead of making matters worse. His way of helping them, however, is rather Flammonde-like, and he patronizes everybody from the school sergeant to the headmaster. Though he says that he is a Socialist, and calls everyone "Comrade," the term is as often condescending or insulting as it is cordial. Finally, Psmith is one of Wodehouse's nonstop talkers; were it not for his vein of irony, one might mistake Psmith's fluency for logomania. Sometimes his constant chitchat has a strategic purpose, for Psmith, though a decent enough cricket player and a tough enough fighter when obliged to brawl, prefers to dominate groups and to get his way with words. But if there is no purpose, the talk flows, and if Psmith has nothing to talk about, he will make up something.

With *Mike and Psmith*, Wodehouse is done with the public school novel. There will be no more schoolboy heroes and no more public school backgrounds, except for purposes of farce (reunions of old boys, for example, in which bishops climb up and down the waterspouts of the dormitories). But in the next novel, *Psmith in the City*, the ties to the school are still strong. There are no accounts of school matches, but at the end of the novel Mike plays in a county match when one of his brother Joe's teammates falls ill. At the start of the book, Mike's father has lost most of his money, and Mike is going to work in a London bank instead of going to a university. He takes a room in Dulwich, not only because he believes that it will be cheaper than one in London, but also because there is a school in Dulwich, and a school means cricket. The sight of the cricket field, however, only depresses him. "Up to now the excitement of a strange adventure had borne him up; but the cricket-field and the pavilion reminded him so sharply of Wrykyn. They brought home to him with a cutting distinctness the absolute finality of the break with the old order of things. Summers would come and go, matches would be played on this ground with all the glory of big scores and keen finishes; but he was done. . . . Top of the Wrykyn averages two years. But didn't do anything after he left. Went into the City or something."

Mike, however, gets a warm welcome from the other clerks in the bank when they learn that he is one of the cricket-playing Jacksons (for the bank, like corporations in our own time, has teams). Another good thing about the bank (Mike does not find very many up to the day he leaves) is that there is a kind of spirit in it that somewhat resembles a school spirit. Everyone is working for one purpose, is doing, in a sense, one kind of work. Yet it is impossible for Mike to love the bank as he loved his school: "There is a cold impersonality about a bank. A school is a living thing." When, at the close of the novel, Mike and Psmith walk out of the bank during working hours, Mike to play cricket at Lord's and Psmith to watch him, their defiance of the bank manager is like a victory over a bad schoolmaster.

Psmith, however, dominates the novel even more than he does the earlier one. As a consequence, many of the ties with school are cut, and new ones are established in their stead. Like Mike, Psmith works in the bank, but not out of any financial need. In his patronizing way, he once commented upon the bridge-playing of the bank manager, Mr. Bickersdyke, when Bickersdyke was staying with the Psmith family in Shropshire. To get revenge, Bickersdyke suggested that it would do Psmith a world of good to have a job in the City. Psmith's father, a man of enthusiasms as sudden and transient as they are passionate, agreed. Psmith, however, does not live like an ordinary bank clerk. He is ensconced in a very comfortable bachelor flat, and from this headquarters he ranges the London clubs (his father takes out memberships for him in a dozen, from the Senior Conservative to the Drones), the theaters, and the restaurants. Thus begin the countless suppers at the Savoy that the later heroes of Wodehouse, romantic and comic alike, will consume. At this point, there are no girls, but there are cigars and wine in plenty. Psmith, as Richard Usborne says, takes us from the cricket field to Piccadilly.

The note of snobbery is stronger in *Psmith in the City* than it is in the school stories, perhaps because there are more sounding boards for it. In the school stories, the lower classes are almost by definition low comedians, court fools without wit. The fact that they speak a language inferior to that of the schoolboys is in itself enough to prevent their affairs, including their love affairs, from being taken seriously. Thus it is when Psmith encounters the parlor-maid and the postman at his housemaster's door: "Psmith stood by politely till the postman, who had just been told it was like his impudence, caught sight of him, and, having handed over the letters in an ultra-formal and professional manner, passed away."

In *Psmith in the City*, the idioms and accents of tram conductors and policemen are more barbarous than those of postmen and parlor-maids; they are also exploited more extensively and treated with greater irony: "The conductor deposed that he had bin on the point of pushing on, seeing as how he'd hung abart long enough, when he see'd them two gents, the long'un with the heye-glass (Psmith bowed) and t'other 'un a-legging of it dahn the road toward him"; "Lucidly and excellently put," says Psmith.

For the first time in the novels, the lower classes appear in really large crowds, on Clapham Common, for instance, listening to a speaker who himself scatters aitches "as a fountain its sprays in a strong wind." The electorate in Kenningford, S. E., Wodehouse says, contains a group of Liberals and a group of Unionists, but it also contains a group (presumably the largest of the lot) that regards elections simply as an opportunity for raising hell. If the people in this group vote at all, they vote irresponsibly, casting their ballots for the man who tells the best stories about his opponent. Psmith uses the expression "the many-headed" to describe the crowd on Clapham Common, and both of the boys use the school term "bargee." This term now connotes not only a member of the lower orders, but also a stupid lout, a loafer, a vulgarian in a cloth cap, a roughneck who likes to start riots in public places.

There is, in short, a new notion of the lower classes, that of the mob, together with a comtempt for the mob, and also a certain fear of it. Mike and Psmith are forced to flee from a mob to the tram of the conductor who deposed above. Fighting at any reasonable odds, however, the public school boys are still superior, for the boxing style of the lower classes is unscientific and inelegant. That of the fellow whom Psmith fights is, Wodehouse says, a combination of windmill and turtle.

The sense of belonging to the public school world is also stronger in the city than in the school itself. Since the school walls no longer separate the boys from the rest of the world, perhaps it is necessary to erect walls of another sort. In any case, Mike is pleased to find that most of the men in the bank (with the exception of a few Scotsmen) are old public school men. In the first week alone, he discovers two Old Wrykynians: "it was pleasing to have them about, and to feel that they had been educated at the right place." But the bank manager is evidently not a public school man. Certainly Mr. Bickersdyke's cricket is no better than his bridge, and Psmith refers to him as a "bargee."

For a self-made man to order an Old Wrykynian like Mike and an Old Etonian like Psmith about the bank is intolerable, as bad as it would be for the "usher" type of schoolmaster to nag them in their studies. Psmith, therefore, persecutes Bickersdyke without mercy, patronizing him in the bank, trailing after him at his club, humiliating him at a public meeting when he is standing for Parliament. Bickersdyke plans to get revenge by firing Psmith in front of half of the bank personnel, but Psmith forestalls the plan by resigning. Bickersdyke would murder Psmith with pleasure, but Psmith, with his usual irony, professes regret and surprise when, at the end of the novel, he recalls his relationship with the bankers: "it seemed to me sometimes, during our festive evenings together at the club, that all was not well. From little, almost imperceptible signs I have suspected now and then that he would just as soon have been without my company."

PSMITH IN AMERICA

In the next Psmith novel, *Psmith Journalist* (1915), Mike and Psmith have just finished their first year at Cambridge. Mike has scored a century against Oxford, and Psmith has condescended to play a bit of nonchalant cricket. Though Psmith is kind enough to regard Cambridge as a pleasant place, he also considers that it might conceivably be rather more lively. When Mike leaves for a tour of what Wodehouse calls "the cricket-playing section of the United States," Psmith accompanies him in the hope that New York will provide "a tolerably spacious rag." One would expect *Psmith Journalist* to be a much better book than *Psmith in the City*, which is a good one. Between the two books, Wodehouse published five others, including the first volume in the Blandings Castle cycle. If the reader did not know that still better books followed, he might suppose that when Wodehouse came to write *Psmith Journalist,* he was already at the top of his form. The intervening books apart, there is an extremely good reason why *Psmith Journalist* ought to be a better book than its predecessor. Mike soon disappears on his cricket tour and returns for only two or three brief intervals, so that the novel is almost wholly Psmith's.

Nonetheless, *Psmith Journalist* is not superior to *Psmith in the City*, but much inferior. Though Psmith is older by a year and Wodehouse is older by five, though the other characters are adults, the entire novel is more juvenile than any of the school novels. Wodehouse now has a greater knowledge of the world, but the book is more provincial than the ones that went before. He tries to deal with real things, but the result is less realistic than any of this other work. No doubt the unfamiliar background of Broadway and gangsters made the earlier editions of the novel successful. But one cannot imagine American boys reading the book today, and one can scarely understand how it has been reprinted again and again in England, most recently in 1950.

After five or six years in the United States, the Wodehouse of *Psmith Journalist* sees the country as an Englishman who had only read of it might see it. He points out that the apartment of the newspaperman Billy Windsor contains a typewriter (since no one in New York ever uses a pen), that the settee becomes a bed by night, that on the walls are hides, knives, and other mementos of Billy's prairie days, including the head of a young bear over the door. Then he says that a small New York apartment is much like a public school study. Likewise, he talks as if nurseries were as common in American houses as in English ones, and as if there were a kind of journalist whose title is "sub-editor." He does not even come near the actual language of his characters. For instance, prize fighters say "chaps," and "I shouldn't be able to," but at other times they are excessively illiterate. So are office boys and gangsters, whose "dat's," "der's," and "dis's" are tedious to read, and whose strongest oaths ("by Gum!") make ordinary euphemisms sound like salty talk.

At this period, Wodehouse regards America in terms of a somewhat sappy adventure and romance. Though Bill Windsor lives in New York City and works as the managing editor of a wretched magazine called *Cozy Moments* (in British fashion, Wodehouse calls it a paper), he was born on a Wyoming ranch. At the time of the novel's action, he is only twenty-five, but he has already worked on a Wyoming newspaper (where it is the custom of editors to keep guns on their desks) and on a paper in the feud country of Kentucky. In this school of journalism, he has lost one ear lobe and acquired a long scar across his left shoulder. He would look more natural, says Wodehouse, riding a broncho or cooking his dinner over a campfire than sitting in an editor's chair.

Wodehouse also sees the United States in terms of a sentimental moral contrast between the frontier and the city. Wyoming has given Billy Windsor muscles as tough as steel, but a heart as soft as a grape. Before the story proper even opens, he has rescued Pugsy Maloney, the office boy, from a beating and perhaps death in the street. Pugsy, in turn, rescues a lost cat from its tormentors. To restore the cat's tissues, as Psmith would say, Billy gives Pugsy a dollar to buy a bottle of milk and tells him to keep the change (milk costs five cents). As far as Billy is concerned, the whole East is corrupt, and one must go to Wyoming to get a square deal, presumably with gun and knife. Yet he is as fascinated by New York as he is repelled by it, and his ambition is to get a job on one of the big dailies.

Like Billy, Wodehouse himself is both repelled and attracted by New York. He is shocked by corrupt politicians and crooked elections, horrified by violence so incredible that it requires a preface for the benefit of British readers. "The conditions of life in New York are so different from those in London that a story of this kind calls for a little explanation. . . . Not all [of the inhabitants of New York] eke out a precarious livelihood by murdering one another, but there is a definite section of the population which murders—not casually, on the spur of the moment, but on definitely commercial lines at so many dollars a murder. The 'gangs' of New York exist in fact. I have not invented them."

But violence and evil are at the same time attractive. Broadway, says Wodehouse is "the Great White Way, the longest, straightest, brightest, wickedest street in the world." Early in the novel Wodehouse deplores the great play that newspapers make over murder, gangsters, and so on, but when Psmith takes over *Cozy Moments*, he turns it into a tabloid of the most sensational sort. If Wodehouse pictures a New York of monstrous gangs, he also pictures one of brutal police. To prod people with their nightsticks is virtually a compulsion of the law officers in *Psmith Journalist*. In the middle of the night they drag innocent citizens to the police station in their pyjamas, and anyone who does not snap to it is stimulated by a short jab.

Wodehouse's conception of the gang leader is remarkably naïve. Bat Jarvis is the head of one of the four biggest gangs in New York, but he has all the earmarks of a small-time hoodlum. As a blind for his criminal activities, he keeps a pet shop. Even as a petty criminal, Bat is no more believable than the hoodlums in Damon Runyon. A sentimental thug and particularly fond of cats, he is so grateful to Billy Windsor for returning his lost cat to him that he vows to do anything to help if Windsor should ever be in trouble. When Windsor and Psmith run up against another gang, Bat is as good as his word. No one since Dick Whittington has ever got so much profit from a cat. An older and more sophisticated Wodehouse was to transform Bat Jarvis into such intentionally comic figures as Soup Slattery, the amiable safe-cracker.

Evidently, Wodehouse was even more appalled by New York slums than he was by New York gangs. "The New York slum . . . is unique. The height of the houses and the narrowness of the streets seem to condense its upleasantness. All the smells and noises . . . are penned up in a sort of canyon, and gain in vehemence. . . . On the lower floors one could see into dark, bare rooms. These were the star apartments . . . for they opened on to the street and so got a little light and air. The imagination jibbed at the thought of the back rooms." Indeed, Wodehouse gets sufficiently interested in the slum question to work up some of the material on it, the dodges of slum landlords, the way they hide behind their agents and their stooges, and so on. He even turns Psmith from a *flâneur* into a crusader. Having seen the dreadful slums, Psmith is at last deeply moved by something: "Here he had touched the realities. There was something worth fighting for. His lot had been cast in pleasant places, and the sight of actual raw misery had come home to him with an added force from that circumstance."

The sympathy for the dwellers in the slums and the indignation against those who exploit them are admirable, but Wodehouse's remedy for the slums is about as adequate as a Band-Aid on a cancer. Psmith writes a series of articles denouncing the slum landlord, and the landlord's strong men threaten and then try to murder Psmith and Windsor. At this point, Bat Jarvis calls in his gang to support the Psmith-Windsor cause. Unable to intimidate Psmith, the landlord surrenders to Psmith's terms. And what are they? To write a check sufficient to cover the costs of repairs to the buildings that he owns. Having brought the villain to his knees, Psmith changes *Cozy Moments* back to its original character (Windsor has got his job on a big newspaper) and sails for England to resume his studies at Cambridge.

Psmith Journalist was an ill-advised project because Wodehouse had no talent for realism and because he was not well acquainted with the kind of people he was writing about. Later, he was to do his best work by writing quite unrealistically about the kind of people he knew better. The saving grace of *Psmith Journalist* is Psmith, whose character it would take more than an Atlantic crossing and a few encounters with gangsters to change. Psmith comes to New York because he is looking for excitement, and the city, especially as Wodehouse sees it, is not, of course, without excitement. But Psmith makes sure that he will have some by arranging for some. It is through his connection with Billy Windsor and *Cozy Moments* that he has his adventures with the underworld.

The proprietor of *Cozy Moments* founded it as an antidote to yellow journalism. Aside from yellow journalism, what a sufficient antidote to *Cozy Moments* would be, it would be difficult to say. Edited by J. Felkin

Wilberfloss, it includes, among other atrocities, "Moments in the Nursery," conducted by Luella Granville Waterman; "Moments among the Masters," conducted by Willberfloss himself and plagiarized outright from the great literature of the past, and "Moments with Budding Girlhood," conducted by Julia Burdett Parslow. When Psmith attaches himself to *Cozy Moments* as unpaid editor, he revamps the magazine in accord with the plan that he outlines to Billy Windsor: "my idea is that *Cozy Moments* should become red-hot stuff. I could wish its tone to be such that the public will wonder why we do not print it on asbestos. We much chronicle all the live events of the day, murders, fires, and the like in a manner which will make our readers' spines thrill. Above all, we must be a search-light showing up the dark spots in the souls of those who would endeavor in any way to do THE PEOPLE in the eye."

Psmith's feat of changing *Cozy Moments* into a paper that concentrates on sports, sensational news, and crusades and then changing it back to its original soppiness is probably the working out of a fantasy that the young Wodehouse had about some of the dreadful magazines for which he supplied copy. In later novels he frequently gives his heroes jobs on magazines that are, as he would say, unfit for human consumption. Even Bertie Wooster does a piece for his Aunt Dahlia's paper, *Milady's Boudoir*. After *Psmith Journalist*, however, Wodehouse is content to leave such rotten publications as they are, probably considering that it serves them jolly well right.

MIKE AND PSMITH AS ANTECEDENTS

The Mike and Psmith stories are extremely important in the career of Wodehouse, not only because they provide a bridge whereby the action is brought out of the school world and into the wider world of London and the counties, and New York as well, but also because they provide the qualities of character that go to make up the heroes of the novels that follow. The heroes of the light romantic novels are a composite of Mike and Psmith, a synthesis of the shy, tongue-tied athlete and the bold, articulate adventurer. Like Mike, these young fellows are endowed with extraordinary physical prowess. If they no longer play cricket or football, still they are capable of standing up to a whole street of villagers or London proletarians, disarming gunmen, climbing up walls and in and out of windows, swinging from one beam to another, and so on. It was appropriate that in the dramatization of *A Gentleman of Leisure*, a novel published in 1910, Douglas Fairbanks played the hero, Jimmy Pitt. The virility of Wodehouse's romantic heroes is indicated by their names, which are always manly and more often than not monosyllabic (Joe, Sam, George). Wodehouse would no longer even dream of giving a hero a name like Jeremy Garnet.

Like Psmith, the heroes of the romantic novels are impudent, resourceful, talented in intrigue, ruthless, and almost incapable of being ruffled. They stop at no strategem to win the girls they love; they lightly patronize their employers (when they have any); and they generally go through the world (as one of them says of himself, quoting a popular song) with their hats on the sides of their heads. Like both Mike and Psmith, they are bound, in spite of their sometimes unconscionable behavior, to a few moral commandments that derive from the public school code. For instance, one does not let a friend down, and one does not sneak. If one may cheerfully lie to a girl to win her, one cannot even consider breaking the engagement if one later discovers that he does not love her.

More important, certain qualities in Psmith help to make up the characters of the nonheroes of the comic novels, like Freddie Threepwood and Bertie Wooster. For one thing, these fellows inherit Psmith's preference for London over the country. Freddie devotes the greatest part of his energies to schemes to foil his father and get up to the Metropolis. Bertie has a flat in Berkley Square, and in his perambulations through the city confines himself to the areas where the theaters, clubs, and fashionable restaurants are found. When he leaves the city to stay at a country house, he always returns to London with relief, and probably with one or two new wounds. For, although the sun may shine upon Bertie when he sets out from London in his two-seater, the journey is a perilous one; the country combines great dullness with danger. The non-heroes also inherit Psmith's languidness. They like to sink into soft chairs, stretch out their legs, and smoke, thinking of nothing in particular by the hour. Even in repose, they need frequent draughts of whisky, tea, or other refreshment to sustain them. When they walk, they "toddle" or "totter."

Another legacy from Psmith is their concern for dress, but whereas Psmith is blessed with fastidiousness, Bertie is cursed with bad taste. Psmith says that he quit playing cricket once and for all because, in a village match, he was caught at point by a man wearing braces and has never got over the shock to his system. Bertie's wardrobe is enormous, but were it not for his valet, Jeeves, it is doubtful if any one piece of apparel would match any other, and some articles are absolutely execrable in themselves.

The snobbery of Psmith is somewhat modified in Bertie and his peers. Though they use the same term for the lower classes that Psmith does, "the many-headed," the contempt seems to have gone out of it. When Bertie addresses working people with such expressions as "my jolly old barmaid," he is not condescending like Psmith, but speaking quite amiably in the idiom of the silly-ass Englishmen. Still, Bertie does not particularly like or admire people in the classes below his own, and he does not even have Psmith's rather anthropological interest in them as representatives of inferior cultures. The egotism of Psmith, which is less an actual preoccupation with the self than it is a conscious parody, a sustained stunt, becomes in Bertie a true absorption in a childish notion of himself which he has derived from the clichés of melodrama. Having arrived at Clapham Common in a cab, but been forced to flee from it in a tram, Psmith says to Mike, "Do you realize the thing that has happened? I am riding in a tram. I,

Psmith, have paid a penny for a ticket . . . If this should get about the clubs. I tell you . . . no such crisis has ever occurred before in the course of my career." Bertie likes to tell the reader that those who know the man Wooster well are aware of this or that quality, that on such and such an occasion he was a thing of fire and chilled steel, that he meant a sharp remark to sting, and so forth.

In yet another way, Psmith is of great importance to the later novels. Speech is vital to Wodehouse's fiction; and Richard Usborne points out that by isolating the elements of Psmith's incessant talk, Wodehouse obtains three different conversational styles for other characters. In part, Psmith's speech is formal, literary, even pompous. It is larded with quotations and allusions, seasoned with archaic phrases and bits of pedantry. Whatever he may be talking about, Psmith prefers circumlocution to conciseness and elegant variation to simple Anglo-Saxon.

But the speech of Psmith is also a travesty of all this. He pushes the poetry around, mixes slang with classy diction, and indulges in conscious malapropisms. While still a schoolboy, he has his style fairly well developed. As Mike and Adair are about to fight in Psmith's study, Psmith says: "My dear young friends, if you *will* let your angry passions rise, against the direct advice of Doctor Watts, I suppose you must. But when you propose to claw each other . . . in the midst of a hundred fragile and priceless ornaments, I lodge a protest. . . . I don't want all the study furniture smashed. I know a bank where the wild thyme grows, only a few yards down the road, where you can scrap all night if you want to. How would it be to move on there? Any objections? None. Then shift ho! And let's get it over with."

The first type of speech derived from Psmith's is that of Wodehouse's clever people, the young heroes of the light romantic novels (whether British or American, they speak the same language) and such perennial undergraduates as Uncle Fred and Lancelot Threepwood. Their idiom is Psmith's transformed into a more sophisticated one. They are no less fluent than he, and they have a faster tempo. They also patronize right and left, not with Psmith's sometimes lymphatic stateliness, but with a cool and impudent wit. Like Psmith, they quote, but whereas Psmith's intonation is an equivalent of quotation marks, they—more subtle—have mastered the art of throwing away quoted lines.

The second type of speech drawn from Psmith's is that of Wodehouse's morons. A kind of shaky translation from Psmith, it is the tongue of Bingo Little and Freddie Threepwood; it is, indeed, the patois of the Drones Club, and it is brought to perfection by the noblest Drone of them all, Bertie Wooster. Bertie loves words as much as any of the clever heroes, and he shoots words out as rapidly as they, but they are professionals, and he is a bemused amateur. Though he can quote with the best of them, his notions as to the sources of his quotations are, more often than not, foggy. "Not one of my things," he will say by way of acknowledgment, "one of Jeeves'," and the reader will recognize that Jeeves has himself quoted from Shakespeare. If Bertie knows more words than any other character in Wodehouse (and he probably does), he does not always know their meanings. Recognizing his own unreliability, he often interpolates, "If that is the word I want." As for the deliberate incongruity in Psmith's speech, in Bertie's it becomes a sheer and inspired inability to discriminate, and Bertie is as likely to say, "And that right speedily," in any spot of conversation as he is to say, "And look slippy about it."

The third type of speech is that of Jeeves. Whether Jeeves is bringing Bertie breakfast or a hangover remedy, laying out his clothes or outlining a scheme for blackmail, his speech stems from the formal strain in Psmith's. It is superbly suited to his wisdom (it is right that an oracle should have a certain linguistic dignity) and it serves to make him thoroughly respectful and, at the same time, completely unapproachable.

A fourth style deriving from Psmith's is Wodehouse's own. The voice of Psmith is first heard in the last of the school novels and next in *Psmith in the City*. From then on, with negligible exceptions, Wodehouse will never write in the lucid but straightforward narrative style of the school stories. Instead, the style of the author, without losing its clarity, will take on the quotation and allusion, the paraphrase and parody, the incongruous mixture of vocabularies with which some of the earlier schoolboys experimented and which Psmith exploited to create his own idiom. But Wodehouse will purge and refine the schoolboy cleverness, the loquacity and affectation of Psmith into a style that is light, lucid, concise, witty, allusive—one of the most skillful styles and one of the best suited to its purpose in twentieth-century British fiction.

The Early Stories
of Katherine Mansfield

Kate Fullbrook

If Katherine Mansfield's idea of the artist transcended both sex and gender, her fiction is nevertheless focused on enactments of the roles of men and women; it trains a clear intelligence on the psychological effects of gender barriers and enclosure. Her theoretical idea of the artist allowed her the sense of distance, and, indeed, estrangement from those sexual constructions that she needed in order to devise fictions in which her characters' identities are riddled with gender codes as if with an unshakeable disease. This may sound like overstatement, but close scrutiny of the stories reveals Katherine Mansfield's continual, even obsessive attention to the defining and distorting part that gender plays in the relationships between individuals and in shaping society.

It is often said that fiction concerns itself most closely with manners and morals. It would be better to say that the history of fiction is *part* of the history of manners and morals in that it is one major way to codify and enact in language the ethical judgements that are features of a given time and place. As moralist, the artist often serves as a kind of outlaw, not only recording the dominant values of his or her culture, but pushing beyond the compromise of typical practice by dramatising hypothetical moral codes, or, by dramatising what the world would look like if the stated values of the culture were substituted for hidden codes which actually determine behaviour but which are left, at least partially, unspoken. Thus hypocrisy, double-dealing—the "textual corruption" that falsifies the area between the theory and practice of ethical codes—is often precisely the subject that lies at the core of the rebellious author's work.

Katherine Mansfield is one of these rebels, and the central characters in her fiction are often themselves outlaws. But they are outlaws of a par-

473

ticular kind; their rebelliousness does not lie so much in overt gestures as in processes of the mind and in the moments that crystallise out of consciousness to reveal to them the discrepancies between their underlying natures and the fixed social masks which they, often confidently, wear. This is not the kind of fiction in which heroic individuals pit themselves against an obviously unjust society, but a fiction in which the individual discovers herself as socially constructed, or is revealed to the reader as socially constructed, and yet possessed of previously unrecognized and unregarded elements of consciousness whose very presence indicates the potential difference of the self from how it has been perceived. The radical incompleteness and selectivity of social definition is thereby revealed.

To emphasise the discontinuity of these moments of truly existential wonder and terror, Katherine Mansfield, sharing in the central modernist impulse in relation to the formal structuring of fiction, moved further and further away from plot as the organising principle in her writing. As Clare Hanson notes in *Short Stories and Short Fictions, 1880–1980*, both the view of causal relations embodied in the conventional plot and the neat "finality" of the traditional ending seemed, for the modernists in general and Katherine Mansfield in particular, "to convey the misleading notion of something finished, absolute, and wholly understood." Katherine Mansfield's ideas ran counter to those that stood behind the shape of the traditional short story. However, although she always hoped to write a novel, she chose the short-story form itself as the most appropriate vehicle for the expression of this view of the world. For, as Hanson again rightly argues, the short story, like the short and fragmented poetry also typical of the period, formally suited the modernist view of the discovery of meaning and of the self—brief, unpredictable, discontinuous, tied in no orderly way to rational or sequential experience.

But, by necessity, art is the imposing of order on what may appear (indeed, what may *be*) amorphous and formless. The modernists still needed a basis of order to replace the comforting linearity of plot. The solution was to follow the late nineteenth-century symbolist lead into adopting the logic of the image and of the symbol as the means for formal unification of their work. That Katherine Mansfield herself did so must be seen as part of what she was attempting to say in her fiction. As Pierre Macherey insists, any "project of writing begins inevitably by taking the form of an ideological imperative—something to *say*." The problem for the writer

> is not that of being restricted by rules—or the absence of such a restriction—but the necessity of inventing forms, or forms derived from a principle which transcends the enterprise itself, but forms which can be used immediately as the means of expression of a determinate content; likewise the question of the value of these forms cannot reach beyond the immediate issue.
>
> (*A Theory of Literary Production*, trans. by Geoffrey Wall)

Form, Macherey goes on to argue "takes the shape or changes in response to a new imperative of the idea." The "imperatives" behind Katherine Mansfield's fiction can be enumerated as the rejection of traditional accounts of the unified self, the need to expose their inadequacy, a special urge to record the damage that these accounts had done to women, and the desire to explore the possibilities that a new view of the self might mean for the transformation of individuals. The forms that Katherine Mansfield uses in her short stories are constantly straining to enact these ideas.

Katherine Mansfield evolved for these uses a story form whose surface is deceptively clear but whose images signal crises for the individual which are in fact crises for the entirety of the ideological fabric that holds the individual in her masked place. The only way to read such stories, to "get at" them, is to be alert to their obliqueness, untrustworthy surfaces, and lack of overt narrative instruction for the reader at the same time as paying attention to the urgent signs of meaning that are dissolved all through the text rather than being concentrated at climactic points. The method itself is a part of the commentary on the world that sees experience as not easily readable but difficult, obscure, and very likely to be other than it seems.

From all this it should be obvious what Katherine Mansfield's technique has to do with her presentation of women. If the traditional view of women is that they should be, in several senses of the word, "selfless," yet at the same time completely enclosed by strict social definitions, the implications of Katherine Mansfield's ideas of the self blow any fixed notion of "women" to pieces. Gender at once becomes an elaborate joke and an obviously *invented* prison. Katherine Mansfield both charts the dimensions of this prison and considers ways to dismantle it. The fiction repeatedly circles around a number of questions relating to women: What does it mean to be defined as female? What does such definition do to the way women experience themselves and the world? Is an alternative definition possible and what might it be like? How is the girl-child tamed into womanhood? And, most importantly, what does it feel like to be a woman alone; what happens to a "relative creature" when there is no one to be relative to?

"I do believe," Katherine Mansfield wrote to Ottoline Morrell in 1919, "that the time has come for a 'new word' but I imagine that the new word will not be spoken easily. People have never explored the lovely medium of prose. It is a hidden country still—I feel that so profoundly." Katherine Mansfield's own evolution of a "new word" for the short story was accomplished in a remarkably short period of time. There are less than fourteen years between her first important story, "The Tiredness of Rosabel," which she wrote in 1908 when she was nineteen, and her last, "The Canary," in 1922. While Katherine Mansfield's method was not fully developed until the completion of "Prelude," which she worked on from 1915 to 1917, her early fiction has its own intrinsic interest, both as an initial statement of what were to become her most characteristic concerns, and for the success of some of the writing. The early fiction is both more overtly aggressive and more obviously politically embattled than the later work.

Very broad satire is favoured and a utopian impulse underlies many of the stories. A keen eye for injustice and a profound feeling for the isolation of individuals inform these stories that swing between Chekhovian realism and the modes of the parable or the fable.

"The Tiredness of Rosabel" marks the start of Katherine Mansfield's mature writing. Although it was composed in 1908 it was not published until 1924 in the posthumous volume, *Something Childish*, which included many of Katherine Mansfield's previously uncollected early stories. The subject is a crucial one for feminist writers—the contrast between the material conditions and the dream life of a working girl. In the story, Katherine Mansfield works the same ground as that in Henry James's fine *nouvelle* of 1898, *In the Cage*, uncovering the fantasies that support and make tolerable the otherwise crushing conditions of exploitation which entrap the girl. Katherine Mansfield stresses the connection between the economic function of her tired Rosabel, a milliner at the end of a long day, and her daydreams which pathetically uphold the whole sexual and social structure that degrades her.

The story begins with an account of Rosabel's return from the shop to her sad fourth-floor room. The girl, for all the expendable anonymity of her position in society, has a hunger for beauty for which she pays heavily—she buys a bunch of violets in spite of only being left with enough money for a meagre tea. As she drags through London on her way home, the city is presented in two series of images, both representing the girl's perceptions. The first series stresses crowding, ugliness and dirt, and is summed up by a description of Rosabel's wet feet, and her skirt and petticoat's coating of "black greasy mud." The other is a function of the girl's consciousness too, which oscillates between her unhealthy lack of basic material needs (her first daydream is of food: "roast duck and green peas, chestnut stuffing, pudding with brandy sauce") and her lack of excitement, pleasure and beauty. Rosabel's mind provides her with what is palpably not there to satisfy her in the physical world. She interprets the scene she sees through the steamed windows of a crowded bus as magical: everything seems "blurred and misty, but light striking on the panes turned their dullness to opal and silver, and the jewellers' shops seen through this, were fairy palaces." What is important here is Rosabel's consciousness as she infuses the wet city with the glamour that satisfies her craving for something other than the life she actually leads.

Katherine Mansfield picks up the symbol of the violets and meshes it with a typical incident in the milliner's working day for the central daydream of the story. The handsome, rich young couple that Rosabel has waited on during the day becomes a starting-point for her tired, slightly feverish fantasies. She imagines herself changing places with the rich woman; the handsome young man brings her masses of Parma violets, feeds her luxuriously, keeps her warm, dry, loves her, marries her. Katherine Mansfield inserts a brilliantly placed aside into the daydream at the moment of sexual surrender—"(The real Rosabel, the girl crouched on the floor in the dark, laughed aloud and put her hand up to her hot mouth.)" Having drawn her emotional sustenance from her dream, Rosabel pulls her grimy quilt around her neck and goes to sleep, waking only to smile as she shivers in the "grey light" of dawn in the "dull room."

The intersection of the daydream's comforts with Rosabel's real needs makes the fantasy more than a condescending excursion into the clichés of "silver-spoon" romance, though the fact that Katherine Mansfield used these clichés to populate her character's mind is itself as much her comment on the power of entrenched imaginative forms to control the contents of consciousness as it is an attack on the final cruelty of such images as drugs for the minds of oppressed women. The young Katherine Mansfield recognised the *function* of trash romance for women (whose elements have not significantly changed), which invites dreams of being the perfect beneficiaries of the sexual system that in fact victimises them. Rosabel is part of a complex social system in which she works and suffers so that rich women may catch their rich men. But there are other impulses revealed as well. Rosabel's need for beauty in her life is as real to her as her need for food. The crudities of her daydream are the semi-conscious expression of needs that are reflected in buying the violets and in her vision of the opalescent city for which there is no outlet for her except in dreams. The discontinuity between what Rosabel "knows" at one level and what she "dreams of" on another level of her consciousness is, as much as the wet clothes and lack of food, part of the reason for the fever, the slight hysteria that the narrator implies is the representative state of the trapped working girl, "the girl crouched on the floor in the dark." The inaccessibility of the meaning of the story, with its two disparate sets of images that only the reader can pull together, to the consciousness of the central character forms a crucial aspect of the story's meaning. It marks Katherine Mansfield's engagement from the first with experimental narration as part of her commitment to speak truly of the lives of women.

The theme of exploitation of women, along with the theme of women's fantasies of possible escape from it, also appear in the early story "The Child-Who-Was-Tired," published in 1910 and based closely on a tale by Chekhov, whom Katherine Mansfield regarded as her most important predecessor as a short-story writer. Again, there is an emphasis on fatigue as central to women's experience, and again fatigue acts as a catalyst for a utopian dream. But if Rosabel's utopia consisted of a stereotyped victory in an unchallenged vision of marriage as the way to material security and aesthetic satisfaction, the dream in this story is more troubled, more diffuse, while just as closely related to the conscious experience of the dreamer.

The story itself is simple, both its portrayal of viciousness and in the direct response to it. The "child" of the title is introduced in the first lines. She dreams of walking down "a little road that led to nowhere" when a hand grabs her, and slaps and shakes her awake. The little girl pleads for sleep, but is tortured awake by her "employer," a brutal woman who treats the child like a slave. The woman and her husband, while giving the child a life of threats and insults, pride themselves on their charity in taking her. The little girl is disgracefully "free-born," illegitimate, and she has been "rescued" from her natural mother who tried to kill her. The irony of this release into slavery is picked up in the ending of the story in which the child, driven by animal need for sleep, and half-pitying the incessant crying of the cruel couple's baby which is in her charge, smothers the infant, as she explains the desirability of death to it—" 'You'll not cry any more nor wake up in the night' ". The baby dead, the child falls immediately to the floor, back into the dream of the little road, having given the one gift her own mother tried to give her—the gift of oblivion. Throughout the story, the brutal couple take pains to represent the child as mad while driving her to an insanity which will bring them perfect poetic retribution through the murder of their own child.

The fairy-tale quality of the story allows Katherine Mansfield to stress the mirroring and doubling which signal the most important meanings of the tale. The child is a double of her natural mother, but succeeding rather than failing to rid herself of the unwanted baby which is the immediate source of her suffering. But the child is also the double of the crying infant, smothered by false parents. The cruel couple, wicked step-parents, are themselves murderers of the spirit of the girl. From one point of view, "The Child-Who-Was-Tired" is a classic parable about oppression in its crudest forms, specifically about the oppression of women and children who live outside the protection of patriarchal law. Psychologically, the story drives toward the moment of psychic assertion when the tormented individual refuses or deforms the role assigned to her by others, yet bases her revolt on a revision of forms she already knows.

The question of the "madness" of the girl's act of murder is, of course, an important one. Like Hardy's Little Father Time who kills his siblings in *Jude the Obscure*, the child as murderer here is a fictional enactment of a pessimistic view of the future for a society that defines those outside its structures as less than human. The death of the baby is a symbol of the death of the future. But one must note too that the child brings death to the baby as a kindly, precious gift. The action of the child who is already outside the law because of her illegitimate birth is, as well, a heroic gesture of defiance at the law that offers her nothing. None of this is understood by the girl who simply takes what she needs because, finally, she must have peace, which she is willing to share profoundly with her victim. Again the reader has access to meanings unavailable to the characters. It is not the child who is mad, but the culture which attempts to immobilise her beneath an iron mask whose weight she cannot bear. The "road to nowhere" in her dream both images the truth of her vulnerable condition and is a figure of utopia, a place that is literally "nowhere," in which everything is unlike the world she inhabits. The story is finally "about" the results of oppression on the unconscious and its eruption into the world in the face of suppressed need.

"The Child-Who-Was-Tired" is simultaneously a cautionary tale, a gesture of protest, and an account of the function of the psyche. The fantastical elements—the nameless characters, the timeless setting, the extremity of the action—emphasise the generality of the paradigmatic relationships in the story. As in "The Tiredness of Rosabel" the experience of the main female figure is that of life as ordeal, and once again the material and emotional conditions of that life are refracted through dreams that are ultimately, in some ways, self-destructive. The terrible irony in "Rosabel" is that the girl's dream of escape actually validates the system that entraps her; the "doubling" technique in "The Child" invites a reading where the vengeance in the girl's act of murder must also be interpreted as suicide. Both stories are less concerned with overt action than with meanings generated in semi-conscious states. And for the characters these meanings are culturally-grounded confusions that promote hysteria and self-destruction.

If these two stories present the dream states of female characters that free the dreamers only into distorted repetitions of their own experience, another story of 1910, "How Pearl Button Was Kidnapped," provides an alternative utopian, rather than dystopian, dream.

"Pearl Button" is almost pure allegory. Again, this is a commentary on a child's freedom revoked by adults. It specifically treats the forces that construct stereotyped roles for women and the difficulty of escape from those roles. Pearl Button is a conventional little girl, swinging alone on a gate outside her parents' house, "the House of Boxes—an obvious image of confinement—singing a "small song," and watching the dust of the street blown by the "little winds" of a "sunshiny day." The diminutive vocabulary and the cadences of the prose are those of the child's mind itself, and the world is seen as she sees it, once again claiming fairy-tale licence for the tale.

> Two big women came walking down the street. One was dressed in red and the other was dressed in yellow and green. They had pink handkerchiefs over their heads, and both of them carried a big flax basket of ferns. They had no shoes and stockings on, and they came walking along, slowly, because they were so fat, and talking to each other and always smiling.

These two rather unusual fairy godmothers are dark, frightened of the House of Boxes, but friendly to Pearl. Their gay clothing and freedom from restraint signalled by their unshod feet, contrast strongly with Pearl's tidy "feminine" pinafore frill, and with the life of Pearl's mother, who, as Pearl tells them, is " 'in the kitchin, ironing-because-its-Tuesday.' " The girl acccepts the women's invitation to join them, and anticipating some sort of constraining order among all adults, wonders what they have in their House of Boxes. But instead of being told their rules Pearl is cuddled and taken to a log house, undivided by walls, which is full of dark people, both men and women, who seem to be engaged in only pleasant things. Taken by them to the sea, Pearl is at first frightened by its immensity; but the people comfort her, strip her of most of her confining clothes, and lead her to the sand to join them in digging for shells, smiling all the time: " 'Haven't you got any Houses of Boxes?' she said. 'Don't you all live in a row? Don't the men go to offices? Aren't there any nasty things?' " It seems there are not. Nastiness reappears only with the arrival of the rescue-party from the world of Boxes. Pearl screams as "Little men in blue coats—little men came running, running towards her with shouts and whistlings—a crowd of little blue men to carry her back to the House of Boxes." The police, emphatically male guardians of conventional regimentation, arrive to turn the idyll into nightmare.

The salient features of this story belong to the romantic tradition that glorifies the "naturalness" and "freedom" of the savage over the inhibitions and pleasure-denying aspects of mechanical civilisation. The story is clear in uniting the nonwhite and the as yet unsubdued girl-child as natural allies against the authority of patriarchy represented by the police. The world of the "dark people," who are also the "people" of the unconscious, is kind, vivid, open to pleasure, unregulated in the relations between the sexes. The dangerous blue of the police is contrasted with the magical blue of the sea which turns to crystal clarity in Pearl's cupped hands, a dream-like reflection of the beauty of the free unconscious when innocent of the strictures embodied by the orderly town.

Katherine Mansfield is using her "dark people" for the same purpose as Dickens's circus people in *Hard Times*, and George Eliot's and D. H. Lawrence's gypsies. What is significant about all these "wild" people is that they serve as foils to the conventional life that surrounds them. Representing liberty over enslavement, the unconscious over consciousness, free pleasure over artificially constructed pain, nature over civilisation, spontaneity over conformity, sexual response over rejection of sexuality, these untamed people stand as testaments to all the positive values that established society refuses. Pearl, who is not kidnapped at all, rather *escapes* from the world of masks into the world of freedom, only to be forced by the police, as if she was a criminal, to abandon her loosely structured utopia to be schooled into the rigid categories of women "ironing-because-it's-Tuesday" and men who inevitably "go to offices." The story should be bracketed with Mark Twain's *Huck Finn* and Henry James's *What Maisie Knew* as a treatment of the child as the image of humanity fettered rather than freed by culture. "Pearl Button" is only a little over four pages long, but its poetic deftness, its original handling of traditional themes, and its firm sense of direction and alliance, make it important in Katherine Mansfield's development.

Two more stories about children from the early period deserve attention. "New Dresses" (1911) and "The Little Girl" (1912), are both only partially successful. But both anticipate, in interesting ways, the major stories that follow them. They are family stories and one of the most notable features of Katherine Mansfield's typical portrayal of family politics is that she adds to the usual configuration of mother, father and child, a fourth element in the figure of the grandmother. Katherine Mansfield's grandmothers are almost always widows and almost always residents in their daughters' houses. At times they are presented as matriarchs of profound strength, without whose presence the rest of the family could not function. At other times they are barely tolerated by the younger adults who treat them as superannuated fossils whose existence is best ignored. They are always crucial for the girl-child. And Katherine Mansfield shows them as loving beyond the powers of those who are still personally locked in the details of the sexual alternation of repulsion and desire.

Further, the grandmother is always a figure of justice in the stories, an impartial observer whose judgements, while often slighted, always run true. While remaining important to her adult daughter, the grandmother is usually of most significance to her granddaughter, who depends on the wisdom of the old woman to survive as an individual under the pressure placed upon her by her parents. There is often something almost penitent about the grandmother as she watches her usually frustrated daughter entrapped by marital subservience. It is almost as if, having sold her daughter into the slavery of convention, the old woman has decided to work differently for the child, while recognising too the forces of culture and temperament which will change her purposeful manoeuvres into something unforeseen. She offers a model of a different *kind* of relationship to those based on class or sexual power struggles. The grandmother is unselfish, a respecter of persons by necessity and through knowledge. She serves the same purpose for the reader as she does for the child—she is the single, dependable source of love in the stories, and a shrewd perceiver of hidden motives.

"New Dresses" is a broad feminist satire, in which Katherine Mansfield uses the doubling strategies already seen in "The Child-Who-Was-Tired" to outline a psychological map of the modern family. The grandmother in the story shares her role with a kindly old man, Dr Malcolm, both of whom take the part of Helen, the little girl who is the scapegoat of the family. The issue at hand is that of new dresses for Helen and her sister, Rose. Anne, Helen's mother, has spent too much money on the cloth, and she nervously tries to displace her anxiety about her husband's reaction to her spending onto her child. Anne's favourite pastime is, in fact, complaining about Helen and her unladylike ways. Helen is grubby, Helen is disrespectful, Helen looks at her brother—known simply as "Boy"—in a "peculiar way." Helen also stutters, and Anne means to take her to the doctor about it, " 'if only to give her a good fright.' " Helen is perceived by Anne and her husband, Henry, as uncooperative in assuming the docility and passivity they expect from a girl.

The grandmother understands this, and implies an unstated link to her daughter after Anne makes the threat to frighten Helen with the male authority of the doctor. " 'Anne,' " she says, " 'you know she's always stuttered. You did just the same when you were her age, she's highly strung.' " Via the grandmother, Katherine Mansfield signals Anne's unwanted and unresolved identification with her rebellious daughter. For Anne, Helen is the self she has lost, the possible other if stammering self that has been submerged in her marriage to Henry, and which she now expresses only in furtive overspending and in constant denigration of rebellious traits in Helen. Anne's persecution of Helen is a devious persecution of abandoned parts of her own potentiality which she unconsciously craves to unloose, while her conscious self holds her in check by refusing to admit the real ignominy of her particular kind of marriage.

The humiliating nature of the marriage is revealed with the arrival of Henry, whom Katherine Mansfield presents in a series of masculine clichés as he returns beery and reeking of cigars after a jolly night out at the Political League. Henry, a caricatured patriarch, quickly seizes his opportunity to criticise his wife's talents as resident consumer in a crude speech in which Katherine Mansfield satirises the major features of sexist domination point by point:

> "Good God! Anybody would think you'd married a millionaire. You could buy your mother a trousseau with that money. You're making yourself the laughing-stock for the whole town. How do you think I can buy Boy a chair or anything else—if you chuck away my earnings like that? Time and again you impress upon me the impossibility of keeping Helen decent; and then you go decking her out the next moment in thirty-five shillings' worth of green cashmere . . ."
> On and on stormed the voice.

This parody of patriarchal rage turns on a series of double binds as well as mutual blackmail. The source of Henry's power is money and he emphasises this in a way that calls the entire community to witness his rights. "Boy" is identified as the only important child with maximum rights to his father's wealth. The sarcastic cut against the grandmother indirectly sneers at her probable lack of use for a trousseau and her dependent female status. Henry indulges in creating an undercurrent of threat as well as pleasuring in his righteous anger. But, most interestingly, Anne's attitude to Helen is thrown up as a reason for her to be contrite. If Anne will continue to condemn all that Helen stands for—and punish Helen accordingly—all might be well.

The satirical presentation of schooling into male and female roles continues. The next day Boy bangs tediously on his high chair while Henry proudly looks on. He encourages his son despite, or rather in defiance of, his wife's annoyance—" 'Go it, old man. Tell mother boys like to kick up a row.' " Anne again displaces her feelings by warming to the sight of the girls—"She could not help thrilling, they looked so very superior." Anne settles for the soothing thought of class supremacy that goes along with acceptance of her subservience, and in a further displacement tells herself she's pleased because the girls look "worthy" of their father. She silently tries to convey her submission to Henry: "It was for your sake I made the dresses; of course you can't understand that, but *really* Henry."

Katherine Mansfield stresses the sadism in patriarchal "love" as Henry goes to bully Helen in the girls' bedroom after she has torn her new dress in rough play inconsistent with the role her parents have planned for her, and hidden the evidence of her "crime." Helen hears Henry

> come creaking into their room and hid under the bedclothes. But Rose betrayed her.
>
> "Helen's not asleep," piped Rose.
>
> Henry sat by the bedside, pulling his moustache.
>
> "If it were not Sunday, Helen, I would whip you. As it is, and I must be at the office early to-morrow, I shall give you a sound smacking after tea in the evening . . . Do you hear me?"
>
> She grunted.
>
> "You love your father and mother, don't you?"
>
> No answer.
>
> Rose gave Helen a dig with her foot.
>
> "Well," said Henry, sighing deeply, "I suppose you love Jesus?"
>
> "Rose has scratched my leg with her toe-nail," answered Helen.
>
> Henry strode out of the room.

Katherine Mansfield associates punishment, religious coercion, and conventional obedience to parents as facets of the same sick structure bent on extinguishing Helen's autonomy. At the same time she allows her reader a pleasurable snicker of sympathy with the child's resistance to that structure. Katherine Mansfield uses humour here as a weapon of revolt and release, a typical strategy in women's writing from Jane Austen to Margaret Atwood, and does so in ways that are very much part of a recognisable tradition of subversion of sexist hegemony.

"New Dresses" ends with the old people trying to make amends to Helen. Dr Malcolm arrives at the house with a copy of the torn dress while the grandmother tells him she is going to comfort Helen with a new doll to make up for her whipping. The old, conventionally "wise" people distance themselves from the imposition of female docility and take their own subversive stands against the parents and in support of the girl's rebelliousness.

The interest in "New Dresses," which is a qualified success despite its overly diagrammatic satire of the patriarchal family, is in Katherine Mansfield's ferocious comedy, her presentation of Anne's confused consciousness, and in the evocation of the sadistic edge in the schooling into gender.

By now it should be clear how closely Katherine Mansfield's early fiction is engaged in feminist issues and how various her experiments with strategies for writing about those issues were. Her repeated attention to the formation of female consciousness is especially sensitive and in a number of her early stories she confronts the question of how, given the cruelty of sexist relations between men and women, the roots of female desire for a male are ever established. That men are to be feared is clear from her treatment of patriarchy; that they might be loved is by no means self-evident.

Katherine Mansfield's attitude toward this subject is often related to her own love-hate relationship with her father, who, by all accounts, seems to have been the epitome of the Victorian bourgeois *paterfamilias* and simultaneously a man of some imagination and generosity. But given the analysis of the *general* state of relations between men and women in the fiction, Katherine Mansfield's interest does not demand an explanation so exclusively tied to her family background.

Some of the devices in "New Dresses" surface again in "The Little Girl," another early story about the education of a female child. The story marks the first appearance of a recurring figure in Katherine Mansfield's fiction—Kezia, the girl-child in quest. Again, the family configuration of mother, father, grandmother and girl is drawn, and the story traces the psychological process of Kezia's shift from pure fear of her father to positive response to him via her imagining of aspects of commonality in their experience.

To Kezia, her father is "to be feared and avoided," and she is relieved when he is out of the house. Again, the girl is portrayed as stuttering and liable to punishment for unintentional crimes. Kezia falls foul of her father while making his birthday present, a pin cushion which she unfortunately stuffs with shredded bits of his papers. She is, of course, punished. Whipped by her father she goes to her grandmother for comfort and explanation:

> "What did Jesus make fathers for?" she sobbed.
> "Here's a clean hanky, darling, with some of my lavender water on it. Go to sleep, pet; you'll forget all about it in the morning. I tried to explain to father, but he was too upset to listen tonight."
> But the child never forgot. Next time she saw him she whipped both hands behind her back, and a red colour flew to her cheeks.

Grandmother's policy of appeasement does not work; but what does is the father's offer of succour rather than hostility. In the absence of her mother and grandmother, Kezia has her repeated nightmare about "the butcher with a knife and rope," a dream of terror about the male as devourer. Since the women are gone, Kezia accepts the comfort of her father who falls asleep beside her.

Poor father! Not so big, after all—and with no one to look after him. . . . He was harder than the grandmother, but it was a nice hardness. . . . And every day he had to work. . . . She had torn up all his beautiful writing. . . . She stirred suddenly, and sighed.

"What's the matter?" asked father. "Another dream?"

"Oh," said the little girl, "my head's on your heart; I can hear it going. What a big heart you've got, father dear."

The ending plays too hard on what is, finally, a fairly sticky sentimentality, but what Katherine Mansfield is trying to do here is interesting. This is a story of generational and sexual *rapprochement* based on Kezia's imagining of commonality with her father rather than on recognition of his superiority or his power. She draws close to him as she perceives him as like herself— suffering, isolated, pitiable and, intriguingly, yet unthreateningly, different. The sexual element, while submerged, is important, and suggests an account of the genesis of female desire quite different from the Freudian or Jungian accounts which still dominate discussion of the subject. Katherine Mansfield here is tentatively positing a female sexuality whose basis is reflective, based on similarity rather than difference. Although sexual difference appears as one factor in the account, it is not the main factor, and the "hardness" of the father elicits curiosity in the girl rather than either respect or fear. What this story gives the reader is an opening into a new account of the links between male and female Katherine Mansfield was to return to in her later fiction.

Except for "The Child-Who-Was-Tired" all the early stories considered so far did not see book publication until 1924. For her contemporaries, Katherine Mansfield was pre-eminently the author of her short-story collection of 1911, *In a German Pension*. This volume became something of a *bête noire* for Katherine Mansfield, locking her into a reputation for thematic and stylistic practices which she felt she outgrew. The *Pension* stories, without exception, treat the poverty, absurdity and bitterness of conventional male/female relations and do so with an aggressive satire that is less obvious in Katherine Mansfield's later work. In 1920 she disowned the collection, writing to Murry who wanted to have it reprinted that:

I cannot have the *German Pension* republished under any circumstances. It is far too *immature* and I don't even acknowledge it today . . . it's not good enough . . . It's positively juvenile, and besides, it's not what I mean, it's a lie.

But she sarcastically gave in regarding reprinting ten days later:

Very well, Isabel about the *Pension*. But I must write an introduction saying that it is early early work, or just that it was written between certain years, because you know, Betsy love, it's nothing to be proud of.

Again in 1922 she warned her agent off the book saying that she had "just begun to persuade the reviewers that I don't like ugliness for ugliness' sake," and that the collection was full of "youthful extravagance of expression and youthful disgust."

C. A. Hankin believes that Katherine Mansfield's reasons for distancing herself from the volume were based on her private life. Hankin argues that a distaste for the "physical subjects" that dominate the book was grounded on Katherine Mansfield's ambivalence about her bisexuality, while her desire to destroy "the personality and the past she wanted buried" led her to turn on the literary productions of her earlier years. One can, of course, only speculate about Katherine Mansfield's motives, but here it is more useful to turn to her literary development than to the details of her life. The sharp satire of the *Pension* volume differs greatly from the lyrical technique that had become Katherine Mansfield's characteristic method by the 1920s. Further, after World War I, the stories were open to simple nationalist readings that could identify the Germans alone as guilty of the abuses she savages. Far from abandoning the attitudes in the *Pension* stories to a past she had left behind, Katherine Mansfield had refined them. She was unfair to the collection. While it does not have the sinuousness, the half-tones and muted gestures of her later fiction, it succeeds on its own terms as biting caricature of brutality, mutual exploitation and moral blindness.

The Germans in the stories are rank and rowdy animals, unconscious of their idiotic parodies of civilised behaviour. " 'There is nothing like cherries for producing free saliva after trombone playing,' " a gallant Herr Professor tells the young woman narrator in "The Modern Soul" (1911). As he chews and spits out the stones he does not wonder at her refusal of his offer to share them: " 'It is your innate female delicacy. . . . Or perhaps you do not care to eat the worms. All cherries contain worms.' " The Professor, a good representative of the men in the volume, thinks himself irresistible. The women at the spa in which many of the stories are set, entice and pursue the men with equally clumsy gestures. The comedy is robust, inventive, absurdist: it is like watching beached walruses at play.

A few of the stories, however, are unremittingly sombre. "Frau Brechenmacher Attends a Wedding" (1911), the best piece in the collection, is a dark continuation of the themes established in the comic *Pension* stories. Its success, comments Sylvia Berkman, derives from its "emotional violence—a savage pity expressed in terms of a harshness that drives the narrator to underline every revolting detail." The story certainly exudes anger about the historical and cultural position of women and with the processes that deny them autonomy and press them to court their own enslavement, while their male partners debase themselves as part of the same process. The anger that informs the story, and is captured in its bluntness, is part of its excellence. Katherine Mansfield is one of the first writers in the twentieth century to address straightforwardly the anger of women at the injustice of their treatment, and express it in a prose that refuses to soften the accounts of the varieties of women's emotional response to their subjection.

"Frau Brechenmacher" begins with the familiar scene of an adult woman training her little girl for female servitude. The Frau and her daughter work frantically to prepare demanding Herr Brechenmacher's clothes for a wedding. When the man arrives he faults their work and his wife's appearance, and sends her into the dark passage to dress while he preens himself in front of the only mirror. The Frau gives the lamp and her shawl to her daughter, passing the standard of womanhood to the prematurely adult creature who has already been denied a childhood. The girl is left to guard the four smaller children who represent both her mother's fate and her own only possible future. The wedding is a farce. The bride, who has been "wild," and who has brought along her illegitimate daughter as a last gesture of defiance, is dressed in white, "giving her the appearance of an iced cake all ready to be cut and served in neat little pieces to the bridegroom," while the air of the *Festsaal* is appropriately fetid, filled with the "familiar festive smell" of "beer and perspiration." When Herr Brechenmacher presents the communal gift it winds up to be a sexual insult—a silver coffee pot containing "a baby's bottle and two little cradles holding china dolls." The matrons watch the proceedings from the sides of the hall like cattle, quietly bemoaning but never challenging their lot, " 'Girls,' " says meek Frau Brechenmacher, " 'have a lot to learn.' " She has learned her own lesson only too well; home again with her drunken husband, he reminds her of their wedding night.

> Herr Brechenmacher yawned and stretched himself, and then looked up at her, grinning.
>
> "Remember the night we came home? You were an innocent one, you were."
>
> "Get along! Such a time ago I forget." Well she remembered.
>
> "Such a clout on the ear as you gave me . . . But I soon taught you."
>
> "Oh, don't start talking. You've too much beer. Come to bed."
>
> He tilted back his chair, chuckling with laughter.
>
> "That's not what you said to me that night. God, the trouble you gave me!"

The Frau goes to bed after looking at the children.

> "Always the same," she said—"all over the world the same; but, God in heaven—but *stupid*."
>
> Then even the memory of the wedding faded quite. She lay down on the bed and put her arm across her face like a child who expected to be hurt as Herr Brechenmacher lurched in.

The story is close to the drama in the vividness of its apprehension of the characters, and the recurrent theme is that of men hurting and maiming women. Marriage is equivalent to ritual slaughter here and the triple sacrifice of the matron, the bride and the little girl presents a barbaric picture of the life-cycle of women. Especially cruel is the heavy sense of imprisonment of the matrons which is only lifted to allow them to witness the humiliation of yet another woman at the wedding. The women are perceived purely as objects by their men—as servants, providers of rough pleasure and as breeding machines. Frau Brechenmacher's mask is heavy, and beneath it she is a tangle of inadmissible fears. She must hide her terror that others are laughing at her, her sense of weakness, her terror of her husband, and she is so caught in her own horrors that she cannot even think of communicating with the other women. All the wives are masks speaking to masks, dumb in their captivity under bestial sexual norms. The tale ends as it began, with the expected violation of a child, the torturing of Frau Brechenmacher's unconscious. The Frau asserts her humanity only through her fear, her stoicism and her silence.

The story, like many of Katherine Mansfield's, is shaped by contradictory pressures. The narrative itself, with its sympathetic, revelatory, outraged view of Frau Brechenmacher's trouble, exists on a completely different ideological plane from that of the world it describes. The method is related to irony but goes beyond it to suggest a fracturing in the realm of values that is signalled by the distance of the ethical commitment of the narration from the world it realistically describes. The story reveals its rage, as Berkman says, in its selection of detail, its unglossed accusations that derive from the brutality of the symbolic objects and actions described. Meaning is made through an indirectness that permeates the entirety of the narrative. Frau Brechenmacher's reactions to her situation—fear, submission, docility—while offered as typical, are rejected by the anger of the prose that reveals them. It is the *manner* of writing that posits an alternative response to the familiar situation of the woman in the story. Katherine Mansfield is testing a kind of writing that is suited to suggesting complex responses to the reader while the narrative surface remains simple. It is obvious how useful this kind of narrative is in the hands of a woman writing out of a sense of the difference of women's potential from her traditional subjection and enforced simplicity. It neither denies the sordidness of women's history nor accepts it as the only paradigm for the future; it initiates a new register in women's satire.

Two stories in the *Pension* collection look closely at the intersection of psychology and biology in men and women's reactions to women's fertility. "At Lehmann's" (c. 1911) studies the awakening of a young girl to the meaning of her sexuality, while "A Birthday" (1911) portrays a man's response to his wife's labour. Both the stories contain protests against the idea of biologically determined destinies for women; both refuse to see women only as agents of reproduction.

Sabina, the jolly young waitress in "At Lehmann's," is happy in her exploitative job and completely ignorant of her sexuality. The narrative is filtered through her consciousness as she good-naturedly does the cook's work as well as her own, wonders about gargantuan Frau Lehmann's pregnancy, and feels stirrings of incomprehensible response to a potential seducer who frequents the café. The seducer is impersonalised in the narrative, as he is in Sabina's mind, and known simply as the "Young Man." Sabina's response to him is both impersonal and unconscious, signalled in the text by actions that become symbols as she lets herself be lured into the secret warmth of the ladies' cloakroom, and stokes the fire high. The Young Man is puzzled by her but moves in to take his advantage:

> "Look here," he said roughly, "are you a child, or are you playing at being one?"
> "I—I—"
> Laughter ceased. She looked up at him once, then down at the floor, and began breathing like a frightened little animal.
> He pulled her closer still and kissed her mouth.
> "Na, what are you doing?" she whispered.
> He let go her hands, he placed his on her breasts, and the room seemed to swim round Sabina. Suddenly, from the room above, a frightful, tearing shriek.
> She wrenched herself away, tightening herself, drew herself up.
> "Who did that—who made that noise?"
>
> In the silence the thin wailing of a baby.
> "Achk!" shrieked Sabina, rushing from the room.

This ending of the story demands a symbolist reading as the association between lovemaking, the screams of the woman in childbirth, and the baby that wails its way into the world coalesce in the narrative to warn Sabina, without her conscious understanding, of her danger. Just precisely what Sabina "knows" at the end of "At Lehmann's" is uncertain; what the reader knows is that Katherine Mansfield has joined together images of male assault, female desire, pain, bewilderment and violence as the important aspects of a typical sexual initiation for women.

"A Birthday" traces a man's reaction to childbirth and fatherhood. The story follows the mind of Andreas Bitzer as his wife suffers through the last stages of labour. The narrative concentrates on the husband's egoism and self-regard, and mocks his self-pity and annoyance with his wife's thoughtlessly interrupting his comfortable existence by giving birth to his third child. As in "New Dresses" a corrective voice is given to an old doctor as Andreas whines about his wife's "weakness."

> "Pity—this weather," said Doctor Erb.
> "Yes, it gets on Anna's nerves, and it's just nerve she wants."
> "Eh, what's that?" retorted the doctor. "Nerve! Man alive! She's got twice the nerve of you and me rolled into one. Nerve! she's nothing but nerve. A woman who works as she does about the

house and has three children in four years thrown in with the
dusting, so to speak. . . !"

"Now *he's* accusing me," thought Andreas. "That's the second
time this morning—first mother and now this man taking advantage of my sensitiveness."

Andreas's ill-expressed and ill-channelled but real feelings of helplessness
are only partly concealed by his mental bluster. His insensitivity, which he
mistakes for delicacy, announces his own vulnerability. Under the cover
of complaints Andreas tries to admit to himself neither his feelings of dependence on his wife nor his knowledge that he has used her too hard.
When the wife, after much pain, gives birth to the son he desires, Andreas
seemingly irrelevantly says, " 'Well, by God! Nobody can accuse *me* of not
knowing what suffering is.' " Katherine Mansfield makes this bundle of
constructs that represents a typical husband ridiculous, a parody of masculine selfishness and vanity. But there is also a shred of pity in the story
for a character who needs so desperately to be validated by the constant
presence of an enslaved wife, whose conformity to a particular male stereotype makes him a silly and vulnerable fool, and who yet shares in the
paralysing terror of isolation that she sees as the most central feature of
the human condition.

If Katherine Mansfield demonstrates a pervasive interest in recording
the experience of women in her early work as well as an interest in discovering new ways to speak of that experience, the *Pension* stories also
make it clear that she had no use for self-declared "progressive" theories
about women which claim that the signs of women's oppression are actually
innate feminine virtues. In terms of locating herself in relation to the feminist movement of her time, "An Advanced Lady" (c. 1911) is one of her
most important stories. In this tale Katherine Mansfield parodies the plat-
itudes of a traitorous "feminism," pernicious in that its claims promote
further entrapment of women. In the story the Advanced Lady herself goes
for a walk with other residents in her hotel including the sceptical narrator.
The Lady has left her daughter behind to sit alone in her room while she
herself holds forth to the other guests about the book she is writing:

> "The trouble is to know where to stop. My brain has been a
> hive for years, and about three months ago the pent-up waters
> burst over my soul, and since then I am writing all day until late
> into the night, still ever finding fresh inspirations and thoughts
> which beat impatient wings about my heart."
>
> "Is it a novel?" asked Else shyly.
>
> "Of course it is a novel," said I.
>
> "How can you be so positive?" said Frau Kellermann, eyeing
> me severely.
>
> "Because nothing but a novel could produce an effect like that."
>
> "Ach, don't quarrel," said the Advanced Lady sweetly. "Yes it

is a novel—upon the Modern Woman. For this seems to me the woman's hour. It is mysterious and almost prophetic, it is the symbol of true advanced women; not one of those violent creatures who deny their sex and smother their frail wings under . . . under—"

"The English tailor-made?" from Frau Kellermann.

"I was not going to put it like that. Rather, under the lying garb of false masculinity!"

"Such a subtle distinction!" I murmured.

"What then," asked Fräulein Elsa, looking adoringly at the Advanced Lady—"whom then do you consider the true woman?"

"She is the incarnation of comprehending Love!"

" 'That theory of yours about women and Love,' " says the disgusted narrator near the end of the story, " '—it's as old as the hills—oh, older!' " " 'I too,' " she says, " 'would like to write a book on the advisability of caring for daughters and taking them for airings and keeping them out of kitchens!' " In effect, this is precisely what Katherine Mansfield herself is doing in the *Pension* stories.

The ideology in Katherine Mansfield's early writing is decidedly and overtly feminist and I can only comment that it is peculiar that this observation is not already a commonplace of Katherine Mansfield criticism. If, as Virginia Woolf suggests in *A Room of One's Own*, one of the tasks of the committed woman writer is to begin to transcribe "the accumulation of unrecorded life" that comprises most of women's lost history, then Katherine Mansfield surely saw herself from the beginning as one of those who broke that silence.

Although the concerns of Katherine Mansfield's early stories—whether fabular, satirical or realist—foreground women's experience, it is important, too, to note that they are not *limited* to it. No one could claim that issues of injustice, isolation, sexual unease or cruelty were the particular property of one sex, race or class. What is important is that Katherine Mansfield uses ordinary women's experiences as the starting-points from which to survey the world in general, and does so with a confidence that was to remain constant in her writing.

Chronology

1834 William Morris born, son of a wealthy stockbroker. Educated at Marlborough College and Exeter College, where he meets Edward Burne-Jones, with whom he becomes involved in Pre-Raphaelite Brotherhood. Upon coming of age, he inherits £900 a year from his father's estate, and the following year is articled to a London architect although he soon turns to painting and poetry. In 1861 he founds the firm of Morris, Marshall, Faulkner & Co., producing furniture, tiles, fabrics, and stained glass.

1837 Queen Victoria ascends the throne.

1839 Walter Pater born, son of a London doctor. He is educated at King's School, Canterbury, and Queen's College, Oxford; upon graduation, he remains in Oxford, tutoring private students in Classics. In 1864 he is elected Fellow of Brasenose College, Oxford; a year later he tours Italy, returning to Oxford, where he teaches until 1885.

1840 Thomas Hardy born in Higher Bockhampton, Stinsford, Dorset, to a stonemason. Educated locally and in Dorchester, he is then apprenticed to an architect, later moving to London to work for architect and church restorer Arthur Blomfield. In 1867 Hardy returns to Dorset and begins work on his first novel, *The Poor Man and the Lady*, which is rejected for publication. After his works begin to be published, Hardy supports himself as a writer.

1847 Abraham Stoker (Bram Stoker) born in Dublin to a civil servant. After graduating from Trinity College, Dublin, he takes a job with the Civil Service, and later begins working as a drama critic with the *Dublin Mail*. Stoker then meets and becomes close friends with the actor Henry Irving, taking a position as his acting manager and personal secretary, a post he holds until Irving's death.

1850 Robert Louis Stevenson born, son of a prosperous Edinburgh engineer. He attends local schools and Edinburgh University, before being articled to a law firm. Chronic ill health forces him to spend each winter in warmer climates. Stevenson begins his literary career as an essayist and travel writer with *An Inland Voyage* (1878). After further travel, Stevenson finally settles in Samoa, where he lives the rest of his life.

1854   Oscar Wilde born in Dublin to William Wilde, a prominent oculist, and Jane Elgee Wilde, a writer (under the pseudonym of "Speranza"). He is educated at the Portora Royal School, Trinity College, Dublin, and Magdalen College, Oxford, where his professors include Walter Pater. After graduating with a B.A. in Greats (Classics) with First Class Honours, Wilde publishes *Poems* (1881) and embarks on a lecture tour of America as a self-styled "Professor of Aesthetics." Wilde later works as an editor of *Woman's World* and as a playwright.

1857   George Gissing born, son of a pharmacist. Educated on scholarships at private schools, he attends Owens College, Manchester, where he excels in Classics, but is expelled for stealing. After a trip to America, Gissing moves to London, where he tutors in Latin and Greek and begins his literary career by publishing *Workers in the Dawn* (1880) at his own expense. He soon begins supporting himself with his steady literary output.

Józef Teodor Konrad Korzeniowski (Joseph Conrad) born in Berdyczew, Poland, to Apollo Korzeniowski, an estate-manager (and sometime writer) and political activist. Conrad follows his parents into political Russian exile, during which his mother dies. Conrad and his father return to Poland in 1869. Conrad later leaves Cracow for Marseilles, where he becomes a sailor, rising in time to position of commander. Later, Conrad becomes a naturalized British citizen; shortly thereafter, he begins writing *Almayer's Folly*, his first novel, and soon gives up his sailing career.

1858   E(dith) Nesbit born in London, daughter of an agricultural chemist and professor. Given desultory schooling in France, Germany, and England, she writes fiction and poetry from an early age. Nesbit later marries Hubert Bland, a founder of the Fabian Society. Though she publishes novels frequently, it is not until *The Treasure Seekers* (1899) that she finds her natural métier for fantasy.

1859   Arthur Conan Doyle born in Edinburgh, son of a civil servant. He studies medicine at the University of Edinburgh, where one of his professors is Dr. Joseph Bell, primary model for Sherlock Holmes. In 1882 Doyle opens his own opthalmology practice in Southsea, writing fiction to supplement his meager income. After the success of the early Sherlock Holmes adventures, he retires from medicine to write fulltime.

1865   Rudyard Kipling born in Bombay, son of an artist and teacher. At six, he travels to England for schooling, boarding at the "House of Desolation" in Southsea before attending the United Services College, Westward Ho! He then returns to India to become a reporter for the *Civil and Military Gazette* (Lahore) and the *Pioneer* (Allahabad) and publishes articles, poems, and tales. In 1889 Kipling sails to England, where he lives for the rest of his life.

1866   H(erbert) G(eorge) Wells born in Bromley, Kent, to a shopkeeper and a lady's maid. After studying at Midhurst Grammar School, he is apprenticed to a draper in Southsea, but wins a scholarship to the Normal School of Science in South Kensington, where he studies under T. H. Huxley. Wells leaves without taking a degree to begin a career as teacher and journalist.

1867   (Enoch) Arnold Bennett born in Hanley, Staffordshire, one of the "Five Towns," to Enoch Bennett, shopkeeper and solicitor. Educated locally, Bennett later studies for law but fails necessary qualifying exams. In 1889 Bennett moves to London to take a job as shorthand clerk to a firm of solicitors, where he begins writing short fiction. In 1895 the *Yellow Book* publishes "A Letter Home," his first significant work.
John Galsworthy born in Kingston Hill, Surrey, son a of wealthy businessman. He attends Harrow, then New College, Oxford, reading law, and is admitted to the bar shortly after graduation. Supported by his father, Galsworthy travels extensively abroad; while sailing back from Australia, he befriends Joseph Conrad, who is first mate aboard the ship. After a desultory attempt to assist in his father's business, Galsworthy devotes his time to writing fiction.

1871   Hardy publishes *Desperate Remedies*, his first novel to be printed, at his own expense.

1872   Hardy publishes *Under the Greenwood Tree. A Pair of Blue Eyes* begins serial publication (book 1873).
(Henry) Max(imilian) Beerbohm born in Kensington, London, son of a prosperous merchant. Educated at Charterhouse and Merton College, Oxford, he leaves the university without taking a degree and moves to London, having already published a series of caricatures and essays in such magazines as the *Strand* and the *Yellow Book*. Beerbohm later succeeds George Bernard Shaw as drama critic for the *Saturday Review*.

1873   Hardy begins serializing *Far from the Madding Crowd* (book 1874). Pater publishes *Studies in the History of the Renaissance*.

1874   G(ilbert) K(eith) Chesterton born in Kensington, London, son of a businessman and investor. He attends St. Paul's School and the Slade School of Art, where he suffers a spiritual and intellectual crisis. Abandoning painting, Chesterton begins work as a journalist and freelance poet, first coming to public notice through his opposition to the Boer War.

1876   Hardy publishes *The Hand of Ethelberta*.

1878   Hardy publishes *The Return of the Native*.

1879   E(dmund) M(organ) Forster born in London, son of an architect who dies before his son is two. As a child, Forster inherits £8,000 upon the death of his aunt. Forster is educated at Tonbridge School and King's College, Cambridge, where he graduates in Classics and history; afterwards, he travels for a year in Greece and Italy. Upon returning to England, he contributes essays and short stories to the

Independent Review. Forster later travels twice to India, where he serves for a period as secretary to the Maharajah of Dewas Senior. Later, Forster lives at Cambridge, where he is elected Fellow of King's College.

1880   Hardy publishes *The Trumpet-Major.*
Eliza Lynn Linton publishes *The Rebel of the Family.*

1881   Hardy publishes *A Laodicean.*
Stevenson begins serial publication of *Treasure Island* in *Young Folks* (book 1883).
P(elham) G(renville) Wodehouse born in Guildford, son of a Civil Service officer and judge stationed in Hong Kong. Educated at Dulwich College, after which he becomes a clerk in the London branch of the Hong Kong and Shanghai Bank. After the success of his early novels, Wodehouse quits the bank. Later he moves to New York and Los Angeles. After political difficulties during World War II, Wodehouse returns to America, where he lives and writes until his death.

1882   Hardy publishes *Two on a Tower.*
Stevenson publishes *New Arabian Nights.*

1883   Olive Schreiner publishes *The Story of an African Farm* in England, under the pseudonym of "Ralph Iron."
Eliza Lynn Linton publishes collected essays in *The Girl of the Period.*

1884   Gissing publishes *The Unclassed.*
The Society of Authors established.

1885   Gissing publishes *Isabel Clarendon.*
Pater publishes *Marius the Epicurean: His Sensations and Ideas.*
Stevenson publishes *A Child's Garden of Verses.*

1886   Gissing publishes *Demos.*
Hardy publishes *The Mayor of Casterbridge.*
Kipling publishes *Departmental Ditties,* a collection of poems.
Stevenson publishes *The Strange Case of Dr. Jekyll and Mr. Hyde; Kidnapped* appears in *Young Folks* (book published same year).

1887   Gissing publishes *Thyrza.*
Hardy publishes *The Woodlanders.*
Pater publishes *Imaginary Portraits.*
Arthur Conan Doyle publishes "A Study in Scarlet," the first Sherlock Holmes adventure, in *Beeton's Christmas Annual.*

1888   Gissing publishes *A Life's Morning.*
Hardy publishes *The Wessex Tales.*
Kipling publishes *Plain Tales from the Hills,* followed by the other Indian Railways Series titles: *Soldiers Three, The Story of Gadsby's, In Black and White, Wee Willie Winkie, The Phantom 'Rickshaw,* and *Under the Deodars.*
Stevenson serializes *The Master of Ballantrae* in *Scribner's* (book 1889); *The Black Arrow* is published.
Wilde publishes *The Happy Prince and Other Tales.*
Kathleen Mansfield Beauchamp (Katherine Mansfield) born in Wel-

lington, New Zealand. Educated in Wellington and then in England at Queen's College, London. She works at various literary magazines in England with her husband, John Middleton Murry, while publishing sketches and short stories. Travels frequently to France and Switzerland because of her tuberculosis.

1889   Doyle publishes *Micah Clarke,* a historical novel.
Gissing publishes *The Nether World.*
Kipling publishes *Sea to Sea.*
Pater publishes *Appreciations.*
The Dial begins publication.
Stevenson publishes *The Wrong Box,* co-written with his stepson, Lloyd Osbourne.
Mona Caird publishes *The Wing of Azrael.*
Several publishers reject the first installments of Hardy's *Tess of the D'Urbervilles.*

1890   Doyle publishes "The Sign of the Four" in *Lippincott's Monthly Magazine;* published in book form as *The Sign of Four.*
Gissing publishes *The Emancipated.*
Kipling publishes *The Light That Failed* (British publication 1891).
Morris publishes *News from Nowhere,* starts the Kelmscott Press.
Schreiner publishes *Dreams.*
Wilde publishes "The Picture of Dorian Gray" in *Lippincott's Monthly Magazine.*

1891   Gissing publishes *New Grub Street.*
Hardy publishes *Tess of the D'Urbervilles* and *A Group of Noble Dames.*
Morris publishes *The Story of the Glittering Plain.*
Wilde publishes an expanded *Picture of Dorian Gray* in book form; he also publishes *Intentions* (essays), *Lord Arthur Savile's Crime and Other Stories,* and *A House of Pomegranates.*
Doyle publishes *The White Company,* first in *Cornhill Magazine,* then as a book.
Copyright law passed which protects British works published in U.S.

1892   Doyle publishes *The Adventures of Sherlock Holmes,* a collection of stories that first appeared in the *Strand.*
Gissing publishes *Born in Exile.*
Hardy publishes the first version of *The Well-Beloved* serially.
Kipling publishes *Naulahka* and *Barrack-Room Ballads.*
Stevenson publishes *The Wrecker.*

1893   Frank Frankfort Moore publishes "*I Forbid the Banns.*"
George Egerton (Mary Chavelita Dunne Clairmonte Bright) publishes *Keynotes,* a collection of short stories.
Gissing publishes *The Odd Women.*
Sarah Grand publishes *The Heavenly Twins.*
Kipling publishes *Many Inventions.*
Schreiner publishes *Dream Life and Real Life.*
Doyle publishes "The Final Problem" in *The Strand,* killing Sherlock Holmes.

1894   Doyle publishes *The Memoirs of Sherlock Holmes.*
Kipling publishes *The Jungle Book.*

Morris publishes *The Wood beyond the World*.
The Yellow Book begins publication.
Mona Caird publishes *The Daughters of Danaus*.
Iota (Kathleen Mannington Caffyn) publishes *A Yellow Aster*.
Pater dies in Oxford on July 30.
Stevenson publishes *The Ebb-Tide*. On December 3 he dies at his home in Samoa of a ruptured blood vessel.

1895   Grant Allen publishes *The Woman Who Did*.
Conrad publishes *Almayer's Folly*.
Kipling publishes *The Second Jungle Book*.
Morris publishes *The Well at the World's End*.
Wells publishes *The Time Machine*.
The Savoy begins publication.
Hardy publishes *Jude the Obscure*; its hostile reception leads him to abandon fiction and to write only poetry.
Wilde tried for sexual offenses; sentenced to two years of hard labor at Reading Gaol.

1896   Conrad publishes *An Outcast of the Islands*.
Beerbohm publishes *The Works of Max Beerbohm*, his first book; he begins a series of articles for *The Daily Mail*.
Wells publishes *The Island of Doctor Moreau*.
Doyle publishes *Rodney Stone*.
Pater's unfinished *Gaston de Latour* published posthumously.
Stevenson's unfinished *Weir of Hermiston* published posthumously.
Morris dies October 3 at his home in London of congestion of the lungs.

1897   Conrad serializes *The Nigger of the "Narcissus"* in the *New Review*; in December it is published in book form.
Galsworthy publishes *From the Four Winds*, a collection of short stories.
Hardy publishes the second version of *The Well-Beloved*.
Kipling publishes *Captains Courageous*.
Morris's *The Water of the Wondrous Isles* and *The Sundering Flood* published posthumously.
Stevenson's fragmentary *St. Ives* published posthumously.
Stoker publishes *Dracula*.
Wells publishes *The Invisible Man: A Grotesque Romance*.
Beerbohm publishes *The Happy Hypocrite*.

1898   William Barry publishes *The Two Standards*.
Bennett publishes *A Man from the North*.
Kipling publishes *The Day's Work*.
Wells publishes *The War of the Worlds* and *Tales of Space and Time*.
Galsworthy publishes *Jocelyn*.

1899   Conrad begins serializing *Heart of Darkness* and *Lord Jim* in *Blackwood's Magazine*.
Gissing publishes *The Crown of Life*.
Kipling publishes *Stalky & Co.*
Nesbit publishes *The Treasure Seekers*.
Beerbohm publishes *More*.
Wells publishes *When the Sleeper Wakes*.

1900   Galsworthy publishes *Villa Rubein*.
        Wells publishes *Love and Mr. Lewisham*.
        Wilde dies on November 30 of cerebral meningitis in Paris, and is
        buried there.

1901   Queen Victoria dies; Edward VIII ascends the throne.
        Galsworthy publishes the first Forsyte story in the collection *Man of
        Devon*.
        Chesterton publishes *The Defendant*.
        Kipling publishes *Kim*.
        Nesbit publishes *The Wouldbegoods*.
        Wells publishes *The First Men in the Moon*.
        Doyle publishes *The Hound of the Baskervilles* serially in *The Strand*
        (book 1902).

1902   Bennett publishes *The Grand Babylon Hotel* and *Anna of the Five Towns*.
        Conrad publishes *Typhoon; Heart of Darkness* appears in book form.
        Gissing serializes *The Private Papers of Henry Ryecroft* in the *Fortnightly
        Review*, under the title *An Author at Grass*.
        Kipling publishes *Just-So Stories*.
        Wodehouse publishes *The Pothunters*.
        Doyle knighted.

1903   Doyle resurrects Sherlock Holmes in ''The Empty House'' for *The
        Strand*.
        Conrad publishes *Typhoon and Other Stories*.
        Gissing dies on December 28 of pneumonia in Ispore, France, and is
        buried there.

1904   Chesterton publishes *The Napoleon of Notting Hill*.
        Conrad publishes *Nostromo*.
        Galsworthy publishes *The Island Pharisees* (revised 1908).
        Kipling publishes *Traffics and Discoveries*.
        Nesbit publishes *The Phoenix and the Carpet*.
        Wodehouse publishes *William Tell Told Again*.

1905   Bennett publishes *Tales of the Five Towns*.
        Chesterton publishes *The Club of Queer Trades*.
        Forster publishes *Where Angels Fear to Tread*.
        Wells publishes *A Modern Utopia* and *Kipps: The Story of a Simple Soul*.
        Doyle publishes *The Return of Sherlock Holmes*.

1906   Conrad serializes *The Secret Agent*.
        Galsworthy publishes *The Man of Property*, the first volume of a trilogy
        collectively entitled *The Forsyte Saga*. The other two novels are *In
        Chancery* (1920) and *To Let* (1921).
        Kipling publishes *Puck of Pook's Hill*.
        Wells publishes *In the Days of the Comet*.
        Wodehouse publishes *Love among the Chickens*.
        Doyle publishes *Sir Nigel*.

1907   Bennett publishes *The Grim Smile of the Five Towns*.
        Conrad publishes an extended version of *The Secret Agent* in book
        form.
        Forster publishes *The Longest Journey*.

Galsworthy publishes *The Country House.*
Nesbit publishes *The Railway Children.*
Kipling is awarded the Nobel Prize for literature.

1908   Bennett publishes *Buried Alive* and *The Old Wives' Tale.*
Chesterton publishes *The Man Who Was Thursday: A Nightmare* and *Orthodoxy.*
Forster publishes *A Room with a View.*

1909   Galsworthy publishes *Fraternity.*
Nesbit publishes *Harding's Luck.*
Stoker publishes *The Lady of the Shroud.*
Wells publishes *Tono-Bungay* and *Ann Veronica.*
Wodehouse publishes *The Swoop* and *Mike.*
Beerbohm publishes *Yet Again.*

1910   Edward VIII dies; George V becomes King of England.
Bennett publishes *Clayhanger,* the first volume of a trilogy that includes *Hilda Lessways* (1911) and *These Twain* (1916).
Chesterton publishes *The Ball and the Cross.*
Forster publishes *Howards End.*
Kipling publishes *Rewards and Fairies.*
Wells publishes *The History of Mr. Polly.*
Wodehouse publishes *Psmith in the City* and *A Gentleman of Leisure.*
Hardy accepts the Order of Merit, after having refused knighthood.

1911   Beerbohm publishes *Zuleika Dobson.*
Chesterton publishes *The Innocence of Father Brown.*
Conrad publishes *Under Western Eyes.*
Forster publishes *The Celestial Omnibus and Other Short Stories.*
Galsworthy publishes *The Patrician.*
Mansfield publishes *In a German Pension.*
Schreiner publishes *Women and Labour.*
Stoker publishes *The Lair of the White Worm.*
Wells publishes *The New Machiavelli.*

1912   Beerbohm publishes *A Christmas Garland,* a collection of parodies.
Bennett publishes *The Matador of the Five Towns.*
Conrad publishes *'Twixt Land and Sea; Chance* is serialized in the *New York Herald.*
Forster begins work on *A Passage to India.*
Chesterton publishes *Manalive.*
Stoker dies on April 20 of syphilis at his home in Ireland.

1913   Chesterton publishes *The Wisdom of Father Brown* and *The Flying Inn.*
Galsworthy publishes *The Dark Flower.*

1914   World War I begins, August 4.
Conrad publishes a revised *Chance* in book form.
Doyle publishes *The Valley of Fear* serially in the United States, then serially in *The Strand* (book 1915).

1915   Conrad publishes *Victory.*
Wodehouse publishes *Psmith Journalist.*
Nesbit awarded Civil Service pension.

1917   Conrad publishes *The Shadow-Line* and writes prefaces to an edition of his collected works.
Kipling publishes *A Diversity of Creatures*.
Doyle publishes *His Last Bow*.

1918   Bennett publishes *The Roll-Call*.
Galsworthy offered, but refuses, knighthood.
Mansfield's "Prelude" published by the Hogarth Press.
World War I ends, November 11.

1919   Beerbohm publishes *Seven Men*.
Kipling publishes *The Years Between*.
Wodehouse publishes *My Man Jeeves*.
Conrad publishes *The Arrow of Gold*.

1920   Conrad publishes *The Rescue*.
Galsworthy publishes *In Chancery*.
Mansfield publishes *Bliss and Other Stories*.
Wells publishes *The Outline of History* and visits Lenin in Russia.
Beerbohm publishes *And Even Now*.

1921   Galsworthy publishes *To Let*.
Wodehouse publishes *Jill the Reckless*.

1922   Chesterton publishes *The Man Who Knew Too Much*.
Mansfield publishes *The Garden Party*.
Galsworthy's *The Forsyte Saga* published as a trilogy.
Bennett publishes *Mr. Prohack*.
Forster publishes *Alexandria: A History and a Guide*.

1923   Wells publishes *Men Like Gods*.
Kipling publishes *Land and Sea Tales for Scouts and Guides*.
Bennett publishes *Riceyman Steps*.
Mansfield publishes *The Dove's Nest*. On January 12 she dies of tuberculosis, in Fontainebleau, France, and is buried there.

1924   Forster publishes *A Passage to India*.
Galsworthy publishes *The White Monkey*.
Mansfield's *Something Childish* published posthumously.
Conrad offered, but declines, knighthood. On August 3 he dies of a heart attack, and is buried in Canterbury.
Nesbit dies May 4, after a long illness, at her home outside London.

1925   Chesterton edits *G. K.'s Weekly* until his death.
Wodehouse publishes *Carry On, Jeeves*.
Conrad's *Tales of Hearsay* and the incomplete *Suspense* published posthumously.

1926   Kipling publishes *Debits and Credits*.
Galsworthy publishes *The Silver Spoon*.
Chesterton publishes *The Incredulity of Father Brown*.

1927   Chesterton publishes *The Secret of Father Brown*.
Forster publishes *Aspects of the Novel*.
Doyle publishes *The Case-Book of Sherlock Holmes*.

1928   Forster publishes *The Eternal Moment and Other Stories*.
            Galsworthy publishes *Swan Song*.
            Hardy dies of cardiac syncope at his home. His ashes are placed in Westminster Abbey, and his heart is buried next to his first wife in the Stinsford cemetery. Florence Hardy publishes the first part of Hardy's autobiography, *The Early Life of Thomas Hardy 1880–1891*.

1929   Galsworthy publishes *A Modern Comedy*, a trilogy resuming the history of the Forsyte family; it contains *The White Monkey, The Silver Spoon, Swan Song* and two interludes. He is awarded the Order of Merit.

1930   Kipling publishes *Thy Servant a Dog*.
            Florence Hardy publishes *The Later Years of Thomas Hardy, 1892–1928*, the last four chapters of which are her own composition.
            Doyle dies July 7 of heart disease at his home in Windlesham.

1931   Galsworthy publishes *On Forsyte 'Change*, a collection of stories.
            Bennett dies March 26 of typhoid fever at his home in London.

1932   Kipling publishes *Limits and Renewals*.
            Galsworthy wins the Nobel Prize for literature.

1932–33   *The Journals of Arnold Bennett 1896–1928* published posthumously.
            Galsworthy dies on January 31, probably of a cerebral tumor; his ashes are scattered over the South Downs.

1934   Wells publishes *Experiment in Autobiography*.

1935   Galsworthy's *The End of the Chapter* published posthumously, containing *Maid in Waiting, The Flowering Wilderness*, and *Over the River*.
            Chesterton publishes *The Scandal of Father Brown*.

1936   Chesterton publishes his *Autobiography*. On June 14 he dies of heart disease at his home in Beaconfield.
            Kipling dies on January 18, in London, of a hemorrhaged ulcer; his ashes are laid in Poet's Corner, Westminster Abbey.

1937   Kipling's autobiography, *Something of Myself*, published posthumously.

1938   Wodehouse publishes *The Code of the Woosters*.

1939   World War II begins.
            Forster publishes *What I Believe*.
            Wodehouse publishes *Uncle Fred in the Springtime*.
            Beerbohm knighted.

1945   The *Collected Stories of Katherine Mansfield* published.
            Wells publishes *Mind at the End of Its Tether*.
            World War II ends.

1946   Wells dies August 13 in London; his ashes are scattered over the sea.

1948   The *Collected Short Stories* of E. M. Forster published.

1951   Forster publishes *Two Cheers for Democracy*, a collection of essays.

1953   Forster publishes *The Hill of Devi.*

1956   Beerbohm dies at his home in Rapallo, Italy, on May 20.

1969   Forster awarded the Order of Merit.

1970   Forster dies on June 7 at a friend's house in Coventry, at the age of ninety-one.

1971   Forster's *Maurice* published posthumously.

1972   Forster's *The Life to Come,* a collection of short stories, published posthumously.

1975   Wodehouse knighted; he dies at his home in Long Island at the age of ninety-three, the author of ninety-eight novels. His last, the incomplete *Sunset at Blandings,* is published posthumously.

Contributors

Harold Bloom, Sterling Professor of the Humanities at Yale University, is the author of *The Anxiety of Influence*, *Poetry and Repression*, and many other volumes of literary criticism. His forthcoming study, *Freud: Transference and Authority*, attempts a full-scale reading of all of Freud's major writings. A MacArthur Prize Fellow, he is general editor of five series of literary criticism published by Chelsea House. During 1987–88, he served as Charles Eliot Norton Professor of Poetry at Harvard University.

Carole Silver is Associate Professor of English at Yeshiva University. She is the author of *The Romance of William Morris* and, with Judith S. Neaman, of *Kind Words: A Thesaurus of Euphemism*.

Mary Jacobus is Professor of English at Cornell University. She is the author of *Tradition and Experiment in Wordsworth's* Lyrical Ballads and editor of *Women Writing and Writing about Women*.

Penny Boumelha is the author of *Thomas Hardy and Women: Sexual Ideology and Narrative Form* and *Charlotte Brontë*.

Geoffrey Wall is Lecturer in English at the University of York. He is translator of Pierre Macheray's *Theory of Literary Production*.

Alastair Fowler is Regius Professor of Rhetoric and English Literature at the University of Edinburgh. His books include *Triumphal Forms* and, most recently, *Kinds of Literature*: *An Introduction to the Theory of Genres and Modes*.

Regenia Gagnier is Assistant Professor of English at Stanford University. She is the author of *Idylls of the Marketplace: Oscar Wilde and the Victorian Public*.

John Goode is the author of *George Gissing*: *Ideology and Fiction* and, with David Howard and John Lucas, *Tradition and Tolerance in Nineteenth Century Fiction*. He is editor of *The Air of Reality: New Essays on Henry James* and George Gissing's *The Nether World*.

Aaron Fogel is Assistant Professor of English at Boston University. He is the author of *Coercion to Speak: Conrad's Poetics of Dialogue.*

Robert Penn Warren is our most distinguished living man-of-letters. His best-known novels are *All the King's Men* and *World Enough and Time.* His other crucial books include *Selected Poems* and *Selected Essays.*

Fredric Jameson is Professor of French Literature at Johns Hopkins University. His books include *The Political Unconscious: Narrative as a Socially Symbolic Act, The Prison-House of Language,* and *Marxism and Form.*

Stephen Knight is Professor of English at the University of Sydney. His books include *Form and Ideology in Crime Fiction, The Structure of Sir Thomas Malory's Arthuriad, Rhyming Craftily: Meaning in chaucer's Poetry,* and *The Poetry of the Canterbury Tales.*

Robert L. Caserio is Associate Professor of English at the University of Utah. He is the author of *Plot, Story, and the Novel: From Dickens and Poe to the Modern Period.*

Stephen Prickett is Reader in English at the University of Sussex. His books include *Coleridge and Wordsworth: The Poetry of Growth, Romanticism and Religion: the Tradition of Coleridge and Wordsworth in the Victorian Church,* and the novel *Do It Yourself Doom.*

Frank McConnell, Professor of English at the University of California, Santa Barbara, is the author of *The Science Fiction of H. G. Wells, The Bible and the Narrative Tradition,* and *The Spoken Seen: Film and the Romantic Imagination.*

John Lucas is Professor of English at Loughborough University and has written widely on nineteenth-century poetry and fiction. His most recent book is *Modern English Poetry from Hardy to Hughes.*

James Gindin, Professor of English at the University of Michigan, is the author of *John Galsworthy's Life and Fiction: An Alien's Fortress* and *Harvest of a Quiet Eye: The Novel of Compassion.*

Robert Viscusi teaches English at the Humanities Institute of Brooklyn College. He is the author of *Max Beerbohm, or The Dandy Dante: Rereading with Mirrors.*

Stephen Medcalf is Reader in English at the University of Sussex. He is editor of *The Later Middle Ages.*

Barbara Rosecrance is Assistant Professor of English at Cornell University and has been an assistant editor of *Partisan Review.* She has written on Forster, early modern British literature, and the poetry and music of the Renaissance.

Richard Voorhees is Professor of English at Purdue University and has written *P. G. Wodehouse* and *The Paradox of George Orwell.*

Kate Fullbrook, Senior Lecturer in English at Bristol Polytechnic, is the author of *Katherine Mansfield.*

Bibliography

GENERAL

Allen, Walter. *The English Novel*. New York: Dutton, 1955.

Altick, Richard D. *Victorian Studies in Scarlet*. New York: Norton, 1970.

Auerbach, Nina. *Communities of Women: An Idea in Fiction*. Cambridge, Mass.: Harvard University Press, 1978.

———. *Woman and the Demon: The Life of a Victorian Myth*. Cambridge, Mass.: Harvard University Press, 1982.

Basch, Françoise. *Relative Creatures: Victorian Women in Society and the Novel*. Cambridge: Cambridge University Press, 1974.

Bellamy, William. *The Novels of Wells, Bennett, and Galsworthy 1890–1910*. London: Routledge & Kegan Paul, 1971.

Buckley, Jerome H. *Season of Youth: The Bildungsroman from Dickens to Golding*. Cambridge, Mass.: Harvard University Press, 1974.

Calder, Jenni. *Women and Marriage in Victorian Fiction*. Oxford: Oxford University Press, 1976.

Cawelti, John G. *Adventure, Mystery, and Romance*. Chicago: University of Chicago Press, 1978.

Chesterton, G. K. *The Victorian Age in Literature*. London: Williams & Norgate, 1913.

Cockshut, A. O. J. *Man and Woman: A Study of Love in the Novel 1740–1940*. London: Collins, 1977.

Cox, Don Richard, ed. *Sexuality and Victorian Literature*. Knoxville: University of Tennessee Press, 1984.

Crofte-Cooke, Rupert. *Feasting with Panthers: A New Consideration of Some Late Victorian Writers*. New York: Holt, Rinehart & Winston, 1968.

Cross, Nigel. *The Common Writer: Life in Nineteenth-Century Grub Street*. Cambridge: Cambridge University Press, 1985.

Cunningham, Gail. *The New Woman and the Victorian Novel*. London: Macmillan, 1978.

Cunningham, Valentine. *Everywhere Spoken Against: Dissent in the Victorian Novel*. Oxford: Oxford University Press, 1975.

Dabydeen, David, ed. *The Black Presence in English Literature*. Manchester: Manchester University Press, 1985.

Daiches, David. *Some Late Victorian Attitudes*. New York: Norton, 1969.

Dowling, Linda. *Language and Decadence in the Victorian Fin de Siècle*. Princeton: Princeton University Press, 1986.

Faber, Richard. *Proper Stations: Class in Victorian Fiction*. London: Faber & Faber, 1971.

Fleishman, Avrom. *Figures of Autobiography: The Language of Self-Writing in Victorian and Modern England*. Berkeley: University of California Press, 1983.

Fletcher, Ian, ed. *Decadence and the 1890s*. New York: Homes & Meier, 1978.

Gide, André. *Journals 1889–1949*. Harmondsworth: Penguin, 1967.

Gross, John. *The Rise and Fall of the Man of Letters*. London: Weidenfeld & Nicolson, 1969.

Hardy, Barbara. *The Appropriate Form: An Essay on the Novel*. London: Athlone Press, 1964.

———. *Forms of Feeling in Victorian Fiction*. London: Peter Owen, 1985.

———. *Tellers and Listeners: The Narrative Imagination*. London: Athlone Press, 1975.

Heilbrun, Carolyn G. *Towards a Recognition of Androgyny: Aspects of Male and Female in Literature*. New York: Knopf, 1973.

Henkin, Leo J. *Darwinism in the English Novel 1860–1910*. New York: Corporate Press, 1940.

Henkle, Roger B. *Comedy and Culture: England 1820–1900*. Princeton: Princeton University Press, 1980.

Hough, Graham. *Selected Essays*. Cambridge: Cambridge University Press, 1977.

Hynes, Samuel. *Edwardian Occasions*. New York: Oxford University Press, 1972.

———. *The Edwardian Turn of Mind*. Princeton: Princeton University Press, 1968.

Jackson, Holbrook. *The Eighteen Nineties: A Review of Art and Ideas at the Close of the Nineteenth Century*. London: Grant Richards, 1913.

Jacobus, Mary. "The Difference of View." In *Women Writing and Writing about Women*, edited by Mary Jacobus. London: Croom Helm, 1979.

Kanner, S. Barbara. "The Women of England in a Century of Social Change, 1815–1914: A Select Bibliography." In *A Widening Sphere: Changing Roles of Victorian Women*, edited by Martha Vicinus. Bloomington: Indiana University Press, 1977.

Katanka, Michael, ed. *Writers and Rebels: From the Fabian Biographical Series*. Totowa, N.J.: Rowman & Littlefield, 1976.

Kettle, Arnold B. *An Introduction to the English Novel*. Vol. 2. Atlantic Highlands, N.J.: Humanities Press, 1974.

Leavis, F. R. *The Great Tradition*. London: Chatto & Windus, 1948.

Leavis, L. R. "The Late Nineteenth-Century Novel and the Change toward the Sexual—Gissing, Hardy, and Lawrence." *English Studies* 66 (1985): 36–47.

Lester, J. A., Jr. *Journey through Despair 1880–1914: Transformations in British Literary Culture*. Princeton: Princeton University Press, 1968.

Levenson, Michael. *A Genealogy of Modernism: A Study of English Literary Doctrine 1908–1922*. Cambridge: Cambridge University Press, 1984.

Levine, George. *The Realistic Imagination: English Fiction from* Frankenstein *to* Lady Chatterley. Chicago: University of Chicago Press, 1981.

Lucas, John. *The Literature of Change: Studies in the Nineteenth-Century Provincial Novel*. New York: Harper & Row, 1977.

———, ed. *Literature and Politics in the Nineteenth Century*. London: Methuen, 1971.

Miller, D. A. *Narrative and Its Discontents: Problems of Closure in the Traditional Novel*. Princeton: Princeton University Press, 1981.

Miller, J. Hillis. *Fiction and Repetition: Seven English Novels*. Cambridge, Mass.: Harvard University Press, 1982.

Minney, R. J. *The Edwardian Age*. London: Cassell, 1964.

Moers, Ellen. *The Dandy: Brummell to Beerbohm*. New York: Viking, 1960.

Myers, W. L. *The Later Realism*. Chicago: University of Chicago Press, 1927.

Polhemus, Robert M. *Comic Faith: The Great Tradition from Austen to Joyce*. Chicago: University of Chicago Press, 1980.

Priestley, J. B. *The Edwardians*. London: Heinemann, 1970.

Rathburn, Robert C., and Martin Steinmann, Jr., eds. *From Jane Austen to Joseph Conrad*. Minneapolis: University of Minnesota Press, 1958.

Rose, Jonathan. *The Edwardian Temperament 1895–1919*. Athens: Ohio University Press, 1986.

Sheridan, Daniel. "Later Victorian Ghost Stories: The Literature of Belief." *Gothic* 2, no. 2 (1980): 33–39.

Showalter, Elaine. *A Literature of Their Own: British Women Novelists from Brontë to Lessing*. Princeton: Princeton University Press, 1977.

Siegel, Sandra. "Literature and Degeneration: The Representation of 'Decadence.' " In *Degeneration: The Dark Side of Progress*, edited by J. Edward Chamberlin and Sander L. Gilman. New York: Columbia University Press, 1985.

Smith, Warren S. *The London Heretics 1870–1914*. London: Constable, 1967.

———, ed. *British Novelists, 1890–1929: Traditionalists*. Detroit: Gale, 1985.

Stewart, Garrett. *Death Sentences: Styles of Dying in British Fiction*. Cambridge, Mass.: Harvard University Press, 1984.

Swinnerton, Frank. *The Georgian Literary Scene*. London: Heinemann, 1935.

Vann, J. Don. *Victorian Novels in Serial*. New York: Modern Language Association of America, 1985.

Vicinus, Martha. *The Industrial Muse: A Study of Nineteenth-Century British Working Class Literature*. New York: Harper & Row, 1974.

Wagenknecht, Edward. *Cavalcade of the English Novel: From Elizabeth to George VI*. New York: Holt, 1943.

Walkovitz, Judith R. "Jack the Ripper and the Myth of Male Violence." *Feminist Studies* 8 (1982): 543–74.

Walvin, James. *A Child's World: A Social History of English Childhood 1800–1914*. Harmondsworth: Penguin, 1982.

Willey, Basil. *More Nineteenth-Century Studies: A Group of Honest Doubters*. London: Chatto & Windus, 1963.

Williams, Raymond. *The Country and the City*. New York: Oxford University Press, 1973.

———. *Culture and Society 1780–1950*. New York: Columbia University Press, 1983.

———. *The English Novel from Dickens to Lawrence*. London: Chatto & Windus, 1970.

———. "The Metropolis and the Emergence of Modernism." In *Unreal City: Urban Experience in Modern European Literature and Art*, edited by Edward Timms and David Kelley. New York: St. Martin's Press, 1985.

Wilt, Judith, "The Imperial Mouth: Imperialism, the Gothic, and Science Fiction." *Journal of Popular Culture* 14, no. 4 (1981): 618–28.

Woolf, Leonard. *Beginning Again: An Autobiography of the Years 1911–1918*. London: Longmans, 1964.

Woolf, Virginia. *The Diary of Virginia Woolf*. Edited by Anne Olivier Bell and Andrew McNeillie. Vols. 1–3. London: Hogarth Press, 1977, 1978, 1980.

Yeazell, Ruth Bernard, ed. *Sex, Politics, and Science in the Nineteenth-Century Novel*. Baltimore: Johns Hopkins University Press, 1985.

WILLIAM MORRIS

Blench, J. W. "William Morris's *Sigurd the Volsung:* A Re-appraisal." *Durham University Journal* 30 (1968): 1–17.

Bono, Barbara J. "The Prose Fictions of William Morris: A Study in the Literary Aesthetic of a Victorian Social Reformer." *Victorian Poetry* 13, nos. 3–4 (1975): 43–59.

Brantlinger, Patrick. "*News from Nowhere:* Morris's Socialist Anti-Novel." *Victorian Studies* 19 (1974): 35–49.

Calhoun, Blue. *The Pastoral Vision of William Morris: The Earthly Paradise.* Athens: University of Georgia Press, 1975.

Chandler, Alice. *A Dream of Order: The Medieval Ideal in Nineteenth-Century English Literature.* Lincoln: University of Nebraska Press, 1970.

Cole, G. D. H., ed. *William Morris: Studies in Prose, Stories in Verse, Shorter Poems, Lectures, and Essays.* London: Nonesuch Press, 1948.

Ellison, R. C. " 'The Undying Glory of Dreams': William Morris and the Northland of Old." In *Victorian Poetry,* edited by Malcolm Bradbury and David Palmer, 139–75. London: Edward Arnold, 1972.

Faulkner, Peter, ed. *William Morris: The Critical Heritage.* London: Routledge & Kegan Paul, 1973.

Fredeman, William E. *Pre-Raphaelitism: A Bibliocritical Study.* Cambridge, Mass.: Harvard University Press, 1965.

Grennan, Margaret. *William Morris: Medievalist and Revolutionary.* New York: King's Crown, 1945.

Henderson, Philip. *William Morris: His Life, Work, and Friends.* New York: McGraw-Hill, 1967.

Hollow, John. "William Morris and the Judgment of God." *PMLA* 86 (1971): 446–51.

Journal of the William Morris Society, 1974–.

Kirchhoff, Frederick. *William Morris.* Boston: Twayne, 1979.

————, ed. *Studies in the Late Romances of William Morris: Papers Presented at the Annual Meeting of the Modern Language Association.* New York: William Morris Society, 1976.

Lewis, C. S. "William Morris." In *Rehabilitations and Other Essays.* London: Oxford University Press, 1939.

Lewis, Peter, ed. *William Morris: Aspects of the Man and His Work.* Loughborough, U.K.: Loughborough Victorian Studies Group, University of Technology, 1978.

Lindsay, Jack. *William Morris: His Life and Work.* London: Constable, 1975.

————. *William Morris, Writer.* London: William Morris Society, 1961.

Marshall, Roderick. *William Morris and His Earthly Paradises.* Tisbury, U.K.: Compton Press, 1979.

Mathews, Richard B. *An Introductory Guide to the Fantasy Writing of William Morris.* London: William Morris Center, 1976.

Oberg, Charlotte H. *A Pagan Prophet: William Morris.* Charlottesville: University Press of Virginia, 1978.

Silver, Carole. *The Romance of William Morris.* Athens: Ohio University Press, 1982.

————, and Joseph Dunlap, eds. *Studies in the Late Romances of William Morris.* New York: William Morris Society, 1976.

Stransky, Peter. *William Morris.* Oxford: Oxford University Press, 1983.

Talbot, Norman. "Women and Goddesses in the Romances of William Morris." *Southern Review* (Australia) 3 (1969): 342–55.

Thompson, E. P. *William Morris: Romantic to Revolutionary.* Rev. ed. London: Merlin Press, 1977.

Thompson, Paul. *The Work of William Morris.* New York: Viking Press, 1967.

WALTER PATER

Benson, Arthur Christopher. *Walter Pater*. London: Macmillan, 1906.

Bloom, Harold, ed. *Modern Critical Views: Walter Pater*. New York: Chelsea House, 1985.

Child, Ruth C. *The Aesthetic of Walter Pater*. New York: Macmillan, 1940.

Crinkley, Richmond. *Walter Pater: Humanist*. Lexington: University Press of Kentucky, 1970.

Currie, Robert, "Pater's Rational Cosmos." *Philological Quarterly* 59 (1980): 95–104.

DeLaura, David J. *Hebrew and Hellene in Victorian England*. Austin: University of Texas Press, 1969.

Dellamora, Richard. "Pater's Modernism: The Leonardo Essay." *University of Toronto Quarterly* 47 (1977–78): 135–50.

Evens, Lawrence, ed. *The Letters of Walter Pater*. Oxford: Clarendon Press, 1970.

Fletcher, ian. *Walter Pater*. London: Longmans, Green, 1959.

Hough, Graham. *The Last Romantics*. London: Duckworth, 1949.

Johnson, R. V. *Walter Pater: A Study of His Critical Outlook and Achievement*. Melbourne: Melbourne University Press, 1961.

Knoepflmacher, U. C. *Religious Humanism and the Victorian Novel: George Eliot, Walter Pater, and Samuel Butler*. Princeton: Princeton University Press, 1965.

Lenaghan, R. T. "Pattern in Pater's Fiction." *Studies in Philology* 18 (1961): 69–91.

Levy, Michael. *The Case of Walter Pater*. London: Thames & Hudson, 1978.

Meisel, Perry. *The Absent Father: Virginia Woolf and Walter Pater*. New Haven: Yale University Press, 1980.

Monsman, Gerald Cornelius. *Pater's Portraits: Mythic Pattern in the Fiction of Walter Pater*. Baltimore: Johns Hopkins University Press, 1980.

———. *Walter Pater*. Boston: Twayne, 1977.

———. *Walter Pater's Act of Autobiography*. New Haven: Yale University Press, 1980.

———. "Walter Pater: An Imaginative Sense of Fact." *Prose Studies* 4 (1981): 1–11.

Peters, Robert. "The Cult of the Returned Apollo: Walter Pater's *Renaissance* and *Imaginary Portraits*." *Journal of Pre-Raphaelite Studies* 2, no. 1 (November 1981): 53–69.

Seiler, R. M., ed. *Walter Pater: The Critical Heritage*. London: Routledge & Kegan Paul, 1980.

Sharp, William. *Papers Critical and Reminiscent*. Heinemann, 1912.

Stein, Richard L. *The Ritual of Interpretation: The Fine Arts as Literature in Ruskin, Rossetti, and Pater*. Cambridge, Mass.: Harvard University Press, 1975.

Wright, Thomas. *The Life of Walter Pater*. 2 vols. London: Everett, 1907.

THOMAS HARDY

Abercrombie, Lascelles. *Thomas Hardy: A Critical Study*. London: Martin Secker, 1912.

Alcorn, John. *The Nature Novel from Hardy to Lawrence*. New York: Columbia University Press, 1977.

Bayley, John. *An Essay on Hardy*. Cambridge: Cambridge University Press, 1978.

Beach, Joseph Warren. *The Technique of Thomas Hardy*. Chicago: University of Chicago Press, 1922.

Bloom, Harold, ed. *Modern Critical Interpretations: Thomas Hardy's* Jude the Obscure. New Haven: Chelsea House, 1987.

———, ed. *Modern Critical Interpretations: Thomas Hardy's* The Mayor of Casterbridge. New Haven: Chelsea House, 1988.

————, ed. *Modern Critical Interpretations: Thomas Hardy's* The Return of the Native. New Haven: Chelsea House, 1987.

————, ed. *Modern Critical Interpretations: Thomas Hardy's* Tess of the D'Urbervilles. New Haven: Chelsea House, 1987.

————, ed. *Modern Critical Views: Thomas Hardy.* New Haven: Chelsea House, 1987.

Blunden, Edmund. *Thomas Hardy.* London: Macmillan, 1942.

Bonica, Charlotte. "Nature and Paganism in Hardy's *Tess of the D'Urbervilles.*" *ELH* 49 (1982): 849–62.

Boumelha, Penny. *Thomas Hardy and Women: Sexual Ideology and Narrative Form.* Brighton: Harvester Press, 1982.

Brooks, Jean R. *Thomas Hardy: The Poetic Structure.* Ithaca: Cornell University Press, 1971.

Brown, Suzanne Hunter. " 'Tess' and *Tess:* An Experiment in Genre." *Modern Fiction Studies* 28 (1982): 25–44.

Carpenter, Richard. *Thomas Hardy.* New York: Twayne, 1964.

Casagrande, Peter J. *Unity in Hardy's Novels.* Lawrence: Regents Press of Kansas, 1982.

Childers, Mary. "Thomas Hardy, the Man Who 'Liked' Women." *Criticism* 23 (1981): 317–34.

Cox, R. G., ed. *Thomas Hardy: The Critical Heritage.* London: Routledge & Kegan Paul, 1970.

Drabble, Margaret, ed. *The Genius of Thomas Hardy.* New York: Knopf, 1976.

Draper, Ronald P., ed. *Hardy: The Tragic Novels: A Casebook.* London: Macmillan, 1975.

Emmet, V. J., Jr. "Marriage in Hardy's Last Novels." *Midwest Quarterly* 10 (1969): 331–48.

Gerber, Helmut E., and W. Eugene Davis, eds. *Thomas Hardy: An Annotated Bibliography of Writings about Him.* DeKalb: Northern Illinois University Press, 1973.

Gregor, Ian. *The Great Web: The Form of Hardy's Major Fiction.* London: Faber & Faber, 1974.

Guérard, Albert J. *Thomas Hardy: The Novels and Stories.* Cambridge, Mass.: Harvard University Press, 1949.

————, ed. *Hardy: A Collection of Critical Essays.* Englewood Cliffs, N.J.: Prentice-Hall, 1963.

Hardy, Florence Emily. *The Life of Thomas Hardy 1840–1928.* London: Macmillan, 1962.

Hornback, Bert A. *The Metaphor of Chance: Vision and Technique in the Works of Thomas Hardy.* Athens: Ohio University Press, 1971.

Howe, Irving. *Thomas Hardy.* New York: Macmillan, 1967.

Johnson, Bruce. *True Correspondence: A Phenomenology of Thomas Hardy's Novels.* Tallahassee: University Presses of Florida, 1983.

Johnson, Lionel. *The Art of Thomas Hardy.* New York: Dodd, Mead, 1894.

King, Jeannette. *Tragedy in the Victorian Novel: Theory and Practice in the Novels of George Eliot, Thomas Hardy, and Henry James.* Cambridge: Cambridge University Press, 1980.

Kramer, Dale. *Thomas Hardy: The Forms of Tragedy.* Detroit: Wayne State University Press, 1975.

Laird, J. T. "New Light on the Evolution of *Tess of the D'Urbervilles.*" *Review of English Studies* 31 (1980): 414–35.

LaValley, Albert J. *Twentieth-Century Interpretations of* Tess of the D'Urbervilles: *A Collection of Critical Essays.* Englewood Cliffs, N.J.: Prentice-Hall, 1969.

Lawrence, D. H. *Study of Thomas Hardy.* In *Phoenix: The Posthumous Papers of D. H. Lawrence.* New York: Viking Press, 1972.

Lodge, David. "Tess, Nature, and the Voices of Hardy." In *Language and Fiction: Essays in Criticism and Verbal Analysis of the English Novel.* London: Routledge & Kegan Paul, 1967.

Meisel, Perry. *Thomas Hardy: The Return of the Repressed.* New Haven: Yale University Press, 1972.

Miller, J. Hillis. *Thomas Hardy: Distance and Desire.* Cambridge, Mass.: Harvard University Press, 1970.

Millgate, Michael. *Thomas Hardy: A Biography.* New York: Random House, 1982.

———. *Thomas Hardy: His Career as a Novelist.* New York: Random House, 1971.

———, and Richard Little Purdy, eds. *The Collected Letters of Thomas Hardy.* 3 vols. to date. Oxford: Oxford University Press. 1978–.

Morrell, Roy. *Thomas Hardy: The Will and the Way.* Kuala Lumpur: University of Malaya Press, 1968.

Page, Norman, ed. *Thomas Hardy: The Writer and His Background.* London: Bell & Hyman, 1980.

Pinion, F. B., ed. *A Hardy Companion: A Guide to the Works of Thomas Hardy and Their Background.* New York: St. Martin's Press, 1968.

Poole, Adrian. "Men's Words and Hardy's Women." *Essays in Criticism* 31 (1981): 328–45.

Sherman, G. W. *The Pessimism of Thomas Hardy.* Rutherford, N.J.: Fairleigh Dickinson University Press, 1976.

Starzyk, Lawrence J. "The Coming Universal Wish Not to Live in Hardy's 'Modern' Novels." *Nineteenth-Century Fiction* 26 (1972): 419–35.

Stewart, J. I. M. *Thomas Hardy: A Critical Biography.* New York: Dodd, Mead, 1971.

Thomas Hardy Annual, 1983–.

The Thomas Hardy Society Review, 1975–

The Thomas Hardy Yearbook, 1970–.

Thurley, Geoffrey. *The Psychology of Hardy's Novels.* St. Lucia, Australia: University of Queensland Press, 1975.

Vigar, Penelope. *The Novels of Thomas Hardy: Illusion and Reality.* London: Athlone Press, 1974.

Woolf, Virginia. "Half of Thomas Hardy." In *The Captain's Death Bed and Other Essays,* 62–68. New York: Harcourt, Brace & World, 1950.

———. "Novels of Thomas Hardy." In *The Second Common Reader,* 266–80. New York: Harcourt, Brace & World, 1932.

Zabel, Morton Dauwen. "Hardy in Defense of His Art: The Aesthetic of Incongruity." *Southern Review* 6 (1940–41): 125–49.

BRAM STOKER

Astle, Richard. "Dracula as Totemic Monster: Lacan, Freud, Oedipus, and History." *Sub-Stance* 8, no. 4 (1980): 96–102.

Bentley, C. F. "The Monster in the Bedroom: Sexual Symbolism in Bram Stoker's *Dracula.*" *Literature and Psychology* 22 (1972): 27–34.

Bierman, Joseph. "Dracula: Prolonged Childhood and the Oral Triad." *American Imago* 29 (1972): 180–98.

Byers, Thomas B. "Good Men and Monsters: The Defenses of *Dracula.*" *Literature and Psychology* 31 (1981): 24–31.

Clements, William M. "Formula as Genre in Popular Horror Literature." *Research Studies* 49 (1981): 116–23.

Demetrakopoulos, Stephanie. "Feminism, Sex Role Exchanges, and Other Subliminal Fantasies in Bram Stoker's *Dracula.*" *Frontiers: Journal of Women's Studies* 2 (1977): 104–13.

Farson, Daniel. *The Man Who Wrote Dracula: A Biography of Bram Stoker*. New York: St. Martin's Press, 1975.

Griffin, Gail B. " 'Your Girls That You All Love Are Mine': *Dracula* and the Victorian Male Imagination." *International Journal of Women's Studies* 7 (1980): 545–65.

Hennelly, Mark M., Jr. "*Dracula:* The Gnostic Quest and Victorian Wasteland." *English Literature in Transition 1880–1920* 20 (1977): 13–26.

Irving, Henry. *Personal Reminiscences of Henry Irving*. 2 vols. New York: Macmillan, 1906.

MacGillivray, Royce. "*Dracula:* Bram Stoker's Spoiled Masterpiece." *Queen's Quarterly* 79 (1972): 518–27.

Miyoshi, Masao. *The Divided Self*. New York: New York University Press, 1969.

Neuberg, Victor E. *Popular Literature: A History and Guide*. Harmondsworth: Penguin, 1977.

Richardson, Maurice. "The Psychoanalysis of Ghost Stories." *Twentieth Century* 166 (1959): 419–31.

Roth, Phyllis A. *Bram Stoker*. Boston: Twayne, 1982.

Seed, David. "The Narrative Method of *Dracula*." *Nineteenth-Century Fiction* 40 (1985): 61–75.

Senf, Carol A. "*Dracula:* Stoker's Response to the New Woman." *Victorian Studies* 26 (1982): 33–49.

Temple, Philip. "The Origins of 'Dracula.' " *Times Literary Supplement*, 4 November 1983, p. 1216.

Wasson, Richard. "The Politics of *Dracula*." *English Literature in Transition 1880–1920* 9 (1966): 24–27.

Weissman, Judith. "Women and Vampires: *Dracula* as a Victorian Novel." *Midwest Quarterly* 18 (1977): 392–405.

Wilt, Judith. *Ghosts of the Gothic: Austen, Eliot, and Lawrence*. Princeton: Princeton University Press, 1979.

Wolf, Leonard, ed. *The Annotated Dracula*. New York: Clarkson N. Potter, 1975.

ROBERT LOUIS STEVENSON

Balfour, Graham. *The Life of Robert Louis Stevenson*. London: Methuen, 1915.

Butts, Dennis. *R. L. Stevenson*. The Bodley Head Monographs Series. London: Bodley Head, 1966.

Calder, Jenni. *RLS: A Life Study*. London: Hamish Hamilton, 1980.

———, ed. *The Robert Louis Stevenson Companion*. Edinburgh: Paul Harris, 1980.

———, ed. *Stevenson and Victorian Scotland*. Edinburgh: Edinburgh University Press, 1981.

Chesterton, G. K. *Robert Louis Stevenson*. London: Hodder & Stoughton, 1927.

Daiches, David. *Robert Louis Stevenson*. Norfolk, Conn.: New Directions, 1947.

———. *Robert Louis Stevenson and His World*. London: Thames & Hudson, 1973.

———. *Stevenson and the Art of Fiction*. New York: Privately printed, 1951.

Egan, Joseph J. "Dark in the Poet's Corner: Stevenson's 'A Lodging for the Night.' " *Studies in Short Fiction* 7 (1970): 402–8.

———. " 'Markheim': A Drama of Moral Psychology." *Nineteenth-Century Fiction* 20 (1966): 377–84.

Eigner, Edwin. *Robert Louis Stevenson and Romantic Tradition*. Princeton: Princeton University Press, 1966.

Furnas, J. C. *Voyage to Windward: The Life of Robert Louis Stevenson*. New York: William Sloane Associates, 1951.

Hammond, J. R. *A Robert Louis Stevenson Companion*. New York: Macmillan, 1984.

Hart, James A. *Robert Louis Stevenson: From Scotland to Silverado*. Cambridge, Mass.: Harvard University Press, 1966.

Hennessy, James Pope. *Robert Louis Stevenson*. London: Jonathan Cape, 1974.

Kiely, Robert. *Robert Louis Stevenson and the Fiction of Adventure*. Cambridge, Mass.: Harvard University Press, 1964.

Knight, Alanna. *The Passionate Kindness: The Love Story of Robert Louis Stevenson and Fanny Osbourne*. Aylesbury, U.K.: Milton House, 1974.

McKay, George L., ed. *The Stevenson Library of E. J. Beinecke*. 6 vols. New Haven: Yale University Library, 1951–64.

Mackay, Margaret. *The Violent Friend: The Story of Mrs. Robert Louis Stevenson*. Garden City, N.Y.: Doubleday, 1968.

McLaren, Moray. *Stevenson and Edinburgh*. London: Chapman & Hall, 1950.

Maixner, Paul, ed. *Robert Louis Stevenson: The Critical Heritage*. London: Routledge & Kegan Paul, 1981.

Rivière, Jacques. *The Ideal Reader*. Edited and translated by B. A. Price. London: Harvill Press, 1962.

Robson, Wallace. "The Sea Cook." In *On the Novel: A Present for Walter Allen on His Sixtieth Birthday from His Friends and Colleagues*, edited by B. S. Benedikz. Totowa, N.J.: Rowman & Littlefield, 1971.

Saposnik, Irving S. *Robert Louis Stevenson*. New York: Twayne, 1974.

Shearer, Tom. "A Strange Judgement of God's? Stevenson's *The Merry Men*." *Studies in Scottish Literature* 20 (1985): 71–87.

Simpson, K. G. "Realism and Romance: Stevenson and Scottish Values." *Studies in Scottish Literature* 20 (1985): 231–47.

Smith, Janet Adams, ed. *Henry James and Robert Louis Stevenson: A Record of Friendship and Criticism*. London: Rupert Hart-Davis, 1948.

Stern, G. B. *Robert Louis Stevenson*. London: Longmans, Green, 1952.

Stevenson, Robert Louis. *The Letters of Robert Louis Stevenson to His Family and Friends*. Edited by Sidney Colvin. Rev. ed. London: Methuen, 1911.

Swearingen, Roger G. *The Prose Writings of Robert Louis Stevenson: A Guide*. London: Macmillan, 1980.

Thorpe, Douglas. "Calvin, Darwin, and the Double: The Problem of Divided Nature in Hogg, MacDonald, and Stevenson." *Newsletter of Victorian Studies Association of Western Canada* 11 (1985): 6–22.

OSCAR WILDE

Beckson, Karl. "Wilde's Autobiographical Signature in *The Picture of Dorian Gray*." *Victorian Newsletter* 69 (1986): 30–31.

———, ed. *Oscar Wilde: The Critical Heritage*. London: Routledge & Kegan Paul, 1970.

Bloom, Harold. *Modern Critical Views: Oscar Wilde*. New York: Chelsea House, 1985.

Cohen, Philip K. *The Moral Vision of Oscar Wilde*. Cranbury, N.J.: Associated University Presses, 1978.

Douglas, Lord Alfred. *Oscar Wilde: A Summing Up*. London: Duckworth, 1940.

Ellmann, Richard. "Romantic Pantomime in Oscar Wilde." *Partisan Review* 30 (1963): 342–55.

———, ed. *Oscar Wilde: A Collection of Critical Essays*. Englewood Cliffs, N.J.: Prentice-Hall, 1969.

Ericksen, Donald H. *Oscar Wilde*. Boston: Twayne, 1977.

Fletcher, Ian, and John Stokes. "Oscar Wilde." In *Anglo-Irish Literature: A Review of Research*, edited by Richard J. Finneran, 48–137. New York: Modern Language Association of America, 1976.

Gide, André. *Oscar Wilde: In Memoriam*. New York: Philosophical Library, 1949.

Gilman, Richard. *Decadence: The Strange Life of an Epithet*. New York: Farrar, Straus & Giroux, 1979.

Gordon, Jan B. " 'Parody as Initiation': The Sad Education of *Dorian Gray*." *Criticism* 9, no. 4 (1967): 355–71.

Hardwick, Michael. *The Osprey Guide to Oscar Wilde*. Reading, U.K.: Osprey, 1973.

Harris, Frank. *Oscar Wilde: His Life and Confessions*. New York: Frank Harris, 1916. 2 vols.

Hart-Davis, Rupert, ed. *The Letters of Oscar Wilde*. New York: Harcourt, Brace & World, 1962.

Hyde, H. Montgomery. *Oscar Wilde: A Biography*. New York: Farrar, Straus & Giroux, 1975.

Jullian, Phillippe. *Oscar Wilde*. Translated by Violet Wyndham. New York: Holt, Rinehart & Winston, 1976.

Lawler, Donald L., and Charles E. Knott. "The Context of Invention: Suggested Origins of *Dorian Gray*." *Modern Philology* 73 (1976): 389–98.

Manganiello, Dominic. "Ethics and Aesthetics in *The Picture of Dorian Gray*." *Canadian Journal of Irish Studies* 9, no. 2 (1983): 25–33.

Meyers, Jeffrey. "*The Picture of Dorian Gray*." In *Homosexuality and Literature 1890–1930*, 20–31. Montreal: McGill–Queen's University Press, 1977.

Murray, Isobel. "Some Elements in the Composition of *The Picture of Dorian Gray*." *Durham University Journal* 64 (1972): 220–31.

Nassar, Christopher S. *Into the Demon Universe: A Literary Exploration of Oscar Wilde*. New Haven: Yale University Press, 1974.

Paglia, Camille. "Oscar Wilde and the English Epicene." *Raritan* 4, no. 3 (1985): 85–109.

Pearson, Hesketh. *The Life of Oscar Wilde*. London: Methuen, 1946.

Pine, Richard. *Oscar Wilde*. Dublin: Gill & Macmillan, 1983.

Poteet, Lewis J. "*Dorian Gray* and the Gothic Novel." *Modern Fiction Studies* 17 (1971): 239–48.

Powell, Kerry. "The Mesmerizing of *Dorian Gray*." *Victorian Newsletter* 65 (1984): 10–14.

———. "Oscar Wilde 'Acting': The Medium as Message in *The Picture of Dorian Gray*." *Dalhousie Review* 58 (1978): 104–15.

Roditi, Edouard. *Oscar Wilde*. Norfolk, Conn.: New Directions, 1947.

San Juan, Epifanio, Jr. *The Art of Oscar Wilde*. Princeton: Princeton University Press, 1967.

Shewan, Rodney. *Oscar Wilde: Art and Egotism*. London: Macmillan, 1977.

Sullivan, Kevin. *Oscar Wilde*. New York: Columbia University Press, 1972.

Winwar, Frances. *Oscar Wilde and the Yellow 'Nineties*. New York: Harper & Brothers, 1940.

GEORGE GISSING

Adams, Ruth M. "George Gissing and Clara Collet." *Nineteenth-Century Fiction* 11 (1956): 72–77.

Bowlby, Rachel. *Just Looking: Consumer Culture in Dreiser, Gissing, and Zola*. New York: Methuen, 1985.

Coustillas, Pierre. "Gissing's Feminine Portraiture." *English Literature in Transition 1880–1920* 6 (1963): 130–41.

———. "Gissing's Short Stories: A Bibliography." *English Literature in Transition 1880–1920* 7 (1964): 59–72.

———. "Gissing's Short Stories: A Bibliography." *English Literature in Transition 1880–1920* 7 (1964): 59–72.

———. *Politics in Literature in the Nineteenth Century*. Lille: Centre d'Etudes Victoriennes, Université de Lille, 1974.

———, ed. *Collected Articles on George Gissing*. New York: Frank Cass, 1968.

———, and Colin Partridge, eds. *George Gissing: The Critical Heritage*. London: Routledge & Kegan Paul, 1972.

Fernando, Lloyd. *"New Women" in the Late Victorian Novel*. University Park: Pennsylvania State University Press, 1977.

Gettman, Royal A., ed. *George Gissing and H. G. Wells: Their Friendship and Correspondence*. Urbana: University of Illinois Press, 1961.

Gissing, George. *George Gissing on Fiction*. Edited by Jacob and Cynthia Korg. London: Methuen, 1978.

———. *Letters of George Gissing to Members of His Family*. Edited by Algernon and Ellen Gissing. London: Methuen, 1927.

———. *London and the Life of Literature in Late Victorian England: The Diary of George Gissing*. Edited by Pierre Coustillas. Brighton: Harvester Press, 1978.

The Gissing Newsletter, 1964–.

Goode, John. *George Gissing: Ideology and Fiction*. New York: Barnes & Noble, 1978.

Grylls, David. *The Paradox of Gissing*. London: Allen & Unwin, 1986.

Halperin, John. *Gissing: A Life in Books*. Oxford: Oxford University Press, 1982.

Jameson, Fredric. *The Political Unconscious: Narrative as a Socially Symbolic Act*. Baltimore: Johns Hopkins University Press, 1981.

Keating, P. J. *The Working Classes in Victorian Fiction*, 32–40. London: Routledge & Kegan Paul, 1971.

Korg, Jacob. *George Gissing: A Critical Biography*. Seattle: University of Washington Press, 1963.

———. "George Gissing: Humanist in Exile." In *The Victorian Experience: The Novelists*, edited by Richard A. Levine. Athens: Ohio State University Press, 1976.

Linehan, Katherine Bailey. "*The Odd Women*, Gissing's Imaginative Approach to Feminism." *Modern Literature Quarterly* 40 (1979): 358–75.

Poole, Adrian. *Gissing in Context*. Totowa, N.J.: Rowman & Littlefield, 1975.

Selig, Robert L. "A Sad Heart at the Late-Victorian Culture Market: George Gissing's *In the Year of Jubilee*." *Studies in English Literature 1500–1900* 9 (1969): 703–20.

Spiers, John, and Pierre Coustillas. *The Rediscovery of George Gissing*. London: National Book League, 1971.

Tindall, Gillian. *The Born Exile: George Gissing*. London: Temple Smith, 1974.

JOSEPH CONRAD

Baines, Jocelyn. *Joseph Conrad: A Critical Biography*. New York: McGraw-Hill, 1960.

Beach, Joseph Warren. "Impressionism: Conrad." In *The Twentieth-Century Novel: Studies in Technique*, 337–65. New York: Appleton-Century, 1932.

Berman, Jeffrey. *Joseph Conrad: Writing as Rescue*. New York: Astra Books, 1977.

Blackmur, R. P. *Eleven Essays in the European Novel*. New York: Harcourt, Brace & World, 1964.

Bloom, Harold, ed. *Modern Critical Interpretations: Joseph Conrad's* Heart of Darkness. New Haven: Chelsea House, 1987.

———, ed. *Modern Critical Interpretations: Joseph Conrad's* Lord Jim. New Haven: Chelsea House, 1987.

———, ed. *Modern Critical Interpretations: Joseph Conrad's* Nostromo. New Haven: Chelsea House, 1987.

————, ed. *Modern Critical Views: Joseph Conrad*. New Haven: Chelsea House, 1986.

Brown, Robert. "Integrity and Self-Deception." *Critical Review* 25 (1983): 115–31.

Conradiana: A Journal of Joseph Conrad Studies, 1968–.

Crews, Frederick. "The Power of Darkness." *Partisan Review* 34 (1967): 507–25.

Daleski, H. M. *Joseph Conrad: The Way of Dispossession*. London: Faber & Faber, 1977.

Ehrsam, T. G. *A Bibliography of Joseph Conrad*. Metuchen, N.J.: Scarecrow Press, 1969.

Ellmann, Richard, and Charles Feidelson, eds. *The Modern Tradition*. New York: Oxford University Press, 1965.

Fleishman, Avrom. *Conrad's Politics*. Baltimore: Johns Hopkins University Press, 1967.

Fogel, Aaron. *Coercion to Speak: Conrad's Poetics of Dialogue*. Cambridge, Mass.: Harvard University Press, 1985.

Ford, Ford Madox. *Joseph Conrad: A Personal Remembrance*. Boston: Little, Brown, 1924.

Galsworthy, John. "Reminiscences of Conrad." In *Castles in Spain and Other Screeds*, 99–126. New York: Scribner's, 1927.

Gekoski, R. A. *Conrad: The Moral World of the Novelist*. New York: Harper & Row, 1978.

Gillon, Adam. *The Eternal Solitary*. New York: Bookman Associates, 1960.

————. *Joseph Conrad*. Boston: Twayne, 1982.

Gillon, Adam, and Ludwik Kryzanowski, eds. *Joseph Conrad: Commemorative Essays*. New York: Astra Books, 1975.

Guérard, Albert J. *Conrad the Novelist*. Cambridge, Mass.: Harvard University Press, 1958.

————. *Joseph Conrad*. New York: New Directions, 1947.

Hagan, John, Jr. "The Design of Conrad's *The Secret Agent*." *ELH* 22 (1955): 148–64.

Harkness, Bruce, ed. *Conrad's* Heart of Darkness *and the Critics*. Belmont, Calif.: Wadsworth, 1960.

Hay, Eloise Knapp. "Joseph Conrad and Impressionism." *Journal of Aesthetics and Art Criticism* 34 (1975): 137–44.

————. *The Political Novels of Joseph Conrad*. Chicago: University of Chicago Press, 1963.

James, Henry. *Notes on Novelists*. New York: Scribner's, 1914.

Jean-Aubry, Gérard. *Joseph Conrad: Life and Letters*. London: Heinemann, 1927.

————. *The Sea-Dreamer: A Definitive Biography of Joseph Conrad*. Translated by Helen Sebba. Garden City, N.Y.: Doubleday, 1957.

Johnson, Bruce M. *Conrad's Models of Mind*. Minneapolis: University of Minnesota Press, 1971.

Joseph Conrad Today: The Newsletter of the Joseph Conrad Society of America, 1975–.

Karl, Frederick R. *Joseph Conrad: The Three Lives*. New York: Farrar, Straus & Giroux, 1979.

————. *A Reader's Guide to Joseph Conrad*. Rev. ed. New York: Noonday Press, 1969.

————, ed. *Joseph Conrad: A Collection of Criticism*. New York: McGraw-Hill, 1975.

Kermode, Frank. "Secrets and Narrative Sequence." *Critical Inquiry* 7 (1980): 83–101.

Kirschner, Robert. Heart of Darkness: *The Psychologist as Artist*. Edinburgh: Oliver & Boyd, 1968.

La Bossière, Camille R. *Joseph Conrad and the Science of Unknowing*. Fredericton, N.B., Canada: York Press, 1979.

McLauchlin, Juliet. *Conrad:* Nostromo. London: Edward Arnold, 1969.

————. "Conrad's 'Three Ages of Man': The 'Youth' Volume." *Polish Review* 20 (1975): 189–202.

Meyer, Bernard C. *Joseph Conrad: A Psychoanalytic Biography*. Princeton: Princeton University Press, 1967.

Miller, J. Hillis. *Poets of Reality: Six Twentieth-Century Writers*. Cambridge, Mass.: Harvard University Press, 1965.

Moser, Thomas. *Joseph Conrad: Achievement and Decline*. Cambridge, Mass.: Harvard University Press, 1957.

Mudrick, Marvin, ed. *Conrad: A Collection of Critical Essays*. Englewood Cliffs, N.J.: Prentice-Hall, 1966.

Nettels, Elsa. *James and Conrad*. Athens: University of Georgia Press, 1977.

Palmer, John A. *Joseph Conrad's Fiction: A Study in Literary Growth*. Ithaca: Cornell University Press, 1968.

————, ed. *Twentieth-Century Interpretations of* The Nigger of the "Narcissus": *A Collection of Critical Essays*. Englewood Cliffs, N.J.: Prentice-Hall, 1969.

Said, Edward W. *Joseph Conrad and the Fiction of Autobiography*. Cambridge, Mass.: Harvard University Press, 1966.

Sherry, Norman. *Conrad's Eastern World*. Cambridge: Cambridge University Press, 1966.

————, ed. *Conrad: The Critical Heritage*. London: Routledge & Kegan Paul, 1973.

————, ed. *Joseph Conrad: A Commemoration*. New York: Harper & Row, 1977.

Stallman, Robert W., ed. *The Art of Joseph Conrad: A Critical Symposium*. East Lansing: Michigan State University Press, 1960.

Tanner, Tony. "Nightmare and Complacency: Razumov and the Western Eye." *Critical Quarterly* 4 (1962): 197–214.

Tennant, Roger. *Joseph Conrad: A Biography*. New York: Atheneum, 1981.

Thornburn, David. *Conrad's Romanticism*. New Haven: Yale University Press, 1974.

Van Ghent, Dorothy. *The English Novel: Form and Function*. Harper & Brothers, 1961.

Watt, Ian. *Conrad in the Nineteenth Century*. Berkeley: University of California Press, 1979.

————, ed. The Secret Agent: *A Selection of Critical Essays*. London: Macmillan, 1973.

Watts, Cedric. *Conrad's* Heart of Darkness: *A Critical and Contextual Discussion*. Milan: Mursia International, 1977.

Whitehead, Lee M. "Recent Conrad Criticism." *Dalhousie Review* 61 (1981–82): 743–49.

Wills, John Howard. "A Neglected Masterpiece: Conrad's 'Youth.' " *Texas Studies in Literature and Language* 4 (1963): 591–601.

Yelton, D. C. *Mimesis and Metaphor: An Inquiry into the Genesis and Scope of Conrad's Symbolic Imagery*. The Hague: Mouton, 1967.

Zabel, Morton Dauwen. *Craft and Character in Modern Fiction*. New York: Viking Press, 1957.

Zyla, W. T., and W. M. Aycock, eds. *Joseph Conrad: Theory and World Fiction*. Lubbock: Texas Tech University, 1974.

E. NESBIT

Bell, Anthea. *E. Nesbit*. London: Bodley Head, 1960.

Blount, Margaret. *Animal Land: The Creatures of Children's Fiction*. New York: Morrow, 1975.

Crouch, Marcus. "The Nesbit Tradition." *Junior Bookshelf* 22 (1958): 195–98.

————. *Treasure Seekers and Borrowers: Children's Books in Britain*. London: The Library Association, 1962.

Darton, F. J. Harvey. "The Eighties and To-day: Freedom." In *Children's Books in*

England: Five Centuries of Social Life, 299–326. Cambridge: Cambridge University Press, 1932.

Ellis, Alec. "The Golden Years of Children's Literature, Part 2: 1890–1920." In *A History of Children's Reading and Literature*, 119–27. Oxford: Pergamon, 1968.

Evans de Alonso, Jean. "E. Nesbit's Well House, 1915–1921: A Memoir." In *Children's Literature: The Great Excluded*, edited by Francelia Butler and Bennett A. Brockman, 147–52. Vol. 3. Storrs, Conn.: Children's Literature Association, 1974.

Eyre, Frank. *Twentieth-Century Children's Books*. London: Longmans, Green, 1952.

Green, Roger Lancelyn. "E. Nesbit." In *Tellers of Tales*, 206–15. Rev. ed. London: Kaye & Ward, 1969.

Jackson, Rosemary. "Victorian Fantasies." In *Fantasy: The Literature of Subversion*, 141–56. London: Methuen, 1981.

Lochhead, Marion. "An Edwardian Successor: E. Nesbit." In *The Renaissance of Wonder*, 56–69. Edinburgh: Canongate, 1977.

Manlove, C. N. "The Union of Opposites in Fantasy: E. Nesbit." In *The Impulse of Fantasy Literature*, 45–69. Kent, Ohio: Kent State University Press, 1983.

Moore, Doris Langley. *E. Nesbit: A Biography*. London: Ernest Benn, 1933.

Nesbitt, Elizabeth. "A Rightful Heritage 1890–1920." In *A Critical History of Children's Literature*, edited by Cornelia Meigs, 328–62. Rev. ed. New York: Macmillan, 1969.

Smith, Barbara. "The Expression of Social Values in the Writing of E. Nesbit." In *Children's Literature: The Great Excluded*, edited by Francelia Butler and Bennett A. Brockman, 153–64. Vol. 3. Storrs, Conn.: Children's Literature Association, 1974.

Streatfield, Noel. *Magic and the Magician: E. Nesbit and Her Children's Books*. London: Ernest Benn, 1958.

ARTHUR CONAN DOYLE

Baker, Michael. *The Doyle Diary*. London: Paddington Press, 1978.

The Baker Street Journal, 1950–.

Baring-Gould, William S. *Sherlock Holmes of Baker Street: A Life of the World's First Consulting Detective*. New York: Clarkson N. Potter, 1962.

————, ed. *The Annotated Sherlock Holmes*. New York: Clarkson N. Potter, 1967.

Brooks, Peter. *Reading for the Plot*. New York: Random House, 1985.

Brown, Ivor. *Conan Doyle*. London: Hamish Hamilton, 1972.

Carr, John Dickson. *The Life of Sir Arthur Conan Doyle*. London: John Murray, 1949.

Clausen, Christopher. "Sherlock Holmes, Order, and the Late-Victorian Mind." *Georgia Review* 38 (1984): 104–23.

Cox, Don Richard. *Arthur Conan Doyle*. New York: Frederick Ungar, 1985.

De Waal, Ronald Burt. *The World Bibliography of Sherlock Holmes and Dr. Watson*. New York: Bramhall House, 1974.

Doyle, Adrian Conan, and P. Weil-Nordon, eds. *Sir Arthur Conan Doyle, Centenary 1859–1959*. London: John Murray, 1959.

Eco, Umberto, and Thomas A. Sebeok, eds. *The Sign of Three: Dupin, Holmes, Peirce*. Bloomington: Indiana University Press, 1983.

Farrell, Kirby. "Heroism, Culture and Dread in *The Sign of Four*." *Studies in the Novel* 16 (1984): 32–51.

Green, Richard Lancelyn, and John Michael Gibson. *A Bibliography of A. Conan Doyle*. Oxford: Clarendon Press, 1983.

Hall, Trevor. *Sherlock Holmes: Ten Literary Studies*. New York: St. Martin's Press, 1969.

Hardwick, Michael, and Mollie Hardwick. *The Man Who Was Sherlock Holmes*. London: John Murray, 1964.

———. *The Sherlock Holmes Companion*. London: John Murray, 1962.

Harrison, Michael. *The London of Sherlock Holmes*. New York: Drake, 1972.

———. *The World of Sherlock Holmes*. London: Frederick Muller, 1973.

Higham, Charles. *The Adventures of Conan Doyle: The Life of the Creator of Sherlock Holmes*. London: Hamish Hamilton, 1976.

Hutter, Albert. "Dreams, Transformation, and Literature: The Implications of Detective Fiction." *Victorian Studies* 18 (1974): 181–210.

Kalikoff, Beth. *Murder and Moral Decay in Victorian Popular Literature*. Ann Arbor, Mich.: UMI Research Press, 1986.

Klinefelter, Walter. *Sherlock Holmes in Portrait and Profile*. Syracuse: Syracuse University Press, 1963.

Lamond, John. *Arthur Conan Doyle: A Memoir*. London: John Murray, 1931.

Locke, Harold. *A Bibliographical Catalogue of the Writings of Sir Arthur Conan Doyle*. Tunbridge Wells, U.K.: D. Webster, 1928.

Nordon, Pierre. *Conan Doyle*. London: John Murray, 1966.

Ousby, Ian. *Bloodhounds of Heaven: The Detective in English Fiction from Godwin to Doyle*. Cambridge, Mass.: Harvard University Press, 1976.

Pearson, Hesketh. *Conan Doyle: His Life and Art*. London: Methuen, 1943.

Rosenberg, Samuel. *Naked is the Best Disguise*. Indianapolis: Bobbs-Merrill, 1974.

Starrett, Vincent. *The Private Life of Sherlock Holmes*. New York: Macmillan, 1933.

Watson, Colin. *Snobbery with Violence: Crime Stories and Their Audience*. London: Eyre & Spottiswoode, 1971.

RUDYARD KIPLING

Amis, Kingsley. *Rudyard Kipling and His World*. London: Thames & Hudson, 1975.

Auden, W. H. "The Poet of the Encirclement." *New Republic* 109 (1943): 579–81.

Babbitt, Irving. "Romanticism and the Orient." *Bookman* (New York) 74 (1931–32): 349–57.

Bloom, Harold, ed. *Modern Critical Interpretations: Rudyard Kipling's* Kim. New Haven: Chelsea House, 1987.

———, ed. *Modern Critical Views: Rudyard Kipling*. New Haven: Chelsea House, 1987.

Bodelsen, C. A. *Aspects of Kipling's Art*. New York: Barnes & Noble, 1964.

Bratton, Jacqueline S. "Kipling's Magic Art." *Proceedings of the British Academy* 64 (1968): 209–32.

Bromwich, David. "Kipling's Jest." *Grand Street* 4 (1985): 150–79.

Chaudhuri, Nirad C. "The Finest Story about India—in English." *Encounter* 8, no. 4 (April 1957): 47–53.

Dobrée, Bonamy. "Kipling the Visionary." *Kipling Journal* 23 (April 1956): 3–5.

———. *Rudyard Kipling: Realist and Fabulist*. London: Oxford University Press, 1972.

Draudt, Manfred. "Reality or Delusion? Narrative Technique and Meaning in Kipling's 'The Man Who Would Be King.' " *English Studies* 65 (1984): 316–26.

Eliot, T. S., ed. *A Choice of Kipling's Verse*. London: Faber & Faber, 1941.

Feeley, Margaret Peller. "The *Kim* That Nobody Reads." *Studies in the Novel* 13 (1981): 266–81.

Gilbert, Elliot L. *The Good Kipling*. Athens: Ohio University Press, 1972.

———. "Silence and Survival in Rudyard Kipling's Art and Life." *English Literature in Transition 1880–1920* 29 (1986): 115–26.

———, ed. *Kipling and the Critics*. New York: New York University Press, 1965.

Gross, John, ed. *Rudyard Kipling: The Man, His Work, and His World*. London: Weidenfeld & Nicolson, 1972.

Howe, Irving. "The Pleasures of *Kim*." In *Art, Politics, and Will: Essays in Honor of Lionel Trilling*, edited by Quentin Anderson, Stephen Donadio, and Steven Marcus. New York: Basic Books, 1977.

Islam, Shamsul. *Chronicles of the Raj: A Study of Literary Reaction to the Imperial Idea towards the End of the Raj*. London: Macmillan, 1979.

―――. "The Kipling and Hemingway Codes: A Study in Comparison." *Explorations* 2, no. 2 (Winter 1975): 22–28.

―――. *Kipling's "Law": A Study of His Philosophy of Life*. London: Macmillan, 1975.

Jarrell, Randall. *Kipling, Auden, & Co.: Essays and Reviews 1935–1964*. New York: Farrar, Straus & Giroux, 1961.

Lewis, C. S. "Kipling's World." In *Literature and Life: Addresses to the English Association*, edited by H. Idris Bell et al. London: George G. Harrap, 1948.

McLuhan, Herbert Marshall. "Kipling and Forster." *Sewanee Review* 52 (1944): 332–43.

Mason, Philip. *Kipling: The Glass, the Shadow, and the Fire*. London: Jonathan Cape, 1975.

Meyers, Jeffrey. "The Idea of Moral Authority in 'The Man Who Would Be King.' " *Studies in English Literature 1500–1900* 8 (1968): 711–23.

Moore, Katharine. *Kipling and the White Man's Burden*. London: Faber & Faber, 1968.

Moss, Robert F. *Rudyard Kipling and the Fiction of Adolescence*. London: Macmillan, 1982.

Norton, Charles Eliot. "The Poetry of Rudyard Kipling." *Atlantic Monthly* 79 (January 1897): 111–15.

Orwell, George. "Rudyard Kipling." In *Dickens, Dali, and Others*. New York: Harcourt, Brace & World, 1946.

Roskies, D. M. E. "Telling the Truth about Kipling and Freud." *English* 31 (1982): 1–17.

Rutherford, Andrew, ed. *Kipling's Mind and Art*. Stanford: Stanford University Press, 1964.

Scheerer, Constance. "The Lost Paradise of Rudyard Kipling." *Dalhousie Review* 61 (1981): 27–36.

Seed, David. "Disorientation and Commitment in the Fiction of Empire: Kipling and Orwell." *Dutch Quarterly Review of Anglo-American Letters* 14 (1984): 269–80.

Shahane, Vasant A. *Rudyard Kipling, Activist and Artist*. Carbondale: Southern Illinois University Press, 1973.

Shanks, Edward. *Rudyard Kipling: A Study in Literature and Political Ideas*. New York: Doubleday, Doran, 1940.

Shippey, Thomas A., and Michael Short. "Framing and Distancing in Kipling's 'The Man Who Would Be King.' " *Journal of Narrative Technique* 2 (1972): 75–87.

Stevenson, Lionel. "The Ideas in Kipling's Poetry." *University of Toronto Quarterly* 1 (1931): 467–89.

Stewart, David H. "Orality in Kipling's *Kim*." *Journal of Narrative Technique* 13 (1983): 47–57.

Stewart, J. I. M. "Fluid at the Centre."*Encounter* 45, no. 3 (September 1975): 62–66.

―――. *Rudyard Kipling*. New York: Dodd, Mead, 1966.

Sullivan, Zoreh T. "Kipling the Nightwalker." *Modern Fiction Studies* 30 (1984): 217–36.

Tompkins, J. M. S. *The Art of Rudyard Kipling*. London: Methuen, 1959.

Trilling, Lionel. *The Liberal Imagination*. New York: Viking Press, 1951.

Wilson, Angus. *The Strange Ride of Rudyard Kipling.* New York: Viking Press, 1977.

Wilson, Edmund. *The Wound and the Bow.* Boston: Houghton Mifflin, 1941.

Yeats, A. W. "The Genesis of 'The Recessional.' " *University of Texas Studies in English* 31 (1952): 97–108.

———. "Kipling, Twenty Years After." *Dalhousie Review* 36 (1956): 59–64.

H. G. WELLS

Amis, Kingsley. *New Maps of Hell: A Survey of Science Fiction.* New York: Harcourt, Brace & World, 1960.

Ash, Brian. *Who's Who in H. G. Wells.* London: Hamish Hamilton, 1979.

Becker, Carl L. *Everyman His Own Historian.* New York: F. S. Crofts, 1935.

Belgion, Montgomery. *H. G. Wells.* London: Longmans, Green, 1953.

Bergonzi, Bernard. *The Early H. G. Wells: A Study of the Scientific Romances.* Toronto: University of Toronto Press, 1961.

———, ed. *H. G. Wells: A Collection of Critical Essays.* Englewood Cliffs, N.J.: Prentice-Hall, 1976.

Bloom, Robert. *Anatomies of Egotism: A Reading of the Last Novels of H. G. Wells.* Lincoln: University of Nebraska Press, 1974.

Borges, Jorge Luis. "The First Wells." In *Other Inquisitions 1937–52,* translated by Ruth L. Simms. Austin: University of Texas Press, 1964.

Brome, Vincent. *H. G. Wells.* London: Longmans, Green, 1951.

Brooks, Van Wyck. *The World of H. G. Wells.* New York: Mitchell Kennerly, 1915.

Costa, Richard Hauer. *H. G. Wells.* Rev. ed. Boston: Twayne, 1985.

Dickson, Lovat. *H. G. Wells: His Turbulent Life and Times.* New York: Atheneum, 1969.

Edel, Leon, and Gordon N. Ray, eds. *Henry James and H. G. Wells.* Urbana: University of Illinois Press, 1958.

Hammond, J. R. *Herbert George Wells: An Annotated Bibliography of His Works.* New York: Garland, 1977.

———. *An H. G. Wells Companion: A Guide to the Novels, Romances, and Short Stories.* London: Macmillan, 1979.

———, ed. *H. G. Wells: Interviews and Recollections.* London: Macmillan, 1980.

Haynes, Roslynn D. *H. G. Wells: Discoverer of the Future.* London: Macmillan, 1980.

Hillegas, Mark R. *The Future as Nightmare: H. G. Wells and the Anti-Utopians.* New York: Oxford University Press, 1967.

Huntington, John. *The Logic of Fantasy: H. G. Wells and Science Fiction.* New York: Columbia University Press, 1982.

Kemp, Peter. *H. G. Wells and the Culminating Ape.* New York: St. Martin's Press, 1982.

Lodge, David. "*Tono-Bungay* and the Condition of England." In *The Language of Fiction: Essays in Criticism and Verbal Analysis of the English Novel.* New York: Columbia University Press, 1966.

McConnell, Frank. *The Science Fiction of H. G. Wells.* New York: Oxford University Press, 1981.

Maugham, W. Somerset. "Some Novelists I Have Known." In *The Vagrant Mood.* Garden City, N.Y.: Doubleday, 1953

Nicholson, Norman. *H. G. Wells.* Denver: Alan Swallow, 1950.

Orwell, George. "Wells, Hitler, and the World State." In *Collected Essays,* 160–66. London: Secker & Warburg, 1946.

Parrinder, Patrick. *H. G. Wells.* Edinburgh: Oliver & Boyd, 1970.

———, ed. *H. G. Wells: The Critical Heritage.* London: Routledge & Kegan Paul, 1972.

————, and Robert M. Philmus, eds. *H. G. Wells's Literary Criticism*. Brighton, U.K.: Harvester, 1980.

Philmus, Robert M. *Into the Unknown: The Evolution of Science Fiction from Francis Godwin to H. G. Wells*. Berkeley: University of California Press, 1970.

————, and David Y. Hughes. *H. G. Wells: Early Writings in Science and Science Fiction*. Berkeley: University of California Press, 1975.

Pritchett, V. S. *The Living Novel*. New York: Reynal & Hitchcock, 1947.

Reed, John R. *The Natural History of H. G. Wells*. Athens: Ohio University Press, 1982.

Schorer, Mark. "Technique as Discovery." In *Forms of Modern Fiction*, edited by William Van O'Connor, 9–29. Minneapolis: University of Minnesota Press, 1948.

Wagar, W. Warren. *H. G. Wells and the World State*. New Haven: Yale University Press, 1961.

————, ed. *H. G. Wells: Journalism & Prophecy 1893–1946*. Boston: Houghton Mifflin, 1965.

Wells, H. G. *Experiment in Autobiography: Discoveries and Conclusions of a Very Ordinary Brain*. New York: Macmillan, 1934.

West, Anthony. *H. G. Wells: Aspects of a Life*. New York: Random House, 1984.

Wilson, Colin. *The Strength to Dream: Literature and the Imagination*. Boston: Houghton Mifflin, 1962.

Woolf, Virginia. "Mr. Bennett and Mrs. Brown." In *Collected Essays*, Vol. 1, 319–37. New York: Harcourt Brace Jovanovich, 1967.

ARNOLD BENNETT

Allen, Walter. *Arnold Bennett*. London: Home & Van Thal, 1948.

Barker, Dudley. *Writer by Trade: A View of Arnold Bennett*. London: Allen & Unwin, 1966.

Bennett, Arnold. *The Journal*. New York: Viking Press, 1932–33. 3 vols.

————. *Sketches for Autobiography*. Edited by James Hepburn. London: Allen & Unwin, 1979.

Bennett, Dorothy Cheston. *Arnold Bennett: A Portrait Done at Home Together with 170 Letters from A. B.* New York: Claude Kendall & Willoughby Sharp, 1935.

Broomfield, Olga R. R. *Arnold Bennett*. Boston: Twayne, 1984.

Craig, Randall. "*Choses vues*: Arnold Bennett and Impressionism." *English Literature in Transition 1880–1920* 24 (1981): 196–205.

Darton, F. J. Harvey. *Arnold Bennett*. London: Nisbet, 1915.

Drabble, Margaret. *Arnold Bennett: A Biography*. London: Weidenfeld & Nicolson, 1974.

Hall, James. *Arnold Bennett: Primitivism and Taste*. Seattle: University of Washington Press, 1959.

Hepburn, James. *The Art of Arnold Bennett*. Bloomington: Indiana University Press, 1963.

Johnson, L. G. *Arnold Bennett of the Five Towns*. London: C. W. Daniel, 1924.

Lafourcade, Georges. *Arnold Bennett: A Study*. London: Frederick Muller, 1939.

Lucas, John. *Arnold Bennett: A Study of His Fiction*. London: Methuen, 1974.

Miller, Anita. *Arnold Bennett: An Annotated Bibliography 1887–1932*. New York: Garland, 1977.

Pound, Reginald. *Arnold Bennett: A Biography*. London: Heinemann, 1952.

Roberts, Thomas R. *Arnold Bennett's Five Towns Origins*. Stoke-on-Trent, U.K.: Libraries, Museums, and Informations Committee, 1961.

Roby, Kinley E. *A Writer at War: Arnold Bennett 1914–1918.* Baton Rouge: Louisiana State University Press, 1972.

Simon, J. B. *Arnold Bennett and His Novels.* Oxford: Basil Blackwell, 1936.

Smith, Pauline. *A. B.: A Minor Marginal Note.* London: Jonathan Cape, 1933.

Swinnerton, Frank. *Arnold Bennett: A Last Word.* London: Hamish Hamilton, 1978.

Wain, John. *Arnold Bennett.* New York: Columbia University Press, 1967.

West, Geoffrey. *The Problem of Arnold Bennett.* London: Joiner & Steele, 1933.

West, Rebecca. *Arnold Bennett Himself.* New York: John Day, 1931.

Woolf, Virginia. "Mr. Bennett and Mrs. Brown." In *Collected Essays,* Vol. 1, 319–37. New York: Harcourt Brace Jovanovich, 1967.

Wright, Walter. *Arnold Bennett: Romantic Realist.* Lincoln: University of Nebraska Press, 1971.

JOHN GALSWORTHY

Banerjee, Jacquelyn. "Galsworthy's 'Dangerous Experiment.' " *Anglo-Welsh Review* 24 (1980): 134–43.

Barker, Dudley. *The Man of Principle: A View of John Galsworthy.* London: Heinemann, 1963.

Core, George. "Author and Agency: Galsworthy and the Pinkers." *Library Chronicle of the University of Texas* 6 (1979): 61–73.

Dupont, V. *John Galsworthy, the Dramatic Artist.* Paris: Didier, 1942.

Dupré, Catherine. *John Galsworthy: A Biography.* London: Collins, 1976.

Eaton, Harold T. *Reading Galsworthy's Forsyte Saga.* New York: Scribner's, 1936.

Fisher, J. *The World of the Forsytes.* London: Secker & Warburg, 1976.

Frazer, June M. "Galsworthy's Narrative Technique in *The Man of Property.*" *English Literature in Transition 1880–1920* 19 (1976): 283–98.

Galsworthy, John. *Letters from John Galsworthy 1900–1932.* Edited by Edward Garnett. London: Jonathan Cape, 1934.

Gindin, James. *The English Climate: An Excursion into a Biography of John Galsworthy.* Ann Arbor: University of Michigan Press, 1979.

———. *John Galsworthy's Life and Art: An Alien's Fortress.* Ann Arbor: University of Michigan Press, 1987.

Higdon, David Leon. "John Galsworthy's *The Man of Property:* 'Now in the Natural Course of Things.' " *English Literature in Transition 1880–1920* 21 (1978): 149–57.

Holloway, D. *John Galsworthy.* International Profiles Series. London: Morgan-Grampian Books, 1968.

Kaye-Smith, Sheila. *John Galsworthy.* London: Nisbet, 1916.

Keating, Peter. "Life with Nemesis." *Times Literary Supplement,* 16 July 1976, 866–67.

MacDorman, Kathryne S. "Tarnished Brass: The Imperial Heroes of John Galsworthy and H. G. Wells." *North Dakota Quarterly* 50 (1982): 37–45.

Marrot, H. V. *Bibliography of the Works of John Galsworthy.* New York: Scribner's, 1928.

———. *Life and Letters of John Galsworthy.* London: Heinemann, 1935.

Mooti, Farouk Abdel. "Galsworthy's Narrative Modes." *Journal of English* 11 (1983): 71–87.

Mottram, R. H. *For Some We Loved: An Intimate Portrait of Ada and John Galsworthy.* London: Hutchinson, 1956.

———. *John Galsworthy.* London: Longmans, 1953.

Sauter, Rudolf. *Galsworthy the Man: An Intimate Portrait by His Nephew.* London: Peter Owen, 1967.

Smit, J. Henry. *The Short Stories of J. Galsworthy*. Rotterdam: D. Van Sijn & Zonen, 1948.

Stevens, Earl E., and H. Ray Stevens. *John Galsworthy: An Annotated Bibliography of Writings about Him*. Chicago: Northern Illinois University Press, 1979.

Stevens, H. Ray. "Galsworthy's *Fraternity*: The Closed Door and the Paralyzed Society." *English Literature in Transition 1880–1920* 19 (1976): 283–98.

MAX BEERBOHM

Auden, W. H. "One of the Family." In *Forewords and Afterwords*. New York: Random House, 1973.

Behrman, S. N. *Portrait of Max: An Intimate Memoir*. New York: Random House, 1960.

Burdett, Osbert. *The Beardsley Period*. London: John Lane, 1925.

Cecil, David. *Max: A Biography*. London: Constable, 1964.

Danson, Lawrence. "Max Beerbohm and *The Mirror of the Past*." *Princeton University Library Chronicle* 43 (1982): 77–153.

Dupee, F. W. "Beerbohm: The Rigors of Fantasy." *New York Review of Books*, 9 June 1966, 12–17.

Felstiner, John. "Changing Faces in Max Beerbohm's Caricature." *Princeton University Library Chronicle* 33 (1972): 73–88.

——. *The Lies of Art: Max Beerbohm's Parody and Caricature*. New York: Knopf, 1972.

——. "Max Beerbohm and the Wings of Henry James." *Kenyon Review* 29 (1967): 449–71.

Grushow, Ira. *The Imaginary Reminiscences of Sir Max Beerbohm*. Athens: Ohio University Press, 1984.

Hart-Davis, Rupert. *A Catalogue of the Caricatures of Max Beerbohm*. Cambridge, Mass.: Harvard University Press, 1972.

Layard, George Soames. "Max Beerbohm; or, Art and Semolina." *Bookman* (London) (August 1911): 201–8.

Lynch, Bohun. *Max Beerbohm in Perspective*. London: Heinemann, 1921.

McElderry, Bruce R., Jr. *Max Beerbohm*. New York: Twayne, 1972.

Mix, Katherine Lyon. *Max and the Americans*. Brattleboro, Vt.: Stephen Greene, 1974.

——. "Max on Shaw." *Shaw Review* 6 (1963): 100–104.

Pritchett, V. S. "Max Beerbohm: A Dandy." In *The Tale Bearers*. New York: Random House, 1980.

Riewald, J. G., ed. *Beerbohm's Literary Caricatures, from Homer to Huxley*. Hamden, Conn.: Archon, 1977.

——, ed. *The Surprise of Excellence: Modern Essays on Max Beerbohm*. Hamden, Conn.: Archon, 1974.

Viscusi, Robert. *Max Beerbohm, or The Dandy Dante: An Exercise in Rereading*. Baltimore: Johns Hopkins University Press, 1986.

Wilson, Edmund. "An Analysis of Max Beerbohm." In *Classics and Commercials: A Literary Chronicle of the Forties*. New York: Farrar, Straus, 1950.

——. "A Miscellany of Max Beerbohm." In *The Bit between My Teeth: A Literary Chronicle of 1950–1965*. New York: Farrar, Straus & Giroux, 1965.

G. K. CHESTERTON

Belloc, Hilaire. "Gilbert Chesterton." In *One Thing and Another*. London: Hollis & Carter, 1955.

————. *On the Place of Gilbert Chesterton in English Letters.* London: Sheed & Ward, 1940.

Bergonzi, Bernard. "Before 1914: Writers and the Threat of War." *Critical Quarterly* 6 (1964): 126–34.

————. "Chesterton and/or Belloc." *Critical Quarterly* 1 (1959): 64–71.

Borges, Jorges Luis. "On Chesterton." In *Other Inquisitions 1937–52*, translated by Ruth L. Simms. Austin: University of Texas Press, 1964.

Boyd, Ian. *The Novels of G. K. Chesterton: A Study in Art and Propaganda.* New York: Barnes & Noble, 1975.

Bradbrook, B. R. "The Literary Relationship between G. K. Chesterton and Karel Capek." *Slavonic and East European Review* 39 (1961): 327–38.

Cammaerts, Emile. *The Laughing Prophet: The Seven Virtues and G. K. Chesterton.* London: Methuen, 1937.

The Chesterton Review, 1974–.

Clarke, Margaret. "Chesterton the Classicist." *Dublin Review* 118 (1955): 51–67.

Clipper, Lawrence J. *G. K. Chesterton.* New York: Twayne, 1974.

Dale, Alzina Stone. *The Outline of Sanity: A Biography of G. K. Chesterton.* Grand Rapids, Mich.: Eerdmans, 1982.

Hart, Jeffrey. "In Praise of Chesterton." *Yale Review* 53 (1964): 49–60.

Hollis, Christopher. *Gilbert Keith Chesterton.* London: Longmans, Green, 1954.

————. *The Mind of Chesterton.* Coral Gables: University of Miami Press, 1970.

Kenner, Hugh. *Paradox in Chesterton.* New York: Sheed & Ward, 1947.

Knox, Ronald A. "Chesterton in His Early Romances." *Dublin Review* 99 (1936): 351–65.

————. "Father Brown." In *Literary Distractions.* New York: Sheed & Ward, 1958.

Lea, F. A. *The Wild Knight of Battersea.* London: James Clarke, 1945.

Mason, Michael. *The Centre of Hilarity.* London: Sheed & Ward, 1959.

Rauch, Rufus William, ed. *A Chesterton Celebration.* Notre Dame, Ind.: University of Notre Dame Press, 1983.

Shaw, George Bernard. "The Chesterbelloc: A Lampoon." In *Pen Portraits and Reviews.* London: Constable, 1932.

Ward, Maisie. *Gilbert Keith Chesterton.* New York: Sheed & Ward, 1943.

————. *Return to Chesterton.* London: Sheed & Ward, 1952.

Wells, H. G. "About Chesterton and Belloc." In *An Englishman Looks at the World.* London: Cassell, 1914.

Wills, Garry. *Chesterton, Man and Mask.* New York: Sheed & Ward, 1961.

E. M. FORSTER

Bedient, Calvin. *Architects of the Self: George Eliot, D. H. Lawrence, and E. M. Forster.* Berkeley: University of California Press, 1972.

Beer, Gillian. "Negation in *A Passage to India*." *Essays in Criticism* 30 (1980): 151–66.

Beer, J. B. *The Achievement of E. M. Forster.* New York: Barnes & Noble, 1962.

Bell, Quentin. *Bloomsbury.* London: Weidenfeld & Nicolson, 1968.

Bloom, Harold, ed. *Modern Critical Interpretations: E. M. Forster's* A Passage to India. New Haven: Chelsea House, 1987.

————, ed. *Modern Critical Views: E. M. Forster.* New Haven: Chelsea House, 1987.

Bodenheimer, Rosemarie. "The Romantic Impasse in *A Passage to India*." *Criticism* 22 (1980): 40–56.

Bowen, Elizabeth. "E. M. Forster." In *Collected Impressions*, 119–26. London: Longmans, Green, 1950.

Bowen, Roger. "A Version of Pastoral: E. M. Forster as Country Guardian." *South Atlantic Quarterly* 75 (1976): 36–54.

Bradbury, Malcolm, ed. *E. M. Forster:* A Passage to India. London: Macmillan, 1970.

Brower, Reuben A. *The Field of Light.* New York: Oxford University Press, 1951.

Brown, E. K. *Rhythm in the Novel.* Toronto: University of Toronto Press, 1950.

Cammarota, Richard S. "Musical Analogy and Internal Design." *English Literature in Transition 1880–1920* 18 (1975): 38–46.

Colmer, John. *E. M. Forster: The Personal Voice.* London: Routledge & Kegan Paul, 1975.

Crews, Frederick. *E. M. Forster: The Perils of Humanism.* Princeton: Princeton University Press, 1962.

Das, G. K., and John Beer, eds. *E. M. Forster: A Human Exploration (Centenary Essays).* London: Macmillan, 1979.

Dowling, David. *Bloomsbury Aesthetics and Novels of Forster and Woolf.* London: Macmillan, 1985.

Faulkner, Peter. *Humanism in the English Novel.* London: Elek/Pemberton, 1976.

Furbank, P. N. *E. M. Forster: A Life.* 2 vols. London: Secker & Warburg, 1977.

Gardner, Philip, ed. *E. M. Forster: The Critical Heritage.* London: Routledge & Kegan Paul, 1973.

Gillie, Christopher. *A Preface to Forster.* London: Longman Group, 1983.

Gransden, K. W. *E. M. Forster.* Edinburgh: Oliver & Boyd, 1962.

Herz, Judith Scherer, and Robert K. Martin, eds. *E. M. Forster: Centenary Revaluations.* Toronto: University of Toronto Press, 1982.

Langbaum, Robert. "A New Look at E. M. Forster." *Southern Review* 4 (1968): 33–49.

Leavis, F. R. "E. M. Forster." *Scrutiny* 7 (1938): 185–202.

McConkey, James. *The Novels of E. M. Forster.* Ithaca: Cornell University Press, 1957.

McDowell, Frederick P. W. "By and about Forster: A Review Essay." *English Literature in Transition 1880–1920* 15 (1972): 319–31.

———. *E. M. Forster.* Rev. ed. Boston: Twayne, 1982.

Meyers, Jeffrey. "The Politics of *A Passage to India.*" *Journal of Modern Literature* 1 (1971): 329–38.

Natwar-Singh, K., ed. *E. M. Forster: A Tribute.* New York: Harcourt, Brace & World, 1964.

Page, Norman. *E. M. Forster's Posthumous Fiction.* Victoria, B.C., Canada: University of Victoria Press, 1977.

Pradhan, S. V. "*A Passage to India:* Realism versus Symbolism, A Marxist Analysis." *Dalhousie Review* 60, (1980): 300–317.

Pritchett, V. S. "Mr. Forster's Birthday." In *The Living Novel and Later Appreciations.* New York: Random House, 1964.

Rosecrance, Barbara. *Forster's Narrative Vision.* Ithaca: Cornell University Press, 1982.

Rutherford, Andrew, ed. *Twentieth-Century Interpretations of* A Passage to India: *A Collection of Critical Essays.* Englewood Cliffs, N.J.: Prentice-Hall, 1970.

Schwarz, Daniel R. "The Originality of E. M. Forster." *Modern Fiction Studies* 29 (1983): 623–41.

Shahane, V. A., ed. *Perspectives on E. M. Forster's* A Passage to India: *A Collection of Critical Essays.* New York: Barnes & Noble, 1968.

Shusterman, David. *The Quest for Certitude in E. M. Forster's Fiction.* Bloomington: University of Indiana Press, 1965.

Spender, Stephen. "Personal Relations and Public Powers." In *The Creative Element: A Study of Vision, Despair, and Orthodoxy among Some Modern Writers.* London: Hamish Hamilton, 1953.

Stallybrass, Oliver, ed. *Aspects of E. M. Forster: Essays and Recollections Written for His Ninetieth Birthday, January 1, 1969.* New York: Harcourt, Brace & World, 1969.

Stone, Wilfred. *The Cave and the Mountain: A Study of E. M. Forster.* Stanford: Stanford University Press, 1966.

———. " 'Overleaping Class,' Forster's Problem in Connection." *Modern Language Quarterly* 39 (1978): 386–404.

Summers, Claude J. *E. M. Forster.* New York: Ungar, 1983.

Thomson, George H. *The Fiction of E. M. Forster.* Detroit: Wayne State University Press, 1967.

Trilling, Lionel. *E. M. Forster: A Study.* London: Hogarth Press, 1944.

Turk, Jo M. "The Evolution of E. M. Forster's Narrator." *Studies in the Novel* 5 (1973): 428–39.

Warren, Austin. "The Novels of E. M. Forster." In *Rage for Order*, 119–41. Chicago: University of Chicago Press, 1948.

Wilde, Alan. *Art and Order: A Study of E. M. Forster.* New York: New York University Press, 1964.

———. "Depths and Surfaces: Dimensions of Forsterian Irony." *English Literature in Transition 1880–1920* 16 (1973): 257–73.

P. G. WODEHOUSE

Aldridge, John W. "P. G. Wodehouse: The Lesson of a Young Master." In *Time to Murder and Create: The Contemporary Novel in Crisis.* New York: David McKay, 1966.

Appia, Henry. "O Rare P. G. Wodehouse." *Études Anglaises* 26 (1973): 22–34.

Bowen, Barbara C. "Rabelais and P. G. Wodehouse: Two Comic Works." *L'Esprit Créateur* 16 (1976): 63–77.

Cannadine, David. "Another 'Last Victorian': P. G. Wodehouse and His World." *South Atlantic Quarterly* 77 (1978): 470–91.

Cazalet-Keir, Thelma, ed. *Homage to Wodehouse.* London: Barrie & Jenkins, 1973.

Clarke, Gerald. "P. G. Wodehouse." In *Writers at Work: The* Paris Review *Interviews, 5th Series,* 1–19. New York: Viking, 1981.

Connolly, Joseph. *P. G. Wodehouse: An Illustrated Biography with Complete Bibliography and Collector's Guide.* London: Orbis, 1979.

Edwards, Owen Dudley. *P. G. Wodehouse: A Critical and Historical Essay.* London: Martin Brian & O'Keefe, 1977.

French, R. B. D. *P. G. Wodehouse.* Writers and Critics. New York: Barnes & Noble, 1967.

Hall, Robert A. *The Comic Style of P. G. Wodehouse.* Hamden, Conn.: Archon, 1974.

Jasen, David A. *A Bibliography and Reader's Guide to the First Editions of P. G. Wodehouse.* Hamden, Conn.: Archon, 1970.

———. *The Theatre of P. G. Wodehouse.* London: B. T. Batsford, 1979.

Lancaster, Osbert. "Great Houses of Fiction Revisited: Blandings Castle." In *Scene Changes.* London: John Murray, 1978.

Medcalf, Stephen. "The Innocence of P. G. Wodehouse." In *The Modern English Novel: The Reader, the Writer, and the Work,* edited by G. D. Josipovici, 186–205. New York: Barnes & Noble, 1976.

Mikes, George. "P. G. Wodehouse." In *Eight Humorists,* 153–75. London: Allan Wingate, 1954.

Muggeridge, Malcolm. "The Wodehouse Affair." In *Tread Softly for You Tread on My Jokes,* 83–93. London: Collins, 1966.

Olney, Clarke. "Wodehouse and the Poets." *Georgia Review* 16 (1962): 392–99.

Orwell, George. "In Defence of P. G. Wodehouse." In *Collected Essays*, 248–64. London: Secker & Warburg, 1961.

Sharma, M. N. *Wodehouse the Fictionalist*. Meerut, India: Munakski Prakashan, 1980.

Sheed, Wilfrid. "P. G. Wodehouse: *Leave It to Psmith*." In *The Good Word and Other Words*, 215–22. London: Sidgwick & Jackson, 1979.

Stephenson, William. "The Wodehouse World of Hollywood." *Literature/Film Quarterly* 6 (1978): 190–203.

Stevenson, Lionel. "The Antecedents of P. G. Wodehouse." *Arizona Quarterly* 5 (1959): 226–34.

Usborne, Richard. *Wodehouse at Work to the End*. Rev. ed. London: Barrie & Jenkins, 1976.

Voorhees, Richard J. *P. G. Wodehouse*. New York: Twayne, 1966.

Wallace, Malcolm T. "The Wodehouse World I: Classical Echoes." *Cithara* 12 (1973): 41–57.

Wind, Herbert Warren. *The World of P. G. Wodehouse*. New York: Praeger, 1972.

KATHERINE MANSFIELD

Allen, Walter. "Katherine Mansfield." In *The Short Story in English*, 165–75. Oxford: Oxford University Press, 1981.

Alpers, Antony. *Katherine Mansfield*. London: Jonathan Cape, 1954.

———. *The Life of Katherine Mansfield*. New York: Viking Press, 1980.

Baker, Ida Constance (L. M.). *Katherine Mansfield: The Memories of L. M.* London: Michael Joseph, 1971.

Beachcroft, T. O. *The Modest Art: A Survey of the Short Story in English*. London: Oxford University Press, 1968.

Berkman, Sylvia. *Katherine Mansfield: A Critical Study*. London: Oxford University Press, 1952.

Bowen, Elizabeth. "A Living Writer." *Cornhill Magazine* 1010 (Winter 1956–57): 119–34.

Carswell, John. *Lives and Letters: A. R. Orage, Beatrice Hastings, Katherine Mansfield, John Middleton Murry, S. S. Koteliansky 1906–1957*. London: Faber & Faber, 1978.

Carter, Angela. "The Life of Katherine Mansfield." In *Nothing Sacred*, 158–61. London: Virago, 1982.

Daiches, David. "Katherine Mansfield and the Search for Truth." In *The Novel and the Modern World*, 65–79. Chicago: University of Chicago Press, 1939.

Daly, Saralyn R. *Katherine Mansfield*. New York: Twayne, 1965.

Foot, John. *The Edwardianism of Katherine Mansfield*. Wellington, New Zealand: Brentwood's Press, 1969.

Fullbrook, Kate. *Katherine Mansfield*. Bloomington: Indiana University Press, 1986.

Gordon, Ian A. *Katherine Mansfield*. London: Longmans, Green, 1954.

Gurr, Andrew. *Writers in Exile: The Literary Identity of Home in Modern Literature*. Brighton: Harvester Press, 1981.

Hankin, C. A. *Katherine Mansfield and Her Confessional Stories*. London: Macmillan, 1983.

Hanson, Clare. *Short Stories and Short Fictions 1880–1980*. London: Macmillan, 1985.

———, and Andrew Gurr. *Katherine Mansfield*. London: Macmillan, 1981.

Hayman, Ronald. *Literature and Living: A Consideration of Katherine Mansfield and Virginia Woolf*. London: Covent Garden Press, 1972.

Hormasji, Nariman. *Katherine Mansfield: An Appraisal*. London: Collins, 1967.

Isherwood, Christopher. "Katherine Mansfield." In *Exhumations: Stories, Articles, Verses*, 64–72. London: Methuen, 1966.

Kaplan, Sydney Janet. "Katherine Mansfield's 'Passion for Technique.' " In *Women's Language and Style*, edited by Douglas Buttruff and Edmund L. Epstein, 119–31. Akron, Ohio: University of Akron, 1978.

Lawlor, P. A. *The Loneliness of Katherine Mansfield*. Wellington, N.Z.: Beltane Book Bureau, 1950.

Maglander, Marvin. *The Fiction of Katherine Mansfield*. London: Feffer & Simons, 1971.

Mantz, Ruth, and John Middleton Murry. *The Life of Katherine Mansfield*. London: Constable, 1933.

Meyers, Jeffrey. *Katherine Mansfield: A Biography*. London: Hamish Hamilton, 1978.

Modern Fiction Studies 24, no. 3 (1978). Special Katherine Mansfield issue.

Moore, James. *Gurdjieff and Mansfield*. London: Routledge & Kegan Paul, 1980.

Morrell, Ottoline. *Ottoline at Garsington: Memoirs of Lady Ottoline Morrell: 1915–1918*. Edited by Robert Gathorne-Hardy. London: Faber & Faber, 1974.

Murry, John Middleton. *Katherine Mansfield and Other Literary Studies*. London: Constable, 1959.

O'Connor, Frank. *The Lonely Voice: A Study of the Short Story*. London: Macmillan, 1963.

O'Sullivan, Vincent. *Katherine Mansfield's New Zealand*. London: Frederick Muller, 1975.

Walsh, William. *A Maniford Voice: Studies in Commonwealth Literature*. London: Chatto & Windus, 1970.

Willey, Margaret. *Three Women Diarists*. London: Longmans, Green, 1964.

Woolf, Virginia. *The Letters of Virginia Woolf*. Edited by Nigel Nicolson and Joanne Traumann. Vols. 2–4. London: Hogarth Press, 1976, 1977, 1978.

Acknowledgments

"William Morris: The World beyond the World" (originally titled "The World beyond the World") by Carole Silver from *The Romance of William Morris* by Carole Silver, © 1982 by Carole Silver. Reprinted by permission of Ohio University Press.

"The Place of Pater: *Marius the Epicurean*" by Harold Bloom from *The Ringers in the Tower: Studies in Romantic Tradition* by Harold Bloom, © 1971 by The University of Chicago Press. Reprinted by permission.

"Hardy's Tess: The Making of a Pure Woman" (originally titled "Tess: The Making of a Pure Woman") by Mary Jacobus from *Tearing the Veil: Essays on Femininity*, edited by Susan Lipshitz, © 1978 by Routledge & Kegan Paul, Ltd. Reprinted by permission.

"Women and the New Fiction 1880–1900" by Penny Boumelha from *Thomas Hardy and Women: Sexual Ideology and Narrative Form* by Penny Boumelha, © 1982 by Penny Boumelha. Reprinted by permission of Barnes & Noble Books and The Harvester Press, Ltd.

" 'Different from Writing': *Dracula* in 1897" by Geoffrey Wall from *Literature and History* 10, no. 1 (Spring 1984), © 1984 by Thames Polytechnic, London. Reprinted by permission of the publisher and the author.

"Parables of Adventure: The Debatable Novels of Robert Louis Stevenson" by Alastair Fowler from *Nineteenth-Century Scottish Fiction: Critical Essays*, edited by Ian Campbell, © 1979 by Alastair Fowler. Reprinted by permission of the author.

"The Artist and the Critics: Advertising, *Dorian Gray*, and the Press" (originally titled "Dandies and Gentlemen: or 'Dorian Gray' and the Press") by Regenia Gagnier from *Idylls of the Marketplace: Oscar Wilde and the*

533

Victorian Public by Regenia Gagnier, © 1986 by the Board of Trustees of the Leland Stanford Junior University. Reprinted by permission of Stanford University Press and Scolar Press.

"Novelist of the Modern City: George Gissing's Early Fiction" (originally titled "The Evolution of the Gissing Novel") by John Goode from *George Gissing: Ideology and Fiction* by John Goode, © 1978 by John Goode. Reprinted by permission of Vision Press.

"Ideas of Dialogue and Conrad's Forced Dialogue" by Aaron Fogel from *Coercion to Speak: Conrad's Poetics of Dialogue* by Aaron Fogel, © 1985 by the President and Fellows of Harvard College. Reprinted by permission of Harvard University Press.

" 'The Great Mirage': Conrad and *Nostromo*" by Robert Penn Warren from *Selected Essays* by Robert Penn Warren, © 1951 by Random House, Inc., © 1958 by Robert Penn Warren. Reprinted by permission of Random House and William Morris Agency.

"The Form of Content: *Lord Jim*" (originally titled "Romance and Reification: Plot Construction and Ideological Closure in Joseph Conrad") by Fredric Jameson from *The Political Unconscious: Narrative as a Socially Symbolic Act* by Fredric Jameson, © 1981 by Cornell University Press. Reprinted by permission of Cornell University Press and Methuen & Co.

" '...A Great Blue Triumphant Cloud'—*The Adventures of Sherlock Holmes*" by Stephen Knight from *Form and Ideology in Crime Fiction* by Stephen Knight, © 1980 by Stephen Knight. Reprinted by permission of Indiana University Press.

"Kipling in the Light of Failure" by Robert L. Caserio from *Grand Street* 5, no. 4 (Summer 1986), © 1986 by Robert L. Caserio and Grand Street Publications, Inc. Reprinted by permission.

"World within Worlds: Kipling and Nesbit" by Stephen Prickett from *Victorian Fantasy* by Stephen Prickett, © 1979 by Stephen Prickett. Reprinted by permission of The Harvester Press.

"Evolutionary Fables: *The Time Machine*" (originally titled "Evolutionary Fables: *The Time Machine* and *The Island of Dr. Moreau*") by Frank McConnell from *The Science Fiction of H. G. Wells* by Frank McConnell, © 1981 by Oxford University Press. Reprinted by permission of the author.

" 'Absolute Realism': Arnold Bennett" (originally titled "Absolute Realism") by John Lucas from *Arnold Bennett: A Study of His Fiction* by John Lucas, © 1974 by John Lucas. Reprinted by permission of Methuen & Co.

"Galsworthy's *Man of Property*: 'I Feel More Like a Sort of Chemist' " by

James Gindin from *John Galsworthy's Life and Art: An Alien's Fortress* by James Gindin, © 1987 by James Gindin. Reprinted by permission of The University of Michigan Press and Macmillan Publishers, Ltd.

"Max Beerbohm, or The Dandy Dante: *Zuleika Dobson*" (originally titled "Things Transmutable, or Parallelogrammatology" & "Completing His Antithesis and Leaving the Room") by Robert Viscusi from *Max Beerbohm, or The Dandy Dante: Rereading with Mirrors* by Robert Viscusi, © 1986 by The Johns Hopkins University Press. Reprinted by permission.

"The Achievement of G. K. Chesterton" by Stephen Medcalf from *G. K. Chesterton: A Centenary Appraisal*, edited by John Sullivan, © 1974 by Stephen Medcalf. Reprinted by permission.

"The Postponement of England's Decline: *Howards End*" (originally titled "*Howards End*") by Barbara Rosecrance from *Forster's Narrative Vision* by Barbara Rosecrance, © 1982 by Cornell University Press. Reprinted by permission.

"The Edwardian Wodehouse: Experiments and Transitions" (originally titled "Experiments and Transitions") by Richard Voorhees from *P. G. Wodehouse* by Richard Voorhees, © 1966 by Twayne Publishers, Inc. Reprinted by permission of G. K. Hall & Co.

"The Early Stories of Katherine Mansfield" (originally titled "The Early Stories") by Kate Fullbrook from *Katherine Mansfield* by Kate Fullbrook, © 1986 by Kate Fullbrook. Reprinted by permission of Indiana University Press and The Harvester Press, Ltd.

Index

537